300 BEERS TO TRY BEFORE YOU DIE!

ROGER PROTZ

CAMRA

CAMPAIGN
FOR
REAL ALE

FALL RIVER PRESS

New York

W9-BUU-534

'The daughter of the grain is superior to the blood of the grape'

Charles V, Emperor of the Holy Roman Empire (1500–1558), who was born in Mechelen in the Netherlands (now Belgium) and who demanded regular supplies of beer from his native city

First Published in Great Britain in 2005 by the Campaign for Real Ale Ltd
230 Hatfield Road, St Albans, Hertfordshire AL1 4LW

Second edition 2010
This 2013 edition published by Fall River Press by arrangement with the Campaign for Real Ale Ltd.

www.camra.org.uk

ISBN: 978-1-4351-4388-3

Printed and bound in China

Managing Editor: Simon Hall
Project Editor: Katie Hunt
Editorial Assistance: Emma Haines
Design: Stephen Bere
Cover Design: Dale Tomlinson
Additional Research: Adam Protz
Marketing Manager: Kim Carvey

ACKNOWLEDGEMENTS
The Publisher would like to thank the breweries for their kind permission in reproducing these photographs.
All photographs have been provided by the breweries except:
Beerlabels.com, 18, 55, 143, 173, 200 left, 215, 259, 272
Biertest-online.de, 219
Bob Steel, 63
CAMRA archive, 5, 7, 8, 15, 23 above, 37, 46, 54, 68, 69, 73, 82, 108, 124, 133, 134, 136, 146, 148, 156, 163, 164, 179, 199, 200 right, 220, 225, 238, 239, 252, 256 below, 258, 274, 274, 278
Cephas/Martin Walls, 113
Cephas/Nigel Blythe, 271
Katherine Longly, 245
National Hop Association, 6
Ralph Gant, 207
Vanessa Courtier, 11, 14, 142, 152, 153, 165, 180, 196, 198, 202, 208, 229, 233, 235, 237, 242, 244, 251, 253, 256 above, 260, 269, 285

Contents

Introduction

'Enjoy the journey and keep travelling' I said in the introduction to the first edition of this book. The journey has taken on an added excitement since I wrote those words in 2005. Then there were close to 500 small craft or 'micro' breweries in Britain. By 2009 the number had grown to well over 700. Britain now has more craft breweries per head of population than any major industrial country. In the United States, the craft beer revolution shows no sign of abating. The country has around 1,200 small breweries. In common with Britain, their beers are the only ones reporting growth as the giant national producers see interest in their bland offerings declining at a rate of knots.

Other countries are also challenging the hegemony of the global producers. In Australia, craft breweries are springing up on both the east and west coasts. New Zealand also has a flourishing small brewery sector. In both northern and southern hemispheres beer drinkers and brewers are relishing beer with flavour. They are rejecting global brands that are mere commodities and offer little more than chill and fizz, devoid of the malt and hop character that form the hallmark of good beer.

The revival of beer with style has been aided by the frenzied activities of the global brewers that lead to merger, concentration and brewery closures. The world's biggest brewer now goes by the curious rubric of ABInBev following the merger of Anheuser-Busch of the U.S. and InBev of Belgium and Brazil. Molson of Canada and Coors in the U.S. have merged as MolsonCoors. Carlsberg prefers to be known in Russia and the Baltic States as Baltic Beverages Holding, while South African Breweries and Miller of Milwaukee go by yet another clumsy title: SABMiller. As this book was going to press, Britain's biggest brewer, Scottish & Newcastle, a company with some tradition and heritage, has been renamed—with scant regard for geography—Heineken UK.

It's not surprising that the global brewers scarcely feature in this book. We are concerned here with aroma, flavour, style, a respect for tradition and—above all—creating beers with the finest natural ingredients and respect for both the consumer and the environment. You can make something legally labelled 'beer' from rice, corn grits, sorghum, industrial enzymes and hop oil but you won't find them in these pages.

The journey that started in 2005 has taken on added pace. Interest in such great and revered beer styles as India Pale Ale, porters, stouts, Bocks and Pilsners has intensified. The beers of Belgium— Trappist ales, lambic and gueuze, sour red to name but a few—continue to inspire brewers in other countries. France, in its northern regions, proves it can make rich and tempting alcohol from the grain as well as the grape. Germany shows that, as well as fine interpretations of lager, it also has beers shaped by older traditions in the form of Alt, Kölsch and wheat. In spite of the encroachments of global producers, craft brewers in the Czech Republic and Poland still make lager beers worthy of the name.

There are new beers in this edition for two reasons: some that featured in the first edition have fallen by the wayside and on my travels I have found new beers worthy of inclusion. I know from the correspondence created by the book in 2005 that many readers are willing to make long journeys to seek out great beers. But as far as possible I have included beers here that are available beyond the borders of their countries of origin.

But whether you sample from the comfort of your armchair or from a bar in a foreign land, join the magic carpet ride.

Making beer

We take beer for granted. We assume, as it is an everyday drink rather than one for special occasions, that it is easily and quickly made. It is true that most beers are not matured for long periods, as is the case with single malt whiskies or vintage wines. But there are vintage beers, too, and there are also beers that are matured for long periods. Not all whiskies are stored for 12 or 18 years, while most wines are also meant for everyday consumption.

At its simplest, wine can be made by crushing grapes and allowing the wild yeasts on the skins to turn the juice into alcohol. If you crush an ear of barley, all you will get is dust on your fingers. Long before the brewer can start work, a maltster has to take the grain from the fields and turn it into malt, the vital ingredient that will launch the fascinating journey that ends with a delicious glass of beer in your hand.

Malt

Barley is the preferred grain of brewers. It has a husk, which acts as a natural filter during the mashing stage, and it delivers a clean, sweet, biscuity character to the finished product. Even wheat beers are made with a blend of barley and wheat. Oats and rye are also occasionally used but in small amounts for fear that their oily, creamy or bready notes will overwhelm the essential character of barley malt.

The finest type of barley is known as 'two-row', so called because there are two rows of grain within each ear. The best two-row is called maritime barley, as it grows close to the sea in rich, dark soil. In regions away from the coast, six-row barley is the norm. It produces coarser malt and is often blended with other cereals such as rice or corn. Craft brewers in the United States who want to create specific, refined flavours from their beers will import malt from Britain or mainland Europe and will avoid 'adjuncts', or cheaper grains. Ale brewers prefer winter barleys sown in the autumn with robust, biscuity tastes, while lager brewers prefer the softer notes that are derived from spring varieties.

When barley reaches the maltings, it is thoroughly washed in deep vats to clean it and remove any harmful bacteria. The grain absorbs moisture, vital to encourage germination. When the correct level of moisture has been achieved, the grain is spread on heated floors or placed in large rotating drums. Germination will last from between four to 10 days, depending on the method used.

During germination, the embryo of the plant starts to grow, while tiny roots break through the husk. The process is known as modification. As the embryo grows it triggers complex chemical changes that turn proteins into enzymes, while the starch in the grain becomes soluble. When the embryo has fully grown and the rootlets stand proud of the husk, modification is complete. Ale brewers want a fully modified malt so that enzymes will work quickly to convert starch into sugar during the infusion mashing process. In traditional lager brewing, malt is poorly modified, with substantial amounts of protein remaining. This is caused by the poorer quality of lager malts with a high nitrogen level that require a more thorough decoction mash.

The grain is loaded into a kiln, where the malt is laid out on a mesh floor and heated from below, or in a drum where the heat is applied externally. The heat is gentle at first. It dries the malt, stops germination and preserves the vital enzymes. The heat is then increased. All brewers need pale malt, as it is rich in enzymes, and this type of malt is gently roasted. The heat is increased to produce darker malts such as amber, brown, black, chocolate or roast. Unmalted roasted barley, often used in stout brewing, is also kilned at a high temperature. Some malts are stewed and arrive at the brewery with the starch already converted to malt sugar. Crystal malt, widely used in English ale brewing, is a type of stewed malt. It gives both colour and a pleasing nutty flavour to beer but must be used in small quantities. Similar malts are known as caramel malt or caramalt.

TOP
Brewers call barley 'the soul of beer', as it is the finest grain for brewing, creating a juicy and biscuity flavour as well as essential sugars for fermentation.

ABOVE
Grain has to be malted to start the brewing process.

Hops—described as 'the grapes of brewing'—give bitterness, aroma and flavour to beer. There are many varieties of hops grown throughout the world. Shown here are the classic English Fuggles (top) and Phoenix from the United States (below).

Hops

The hop is a remarkable plant that provides bitterness to beer to balance the sweet, juicy and biscuity nature of malt. It also delivers superb aromas and flavours reminiscent of pine, resins, citrus fruit, fresh-mown grass and floral notes. The Latin name for the hop is *Humulus lupulus*, the wolf plant, because, left to itself, it would run wild across the ground. Hop growers train plants to climb up tall trellises to absorb sun, warmth, wind and rain. The male and female plants grow separately. Most brewers, especially lager makers, prefer unfertilised female hops, while ale brewers want the earthier and more pungent character of fertilised plants. The cone of the plant contains acids, oils and resins that give aroma and flavour to beer, help stabilise the wort during the brewing process and attack bacteria.

Hops are picked in the autumn and dried in oast houses. The cones are laid out on perforated drying room floors and heated from below. Once dry, the hops are packed into large sacks called pockets or taken to a specialist factory and turned into pellets by milling and reducing under great pressure. There is a tendency in giant breweries to use hop extract, which is a thick liquid like damson jam created by crushing the hops. Craft brewers prefer not to use extract, which can give a harsh note at the back of the throat.

There are scores of different hop varieties. Germans call the types that grow in the vast Hallertau region near Munich 'noble hops' as a result of their fine aroma and gentle bitterness. Many lager brewers will buy Saaz hops from the Czech Republic for their superb aroma. American hops, many descended from European stock, are famous for their distinctive and robust citrus fruit character. English hops have resiny aromas and flavours, with a medium bitterness. Hops are grown in many countries, including Russia, Poland, Slovenia—well known for the Styrian Golding—Northern France, Belgium, Australia, New Zealand, Canada, Japan, South Africa, Zimbabwe, South and Central America, Greece, Turkey and parts of Scandinavia.

Just as with grapes, each hop variety will have its own character and distinctive aroma and flavour. Many brewers will blend two or more varieties to achieve the balance of flavour they are looking for. In England, for example, two long-established varieties, the Fuggle and the Golding, are often used in tandem: the Fuggle primarily for bitterness and the Golding for aroma. Several European countries, with England leading the field, have developed new types of hops known as dwarf or hedgerow varieties that grow to only half the height of conventional hops, are easier to pick and are less prone to attack by pests and disease.

Water

Even the strongest beer is made up of 93% water. The quality of water is therefore crucial to brewing. For centuries, long before brewers were able to adjust water to suit their recipes, breweries developed around natural supplies in the form of wells or springs. River water was used before such sources were ruined by pollution.

In a brewery, water is always known as liquor. Its formulation will depend on the minerals present in the rocks and soil of a particular area. Soft water is the result of rain falling on insoluble rock such as slate or granite. Where soluble rock is present, water will pick up such sulphates as calcium and magnesium, also known as gypsum and Epsom salts. It is these salts present in the waters of the Trent Valley that made Burton-on-Trent a key town in the development of brewing. The hard waters help acidify the mash, encourage enzymes to work, ensure the best extraction of aromas and flavours from malt and hops, and discourage astringency. Yeast thrives on magnesium. On the other hand, the soft waters of such famous lager brewing towns as Pilsen emphasise the soft malty character of the beer. The total salts in the waters of Burton amount to 1,226 parts per million. In Pilsen, on the other hand, the figure is just 30.8. Brewers can now adjust their liquor to suit their purposes: many ale brewers 'Burtonise' their waters by adding gypsum and magnesium salts. All brewers thoroughly cleanse their liquor to remove impurities and such agricultural chemicals as nitrates, which can create a haze in beer.

Yeast

It was not until the 18th and 19th centuries that scientists, including Louis Pasteur, were able to explain yeast's role in brewing. Until then, fermentation was looked on as some kind of witchcraft. The foam produced by this strange alchemy was known as 'God-is-good'. Pasteur demonstrated with the aid of a microscope that the production of alcohol was the result of a natural chemical reaction in which yeast cells multiplied as they turned sugars into alcohol and carbon dioxide.

Yeast is a fungus, a single cell plant that can turn a sugary liquid into alcohol and CO_2. There are two basic types of brewer's yeasts: ale and lager. Ale yeast is classified as *Saccharomyces* [sugar fungus] *cerevisiae*, while lager yeast is labelled *Saccharomyces carlsbergensis*, as the first pure strain of lager yeast was isolated at the Carlsberg breweries in Denmark. It is also known today as *Saccharomyces uvarum*. The two types are often referred to as 'top fermenting' and 'bottom fermenting' strains. This is because ale yeast creates a thick collar of foam on top of the fermenting beer, while lager yeast produces a smaller head and sinks to the bottom of the vessel. The terms are misleading, as both yeasts must work at all levels of the liquid to convert malt sugars into alcohol. I prefer the terms warm fermenting and cold fermenting yeasts, for ale yeast will only work at 12˚C (55˚F) and above, while lager yeast is tolerant of cold and will happily work at temperatures as low as 5˚C (40˚F).

Yeast is not a neutral substance. It does more than produce alcohol. As the same strain reproduces itself many times over during fermentation, it does not die out. There is always a fresh supply of refrigerated yeast on hand. A brewery's yeast culture picks up, retains and passes on vital flavour characteristics from one brew to the next. Breweries not only safeguard their cultures but lodge samples in yeast banks. If a brewery has the misfortune to get a yeast infection, fresh supplies can be obtained from the bank.

The role of wild yeast strains in the production of Belgian lambic and gueuze beers is explained in the relevant section of the book (see pages 240–1).

Brewing

In the brewery, the malt is ground, or 'cracked', in a mill. The mill has several settings, and the malt is reduced to flour, coarser grain and the husks. The mixture is known as grist. In an infusion mash system, malt and pure hot liquor are mixed in a large circular vessel known as a mash tun. The thick, porridge-like mixture is left to stand for an hour or two as saccharification takes place. This means that the enzymes in the malt convert starch to sugar. Two principal types of sugar are produced. Maltose is highly fermentable, while dextrin can be only partially fermented by brewer's yeast, and the dextrins left give body and flavour to the beer. The sugars dissolve in the hot liquor and produce an extract called wort. When the brewer is satisfied that full conversion has taken place, he opens the slotted base of the vessel and the wort filters through the spent grain. To make sure no vital sugars are left behind, the spent grains are then sprinkled, or 'sparged', with more hot liquor to wash them out.

The wort is pumped to the copper, a domed vessel made from either copper or stainless steel. Boiling wort gushes up a central tube inside the copper, while hops are added through a hatch in the top of the vessel at specially selected times to extract the maximum aroma and bitterness. They are usually put in at the start of the boil, half way through and just a few minutes before the boil ends. Special brewing sugars may be added during the copper boil for colour, flavour and to encourage a powerful fermentation. At the end of the boil, the 'hopped wort' is filtered through the bed of spent hops into a vessel called a hop back. The liquid is cooled and run into fermenting vessels, which may be round or square, open or covered, where liquid yeast is mixed, or 'pitched'.

Ale fermentation lasts for around seven days. During that time, enzymes in the yeast turn sugar into alcohol and carbon dioxide. Fermentation also creates natural chemical compounds called esters that are similar to fruity aromas. They are present in the atmosphere in the fermentation rooms and may be reminiscent of apples, oranges, pineapples, pear drops, liquorice or molasses. Eventually the

BELOW
A classic lager brewery showing the burnished copper vessels used in the mashing process.

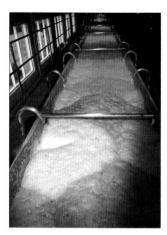

In the Burton 'Union System', yeast is trapped in the troughs above the fermenters. It is a 19th-century method used to clear pale ale of yeast.

yeast will be overcome by the alcohol it has produced. The cells will clump together and rise to the surface. The unfinished, or 'green', beer will spend several days resting in conditioning tanks and purging itself of rougher and unwanted alcohols. Finally, the beer will be run or racked into kegs or casks. It may be filtered and pasteurised or, if it is cask-conditioned real ale, it will be left to mature and enjoy a secondary fermentation in cask. Extra hops may be placed in each cask for additional aroma and flavour, while finings will start to clarify the beer.

In lager brewing, where the malt is less modified than ale malt, a decoction mashing system is used. A third of the mash will be pumped from one vessel to another, heated to a higher temperature and returned to the first vessel. A further third of the mash will receive similar treatment. The aim of the system is to degrade protein in the mash and gelatinise the starch so it can be attacked by enzymes and converted to sugar. When saccharification is complete, the mash will be pumped to a lauter tun with a false bottom, where the liquid is run off and the spent grains are then sparged.

Following the copper boil with hops, the hopped wort is cooled and pumped to fermentation vessels—which are usually enclosed—where yeast is pitched. As a result of a lower temperature, the yeast will work more slowly, and conversion to alcohol may take as long as two weeks. Finally, the liquid goes to the lager cellar and is run into tanks for a long, slow second fermentation and ripening at a temperature just above freezing point. Lager tanks may be upright conical vessels but purists prefer horizontal vessels, where the yeast works more slowly and produces a fuller-flavoured beer. There is a growing tendency to speed up the lagering time but classic beers such as the Czech Budweiser Budvar enjoy 90 days in the cellar. When lagering is complete, the beer will be filtered, as a heavy sediment of yeast and protein will have settled in the tank, and is then racked into kegs. The lagering process removes many of the fruity characteristics associated with ale.

By two very different routes, classic ale and classic lager brewing and fermentation, we now have beer to drink and savour.

Tasting beer

A little care, skill, and appreciation of the art of the brewer is required to appreciate beer at home. First, the glass. You can use a conventional pint or half-pint beer glass, or similar measures in metric countries. You may be lucky enough to have one of the glasses designed to accompany a particular beer. Or you may use any suitable glass container in your home. Whatever you use, it must be scrupulously clean and, above all, it should contain no residue from cleaning agents. If you take a glass from a dishwasher, rinse it thoroughly under running cold water. Washing-up liquids and detergents will not only leave a vile taste in the glass, but will also kill the head on the beer. Avoid pouring and drinking beer in a kitchen area. Oil or fats used in cooking infiltrate a beer glass, leave unpleasant flavours and also kill the head.

There is more to pouring beer into a glass than merely emptying the liquid from one container into the next. Hold the glass and bottle at eye level. Slowly pour the beer into the glass, raising the glass from the horizontal to the vertical as it fills. Let the beer trickle down the side of the glass. When the glass is two-thirds full, raise it to the vertical and pour more quickly: this should give the required healthy head of foam. Don't pour too slowly or the head will fail to materialise. Pouring at eye level is important when a beer contains yeast sediment. You can monitor the passage of the yeast, which will rise from the bottom of the bottle towards the neck, and stop pouring just before it leaves the bottle. If some of the yeast does get into the glass, don't worry: it will do you no harm and is full of healthy nutrients.

If you are pouring a German wheat beer, you cannot avoid the yeast sediment getting into the glass. It's meant to be served that way. A German beer waiter will deliberately rotate the bottle as he or she pours, and will give a final dramatic roll of the bottle to ensure all the yeast enters the glass.

If you are giving a beer tasting at home, you may find that large stemmed glasses intended for red wine are the most suitable containers, as they allow the aroma of the beer to develop, while the stem on the glass enables drinkers to swirl the beer to release the aroma to the full.

Whether you are drinking for pleasure or taking part in a tasting, begin by appreciating the aroma. Depending on the style, you will detect malty and hoppy aromas plus a fruitiness from either the hops or as the result of natural chemical esters created during fermentation.

As the beer passes over the tongue, you will detect more malt, hop and fruit notes. The tongue spots sweetness, bitterness and saltiness. Finally, let the beer slip down the back of the tongue and throat to appreciate the aftertaste or finish. This is an important part of the tasting process, as a beer that starts malty on the aroma may finish with a pronounced degree of hop bitterness, or vice versa.

If you are organising a beer tasting, you will need a good supply of glasses. If you reuse glasses, rinse them thoroughly between beers. You should also have a good supply of uncarbonated mineral water to drink between beers, plus plates with crackers or other kinds of dry biscuits to cleanse the palate further. Many tasters like to have small squares of cheese as well, but these should be of the mild variety, as the likes of blue Stilton or mature Cheddar are too overpowering, especially if you are tasting delicately flavoured beers.

You should involve only one style of beer in a tasting: there is little point in attempting to match, say, pale Pilsners with English barley wines. Using the beers mentioned in this book, you could arrange tastings of Bocks, wheat beers, Belgian ales or English pale ales.

Draught beer can be difficult to handle for a tasting at home. If you know a pub or bar with a friendly landlord and an upstairs room, you could arrange a tasting there. In Britain, many brewers of cask-conditioned beer supply their products for home drinking in polypins containing 18 or 36 pints. Follow the simple instructions on the box to set up the beer, which must be allowed to settle for 24 hours. It is crucial that cask beer is kept in a cool place with a temperature of 11–12˚C (52–55˚F). The Wells and Young's Brewery in Bedford, England, has pioneered cask beer in a take-home can containing eight pints of Bombardier Best Bitter. The cans are easy to set up and serve from, and other brewers may follow the example.

Bottled beers should be kept in a cool place prior to serving. Many brewers will suggest a serving temperature on the bottle label. A simple rule of thumb is that lager beers should be served cold, ales served cool: 8–9˚C (46–48˚F) for lager, 11–12˚C (52–55˚F) for ales. You will have to experiment with your refrigerator and a thermometer to see how long beers should be stored. Beers containing sediment should be stored upright unless the bottles have corks, in which case they should be laid down to keep the corks moist. Sedimented bottles should be opened and left to stand for five or 10 minutes to vent off some of the carbonation created by bottle conditioning and to stop the beer 'fobbing' or gushing out of the container. Strong ales such as barley wines can be served at a slightly higher temperature of around 13–14˚C (55–57˚F) to allow the full aroma and palate to develop.

You will need tasting sheets with the names of each beer and with columns that allow the tasters to give marks out of 10 for appearance (clarity), aroma, palate, finish, and adherence to style. With some styles, you may wish to add marks for colour. Many beers called India Pale Ale, for example, are too dark, while a true Irish Dry Stout should be jet-black but with just a tiny hint of ruby around the edge when held against the light.

Above all... enjoy!

India Pale Ales

India Pale Ale is a conundrum. As the title is often abbreviated to IPA, many people are unaware of the full name. Others call it *Indian* Pale Ale, assuming its origins lie in the subcontinent. To muddy the waters further, many modern IPAs are both too dark and too weak to deserve the title. The first IPAs were truly pale, using no coloured malts, and had robust strengths of 6% or more. I have assembled some beers I believe to be true to the style: to mix the grain, if not the metaphor, I have sorted the wheat from the chaff.

These beers underscore the way in which India Pale Ale transformed brewing on a world scale. Until the Industrial Revolution of the 18th and 19th centuries, all beers were brown in colour, as barley malt was roasted, or 'kilned', by wood fires that tended to scorch the grain. The result was brown malt, which, in turn, produced brown beer. Small amounts of paler malts were made using coal fires, but coal gave off gas that impregnated the malt with unpleasant flavours. As soon as coke—coal without the gas— was developed, pale malt started to be made in substantial quantities.

Brewers in Britain welcomed this development. They could produce attractive, sparkling pale beers, quite different in taste and appeal from darker porters and stouts, using malt that had a higher proportion of the natural enzymes that turn starch into sugar during the brewing process. As a result, it took smaller amounts of pale malt to make beer. This was a significant factor when brewing became a fiercely competitive industry rather than a homespun trade carried out by publicans in their cellars.

The term IPA was coined because the first pale, strong beers were made for export to India and eventually to other parts of the British Empire. An East London brewer called Hodgson, who had easy access to the East India Docks, made the first 'India Ale' at the end of the 18th century. But he was soon supplanted by bigger brewers such as Allsopp, Bass and Worthington, all based in Burton-on-Trent in the English Midlands.

As a result of the Napoleonic Wars (1799–1815), the Burton brewers had lost their lucrative trade in nut-brown ales exported to Russia and the Baltic, and were desperate for new foreign markets. They were able to replicate Hodgson's beer and to improve on it with the help of the spring waters of the Trent Valley, which are rich in the sulphates that tease out the best character from malt and hops.

During the early decades of the 19th century, the Burton brewers built a substantial trade with India and then moved on to Australia, the Caribbean and even the United States with their new pale beers. In order to withstand the rigours of long sea journeys, the brewers realised that the best defence against spoilage was alcohol and hops. The natural acids, resins and tannins in the cone of the hop plant are anti-bacterial and helped keep the beer, which was stored in wooden casks, free from infection. Prodigious amounts of hops—four times as many as in a conventional beer—were used.

The heyday of India Pale Ale was brief. By the end of the 19th century it had been replaced in most of the British colonies by German or German-inspired lager beers, which were less bitter and kept cool by refrigeration. The British brewers turned to an offspring—pale ale—for the domestic market, but IPA lingered on as a speciality for some brewers.

Today IPA is enjoying a resurgence of interest on both sides of the Atlantic, and some—in the finest traditions of the style—even make the sea journey.

Burton Bridge Empire Pale Ale

Source: Burton Bridge Brewery, Burton-on-Trent, Staffordshire, England
Strength: 7.5%
Website: www.burtonbridgebrewery.co.uk

Let us begin at the beginning with a beer from Burton, one that has a terrier-like devotion to the style. Burton Bridge is a micro-brewery behind an inn, or 'brewery tap'. The company owns three other pubs in the small town that was once the centre and great innovator of British brewing. The owners, Geoff Mumford and Bruce Wilkinson, worked for the national group Allied Breweries before launching Burton Bridge in 1982, and have many years' experience of the brewing art.

Empire Pale Ale is matured in cask for a minimum of three months in the brewery to replicate the length of a sea journey from England to India in the 19th century. The beer is then bottled with live yeast and will continue to improve and mature under glass.

In the exact style of Victorian times, it is brewed from Pipkin pale malt and brewing sugar, with no darker grains, and is hopped with English Challenger and Styrian Goldings hops from Slovenia (British brewers often used sailing ships to bring both malt and hops from abroad). A pronounced orange fruit note from the hops and house yeast dominate the aroma and palate. The fruitiness is balanced by biscuity malt and deep, tangy, spicy and resiny hops, with a long and lingering finish with juicy malt, tart fruit and bitter hops.

The beer won the Guardian/CAMRA Bottle-Conditioned Beer of the Year award in 1997. It's worth buying for the 'British Raj' label alone, which shows an army officer and a cricketer enjoying tankards of beer. Both IPA and cricket were introduced to the Indian subcontinent by the Raj; cricket today is the greater passion.

TASTING NOTES
Appearance
Aroma
Taste
Overall score

TASTING NOTES
Appearance
Aroma
Taste
Overall score

Caledonian Deuchars IPA

Source: Caledonian Brewing Company, Edinburgh, Scotland
Strength: 3.8%
Website: www.caledonian-brewery.co.uk

The Caledonian Brewery dates from 1869. It draws on the hard waters that bubble up from red sandstone underground strata known as the Charmed Circle, which made Edinburgh a great brewing centre and enabled it to compete with Burton as a leading producer of IPA.

Robert Deuchar owned a brewery that closed in the 1960s, and Caledonian acquired the name for this pale bronze beer that is both succulent and controversial: Scottish IPAs were darker and maltier than the English style, as can be seen in McEwan's Export, whereas Deuchars is pale with a fine hop character. It's brewed from Scottish Golden Promise malt with a touch of darker crystal: at 12.5 units of colour on the brewers' scale, this is a pale beer by any standards. The hops are English Fuggles and Styrian Goldings. The beer has a luscious citrus fruit note on the aroma balanced by tart, spicy hops. Juicy malt, tart hops and tangy fruit dominate the mouth, followed by a long finish, in which peppery hops linger with pronounced lemon fruit and biscuity malt.

At just 3.8%, the beer has a modest strength for the style; a filtered bottled version is widely available in supermarkets and specialist beer shops at 4.4%. The draught beer was named Champion Beer of Britain by CAMRA in 2002, since when sales have soared.

Some of the character of Caledonian's beers comes from the unique boiling coppers fired by direct gas flame (originally coal). The brewers claim this creates a good 'rolling boil' when hops are added to the sweet extract, draws intense bitterness and aroma from the hops, and stops the sugary extract, or wort, becoming stewed.

Concertina Bengal Tiger

Source: Concertina Brewery, Mexborough, South Yorkshire, England
Strength: 4.6%
Website: None

TASTING NOTES
Appearance
Aroma
Taste
Overall score

As befits the style, you will have to travel to sample Bengal Tiger, as it's available only in a workingmen's club in Mexborough and a few pubs in the immediate area. The club's full title is the Concertina Band Club—known locally as 'The Tina'—and it's the only private club left in Britain that brews on the premises.

As the name suggests, the club was founded (in the 1880s) to enable members to sustain a band based solely on the concertina. The Mexborough band was of high repute: it gave a private performance to King Edward VII and won a thousand guineas prize in a competition at London's Alexandra Palace in 1906. Concertina bands have long since disappeared and the Mexborough club went into decline until Kenneth Pickering bought it in 1986. He encouraged his son Andy, a keen home brewer, to install a brewery in the club cellar.

The brewery was launched in 1992 with equipment from Mansfield Brewery in Nottingham and from Whitbread. It can brew just eight barrels of beer at a time, with a mash tun, copper, four fermenters and settling tanks. Andy uses pale and crystal malts, and Fuggles, Styrian Goldings and Target hops in his beers. He started with Club Bitter and Old Dark Attic but he always wanted to brew an IPA. A member of the club found an image of a Bengal tiger on his computer and he designed a clip for the handpump on the bar. The beer has a complex aroma of biscuity malt, spicy hops and tangy fruit, with a malty/hoppy palate underscored by citrus fruit. Tart fruit, juicy malt and bitter hops dominate the finish.

To sample the beer, you can enter the club at 9a Dolcliffe Road, Mexborough, by signing the visitors' book or pay £2 for a year's membership. The club is open 12–4 and 7–11 Monday to Saturday, and 7–10.30 on Sunday. The club is just off the high street and a few minutes' walk from Mexborough railway station.

Goose Island IPA

Source: Goose Island Beer Company, Chicago, Illinois, USA
Strength: 5.9%
Website: www.gooseisland.com

TASTING NOTES
Appearance
Aroma
Taste
Overall score

John and Gregg Hall, father and son, built a Chicago brew-pub and turned it into a major commercial company, revered by beer lovers throughout the US via the Beer Across America Club, which offers micro-brewed beers to members.

The original brew-pub, with a large bar room with burnished mahogany fittings, is at 1800 North Clybourn, while a second bar and brewery opened in Wrigleyville at 3535 North Clark Street. Goose Island, named after an island in the Chicago River, is best known for its copper-coloured Honkers Ale (see page 90), but the IPA is the standout beer, arguably the finest modern interpretation of the 19th-century style.

The Halls don't stint on ingredients for their beers, using both North American and European malts, and Cascade and Mount Hood hops from the US, Czech Saaz and Styrian Goldings. Water is drawn from Lake Michigan and carbon filtered. Yeast strains for ales, lagers and wheat beers are imported from Europe to ensure the correct aromas and flavours.

The bottle-fermented IPA is true to style in two important particulars: it is truly pale, with just 10 colour units (only fractionally darker than a Pilsner), and heavily hopped, with 58 units of bitterness, making it one of the bitterest beers in the world. It has an entrancing aroma of bitter oranges, spicy hops and a cracker biscuit maltiness. In the mouth a full, rich fruitiness balances the bitter edge of the hops, and there is a superb underlying juicy malt note. The persistent finish has an iron-like intensity from the hops, more bitter, tangy fruit and a lingering, delightful malt character. (For British stockists, contact James Clay & Sons: beersolutions.co.uk.)

Hogs Back BSA

Source: Hogs Back Brewery, Tongham, Surrey, England
Strength: 4.5%
Website: www.hogsback.co.uk

BSA stands for Burma Star Ale. It was first brewed in 1995 as a tribute to the Burma Star Association, which marks the contribution made by soldiers and prisoners of war involved in the Burma campaign in World War Two. Stocks of beer are sold at the Imperial War Museum in London, and a donation from each sale goes to BSA's welfare funds.

Hogs Back is one of Britain's most successful micro-breweries. It was launched in 1992 in restored farm buildings that date from the 18th century. As well as a wide range of cask beers, Hogs Back produces several bottle-fermented beers that stand out from the crowd as a result of both their quality and the gold-embossed labels designed in-house by one of the brewery's partners. Their beers can be bought in local branches of Sainsbury's, at the on-site shop or by mail order: see website.

BSA is brewed from Maris Otter pale malt, with touches of crystal and chocolate malt, which combine to produce a deep bronze colour with a hint of red. The hops are the traditional English ale varieties: Fuggles and Goldings. The result is a beer with a deep and abiding aroma of crisp, nutty malt, orange fruit and spicy, resinous hops, with a palate of biscuity malt, tangy fruit and bitter hops. The finish lingers with pronounced orange fruit notes, rich malt and a firm underpinning of bitter, peppery hops.

The label depicts servicemen at the time of the Burma campaign and carries the moving wartime lines: 'When you go home tell them of us and say— for your tomorrow we gave our today.'

TASTING NOTES
Appearance
Aroma
Taste
Overall score

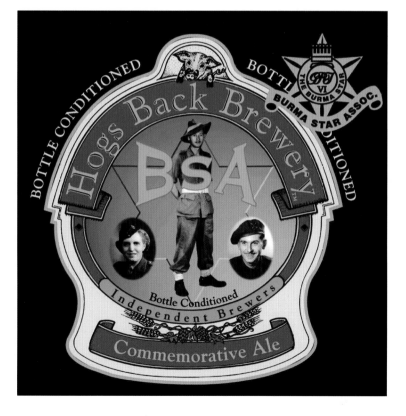

Marston's Old Empire

Source: Marston, Thompson & Evershed, Burton-on-Trent, Staffordshire, England
Strength: 5.7%
Website: www.wdb.co.uk

TASTING NOTES
Appearance
Aroma
Taste
Overall score

Curiously, Marstons has been brewing in Burton since 1834 but never made an IPA until it launched Old Empire in 2003. Even more curious is the fact that the current site is Marston's second in Burton and it was bought from the London brewery Mann Crossman & Paulin, which had moved to Burton specifically to brew IPA for the London market. Marston's concentrated instead on a range of beers led by the world-famous Pedigree pale ale (see page 59) that is still fermented in the 'union rooms' packed with giant oak casks. Yeast from the unions is used to produce Old Empire.

Marston's invited me to give my views on several trial brews and my response was always the same: 'More hops!' The beer that emerged in both cask and bottle has 40 units of bitterness and I would still prefer a tad more.

It is made with Optic pale malt only and has 12 units of colour. The hop varieties are English Fuggles and Goldings and American Cascade. It's a rich and luscious beer. It starts with the usual sulphury note you expect from Burton-brewed beers as a result of the high levels of sulphates in the water. Floral hops, succulent malt, vanilla and light citrus fruit soon break through on the nose, followed by juicy malt, hop resins and tart fruit in the mouth. The long finish is packed with biscuit malt, spicy hops and lemon fruit, and is wonderfully quenching.

It took Marston's more than a century and a half to make an IPA but it was worth waiting for.

Meantime India Pale Ale

Source: Meantime Brewing Company, London, England
Strength: 7.5%
Website: www.meantimebrewing.com

Alastair Hook is not afraid to raise hackles: 'We are the only British brewery to make a true IPA,' he says. It's a claim that may not make him a welcome visitor to Burton-on-Trent but he bases it on the fact that the first 'India Ale' was brewed in London by George Hodgson late in the 18th century. Meantime is in Greenwich, just across the Thames from Bow, from where Hodgson exported his pale ale to India. Alastair feels he can almost reach out and touch brewing history.

For a young man, he has a remarkable brewing pedigree. He trained at two renowned brewing schools, Heriot-Watt in Edinburgh and Weihenstephan in Munich, before running breweries in Kent, London and Manchester. In 1999 he founded Meantime in Greenwich, close to the Meridian. With his background, he has created such classic European styles as Dunkles, Helles, Kölsch and both Belgian and German wheat beers, while his London Porter is produced with the addition of chocolate and coffee.

Meantime IPA is brewed with Maris Otter pale malt and Fuggles and Goldings hops: there are minute amounts of crystal and Munich malts added for colour balance. Alastair says: 'The beer is brewed with as many hops as we can physically get in the copper. We then fill the lauter tun [filtration vessel] with more hops for a further infusion. And then we dry hop with even more hops using our own unique circulation process to ensure maximum contact between the hops and the body of the beer. All this gives us a final hopping rate of well over 2lbs of hops per barrel.' The bitterness units are literally stunning: between 75 and 80.

The bottle-conditioned beer, in an attractive corked and cradled bottle, has a golden colour and a superb aroma of spicy hop resins, tart orange fruit and rich malt. The palate is deep and complex, with peppery hops, tart citrus fruit, juicy malt and a hint of marzipan, followed by a long and bittersweet finish, with rich malt balancing the profound hop bitterness and a continuing marzipan note.

TASTING NOTES
Appearance
Aroma
Taste
Overall score

Pike IPA

Source: Pike Brewery, Seattle, Washington, USA
Strength: 6%
Website: www.pikebrewing.com

TASTING NOTES
Appearance
Aroma
Taste
Overall score

Originally called Pike Place Brewery after its first location in Seattle's restaurant and food market area, the pub and brewery have moved to 1415 First Avenue with a considerably up-rated production of 15,000 barrels a year. The brewery was founded by Charles Finkel's Merchant du Vin company that now specialises in the fruit of the barley rather than the vine: it is the major importer of Samuel Smith's beers into the US from Britain, for example.

Head brewer Drew Cluley has fashioned a stunningly hoppy India Pale Ale, using Chinook, Magnum and Willamette American hop varieties and pale, crystal, Munich and cara malts. Munich malt gives the signature red/bronze colour to the famous Oktoberfest beers of the Bavarian capital, while cara malt is similar to crystal, a stewed malt that gives a nutty flavour to beer.

The finished beer has an appealing burnished brass colour with a massive burst of floral hops and grapefruit, typical in particular of the characteristics of the Chinook. Underlying the hops is a rich, nutty and cracker biscuit maltiness. Juicy, quenching malt, citrus fruit and bitter hops combine in the mouth, followed by a punchy finish with creamy malt, earthy, resinous hops and tangy fruit. It's a memorable beer and the perfect companion for the fresh food in local restaurants.

Shipyard Fuggles IPA

Source: Shipyard Brewing Co, Portland, Maine, USA
Strength: 5.8%
Website: www.shipyard.com

Shipyard's beers are all about yeast. Alan Pugsley is a young British brewer who trained at the Ringwood Brewery in Hampshire under Peter Austin, renowned as the father of British micro-brewing: Ringwood was one of the earliest new-wave micros in the late 1970s. When Pugsley moved to the United States, he reached an agreement with Ringwood to reproduce its Old Thumper strong ale—one-time winner of CAMRA's Champion Beer of Britain award—along with the Hampshire brewery's yeast when he created Shipyard Brewing in 1992.

The Ringwood yeast strain gives a rich and rewarding fruitiness to Pugsley's beers. The current brewery, which is the second site used, is close to the home of the poet Henry Wadsworth Longfellow, as well as the city's historic shipyard. An IPA makes sense in a city with such powerful links to the sea.

Fuggles IPA is a 'single varietal' beer, which means it is brewed with just one hop, the English Fuggle. The hops give a characteristic earthy, resinous, spicy and piny aroma and flavour to the beer. The grains are pale, crystal and malted wheat that combine to produce a biscuity, nutty and creamy note. Malt and hops are underscored by the distinctive orange fruitiness of the Ringwood yeast culture. This is a much-travelled culture: before Peter Austin founded Ringwood and then travelled the world building small breweries, he was head brewer at the Hull Brewery in North-east England and brought samples of their yeast south with him. The giant American brewer Miller has taken a stake in Shipyard: let us hope the character of the beers is not dumbed down.

TASTING NOTES
Appearance
Aroma
Taste
Overall score

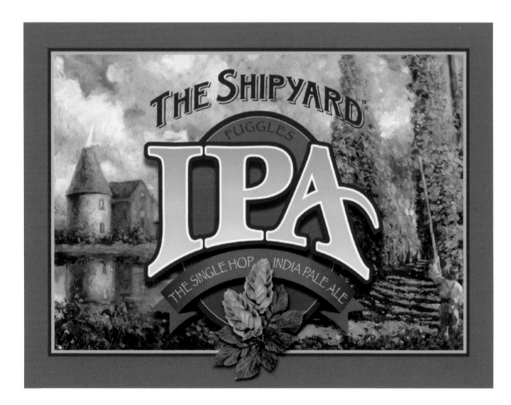

Thornbridge Jaipur IPA

Source: Thornbridge Brewery, Bakewell, Derbyshire, England
Strength: 5.9%
Website: www.thornbridgebrewery.co.uk

TASTING NOTES
Appearance
Aroma
Taste
Overall score

Thornbridge is another example of the remarkable success of Britain's small craft breweries. It was founded in 2005 using a 10-barrel plant at Thornbridge Hall, a once stately home that had fallen into disrepair but has been revived by Jim and Emma Harrison, who had made fortunes from industry and commerce. Jim, as well as being a sharp businessman, has a genuine passion for beer. He was given sound brewing advice by Dave Wickett at Kelham Island Brewery in Sheffield. As a result, Jim developed a number of fine beers with the skills of brewers Stefano Cossi from Italy and Kelly Ryan from New Zealand.

Jaipur IPA has been the brewery's great success. It won an amazing 48 awards from beer festivals and competitions in just four years and was the springboard for a new, enlarged brewery in the summer of 2009. It's based at Crompton Mill near Bakewell. The mill, in breathtakingly beautiful countryside in the Derbyshire Peak District, was the unlikely setting for Richard Arkwright's factory in the late 18th century. He harnessed the power of the River Derwent to make a spinning frame driven by water that helped power the industrial revolution.

The new brewery cost £1.6 million and will enable Thornbridge to produce 30,000 barrels of a beer year. It has its own bottling line that will allow IPA and other beers to be made available in bottle-conditioned form. With Stefano's background and contacts, the brewing kit was built in Italy and is a flexible one using mash mixers, lauter tuns and conical fermenters that will permit both ale and lager to be produced.

Stefano and Kelly use English malts and hops in most of their brews and Maris Otter pale malt is the bedrock of Jaipur. But the hops for the IPA are two American varieties, Cascade and Chinook. American hops in such a quintessentially English beer as India Pale Ale may seem odd but in fact Stefano and Kelly are following the 19th-century habit of British brewers, who imported both grain and hops from the United States.

As a result of the American influence, there is a luscious tropical fruit and grapefruit character to the beer on the nose and the palate. A delightful resinous hop note and tangy fruit are balanced by juicy malt in the mouth while the long finish has citrus fruit, sweet grain and bitter hops, finally ending dry. This is one of the finest examples of revivalist British IPAs and richly deserves its many awards.

Worthington's White Shield

Source: Coors Brewers, Burton-on-Trent, Staffordshire, England
Strength: 5.6%
Website: www.coorsbrewers.com

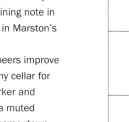

We finish this section with the granddaddy of IPAs. William Worthington was one of the great Burton brewing entrepreneurs of the 19th century who joined the scramble to export new pale ales to India and further afield.

Worthington's main claim to fame was the high quality of its bottled beers, a sector of the market that boomed when commercial glass-blowing developed in Victorian times. At one time, bottled beer accounted for more than half of Worthington's production. Although Worthington merged with Bass in the 1920s, its bottled beers continued to appear under its own name. In the 'keg revolution' days of the 1970s, when it was often difficult to find real draught beer in British pubs, White Shield, with its natural sediment of yeast, kept legions of beer lovers happy.

White Shield was shunted around various regional breweries when Bass lost interest in brewing, but it has now come home to Burton. The American brewing giant Coors bought the old Bass complex in 2000. This includes a small brewing plant in a former engine shed. The brewery, run by master brewer Steve Wellington, re-creates old Bass beers from the past, but White Shield is by far the biggest product. The brand has become so successful that in 2009 Coors moved production to its new brewery to cope with demand.

It's brewed from pale malt with a tiny amount of crystal and hopped with English Challenger, Fuggles and Goldings. It is interesting to note that, as the classic IPA, it has 26 units of colour, making it quite dark for the modern interpretation of the style. The hops create 40 units of bitterness. This wonderfully enticing and complex beer has spices, peppery hops, light apple fruit and sulphur on the nose, with juicy malt, tart and tangy hops, hop resins and spices in the mouth. The lingering finish has a bitter hop character but is balanced by rich malt and apple fruit: apple is a defining note in Burton pale ales and is also found in Marston's Pedigree (see page 59).

To prove that bottle-fermented beers improve with age, I kept a White Shield in my cellar for 10 years. When opened, it was darker and fruitier than a young version, with a muted hop bitterness. Buy some and lay some down.

TASTING NOTES
Appearance
Aroma
Taste
Overall score

Pilsners

Pilsner, in common with India Pale Ale, transformed brewing in the 19th century, but its impact was more profound and enduring. The name comes from the Bohemian city of Pilsen, now the great industrial heartbeat of the modern Czech Republic. It was not the first lager beer but it was the original golden beer made by the new system of cold fermentation and ageing. For centuries, brewers in central Europe had struggled to keep beer free from infection during hot summers. In Bavaria, beers were stored in deep, icy caves in the Alps. (The German word for 'store' is *lager*.) The cold kept wild yeasts and bacteria at bay, and fermentation was slower due to the low temperatures.

This empirical method was turned into a commercial system as a result of the Industrial Revolution and the invention of ice-making machines. Following primary fermentation, beer was stored in cellars deep beneath breweries and kept cold by ice packed in rooms above. The yeast worked slowly, turning remaining sugars into alcohol with a lively, natural carbonation.

The first commercial lager beers, which were brewed in Munich and surrounding areas of southern Germany, were dubbed 'Bavarian beer'. They were dark brown in colour, as the method for brewing pale malt that had been developed in England had not yet reached central Europe.

Change was sudden in the 1840s. The spark came in neighbouring Bohemia when the disgruntled citizens of Pilsen poured an entire batch of the local brewery's beer down the drains. It was sour and undrinkable, and a clamour went up to open a brewery that would use the new methods developed in Munich. Local businessmen and tavern owners clubbed together to raise the funds to build the Burghers' [Citizens'] Brewery. A modern malt kiln was imported from England to enable pale malt to be made, while a Bavarian brewer called Josef Grolle, who was skilled in the arts of lager brewing, was hired.

Grolle's first brew appeared in 1842 and it was a sensation. Its golden appearance and clarity in the glass were appealing, while its complexity of aromas and flavours, at once rich and malty yet enticingly hoppy and bitter, entranced all who drank it.

The beer was called in the German fashion Pilsner, meaning 'from Pilsen', just as a Hamburger steak came originally from Hamburg and a Frankfurter sausage from Frankfurt. Pilsner's reputation spread rapidly, aided by canals and a new railway system that carried supplies to all the great cities of the Austrian Empire, across into Bavaria and up the Elbe to Hamburg and beyond. A Pilsen Beer Train left every morning for Vienna. The beer became a cult drink in Paris, and by 1874 the style had reached the United States.

While the conservative Bavarians were slow to switch from dark to golden lagers, brewers in other parts of Germany met the consumer demand for the new pale style. A sudden rush of competing Pilsner beers forced the Bohemian brewery in 1898 to register its beer as Pilsner Urquell (*Urquell* means 'original source' in German); it is known in Czech as Plzensky Prazdroj.

But the brewery stable door had been left open too long and the dray horses had bolted. Just before World War One, the Czechs took several German brewers to court in an attempt to stop them using the term Pilsner. The result was a compromise. The Germans agreed either to shorten the term to Pils or to state the place of origin on their label to avoid any suggestion the beer came from Pilsen. The Rhineland brewery Bitburger, the first to brew a German Pilsner, has ever since called its beer Bitburger Pils. Others have adapted the spelling slightly to Pilsener. These tinkerings had little effect. Most of the world thought Pilsner was a German beer, a misconception deepened by the Cold War, when Czechoslovakia disappeared behind the Iron Curtain as a Soviet satellite.

As lager brewing spread throughout the world, more and more Pils beers appeared. Many are travesties of the original. They are often too pale— a true Czech Pilsner is burnished gold with a hint of colour in its cheeks. A true Pilsner is never bland but has the classic signature of a floral, hoppy aroma and a dry and bitter—often intensely bitter—finish.

My first visit to Pilsner Urquell in the 1980s was a revelation. Both primary fermentation and lagering were in wooden vessels. Secondary fermentation and ageing took place in giant oak casks deep below ground in sandstone cellars. The casks were lined with pitch, which helped create a natural carbonation and a rich aroma and flavour. I learnt at both Pilsner Urquell and other Czech breweries that ageing beer in horizontal tanks or casks leads to a slower second fermentation, with some unfermented sugars left in the beer for fullness of palate. Today many

brewers have switched to upright conical tanks with faster and shorter ageing. The result, even at Pilsner Urquell, is beer with diminished character.

For this section of the book, I have chosen a handful of beers that I consider to be true to style, but I had to think long and hard before including the 'Original Source Pilsner'.

ABOVE
A Belle Epoque promotion for the original golden lager from Pilsen.

LEFT
Christoffel bier from the Netherlands is a fine example of a full-bodied modern Pilsner.

Bitburger Pils

Source: Bitburger Brauerei Theo Simon, Bitburg/Eifel, Germany
Strength: 4.8%
Website: www.bitburger.de

TASTING NOTES
Appearance
Aroma
Taste
Overall score

Bitburger not only brews a fine example of a Pilsner beer but it also played a central role in the development of the style. It was the first brewery outside Bohemia to label a beer Pilsner, an act that infuriated the Czechs. The result was a court case just before World War One that led to an agreement that German brewers would include the place of origin on the label of their Pilsner beers to avoid any suggestion that the beers came from Pilsen.

Bitburger and most other German brewers went a step further and shortened Pilsner to Pils. For decades the label has made it clear the beer comes from Bitburg, a small town in the Eifel lake district, close to both the Luxembourg border and the historic city of Trier, birthplace of Karl Marx.

The company was founded in 1817 by Theo Simon, whose head, topped by a smoking cap, still adorns the label. It was a humble farmhouse brewery that at first made warm fermenting beers, but by 1884 was producing a golden lager, using ice from the lakes for cold conditioning. Its fortunes were boosted when a rail line was built to supply the Prussian army with cannons from the steelworks at Saarbrücken. The Simon family, which still owns the company, used the rail links to export its beer to northern Germany. The original brewery, with fine copper vessels, is in the centre of Bitburg and continues to make some beer, but the main production unit, built in the 1980s, is on a greenfield site outside the town.

Enormous care is devoted to selecting the finest raw ingredients: Alexis, Arena and Steiner spring barleys, and Hersbrucker, Hüller, Perle and Tettnang hops, plus a small amount of the locally grown Holsthum variety. The beer has three hop additions in the kettle and 38 units of bitterness.

Bitburger is lagered for six to eight weeks and emerges with a rich toasted malt nose balanced by floral hops and light citrus fruit. Juicy malt and tangy hops dominate the palate, while the long finish has a delicious bitter-sweet note of biscuity malt, piny hops and light fruit before finally becoming dry.

Bitburger Pils is widely exported and uses the famous advertising line '*Bitte Ein Bit*'— a Bit Please.

Brand-UP

Source: Brand Bierbrouwerij, Wijlre,
Netherlands
Strength: 5.5%
Website: www.brand.nl

Brand is the oldest brewery in the Netherlands,
dating from 1340, when it was part of the estate
of the local lord. According to legend, the peasants
on the estate spent more time drinking beer than
attending church services and the brewery was
sold. It came under the control of the Brand family
in 1743—what happened in the intervening
centuries is unclear—and the brewery was
modernised in the 19th century to switch to cold
fermentation. In the 1970s, the company became
the official supplier of beer to the Dutch royal
family, which enabled it to be called the Royal
Brand Brewery, though it lost the title in 1990.
In 1989, Brand became part of the Heineken
group but it enjoys considerable autonomy.

Brand makes a Premium Pilsener, brewed
from 90% pale malt and 10% maize and aged for
42 days. But, unusually, Brand makes a second
Pilsner. Brand-UP is not a soft drink: UP stands
for Urtyp Pilsner, or Original Pilsner. The name
is not designed to cause confusion with Pilsner
Urquell but to emphasise that it's true to the
style. Several Dutch and German brewers use
Ur in their beer names to stress their originality
or dedication to style.

Brand-UP is an all-malt brew and is hopped with
German Hersbrucker, Spalt and Tettnang hops,
varieties known as 'noble hops' as a result of
their fine and delicate aromas. The beer is aged
for up to 56 days, and has 36 to 38 bitterness
units. It has a superb floral hop aroma with gently
toasted malt and lemon fruit, with hop resins,
juicy malt and tart fruit in the mouth. The finish
is long, finely balanced between hop bitterness,
citrus fruit and mellow malt. On a visit to
Maastricht, I introduced some sceptical CAMRA
members to Brand-UP and they were entranced.
Brand beers are fresh and unpasteurised. The
head brewer says: 'Pasteurisation serves to
lengthen the shelf life of a beer but only marginally
and at enormous costs to the taste and aroma of
the beer.' Amen to that.

Christoffel Blond

Source: Bierbrouwerij St Christoffel,
Roermond, Netherlands
Strength: 6%
Website: www.christoffelbier.nl

By alphabetical good fortune, the Brand brewery
is followed by a second brewery in Dutch Limburg
that was founded by a member of the Brand
family. Leo Brand studied at the world-famous
brewing faculty of Weihenstephan near Munich
and then worked in the German brewing industry.
In 1986, he returned home to launch his own
brewery behind his house in the old coal-mining
town of Roermond, where St Christopher is the
patron saint. Brand moved to a new site in 1995
but kept the handsome domed and brick-clad
copper kettle that he had found in a barn. He
brewed strictly to the German *Reinheitsgebot*,
the 16th-century Purity Law that permits only
malted barley or wheat, hops, yeast and water:
no sugars, chemicals or cheap 'adjuncts' such
as rice or corn are permitted.

Brand was so dissatisfied with many beers
labelled Pilsner that he called his interpretation
Christoffel Bier, which was later changed to the
even more undistinguished Blond. Don't let
the name put you off: this is one of the finest
modern Pilsners, bursting and booming with hop
character and a massive 45 units of bitterness.
It's brewed from pale barley malt only and hopped
with Hallertau and Hersbrucker hops that give
a superb piny and resinous aroma, with toasted
malt and spicy hops in the mouth, followed by
a finish of great length that becomes dry and
bitter, with hints of iodine, rich malt and a late
burst of citrus fruit.

When some drinkers complained the beer
was too bitter, Leo Brand declared: 'I am not
brewing to please everyone!' With that dedication
to quality ringing in drinkers' ears, he retired in
2001, but his successors have remained true
to his beliefs.

TASTING NOTES
Appearance
Aroma
Taste
Overall score

TASTING NOTES
Appearance
Aroma
Taste
Overall score

Grolsch Pilsener

Source: Grolsche Bierbrouwerij, Nederland, Boeklo, Netherlands
Strength: 5%
Website: www.grolsch.nl

TASTING NOTES
Appearance
Aroma
Taste
Overall score

This book proves, I hope, that small is beautiful. Grolsch is one of the few large breweries to figure in these pages but in Dutch terms it is a minnow compared to the global giant Heineken/Amstel. It has won a deserved international reputation for the quality of its beers by concentrating on good brewing practice and the finest raw materials.

In 2004, Grolsch moved from it historic sites at Enschede and Groenlo to a new brewery at Boeklo. Brewing water is pumped 7km (4 miles) from Enschede to ensure consistency of product, and Perle hops are sourced from the German

hop-growing area of Hallertau. The only significant change to the beer is that the brewery has phased out the use of a small amount of corn [maize].

In spite of the company's close proximity to the German border, it has concentrated on Dutch and international sales. But it is now keen to build sales in Germany, where it wants to adhere to the *Reinheitsgebot*, or Pure Beer Law, that forbids the use of any grains apart from malted barley and wheat.

Grolsch can trace its history back to 1615, but the modern company was the result of a merger in 1922 of two separate breweries in Enschede and Groenlo. It's now the second biggest brewing group in the Netherlands after Heineken/Amstel, though that's a bit like saying Manchester United and Oldham Athletic are both professional football clubs in North-west England. Grolsch is no slouch, though. The new site can produce 3.4m hectolitres (74.8m gallons) of beer a year: 600 bottles and 550 kegs are filled every hour.

The Pilsener is made from a complex blend of spring barleys grown in Belgium, England, France, Germany and the Netherlands. It is lagered for 10 weeks and has 27 units of bitterness. It has a grassy hop resins aroma balanced by lightly toasted malt, with a good tingle of hop bitterness and juicy malt on the tongue followed by a quenching, dry and gently bitter finish with a good underpinning of malt.

The beer is best known for its traditional 'swing-top' stoppered bottle. Drinkers in Britain are advised to drink this version, as conventional bottles and draught versions are brewed under licence by Coors in Burton-on-Trent. The swing-top beer is not pasteurised, which adds to its appeal and freshness. The survival of this delightfully old-fashioned bottle is due to consumer preference in the area of the Netherlands where Grolsch is based. People there have a reputation for being careful with their cash and prefer to drink only half a bottle at a time and reseal it to keep it in good condition for the following day.

Jever Pilsener

Source: Friesische Brauhaus zu Jever, Friesland, Germany
Strength: 4.9%
Website: www.jever.de

The old moated town of Jever (pronounced 'Yay-ver') and its brewery are in German Friesland, the region with a group of islands divided among Germany, Denmark and the Netherlands. The islands, which once formed an independent buffer state, were the setting for the first modern spy story, Erskine Childer's *The Riddle of the Sands*.

The Frisians enjoy bitter drinks, and Jever Pilsener, with a redoubtable 44 units of bitterness, satisfies their tastes: the word '*Herb*' on the label means bitter. The brewery was founded in 1848 by Diedrich Konig and would be dubbed a micro today. It soon passed to Theo Fetkoter, who not only expanded the business but also drew water from a nearby well. The well is still used today, and its silky softness helps create the beer's taste and allows the aroma and bitterness of the hops to shine through.

The brewery has had a seesaw history. It has been taken over several times and is now part of the Brau & Brunnen brewing group. During World War Two, it was starved of raw materials. It recovered and was able to expand as a result of the growing popularity of Pilsner beers.

Jever Pilsener is made from pale malt and is hopped with Hallertau and Tettnang German varieties. First-time drinkers should be warned that this beer has an uncompromising and shattering bitterness. It has a herbal, grassy and resinous aroma balanced by toasted malt and a faint hint of honey sweetness. Bitter hops burst on the tongue, while the finish has an iron-like bitter intensity with only a small walk-on part for malt.

The beer is the perfect companion for the fish dishes that dominate the cuisine in Friesland.

TASTING NOTES
Appearance
Aroma
Taste
Overall score

Malt Shovel James Squire Original Pilsener

Source: Camperdown, New South Wales, Australia
Strength: 5%
Website: www.malt-shovel.com.au

Only the Australians would name a brewery and its beers after a convict, recalling their colonial past and the infamous British practice of transporting 'criminals', often on trumped-up charges, Down Under. James Squire from Kingston in Surrey was arrested in 1785 and transported for the heinous crime of stealing chickens. While he was still a convict, he started to brew ale for the governor of New South Wales. When he was freed he was encouraged to brew commercially to counteract the illicit importing of rum. By 1805 Squire had successfully grown the first hops in the country and a year later he had opened a new brewery on the shores of the Parramatta River at Kissing Point. He followed this by building the Malt Shovel Tavern between Parramatta and Sydney. He is commemorated as the father of Australian brewing.

Chuck Hahn, an American with a love of Pilsner beers, built the modern Malt Shovel Brewery, which is now part of the Lion Nathan group. Unlike most Australian lagers, which are brewed with substantial amounts of cane sugar and are syrupy sweet as a result, Hahn's Original Pilsener uses pale and Munich malts without any brewing sugars. The hop varieties are Belgian and Czech Saaz. The delectable beer has a floral, herbal and spicy hop aroma, with mellow malt and tart hops in the mouth, and a lingering quenching finish that finally becomes dry with hop bitterness dominating. Hahn pays tribute to 'the industrious people of Plzen [Pilsen]' on the bottle label.

There are three James Squire brewpubs in Australia: two in Melbourne and one in Sydney. A fourth is planned for Perth.

TASTING NOTES
Appearance
Aroma
Taste
Overall score

Perla Chmielowa Premium Pils

Source: Lublin Breweries, Poland
Strength: 5%
Website: www.perla.pl

TASTING NOTES
Appearance
Aroma
Taste
Overall score

The history of the Lublin breweries has been as tumultuous and even as tragic as that of Poland itself. The group has two plants, one in Lublin, the second in Zwierzyniec. The brewery in Lublin, in the heart of Poland's hop-growing region, was founded by Karl Rudolf Vetter who bought a deserted monastery in 1844. A year later he opened a distillery on the site and followed it in 1846 with a brewery: he was restoring the monastic traditions of making beer and distilled spirits.

The second plant in Zwierzyniec has an even older ancestry. It dates from the 16th century and in 1806 started to produce English-style ales and porters: at the time there was great interest in Poland, Russia and the Baltic States in ales from England. As a result, strong Baltic porters and stouts became a major feature of the brewing industries in those countries.

In 1912, the breweries were bought by Sender Zylber, who also owned a brick works in the town. The Zylber family modernised the Lublin plant to make Pilsner-style lager. During World War Two the occupying German army took over the breweries and the Zylbers were sent to the Lublin ghetto. Some were moved to concentration camps, others were shot when the ghetto was razed by the retreating Nazis.

Following the war, the two breweries were taken in to state ownership by the communist regime in 1948. They returned to the private sector in the 1990s and now form a joint stock company. The group produces more than one million hectolitres a year and has avoided being bought by one of the global giants that have snapped up many breweries following the fall of communism.

Perla—Pearl—is the group's leading brand. It's brewed with pale barley malt and the pick of fragrant Lublin hops. 'Chmielowa' in the beer's name means hop in Polish. The beer has a toasted malt, floral hops and citrus fruit aroma. The palate is quenching, with juicy malt, bitter hop resins and lemon fruit. The finish becomes more hoppy and bitter but the hop character is balanced by rich grain and tangy fruit. It's a distinctive beer, hoppy and bitter by modern lager standards and one to treasure as the Pilsner-style beers of central and eastern Europe are dumbed down by international owners.

Pilsner Urquell

Source: Pilsner Urquell Brewery/Plzensky Prazdroj Pivovar, Pilsen,
Czech Republic
Strength: 4.4%
Website: www.pilsnerurquell.com

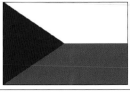

TASTING NOTES
Appearance
Aroma
Taste
Overall score

On my most recent visit to Prague, I dropped into the Café Slavia, a famous haunt of writers and artists. It stands across the road from the impressive bulk of the National Opera House that was built by public subscription in the 19th century in order that operas could be performed in Czech when German was the official colonial language of Bohemia. As my first beer arrived, the heavens opened and Prague was drenched in heavy rain for several hours. I had no choice but to spend the afternoon drinking Pilsner Urquell. There are worse ways to lose a few hours and there is no doubt it is still a fine beer. But it's not the beer it used to be. As it's the original Pilsner, once the benchmark for how a true golden lager should taste, it's worth asking the question: why?

At first, all is strictly and reassuringly traditional in Pilsen. The brewery entrance is a stupendous 19th-century Napoleonic arch (see picture, page 30) that proclaims the pride and pomp of the industrial age. In the brewhouse, malt is mashed in an intricate system of linked, burnished copper vessels. The system is known as triple decoction. Once mashing is underway, one third of the grain is transferred from the first vessel to a second, where the temperature is raised, and the grain is then returned to its first home. Another portion of grain is then moved to a third vessel where the temperature is raised still higher before the grain returns to the first vessel. The system ensures that enzymes in the grain fully convert starch to sugar, while protein that would cause a haze in the finished beer is degraded.

When mashing is complete, the sweet extract, or wort, is pumped to direct-flame boiling coppers where whole flower Zatec hops are added three times. The copper boil is protracted, around 2½ hours (90 minutes are the norm in most breweries). This long boil extracts as many acids, resins and tannins as possible to give the beer a fine aroma and palate, as well as ensuring the clarity of the beer. The hops create 40 units of bitterness.

Before major change arrived in the early 1990s, the hopped wort was transferred to 30-hectolitre (660-gallon) open oak tuns for primary fermentation. Then the 'green', or unfinished, beer was taken underground to deep, dank, cold sandstone cellars where ageing and secondary fermentation took place in 35-hectolitre (770-gallon) horizontal oak casks. The casks were lined with pitch; periodically each cask was taken to the brewery yard to be relined, the air rich with the autumnal, piny smell of the burning pitch.

In the early 1990s, following the fall of the communist regime and the privatisation of the brewery, the oak vessels were replaced in stages by conical steel fermenting vessels. Today a few of the old wooden vessels are confined to a small on-site museum as an example of the quaintness of the past.

We are now getting close to unravelling the mystery of the beer's change of character. The long ageing in pitch-lined wooden vessels,

allied to the soft spring waters used by the brewery, gave the beer a complex aroma and palate that was malty, creamy and buttery but underscored by a deep, firm bitterness and a fine floral, herbal, resinous hop aroma. Fermentation in conicals is faster and turns more malt sugars to alcohol; the result is a more austere beer in the North German style, with pronounced bitterness but a lack of the old malty complexity.

There is also controversy surrounding the length of time the beer is now aged. Pilsner Urquell claims that ageing lasts for 40 days and that has always been the case. But I am not alone in disputing this. In his *Beer Companion* (1993), Michael Jackson wrote: 'The beer is said to be lagered for between two and three months.' In two of my books, *The European Beer Almanac* and *The Ultimate Encyclopedia of Beer*, published in the early and mid-1990s respectively, I said even more emphatically that the beer was aged for 70 days. Michael and I did not make up the figures: we were given the information when we visited the brewery—separately—in the 1980s. Did the communists dupe us? Unlikely. The regime was proud of Pilsner Urquell and welcomed visitors, who were shown films in different languages about the history of the brewery and the brewing processes.

It's not a case of 'You pays your money and you takes your choice'. Younger drinkers can never taste the old Pilsner Urquell. Enjoy what is on offer. I can only regret that you will never have the opportunity to drink the original, the classic, the peerless Pilsner.

PS: The global brewing giant SABMiller now owns Pilsner Urquell. SAB stands for South African Breweries, which has merged with the American brewer Miller (brewer of Miller Lite, 'a fine Pilsener beer'!). Pilsner Urquell is now brewed under licence in Poland and may also be made in Russia. How can the 'Original Pilsner' be made anywhere else than at source? By the river of Pilsen, there I sat down, yea, I wept when I remembered Urquell.

Spendrup's Old Gold

Source: Spendrup's Bryggeri AB, Varby, Stockholm, Sweden
Strength: 5%
Website: www.spendrups.se

While Jens and Ulf Spendrup are the fourth generation of the family to run a brewing business that bears their name, the modern company is the result of a merger of several brewers that formed a major independent counter to the might of Sweden's brewing giant Pripps.

Brewing is a difficult business in a country where beer is heavily taxed. Until Sweden joined the European Union in 1995, beer could be bought for home consumption only in state-owned shops. Stronger beers were taxed almost to oblivion and could not be sold in bars and restaurants; this restriction has now been relaxed. Pripps enjoyed government patronage as a nationalised industry and responded by producing astonishingly bland and undistinguished pale lagers (its main brand is called Bla, which means blue in Swedish, but could be taken as a consumer comment on the quality of the beer). The group was privatised in the 1990s and is now part-owned by the Volvo car group.

Spendrups has carved out an important niche in the market by concentrating on top-quality, all-malt golden lagers sold in attractive packaging. The group has several plants in Sweden, including a large, modern but attractive facility with copper vessels in the Stockholm suburbs, with fine views over a tree-fringed lake.

Spendrup's Old Gold is firmly in the Pilsner camp, to the extent of enjoying the burnished colour of a true member of the family. It's hopped with German varieties and has a luscious toasted malt, floral hops and light citrus fruit aroma. Juicy malt and bitter, spicy hops dominate the palate, while the lingering finish is finely balanced between creamy malt, tangy hop resins and tart lemon fruit.

This is a beer that deserves wider recognition and approval. The packaged version comes in a distinctive ridged brown bottle.

Trumer Pils
Source: Trumer Brauerei, Obertrum, Salzburg, Austria
Strength: 4.9%
Website: www.sigl.co.at

TASTING NOTES
Appearance
Aroma
Taste
Overall score

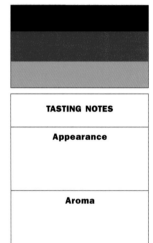

TASTING NOTES
Appearance
Aroma
Taste
Overall score

Trumer Pils is widely regarded as the finest Pilsner brewed in Austria. The independent, family-owned Sigl brewery has been producing beer since 1601 in a scenic Alpine location with access to an inexhaustible supply of fine brewing water from the surrounding mountains.

Austria was part of the 'golden triangle' of brewing innovation in central Europe: lagering techniques were pioneered in Munich, the first golden beer made by cold fermentation came from Pilsen, while the great Austrian brewer Anton Dreher produced the 'Vienna Red' style of lager beer that still finds expression in the March beers brewed in Munich and stored until the Oktoberfest.

Sigl's Trumer Pils is made with pale German malting barley and hops from Austria and the German Hallertau region. The hops create 26 units of bitterness, comparatively low for the style, but the softness of the water and the light malt character enable a delicate bitterness to permeate the beer from aromas to finish.

To avoid any harsh flavours from the malt, the husk is removed from the grain before mashing begins. The beer is kräusened during the ageing period: this means that a portion of unfermented, sugary wort is added to the lagering tanks to encourage a strong secondary fermentation. The beer that emerges from the long brewing and fermenting process—it is aged for six weeks— has a rich aroma of toasted malt, cornflour, noble hops and lemon fruit, with juicy malt and gently bitter hops in the mouth, and a quenching finish dominated by tart citrus fruit, spicy and bitter hops and sweet malt. It's an exceptional beer but, as I have criticised the owners of Pilsner Urquell for brewing the beer under licence, I must report that since 2004 Trumer Pils has also been brewed in Berkeley, California. It's made under the strict supervision of Sigl brewmasters using exactly the same ingredients, with the exception of the water, which flows from the Sierra Nevada mountain range rather than the Alps.

Weihenstephaner Pilsner
Source: Weihenstephan Brauerei, Freising, Munich, Germany
Strength: 5.1%
Website: www.weihenstephaner.de

Signs throughout the brewery, repeated on bottle labels, proclaim that Weihenstephan is the '*Ältester Brauerei der Welt*' (the oldest brewery in the world). *Weihenstephan* means Holy Stephen, and a religious community was built on a hill near Munich in 724 by Irish Benedictines to commemorate St Stephen, the first Christian martyr. The monks built a brewery in 1040 to sell beer locally to aid their work in the community, but it's likely they were making beer much earlier, as they were growing hops by 768.

The location was ideal for brewing, as beer could be stored in cellars dug into the hill. The monastery that developed on the site has been sacked and attacked many times over the centuries. It was secularised in 1815 and owned first by the Bavarian royal family and now by the state. The site today includes a brewery and the world-famous brewing faculty of Munich University that runs training courses for students from around the world. Directed by Professor Ludwig Narziss, the faculty works closely with the German health service to evaluate the healthy properties of beer. It has carried out important research in to the contribution that hops can make to help prevent cancer.

The brewery is best known for its wheat beers but it produces superb lagers as well, and the Pilsner is one the finest of the breed. It is brewed from German pale barley malt and hops from the neighbouring Hallertau region. The beer is wonderfully refreshing, with a malty and biscuity aroma balanced by tart lemon citrus fruit and spicy hops. Juicy malt, tangy fruit and hop resins dance on the tongue, while the finish is lingering and beautifully balanced between rich malt, bitter hops and fruit. Magnificent.

Brown & Mild Ales

Brown beers provide a link to two quite disparate brewing periods: the bucolic pre-industrial age and the smoke-stacked period of the late 18th and early 19th centuries. As I explained in the section on India Pale Ale (see page 10), before the Industrial Revolution most beers were brown in colour. Malt was cured in kilns in which wood provided the fuel: wood was cheap and plentiful, whereas coal and coke were taxed and expensive. The beers of the time had a smoky aroma and palate, sometimes with a touch of lactic sourness that resulted from long periods of maturation in giant oak vessels known as tuns.

Beers that most closely recall this method of brewing are the well-matured oud bruin, or old brown, beers of the East Flanders region of Belgium and which feature powerfully in its cuisine. And as many beer styles cross-pollinate, there is a further link with the well-matured 'country' beers that survive in the shape of Greene King's Strong Suffolk Ale and the 'sour red' beers of West Flanders.

Brown beers of the pre-industrial age that were stored for only a short time were often known as mild ale, as they lacked the sour bite of beers aged for lengthy periods. This type of mild ale was one of the constituents of the early porters and stouts. The term was resurrected in the later 18th and 19th centuries when brewers were anxious to reduce the cost of maturing beer in wood. A demand from industrial workers for a sweeter, lighter and cheaper beer than porter and stout coincided with the commercial needs of the brewers. A new type of mild ale was born. It was brewed at first using brown, well-cured malt but this was replaced in the 19th century by pale malt, which by then had become more widely available, and blended with such darker grains as crystal, black and chocolate malts. Brewing sugar and caramel were also used to give the beer the sweetness demanded by drinkers who wanted to restore the energy lost after long shifts in the sapping heat of factories and mines.

Mild ale, in common with the dark, or dunkel, lager beers of Bavaria, became the dominant beer style of the industrial age. While most modern milds are low in strength, the term 'mild' has nothing to do with weakness. It was used to define a style that, compared to pale ale, was sweeter and low in hop bitterness. In 1871, in Herbert's *Art of Brewing*, the typical gravity of mild was given as 1070 degrees, which is around 7% alcohol in modern measurement. At the turn of the 20th century the average strength of beer was 5.5% at a time when mild was the dominant style. This potent type of mild is still occasionally available, as can be seen in the remarkable Sarah Hughes' Dark Ruby, brewed in the West Midlands.

In Britain, mild did not lose its hegemony until the 1950s, when heavy industry went into decline and paler beers became the fashion. Mild's decline was hastened by its perceived old-fashioned, cloth-cap image. Several brewers responded to this problem

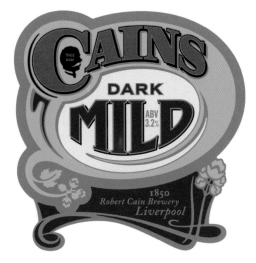

LEFT
Cain's Dark Mild is an excellent example of a Merseyside interpretation of the style that was hoppier than the norm to compete with Guinness imported from Dublin.

In England, brown ale means a bottled version of mild. It is also the name for a stronger type of brown beer confined to the North-east corner of the country. Brewers in such important industrial centres as Newcastle and Sunderland responded to the popularity of the pale ales and bitters of London and the Midlands with strong but darker russet-coloured beers called brown ales. They are sweeter than pale ale but with more hop bitterness than traditional milds. North-east brown ale is represented in this section by Double Maxim, which originated in Sunderland and, to my mind, is a finer example of the style than a better-known beer from Tyneside.

by dropping the term 'mild' but continuing to brew beers that belong firmly to the mild family: see for example Banks's Original and McMullen's AK. The latter also stands as a reminder that not all members of the mild clan are dark in colour. In the 19th and early 20th centuries, many brewers produced several mild ales, among them light milds that were similar to pale ales or bitters in colour but which lacked their hop bite.

In some areas of England, mild has never gone away. Banks's Original is the main brand made by the country's leading regional brewer. Other brewers in the Black Country district of the West Midlands also remain major mild producers. South Wales and Merseyside may have lost their industries but dark milds nevertheless remain popular drinks in those regions. In general, mild has seen a small resurgence due to the rapid expansion of the micro-brewing sector, where brewers rather than accountants decide the beer portfolio and there is a keen determination to maintain Britain's rich heritage of beer styles. That determination has crossed 'the Pond' and several American small craft brewers now fashion brown ales, although the term 'mild' is not used in the United States.

Banks's Original

Source: Wolverhampton & Dudley Breweries, Wolverhampton, West Midlands, England
Strength: 3.5%
Website: www.wdb.co.uk

This beer was called 'Mild Ale' until the 1990s when Wolverhampton & Dudley, the biggest regional brewing group in Britain, decided the word 'mild' would not appeal to younger drinkers and brought in the meaningless Original. But let's not quibble. This is a brilliant example of the Black Country style and is by far the biggest selling mild ale in Britain. The name Black Country comes from the time when factories belched black smoke into the atmosphere and industrial workers favoured a dark beer to quench their legendary thirsts.

In the 1890s a number of Black Country breweries, including Banks's of Wolverhampton and Hanson's of Dudley, merged at a time when mild was far and away the leading beer style of the region. The group, which now includes Marston's of Burton-on-Trent, remains a major mild ale producer, with Hanson's Mild Ale also in its portfolio, although the Dudley brewery is long closed.

Banks's has a fine traditional brewery in the centre of Wolverhampton. It malts its own contract-grown Maris Otter barley and also has its own hop 'yards', or fields, in Worcestershire where it grows Fuggles. The brewery even makes its own finings to clear beer: a section of the brewery has a stock of swim bladders from the sturgeon and other fish that are boiled on the premises. Banks's Original is comparatively light in colour—tawny or amber—registering 40 units. It's brewed from pale malt and caramel and hopped with Fuggles and East Kent Goldings: the hops contribute 25 units of bitterness. The beer has a rich vine fruits aroma with a gentle underpinning of hops. Sweet malt, dark, burnt fruit and hops mingle on the tongue, while vinous fruit contributes a port wine character to the finish, which also has a hint of vanilla and a gentle, fading hop bitterness. It's the caramel—burnt sugar—that gives Banks's Original its distinctive fruity and vinous appeal. They call it 'empty glass beer' in the locality: as soon as you finish one pint, you'll want another.

Banks's Original is the brewery's flagship beer, accounting for 60% of production. It's available in bottle, but this is a beer to savour in cask-conditioned draught form.

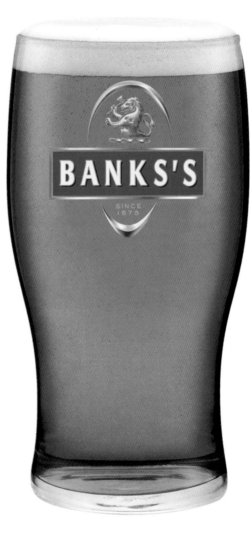

TASTING NOTES
Appearance
Aroma
Taste
Overall score

TASTING NOTES

Appearance
Aroma
Taste
Overall score

Bateman's Dark Mild

Source: George Bateman & Son, Salem Bridge Brewery, Wainfleet All Saints, Lincolnshire, England
Strength: 3%
Website: www.bateman.co.uk

Bateman's is one of the most idyllic breweries in Britain. It stands on the banks of a small river and is dominated by a windmill that recalls the time when grain was milled on the site. George Bateman opened his brewery in 1874 and it is still run by members of his family, including Stuart and Jaclyn Bateman. When the brewery was threatened by closure in the 1980s, George Bateman, his wife Pat and children Stuart and Jaclyn threw themselves into a battle to save the company. They were victorious in 1986 and, as though some divine hand had written the script, won CAMRA's Champion Beer of Britain competition that year.

Bateman's has won several awards in the competition since then, including a gold for Dark Mild in 1997. The beer is now widely available in cask form: several other regional breweries that had phased out their own milds take Bateman's beer in their pubs. While it has a modest strength, it is packed with rich malt and dark fruit notes and is unusually bitter for the style due to the blending of Challenger and Goldings hop varieties. The colour rating is 124, the bitterness units 24. The grains are Maris Otter pale malt, crystal malt and wheat malt, with small amounts of wheat syrup and caramel. It has a rich biscuity malt, burnt fruit and hazelnut aroma, with dark chewy malt, raisin fruit and hop resins in the mouth. The finish is far from sweet: it is dry with dark malt and caramel notes balanced by tangy hops.

The brewery includes a visitor centre and the Brewing Experience that follows all the stages of making beer. Dummies of brewery workers include look-alikes of Luciano Pavarotti and Bill Clinton: the former American president is cast in the role of cask sniffer. Wainfleet is on the Peterborough to Skegness railway line.

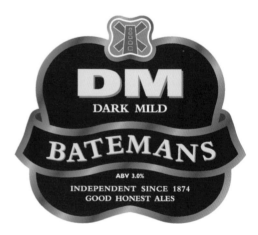

Batham's Mild Ale

Source: Batham's Delph Brewery, Brierley Hill, West Midlands, England
Strength: 3.5%
Website: www.bathams.co.uk

Batham's small brewery, with its 'brewery tap', the Vine pub next door, is a shrine for lovers of Black Country mild. The fascia of the pub bears a quotation from Shakespeare's *Two Gentlemen of Verona*: 'Blessings of your heart, you brew good ale', and the brewery richly deserves the Bard's accolade. The pub is best known by its nickname of the Bull and Bladder: a butcher's shop and slaughterhouse were part of the site when Daniel Batham took over the brew-pub in 1881 after he had lost his job in the local coal-mining industry.

Batham's had been in business for 70 years before it first brewed a bitter. Its success was rooted in its dark mild. Today, the brothers Tim and Matthew Batham are the fifth generation to run the brewery and its 10 pubs. Tim is the brewer and is justly proud of the small plant run on strict utilitarian Victorian 'tower brewery' lines, with the brewing process flowing logically from floor to floor without the aid of pumps. The hot liquor tank feeds the mash tun with water from the public supply that has been 'Burtonised', or hardened with the addition of gypsum salts. The malt is Maris Otter pale: the mild's colour comes from the use of caramel. Herefordshire Northdown and East Kent Goldings hops are added in the copper. After the boil, the hopped wort is cooled and pumped to wooden fermenting vessels, some of which are more than 100 years old. Mild and bitter are 'parti-gyle beers': additional brewing water or liquor is added to

the 4.3% Best Bitter to reduce it to 3.5% for the mild. Caramel is added in the fermenter and Tim adds twice the rate of yeast for mild as he does for the bitter. The acidity of the wort is lower in the mild than the bitter as a result of breaking it down with liquor and it is vital to get a vigorous fermentation going as quickly as possible.

Batham's Mild Ale is remarkable in several ways. A mild ale brewer would normally prefer soft to hard water, so the addition of gypsum to the brewing liquor gives the beer a flinty dryness missing from most milds. The beer is also dry hopped, which means additional Goldings are added to each cask of beer. The result is a mild with a pronounced bitter hop character. Finally, the combination of caramel and the Whitbread B yeast strain brings a rich blackcurrant fruit note to the aroma and palate. The ruby red beer, fruity, biscuity, hoppy and quenching, is best enjoyed in the Vine, a great Black Country institution, where regular live jazz concerts are staged in a large back room.

Brains Dark

Source: S A Brain, the Cardiff Brewery, Cardiff, Wales
Strength: 3.5%
Website: www.sabrain.com

TASTING NOTES
Appearance
Aroma
Taste
Overall score

Brains Dark is a Welsh legend. Visitors to Cardiff are immediately regaled by the brewery's products, as almost every pub seems to carry the name, while brewery drays, posters and bus sides inform all and sundry that 'It's Brains You Need'. As Cardiff develops into a modern metropolis, based on commerce rather than heavy industry, Dark still charms and refreshes beer lovers. It is now sold far from its home base as a result of winning many awards, including the Best Mild category in CAMRA's 2004 Champion Beer of Britain competition.

Samuel Arthur Brain took over a small brewery in central Cardiff in 1882. It expanded rapidly to keep pace with the astonishing development of Cardiff from an insignificant small town into a major port and city. The success of the brewery was based on its Dark Mild. It was known for many years as Red Dragon Dark, using the Welsh national symbol, and it's disappointing that this commitment to nationhood has been dropped at a time when Wales has gained its own elected assembly. With 212 pubs, Brains is a major force in beer retailing in Wales and English counties that border the principality. It marked its commitment to brewing in 1999 when it moved from the city centre to the substantially bigger site vacated by Welsh Brewers, a subsidiary of Bass.

Dark remains a vibrant member of the beer portfolio, its signature being a rich chocolate character due to the generous use of chocolate malt, a grain that resembles coffee beans in appearance and which imparts a delightful aroma and palate. Pale malt, from Regina and Pearl varieties, are blended with chocolate malt. Brewing sugar and caramel are also used, and the beer is primed in cask with brewing sugar to encourage a powerful second fermentation. The colour rating is 110. The hop varieties are Challenger, Fuggles and Goldings, and the units of bitterness are 22. Light hops and rich chocolate dominate the aroma, while the palate encounters more chocolate, hops, dark malt and nuttiness. The finish is bitter-sweet, quenching, with a good, gentle underpinning of hops and a vinous note from the caramel.

Brooklyn Brown Ale

Source: Brooklyn Brewery, Brooklyn, New York City, USA
Strength: 5.6%
Website: www.brooklynbrewery.com

Brooklyn Brown Ale is the beer that launched the modern style version in the United States. The brewery was the brainchild of Steve Hindy and Tom Potter, journalist and banker respectively. At first the F X Matt Brewery in upstate New York brewed for them, but Hindy and Potter opened a dedicated brewing plant in Brooklyn in 1996.

Before Prohibition and the Great Depression, Brooklyn had been a major brewing area, dominated by German styles, but one by one all the breweries had closed. Hindy and Potter called on a veteran brewer named Bill Moeller, a man with German ancestry, to fashion first a Brooklyn Lager (see page 276) and then Brooklyn Brown Ale. The Brown Ale was meant to be a seasonal beer but its popularity caused it to become a regular brew.

The brewmaster at Brooklyn is Garrett Oliver, a celebrated beer connoisseur in the US, a man dedicated to re-creating classic styles. He gives regular seminars and is the author of the magnificent book on matching beer and food, *The Brewmaster's Table*. Since he arrived at the brewery in 1996, he has tweaked Brown Ale considerably and it is now very much his own beer.

Garrett is a fan of English brown and mild ales, but while he finds them light and refreshing, he looks for greater depth and complexity in his own beer. In particular, he wants some roasted malt character missing from most English interpretations of the style. He is also aided by a robust strength, something English milds have not enjoyed for many years. He blends English pale ale malt with Belgian aromatic malts and American caramel, chocolate malt and roasted barley. The colour rating is 35. The hops are all home-grown varieties: Cascade, American Fuggles and Willamette, which create 28 bitterness units. The finished beer has a burnished mahogany colour and a rich and inviting aroma of chocolate, dark, burnt fruit, roasted barley and tangy hops. Caramel, roast and chocolate dominate the palate,

followed by a finish that is dry from the malts and roast, with a continuing chocolate note and a solid underpinning of tart hops.

Garrett recommends the beer as a companion for steaks, venison, ham and roasted pork and also for such cheeses as Cheddar, Gouda, Gruyère and Stilton.

TASTING NOTES
Appearance
Aroma
Taste
Overall score

TASTING NOTES

Appearance	
Aroma	
Taste	
Overall score	

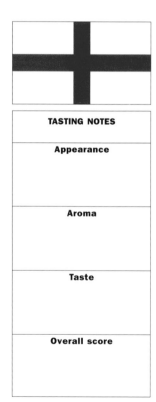

TASTING NOTES

Appearance	
Aroma	
Taste	
Overall score	

Buckerfield's Appleton Brown Ale

Source: Buckerfield's Brewery, Swan's Hotel, Victoria, British Columbia, Canada
Strength: 5%
Website: www.swanshotel.com

Swan's Hotel in the centre of Victoria is a hotel in the grand manner, with many Art Nouveau flourishes, spacious rooms, deep leather sofas, an English-style pub, an art collection and its own brewery. It was fashioned in the 1980s from old grain and grocery warehouses by Michael Williams, a shepherd from Shropshire, England, who emigrated to Victoria, the most English of Canadian towns with its black taxis and red buses.

Williams trained dogs and bought grain from the warehouses that had been created in the 1800s to help feed the hordes of prospectors who used the town as a base while they searched for gold in the Klondike. Eventually, Williams was able to buy the buildings and transform them into Swan's Hotel, so called, he said, because the site had been an ugly duckling. As well as the on-site pub, complete with imported English handpumps to serve cask-conditioned beer, Williams got Frank Appleton to design a small brewery for him and then named one of his beers in the designer's honour.

The malts and yeast are imported from England, though the hops are grown in Washington State. Williams knew he couldn't sell beer with the low strength of an English mild, so Appleton Brown Ale has a robust strength and flavour. It's brewed using pale, crystal and chocolate malts with a touch of roasted barley. The hops are Cascade and Willamette in pellet form. The beer has a pronounced aroma of apple fruit and cinnamon, with dark fruit in the mouth and a creamy, bitter-sweet finish. There is a generous tart and fruity hop character underpinning the malt flavours and a pleasing, chewy and burnt note from roasted barley.

Michael Williams was a generous and engaging host when I visited Swan's in the 1990s, and I was saddened to hear that he has since died. He has left Swan's and Buckerfield's to the local university, which benefits from the profits made.

Cains Dark Mild

Source: Robert Cain & Co, Liverpool, England
Strength: 3.2%
Website: www.cainsbeers.com

Robert Cain came from Cork in Ireland to Liverpool and opened a striking red-brick Victorian brewery in 1850 that became one of the top 50 industrial companies in Britain. After several changes of ownership and closure for a while, Cains was bought in 2002 by two young entrepreneurs, Ajmail and Sudarghara Dusanj, who have restored the fortunes of the brewery and produced a special beer to mark the fact that Liverpool was the European City of Culture in 2008.

Throughout its roller-coaster life, Dark Mild has been the bedrock of Cain's success and is now promoted with renewed vigour by the Dusanj brothers. The beer has a fascinating history. As a result of Liverpool's large Irish community, Guinness Stout has always had a big following there. Even when Guinness had a London brewery, the stout sold on Merseyside was brewed in Dublin. But Guinness was comparatively expensive and beyond the reach of impoverished Liverpudlians in the late 19th and early 20th centuries. As a result, Cains and other local brewers fashioned dark milds that were similar in character to Guinness while being considerably weaker and cheaper. The key ingredient was roasted barley, which gives a burnt, slightly acrid and bitter fruit flavour to beer. Cains has continued this tradition.

Dark Mild is brewed from a blend of Maris Otter pale barley malt, roasted barley and chocolate malt. The colour is 140. The hops are Styrian Goldings for aroma and Target for bitterness, with 23 bitterness units. To encourage a good hop character, Styrians are added late in the copper boil and also to each cask of beer as it leaves the brewery. The result is a distinctive beer with greater hop bitterness than is the norm for the style. It has a pronounced dark fruit, chocolate, roasted grain and bitter hops aroma, with roast and fruit dominating the palate. The finish is smooth, chocolaty and grainy but with a solid underpinning of hops.

Double Maxim

**Source: Double Maxim Beer Co,
Houghton le Spring, Co
Durham, England
Strength: 4.2%
Website: www.dmbc.org.uk**

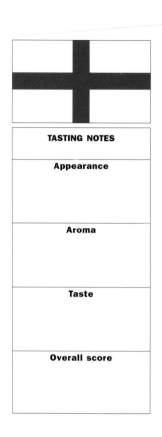

Double Maxim is a stalwart of Sunderland and Wearside, a fine example of a strong North-east brown ale. Following the closure of Vaux of Sunderland in 1999, two Vaux directors, Doug Trotman and Mark Anderson, and former head brewer Jim Murray, bought the brand, and sell the beer nationally as a bottled product. They are still based close to Wearside. Cuthbert Vaux founded his brewery in Sunderland in 1837 to meet the demands of shipbuilders and miners in the area. A beer called Maxim Ale was brewed to mark the activities of Captain Ernest Vaux, who had led a raid during the Boer War in South Africa using a Maxim machine gun. A stronger version of the beer, called Double Maxim, was introduced in 1938, no doubt to offer some choice and competition to the high-profile Newcastle Brown Ale brewed since 1927 on neighbouring Tyneside.

The beer is brewed with pale and crystal malts with a touch of caramel and is primed with sugar to encourage a powerful fermentation. Fuggles are the only hops used, giving the beer a superb earthy, spicy and resinous aroma. It is fruity—plums and apricots—and nutty in the mouth, and comes dry in the finish with some tart fruit and spicy hop notes. It has 22 units of bitterness. It's good news that this important North-east beer is still brewed. After years of lobbying by CAMRA, Vaux relented in the 1990s and produced a cask-conditioned version of Double Maxim, and the new company produces the beer in both cask and bottled versions.

TASTING NOTES

Appearance
Aroma
Taste
Overall score

Elgood's Black Dog Mild

Source: Elgood & Sons, Wisbech, Cambridgeshire, England
Strength: 3.6%
Website: www.elgoods-brewery.co.uk

Elgood's, in the North Brink area of Wisbech alongside the River Nene, is one of the finest brewery sites in Britain. It dates from 1795 and was one of the first classic Georgian breweries to be built outside London. It came under the control of the Elgoods in 1878, and the fifth generation of the family runs the company today. Managing director Belinda Sutton is an Elgood and one of the few women to direct a major brewery in Britain. As well as an attractive brewhouse and fermenting rooms, Elgood's also has magnificent grounds and gardens administered by one of Belinda's sisters. It is possible to tour both the brewery and gardens: see the website for information.

Black Dog Mild is a reminder that mild ales were not just brewed to refresh industrial workers—agricultural workers also needed refreshment, and dark milds, with both sweetness and bitterness, were in great demand in the fenlands of Cambridgeshire between the 18th and mid-20th centuries.

Black Dog, which takes its name from the brewery's logo of a dark hound with a key in its mouth, was a finalist in CAMRA's Champion Beer of Britain competition in 2004 and has won many other CAMRA awards. Its signature comes from the use of roasted barley, which gives the beer a chewy, grainy appeal. The malts are Maris Otter pale and crystal, with some flaked maize and torrefied wheat, which are used mainly to give the beer a good collar of foam: they are virtually identical to cornflakes and popcorn respectively, and in the wrong hands (i.e. some American and Australian lager brewers) are used in large quantities for cheapness and clarity. Clarity in Black Dog is not a major consideration with a colour rating of between 80 and 100. Fuggles hops contribute 25 units of bitterness. The beer has a pleasing aroma of roasty and toasty grain balanced by the familiar earthy hop resins imparted by Fuggles. Dark malt, vinous fruit, roasted grain and light hops dominate the mouth, while the lingering finish is finely balanced between fruit, hops and dark grain.

Highgate Dark Mild

Source: Highgate Brewery, Walsall, West Midlands, England
Strength: 3.4%
Website: www.highgatebrewery.com

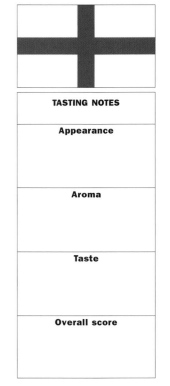

The Highgate Brewery stands as testament to the importance of mild ale to the Midlands region of England. The imposing red-brick brewery—standing somewhat incongruously on rising ground in a residential area of Walsall—was opened in 1898 with a capacity of 100,000 barrels a year to make just dark mild for workers engaged in the local leather industry. In 1938, Highgate was taken over by the giant Birmingham brewery of Mitchells & Butlers, another major mild producer. M&B planned to close Highgate but kept it open during World War Two, when every brewery received rations of malt and hops, and the Birmingham brewery didn't want to lose the raw materials earmarked for Walsall. When M&B became part of Bass, Highgate continued to brew as the smallest plant in the Bass group. It was bought by its management in 1995 and was acquired by new owners in 2009.

Much of the equipment in the spacious and spick-and-span brewery still dates from Victorian times. Mashing takes place in two ancient tuns, originally made of wood, relined with stainless steel but retaining hand-raised wooden lids. Boiling is carried out in two burnished and cherished coppers with internal heating columns topped by funnels known as Chinese Hats. The splendid fermenting room is packed with a variety of round and square wooden vessels. Head brewer Neil Bain describes the Highgate house yeast as 'a beast': unusually, it is a four-strain type, with each strain attacking elements of the brewing sugars at different times.

The recipe for Highgate Dark Mild calls for 2 tonnes/tons of Pearl pale malt, 65kg (143lbs) of black malt and 15–20kg (33–44lbs) of crystal malt for every 100 barrels brewed. Maltose syrup and caramel are also used to increase fermentability and colour. The colour rating is 70. Brewing liquor, rich in iron, is drawn from a bore hole on the site. Whole hops are Goldings and Progress, which create 22 units of bitterness. The finished beer has a complex aroma of dark fruit, chocolate and liquorice with chewy dark grain, chocolate and light, spicy hops in the mouth. The lingering finish is malty and fruity with a good underpinning of hops. Dark Mild is the base from which Highgate's strong winter beer, Old, is brewed.

TASTING NOTES
Appearance
Aroma
Taste
Overall score

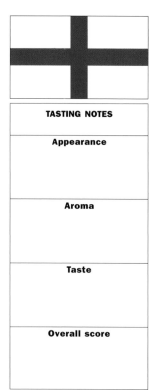

Holt's Mild Ale

Source: Joseph Holt, Derby Brewery, Cheetham, Manchester, England
Strength: 3.2%
Website: www.joseph-holt.com

TASTING NOTES
Appearance
Aroma
Taste
Overall score

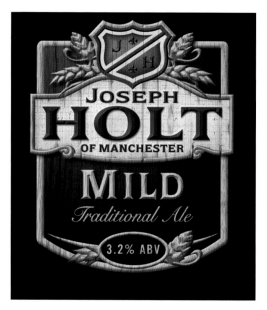

Joseph Holt is a phenomenon. Year in and year out, it is one of the most successful and profitable breweries in Britain, but it has achieved this success by remaining determinedly independent and family-owned. In the 1990s, it withdrew from the London Stock Exchange for fear it might put its independence at risk. The company owns 127 pubs, a considerable estate, but all within a 25-mile radius of the brewery. It still supplies its pubs with its bitter in giant 54-gallon hogsheads and refuses to supply beer festivals that are outside its trading area. It neither seeks nor requires publicity. In 1992, I was the first journalist ever allowed through the doors, and I asked about the Holt's advertising policy. I was met with a bemused look from company secretary Tom Dempsey. 'Do you mean our beer mats?' he asked.

Joseph Holt, the son of a weaver, founded the brewery in 1849. As the population of Manchester exploded in the middle of the 19th century from 70,000 to more than 300,000 due to the demand for cotton, brewers set up in business to meet the insatiable demand for refreshing mild ale. Joseph went to work as a carter for a Manchester brewery and then, supported by wife, Catherine, opened two small breweries of his own before moving to the present site. While considerable sums have been spent upgrading the business in recent years—it now has something as modern as a website and even makes its own lager—it nevertheless remains firmly traditional, still using many brewing vessels from the 19th century.

The mild is sensational. At a small beer festival in the North-west some years ago, surrounded by a fine choice of local beers, I drank nothing but this remarkable dark and bitter ale. It is yet another example of the more bitter style of mild made in the North-west, with Goldings and Northdown whole cone hops creating 30 units of bitterness. It is brewed with Halcyon and Alexis pale malt, crystal malt, flaked maize and dark invert sugar. Chocolate, liquorice, tart fruit and peppery hops coat the tongue, while the long finish is dry and bitter, but quenching with tart fruit and chocolate notes.

Hydes Dark Mild

Source: Hydes Anvil Brewery, Manchester, England
Strength: 3.5%
Website: www.hydesbrewery.com

The demand for mild is still so strong in the Manchester area that Hydes produces three versions of the style: Light Mild, Traditional Mild and Dark Mild, all 3.5%. The family-owned company, which has 72 pubs, dates from 1863, when Alfred and Ralph Hyde bought a small brewery from their grandfather, Thomas Shaw. In step with the development of Manchester into a vast, thriving and humming industrial city, the Hydes moved three times before settling on the present site in the Moss Side district. The name was changed to Hydes Anvil Brewery in 1944 to incorporate the anvil trademark, a sign of strength, craftsmanship and durability. The brewery has enjoyed considerable expansion in recent years, installing new brewing, fermenting and conditioning capacity to increase annual production from 60,000 barrels to 100,000.

The milds are essentially the same brew with the addition of darker grains for colour and flavour. The classic Dark Mild is distinct from Light and Traditional due to the use of chocolate malt. The recipe comprises Fanfare pale ale malt, crystal malt and chocolate malt, with a colour rating of 115. It is a single hop varietal beer, using just Fuggles, which create 23 units of bitterness. The aroma is roasty and chocolaty, with juicy malt and gentle, spicy hops. Rich smoky, roasted grain and chocolate fill the mouth, while the finish is bitter-sweet, with dark, roasted malt, tart fruit and light hop notes.

TASTING NOTES

Appearance

Aroma

Taste

Overall score

Liefman's Oud Bruin

Source: Liefman's Brouwerij, Oudenaarde, Belgium
Strength: 5%
Website: www.liefmans.be

The Oud Bruin, or Old Brown, beers of East Flanders are a powerful link to the long-matured brown ales that were the dominant feature of brewing before the industrial revolution of the late 18th and 19th centuries. The region also has another claim to fame: it is home to one of the great beer-based culinary dishes, *carbonade flamande*, the classic beef stew, in which the meat is tenderised with Old Brown beer. The fact that Old Brown beers are also known as 'provision beers' stresses the point that their roots lie in pre-industrial societies where agricultural workers needed hearty food and drink to sustain them in their labours.

Oudenaarde is the historic capital of East Flanders, on the River Scheldt that flows to Ghent and Antwerp. The town has striking Gothic architecture and was once the capital of the whole of ancient Flanders. It was central to the textile industry and was the birthplace of Jean Gobelin, the celebrated tapestry designer. Another famous citizen was the 11th-century Benedictine monk Arnold of Oudenaarde, who was a brewer and one of two Saint Arnolds from the area referred to as the patron saint of brewers.

Liefman's brewery has some history, too. It opened in 1679, which places it at the dawn of modern brewing and predates the early porter brewers of England who created a commercial industry there. While the current vessels at Liefman's do not date from the 17th century, the practice of long maturation and multistrain yeast cultures are a powerful reminder of ancient brewing methods that impart a characteristic bitter-sweet flavour with a hint of sourness. In the 1970s, when the owner of the brewery died

TASTING NOTES

Appearance

Aroma

Taste

Overall score

suddenly, it was taken over by the brewer's secretary, Rose Blancquaert-Merckx, who was known to everyone in the brewery and the town as 'Madame Rose'. A former ballet dancer, she occasionally surprised visitors by kicking off her shoes and dancing inside one of the brewery vessels. Her passion and verve helped build awareness of Liefman's beers, and the passion continued when she retired.

Madame Rose's retirement coincided with the takeover of Liefman's by the Riva brewing group, best known for its Dentergems spiced wheat beer. For reasons I have never grasped, Riva decided to mash and boil Liefman's beers at its own brewery in Dentergem. The liquid is then trunked back to Oudenaarde where it is fermented, matured, blended and bottled with live yeast to encourage a second fermentation. For a few years, Oudenaarde was closed but Riva plans to reopen it and restore brewing there.

For Oud Bruin, Pilsner malts are blended with Munich and Vienna malts and a touch of roasted barley. Whitbread Goldings Variety—actually a type of Fuggle—is the main bittering hop with German and Czech varieties: they contribute 20 units of bitterness. The house yeast strain is carefully stored and cultured in the brewery but it came originally from the Rodenbach brewery in Roeselare, famous for its 'sour red' beer: it is the yeast that gives the lactic edge to Liefman's beers.

Another characteristic is the brewing liquor: instead of adding the traditional sulphites beloved by ale brewers, Liefman's uses sodium bicarbonate, which adds a softness to the beer and presumably guards against any ill effects from too generous portions of *carbonade flamande* in the town's restaurants.

After primary fermentation, Oud Bruin is matured for four months in metal tanks, an astonishing period for an ale and, again, a powerful link to brewing practices from earlier times. The beer that emerges from this long process has a rich aroma of dark fruits, roasted grain, a hint of chocolate and peppery hops. Sweetness is evident in the mouth but is balanced by the lactic note and the hops. The lingering finish is bitter-sweet, with rich, dark malts, spicy hops and the persistent hint of sourness.

Liefmans

speciaal bier voor speciale mensen!

A stronger version of Oud Bruin is known as Goudenband (Gold Riband). This 6% beer is the result of blending Oud Bruin with a stronger beer that has matured for between six and eight months. Both beers are centrifuged to remove the yeast and then reseeded with a dosage of fresh yeast and priming sugar to encourage fermentation in bottle. The bottles are matured for a further three months in the brewery's cellars before being released.

Goudenband has the characteristic Liefman's sourness but is balanced by an even greater fruitiness and spicy hop than Oud Bruin. It has 60 colour units and 20 units of bitterness. If bottles are laid down for several years, the beer will take on a pronounced 'sour wine' note that some drinkers compare to dry Spanish sherry.

There are more joys yet. Once a year, the brewery adds cherries or raspberries to Goundenband, which is then fermented for a further two months, creating beers with strengths of 7.1% for the cherry beer and 5.1% for the raspberry version. When young, these beers are fruity, even cloying, but laid down for a year or more, the sweetness diminishes and the sourness breaks through, making them wonderfully refreshing.

All the Liefman's beers, presented in attractive stoppered bottles and wrapped in coloured tissue paper, should be treasured as remarkable examples of the rich tapestry of beer and brewing history.

McMullen's AK

Source: McMullen & Sons, Hertfordforshire, England
Strength: 3.7%
Website: www.mcmullens.co.uk

McMullen's AK is, like Winston Churchill's description of Soviet Russia, 'a riddle wrapped in a mystery inside an enigma'. It is that rare beer in modern times: a light mild, and a splendidly full-bodied, full-tasting member of a much-depleted style. But where does the curious name come from? There is nothing in the brewery's records or archives, even though it's the company's biggest-selling brand that has existed since at least the late 19th century.

AK was once widely used as a brand name, most notably by the large Kentish brewery Fremlins. One suggestion for the name comes from brewing historian Martyn Cornell who argues that the 'K' may derive from a medieval Dutch beer called Koyt, which came in two strengths: Single and Double Koyt. Single in old Dutch was Ankel, therefore the weaker of the beers would have been branded AK. Flemish weavers who settled in Kent in the 15th century brought with them a considerable thirst for beer and may have handed on the AK designation to local brewers.

My own theory is more prosaic but is also based on the system of branding casks with letters long before beer mats, bar towels and pump clips were in use. For centuries, a widely used form of branding was the 'X' to denote strength, still in use (and even abuse) today with such beers as Castlemaine 4X. It was a simple system: the more Xs on the cask, the stronger the beer. In Victorian times, two main beer styles developed: mild and pale ale or bitter. Pale ale casks continued to be branded with Xs. If you split an X vertically, you get a K, which became the 19th-century method of branding mild. At a time when many breweries produced several versions of mild, AK meant either the weakest mild or it was used to distinguish light mild from dark.

McMullen, a family with Irish connections, dropped the term 'mild' in the 1990s in an attempt to rebrand AK for the modern market. The brewery dates from 1827 when Peter

McMullen, a cooper, decided it would be more sensible and profitable to put his own beer in the casks he built. Today, the striking red-brick Victorian site supplies beer to 134 pubs in Hertfordshire, Essex and London.

AK is brewed with water from an artesian well beneath the brewery, Halcyon pale malt, a tiny amount of chocolate malt, flaked maize and maltose syrup. The single hop variety is Whitbread Goldings. The colour is 24, the bitterness 22. There is another Whitbread connection: the yeast culture is known as Whitbread B and originated in the Mackeson Milk Stout brewery in Kent. It imparts a rich and fruity character to the beer. AK has a floral and spicy hop nose with juicy malt and tart orange fruit. Biscuity malt, tangy fruit and delicate hop resins dominate the mouth while the finish is dry with a good malty character balanced by orange fruit and hop resins. It's a great beer by any name.

TASTING NOTES
Appearance
Aroma
Taste
Overall score

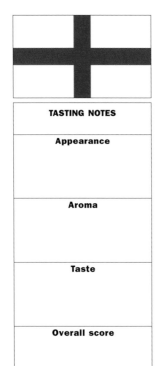

Manns Original Brown Ale

Source: Marston, Thompson & Evershed Brewery, Burton-on-Trent, Staffordshire, England
Strength: 2.8%
Website: www.wdb.co.uk

For once, the overused word 'original' is apt. The large East London brewer Mann Crossman & Paulin launched the beer in 1902 as a mixer with draught mild. Drinkers at the time complained that draught mild was rough and badly kept, and the head brewer at Manns, Thomas Wells Thorpe, introduced the first example of bottled mild, which he dubbed brown ale, as an antidote. At just 2.8%, it was extremely low in alcohol for the time but its sweetness and smoothness took the edge off the harshness of the stronger draught versions available. Thorpe described it as 'the sweetest beer in London'.

Many brewers followed Manns but the Cockney beer dominated the market. Manns was taken over by the giant brewing group Watneys in 1958 and the Whitechapel brewery eventually closed. But Manns Brown had such a large following that Watneys continued to brew it. For a while it was produced at another Watneys subsidiary, Ushers of Trowbridge in Wiltshire, where it accounted for an astonishing 200,000 barrels a year. Ushers, too, closed and for several years Manns Brown has been brewed at the Burtonwood brewery in North-west England, a long way removed from its Cockney heartland. But the Cockney traditions of the beer had been diluted in the 1990s when it was promoted with the aid of the *Daily Mirror* cartoon character Andy Capp, who came from Sunderland and was more likely to sup copious amounts of Double Maxim than ale from London.

The drinks group Refresh UK, which also owns the Brakspear and Wychwood breweries in Oxfordshire, was bought by Marston's, who brew it in Wolverhampton. It is promoted with some zeal, though Marston's doesn't stress the point that it was the favourite tipple of the vast and exploding Mr Creosote in *Monty Python's The Meaning of Life*.

Manns now commands a 90% share of the sweet brown ale market. Brewed with pale and crystal malts and a touch of roasted barley and wheat malt, and hopped with Target, it has a sweet toffee and light sultana fruit aroma, with more toffee, coffee, dark fruit and roasted grain in the mouth. The finish is sweet but not cloying, and is dominated by rich malt and vine fruits, with only the lightest hint of hops.

Mighty Oak Oscar Wilde

Source: Mighty Oak Brewing Co, Maldon, Essex, England
Strength: 3.7%
Website: www.mightyoakbrewery.co.uk

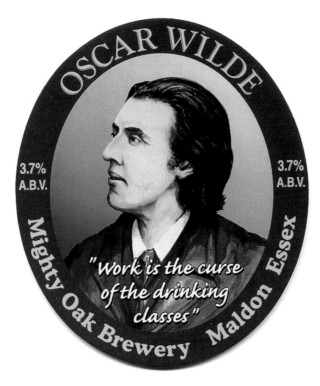

TASTING NOTES

Appearance

Aroma

Taste

Overall score

Oscar Wilde, an archetypal 'champagne socialist', is an unlikely drinker of dark mild. But this is Cockney rhyming slang and Oscar Wilde stands for mild, though I cannot recall from my East End youth ever hearing anyone order 'a pint of Oscar'. Perhaps I frequented the wrong pubs.

Mighty Oak is an award-winning micro-brewery founded in 1996 by John Boyce and his partner Ruth O'Neill. John worked for many years at the now-closed Ind Coope brewery in Romford, while Ruth is that most useful of people in a brewery: an accountant.

In the brewery's short history, it has moved to bigger premises and increased production to 70 barrels a week to supply pubs in London and the surrounding counties. John Boyce will remember from his previous employment that Ind Coope brewed a mild ale, as did the great brewers close by in East London, which was the base—as a result of good water supplies—for the likes of Charrington, the previously mentioned Manns, and Truman: Truman brewed Trubrown, the first mild ale to be advertised on British television in the 1950s.

Oscar Wilde is strong for the style and has a good hop character. It's brewed with Maris Otter pale malt, crystal malt and chocolate malt. The only hop is Challenger, which creates 21 units of bitterness. It has smoky malt and espresso coffee on the aroma with dark fruit notes and hop resins. Coffee and chocolate flavours dominate the mouth with dark and bitter fruit and the tang of hops. The long finish has tart and bitter hops, vinous fruit, chocolate and dark malt.

Would you Adam and Eve it, it's a great pint of pig's ear.

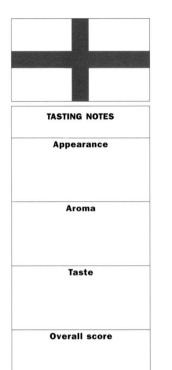

Moorhouse's Black Cat

Source: Moorhouse's Brewery, Burnley, Lancashire, England
Strength: 3.4%
Website: www.moorhouses.co.uk

TASTING NOTES

Appearance

Aroma

Taste

Overall score

Black Cat gave an enormous boost to the mild ale sector in England when it won CAMRA's Champion Beer of Britain award in 2000. Its success proved that mild ale was a beer style fit for a new millennium. The championship was also a boon for a company that had had a helter-skelter existence since a Burnley businessman, William Moorhouse, launched it in 1865. He concentrated at first on making mineral waters but his success prompted him to build a bigger site and add beer and 'hop bitters' to his portfolio.

Hop bitters were in vogue in the late 19th and early 20th century as a result of lobbying against the 'demon drink' by a powerful temperance movement. Moorhouse's hop bitters were less than 2% alcohol and were sold in special Temperance Halls set up to wean working people in Burnley's mills away from strong liquor.

When the descendants of William Moorhouse sold the business in 1978, it went through several hands and was on the point of closing in 1985 when Bill Parkinson had a pint of Moorhouse Bitter and—like the American who loved his Remington razor so much he bought the company—made a bid for the brewery and owned it within seven days.

Mr Parkinson had made his fortune from Lifting Gear Hire, a heavy engineering firm that, for example, supplied the equipment to lift the stricken Russian submarine *Kursk* from the bottom of the Barents Sea. He has since invested more than £1 million in the company and added new brewing equipment with the aim of boosting production to 20,000 barrels a year.

Moorhouse's is best known for its strong bitter, Pendle Witches Brew (see page 106), named after the terrifying old crones who inhabited the Pendle Moors outside Burnley in the 16th and 17th centuries. But Black Cat has also established itself as a major national brand, winning an award in the International Brewing competition in 1998, the overall CAMRA championship in 2000, and silver and bronze awards in the same competition in 2001 and 2002.

It's a brilliant example of a North-west dark mild, brewed with Halcyon pale malt, chocolate malt, invert sugar and flaked maize. The only hop is Fuggles. It has a succulent aroma of dark, roasted grain, bitter chocolate and light hop resins. Chocolate dominates the palate but there are also notes of dark fruit and light, spicy hops. The finish has some dark fruit notes, with a continuing chocolate presence and gentle hops. Above all, it is wonderfully refreshing.

Sarah Hughes Dark Ruby

Source: Sarah Hughes Brewery, Beacon Hotel, Sedgley, West Midlands, England
Strength: 6%
Website: None

This is the way dark milds used to be in the 19th and early 20th centuries: strong. I have seen the beer described as 'old ale' but I disagree and regret that brewery owner John Hughes has pandered to this view by dropping 'mild' from the title.

When the Beacon Hotel was built in 1850 the site included its own tiny 'tower' brewery in the yard at the rear. Sarah Hughes bought the hotel in 1921 and ran it for 30 years, handing it over to her son and daughters when she retired. She died in 1951. The brewery had always made just one beer: the strong dark mild. The Hughes family closed the brewery in 1958 but Sarah's grandson, John, decided to reopen it in 1987. All the old wooden vessels had rotted away and were replaced by stainless-steel ones faced with wood. John had the good fortune to discover Sarah's recipe for her mild in an old cigar box locked in a bank security vault.

To watch the brewing process, you have to clamber up narrow wooden stairs to the top of the building. Maris Otter pale malt is blended with 10% crystal malt. After mashing, the extract is dropped a few feet into a tiny underback and from there into the original open-topped copper where it is boiled with Fuggles and Goldings. It then falls to a hopback for clarification and then into five fermenters converted from cellar tanks from the old Ansells brewery in Birmingham. John Hughes won't reveal the source of his yeast but says it comes from another Black Country brewery, which narrows the field.

John has lovingly restored the hotel and turned it into a shrine to Victoriana, complete with tap room, smoke room and snug, all with open fires and tiled floors. Each room is supplied with beer from a central servery, with glasses pushed through a hatch. Every item is Victorian, including the gas lamps, wallpaper and out-of-tune piano.

Dark Ruby, brewed by Guy Perry, has a rich and fruity nose with blackcurrant dominating, laced with earthy Fuggles hop resins. The palate is amazingly complex, summoning up every dark fruit imaginable: it is like chewing all the dark sweets from a tube of Maynard's Wine Gums. The finish is dry, with spicy and peppery hops balancing the tart, tangy, bitter fruits and dark malt. As well as being available on draught, Dark Ruby also comes in bottle-fermented form and is suitable for vegans.

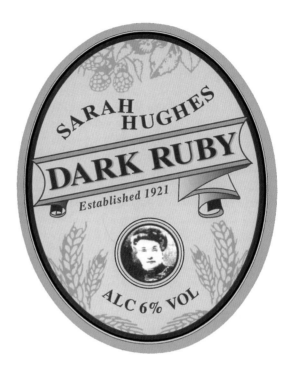

TASTING NOTES
Appearance
Aroma
Taste
Overall score

Pale Ales

The boundary between pale ale and bitter is—unlike the beers themselves—often a hazy one. Some books on beer do not trouble to make the distinction, merging the two styles. Even brewers are sometimes confused. Marston's Pedigree is a classic Burton pale ale, and I include it in this section, but it's marketed as a bitter.

Pale ale should live up to its name: the earliest versions were brewed only with pale malt and brewing sugar, whereas bitter made use of a new type of malt called crystal that gives a bronze or copper colour to the finished beer. Both styles are bitter in the sense that hop rates are generous, and brewers tend to choose varieties that impart tangy, spicy, peppery, citrus fruit and resiny aromas and flavours. But, to paraphrase the old philosophy joke, we must not put Descartes before the dray horse. Pale ale predates bitter by some years. While there are some references to 'bitter beer' in 19th-century books, the word was used as a descriptor rather than as a generic term. Bitter, as is made clear in the next section (see pages 66–7), developed as a style at the turn of the 20th century. Pale ale appeared much earlier.

The success of India Pale Ale abroad encouraged the Burton brewers to make IPA available to the home market, a task made easier by the new railway system that was faster and more direct than coaches and canals. But many drinkers found IPA too strong and too bitter. British brewers hurried to produce a type of pale ale that would better suit the domestic market, with less alcohol and fewer hops. They were aided by dynamic changes in brewing practice made possible by better-quality malt, hops and refrigeration. Louis Pasteur in France and Emil Christian Hansen in the Carlsberg laboratories in Copenhagen developed a scientific understanding of yeast that led to pure cultures being developed, with improved fermentations free from infection. The brewers were anxious to move away from the expense of storing or vatting beer for long periods, a system that became out of date with new yeasts that packed down quickly and allowed beer to 'drop bright' within weeks rather than months. When tax was lifted on glass in the late 19th century, brewers were able to produce bottled beer for the first time in substantial quantities.

Bottled pale ale acquired snob appeal as British society changed dramatically with the growth of a new and large middle class. Pale ale was not cheap and its price was pitched above those for mild and porter. Richard Wilson, writing in *The British Brewing Industry 1830–1980*, argues that 'Quality and cost... made it [Burton pale ale] a status drink for the expanding lower middle class of clerks and shopkeepers, the armies of rail travellers and those "aristocrats of labour" [skilled workers] whose standards of living rose appreciably after 1850'. Wilson described bottled pale ale as 'the high-fashion beer of the railway age'. It was consumed at home by 'respectable' middle-class drinkers who did not wish to rub shoulders with the hoi polloi in common ale houses. Here was the dividing point: pale ale, unlike the milds and porters of the time, and the bitters or 'running beers' that came later, became identified as a bottled, rather than a draught, product. The gap became wider as large brewers, such as Whitbread in London, made bottled pale ale a leading brand in their portfolios and eventually filtered and pasteurised them for ease of home delivery and consumption.

Confusion and the blurring of the distinction between pale ale and bitter took place in the 20th century as draught bitter increased rapidly in popularity. While the likes of Bass and Worthington continued to produce sedimented pale ales in bottle, many brewers preferred to cut costs by bottling filtered and pasteurised versions of their bitters and labelling them light ale or pale ale. The result has been that a style pioneered in Britain, and a descendant of the revolutionary IPAs of the early 19th century, is now confined to just a handful of beers. For this reason, the beers represented in this section are largely 'New World' pale ales brewed in the United States. In the US, in particular, there is a passion for faithfully and passionately re-creating great beer styles. As the term bitter is rarely used in the US, American pale ales bursting with rich malt and hop character have rescued and revived a style that has been largely bowdlerised out of all recognition in the land of its birth.

Anchor Liberty Ale

Source: Anchor Brewing Co, San Francisco, California, USA
Strength: 6%
Website: www.anchorbrewing.com

TASTING NOTES
Appearance
Aroma
Taste
Overall score

Liberty Ale is a revolutionary beer. It was first brewed in 1975 to commemorate the 200th anniversary of Paul Revere's ride from Boston to Lexington to warn the American rebels that the British Redcoats were marching to arrest them: his ride signalled the start of the War of Independence. And Liberty Ale sparked the resurgence of pale ale brewing in the US, a style that was almost totally extinguished by Prohibition in the 1920s.

The Anchor Brewery is best known for its Steam Beer (see page 238), but Liberty Ale stands free of its shadow. Ironically, Fritz Maytag, the man who saved Anchor from closure and turned it into one of the most highly regarded craft breweries in the US, was prompted to brew his pale ale following an extensive tour of Britain.

Marston's Pedigree from Burton-on-Trent, the home of pale ale, Timothy Taylor's Landlord from Yorkshire and Young's Special Bitter from London inspired him to produce a pale, sparkling and hoppy ale.

However, inspiration did not lead to subservience. Maytag's beer is strong, straw-coloured, an all-malt beer without additional sugars, and massively hopped. It's an all-American, love-me-or-leave-me beer, and it's the hops that give Liberty its profound character. Unlike the restrained spicy and peppery notes of traditional English varieties, Cascade hops from Washington State distend the nostrils with their assault of pine and grapefruit.

When I saw the hop store at Anchor I was astonished by the fresh vibrant green of the hops. When I flew from California to the Yakima Valley hop-growing region of Washington State, below the Cascade mountains, I discovered the secret of the hops and their intense aromas and flavours: plenty of rain but also blazingly hot summers that encourage the hops to swell on the bine and develop their rich fruity/citrus character. Cascade hops are used in abundance in Liberty Ale, both in the fermenters and in the maturation tanks. They dominate the nose and palate but are complemented by juicy malt from two-row barley. Many big American brewers use six-row barley (i.e. six rows of grain in each ear of grain), but craft brewers prefer the smoother, biscuity flavour of two-row varieties. The finish of Liberty is long and lingering, becoming dry and bitter but with a fine balancing act of malt and citrus fruit. An awesome ale.

Boston Ale

Source: Boston Beer Company, Boston, Massachusetts, USA
Strength: 5%
Website: www.samueladams.com

TASTING NOTES
Appearance
Aroma
Taste
Overall score

This is another beer with revolutionary credentials. The brewery has a split personality: officially it's the Boston Beer Company, but Boston Ale and its other brands all carry the name of Samuel Adams, as does the website.

Adams was a brewer (some records suggest maltster) in Boston. He was an active campaigner for American independence, he was involved in the Boston Tea Party and was a signatory to the Declaration of Independence, drafted by another keen beer drinker, Ben Franklin.

Adams, holding a foaming tankard, stares sternly from the label of Boston Ale, which is subtitled Stock Ale. Stock was an 18th-century English term meaning strong ale matured for a year or more that was used for blending with younger beers. In New England it took on a different meaning and indicated a beer similar to an IPA that was vatted for several months.

Jim Koch, who is descended from a family of German immigrants that ran several breweries, founded the Boston Beer Company. His forebears include Louis Koch, whose brewery in St Louis, Missouri, fell victim to another St Louis brewery, Anheuser-Busch, manufacturer of American Budweiser. Jim Koch's father went out of business in Ohio during a bout of merger mania in the 1950s. Jim, a graduate of Harvard, became a successful management consultant but brewing was in his genes. In 1985, he launched Samuel Adams Boston Lager, produced under contract. In 1988 he moved into the former Haffenreffer brewery in Boston, where he launched Boston Ale.

Boston Ale is brewed from two-row pale barley malt and caramel malt: the last named is similar to English crystal malt. The hops are German Spalt and English Fuggles and Goldings. Hops are added three times during the copper boil and there is a massive addition of Goldings in the maturation tank. The pale bronze beer has rich biscuity malt, tart fruit and perfumy, spicy hops on the aroma. Juicy malt, tangy fruit and hop resins fill the mouth while the finish is malty and fruity and dries to a long, hop-bitter finale. The beer is based on a family recipe and is kräusened. This means that some sugar-rich and unfermented wort is added to the maturation tank to encourage a strong second fermentation: it's a method borrowed from classic lager brewing. Boston now brews one million barrels a year in plants strategically placed around the US and is the biggest craft brewery in the country.

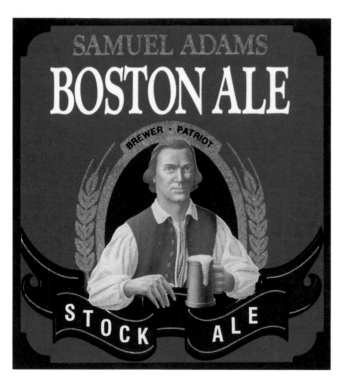

BridgePort Blue Heron

Source: BridgePort Brewery, Portland, Oregon, USA
Strength: 4.9%
Website: www.bridgeportbrew.com

BridgePort has a striking façade. It's based in a warehouse built in 1888 for the Portland Cordage Co that made rope for ships using the Columbia and Willamette rivers that service the town and which are criss-crossed by bridges. The exterior is covered in climbing plants, including some hop bines from the surrounding Oregon hop fields.

When I first visited, the American-Italian Ponzi family owned the brewery. They had made their money from wine but spotted a niche in the market in the 1980s as craft brewing began to blossom in the US, in the Pacific North-west in particular. Their investment had made it possible to install a modern stainless-steel brewhouse open to view for drinkers in the spacious bars in the refurbished building. The beers included a cask-conditioned ale called Coho, a rarity in the US at the time. There was alarm in beer-loving circles when the Ponzis sold the business in 1995 to Gambrinus of Texas, best known for importing the Mexican lager Corona into the US. But to date the new owners have invested massively in BridgePort and expanded the range of naturally conditioned beers.

Blue Heron, named after the emblem of Oregon State, remains one of the flagship beers. It's brewed from barley grown in the Northwest region and has a complex grist of pale, crystal, black and chocolate malts. The dark grains are used in tiny proportions to give subtle nuances of aroma and flavour, and to imbue the finish with a burnished bronze colour. The hops come from the Willamette area: the Willamette is an offspring of the English Fuggle but has developed its own character in

American soil. Surprisingly, Blue Heron has only 18 units of bitterness, extremely low for a pale ale, but nevertheless the hops give a fine sappy and citrus fruit aroma and palate to the beer, balanced by soft, creamy malt in the mouth, and a long finish with pronounced hop resins, tart fruit and juicy malt. It's a splendidly refreshing beer.

TASTING NOTES
Appearance
Aroma
Taste
Overall score

Coopers Sparkling Ale

Source: Coopers Brewery, Adelaide, Australia
Strength: 5.8%
Website: www.coopers.com.au

TASTING NOTES
Appearance
Aroma
Taste
Overall score

Coopers was for long an oddity in Australia. It produced ale when sensible brewers made lagers for a torrid climate. Its flagship brand Sparkling Ale often didn't sparkle: the beer was naturally conditioned with live yeast in keg and bottle, and threw such a heavy sediment that in the glass it was often cloudy. (When a rival Adelaide brewer launched its own sparkling ale, it used the slogan 'A new cloud on the horizon'.) And then, in the 1970s, in step with the 'real ale revolution' in Britain, beer connoisseurs bored with bland lagers discovered Coopers and turned Sparkling Ale into a cult drink. It is no longer confined to South Australia but is a national brand and is also widely exported.

Coopers is now revered rather than reviled, and is the only major brewery in Australia that is still in family hands. The founder was a most unlikely brewer. Thomas Cooper came from the Skipton area of Yorkshire. He emigrated with his wife to Australia in 1852. Cooper was a Methodist lay preacher who disapproved of drinking but his wife was the daughter of an innkeeper and she made beer at home. Cooper worked as a shoemaker and a dairyman but one day turned his hand to brewing when his wife was taken ill. His friends were so impressed with his home brew that they encouraged him to open a commercial brewery, which he did in 1862. When his first wife died, Cooper remarried and fathered 16 children. Today, members of the fourth and fifth generations of the family run the business. They have their own maltings near Adelaide where two-row barley varieties are turned into pale, crystal and roasted malts, while Pride of Ringwood hops come from Tasmania.

For many years, the beers were fermented in a system similar to the 'double drop' method widely used in England in the 19th century (see Brakspear Bitter, page 70). Primary fermentation was in wooden casks made from jarrah hardwood. The beer was then dropped into 108-gallon wooden puncheons where a cleaner fermentation continued. This historic system has been replaced by stainless-steel conical vessels, and some devotees feel the beer has lost a little of its character as a result.

Sparkling Ale is nevertheless a wonderfully complex and rewarding beer. It is brewed from pale and crystal malts with around 18% cane sugar. Cane sugar is used widely in Australian brewing and has been since the early settlers arrived, when it was used to make a rough kind of ale before barley was cultivated. In the wrong hands, too much cane sugar can create a sweet, cloying beer, but Cooper's vigorous ale yeast attacks the sugar and turns it into alcohol.

Pride of Ringwood hop pellets create 27 units of bitterness. The gold/amber beer (10 colour units) is intensely fruity, with apple and banana dominating. The hops give a tempting peppery note to the aroma and a good underpinning of bitterness through the palate to the finish. Citrus fruit also makes an appearance in the long finish with juicy malt and spicy hops. After primary fermentation, the beer is filtered and a dosage of sugary wort is added to encourage a secondary fermentation. Both kegs and bottles are then conditioned in the brewery for six weeks before being released to the trade.

De Koninck

Source: De Koninck Brouwerij, Antwerp, Belgium
Strength: 5%
Website: www.dekoninck.be

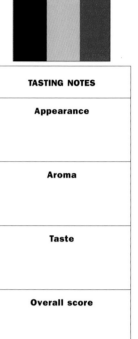

TASTING NOTES
Appearance
Aroma
Taste
Overall score

De Koninck means 'the king' and it is unquestionably the monarch of all it surveys in Antwerp. Large banners drape from buildings displaying a glass of the amber beer. Blow-ups of the glass hang from the ceilings of bars. The beer is so celebrated in the Flemish region of Belgium that nobody has to order it by name. Drinkers merely mention the word *bolleke**, which means little goblet, and a beer swiftly arrives on the bar top or table. 'The king' is not idle boasting but the name of the man, Joseph Henricus De Koninck, who opened a small brew-pub and beer garden in Antwerp in 1833. Following World War One, the Van Den Bogaert family joined the business, and Modeste Van Den Bogaert and his son are now in charge.

On my first visit, the brewery, despite being based on the outskirts of a mighty city, was charmingly rustic, with the beer made in traditional vessels, including a brick-clad boiling copper. When I returned a few years later, these vessels had become part of a small museum. Brewing now takes place in a modern brewhouse that appears to have been designed by draughtsmen from Cape Canaveral: the new stainless-steel copper, sited on a gantry, seems on the point of departure for a moon landing.

For once, change has not impaired the character of the beer. It's ale, made by warm fermentation and, in common with many Belgian pale ales, was inspired by the English versions. But it does more than merely pay homage to them. De Koninck is made with Pilsner and darker Vienna malts with no brewing sugars. The hops are exclusively Saaz, most from the Czech Republic but some grown in Belgium; they are added three times during the boil. The finished beer (22 colour units, 23 bitterness) has an enticing amber colour, a dense rocky head of foam and an entrancing aroma of biscuity malt, hop resins and a spicy, cinnamon-like note. The spice comes from the house yeast. I asked Modeste Van Den Bogaert if the yeast was single strain or multi-strain. He answered enigmatically, 'Perhaps', which is the reply he gives to most questions. Juicy malt, tangy hops, spice and citrus fruit dance on the tongue while the persistent finish becomes dry but is preceded by further delights of toasted malt, spice and fruit. The beer is superb in bottle but is best drunk—filtered but unpasteurised—on draught. It is conditioned in the brewery for two weeks before being released. The Café Pelgrim opposite the brewery not only serves De Koninck but also has a bucket of fresh yeast delivered every day for those drinkers who enjoy a shot of the bitter, frothy liquid as a tonic.

*Antwerp waiters and bar staff feign not to know why the word *bolleke* causes such amusement to British visitors. But the servers take great delight, and with perfectly straight faces, in asking tourists 'not to drop one' as they hand round glasses of De Koninck.

Doc Hadfield's Pale Ale
Source: Spinnakers Brewpub, Victoria, British Columbia, Canada
Strength: 4.2%
Website: www.spinnakers.com

When I arrived at Spinnakers, I enjoyed a splendid lunch and sampled the beer range, then went outside to walk on the beach that fronts the pub, restaurant, brewery and guest house complex. I could have been in Cornwall, with the fine sand and dark rocks, but thoughts of home were quickly dispelled when I suggested to Paul Hadfield that I would take a stroll in the woods behind Spinnakers. 'Don't,' he advised. 'Bears!' Victoria may be frightfully British but Newquay it isn't.

Victoria also had a long fight to establish a brew-pub, the first in the whole country. Spinnakers was the dream of Paul Hadfield, an architect, and businessman John Mitchell. Both are from Vancouver, where John had run a bar. He returned from a trip to Britain with 14 ales. When John, Paul and their friends sampled them a whole new world of beer opened before them. In a vast country dominated by two brewing giants and little choice, they were determined to brew their own British-style ales. The local council refused to give permission but, after lobbying by locals, said it would grant a licence only if a majority approved in a referendum. Ninety-five per cent of those voting said 'Yes'. Even then, Paul and John had to wait for an amendment to federal law before they could fire their mash tun and copper. But from opening day in 1984, Spinnakers has been a huge success, with the brewhouse, built by a British company based in Manchester, expanded twice to meet demand.

Malts are imported from Simpsons in England, while the ale yeast strain was acquired from the National Yeast Collection in Norwich. The Pale Ale, brimming with snappy, fruity Cascade hop character, is made from pale malt, with the hops added twice in the brew kettle and then again in the hop back where the beer rests prior to fermentation. It has a piny and citrus fruit aroma balanced by biscuity malt. Hops, malt and fruit dance across the tongue while the long finish becomes dry, spicy and hoppy but with a good balance of tart fruit and juicy malt. It's enough to make a bear turn to drink.

Geary's Pale Ale
Source: D L Geary Brewing Company, Portland, Maine, USA
Strength: 4.5%
Website: www.gearybrewing.com

The two Portlands—Maine and Oregon—stand on east and west coasts of the US, separated by a vast continent, but they share a love of quality beer. Geary's was one of the earliest American micro-brewers and helped kick-start the brewing revolution.

There were only 13 micros in the entire country when David and Karen Geary opened their plant in 1986. David had learned the brewing skills on several short stints in Britain. He pays tribute to the late David Maxwell Stuart, the laird, or lord, of Traquair in the Scottish Borders, who had re-opened the ancient brewhouse in his stately home and passed on the brewing skills to the visiting American. David also visited the Ringwood brewery in Hampshire and returned with a supply of the house yeast. The trip led to Peter Austin, owner of Ringwood, and his brewer Alan Pugsley, building David's plant. Alan later set up the Shipyard brewery in Portland where he also uses the Ringwood yeast strain.

Geary's Pale Ale holds a special place in the affections of American drinkers, for it proved that there was more to beer than cold, bland and fizzy quasi-lagers, and encouraged a new generation of brewers to follow Geary's path. The copper-coloured beer bears the hallmark of the Ringwood yeast strain, a fruity and spicy note. The beer is brewed with pale, crystal and chocolate malts and is generously hopped with Cascade and Mount Hood from the US, Fuggles from England and Tettnang from Germany. It has a massive floral hop, spicy and citrus fruit aroma with biscuity malt, tangy fruit and hop resins on the tongue. The big finish is fruity and malty but is underscored by a lingering spicy hop note.

TASTING NOTES
Appearance
Aroma
Taste
Overall score

TASTING NOTES
Appearance
Aroma
Taste
Overall score

Iceni Boadicea Chariot Ale

Source: Iceni Brewery, Ickburgh, Norfolk, England
Strength: 3.8%
Website: www.icenibrewery.co.uk

Brendan Moore had a dream one night that encouraged him to leave his job in the food industry in 1995 and become a fully-fledged commercial brewer. He is an Ulsterman living in Norfolk and one night he dreamt that Boadicea, Queen of the Iceni tribe in East Anglia 2000 years ago, was stopping transit vans on the A11 road carrying imported foreign beers. She then went to a cave where she drew pints of ale from a well.

Brendan told the landlord of his local pub about his remarkable dream and was advised to accept Boadicea's challenge to save English ale from foreign invaders by taking up brewing. If Boadicea—Boudicca to the invaders of long ago—was able to defeat the Romans in Colchester, London and St Albans, Brendan thought he could make a modest living as a brewer. Naturally his first beer was called Boadicea Chariot Ale.

Brendan has become a major force in East Anglian brewing. He makes a large portfolio of beers, including more than 20 bottle-conditioned ones, many of them named after tribal warriors or Norfolk idioms. There's a visitor centre at the brewery that draws large crowds who can watch the brewing process as well as visiting Brendan's own hop garden. He plans to grow barley on the site and he's a partner in his daughter Frances's Elveden brewery on the Iveagh family's estate at Thetford: the Iveaghs are the ennobled branch of the Guinness family. He's the driving force behind the East Anglian Brewers' Co-operative that buys malt and hops in bulk for craft brewers in the region. The co-op also delivers beer to pubs and farmers' markets from one truck, cutting down on 'beer miles'.

The malted barley used in Chariot Ale comes from Branthill Farm near Wells-next-the Sea in Norfolk. Brendan and the brewers' co-op buy as much malt as possible from farmer Teddy Maufe at Branthill. He not only grows the finest variety of malting barley—Maris Otter—but has also established a 'traceability' scheme that enables brewers to track their malt down to the fields where the barley was grown. This, they believe, allows them to brew beers with consistent aromas and flavours from one year to another and gives Maris Otter as much credibility as the 'terroir' of French grapes. Farmer Maufe also runs two Real Ale shops that sell East Anglian craft brewers' beers to both visitors and by mail order (www.therealaleshop.co.uk).

For Chariot Ale, Brendan uses Maris Otter pale malt and Pilot hops grown in Suffolk. The beer has a deep bronze colour and an aroma rich with hop resins, nutty malt and citrus fruit. Tart fruit, hop resins and cracker-wheat grain build in the mouth. The finish is intensely bitter and hoppy but malt and tart fruit give a sturdy balance.

TASTING NOTES
Appearance
Aroma
Taste
Overall score

Marston's Pedigree

Source: Marston, Thompson & Evershed Brewery, Burton-on-Trent, Staffordshire, England
Strength: 4.5%
Website: www.wdb.co.uk

In any country where a brewer makes pale ale, he or she will genuflect in the direction of Burton-on-Trent. This small and otherwise unremarkable town in the middle of England was the engine room of brewing in the 19th century. Beer from such revered breweries as Allsopp and Bass refreshed all parts of the British Empire and were even acceptable in post-revolutionary America. Burton Pale Ale became a hallmark and a benchmark, and even encouraged the first makers of pale lager beers in Bavaria and Bohemia.

The secret of Burton's success lay not in the town but under it: the springs that bubble to the surface of the Trent Valley are rich in sulphates—

TASTING NOTES
Appearance
Aroma
Taste
Overall score

The Burton Unions at Marston's Brewery in Burton-on-Trent. Fermenting beer rises from the giant oak vessels into the troughs above, where the yeast is trapped.

calcium and magnesium in particular, better known as gypsum and Epsom Salts respectively. The salts enhanced the flavours of the new pale malts developed in the 19th century and also new and improved varieties of hops. The result was IPAs and pale ales with delicious and refreshing juicy malt and bitter hop character.

The Burton brewers also needed to present their new pale beers in the most attractive fashion, especially as glass was replacing pewter as the preferred container for draught beer in pubs.

Beer needed to be clear, sparkling and clear of dregs. Peter Walker, a brewer from Warrington, one of many who set up new plants in Burton to capitalise on the water there, developed a system known as the 'Burton Union'. It was based on a medieval method used by monks. As beer fermented in wooden casks, yeast frothed out of the bung holes of the casks and was collected in buckets below for reuse.

It was a messy system and Walker turned it on its head. He placed troughs above the fermentation casks, and connected troughs and casks with swan-necked pipes. The fermenting wort and yeast rise from the casks up the pipes and drip into the trays above. The troughs are slightly inclined,

enabling the beer to run back into the casks while the yeast is held behind. The method is brilliant in its simplicity: the beer is aerated, encouraging a powerful, continuing fermentation; it is cleared of unnecessary yeast; and the yeast propagated by the system can be stored and used again. Casks and troughs, linked together, were said in Victorian times to be 'held in union', hence the name of the system.

At one time, all the Burton brewers used the union system but it was phased out on the grounds of cost. But Marston's has remained true to the system and spent £1 million in the 1990s adding a third room of union casks. The oak casks, each one holding 144 gallons, have to be repaired at regular intervals, which means Marston's has to employ coopers, and the finest oak has to be imported from Europe and the US. But the company won't compromise, as the flavour of Pedigree is paramount.

Pedigree is a true Burton pale ale, not a bitter. It is brewed from Maris Otter pale malt, which comprises 83% of the recipe, and 17% glucose sugar. The hops are the whole flowers of Fuggles and Goldings. The colour rating is 20, the bitterness units 24. This is an authentic 19th-century Burton pale ale recipe. Maltose, which is the brewing sugar derived from malt, cannot be entirely fermented into alcohol: some maltose is left and gives fullness, or 'body', to the beer. Glucose, on the other hand, can be 'fermented out', giving more alcohol and dryness to the finished beer. The units of bitterness contributed by the hops show how the Victorian brewers responded to public demand for a less bitter and 'narcotic' beer. The gold/bronze Pedigree has a delightful aroma of juicy malt, hop resins and tart fruit, all overlain by a renowned waft of sulphur that comes from the salt-rich water. It's an aroma known locally as 'the Burton snatch'. Biscuity malt, spicy hops and apple fill the mouth: apple fruit is another defining characteristic of Burton pale ale. The finish has earthy, peppery hops, juicy malt, slight saltiness and further hint of apple.

I once described the Marston's union rooms as 'the cathedrals of brewing'. On a subsequent visit I was welcomed to the brewery by a member of staff dressed in the full regalia of a bishop. I hope he'll put in a good word for me with St Peter.

Mendocino Blue Heron Pale Ale

Source: Mendocino Brewing Company, Hopland, California, USA
Strength: 5.5%
Website: www.mendocinobrew.com

TASTING NOTES
Appearance
Aroma
Taste
Overall score

The address—Hopland—is a marketing man's dream. Hops were grown in this area of California until an outbreak of mildew in the 1950s destroyed the plants. As a result, cultivation moved north to Oregon. Mendocino's beers are packed with hop bitterness, aroma and flavour. Most of the hops come from the Pacific North-west but the owners of the brewery have restored pride and tradition by planting new hop bines amid California's vineyards.

Mendocino is a company with a short but stormy history. In the 1970s, Jack McAuliffe launched the New Albion brewery in Sonoma, the first new micro-brewery in the US since Prohibition. McAuliffe served in Britain with the US Navy and acquired a taste and a passion for English ales, as his choice of name for his brewery shows. His beers were good but the enterprise was ahead of its time and lasted for only six years.

Some of the equipment, along with the English yeast strain and two of the brewers, helped set up Mendocino in 1983. The company expanded rapidly to meet the demands for its ales and lagers. But nemesis stalked hubris: a new brewery in Ukiah in 1996 overstretched the company and it was rescued by Vijay Mallya, the billionaire owner of United Breweries of India, best known for Kingfisher lager. The acquisition has enabled Mallya to expand sales of Kingfisher in the US but Mendocino survives as a craft brewery.

Most of the beers are named after birds, including the Blue Heron, which nest in the Russian River area of California. Blue Heron Pale Ale is an all-malt beer that uses only pale malt from two-row barley. The hops are Cascade and Warrior. The beer—colour eight units, bitterness a massive 45 units—has a stunning aroma of pine and tart citrus fruit, with grapefruit dominating. Hops meld with juicy malt on the nose and in the mouth while the finish is long and finishes dry and bitter but with powerful contributions from biscuity malt and citrus fruit. Blue Heron, on draught or bottle fermented, is the perfect companion to the excellent cuisine in the brewery's restaurant.

Palm Spéciale

Source: Palm Brouwerij, Steenhuffel, Belgium
Strength: 5.2%
Website: www.palm.be

TASTING NOTES
Appearance
Aroma
Taste
Overall score

Palm beers are the biggest-selling pale ales in Belgium. Owned by the Van Roy family for 250 years, the brewery is substantial and the company expansive: it now also owns the Rodenbach brewery in Roeselare. But the Steenhuffel site has a country air, recalling its origins as the De Hoorn farm in the 16th century. A brewery has been in operation since 1747 and was called De Hoorn until 1975, when the name changed to Palm to strengthen the identity of its main brands. Pale ales were introduced after 1918, when a member of the family who was a priest suggested the ales should be called Palm as a symbol of peace following World War One.

The brewery is a blend of old and new vessels, with copper ones dating from the late 19th and early 20th centuries in one brewhouse, alongside a new 1990s brewhouse built with stainless-steel equipment. Unusually for an ale, the brewing cycle begins with a decoction mash. The brewery's wells provide soft water high in calcium carbonate. Pale malt is blended with darker malt and a little maize to produce a rich amber-coloured beer: colour is around 14 units. Kent and Styrian Goldings create between 25 and 30 units of bitterness. A complex, three-strain yeast culture ferments the beer to a biscuity dryness with rich orange fruit and peppery Goldings on the aroma, juicy malt, citrus fruit and hops in the mouth, and a finish finely balanced between toasty malt, tart fruit and herbal and spicy hops.

The brewery's beers are marketed with the symbol of the local sturdy, white-maned Brabant working horses. The horses are bred at a stud run by Palm, which also owns the adjoining chateau of Diepensteyn. After a tour of the brewery I was taken to admire the horses and then to enjoy a superb lunch in the chateau, where each dish was matched by a different beer: Palm also brews a spiced wheat beer, a Pils, a 7% ale called Aerts and a seasonal Dobbel, or double, Palm at 5.5%. Groups may tour the brewery and the chateau.

Samuel Smith Old Brewery Pale Ale

Source: Samuel Smith Old Brewery, Tadcaster, Yorkshire, England
Strength: 5.2%
Website: www.samuelsmithbrewery.co.uk

TASTING NOTES
Appearance
Aroma
Taste
Overall score

Sam Smith's is one of the oldest family-owned breweries in England. It is fiercely loyal to its Yorkshire base, but some of its 200 pubs are in London, among them the Olde Cheshire Cheese in Fleet Street, once a haunt of such literary giants as Dr Johnson and Charles Dickens.

Tadcaster has been an important brewing town since the 14th century, sitting on an underground lake of limestone water. The town became known as the 'Burton of the North' as a result of the importance of the water supply. Today there are still three breweries in the town, a former Bass plant now owned by Coors, Sam Smith's and John Smith's. Sam and John came from the same family but a row early in the 20th century led to John walking up the hill and opening his own plant. Now it is part of the Scottish & Newcastle group, a fate that Humphrey Smith, the current chairman of Sam Smith's, would never tolerate. His brewery dates from 1758 and still uses 'Yorkshire square' fermenters. This system, in common with the Burton union system, was designed to separate fermenting beer from yeast and also created the thick collar of foam beloved by Yorkshire drinkers.

The first brewery to use squares was Bentley & Shaw of Huddersfield, and it is thought that the system was the result of work in the 18th century by the Yorkshire scientist Dr Joseph Priestley, who lived next door to a brewery in Leeds. He unravelled the mysteries of 'fixed air', or carbon dioxide, and the absorption of gases in liquids. His research led to the development of carbonated water and later soft drinks.

A few Yorkshire brewers still use squares but Sam Smith is the only one that employs vessels made of Welsh slate: most modern squares are built of stainless steel. A square is a two-storey vessel. The two chambers are connected by a porthole with a raised rim and also by 'organ pipes'. The bottom chamber is filled with wort and yeast. As fermentation gets under way, yeast and wort rise through the porthole into the top chamber. The rim traps the yeast while the wort drains back into the bottom chamber via the organ pipes. The result is a beer with a high level of natural carbonation and a full-bodied, malty body.

Sam Smith's Pale Ale is a notable member of the Yorkshire family of beers. It is brewed from pale malt and 10% crystal malt, and hopped with the traditional English varieties, Fuggles and Goldings. It has 35 colour units and 26 bitterness units. The aroma has a malty, biscuity character with a hint of toffee or butterscotch, and a spicy and herbal note from the hops. The rich palate is dominated by biscuity malt, spicy, herbal hops, butterscotch and a hint of vinous fruit. The finish is long and broad, with delicious juicy malt and a lingering hop bitterness, with touches of fruit and toffee.

ABOVE
The Olde Cheshire Cheese in Fleet Street London, once a haunt of such literary giants as Dr Johnson and Charles Dickens is now a major London outlet for Sam Smith's.

Sierra Nevada Pale Ale

Source: Sierra Nevada Brewing Company, Chico, California, USA
Strength: 5.6%
Website: www.sierranevada.com

TASTING NOTES
Appearance
Aroma
Taste
Overall score

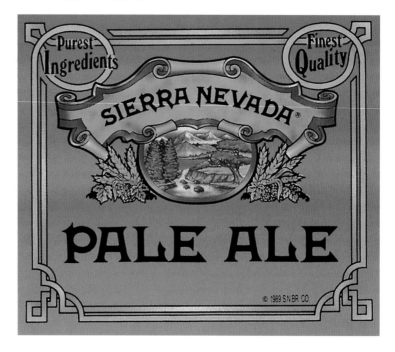

For beer lovers both within and without the US, Sierra Nevada is the benchmark pale ale of modern brewing. It was the inspiration for many of the revivalist pale ales and IPAs that now make beer drinking such a pleasure in North America.

The brewery dates from 1981 and was launched by two keen home-brewers, Ken Grossman and Paul Camusi, in the university town of Chico, where there is a fine supply of water from the Sierra Nevada and Cascade mountain ranges. They started with converted dairy tanks but the success of their venture enabled them to buy a state-of-the-art plant with copper vessels from Germany. That plant has also been replaced, and the current site produces 800,000 barrels a year. It is one of the ironies of modern craft brewing that Sierra Nevada is considered to be a micro in the US but is bigger than many British regional breweries that each make around 25,000 barrels a year.

Sierra Nevada now has a wide range of beers but Pale Ale made the company's reputation.

It has won many awards at the Great American Beer Festival and won a gold medal in the 2004 Brewing International Awards. The bottled version (which is bottle fermented with live yeast) is made from two-row pale malt and caramel [crystal] malt. It is hopped with Magnum and Perle for bitterness and late hopped with Cascade for aroma: it has 37 units of bitterness. The draught version is slightly darker and also a degree or two lower in strength. Pale Ale has a pale bronze colour with a hint of amber, topped by a big fluffy head of foam. The aroma is spicy and peppery from the hops, balanced by biscuit malt and tart citrus fruit from the Cascades. In the mouth there is a superb balance of hop resins, juicy malt and tangy fruit, while the long, deep finish offers a hint of vanilla pods and marzipan before it finally becomes dry, bitter and hoppy but underscored by sweet malt. It is a beautifully balanced beer with an uncompromising hop character.

Younger's Special Bitter

Source: Rogue Ales, Newport, Oregon, USA
Strength: 6.5%
Website: www.rogue.com

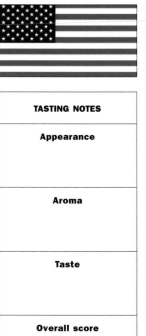

British readers may think this beer has a connection with Younger's, the brewery that became part of the giant Scottish & Newcastle group. But the name is more prosaic: it pays homage to Bill Younger of the Horse Brass pub in Portland, Oregon, an enthusiastic purveyor of Rogue beers.

'Enthusiasm' is the key word at the brewery. Jack Joyce, a former advertising executive with Nike, founded the small craft brewery in 1988 in Ashland, Oregon, and named it after the local Rogue river. Jack had a vision of small batch, well-brewed beer made without preservatives or cheap cereal adjuncts, and that vision married with the skills of brewmaster John Maier, who had previously brewed with the Alaskan Brewery.

When a flood destroyed their original site, they set up shop in Newport and have expanded to a 50-barrel production line. They don't want to get big or take part in mergers and takeovers but want to concentrate on making great beers that boom with hop character from local varieties. Younger's Special Bitter was originally called Rogue Ale and is brewed with two-row pale malt and crystal malt, with imported East Kent Goldings and local Willamette. It has a colour of 17 units and a powerful 35 units of bitterness. It has an overwhelming nose of apricot fruit and floral hops, underscored by rich biscuity malt with a hint of toffee. The palate is full-bodied, with chewy malt, peppery, mouth-puckering hops and tart fruit, while the long and lingering finish has an amazing punch of hops with an almost iodine-like bitterness but wonderfully balanced by biscuity malt and citrus fruit. At 6.5%, this beer might be considered an IPA rather than a pale ale, but Rogue avoids any dispute by brewing an IPA as well.

TASTING NOTES
Appearance
Aroma
Taste
Overall score

Bitters

Bitter was a beer style born as much by the demands of brewers' cash flow as consumer preference. The 19th century was a turbulent time for the British brewing industry. In 1830, a Beer Act allowed anyone to open a pub or beer house on payment of two guineas (£2.40) for a licence. 46,000 new beer houses opened, almost doubling the number of licensed premises in Britain. Nicknamed Tom and Jerry Houses, they were often no more than the front rooms of private houses. Most of the new publicans had no business acumen, let alone the ability to store and serve beer, often in premises without cellars or any rudimentary form of cooling.

BELOW
Brakspear Bitter from Oxfordshire is a classic English copper-coloured beer with a rich hop character.

But the brewers, confronted by thousands of new licensed premises, rushed to dominate them by offering publicans 'loan tie' agreements: in return for loans and discounts, the publicans agreed to take beer only from the donor breweries. This beer retailing experiment in a free market was a disaster. One of the supporters of the Parliamentary Bill that led to the Act, Sydney Smith, wrote: 'Everybody is drunk. Those who are not singing are sprawling. The sovereign people are in a beastly state.'

When the law was tightened to prevent such easy access to beer retailing, many of the new pubs crashed and the brewers lost their investments. In 1896, the London brewer Barclay Perkins was owed £2 million by bankrupt publicans. Allsopp of Burton-on-Trent was so badly affected that it went into receivership and had to be restructured. Undeterred, other brewers rushed to buy the thousands of failed pubs on the market. The property scramble sent prices soaring. The brewers paid extravagant amounts to establish estates of 'tied pubs'.

As many of the breweries had become public companies and were responsible to their shareholders, urgent action was necessary to restore profitability. Brewers and shareholders were no longer prepared to lock up beer—liquid capital—in vats and casks, waiting months and even years for the cash to come in. They moved away from porters, stock ales and IPAs, and developed a new type of draught ale known as 'running beer'. The scientific understanding of yeast was a powerful impetus to producing running ales. Pure strains meant that fermentation could be better controlled. Yeast packed down and cleared in cask within a few days, enabling beer to 'drop bright' and be served within a few days of reaching the pub cellar.

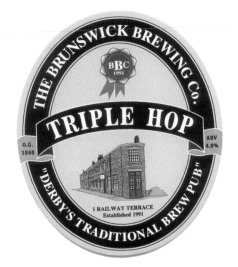

Running beers—today's cask-conditioned beer, or real ale—quickly came to dominate the pub market by the turn of the 20th century. Mild made up a substantial proportion of the draught market, but a lighter beer, an offshoot of pale ale, quickly challenged mild's hegemony. The brewers were conscious that running beers, which enjoyed only a brief secondary fermentation in cask, lacked the smoothness and maturity of vatted beers. The problem was overcome by the development of a new type of malt called crystal. It is stewed malt made by a process similar to making toffee that turns the starch inside each kernel of malt into crystallised sugar. It cannot be fermented by brewer's yeast but adds a rich nutty and biscuity character to beer and a fullness of palate. While crystal has to be blended sparingly with pale and other standard malts (usually not more than 10% of the total), it gave running beers the characteristic bronze and copper colours that became the hallmark of a style dubbed 'bitter' by drinkers to distinguish it from less heavily hopped mild ale.

Bitter became the style of beer that distinguished Britain from every other brewing nation. Visitors from overseas, even though affronted by the assault of hop bitterness on their mouths and throats, find a visit to a British pub and a glass of bitter high on their itineraries. Even though the insipid versions of lager brewed in Britain now vie with ale in popularity, bitter—low in carbonation, malty, nutty and with fruity, spicy and peppery hop notes—remains a staple of pub life.

Bitter comes in different strengths but the differences are often confused by labelling. Standard bitters should come within the band of 3.6–4% alcohol, best bitters 4.1% and above. Nevertheless, as this section shows, some brewers call standard bitters 'best'. Perversely, a few bitters are known as 'ordinary', as in the case of Brakspear's and Young's bitters. Only the English, with their tight-lipped refusal to admit to doing something well, could downplay one of the glories of the beer world with such a dismissive shrug of the shoulders.

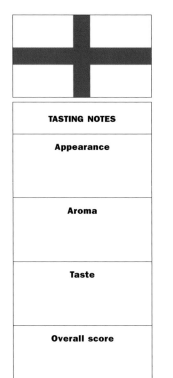

Adnams Bitter

Source: Adnams Sole Bay Brewery, Southwold, Suffolk, England
Strength: 3.7%
Website: www.adnams.co.uk

TASTING NOTES
Appearance
Aroma
Taste
Overall score

Adnams has both history and location on its side. Southwold is on the Suffolk coast, with a whitewashed, inshore lighthouse standing as a stubby sentinel over the small market town. Brewing has been carried on in Southwold for 650 years: in 1345, Johanna de Corby was fined by local magistrates for serving her ale in unmarked tankards. For centuries, brewing took place at the back of the Swan Hotel, a magnificent coaching inn. The brewery grew over time and was bought by George and Ernest Adnams in 1872. In 1902, the Anglo-Irish Loftus family joined them in a long-running partnership: members of both families still control the company today.

When I first visited Adnams in the late 1970s, it enjoyed a fine reputation for its beer but, apart from a small amount of free trade in London and the Home Counties, sales were confined to its own estate of pubs in Suffolk. Enormous demand for the beer saw sales increase dramatically. In 2001, £1.8 million was invested to double fermenting capacity. As a result, Adnams' beers are now available nationally but there has been

no decline in quality. The attitude of chairman Jonathan Adnams and head brewer Fergus Fitzgerald is simple: if you don't like our beers, drink someone else's. Adnams refuses to compromise and produces spectacularly hoppy and tangy beers with a hint of salty sea breeze: they are to beer what Islay is to malt whisky.

Bitter is the flagship product, a pale copper beer brewed with Maris Otter pale and crystal malts, invert sugar and a touch of caramel for colour adjustment (26 colour units). The hops are First Gold, Fuggles and Goldings, used in whole flower form, with dry hopping in cask (33 units of bitterness). The Adnams' yeast culture gives the beer a pronounced orange fruit tang on the nose and palate, with peppery hops and juicy malt. The finish lingers and is finely balanced between biscuity malt, tart citrus fruit and bitter and peppery hops.

I hesitate to call it a beer to die for, as one of the brewery's founders, George Adnams, went to Africa where he was eaten by a crocodile, proof that a career in brewing is the safer option.

Black Sheep Best Bitter

Source: Black Sheep Brewery, Masham, North Yorkshire, England
Strength: 3.8%
Website: www.blacksheepbrewery.com

The wealth of Wensleydale, where the market town of Masham is based, comes from sheep and wool. The name of the brewery is a joke within a joke, reflecting both the rural economy and the fact that founder Paul Theakston is the black sheep of the famous brewing family. Paul was a director of Theakston's brewery in Masham (see Theakston Best Bitter, page 77) until it was taken over by the national group Scottish & Newcastle in 1988. He walked out and founded his own brewery in 1992 in the former maltings of another old Masham brewery, Lightfoot's. He toured Yorkshire and the surrounding counties to buy the finest traditional brewing equipment, including a vast domed copper and Yorkshire square fermenters.

Paul doesn't own a single pub but he has built a free trade of 800 outlets, while the bottled versions of his beers are available nationally. A new brewhouse was built in 2003 and further expansion will increase production to 80,000 barrels a year, an impressive success story for a company that is less than 15 years' old. The site includes a visitor centre, shop and an excellent bistro run by Paul's wife Sue.

Black Sheep Best enjoys a vigorous fermentation with a multi-strain yeast culture and emerges with a pale gold colour (19 units) and a heavy collar of foam in the Yorkshire manner. It is brewed with Maris Otter pale and crystal malts and a tiny amount of roast malt for colour and flavour. The hops are Challenger, Fuggles and Progress; Fuggles are used as a late copper hop (31 units of bitterness). The beer has a spicy and earthy Fuggles character on the nose, balanced by biscuity malt and citrus fruit. Full-bodied, slightly toasted malt fills the mouth with tangy hop resins and tart fruit, followed by a finish bursting with complex malt, fruit and hop notes, finally becoming dry and uncompromisingly bitter. Great Yorkshire beer, baa gum!

TASTING NOTES
Appearance
Aroma
Taste
Overall score

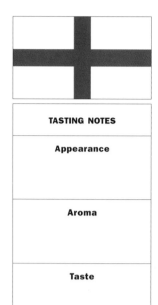

Brakspear Bitter

Source: Brakspear Brewing Co, Witney, Oxfordshire, England
Strength: 3.4%
Website: www.brakspear-beers.co.uk

TASTING NOTES
Appearance
Aroma
Taste
Overall score

Drinkers may call for 'a pint of Ordinary' but Extraordinary would be a better description. It is one of the joys and mysteries of the beer world that so much flavour and complexity can be packed into a beer of such modest strength.

W.H. Brakspear traces its history back to 1779 in the riverside town of Henley-on-Thames. The Brakspears were distantly related to Nicholas Breakspear who, as Adrian IV, became the first and so far only English-born Pope in 1154. The Brakspears pronounce their name in the same way as their illustrious forebear and use the symbol of the bee on his mitre as the company logo. The brewery was founded by Robert Brakspear and briskly expanded by his son William Henry, who built a chain of pubs in Oxfordshire and Buckinghamshire.

The character of the Henley beers owes much to the fascinating 'double drop' fermenting system that is used. The wooden vessels are ranged on two storeys. Fermentation starts in the top bank of vessels and after 16 hours the liquid is literally dropped down into the second storey of vessels below. Dead yeast cells, unwanted protein and other detritus are left behind, encouraging a cleaner and faster fermentation in the second bank of vessels. The result was beers that were full-bodied, quenching and clean tasting, and with a butterscotch note known as diacetyl that is a bi-product of fermentation and which most brewers struggle to keep out of their beers.

In 2002, the brewery, by now a public, listed company, was threatened with closure, as its riverside site was worth a fortune as private housing. In spite of a vigorous campaign by drinkers, the brewery did close but the drinks group Refresh UK, which also owned the Wychwood Brewery in Witney, bought the rights to the beers. Refresh built a new, separate brewhouse alongside the Wychwood plant and installed the double-drop fermenters in a raftered building that was once a maltings. Brakspear Bitter and Special were unveiled in 2004 to great acclaim. The water supply in Witney is almost identical to Henley's and the same recipes are used for the beers. Both breweries are now owned by Marston's.

The Bitter is brewed with Maris Otter pale and crystal malts with invert sugar added in the copper. The hops are whole flower Fuggles and Goldings. The deep bronze beer has 22 units of colour and 38 units of bitterness: this is 'boy's bitter' with hair on its chest. The aroma has pungent, earthy hops, biscuity malt, butterscotch and tart orange fruit. Sappy malt, bitter hop resins and fruit vie for attention on the tongue, while the finish has a wonderfully clean maltiness balanced by tangy fruit, butterscotch and bitter hops.

Brunswick Triple Hop

Source: Brunswick Inn, Derby, England
Strength: 4%
Website: www.brunswickinn.co.uk

The Brunswick is a remarkable inn that was once part of a row of cottages built for railway workers in 1842. The triangular, end-of-terrace pub is at 1 Railway Terrace, just a minute's walk from Derby railway station. The pub closed in 1974 and fell into disrepair but was rescued and restored to its Victorian glory by the Derbyshire Railway Trust. It reopened in the 1980s and has flagstone floors, a warren of small, intimate rooms off a central corridor, old station waiting-room furniture, coal fires, lamps and railway memorabilia by the yard. It's an atmospheric cross between a pub, a country station and a working men's club. Shortly after the reopening, a brewery was added in rooms at the back of the pub and the Brunswick rapidly won a reputation as a classic Victorian ale house serving superb beers.

The range of beers is vast and ever-changing, with monthly, seasonal and one-off brews backing such regulars as Railway Porter and Old Accidental. Triple Hop is the session beer brewed with pale malt only and a pinch of torrefied wheat for clarity and a good head of foam. The three hop varieties used are Challenger, Goldings and Northdown. The beer is pale gold with a rocky head of foam, a pungent, earthy and spicy hop nose with biscuity malt, tart lemon fruit and a hint of sulphur from the water (Derby is just down the road from Burton-on-Trent and also enjoys similar pungent and salty water). The palate has rich, juicy malt, tangy fruit and bitter hop resins, with a lingering finish that becomes exceptionally dry and bitter but balanced by rich malt and citrus fruit. It's a pale, quenching and uncompromisingly bitter beer.

The pub is now owned by Everards, the Leicester-based regional brewery, but the Brunswick enjoys almost complete autonomy under manager and brewer Graham Yates, who can usually be found pulling pints behind the bar in the main corridor when he's not 'mashing in'.

There's good lunchtime food, a family room where children are welcome, and live jazz on Thursday evenings.

Butcombe Bitter

Source: Butcombe Brewery, Cox's Green, Wrington, Somerset, England
Strength: 4%
Website: www.butcombe.com

Butcombe opened for business in 1978 and for the first 18 years of its life was a one-beer brewery, producing only Bitter. It has since added to the range but Bitter accounts for three-quarters of its output.

The founder was Simon Whitmore, who downsized from executive posts with Guinness International and Courage to set up one of the first of the 'new wave' micro-breweries in the 1970s. He sank his redundancy money from Courage into the brewery, built at the back of his house in the countryside. The acclaim for Bitter was so great that he had to expand the site twice to cope with demand. In 2003, after a lifetime in brewing big and small, Simon finally retired and sold the company to a small group of friends led by Guy Newell, who had set up the national wholesaling company The Beer Seller. A new brewery was built in 2005, just a few miles from Butcombe and using the same water supply. The recipes, which avoid any added sugars or colourings, remain unchanged but annual output will rise to 30,000 barrels a year, making Butcombe bigger than several family-owned regional breweries.

Bitter is made from Maris Otter pale malt with 5% crystal (20 units of colour). The hops are Northdown, German Northern Brewer and Yeoman (31–35 units of bitterness). The pale bronze beer has a superb aroma of pungent, spicy hop resins, tart fruit and biscuity malt, followed by full-bodied juicy malt, peppery hops and light fruit in the mouth. The finish is long and deep, beautifully balanced between smooth grain and bitter hops, with a continuing bridge of tart fruit.

Butcombe owns seven pubs, and one warm summer day I enjoyed with Simon Whitmore a pint or two of Butcombe Bitter and a proper ploughman's lunch of tangy, crumbly cheese and fresh crusty bread in the garden of one of them.

TASTING NOTES

Appearance

Aroma

Taste

Overall score

TASTING NOTES

Appearance

Aroma

Taste

Overall score

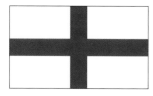

Coniston Bluebird Bitter

Source: Coniston Brewing Co, Coniston, Cumbria, England
Strength: 3.6%
Website: www.conistonbrewery.com

TASTING NOTES
Appearance
Aroma
Taste
Overall score

Coniston sprang to fame—and raised the profile of the entire micro-brewing sector—when Bluebird Bitter won CAMRA's Champion Beer of Britain competition in 1998. The beer became nationally available and, thanks to its success, the Ridgeway Brewery in Oxfordshire produces a stronger, bottle-conditioned version at 4.2%. Coniston enjoys one of the finest locations of any British brewery. It stands at the end of a road that leads up to a Lakeland peak called the Old Man of Coniston. The brewery is fronted by the Black Bull, an ancient coaching inn that dates from the time of the famous Elizabethan sea dog, Sir Francis Drake, conqueror of the Spanish Armada.

It's a more recent mariner, though, who is commemorated in the inn. Donald Campbell used it as his base for his ill-fated assault on the world water speed record on Coniston Water in 1967. There are photos of Campbell and his team on the walls of the inn, and the brewery's main beer is named after his boat, *Bluebird*.

Brewer Ian Bradley, whose parents own the inn, has access to the finest brewing water, with a beck—local dialect for a stream—running alongside and fed by water from the surrounding mountains and fells. Ian uses Maris Otter pale malt and 5% crystal in the beer. Bluebird is a 'single varietal' beer, using just one hop, Challenger. Colour is 21 units, bitterness 22. The pale bronze beer has a rich and enticing aroma of hop resins and elderflower backed by rich, biscuity malt. The palate is full, balanced between juicy malt, tart fruit and bitter hops, followed by a long, smooth and quenching finish that becomes dry, bitter and hoppy but with mellow notes of biscuity malt and fruit.

Ian Bradley lost a leg in a motorcycle accident a few years ago but, with great courage, has overcome his disability to manage the brewery with enormous verve and enthusiasm. As the mood takes him, he will either wear a false leg or hop around the place on his good 'un like yet another sea dog, Long John Silver.

Harveys Sussex Best Bitter

Source: Harvey & Son, Lewes, East Sussex, England
Strength: 4%
Website: www.harveys.org.uk

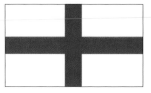

TASTING NOTES
Appearance
Aroma
Taste
Overall score

Lewes is an ancient town close to the sea and the Sussex Downs, and guarded by a castle. It has its own bibulous 'cathedral', the locals' affectionate name for Harvey's brewery. The site was built in 1784 alongside the River Ouse that meanders through the town. It came under the control of John Harvey in 1790 and, in 1880, his family rebuilt the site in red-brick Victorian Gothic style (see picture), though the Georgian fermenting rooms and cellars remain. The architect was the celebrated William Bradford, who also designed the Hook Norton, Shipstone and Tolly Cobbold breweries. His constructions are known as 'tower breweries', as the brewing process flows logically from floor to floor by gravity, without the aid of mechanical pumps.

The seventh generation of the Harvey family is still in evidence at the brewery. In the 20th century, the Jenners, who had run a south London brewery since the mid-18th century before moving to the coast, joined the Harveys. Miles Jenner represents his family today in the role of head brewer. His father arrived in Lewes in 1938 and worked for Harveys for the following 60 years as head brewer, managing director and,

finally, chairman. Miles has been head brewer since 1986 and lives with his family in 'the brewer's house' in the grounds of the brewery. He makes sensational beers that deserve to be better known, but the company has avoided the high-risk strategy of going national and selling its products at deep discounts to the voracious pub groups. Harveys instead concentrates on supplying its 45 pubs as well as the free trade in London and South-east England.

Best Bitter is a classic of the style, a complex and rewarding blend of malt and hops. The malts are Maris Otter and Pipkin pale malts, with crystal malt, flaked maize and brewing sugars. No fewer than four hop varieties—Bramling Cross, Fuggles, Goldings and Progress—are used and added at different stages of the copper boil to extract the desired aromas and bitterness (colour 33 units, bitterness 38 units). The amber beer has a tempting nose of pungent, grassy and spicy hops, biscuit malt and tangy fruit. It fills the mouth with sappy malt, hop resins and citrus fruit, followed by a long and deep finish that becomes dry, bitter and hoppy but beautifully balanced by juicy malt and fruit.

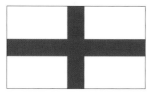

Holden's Black Country Bitter

Source: Holden's Brewery, Woodsetton, Dudley, West Midlands, England
Strength: 3.9%
Website: www.holdensbrewery.co.uk

TASTING NOTES
Appearance
Aroma
Taste
Overall score

In the 19th and early 20th centuries, just about every town and village in the Black Country had a brewery or a pub that brewed on the premises. Their task was to satisfy the enormous demand for refreshment from the army of workers in factories and mines. Most of the small breweries have gone but Holden's, along with its near neighbour Batham's, continues. They have more than just beer in common. Both families are keen supporters of 'The Baggies'—West Bromwich Albion football club—and the breweries' taps or adjacent pubs sport literary quotations above the doors.

As we have seen in the case of Batham's (see page 37), Shakespeare is the inspiration, but Holden's goes one better with a Latin phrase from Horace's *Odes: Nunc Est Bibendum*, or Now Is the Time for Drinking. Wise words indeed, suggesting that Black Country folk were remarkably literate long before education was universal.

The Holden's involvement in brewing goes back four generations when Edwin and Lucy Holden first made beer in the Park Inn. They were so successful that they built a substantial brewery next door, which is one of the neatest and most attractive I have visited, with gleaming metalwork and tiles, and mashing, boiling and fermenting laid out on two floors. The brewery now owns 21 pubs and supplies an additional 60 outlets in the area. The Holdens have renovated, to much acclaim, a Grade II listed railway building in Codsall, where their beers are sold, and have also restored the Park Inn to its full Victorian splendour, with fascinating photographs of the family and its workers over several generations.

Black Country Bitter is a classic, brewed with Maris Otter pale malt and a high proportion of crystal malt (12%) with some torrefied wheat for clarity and head. Fuggles is the only hop variety used and the beer is dry hopped in cask (colour 24, bitterness 26). The beer has a copper colour with crisp, earthy hop resins, biscuity malt and a vinous fruitiness on the nose. Sappy malt, ripe fruit and bitter hops dominate the mouth, with a finish in which the nutty and fruity character of crystal malt plays a full part, balanced by a gentle but persistent earthy hop bitterness. Stonkin' good beer, as they say in the Black Country, echoing Horace.

Holt's Bitter

Source: Joseph Holt, Derby Brewery, Cheetham, Manchester, England
Strength: 4%
Website: www.joseph-holt.com

Holt's Bitter, in common with the brewery's Mild (see page 44) is a beer that takes no prisoners. If you don't like hop bitterness, then you'd be advised to drink a different brew, as this beer puckers the tongue and leaves a furrow down the back of the throat. With 40 units of bitterness, it is one of the bitterest beers regularly brewed in Britain.

Aficionados not only revel in the pungent aroma and flavour of the beer but are also aware they are helping to contribute to a good cause. The Holt family has long been a supporter of Christies Hospital in Manchester, one of the first to specialise in analysing and treating cancer. In the 1930s, the Holts helped sponsor the pioneering work of Dr Ralston Paterson at Christies. Today a donation from every pint of the brewery's beers goes to the hospital.

The Bitter is so popular in Holt's pubs that the brewery still supplies the beer in casks called hogsheads that each holds 54 gallons of beer. Most other breweries have long since phased out such giant casks but it's not unknown at Holt's to send a hogshead to a pub in the morning and for it to return empty to the brewery in the evening.

The Bitter is almost identical to the Mild except that it is stronger, and dark invert sugar in the recipe is replaced by a light version. The grains are Halcyon and Alexis pale malt, crystal malt and black malt, and the hops are Goldings and Northdown. It has a piquant, nostril-widening aroma of spicy and peppery hops, juicy malt and tart fruit. The palate is quenching, dominated by sappy malt, tangy citrus fruit and aggressive bitterness, followed by a persistent finish bursting with snappy and spicy hops, biscuity malt and bitter-sweet fruit.

On my first visit to the brewery, the head brewer refused to reveal any information about the ingredients he used on the grounds of commercial confidentiality. Not long afterwards, though, he spoke at a meeting of one of the CAMRA branches in Manchester and was asked the same question. 'I'll tell you my recipes as long you don't pass them on to that b*****d Roger Protz', he said. The branch duly reported his speech in their newsletter, revealing the recipes to posterity as well as to me.

TASTING NOTES
Appearance
Aroma
Taste
Overall score

Shepherd Neame Master Brew Bitter

Source: Shepherd Neame Brewery, Faversham, Kent, England
Strength: 3.7%
Website: www.shepherd-neame.co.uk

TASTING NOTES
Appearance
Aroma
Taste
Overall score

Shepherd Neame is more than a brewery—it's a living museum of beer. The company dates from 1698 and is Britain's oldest brewery, but it's thought that brewing was carried out on the same site many years earlier. It's known that monks were brewing in an abbey in Faversham from the 12th century, though they would not have made use of Kentish hops, which were not grown until the 15th century, when Flemish weavers settled in the area and planted hop bines, as they couldn't acquire a taste for unhopped English ale.

Shepherd Neame is still run by the Neame branch of the two founding families and they fashion marvellous tangy bitter beers full of the piny and floral aromas of fresh hops plucked every autumn from the surrounding fields.

The brewery and its offices are a maze of wood-panelled rooms, unlined teak mash tuns dating from World War One and a steam engine that can still be used in the event of a power failure. Demand for the beers is so great that the brewhouse was substantially extended at the turn of the present century.

Master Brew Bitter is known among brewers as 'cooking bitter', a dismissive name for a beer of modest strength. But this is a beer of enormous character, due to the generous use of locally grown Goldings and Target hops, which create a punchy 37 units of bitterness. The grains are Halcyon pale and crystal malts and the colour rating is 25. The copper-coloured beer, topped by a lively head of foam, draws the drinker in with a stunning aroma of hop resins, biscuity malt and tangy fruit. Juicy malt, peppery hops and a fruitiness reminiscent of a confectionery from my youth called orange-and-lemon slices fill the mouth. The long and deep finish is beautifully balanced between juicy malt, bitter-sweet fruit and a lingering and persistent peppery and bitter hoppiness.

Triple fff Alton's Pride

Source: Triple fff Brewing Co, Four Marks, Alton, Hampshire, England
Strength: 3.8%
Website: www.triplefff.com

Alton's Pride is a no-nonsense, old-fashioned English traditional bitter. At a time when the cask beer sector of the pub scene in England is becoming flooded with golden ales, it's good to blow the trumpet for a beer rooted in the country's great copper-coloured brewing tradition.

And blowing the trumpet is the correct phrase to use, for Triple fff is a musical term for extra loud, triple fortissimo, both feet on the pedals. Owner and head brewer Graham Trott likes his music good and loud as well as making beer packed with aroma and flavour. He started brewing in 1997 on a five-barrel plant but demand for his beers was so high that in July 2008 he opened a 50-barrel site and then just a few weeks later won the prize of Supreme Champion Beer of Britain for Alton's Pride at the Great British Beer Festival in London.

'It's been magic,' he says. At a time of economic down-turn, with many pubs closing, he still struggles to keep up with demand for Alton's Pride and his other beers. The range includes the memorably-named Pressed Rat & Warthog, taken from a Cream track, Comfortably Numb, a Pink Floyd number, and Stairway from Led Zeppelin's 'Stairway to Heaven'.

Alton's Pride is brewed with Maris Otter pale barley malt and cara gold. Graham thinks he's the only brewer in Britain to use cara gold, which is a stewed malt in the manner of the widely-used crystal malt. It's made in a similar manner to toffee, with each grain of malt containing a tiny ball of caramelised sugar. This type of malt sugar can't be fermented by brewer's yeast but it adds both colour and a nutty, fruity character to beer. Graham says cara gold gives a more subtle flavour to his beer than crystal. The hops are First Gold and Northdown.

The beer has a copper/bronze colour with a powerful aroma of fresh hop resins, nutty malt, a hint of butterscotch and citrus fruit. Fruit, malt and bitter hops vie for attention in the mouth, but hop bitterness dominates the finish, though there

is a continuing contribution from ripe malt and tart fruit and a gentle hint of butterscotch.

You can visit the brewery (01420 561422: tours by arrangement) in a style as traditional as the beers. The full address of Triple fff is Station Approach, and the brewery stands close to the restored Watercress steam train line at Four Marks station. You can continue on the train and enjoy Alton's Pride and the other beers in the range at the Railway Arms in Alton. It all makes for a memorable day out.

TASTING NOTES
Appearance
Aroma
Taste
Overall score

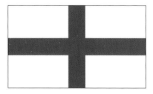

Uley Bitter

Source: Uley Old Brewery, Uley, Gloucestershire, England
Strength: 4%
Website: www.uleybrewery.com

TASTING NOTES
Appearance
Aroma
Taste
Overall score

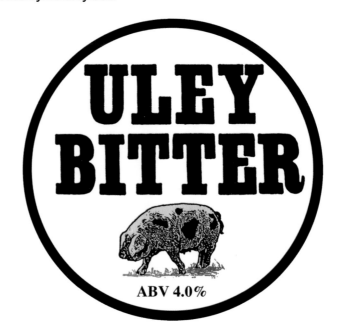

Perhaps it's the alcohol, but laughter and brewing are often intertwined. Chas Wright, who, with his beret, beard and striped jumper, looks like a cross between a pirate and a French onion seller, has a ribald sense of humour. With the exception of his Bitter, his beers have a porcine character, including Old Spot—a local Gloucestershire breed of pig—Pigor Mortis and Pig's Ear, which is Cockney for beer. Chas once chanced his arm and brewed a beer called Oil of Uley. To nobody's surprise, he received a threatening letter from the manufacturer of a well-known brand of beauty products. Chas told the company it could sue him if it wished but he was just a small, struggling brewer with no money in the bank. The threat of legal action was not carried out.

The small town of Uley is in the Cotswolds, and the hills have an abundance of fine brewing water. A natural spring bubbles away at the side of the brewery and provides pure brewing liquor.

Uley is based in part of a brewery called Price's that dates from 1833 when the sylvan area had a thriving pottery industry. When the industry declined, Price's went out of business and the buildings lay derelict for years. Chas Wright set up shop in 1985 and Uley is now one of the longest running of Britain's micro-breweries.

He uses only Maris Otter malt from the specialist maltsters Tuckers, in Devon, and whole Herefordshire hops: he has no truck with additives or brewing sugars. The amber-coloured Bitter has some crystal malt alongside the pale, with Fuggles and Goldings whole flower hops. It has an intense aroma of biscuity malt, with a hint of toffee, tart citrus fruit and peppery, spicy and earthy hops. Rich juicy malt, hop resins and tangy fruit fill the mouth, with a lingering finish that becomes dry and hoppy, but with a good underscore of orange fruit and sappy malt.

Welton's Pridenjoy

Welton's Brewery, Horsham, West Sussex, England
Strength: 2.8%
Website: www.weltons.co.uk

At last, a living example of a South of England 'boy's bitter', so low in alcohol it would have been legal under American Prohibition but bursting with rich malt, hops and fruit character.

Ray Welton is a character, a man with laughter on his lips and a sharp eye for business opportunities, which includes brewing a low-strength beer at a time when all the industry emphasis is on stronger 'premium' products. He has alcohol in his blood, so to speak. His grandfather was a cider maker in Surrey and his father ran a drinks wholesaling company. Ray was taught to brew by the retired head brewer at King & Barnes in Horsham.

Welton's was first based in Dorking but, when King & Barnes closed, Ray moved to Horsham to pick up some of the slack left by the collapse of a substantial regional brewery. He has useful engineering skills that have enabled him to pick up brewing kit on the cheap and refashion it to his own needs. It's not the prettiest micro-brewery in the world but it works and produces a large range of beers. The fermenting vessels are remodelled Carlsberg tanks, the mash tun came from a brew-pub in Croydon, while Ray found the copper on a waste dump with a tree growing inside it. Talk about 'beer from the wood'! 'It's the Steptoe in me,' Ray grins, recalling a British television comedy about a rag-and-bone man.

Pridenjoy is spelt without any spaces, as Ray knows that London regional Fuller's is highly protective of its flagship beer London Pride (see page 89): Ray hopes the lack of spaces will keep m'learned friends at bay. The beer has a remarkably complex recipe, with pale, amber, chocolate, Munich and wheat malts, with Bramling Cross and Northdown hops. It has a superb aroma of peppery hops, vinous fruit and biscuity malt, with sappy malt, hop resins and ripe fruit dominating the mouth. The long finish is indeed a joy, bitter-sweet to start but ending on a high note of tart fruit and bitter hops.

TASTING NOTES
Appearance
Aroma
Taste
Overall score

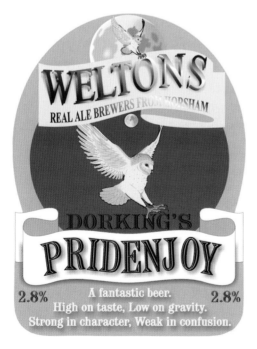

Woodforde's Wherry

Source: Woodforde's Norfolk Ales, Woodbastwick, Norfolk, England
Strength: 3.8%
Website: www.woodfordes.co.uk

TASTING NOTES
Appearance
Aroma
Taste
Overall score

In 1981, Ray Ashworth and David Crease met at the Norwich Homebrewers' Society and decided to turn their passion for craft beer into a commercial venture. Fifteen years later, their first beer, Wherry Best Bitter, was named Champion Beer of Britain at CAMRA's Great British Beer Festival, catapulting the Norfolk brewery on to the national stage.

The brewery takes its name from Parson Woodforde, an 18th-century Norfolk clergyman whose diaries reveal he spent as much time quaffing ale and scoffing food as he did at his devotions. The brewery named in his somewhat dubious honour had a switchback first few years. The original site at Drayton had a poor water supply but a move to the Spread Eagle pub at Erpingham in 1983 proved a disaster when fire gutted the premises. The brewery was rebuilt but demand for the beers made a further move necessary. Ray Ashworth found farm buildings at Woodbastwick near Norwich and took a year to build a suitably sized new plant. Two farm cottages next door were converted into a brewery tap, the Fur & Feather Inn, which serves the full range of Woodforde's beers. The move coincided with the brewery winning a remarkable number of accolades in the Champion Beer of Britain competition. As well as Wherry's award, Woodforde's has won gold and silver trophies for Mardler's Mild, Norfolk Nog strong ale and Headcracker barley wine.

Wherry remains the flagship brand. It takes its name from the famous sailing barges that took grain from Norfolk to other parts of the country and returned with coal. The beer is available in both cask-conditioned and bottle-conditioned form: on draught it's known by the full title of Wherry Best Bitter while in bottle the name is shortened to just Wherry: the rim of yeast in the neck of the bottle confirms it's truly a packaged version of the draught beer.

Woodbastwick has its own water borehole, with 'brewing liquor' that's surprisingly low in nitrates in an agricultural area known as the bread basket of England. The brewery also has the pick of locally-grown Maris Otter malting barley. The success of the brewery, led by Wherry, saw an expansion to the site between 2001 and 2003 that doubled production, with the addition of six new fermenting vessels. A shop and visitor centre (see website) has been added and it's possible to leave with containers of draught beer, bottled beer and home-brewing kits to recreate the Woodforde range.

Wherry is brewed with Maris Otter pale and crystal malts. The hops are English and Styrian Goldings. It has a bronze colour and an aroma reminiscent of orange and lemon slices confectionery, balanced by grassy, herbal hops and a digestive biscuit malt note. Juicy malt, bitter hops resins and tart fruit fill the mouth while the finish has sweet malt, bitter, spicy hops and tangy citrus fruit.

Best Bitters

It is a curiosity of British brewing that brewers will dismiss their bitters as 'ordinary' or 'cooking' but will puff out their chests with pride when discussing the merits of stronger members of the family. '*Best* Bitter', they proclaim, as though the stronger beers live in a different world from their weaker brethren. It is all the more odd when you consider that in many cases Best and Ordinary use identical grains, hops and brewing sugars. In some cases, a brewer will make a strong wort and then add water or 'brewing liquor' to achieve the desired strength for Bitter and Best.

'Bigger Bitter' would never catch on in a world obsessed with marketing and obesity, but that is effectively what we are talking about: beers with bigger aromas and flavours, richer in malt and hops.

I am often asked at public beer tastings and seminars how stronger beers are made. The answer is that a brewer will add more malt and perhaps special sugars to encourage the yeast to produce more alcohol. There is a limit to how much malt can be packed into a mash tun, so brewing sugars are added during the copper boil. A higher level of alcohol will create a rich malt character, with perhaps overtones of vinous fruit, toffee and butterscotch. To balance the maltiness, a generous addition of hops will give a powerful bitterness with pronounced spicy, peppery, grassy and floral notes.

It would be wrong, however, to give the impression that all Best Bitters are merely stronger clones of Bitter. A brewer, given the opportunity to make a beer between 4 and 5% alcohol, may produce something radically different. While his standard Bitter may be copper or amber coloured,

his Best may be straw coloured or pale bronze, using pale malt only. He may use a new balance of hops or just a single one to give a different aroma and flavour, perhaps importing hops from North America or mainland Europe in place of traditional English varieties.

One of the many fascinating developments in brewing in recent years has been the two-way flow of hops between Britain and the United States. While many American craft brewers use English Fuggles and Goldings in their interpretations of pale ale, their British counterparts have learned to treasure the pungent citrussy nature of American varieties.

ABOVE
Honker's Ale is a modern bitter produced by a craft brewery in Chicago.

LEFT
Bishop's Finger comes from Shepherd Neame, the oldest English brewery based in the heart of the Kent hop fields.

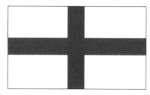

Adnams Broadside

Source: Adnams Sole Bay Brewery, Southwold, Suffolk, England
Strength: 4.7%
Website: www.adnams.co.uk

TASTING NOTES
Appearance
Aroma
Taste
Overall score

Southwold has two faces. There is the town centre with its market place surrounded by some fine Georgian buildings, including Adnams' Swan Hotel, and the harbour area where fishermen still set sail to search for fish and seafood in the North Sea (their produce can be bought fresh from huts alongside the banks of the river Blyth).

While Southwold attracts mainly tourists to its town centre pubs, its workaday aspect can be seen in the Harbour Inn and the Bell across the river in Walberswick, where fisherfolk sink a few pints after a day's gruelling work. After a glass of Bitter, they might move up a notch to Broadside, a beer that commemorates an important piece of history. Southwold traces its roots back to the 15th century, when it was granted a royal charter by Henry VII. In 1672, the English and French fleets combined to defeat the Dutch in the Battle of Sole Bay, off Southwold. Men o' War in those days would place all their guns along one deck of a ship and fire them by turning broadside to the enemy's vessels.

The beer that recalls this famous battle is made from 100% Maris Otter pale malt with just a tiny addition of caramel for colour adjustment. It has 38 units of colour. The hops are First Gold, Fuggles and Goldings, which create 33 units of bitterness. First Gold is one of a new type of 'hedgerow' hops pioneered in England that grow to only half the height of conventional varieties, are easier to pick as a result and are less prone to attack by disease and pests.

Broadside has a superb aroma of tangy fruit, floral and resinous hops and biscuity malt, with the Adnams' hallmark of a whiff of seaside salt. Sappy malt, tart orange fruit and spicy hops fill the mouth, while the finish is deep and long, dominated by tangy fruit, biscuity malt and great depth of hop bitterness. The poet John Masefield, who wrote several epics about the sea and ships, told one young seaman in the poem *Dauber* to 'grow some hair upon thy chest'. He should have advised a regular diet of Broadside to speed the process. A filtered version of Broadside in bottle is considerably stronger at 6.3%.

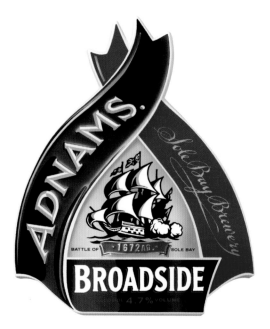

Bateman XXXB

Source: George Bateman & Son, Salem Bridge Brewery, Wainfleet All Saints, Lincolnshire, England

Strength: 4.8%

Website: www.bateman.co.uk

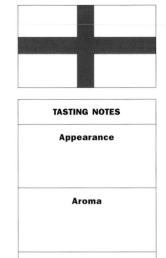

TASTING NOTES
Appearance
Aroma
Taste
Overall score

There is a lot of emotion attached to Bateman's XXXB. As I explained in the section on brown and mild beers (see page 36), the family-owned brewery almost closed in the 1980s as a result of a split in the family, with some members anxious to sell up and retire on the proceeds. Chairman George Bateman and his side of the family finally raised the cash to buy out their relatives and keep the flag flying above the windmill that marks the brewery as you enter the small market town of Wainfleet.

Nobody who was present will ever forget the rousing speech George Bateman made to the annual meeting of CAMRA, when he appealed for support to keep his brewery going. And then, with victory secure, guess which beer won the title of Supreme Champion Beer of Britain at CAMRA's Great British Beer Festival in 1986? As I said to George at the time: 'Who writes your script?'

Within a few years, Bateman's had gone from relative obscurity to national celebrity and XXXB became the flag bearer. The brewery also produces an XB bitter, and the names mark the time before brand images when casks were stamped with Xs to denote strength. In this case the name means a strong triple X bitter.

XXXB is brewed in classic mash tuns, coppers and wooden fermenters with Maris Otter pale malt, crystal malt and wheat malt and a small amount of wheat syrup. The colour is 38 units. Two hop varieties, Challenger and Goldings, create a robust 41 units of bitterness. This superb and complex beer has a rich aroma of biscuity malt, vinous fruit and tangy hop resins. The full-bodied palate is a fine blend of ripe fruit, ripe malt and peppery hops, followed by a big and long finish with a luscious bitter-sweet character that conjures forth creamy fruit with even a hint of banana, biscuity malt and a powerful peppery and earthy bitter hop note.

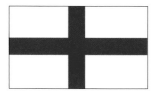

Black Sheep Emmerdale Ale

Source: Black Sheep Brewery, Masham, Yorkshire, England
Strength: 5%
Website: www.blacksheep.co.uk

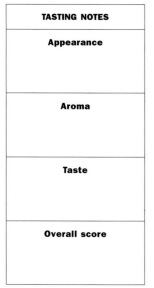

TASTING NOTES
Appearance
Aroma
Taste
Overall score

It is symptomatic of the deep roots that the pub holds in the British way of life that licensed premises form the focus for three famous TV soaps: *Coronation Street* has the Rovers Return, *EastEnders* the Queen Victoria, and *Emmerdale* the Woolpack. *Emmerdale* is set in rural Yorkshire, and Black Sheep saluted the saga's success by naming a beer in its honour in 2003.

Emmerdale Ale is highly distinctive due to the use of Demerara sugar, which accounts for 16% of the recipe. In the 17th and 18th centuries, sugar from the West Indies was widely used in Yorkshire beers at a time when English landlords owned sugar plantations in the Caribbean. Sugar was cheap, as slaves were used to plant and harvest it. When slavery was abolished in the 19th century, sugar had to be bought and sold at a commercial rate and it lost its attraction to brewers. Demerara, a brown crystalline sugar used chiefly in rum production, takes its name from the Demerara River in Guyana that runs into the Atlantic at Georgetown.

Paul Ambler, the head brewer at Black Sheep, gives us a taste of what beers were like three or four centuries ago, though they would have been considerably darker before the advent of pale malt. As well as brown sugar, Emmerdale Ale is brewed with Maris Otter pale malt, crystal malt and torrefied wheat. It has 21 units of colour. Only one hop, Whitbread Goldings Variety, is used, with 36 units of bitterness. In spite of its name, the hop is an offshoot of the Fuggle and was developed by the national brewer Whitbread on its farms in Kent. They are still grown today, even though Whitbread sold its brewing interests in 2000. The beer has an aroma of biscuity malt, leafy and earthy hop resins and a touch of honey sweetness. There is a warming rum-like note in the mouth that blends with tart and bitter hops and juicy malt. The lengthy finish has tangy fruit, spicy hops, creamy malt and a continuing hint of rum. The wheel of history has turned full circle: today Demerara sugar is four times as expensive as barley malt.

Brains SA

Source: S A Brain, The Cardiff Brewery, Cardiff, Wales
Strength: 4.2%
Website: www.sabrain.com

The label for SA shows a red-and-black quartered motif, evoking the image of a rugby shirt. The Welsh are passionate about Rugby Union and beer, a fact underscored by the large number of pubs in the vicinity of both Cardiff Arms Park and the National Stadium. American readers, whose version of armour-plated football developed out of the British oval ball game, will be astonished to learn that rugby is played with a minimum of protective clothing. This could be one reason why beer lovers in Wales claim SA stands for 'Skull Attack', though overconsumption and the resulting hangover are a more likely cause.

The brewery is not keen on the nickname and prefers to suggest that SA is drawn either from the initials of the founder of the company, Samuel Arthur, or for Special Ale. These alternatives cut no ice with the beer's devotees. I wrote a magazine profile about the Welsh National Opera some years ago and interviewed members of the chorus. When they heard about my interest in beer, they waxed lyrical about Skull Attack, which they drank in such copious amounts in Cardiff it was a wonder they could sing in tune.

The beer that gives them so much delight is not, despite its name, especially strong and, in the Welsh tradition, is malt accented, recalling the time when beer was fashioned to meet the needs of coal miners and steel workers. It is brewed with Pearl and Regina pale malts, 8% crystal malt and some brewing sugar. It has 27 colour units. The three hops are all English varieties: Challenger, Fuggles and Goldings (27 units of bitterness). The deep amber beer has a ripe aroma of biscuity malt, a nutty note from the crystal malt and a light but firm spicy hop presence. A digestive biscuit maltiness, a touch of barley sugar sweetness, and a good underpinning of hop resins fill the mouth, followed by a long finish that is bitter-sweet, with sappy malt, light but persistent spicy hops and a pear-drop fruitiness.

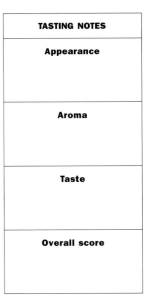

TASTING NOTES
Appearance
Aroma
Taste
Overall score

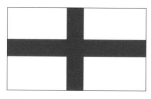

Brewster's Decadence

Source: Brewster's Brewing Co, Grantham, Lincolnshire, England
Strength: 4.4%
Website: www.brewsters.co.uk

TASTING NOTES
Appearance
Aroma
Taste
Overall score

Sara Barton has restored the ancient name and tradition of the brewster or female brewer. In Saxon times, when brewing took place in the home, women would bake bread and make unhopped ale from the same natural ingredients, creating the old saying that ale is 'liquid bread'. It was only when brewing moved from the hearth to commercial taverns that men took charge.

Sara learned her brewing skills with Courage, a once famous national English brewery, but she downsized from giant brewing vessels to a micro kit when she set up in 1998 behind her Leicestershire house in the Vale of Belvoir. In 2006 Sara moved to a bigger site in Grantham where she brews on a 10-barrel kit that came from a former Firkin brew-pub in Liverpool. (Firkins, which took their name from a nine-gallon beer cask, were a chain of lively pub breweries that were sold off in the 1990s.)

The Brewster's kit is a firmly traditional ale system of mash tun, copper and six fermenters. Sara uses Maris Otter pale malt and a touch of caramalt that gives Decadence a hint of amber

and bronze. The hops are American Chinook and the new Nelson Sauvin hop from New Zealand. Nelson Sauvin has taken the beer world by storm and craft brewers are queuing up to use it. The name Sauvin comes from the Sauvignon grape and is so-called as a result of the rich, fruity, citrus note it gives to beer. Anybody who has drunk the Montana wines from New Zealand will know what to expect. Combined with Chinook, Decadence has a profound aroma and palate of grapefruit and passion fruit, balanced by hop resins and cracker-like maltiness.

Sara's beers have a powerful female influence. Decadence was brewed to mark 10 years of Brewster's brewery and her 20 years in the industry. She also has a range of seasonal beers called Wicked Women and a strong ale called Belly Dancer. She won the prestigious title of Rural Businesswoman of the Year from Country Living magazine in 2002 and her cask beers are now available in around 250 pubs in central England and further afield.

Cains Formidable Ale

Source: Robert Cain & Co, Liverpool, Merseyside, England
Strength: 5%
Website: www.cainsbeers.com

TASTING NOTES
Appearance
Aroma
Taste
Overall score

The beer is known as FA for short, which gives free rein to practitioners of demotic English. FA is also short for Football Association, the governing body of English soccer, while the term 'sweet FA' means a total lack of knowledge or understanding of a subject, which many football supporters think sums up the FA's guidance of the game. In this context, F stands for one of the most widely used vulgar words in the language and A is for All. As Merseysiders are among the most passionate of football supporters and have been known to utter the occasional expletive, Cains was on sure ground with the name of the beer.

Unlike Brakspear Bitter and Special, FA is a radically different beer from the company's 4% Bitter, which is a deep copper-coloured member of the family, using chocolate malt and dark cane sugar and with 30 units of colour. FA, on the other hand, is brewed using only Maris Otter pale malt, with a touch of wheat malt for head retention and a small amount of brewing sugar. The result is an exceptionally pale beer with just 14 colour units. Target hops are used for bitterness and the hopped wort, or extract, is late hopped in the copper with Goldings for aroma, and then dry hopped in cask with Northdown. The bitterness units are 30. The beer has a tempting aroma of rich 'wine gums' fruit, juicy malt and floral hops, with orange and lemon fruit dominating the mouth but with a solid backing of biscuity malt and bitter hop resins. The lingering finish enjoys a fine balance of sappy malt, bitter hop resins and bitter-sweet fruit, leaving a tart and tangy impression with a hint of clean sweetness. It is a splendidly refreshing beer.

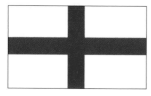

Freeminer Speculation

Source: Freeminer Brewery, Cinderford, Gloucestershire, England
Strength: 4.7%
Website: www.freeminer.com

TASTING NOTES
Appearance
Aroma
Taste
Overall score

Freeminer is one of the most successful and long-established of Britain's new wave of micro-breweries. Don Burgess founded it in 1992 in the remote Royal Forest of Dean, an area made famous by such legendary television plays by Dennis Potter as *Blue Remembered Hills*, *Pennies from Heaven* and *The Singing Detective*. The medieval royal connection to the forest confers certain rights on the men born in the area. Any male born within the Hundred of St Briavels—a hundred being an ancient division of a county—can dig for coal or iron ore in the forest without charge on reaching the age of 21 and working for a year and a day in one of the drift mines dug from the hillsides.

Many of Freeminer's beers carry the names of now defunct mines: as well as Speculation, there are also Deep Shaft, Pot Lid, Shakemantle, Trafalgar and Waterloo, while Strip And At It describes the tough nature of the work.

Freeminer has won several awards for its beers, including two in the Champion Beer of Britain competition and one from the annual Beauty of Hops contest. Several of the beers, including Speculation, are available in bottle-fermented as well as cask form.

Speculation is brewed with Maris Otter pale, crystal and chocolate malts and roasted barley, and hopped with Fuggles and Goldings from Worcestershire. The colour rating is 34 and the bitterness 40. The deep copper-coloured beer has peppery and resiny hops on the nose with sultana fruit, roasted grain and a hint of chocolate. The mouth is filled with rich and pungent flavours of roasted grain, chocolate, bitter hops resins and tangy fruit, followed by a long and complex finish in which hop bitterness starts to dominate but with good contributions from roast grain, chocolate and fruit. A full-bodied, rich and rewarding beer.

Fuller's London Pride

Source: Fuller, Smith and Turner's Griffin Brewery, Chiswick, London, England
Strength: 4.1%
Website: www.fullers.co.uk

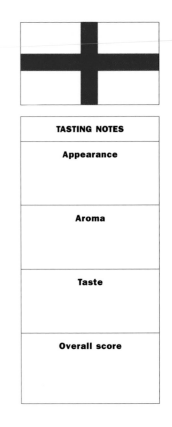

The family-run brewery close to the banks of the Thames is a marvel of the brewing world. Created more than 350 years ago and still run by members of the three founding families, Fuller's has grown from a relatively small London regional to a company owning 238 pubs and hotels, along with 600 national free trade accounts. In spite of its success, the company refuses to compromise, remaining true to traditional brewing methods and the use of the finest raw materials.

London Pride is the flagship beer. Its quality has been recognised in such competitions as the Beer and Cider Competition, where it was named Supreme Champion Beer in 2000 and won gold medals in the two following years, and in the Champion Beer of Britain Competition, where it has twice been named Champion Best Bitter and was the overall Supreme Champion in 1979. Perhaps its most remarkable achievement has been to become the best-selling premium cask bitter in Britain, with sales growing from 80,000 barrels a year in 2000 to 130,000 by 2004.

It is brewed with Optic pale malt (90%), 3% crystal malt and 7% flaked maize. The colour rating is 24. A complex hop recipe involves Challenger, Northdown and Target varieties, with Target used primarily for bitterness, and Challenger and Northdown added late in the copper boil for maximum aroma: 30 units of bitterness. London Pride has the Fuller's yeast signature of a rich orange fruitiness that dominates nose, palate and finish but is superbly balanced throughout by biscuity malt and a firm and very English floral, spicy and resiny hop attack.

It is the genius of British brewers to fashion beers that are complex and also highly quaffable, thanks to low carbonation and the brilliant balance of ingredients. Too malty, and the beer would be cloying; too bitter and it would close down the throat. The balance of London Pride means that several pints will slip down easily but with maximum enjoyment. Raise a glass to head brewer John Keeling and his team.

TASTING NOTES
Appearance
Aroma
Taste
Overall score

Goose Island Honker's Ale

Source: Goose Island Beer Company, Chicago, Illinois, USA
Strength: 5%
Website: www.gooseisland.com

As well as the renowned IPA (see page 15), Goose Island brews a wide range of beers, including Kilgubbin Red Ale to salute the Irish settlers who made their home on Goose Island in Chicago (Kilgubbin is Gaelic for goose). But the brewery's biggest brand is Honker's Ale, brewed in the style of an English bitter. The beer has driven the success of the company that produces 1.6 million cases a year for distribution throughout the US—not bad going for an enterprise that started out as a simple brew-pub.

Head brewer Greg Hall and his brewing team studied at the brewing faculty of the world-famous Siebels Institute in Chicago and have a wide-ranging knowledge of beer styles and ingredients. They source malts and hops from Britain and mainland Europe. Honker's uses malts from the American Midwest and just one hop, the Styrian Golding from Slovenia. Styrians are an offshoot of the English Fuggle. When the Slovenes developed their hop industry, they found that traditional European hop varieties from the German Hallertau region and Czechoslovakia would not grow in Slovenia's soil. Hardy English Fuggles adapted without difficulty and became the main variety grown there. But the Slovenes struggled with the odd name Fuggles and called the hops Goldings after another English variety.

Honker's Ale (14.5 colour, 35 bitterness) has a touch of crystal malt and wheat, and offers a pleasing and tempting pale copper colour. It has a rich almond nut aroma balanced by a cracker biscuit maltiness and a spicy hop note. Juicy malt, a developing tart citrus fruit note and bitter hop resins fill the mouth, while the finish is a fine balance between tangy fruit, biscuity malt and bitter hops, with the almond note reappearing.

Greene King Abbot Ale

Source: Greene King Westgate Brewery, Bury St Edmunds, Suffolk, England
Strength: 5%
Website: www.greeneking.co.uk

To mark its religious connections, Abbot Ale is given 'two Sabbaths' in the fermenters to ensure each brew is properly blessed by whichever god looks after the brewing process.

Bury St Edmunds has long been an important brewing and malting town, with ale making dating from the time of the monks who built a monastery in the area in the seventh century. King Canute, who famously failed to hold back the encroaching tide, founded a Benedictine community in 1020 to commemorate St Edmund. Edmund was the king of East Anglia who was slain in battle with the Danes in the ninth century. His shrine developed into the town of St Emundsbury, later Bury St Edmunds.

Centuries later, Benjamin Greene opened a brewery in 1799 on Westgate and eventually moved into a mansion that had been the home of the last abbot of the town following the dissolution of abbeys and monasteries under Henry VIII. A rival King brewery opened also on Westgate in 1868 and the two companies merged in 1887. The Greenes still play an active role. The chairman in the 1970s and '80s was Sir Hugh Greene, a former Director-General of the BBC. The novelist Graham Greene was fond of beer, mentioned it regularly in his books, and mashed a special ale at the brewery to mark his 80th birthday.

Abbot Ale therefore has a bit of history on its side and is brewed in a highly traditional brewhouse with copper vessels, using Halcyon and Pipkin pale malts, amber and crystal malts and brewing sugar. Colour units are 30. The all-English hop recipe is made up of Challenger, Fuggles and Northdown pellets, which create 26 units of bitterness. After the copper boil, the hopped extract percolates through a deep bed of hops in the hop back for additional aroma and bitterness. The beer has a pronounced biscuity malt, vinous fruit and spicy hops aroma, with more tangy fruit, bitter hop resins and juicy malt in the mouth. The long finish has the fullness and richness of malt and fruit beautifully balanced by a deep hop bitterness.

Hook Norton Old Hooky

Source: Hook Norton Brewery Co, Hook Norton, near Banbury, Oxfordshire, England
Strength: 4.6%
Website: www.hook-norton-brewery.co.uk

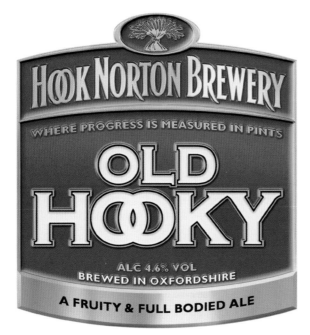

TASTING NOTES
Appearance
Aroma
Taste
Overall score

Hook Norton seems to exist in a time warp. Village and brewery are almost lost down narrow country lanes. The red-brick Victorian tower brewery is powered by a 19th-century steam engine, while mashing, boiling and fermentation take place in superb wood and copper vessels. Local deliveries are made by horse-drawn drays, with the horses kept in stables within the grounds. But the company founded in 1849 by a farmer and maltster, John Harris, and still run by his descendants, the Clarkes, is no slouch when it comes to selling beer. It owns 43 pubs and distributes to a further 500 free trade accounts. It has turned the brewery into a tourist attraction with a museum and visitor centre. The museum tells the fascinating story of how Harris brewed for his farm workers and family but was forced to expand production when gangs of navvies arrived in the area to build a railway line, which has since been axed. The brewery has been expanded and overhauled in recent years to enable production to grow to meet demand—a demand based on cask beer. One of Hook Norton's proud boasts is that it has never sold a drop of keg beer in its life, and its bottled beers account for only a tiny proportion of production.

Brewing water is drawn from a well on site, and only the finest raw materials are used. Old Hooky, despite the name, is not an old ale but a strong bitter. It is brewed from Maris Otter pale and crystal malts, with malted wheat (34 colour units). The hops are Challenger, Fuggles and Goldings, which create 32 units of bitterness. The deep copper-coloured beer has a rich aroma of fresh bread maltiness, fruitiness reminiscent of raisins and sultanas, and tangy hops resins. Fruit, malt and hop bitterness build in the mouth while the finish has a bitter-sweet start with malt and fruit dominating, but hop bitterness provides a firm base that prevents any cloying sweetness.

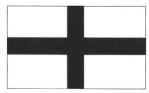

Iceni Fine Soft Day

Source: Iceni Brewery, Ickburgh, near Thetford, Norfolk, England
Strength: 4%
Website: www.icenibrewery.co.uk

TASTING NOTES
Appearance
Aroma
Taste
Overall score

Brendan Moore is an Ulsterman brewing in deepest Norfolk who has helped change the way in which small craft breweries get their beers to market. He supplies around 35 pubs but in general stays clear of a pub trade increasingly dominated by national groups that demand deep discounts from suppliers. Brendan has set up the East Anglian Brewers' Co-operative that delivers to beer festivals and farmers' markets in the region. Bottled beer and gift packs are a major part of Brendan's business, and all his draught beers are available in bottle-fermented form as well. His beers are on sale in the tourist shop in Thetford Forest, which attracts large numbers of visitors, and he grows barley and hops on a plot alongside the brewery as a further tourist attraction.

Brendan was encouraged to turn his home-brewing skills into a commercial venture when he had a dream in which Boudicca, or Boadicea, the legendary Queen of the Iceni tribe who fought many battles with the occupying Romans, urged him to brew good ale in an attempt to stop cheap European lager that was flooding into Britain as a result of the European Union's 'open borders' policy. He may not have stopped cheap Stella arriving in Dover from Calais but he has certainly added to the sum of beer drinkers' pleasures with his potable ales, several of which commemorate the Iceni, while Fine Soft Day is a Norfolk greeting.

In common with all the bottled beers, Fine Soft Day is kräusened with a blend of unfermented sugary extract and yeast to encourage a vigorous second fermentation in bottle. In the case of Fine Soft Day, maple syrup is also added to the brew to give the smoothness and softness demanded by the title. The other ingredients are Halcyon pale malt and caramalt, with Challenger and Fuggles hops. The beer is bronze coloured and has a tempting aroma of peppery hops, citrus/lemon fruit and biscuity malt. Juicy malt, tart fruit and hop resins fill the mouth, while the long finish has a touch of sweetness from the maple syrup but is balanced by an increasing hop bitterness and tangy fruit.

Mordue Workie Ticket

Source: Mordue Brewery, Shiremoor, Tyne & Wear, England
Strength: 4.5%
Website: www.morduebrewery.com

Two brothers, Gary and Matthew Fawson, revived a Geordie brewing tradition when they opened their tiny brewery in 1995, using the name of Joseph Mordue's 19th-century brewery on Wallsend village green. Their world changed two years later when Workie Ticket was named CAMRA's Champion Beer of Britain at the Great British Beer Festival. The brothers were media-friendly and their fame spread quickly as Workie Ticket went on sale in pubs far from its North-east home. In 1998, the Fawsons moved across the road to a new 20-barrel site and they now supply some 150 accounts.

Their beers stress their roots, with such names as Five Bridge Bitter—marking the bridges across the River Tyne in Newcastle—Geordie Pride and the outrageous pun in A'l Wheat Pet. Workie Ticket is a Geordie expression for someone who is workshy or works his ticket. It is not an accusation that can be levelled at the Fawson brothers, who have worked mightily to build the success of their brewery.

Their prize beer and leading brand is brewed with Halcyon pale malt, pale chocolate malt and torrefied wheat. A complex hop recipe is comprised of Challenger, Fuggles and East Kent Goldings. Both colour and bitterness units are in the 30s. The beer has a rich and tempting aroma of creamy malt, vanilla, a hint of chocolate and peppery hops. Pungent hop resins dominate the palate but are balanced by biscuity malt and tart fruit. The lengthy finish is dry and hoppy, but with good contributions from juicy malt, vanilla and tangy fruit.

TASTING NOTES

Appearance

Aroma

Taste

Overall score

Rooster's Yankee

Source: Rooster's Brewing Co, Knaresborough, North Yorkshire, England
Strength: 4.3%
Website: www.roosters.co.uk

Sean Franklin, who runs Rooster's with his wife Alison, put hops on the map in the 1990s when he described them as 'the grapes of brewing'. Until then, brewers and even beer writers thought of hops as a plant that added bitterness to beer and helped prevent infections. Sean's comment made everyone think more carefully about the role of hops in the brewing process. He is a self-confessed 'hop head'. He loves the fascinating diversity of aromas and flavours that hops give to beer, and will blend English varieties—herbal, spicy and peppery—with the more citrus, floral and perfumy character of American and mainland European ones.

All his regular beers are pale in colour: he avoids the use of dark malt, as he wants the hops to dominate and shine through. He pumps nitrogen into his beers during the mashing process to stop oxidation and emphasise their pallor. With Yankee, he says his aim is to develop a powerful Muscat grapes and lychees nose and palate, which is due to the exclusive use of American Cascade hops. They are added at the start of the copper boil and at the end, with a further addition in the hop back, a vessel where the hopped wort rests after the boil. The main grain is Maris Otter pale malt with a touch of crystal. The colour is 12, bitterness 28 units. The beer has a delightful aroma of tropical fruits and light juicy malt. There is light biscuity malt in the mouth but the emphasis is on the pungent grapefruit note from the hops. The finish is long, bitter and hoppy, with continuing citrus fruit. It is a wonderfully refreshing beer.

The Franklins opened the brewery in 1993 and moved to bigger premises in 2001, where they supply 500 outlets.

TASTING NOTES

Appearance

Aroma

Taste

Overall score

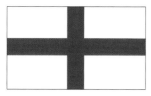

St Austell HSD

Source: St Austell Brewery Co, St Austell, Cornwall, England
Strength: 5%
Website: www.staustellbrewery.co.uk

TASTING NOTES
Appearance
Aroma
Taste
Overall score

HSD stands officially for Hicks Special Draught, named in honour of the founder of the brewery, Walter Hicks. But to legions of West Country drinkers the beer is known affectionately, if somewhat alarmingly, as High Speed Diesel. Careful consumption is strongly advised.

Hicks founded the brewery in 1851 and its current site is built from mellow Cornish stone. It is still run by Hicks's descendants, with his great-great-grandson James Staughton at the helm. St Austell is a powerful presence in Cornwall. It is one of the county's biggest employers, owns 150 pubs and has extensive free trade. In recent years both the brewery and its products have been overhauled. Distribution has expanded into Devon and Somerset, and an attractive visitor centre has been added. Production takes place in a superb brewhouse and fermenting area, with traditional copper and wooden vessels. A Celtic Beer Festival is staged every winter in the brewery's extensive cellars, with beers and ciders from other producers in the region.

HSD is brewed with Maris Otter pale and crystal malts and roasted barley (colour 40 units). The hops are the whole flowers of Fuggles and Goldings, which create 30 units of bitterness. The deep copper-coloured beer has a toasted and biscuity malt aroma with sultana fruit and floral, spicy hops. A digestive biscuit maltiness and ripe dried fruits fill the mouth with a solid underpinning of bitter hop resins. The deep finish has ripe fruit and malt but the initial sweetness is offset by a firm undercurrent of lingering hop resins.

St Peter's Organic Best Bitter

Source: St Peter's Brewery, St Peter South Elmham, near Bungay, Suffolk, England
Strength: 4.1%
Website: www.stpetersbrewery.co.uk

St Peter's brewery enjoys a magnificent setting behind a moated Tudor farmhouse. The farm dates from 1280, with the moat dug to stop an invasion by marauding Vikings. Its Tudor design is the result of the dissolution of nearby Flixton Priory by Cardinal Wolsey, an act that prompted Henry VIII to embark on a widespread wrecking of abbeys and priories to break the back of the church and fill his depleted coffers. Fixtures and fittings from Flixton were taken to St Peter's, which now enjoys a façade of Caen stone from Normandy, a great chimney, latticed windows and a porched entrance complete with a tombstone. Inside, the Great Hall has an imposing raftered ceiling, a 15th-century tapestry depicting manna from heaven, and a carved madonna and child. A dining room has a portrait of St Peter before the Basilica in Rome.

The building now belongs to John Murphy, a marketing expert who advises—clearly with great success—companies and corporations on how to improve their branding and image. He decided to add a brewery at St Peter's, as the poor showing of British beers abroad disappointed him and he decided to fashion his own brands for export. The brewery is fortunate to have its own borehole that draws fine brewing water from an aquifer 90m (300ft) below ground.

St Peter's beers, which include fruit beers and a honey porter, are now exported to the US, Europe, Japan, Scandinavia and Australia. All the beers appear in distinctive green flagon-shaped bottles, which are based on an 18th-century flagon that John Murphy found in a shop in Gibbstown near Philadelphia. Cask-conditioned versions are available in Britain and can be enjoyed in St Peter's London pub, the Jerusalem Tavern at 55 Britton Street, EC1, a faithful re-creation of an 18th-century coffee house. In 2002, the brewery doubled in size to meet demand for the beers, and a new bottling hall and brewing copper have since been added.

Organic Best Bitter has joined the growing number of British beers that use malts and hops grown without agri-chemicals. The grains are Scottish Regina pale and crystal malts, with New Zealand Hallertauer hops. The colour is 34 units, bitterness 35 units.

The pale bronze beer has a biscuity malt and peppery hops aroma, followed by an explosion of spicy, bitter hop resins on the tongue with a good balance of sappy malt and tart fruit. The long finish has good juicy malt and citrus fruit but is dominated by an iodine-like hop bitterness.

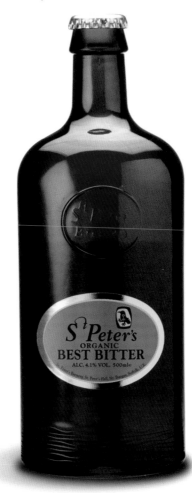

TASTING NOTES
Appearance
Aroma
Taste
Overall score

ABOVE
The Jerusalem Tavern, a London outlet for St Peter's beer.

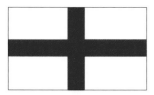

Shepherd Neame Bishop's Finger

Source: Shepherd Neame Brewery, Faversham, Kent, England
Strength: 5%
Website: www.shepherd-neame.co.uk

There was an abbey in Faversham for many centuries and the monks would have brewed ale for their own consumption. It would be historically fascinating if Shepherd Neame's strong bitter had a religious connection, but Bishop's Finger has more prosaic roots. It is named after an ancient roadside signpost shaped liked a clenched hand with the forefinger extended to point visitors in the right direction.

Since the travellers in *The Canterbury Tales* made their way through Kent to their destination, there is something Chaucerian about the bawdy local nickname for the beer: Nun's Delight. The soubriquet is not mentioned in the hallowed halls of the Faversham brewery, where wood-panelled walls and a visitors' reception area housed in a restored medieval hall demand respect and contemplation. In spite of its impressive age, Shepherd Neame is a company with its eye focussed on future success. In 2000 it invested £2.2 million in a new brewhouse that has increased annual production to 200,000 barrels a year. It owns 372 pubs in London and the South-east, and supplies 2,000 free trade accounts.

For many years, Bishop's Finger was available only in bottle but interest from beer lovers encouraged the brewery to produce a cask version as well. It is brewed with Halcyon pale malt and crystal malt, and Goldings and target hops plucked from the surrounding hop fields. It has 41 units of colour and a powerful 43 units of bitterness. It has a rich and tempting aroma of fruit reminiscent of raisins and sultanas, a warm Ovaltine* maltiness and tangy hop resins. Vinous fruit, biscuity malt and peppery hops fill the mouth, while the long finish interweaves between dried fruit, rich malt and a deep and drying hop bitterness.

*For non-British readers, Ovaltine is a bedtime drink made from malted barley and hot milk.

Timothy Taylor's Landlord

Source: Timothy Taylor's Knowle Spring Brewery, Keighley, West Yorkshire, England
Strength: 4.3%
Website: www.timothy-taylor.co.uk

The importance of pure water in the brewing process is underscored by the experience of Timothy Taylor. He was a maltster who opened a small brewery in the wool town of Keighley in 1858 and established new premises in 1863 to use the Pennine waters that flowed from the Knowle Spring. Taylor's grandson, John Taylor, was ennobled as Lord Ingrow and he thinks so highly of the spring water that he bottles it and takes it home to mix with his whisky.

Taylors, based in attractive stone buildings and with highly traditional brewing vessels, brews a wide range of beers, from light and dark milds to strong dark ales, but its flagship is Landlord, which holds the record of winning the CAMRA Champion Beer of Britain no fewer than four times. So successful is the beer that £11 million has been invested in the brewery over the past decade to expand production. Its fortunes were given an unexpected boost in the

Upper Canada Dark Ale

Source: Upper Canada Brewing Co, Toronto, Ontario, Canada
Strength: 5%
Website: www.uppercanada.com

Upper Canada is the settlers' name for Ontario. The brewery of that name was founded in 1985 by Frank Heaps and has grown into a sizeable commercial company with splendid copper brewing vessels. Its first brewer was trained at Weihenstephan in Germany but his successors have been British with a love of ale, though the portfolio includes a lager and a wheat beer. The brewery has sunk deep roots in Toronto's artistic life. Since 2000, Upper Canada has run an annual Writers' Craft Awards for local novelists and short story writers. It also stages art, music and theatre festivals.

Dark Ale has an attractive chestnut hue and is brewed with pale, roasted and black malts, and is hopped with a single variety, English Challenger. It is an all-malt beer, as Upper Canada avoids the use of sugars and cheaper grains. It has a robust roasted grain aroma with a touch of sour fruit and a good attack of bitter, floral hop resins. Rich roasted grain, tart fruit, a hint of bitter coffee and tart hops fill the mouth, while the long finish has a solid base of bitter hops with smoky malt notes and sour fruit.

It's a good quenching beer, one that Upper Canada recommends as a base for Cheddar Cheese Soup, made with carrots, onions, celery, butter, flour, chicken or vegetable stock, Parmesan and grated Cheddar and a generous helping of the beer.

TASTING NOTES
Appearance
Aroma
Taste
Overall score

early 21st century when the singer Madonna, who has a home in England, said Landlord was her favourite beer. With phlegmatic Northern humour, Taylors changed its truck signs from 'Pedigree—loved by Yorkshiremen' to 'Pedigree—loved by Yorkshiremen… and Madonna'.

Landlord is brewed with just one grain, Scottish Golden Promise, with some brewing sugar and a touch of caramel for colour adjustment. The hops are Fuggles, Styrian Goldings and Whitbread Goldings Variety. The intense hop bitterness of the beer is achieved by circulating the hopped wort over a deep bed of Styrians in the hop back. The finished beer has a superb aroma of juicy malt, spicy and earthy hop resins and tart citrus fruit. Tangy fruit, juicy malt and bitter hops pack the mouth, while the long finish is beautifully balanced between biscuity malt, lemon fruit and bitter hops. To confuse the issue, the bottled version of Landlord is called a pale ale. Pale ale or bitter—you pays your money and you takes your choice. Let's just settle for a world classic beer.

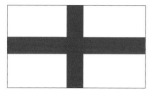

Wadworth 6X

Source: Wadworth & Co, Devizes, Wiltshire, England
Strength: 4.3%
Website: www.wadworth.co.uk

TASTING NOTES
Appearance
Aroma
Taste
Overall score

Wadworth 6X is a fine example of an English bitter in which the blend of malts and hops produces a subtle beer with low carbonation and great drinkability. It comes from one of the handsomest breweries in England, a Victorian red-brick pile constructed on the tower principle, with the stages of the brewing process flowing logically from floor to floor.

Henry Wadworth founded the brewery in 1885 in an ancient market town with a name of Norman-French origin that means boundaries or divisions. Wadworth is still family owned, employs a cooper who fashions wooden casks, uses dray horses to deliver beer to local pubs, as well as traditional coppers and mash tuns. It is not stuck in a time warp, however.

Considerable investment in recent years has enabled production to grow to 200,000 barrels a year, the bulk of which is made up of 6X. The beer is supplied to Wadworth's own estate of 256 pubs and free trade throughout the country.

The name 6X recalls the time when medieval monks blessed casks of ale with Xs, with the number of crosses indicating strength: a true six X would be considerably higher in alcohol than Wadworth's brand. It is brewed with Fanfare pale malt and a small amount (4%) of crystal, with 3% cane sugar (colour 28 units). The complex hop recipe is made up of four English varieties: First Gold, Fuggles, Goldings and Progress, of which the main hop is Fuggles (67%). The hopped extract filters through a bed of Goldings in the hop back after the copper boil (23 bitterness units).

The copper-coloured beer has a tempting aroma of spicy and earthy hop resins, biscuity malt and a hint of vanilla. It fills the mouth with sappy malt, a touch of barley sugar sweetness and a growing bitter and peppery hop note. The long finish is finely balanced between rich, juicy malt, hints of barley sugar and vanilla, and a firm hop bitterness.

Wellington Arkell Best Bitter

Source: Wellington Brewery, Guelph, Ontario, Canada
Strength: 4%
Website: www.wellingtonbrewery.ca

The name Arkell will be familiar to British beer drinkers, as the family of that name runs a respected regional brewery in Swindon, Wiltshire (see page 102). A member of the family emigrated to Canada and founded a community near Guelph in Wellington County. He is honoured by a beer branded Arkell, brewed in a town that is a centre of agriculture, boasts an agricultural university and has long been an important brewing centre.

Wellington Brewery specialises in English-style beers, including an Imperial Stout, County Ale, Special Pale Ale and, inevitably, an Iron Duke. The brewery was founded in 1985 by a group of British beer devotees, and they import malts and hops from Britain and mainland Europe to give their brews authentic flavours. At first they produced their beers in cask-conditioned form but quickly found that many bar owners had no idea how to look after beers that require careful monitoring in the cellar. Filtered keg beers replaced the cask ones, though a few outlets have overcome their initial resistance and now take the naturally conditioned versions.

Arkell Best, which offers more profound aromas and flavour in its cask form, is brewed with pale and crystal malts, and is hopped with Goldings and Styrian Goldings. It has a distinctive peppery Goldings hop aroma, with biscuity malt and a raisin-like fruitiness. It has a firm palate with a rich juicy malt note, ripe fruit and bitter hop resins. The lingering finish has creamy malt and rich fruit but finally becomes dry, bitter and hoppy.

TASTING NOTES
Appearance
Aroma
Taste
Overall score

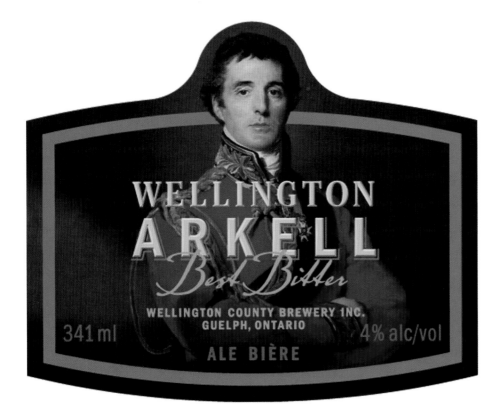

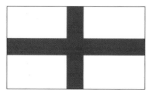

Wells Bombardier

Source: Wells & Young's Brewery, Bedford, England
Strength: 4.3%
Website: www.wellsandyoungs.co.uk

TASTING NOTES
Appearance
Aroma
Taste
Overall score

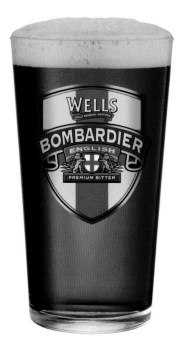

Charles Wells, a merchant seaman, gave up his career to found a brewery in Bedford that is still run by his descendants. It is now the only independent brewing concern in Bedfordshire's county town, the home of John Bunyan. It moved from its original site in 1976 to a modern and highly flexible new brewery that can produce both ale and lager. Part of the site once housed a building where Glenn Miller and his United States Army Orchestra recorded concerts during World War Two. Bing Crosby was among many American entertainers who appeared there with the orchestra. It is now a canning line: *sic transit gloria mundi*!

Wells is the largest independent family-owned brewery in Britain and it merged in 2006 with Young's of Wandsworth in London to form Wells & Young's. It has not ignored its ale brands, though: it has a sizeable pub estate of 255 to supply, as well as extensive free trade.

Adroit marketing has turned Bombardier into one of the country's Top Ten premium cask beers. When it was launched, the beer had an image on its labels of a famous boxer called Bombardier Billy Wells, who has no connection with the brewing family: it was his rank when he was a soldier in the Royal Artillery.

The beer is brewed with Fanfare pale malt, crystal malt and invert sugar: colour 30 units. The hops are Challenger and Styrian Goldings in pellet form: 31 units of bitterness. The rich and complex copper-coloured beer has a superb aroma of wholemeal biscuits, tangy raisin and sultana fruit, floral hops and a touch of sulphur from the water. In the mouth there is a good solid base of hop bitterness, with juicy malt and vinous fruit. The finish has good length, with a final bitter hoppiness but preceded by tangy fruit and rich malt. Export bottled versions of the beer are considerably stronger. The company has pioneered draught cask beer for home consumption with vented cans.

Wolf Granny Wouldn't Like It

Source: Wolf Brewery, Attleborough, Norfolk, England
Strength: 4.8%
Website: www.wolfbrewery.com

TASTING NOTES
Appearance
Aroma
Taste
Overall score

One of the many fine contributions craft brewers have made to British beer drinking is humour. They have got away from simple brand names such as Bitter and Best Bitter and come up with titles that bring a smile of pleasure to the lips as well as the tastebuds. The Wolf Brewery, which started life as the Reindeer brew-pub in Norwich, moved to its new site in 1996 with a 20-barrel plant based in the former Gaymer cider factory and orchards. It's a site with nostalgic appeal for me: I was evacuated from London to Norfolk during World War Two and can still recall as a small child the large cider works alongside the railway line from Norwich to London.

Wolf Witham owns the brewery, and his beers have many lupine connections, including Wolf in Sheep's Clothing, Coyote Bitter and Lupus Lupus. The last named is a pointer to the fact that the Latin name for the hop means 'wolf plant' because, untamed, it will run wild over the countryside. The pump clip and label for Granny Wouldn't Like It show a cartoon representation of Red Riding Hood and the wolf.

The beer is brewed with Halcyon pale, chocolate and wheat malts and hopped with Challenger and Goldings. The amber-red beer has a rich aroma of peppery hops, vinous fruit, biscuity malt and chocolate. The full palate is dominated by wholemeal biscuits, rich fruit, increasing hop bitterness and a hint of chocolate and roasted grain. The chocolate and roast notes persist into the long and deep finish, accompanied by ripe, sweet fruit and a solid underpinning of bitter hop resins.

Wolf Witham is wrong: I know for a fact that my late grandmother would have adored the beer. All Wolf's cask beers are also available in bottle-fermented form.

Extra Strong Beers & Bitters

Extra Strong Bitter is a style that has come in from the cold. Many brewers produced strong ales but were shy of admitting the fact. At the end of a brewery tour I have often been told, in an almost shame-faced manner, 'We do have an interesting high-gravity beer if you'd fancy a small glass.' These were beers for special occasions and only rarely allowed out into pubs and bars.

in the early 20th century when a limited form of prohibition banned the sale of spirits in bars. Brewers responded by producing strong beers that soothed the loss felt by brandy, gin and whisky drinkers.

The success of strong beers has encouraged brewers to pay great attention to the style. One objection to the category in the past was that the beers tended to be sweet and cloying, with a liquid barley sugar flavour. Brewers have turned, yet again, to the hop for help. A generous addition of hops, in the copper, the hop back and even in the cask, tempers the richness and sweetness of beers made with substantial amounts of malt and other grains and sugars. The careful marriage of malt and hops, the balance of sweetness, fruit and bitterness, make this style of beer one that constantly surprises and delights.

Although it just falls outside this category, Courage has a beer called Directors Bitter (4.8%) that was first brewed solely for the directors of the company's plant in Alton in Hampshire. Then, from the late 1970s, one English beer, Fuller's Extra Special Bitter, caught beer drinkers' fancies so much so that it won several awards in CAMRA's Champion Beer of Britain competition. It crossed the Atlantic and became a cult beer in the United States, to such an extent that the Great American Beer Festival now has a category called Extra Special Bitter. In Britain, the title belongs exclusively to Fuller's and it rigorously protects the brand name.

In mainland Europe there is less reticence about strong beers. They are part of the everyday drinking experience. In Belgium, in particular, with its deep-rooted beer culture, strong beers reflect a period

Arkell's Kingsdown Ale

Source: Arkell's Brewery, Kingsdown, Swindon, Wiltshire, England
Strength: 5.2%
Website: www.arkells.co.uk

Arkell's is one of the unassuming family-owned breweries, little known outside their trading areas, that form the backbone of traditional, high-quality brewing in England. John Arkell founded the company in 1843. He came from a farming family and emigrated to Canada, where he helped set up a community in Ontario that still exists today (see Wellington Arkell Best Bitter, page 99). John, however, returned to England and married his fiancée, who had become homesick in the New World.

John started to farm, grew barley, and took the next logical step of building a modest brewery in the Kingsdown area of Swindon. His timing was perfect. The great railway builder and architect Isambard Kingdom Brunel had chosen Swindon as the site for his works as he developed the Great Western railway line. Swindon rapidly grew from a sleepy market town into a thriving industrial one, with many thirsty throats to relieve.

To keep pace with demand, the Kingsdown brewery has been rebuilt and developed several times but it retains its Victorian charm, with an imposing tall chimney and a steam engine that can still be used in the event of a power cut.

Brewing takes place in traditional wood-jacketed mash tuns, copper boiling kettles and open square fermenters. Kingsdown Ale was introduced in 1969 when Swindon Town football club won the Football League Cup. The football team has not had much to celebrate since then but the beer has become a popular member of the brewery's portfolio.

Head brewer Don Bracher makes the beer as a 'parti-gyle' with his premium bitter 3B. This means he makes a strong wort, or extract, then adds brewing water to create the two different beers. Kingsdown is fashioned from Maris Otter pale and crystal malts with a small amount of brewing sugar (30 units of colour). The hops are Fuggles and Goldings, with a late addition of Goldings at the end of the copper boil (36 bitterness units). The generous use of Goldings gives a peppery bitterness to the amber-coloured beer that brilliantly balances biscuity malt and pear drop fruitiness. Hops and fruit offer an enticing aroma, and then fill the mouth alongside juicy malt. The deep and complex finish is bitter-sweet, with sappy malt, ripe fruit and peppery hops working in harmony.

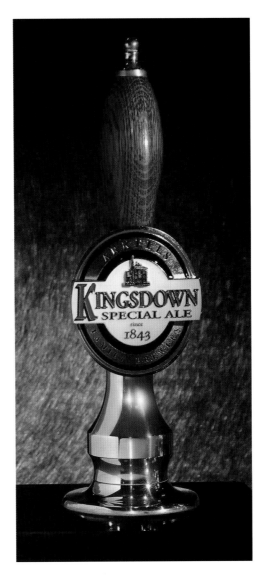

TASTING NOTES
Appearance
Aroma
Taste
Overall score

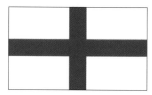

Fuller's ESB

Source: Fuller Smith and Turner's Griffin Brewery, Chiswick, London, England
Strength: 5.5%
Website: www.fullers.co.uk

TASTING NOTES
Appearance
Aroma
Taste
Overall score

This is the beer that gave its name to an international style. While there are many American ESBs, the brand name is now unique to Fuller's in Britain and it defends the name with legal vigour in its home market.

It started life as Winter Beer in 1969 and became a regular brew under its current name two years later. Three times winner of CAMRA's Champion Beer of Britain award, ESB is renowned for its classic Fuller's house style of a deep, rich fruitiness balanced by tangy hops. Some years ago, I described ESB as 'liquid Cooper's marmalade', which to my surprise rather pleased the brewery. In 2004, I was invited—as a beer and marmalade expert—to the Chiswick brewery to taste a revamped version of the beer. The changes were the result of a slight fall in sales. Market research showed that many drinkers rejected ESB on the grounds that it was too strong. It is a curiosity of beer drinking that people will down several glasses of lager of 5% or more but will baulk at an ale of similar strength.

Head brewer John Keeling and his team tackled the problem by keeping the strength at 5.5% but extended the time the beer matures in the brewery before going out to trade. Following fermentation, the beer rests for 21 days in conditioning tanks on a deep bed of Goldings hops. The result is an increased peppery hop note that better balances the beer's intense fruitiness. The brewery has cleverly developed a new branded glass for the beer that looks like an over-sized half-pint measure but actually contains a full pint. It makes a pint of ESB look less daunting to drinkers worried about its strength.

ESB is brewed from 90% Optic pale malt, 3% crystal malt and 7% flaked maize (colour units 30). The complex hop recipe includes Challenger, Goldings, Northdown and Target. The beer is late hopped in the copper with Challenger and Northdown, matured over Goldings that are then used to dry hop in the cask (34 units of bitterness). The finished beer has an explosion of rich malt, marmalade fruit and peppery hops on the nose, with an enormous attack of juicy malt, orange peel and bitter hop resins in the mouth. The deep, complex and lingering finish is beautifully balanced between malt, hops and tangy fruit, finally becoming dry with a good bitter hop resins note. A world classic.

Jennings Sneck Lifter

Source: Jennings Brothers, Cockermouth, Cumbria, England
Strength: 5.1%
Website: www.jenningsbrewery.co.uk

TASTING NOTES
Appearance
Aroma
Taste
Overall score

Cumbria has a substantial number of breweries, 15 at the last count. But most of them are relatively new 'micros' and Jennings is the sole large commercial operator. It dates from 1828, when John Jennings, the son of a maltster, opened a small brewery in the village of Lorton. He was sufficiently successful to have to move in 1874 to bigger premises in Cockermouth, most famous as the home town of Fletcher Christian, leader of the mutiny on the *Bounty*.

The brewery enjoys a spectacular base at the foot of Cockermouth Castle (see picture)— home to the Egremont family that includes the celebrated science fiction writer John Wyndham —and alongside the confluence of the rivers Cocker and Derwent. There are no Jennings left to run the company, but the brewery still has a strong local base, and in 2005 it was bought by the national group Wolverhampton & Dudley Breweries. The modern company owns 120 pubs and has a large trade throughout the North-west and across the Pennines into Northumbria. £1 million was invested in the brewery in 1999 but it remains staunchly traditional in its brewing methods and remains committed to both cask-

conditioned draught beer and the best brewing materials. It draws pure 'brewing liquor' from a well on the site.

Sneck Lifter, Jennings' strongest regular beer, takes its name from a dialect expression for someone who lifts the sneck, or catch, on the door to enter a pub. I have also been told that it means someone who doesn't buy his round of beer and hurries out of the pub by lifting the sneck. The beer is dark for a bitter and some people consider it to be close to a porter, though I doubt the London style ever found its way to such a remote area. It is brewed with Maris Otter pale malt, torrefied wheat, invert sugar and a small amount of black malt (50 colour units). The hops, used in whole flower form, are Fuggles and Goldings, which contribute 40 units of bitterness. It has a rich wholemeal and fresh bread aroma backed by spicy and peppery hops and espresso coffee notes from the black malt. The dark malt character builds in the mouth, adding some dried fruit notes, with a good balancing note of peppery hops. The finish is deep and complex, with a bitter-sweet fruitiness, a hint of coffee and chocolate, and a final lingering hop bitterness.

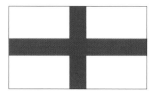

Moorhouse's Pendle Witches Brew

Source: Moorhouse's Brewery, Burnley, Lancashire, England
Strength: 5.1%
Website: www.moorhouses.co.uk

TASTING NOTES
Appearance
Aroma
Taste
Overall score

The journey to Burnley is one of the unsung great railway journeys of the world. I caught a train at Leeds that took a circuitous route past small towns with redundant mills and their tall, forlorn chimneys, then climbed steeply as it made for the peaks of the Pennine hills, England's rocky backbone. Brown moors and hills rose on either side, interspersed by tumbling rivers and streams. Then the train reached the summit and started the long glide down into Burnley, a mill town once so important that it had three railway stations. It was among the Pendle Hills that glower over Burnley that witches are alleged to have practised their dark arts in the 16th century. The reality is that many women, caught up in the turbulence of the times, were wrongly accused of witchcraft. James I had survived the Gunpowder Plot that failed to blow him and the Houses of Parliament to Kingdom Come. He then launched a campaign against such rebellious and staunchly Roman Catholic areas as Lancashire. In his book *Daemonology* he told the prosecuting authorities how to spot the 'devil's mark' on suspects' bodies. In most cases, birthmarks and blemishes were sufficient 'evidence' for women to be arrested. Several women from the Burnley area were tried on trumped-up charges and hanged.

The story should not distract us from the pleasures of the beer that recalls this grim period of English history. Pendle Witches Brew has won awards in CAMRA's Champion Beer of Britain competition and a silver medal in the Brewing International Awards. It is brewed with Halcyon pale malt, crystal malt, invert sugar and torrefied wheat, and hopped with just one variety, Fuggles. A pale bronze beer, it has a fine aroma of biscuity malt, spicy hops, pear-like fruit and a faint hint of vanilla. The mouth is filled with interweaving bitter-sweet flavours of fruit, malt and hop resins. The lengthy finish has some sweetness from malt and fruit but is balanced by a powerful and spicy hop character.

Pauwel Kwak

Source: Brouwerij Bosteels, Buggenhout, Belgium
Strength: 8%
Website: www.karmeliet.be

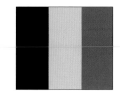

TASTING NOTES
Appearance
Aroma
Taste
Overall score

The idiosyncratic glass in its wooden serving shoe has tended to overshadow the quality of the beer itself. It comes from a family-owned brewery in the Dendermonde area, founded in 1791 by Evarist Bosteels. The company is run today by the sixth generation of the family, Ivo Bosteels and his son Antoine, and is based in the family's former mansion, which includes a small tower brewery.

The brewery's celebrated strong beer takes its name from a tavern keeper called Pauwel Kwak—literally Fat Paul—who owned De Hoorn (the Horn) on the busy road from Ghent to Mechelen. This was in the days of horse-drawn coaches. Mail coaches stopped at the tavern three times a day but the coachmen were not allowed to leave their vehicles for security reasons. So Fat Paul devised a glass with an oval base that the coach driver could place in his stirrup. As coach travel died out, the beer disappeared but Bosteels revived it, using the traditional oval-bottomed glass. As the glass cannot stand on its own, the brewery devised the wooden shoe to hold it.

The brewery has its own well in the grounds that supplies water from a depth of more than 100m (330ft). The water is soft and low in salts, and imparts a mellow note to the beer, which is made from three grains, including wheat. In the Belgian tradition, white candy sugar is added in the brew kettle to encourage a strong fermentation. The brewer does not want too much bitterness and therefore uses Styrian Goldings primarily for aroma. The finished beer is a burnished amber colour, with a dense rocky head of foam, a gentle spicy hop aroma, sappy malt and a big vanilla character from the house yeast. Malt, vanilla and a banana fruit note fill the mouth, while the big finish has a restrained spicy hop note, a rich maltiness and a lingering hint of liquorice, banana and vanilla.

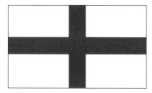

Ridley's Old Bob

Source: Greene King, Westgate Brewery, Bury St Edmunds, Suffolk, England
Strength: 5.1%
Website: www.greeneking.co.uk

TASTING NOTES
Appearance
Aroma
Taste
Overall score

Old Bob is named after a former brewer at Ridley's. The brewery has closed but the beer lives on. This was not the case of a big, bad brewer shutting a smaller one: the Ridley family, for reasons that have never been revealed, were keen to get out of brewing. It was a tragedy, for the brewery, almost lost down country lanes in rural Essex, was a classic 19th-century complex of brownstone buildings topped by an imposing chimney.

It was opened by a farmer, William Ridley, who ran a mill on the site alongside the river Chelmer. His son, Thomas Dixon Ridley, expanded the malting and milling side of the business and then added a tower brewery downstream from the mill in 1842. When I visited the brewery shortly before it closed I was entranced by some of the traditional equipment, including a cast-iron mash tun and eight wooden fermenters. A malt weighing machine dated from the 19th century and was one of the oldest pieces of weighing equipment in the country.

But the brewery's history pales into insignificance when compared to the Ridley family's, which can be traced back to the rugged border country of Northumbria in the 10th century. One of the most famous members of the family was Bishop Nicholas Ridley, who was burnt at the stake during the reign of Mary Tudor when he refused to renege on his Protestant beliefs. The last chairman of the brewery was also named Nicholas, who now lives in tax exile in Monaco.

Greene King bought and closed Ridley's in 2005 but continues to produce both Old Bob and Witchfinder Porter (page 161). I'm not a great believer in moving beers from one production plant to another: even when the same ingredients, including the original yeast culture, are used, the character of the beers often changes. However, Greene King is making a good fist of Old Bob, which is a delicious bottled beer.

It's made with Maris Otter pale malt (75%), crystal malt (12.5%) and torrefied wheat (12.5%).

Torrefied wheat is similar to popcorn and is used to give flavour and a good head to beer as well as reducing haze in the finished product. Old Bob has 45 colour units. It's hopped with Fuggles and Goldings for bitterness, with Styrian Goldings in the hop back for aroma (35 bitterness units). While it's 5.1% in strength, the original gravity—a measurement of malt sugars in the wort prior to fermentation—is 1055 degrees. This indicates that fermentation is stopped before all the malt sugars have turned to alcohol, leaving some sweetness in the beer.

The aroma is rich and redolent of such dried vine fruits as raisins and sultanas, with wholemeal biscuits and a light spicy hop note. Ripe fruit and sweet malt fill the mouth, but spicy and earthy hop notes in the finish prevent the beer from being cloying: the hops balance the dried fruit and biscuit malt character.

Ringwood Old Thumper

Source: Ringwood Brewery, Ringwood, Hampshire, England

Strength: 5.6%

Website: www.ringwoodbrewery.co.uk

TASTING NOTES
Appearance
Aroma
Taste
Overall score

Ringwood is a remarkable success story, one that proves that small craft breweries can succeed against all the odds in a market place increasingly dominated by giant global producers. The brewery was launched in 1978 by the legendary 'father' of micro-brewing, Peter Austin, who went on to build small breweries in the United States, France and even China. On my first visit to the brewery, it was based in an old bakery near the railway station. Ringwood is now owned by Marston's who have invested in the brewery and expanded sales of the beers.

To keep up with demand, a new brewhouse was commissioned in 1994 and a new fermenting room was added a year later. Demand continued to increase and further fermenters were added in 2002. Ringwood now produces around 30,000 barrels of beer a year, making it a regional rather than a micro producer. Best Bitter is its biggest

seller but there is no doubt that the company was put on the map and went on to greater success as a result of winning CAMRA's Champion Beer of Britain competition in 1988 with Old Thumper.

It is brewed from Maris Otter pale malt with small amounts of chocolate and crystal malts and some torrefied wheat (33 units of colour). The hops are a blend of all English varieties, Challenger, Goldings and Progress (32 units of bitterness). The deep bronze beer has a big peppery and spicy hop aroma balanced by biscuity and nutty malt with a hint of tart apple fruit. Rich juicy malt, tangy fruit and bitter hop resins fill the mouth, followed by a long finish that ends dry and bitter but with compensating notes of sappy malt, nuts and fruit. The beer is brewed under licence in the US by Shipyard Breweries (see also next entry).

Shipyard Longfellow Winter Ale

Source: Shipyard Breweries, Portland, Maine, USA
Strength: 5.5%
Website: www.shipyard.com

TASTING NOTES
Appearance
Aroma
Taste
Overall score

Shipyard, as explained in the IPA section (see page 19), was inspired by British micro-brewer Peter Austin and one of his brewers, Alan Pugsley, who is now a partner in the company, in which giant brewer Miller also has a stake.

Winter Ale is a seasonal speciality, one that beer lovers in New England await with keen anticipation. The Shipyard website was inundated in 2004 with requests to know whether the beer had been discontinued, as the brewery had launched a new Winter Ale. Alan Pugsley himself had to take to the airwaves to assure the worried drinkers that Longfellow was on the way. The beer is named after the celebrated poet Henry Wadsworth Longfellow, who lived in Portland, a major fishing harbour and port.

He is most famous for the epic *Hiawatha* but he also wrote poems about the sea, including *The Wreck of the Hesperus*.

Longfellow Winter Ale employs pale, crystal and chocolate malts and roasted barley (colour 44) and is hopped with Cascade, East Kent Goldings, German Tettnanger and Warrior (40 bitterness units). The house yeast strain, imported from Ringwood in England, imparts a typical fruity character. The rich amber beer has a spicy cinnamon and roasted grain aroma, with hints of bitter chocolate and coffee in the mouth, roasted grain, fresh apple and earthy hops. The long finish is deep and complex, with vine fruits, spices, earthy hop resins and roasted grain.

Wild River Extra Special Bitter

Source: Wild River Brewing, Grants Pass, Oregon, USA
Strength: 5.3%
Website: www.wildriverbrewing.com

TASTING NOTES
Appearance
Aroma
Taste
Overall score

The first head brewer at Wild River, Hubert Smith, was a frequent visitor to Britain and I met him regularly at the Great British Beer Festival where he graced my annual beer seminars. He had a passion for strong English pale ales and he poured that passion into his interpretation of Extra Strong Bitter.

Wild River started life as a Pizza Deli in 1975, founded by Jerry and Bertha Miller at Brookings Harbor with the toe-curling slogan, 'Blame us if your life goes to Pizzas'. They flourished in their attractive river setting close to the California border and eventually opened new premises at Cave Junction and Grants Pass. Realising that pizza and strong malty/hoppy beers are a marriage made in heaven, the Millers added in-house brewing facilities first at Cave Junction and then at a bigger plant at Grants Pass, which

has a 15-barrel kit. The breweries produce a wide range of beers, which are also widely distributed in bottle, and include Kölsch, Hefe Weizen and Russian Imperial Stout.

The stand-out beer is the ESB, brewed from pale, Munich, crystal and wheat malts and hopped with American Chinook and English Fuggles. The copper-coloured beer throws a dense, rocky head of foam and has an enthralling, complex aroma of tangy hop resins, tart citrus fruit and biscuity malt. Rich creamy malt fills the mouth with a good balance of earthy hop resins and tart fruit, while the long and deep finish is a fine balance between juicy malt, lemon fruit and a lingering hop-leaf bitterness.

Wychwood Hobgoblin

Source: Wychwood Brewery, Eagle Maltings, Witney, Oxfordshire, England
Strength: 5.2% (bottle); 5% (cask)
Website: www.wychwood.co.uk

Wychwood was set up in 1983 in the maltings of the old Clinch's brewery that dated from the 1800s. The founders of Wychwood were Paddy Glenny and the late head brewer Chris Moss, who was much loved in brewing and CAMRA circles. Chris fashioned the first version of Hobgoblin with a striking label based on the legends and myths of the Royal Forest of Wychwood that covered most of West Oxfordshire in medieval times. In common with the New Forest in Hampshire, Wychwood was reserved for the sovereign and his court to go hunting. Fairies, demons and hobgoblins roamed the forest: hobgoblins were bigger versions of goblins and, despite their terrifying appearance, acted as guardians of farm and country folk, though apparently they could turn nasty if thwarted. Sounds like the Stella drinkers in my local.

Over the years, Hobgoblin has ranged from 4.5% to 5.5%. I have included it in this section because of the strength of the bottled version, though it's a moveable feast. It is brewed from 90% Maris Otter pale malt, with 7% crystal malt and 3% torrefied wheat (40 colour units). The hops are Fuggles and Styrian Goldings, which create 28 units of bitterness. The amber-red beer has a tempting aroma of biscuity malt, vinous fruit and spicy hop resins. Full-bodied malt, sultana fruit and earthy hops coat the mouth, while the complex finish has a bitter-sweet start, with creamy malt and ripe fruit, but spicy hops linger at the back of the tongue.

Sales of Hobgoblin have soared in recent years in recent years to such an extent that the brewery, along with the adjacent Brakspear plant, is now owned by Marston's.

TASTING NOTES
Appearance
Aroma
Taste
Overall score

Old Ales, Barley Wines & Vintage Ales

BELOW

Strong Suffolk from Greene King is one of the few remaining examples of 18th-century 'country beers' matured for long periods in wooden vessels called tuns.

It is tempting—and many beer writers have fallen for the temptation—to list Old Ales and Barley Wines as though they are the same style of strong beer. They are not. The designation Old Ale does not necessarily imply strength (they can be as low as 4.5%), whereas Barley Wine clearly suggests a beer that is a rival to the fermented juice of the grape. Both are English styles and they have quite different histories, though they do have in common the need to be matured for a considerable period.

Old Ales in the 18th century were also known as 'stale' as a result of maturing for many months or years in wooden tuns, where the beer was attacked by wild yeasts and acetified by lactobacilli and tannins in the wood. The sour flavour of stale was much appreciated at the time and lives on in the form of the sour red beers of Belgium (see page 201). Stale was an important constituent of the early types of porter (see page 136) and was also blended with the young, fresh mild ales of the 18th century to give them some semblance of maturity.

Once brewers in the late 19th and early 20th centuries stopped vatting or maturing beer for long periods, old and stale disappeared. Old reappeared as part of the revival of interest in beer styles created by CAMRA and the 'real ale revolution' of the 1970s. Many of the new-wave old ales are reserved for the winter period, others are now brewed all year round. The classic of the style is the remarkable Greene King Strong Suffolk Ale, a genuine old ale or 'country ale' from the 18th century. It is a blend of two beers, one of which is still matured in ancient wooden vats. Some old ales are 'vatted' in the sense that they mature naturally on their yeast under glass. The best-known examples are Gale's Prize Old Ale in its corked bottle and the celebrated Thomas Hardy's Ale, rescued from oblivion by a micro-brewery a few years ago.

Barley wine for centuries was the preserve of the English aristocracy. While the labouring classes made do with cheap brown ales, the nobility drank beer matured for long periods that had the potency of wine. Such beers were also known as October beers—October being considered the best month to make good beer, using the new malts and hops of the harvest—Dorchester beers, malt liquors or malt wines, but by the early 18th century the term barley wine was in vogue. As a result of the interminable wars with France, it was the patriotic duty of noble Englishmen and women to drink the 'wine of the country'. Fine cut-glass goblets adorned the tables of the aristocracy and, deprived of their beloved claret, they turned to beers made as strong as wine. In *Every Man His Own Brewer*, published in London in 1768, the author commented on 'The Method of Manufacturing Pure Malt Wines': 'Laying aside vulgar opinion, that foreign wines are used by the rich, rather from vanity than taste, it must be observed that experience will always be superior to custom. Our business then is to prepare our malt drinks as nearly as possible to answer the like purpose of foreign wines.'

Commercial, or 'common', brewers supplied barley wines to the nobility but the landed gentry had their own breweries in their country mansions. In her book *Country House Brewing in England 1500–1900* (Hambledon Press), Pamela Seabrook paints a fascinating picture of beer making in small brewhouses usually attached to the kitchens of stately homes. Brewing was often one of the many tasks of the butler. An 1820s training manual for butlers said: 'The keys of the wine and ale cellars are specially kept by him, and the management of the wine, the keeping of the stock book, and also of ale in stock, or in brewing, are in his particular charge. This duty he generally performs in the morning before he is dressed to receive company… While these duties and those of brewing are in hand, he leaves the parlour and waiting duties to the under-butler and footman.'

October beers, or barley wines, of the period were exceedingly strong. One recipe called for 23 bushels of malt to make two 54-gallon hogsheads of beer, one bushel being the equivalent of eight imperial gallons. There was considerable dispute over how long the beers should be left to mature. One 18th-century writer considered that a beer brewed in October should be left until spring, when the increase in temperature would encourage a second fermentation. The beer would then be 'very fine, strong, mellow, well-tasted and wholesome' by Michaelmas (i.e. the end of September). But another writer was of the opinion that the beer would be at its best by midsummer, although it would keep for five or even 10 years.

LEFT
The 'double drop' fermenters at Brakspear are crucial to the flavour of the finished beers, which have a renowned butterscotch note.

The decline of the English aristocracy in the 20th century—only Lord Lichfield's estate at Shugborough in Staffordshire has a working brewery today—left the brewing of barley wines to commercial producers. The brand leader in Britain for decades was Whitbread's Gold Label, now reduced to a canned product, while Bass No1 Barley Wine is an occasional brew from a pilot plant in the Coors complex at Burton-on-Trent. The style has crossed the Atlantic, where it is brewed with enthusiasm by craft brewers. It has also been the inspiration for strong Belgian beers (see Bush, page 119).

Brewers enjoy challenges. The opportunity to brew vintage ale moves them from the world of mainstream beers to a level where the adroit blending of massive amounts of malts and hops can produce beers with astonishingly complex and rewarding aromas and flavours. The brewer is more fortunate than the wine maker: as Fuller's shows with its Vintage Ale, it is possible to take different malts, sugar and hop varieties once a year to produce beers that have a recognisable house style but which vary subtly and often sublimely from one vintage to the next.

Anchor Old Foghorn

Source: Anchor Brewing Co, San Francisco, California, USA

Strength: 8.7%

Website: www.anchorbrewing.com

TASTING NOTES
Appearance
Aroma
Taste
Overall score

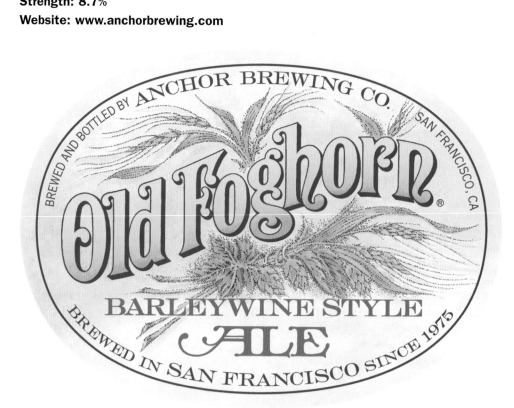

The beer's inspiration is the throaty growl of a ship's horn as it navigates the fog-wreathed waters of San Francisco. Owner Fritz Maytag discovered barley wine on his seminal trip to England, where he also fell in love with well-hopped pale ales (see page 53).

Old Foghorn was introduced in 1975 and has become an American classic, building on the English experience but adding new depths of richness due to an emphatic American hop character. The beer is certainly well matured: it rests on a deep bed of Cascade hops for up to 10 months before it is released to the public. It is brewed from pale and crystal malts, and—unusually—only the 'first runnings' from the mash tun are used. This means the spent grain is not sparged, or washed, with a further addition of hot water to rinse out any remaining malt sugars.

Cascades produce 65 units of bitterness. Fermentation is in deep vessels, where the yeast is regularly roused to prevent it from falling asleep on the job as it creates such a high level of alcohol. The beer is pasteurised but this does not prevent it developing in bottle, and some drinkers prefer to lay down some small nip bottles for several years. It is also available on draught. The burnished mahogany ale has a pronounced ripe fruit aroma reminiscent of apricots and raisins, balanced by a ripe malt loaf note and tangy, bitter hops. Malt and fruit build in the mouth but the crescendo is reached in the finish, which lingers on the tongue and the throat with massive vinous fruit, plump grain and bitter hop resins. It's a sipping beer, to be appreciated like a fine Cognac or single malt whisky, and is a fine companion for blue cheese.

Anker Gouden Carolus Classic

Source: Het Anker Brewery, Mechelen, Belgium
Strength: 8.5%
Website: www.hetanker.be

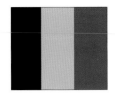

Nuns, emperors, dukes and beer forge a rich heritage at Het Anker brewery. It was the fortuitously named Duke Charles the Stout who decreed in 1471 that nuns in the Low Countries could brew beer for their hospices free from tax. As a result, sisters from a convent in Mechelen, then a linchpin of the Holy Roman Empire, moved to a new site in 1596 where they built the Hospice de Beaune. The buildings included a small brewery where beer was made to comfort the sick and the dying.

The nuns left the hospice in 1865 and seven years later the site was sold to Louis van Breedam. He expanded the brewing operation and called his company Het Anker. The name commemorated the name of Jan In Den Anker, a maltster who opened Mechelen's first brewery in 1369, and it also maintained the religious theme, reminding pious drinkers that hope is the anchor of the soul.

The brewery has remained in the hands of the van Breedam family ever since. In 1939 Charles van Breedam took the fateful decision to stop brewing Pils lager and went back to making warm-fermented ales. The major turning point in Het Anker's fortunes came in 1963 when Michel van Breedam launched a strong beer called Gouden Carolus. The name, Golden Charles, came from a coin minted during the reign of one of the most famous Habsburg emperors, Charles V (1500–1558) who grew up in Mechelen and loved the local beers.

The brewery today is a fascinating blend of old and new. The offices, with a large anchor by the entrance, are based in part of the former convent, a group of mellow stone and gabled buildings. A cobbled yard leads to the brewery run by the young, energetic and enthusiastic general manager Charles Leclef, a Breedam on the distaff side of the family. He has grown beer sales dramatically from just 1,300 hectolitres in 1997 to 14,500 by 2009. Gouden Carolus has been rebranded Classic, as Charles has added

four additional beers to the range: a 9.5% Tripel, an 8% Ambrio, Hopsinjopor (8%, with four hop varieties) and an annual vintage Cuvée van de Keizer (11%), which means the Emperor's Brew. The last-named in brewed every year on 24 February, the birthday of Charles V.

The brewery is a blend of old and new. The vessels in the brewhouse—mash tun, mash filter and copper—date from 1947 while one floor below modern conical fermenters were installed in 2004. Four additional fermenters were due to be installed in 2009. Fermentation last for five days. The beer is then filtered and left in conditioning tanks to ripen. Three-quarters of production is packaged and yeast and sugar are added to encourage a strong second fermentation in bottle.

The success of Gouden Carolus has encouraged Charles Leclef to add a single malt whisky to his range, recalling the time in the 18th century when Het Anker made geneva (gin) as well as beer.

Gouden Carolus Classic is brewed from five malts: Pils, wheat, light and dark caramalt, and roast. The single hop is Golding. The beer has a ruby colour and an enticing aroma of port wine, chocolate and spicy hops. Burnt fruit (raisins) builds in the mouth, with chewy malt and continuing chocolate and spicy hops. The finish has enormous length and is bittersweet with hints of liquorice, roasted grain, dark fruit, chocolate and tangy hops.

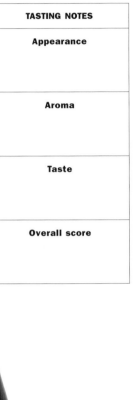

TASTING NOTES
Appearance
Aroma
Taste
Overall score

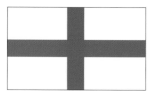

Ballard's Wassail

Source: Ballard's Brewery, Nyewood, West Sussex, England
Strength: 6%
Website: www.ballardsbrewery.org.uk

TASTING NOTES
Appearance
Aroma
Taste
Overall score

Carola Brown is a stalwart of craft brewing in Britain. She launched Ballard's in 1980 at her farm, Cumbers, and moved to an old sawmill in Nyewood in 1988. She was a founder of SIBA, which stood for Small Independent Brewers' Association but is known today as the Society of Independent Brewers. SIBA was created to give small brewers a voice in both the brewing industry and the pub trade. It has achieved remarkable success. It has persuaded the British government to introduce Progressive Beer Duty, which means smaller producers pay less tax on their products than giant national and regional brewers, and has also reached agreements with the powerful pub chains, several of which now buy beer from SIBA members.

Ballard's produces 1,500 gallons of beer a week from a smart and compact brewhouse. It brews only with malt and hops, avoiding sugars and cheaper grains. Several of its draught beers are also available in bottle-fermented form. The bottled versions are filtered, reseeded with fresh yeast and conditioned in the brewery for two weeks before release to trade.

Wassail is both a greeting—from the Middle English *waes aeil*, which means 'good health'—and also an ancient type of spiced or mulled wine drunk to celebrate Christmas Eve and Twelfth Night. Ballard's Wassail has a picturesque label that features Hengist, fifth-century leader of the Jutes, who, with his brother Horsa, brought the first Germanic settlers to England and with them the language that became English. The label also shows Vortigern, King of the Britons, and Rowena, Hengist's daughter, who seduced Vortigern.

The label is as complex as the beer, which is brewed with Pipkin pale and crystal malts and hopped with Fuggles and Goldings. The amber-red beer has a powerful aroma of dried vine fruits, a freshly-baked bread maltiness and earthy and spicy hops. Raisin and sultana fruit, ripe malt and hop resins coat the tongue, while the finish is deep and long, interweaving between rich fruit, malt and tangy, spicy hops.

Blue Anchor Spingo Special

Source: Blue Anchor, Helston, Cornwall, England
Strength: 6.6%
Website: www.spingoales.com

TASTING NOTES
Appearance
Aroma
Taste
Overall score

Beer has been brewed for 600 years or more on the site of the present inn. It started life as a monks' hospice around the year 1400. The monks brewed ale to refresh and sustain themselves, and they chose the site because it had a well with a plentiful supply of fresh water. Even a humble monks' resting place did not escape the dissolution of religious houses under the Tudors. It became a secular inn and took on the name of Blue Anchor at a time when Helston was an important port. The symbol of an anchor is weaved in the thatch on the pub roof.

The Blue Anchor remains gloriously unspoilt and has protected status as a Grade I listed building. The bars have flagstone floors, beamed ceilings and open fires. At the rear of the pub, a two-storey block houses the brewery, which has a mash tun that was installed in the 1920s and was originally a French wine cask. Opposite the tun is a venerable old lagged vessel that doubles as hot liquor tank and boiling copper.

The hopped wort is cooled in an open tray known as a cool ship and is then dropped down one storey into four small fermenting vessels.

The name Spingo was introduced following World War One and was based perhaps on a strong style of beer brewed in Yorkshire called Stingo. Spingo Special is brewed from Pipkin pale malt and Goldings hops. Although only pale malt is used, the beer has an amber-red colour, as some of the malt sugars caramelise during the long copper boil. The aroma is earthy and spicy with rich vine fruits. Peppery hops, biscuity malt and blackcurrant fruit pack the mouth, leading to a complex finish with massive tart fruit notes balanced by malt and bitter hops and hints of caramel and vanilla.

Special versions of Spingo are brewed for Easter and Christmas, and all the beers are available in bottle-fermented as well as draught form. Bottles are available from the pub and specialist shops.

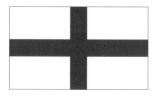

Brakspear Triple

Source: Brakspear Brewing Co, Witney, Oxfordshire, England
Strength: 7.2%
Website: www.brakspear-beers.co.uk

TASTING NOTES
Appearance
Aroma
Taste
Overall score

Triple is one of the best new beers to appear in Britain for many years—it's a glass of the Old Stunning, as Charles Dickens was wont to say. It was first brewed in 2005 to celebrate the return of Brakspear to Oxfordshire: see page 70 for the story of the Brakspear brewery in Henley-on-Thames. Lovingly, piece by piece, the 'double drop' wooden fermentation system was moved from Henley to Witney to allow the yeast culture to reproduce the distinctive aromas and flavours of the beer, including the renowned diacetyl (butterscotch) characteristic.

In 2007, both Brakspear and Wychwood breweries, which share the same site, were bought by Marston's of Burton-on-Trent, which has given the beers of both breweries greater presence in pubs, supermarkets and specialist beer shops.

Triple is not, it must be emphasised, an attempt to brew a Belgian-style Tripel. Tripel means a golden beer, of which Westmalle is the best known example. The Brakspear beer gets its name from the fact that it's hopped three times—twice in the copper and finally in the fermenter, once the beer has dropped into the second storey of vessels. The second reason is that the beer enjoys three fermentations, once in the fermenting hall, a second time during a lengthy period of maturation in conditioning tanks, and finally in the bottle.

The packaging is superb. The 'bee' logo, taken from the mitre of Pope Adrian IV (Nicholas Breakspear), appears twice, once as part of a red seal that appears alongside the individual number on each bottle. If you want to trace when a beer was bottled you can track the number via the Brakspear website.

The beer is brewed with Maris Otter pale malt with crystal and black malts. The hops are English Northdown and American Cascade. Northdowns are used early in the copper boil for bitterness while Cascades are added late for aroma. A further addition of Cascade is made in the fermenters. A fresh yeast culture is used when the beer is bottled.

Triple has a pale amber/copper colour and a complex bouquet of pear drop fruit, oak, liquorice, butterscotch, nutty malt and nose-tingling hop resins. Hop resins and bitterness build in the mouth but are balanced by nutty and slightly toasted grain and ripe fruit. The finish has enormous length, dominated by tart fruit—in which Cascade hops play a major role—juicy malt and bitter hops. The beer is bottle conditioned and, at 7.2 per cent, will improve with age. It's a fine companion for ripe cheese: hold the port wine, Triple and Stilton are a marriage made in heaven.

BridgePort Old Knucklehead

Source: BridgePort Brewery, Portland, Oregon, USA
Strength: 9%
Website: www.bridgeportbrew.com

If you call someone a knucklehead, you will insult them; the British would use bonehead in its place for someone short on brains and thick on top. And yet the dignitaries of Portland queue up to get their face on the label of this annual vintage barley wine. To date they include the Mayor of Portland—some may think that voting for a knucklehead is not confined to one city in Oregon—and the doyen of American beer writers, Fred Eckhardt.

The beer is brewed in the autumn, using the new malts and hops of the harvest, and released in nip bottles in November. I have given 9% as the most recent rating but over the years it has varied from 8.7% to 9.1%. The malts come from the Pacific North-west region and include pale, crystal and a touch of chocolate. The hops are imported East Kent Goldings from England, with locally grown Chinook used for aroma as a late hop during the copper boil. The generous hop rate is important to balance the richness of the malt. At such a high level of alcohol, the beer has a massive fruity and vinous aroma: apple, apricot, pear and even banana can be detected with a hint of grapefruit from the Chinooks. The fruit is balanced by a rich and biscuity malt character and a blast of peppery Goldings. Ripe flavours of malt loaf, spicy hop resins and a persistent jammy fruitiness fill the mouth, while the long and lingering finish has some welcome dryness and bitterness from the hops that offset the continuing vine fruits and ripe malt. Sip carefully or you may emulate the name on the label.

TASTING NOTES
Appearance
Aroma
Taste
Overall score

Broughton Old Jock

Source: Broughton Ales, Broughton, Peebles-shire, Scotland
Strength: 6.7%
Website: www.broughtonales.co.uk

TASTING NOTES
Appearance
Aroma
Taste
Overall score

Broughton, brewery and small town, are in the Scottish Borders, a region of low hills that was fought over for centuries by the English and the Scots. There are still the remains of ancient keeps and small castles, built to halt the advancing British troops. The fortifications have a history of ale brewing, where women known as ale wives made hearty beers from local barley and oats to help sustain their fighting men folk. The tradition is maintained at Broughton, which brews an Oatmeal Stout (see page 141) as well as Old Jock.

The brewery, down a rutted lane and surrounded by fields where sheep graze, was founded in 1979 by David Younger, a member of the Younger brewing clan that once had a major plant in Alloa and was also part of the Scottish & Newcastle dynasty. He was supported by James Collins of the famous Scottish publishing house that became part of the Murdoch empire. There is a literary connection in Broughton, too: it was the birthplace of John Buchan, the adventure story writer, most famous for *The Thirty-Nine Steps*. The town has a Buchan Museum and the brewery produces a Greenmantle Ale in memory of one of his novels.

Old Jock is a member of a Scottish style known as a wee heavy, which indicates a strong bitter beer sold in nip bottles (though Old Jock is also available on draught). It is named in honour of Scottish soldiers, known as Jocks, who, once the Border disputes were settled, fought alongside the English in many battles.

The beer is brewed from Maris Otter pale malt and roasted barley (55 colour units) and hopped with Fuggles and Goldings for aroma and Target for bitterness (30 units of bitterness). It has a dark ruby colour and a rich aroma of roasted grain, vine fruits and spicy hops. Dark fruit, bitter roasted grain and hop resins fill the mouth, followed by a long finish with a good underpinning of bitterness to balance the increasing dominance of rich fruit and malt flavours. The bottled version of the beer has struggled in American markets, where the name is thought to refer to an item of male sportswear.

Bush Ambrée

Source: Brasserie Dubuisson, Pipaix, Belgium
Strength: 12%
Website: www.br-dubuisson.com

Dubuisson is a classic example of a Belgian farm brewery, in an area packed with small brewers, close to Tournai and Lille across the border in France. The brewery stands on the Mons road and, although farming no longer takes place, its origins are clear from the tiled roof and green-painted shutters at the windows.

In 1769, Joseph Leroy, an ancestor of the Dubuisson family that still runs the company, decided to brew at the farm to supply beer to his labourers and the local village. In 1931, Alfred Dubuisson took the decision to stop farming and concentrate on brewing. Two years later he changed the name of his single beer to Bush, which is the English for 'Buisson'. There are two theories for the name change. One says it was a way of paying homage to the British troops who liberated the farm and brewery at the end of World War One. The second says it was done in order to meet the increased competition from British beer imports. As there is a rather big gap between 1918 and 1933, I tend to accept the second theory.

In a country famous for strong beer, Bush is one of the strongest. It is brewed in an attractive brewhouse, with mash tun and copper set in tiled surrounds, the hallmark of many small, traditional Belgian breweries. The beer is brewed with pale malt and caramalt: the last named gives a luscious sweet and nutty character to the beer as well as its amber colour. The hops are East Kent Goldings and Styrian Goldings. The finished beer has a rich barley sugar, nutty and peppery hop aroma, with malt, fruit and hops filling the mouth, and a lingering finish in which the richness of the malt and fruit is balanced by peppery hop resins. It is a warming and alcoholic beer, the perfect aperitif, according to the brewers.

As a result of objections from Anheuser-Busch, the beer is sold in the United States under the name of Scaldis, the Latin name for the Scheldt, Belgium's main river. Anheuser-Busch is best known for American Budweiser and it is difficult to imagine that any self-respecting beer drinker could confuse the two beers.

TASTING NOTES
Appearance
Aroma
Taste
Overall score

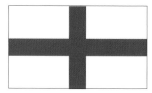

Chiltern 300s Old Ale

Source: Chiltern Brewery, Terrick, near Aylesbury, Buckinghamshire, England
Strength: 4.9%
Website: www.chilternbrewery.co.uk

TASTING NOTES
Appearance
Aroma
Taste
Overall score

Chiltern is an old-established craft brewery founded in 1980 by Richard Jenkinson. He was a City of London businessman who grew tired of the daily commute and decided to settle down in the delightful Buckinghamshire countryside and raise a rare breed of white rabbit. That enterprise failed to get out of the warren, so Richard turned instead to brewing and did so with some success.

He has been joined by the younger generation of his family George and Tom, and sales of the beers encouraged a major investment in 2004 in a new brewhouse and temperature-controlled cold store. The brewery is visitor-friendly, with tours every Saturday at 12 noon and weekday visits by arrangement. There is a small brewery museum and a shop where draught and bottled beers can be taken away, along with beer-based cheeses, pickles and mustards. Richard has a passion for local history, and 300s Old Ale records the ancient practice of dividing English counties into areas known as hundreds, each one controlled by a steward. The Buckinghamshire divisions still have an important role to play in modern times: any Member of Parliament who wishes to resign his or her seat must apply for permission to do so to the Steward of the Chiltern Hundreds.

The beer that pays homage to this curious example of English political practice is brewed from Maris Otter pale malt (86%) and a substantial proportion of crystal malt (14%). The whole flower hops are Challenger for bitterness, and Fuggles and Goldings for aroma. The deep copper colour and the luscious nutty and vinous aroma and palate derive from the generous use of crystal malt. This is balanced by a tart hop and earthy hop resins character with a fine, full-bodied juicy malt note in the mouth. The finish lingers, finely balanced between tart fruit, biscuity malt and a good, solid underpinning of spicy hop resins.

Chiltern beers can be enjoyed in the King's Head in Aylesbury.

Cooper's Extra Strong Vintage Ale

Source: Cooper's Brewery, Adelaide, Australia
Strength: 7.5%
Website: www.coopers.com.au

In March 2009, one of the final pieces in my personal beer jigsaw clicked into place when I fulfilled a 30-year-old ambition to visit Cooper's brewery in Adelaide, South Australia. As I explain in the section on Cooper's Sparkling Ale (page 56), the wooden puncheons used to ferment Cooper's beers are no longer used. But to my great pleasure I found the old vessels on display in a museum attached to the new brewery in Regency Park.

The modern brewhouse, with gleaming stainless steel vessels, was built in far-away Burton-on-Trent. The Cooper family, represented by the fifth generation Glenn and Tim, are determined to maintain traditional brewing methods and they went to the considerable expense of importing brewing kit all the way from the historic home of pale ale brewing in England.

Cooper's has added to its beer range in recent years with mild ale and lager. But the beer that caught my attention when it was launched in Britain in 2007 is Extra Strong Vintage Ale. The family is not shy of challenging Australia's mainstream beer styles. Sparkling Ale is a powerful antidote to bland national lagers. Now, with Vintage Ale, drinkers are confronted by a strong and intensely fruity beer that in its homeland can be consumed on draught as well as in bottle.

Vintage Ale was launched in 1998 and has been produced every year since then with the exception of 2005. When I first met company chairman Glenn Cooper in London in 2007 for the launch of bottle-conditioned Vintage Ale, I suggested the reason he had missed out 2005 was because Australia had lost the Ashes that year. For readers outside Britain, the Ashes is a fiercely-contested cricket tournament staged every two years between England and Australia. In 1882, when Australia first beat England at cricket, a bail—part of the wooden wicket—was ceremonially burnt and the ashes placed in a small urn to mark the death of English cricket.

Ever since, the winner of each series holds the Ashes urn. At the time of writing in 2009, England beat Australia in the latest tournament and I don't yet know whether Cooper's has overcome the shock and will brew a 2009 Vintage Ale.

The strength of 7.5% is nominal and can vary from year to year: it's not an exact science, as live yeast in a bottle can create more alcohol during storage. The beer is brewed with pale and crystal malts and is hopped with Pride of Ringwood from Tasmania. Some vintages have had an addition of hops from other countries, including German Hallertauer and Czech Saaz.

The 2007 vintage has an enormous bouquet of fruit—blood oranges and sherry wine. In the mouth fruit is balanced by a powerful hint of fresh tobacco and hop resins. The finish is long and complex, with rich malt, tangy hops and citrus fruit. Cooper's urges drinkers to lay down some samples of each vintage as they will improve with age.

TASTING NOTES
Appearance
Aroma
Taste
Overall score

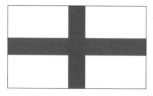

Cottage Norman's Conquest

Source: Cottage Brewing Co, Lovington, near Castle Carey, Somerset, England
Strength: 7%
Website: None

TASTING NOTES
Appearance
Aroma
Taste
Overall score

There are subtle jokes associated with this beer. The original gravity—the measure of the fermentable sugars before fermentation—is 1066, the year of the Norman conquest of England, which is depicted on the label of the bottle-fermented version. Norman is also the name of Chris Norman, who founded the brewery with his wife Helen in 1993.

Chris had been both an airline pilot and a keen home-brewer who took early retirement in order to pursue commercial brewing. Just two years later, the Normans hit the jackpot when Norman's Conquest won CAMRA's Supreme Champion Beer of Britain competition. When I went to see them a few weeks later, I found they ran a truly cottage, or garage, industry from the garden of their home in Somerset. My next visit was as a guest at a party to celebrate 20 years of successful brewing at a new site in a former cheese dairy with a 30-barrel plant that supplies some 1,500 customers.

Several new beers have been added to the range, including some with a steam railway theme, such as Golden Arrow. But Norman's Conquest remains the brewery's best-known product, even though it is made in small batches. The bottled version is filtered, reseeded with yeast and primed with brewing sugar to encourage a secondary fermentation. Drinkers should be patient and wait a couple of months to allow the beer to reach optimum condition, but check the 'best before' date on the label.

Norman's Conquest is brewed with Maris Otter pale, crystal and chocolate malts and hopped with just one variety, Challenger. The deep ruby beer has a digestive biscuit, dark fruits and bitter hop resins aroma. The full-bodied palate has delicious hints of chocolate, bitter orange and vine fruits, juicy malt and tangy hop resins. The long, deep finish offers chocolate, tart fruit, sappy malt, a hint of liquorice and an abiding undercurrent of bitter hop resins. A wonderfully warming yet refreshing sipping beer.

Fuller's Vintage Ale

Source: Fuller, Smith and Turner's Griffin Brewery, Chiswick, London, England
Strength: 8.5%
Website: www.fullers.co.uk

Vintage Ale has been a revelation. It was introduced in 1997 by the company's revered head brewer Reg Drury and continued by his successor John Keeling. The aim was to produce a strong bottle-fermented beer every September using different varieties of malted barley and hops. Fuller's house yeast strain adds the familiar signature of rich orange fruit, but there are subtle and even profound differences between one vintage and the next. The beer will also improve and develop over time, which means that tasting notes based on a young or mature beer will be radically different.

Vintage Ale is based on Fuller's Golden Pride barley wine, which is a pasteurised bottled beer. Vintage comes from the same mash but is conditioned in the brewery for four weeks at the end of fermentation and is then filtered and reseeded with fresh yeast. Some 50,000 bottles are produced every year, individually numbered and presented in an attractive claret box.

In 2004, I enjoyed a tasting of Vintage Ale at the brewery in the company of wine writer Oz Clarke, and we both revelled in the complexity and diversity of aromas and flavours presented to us. We found fresh tobacco, citrus fruits—orange in particular—liquorice, marzipan, vanilla, peppers and spices, to name just a few of the characteristics.

To give an indication of the different recipes used, the 2002 vintage—which marked the Queen's Golden Jubilee—was brewed with Golden Promise malt from Scotland and Goldings hops. Tobacco, cherries, marzipan, oranges and peppery hops were among the aromas and flavours detected. The 2003 vintage was dramatically different, using Optic malt and three hop varieties, Challenger, Northdown and Target. It was paler in colour, with a pronounced amber tone, and a richer malt character, but balanced by tart hop resins on the nose and a big hop bitterness in the finish, with orange and cherry fruit. The 2004 vintage had reverted to a single hop, Goldings again, with Maris Otter malt. Drunk young, the beer had a burnished ruby-red colour, with a massive biscuity malt, peppery hops and orange fruit aroma and palate, and a long, complex finish with vanilla notes adding to the complexity. And it will get better. Who says beer is a simple refresher?

TASTING NOTES
Appearance
Aroma
Taste
Overall score

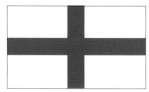

Gale's Prize Old Ale

Source: Fuller, Smith and Turner's Griffin Brewery, Chiswick, London, England
Strength: 9%
Website: www.fullers.co.uk

TASTING NOTES
Appearance
Aroma
Taste
Overall score

This is an old ale in the true sense of the word, with the beer matured in tanks in the brewery for between six and 12 months before it is bottled. It is one of a large portfolio of beers fermented with Gale's hearty, three-strain house yeast that imparts a rich and fruity aroma and flavour, which is most in evidence in Old Ale.

The brewery dated from 1847 when Richard Gale started brewing in the Ship & Bell. His son George expanded the business by buying local inns and farm buildings next to the Ship & Bell. Brewing moved out of the inn and into the farm but this timber building burnt down and was rebuilt. Its tower still dominates the small town 10 miles from Portsmouth though the brewery closed when it was bought by Fuller's.

Soft water feeds the mash tuns and coppers, with separate vessels used to produce Prize Old Ale, which has been brewed since the 1920s, when a new head brewer brought the recipe with him from Yorkshire. Maris Otter pale malt and black malt are used, with around 10% brewing sugar. The hops are Worcestershire Fuggles and East Kent Goldings (colour 90 units, bitterness 53 units). Following the long maturation, the beer is bottled with crown corks: Fuller's has phased out the use of driven corks. The original yeast strain creates a powerful second fermentation in bottle and the declared strength of 9% could rise to as high as 12%.

While the brewery is required to put a 'best before' date on each bottle, the beer will come into its best form after five years and remain drinkable for at least 20. After a few years, the beer takes on a renowned Cognac note. Drunk younger, it is fruity (raisins, sultanas and dates) with a solid underpinning of earthy and spicy hops.

During one visit to the old brewery, I was shown a fermenter where a former brewer committed suicide by jumping into the vessel, where he was overcome by alcohol and carbon dioxide. Is it the origin of the term 'stiff drink'?

Greene King Strong Suffolk Ale

Source: Greene King, Westgate Brewery, Bury St Edmunds, Suffolk, England
Strength: 6%
Website: www.greeneking.co.uk

Strong Suffolk Ale is a potent link with brewing practice in the 18th century. It is a now rare example of a 'country beer', a style that depended on long, slow maturation in wooden casks. The beer that emerged from slow ageing was used to blend with younger beers, and this is still the case at Greene King. The beer, matured for between one and five years in giant, 60-barrel tuns in the Westgate Brewery, is used as the base for St Edmund barley wine and the draught Winter Ale. The most notable and intriguing blend, however, is Strong Suffolk.

The tuns that hold the strong ale component are reached by a daunting clamber up narrow ladders and catwalks in tunnels at the rear of the brewery. It's thought that the tunnels once linked the monastery and the abbot's house, where the brewery now stands. Monks may have taken shelter in the tunnels at the time of the dissolution of the monasteries. The lids of the vats are covered in marl, a dialect word for the sandy gravel that covers much of Suffolk. I was told that the marl keeps wild yeast and other bacteria from infecting the beer. In spite of this protective covering, the 12% beer, known as Old 5X, that emerges from the untreated wooden vessels has a slight lactic sourness and hint of iodine. This beer is not sold commercially but small bottles are sometimes made available to visitors who show an interest in the subject. Old 5X is blended with another beer, the 5% BPA, or Best Pale Ale. This is another brew that is not found outside the brewery but I was given a taste of this rich, creamy and predominantly malty ale.

The two beers are brewed with Halycon and Pipkin pale malts, crystal malt and brewing sugar (100 colour units). The hops used are Northdown for bitterness and Target for aroma (32 units of bitterness). The blended beer has a spicy, oaky, sherry wine and iron-like intensity on aroma and palate with a hint of sourness. The finish is big and complex, with malt, a vinous sweetness and some tannins balanced by bitter and earthy hop resins and the continuing hint of lactic sourness. The beer is filtered and pasteurised, and I have failed to convince the brewery that it would take the beer an extra mile if it were produced in bottle-fermented form.

In 2002, Strong Suffolk was made available as a cask-conditioned draught winter ale, but the experiment has not been repeated. Greene King recommends that Strong Suffolk is a good companion with pickled herring. Tangy cheese, blue Stilton in particular, would be an equally interesting match. The beer is sold in the United States as Olde Suffolk.

TASTING NOTES
Appearance
Aroma
Taste
Overall score

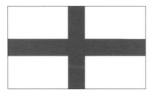

Highgate Old Ale

Source: Highgate Brewery, Walsall, West Midlands, England
Strength: 5.3%
Website: www.highgatebrewery.com

TASTING NOTES
Appearance
Aroma
Taste
Overall score

Highgate has had two changes of ownership in recent years. It was bought by its senior management in 1955, when the former owner, Bass, wanted to close the Victorian site, and then it was sold on to Aston Manor in Birmingham. There were initial worries that Aston Manor, which specialises in packaged beers and ciders, would change Highgate's portfolio of beers, but tradition has survived intact.

In order to survive, Highgate is no longer a dark ale specialist. It has added three bitters to its range but has also won a lucrative contract with Coors of Burton-on-Trent to brew the major West Midlands brand M&B Mild. But Highgate Dark and Old remain the bedrock of the small red-brick brewery, with its impressive wooden mash tuns and fermenters as well as copper boiling kettles.

Highgate Dark and Old are 'parti-gyled', which means a strong beer is made and then watered down with pure, iron-rich brewing liquor from a borehole on the site. Old Ale is made with Pearl pale malt, crystal and black malts, with Fuggles and Progress whole hops. Highly fermentable maltose syrup is added to encourage a powerful fermentation with the complex, four-strain house yeast, with each strain attacking different sugars in the wort. Colour units are 111, bitterness 30. The beer has a rich dark and roasted malt aroma with ripe dried fruits, bitter chocolate and grassy hops. Vinous fruit, luscious flavours of chocolate, liquorice and burnt malt fill the mouth, while the long finish has a good underpinning of gentle hop bitterness to balance the sweetness and richness of the malt character. The draught version of Old Ale is available only in the winter months but a filtered bottled version is sold all year round.

*As this edition was going to press, Highgate Brewery was up for sale again. We can only hope that the classic beers will survive.

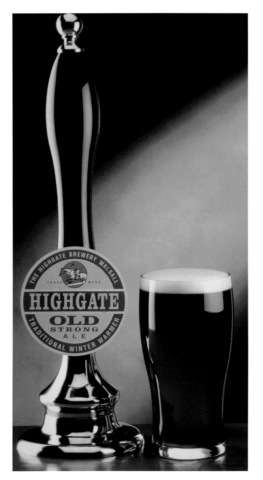

Lees Harvest Ale

Source: J W Lees, Greengate Brewery, Middleton Junction, Greater Manchester, England
Strength: 11.5%
Website: www.jwlees.co.uk

TASTING NOTES
Appearance
Aroma
Taste
Overall score

Brewers are a special breed. Not only do they have rare skills, honed over long years, but they also rise from their beds every day to begin work when most sensible folk are still slumbering. When I was invited to 'start the mash' for the annual brew of Harvest Ale at J W Lees, I booked into a convenient bed and breakfast near the brewery and was picked up the next morning by head brewer Giles Dennis at 5.30am. He was bright, cheerful and alert, while I was barely capable of speech.

In the brewery, I put on the regulation white coat and obediently followed the instructions of Giles and his fellow brewers, pushing the right buttons and pulling the correct levers to deliver malt and hot brewing liquor to the mash tun. Then I was hustled off to the inner sanctum, the brewers' 'sample room', and was taken through a tasting of several vintages of Harvest Ale. This was followed by a sumptuous brewers' breakfast before we returned to the brewhouse to check that the mash had successfully converted malt starch to sugar and we could transfer the wort to the copper for the boil with hops.

Harvests may seem remote from Lees' brewery in the outskirts of Manchester but Middleton Junction was a rural area in 1828, when John Lees, a retired cotton manufacturer, bought the site and started to brew beer as the industrial revolution spawned a thirsty army of cotton workers. His grandson, John Willie Lees, who built a new brewhouse to cope with demand, busily expanded the business. Today, his descendants still run the brewery.

Harvest Ale is brewed every autumn with fresh crops of Maris Otter malt and East Kent Goldings hops from the harvest. Each vintage is then released in 275ml bottles in time for Christmas. The beer is filtered and pasteurised but will develop in bottle.

A 2002 vintage is russet coloured, with an intense peppery aroma from the Goldings (35 bitterness units), a surprising hint of chocolate—no doubt caused by some caramelisation of the brewing sugars during the copper boil—and bitter orange fruitiness. A massive vinous richness reminiscent of Oloroso sherry fills the mouth, underscored by the continuing orange (Seville, of course) note. The finish is deep and long, with fruit, barley sugar, a hint of vanilla and a gentle spicy hop bitterness.

Pike Old Bawdy

Source: Pike Brewing Co, Seattle, Washington, USA
Strength: 10%
Website: www.pikebrewing.com

TASTING NOTES
Appearance
Aroma
Taste
Overall score

The Pike brewery has moved several times in Seattle but it commemorates its first site with this big fruity and oaky barley wine. Charles and Rose Ann Finkel launched their brewery in 1989 in part of the former LaSalle Hotel in Seattle. The hotel had been a notorious brothel or bawdy house, a fact celebrated by a light bulb on the label of the beer. This is a reference to Naughty Nellie, the madam who converted an old seamen's hostel into the luxurious red light LaSalle.

Old Bawdy is a racy beer in every sense of the word. Charles Finkel has established a reputation and won many awards for his devotion to beer and his determination to brew precisely to style. He researched English barley wines in depth before creating his annual vintage, the first of which appeared in 1998. The beer has a whisky connection, for it uses a proportion of peated malt and is aged in oak casks. English brewers of the style centuries ago would have aged their beers in oak, but I'm not aware they imported peated malt from Scotland.

Old Bawdy is brewed with pale malt, crystal and peated, and is massively hopped with Centennial, Chinook, Columbus and Magnum varieties. The hops all come from the Yakima Valley region of Washington State. The first time I visited Pike, I flew the following day over the Cascade Mountains to Yakima and was astonished by the climate change. Seattle, on the coast, is cool and rainy. Yakima, on the other hand, is hot, so hot that the hop fields have to be irrigated to ensure a plentiful supply of water to the plants. The result is hops that are a brilliant green in colour and bursting with resinous and fruity character.

The hops give Old Bawdy a mighty 90 units of bitterness. It has a deep, burnished orange/amber colour and has an entrancing aroma of sweet malt, rich marmalade fruit, oaky/woody notes and assertive citrus hops. Fruit builds in the mouth but is balanced by juicy malt and hop bitterness. The finish is long and deep, with a woody/oaky note underpinning ripe malt, tangy fruit and hop resins. The whisky note makes this a fine late-night beer before retiring to bed—with or without Naughty Nellie.

Robinson's Old Tom

Source: Frederic Robinson Unicorn Brewery, Stockport, Cheshire, England
Strength: 8.5%
Website: www.frederic-robinson.com

It's a brave brewer who names his strong beer after a cat and even puts a cat's face on the label. Imagine the guffaws of laughter if a batch of beer developed a fault and tasted like... I leave the rest to your imagination. But the family-owned Robinson's brewery is a highly professional one that has been producing beer since 1838 and there are few complaints about the quality of its brews.

Frederic Robinson founded his brewery at the Unicorn Inn in the centre of Stockport. The present impressive red-brick brewery was built in the 1920s and it has stayed firmly in family ownership ever since. Five sixth-generation members of the family were appointed to the board in 2003 to ensure continuity.

The beers are notably fruity and this is most in evidence in Old Tom, whose name may stem from the fact that breweries have always kept cats on the premises to kill rodents that would otherwise run riot in malt stores. It is available on draught and in filtered bottled forms, and is brewed with Halcyon pale malt, crystal malt and a small amount of chocolate malt (100 units of colour). The beer is hopped with a single variety, Goldings, and the beer has 35 units of bitterness. Old Tom has a ripe vine fruits aroma with a delicious hint of chocolate as well as peppery hop resins. Port wine, dark malt, chocolate and bitter hops fill the mouth, while the long and complex finish offers an increasing rich vinous fruitiness and a solid underpinning of bitter hops. The draught version of the beer won CAMRA's Champion Winter Beer of Britain award in 2005.

Sierra Nevada Bigfoot Ale

Source: Sierra Nevada Brewing Company, Chico, California, USA
Strength: 9.6%
Website: www.sierranevada.com

TASTING NOTES
Appearance
Aroma
Taste
Overall score

This is a big beast of a beer named after the wild man-cum-animal that is supposed to roam the mountainous regions of California. Even he might stop his rampaging and sleep for a while if he supped a glass of the beer that bears his name.

In the American fashion, Sierra Nevada has taken the English style of barley wine and added its own interpretation, in particular a profound bitter hop character to balance the sweetness of the massive amount of malt used to create the alcohol. 9.6% is nominal: some years the beer has reached more than 12%, and since each vintage is bottle fermented it will increase in strength as a result of a secondary fermentation under glass.

The beer is also produced on draught and should, like its namesake, be approached with caution. For several years, Bigfoot was the strongest beer made in the US but several other brewers have attempted to outbid it.

The beer is brewed with two-row pale malt from the Pacific North-west, imported English crystal malt and an addition of dextrin, a type of malt sugar that cannot be fermented by conventional brewer's yeast and which adds 'body', or mouthfeel, and sweetness. The beer has a complex hop recipe, with Chinook for bitterness, and Cascade and Centennial used at the end of the copper boil. The beer is then dry hopped in the maturation tank with all three varieties grown in Oregon and Washington State. Unusually for a barley wine, it is the hops that dominate, bursting on to the nose with bitter and piny resins and tart citrus fruit. Malt struggles to make an appearance on the aroma but starts to build in the mouth with rich grain and warming alcohol. The finish leaves tyre marks on the back of the throat due to the massive hop attack, but there is a good balancing malty and nutty note from the grain. The beer will improve for around a year in bottle.

Theakston's Old Peculier

Source: T & R Theakston, Masham, North Yorkshire, England
Strength: 5.7%
Website: www.theakstons.co.uk

The beer with the peculiar spelling has a few centuries of history behind it. In the 12th century, Sir Roger de Mowbray from Masham was captured while fighting in the Crusades and held prisoner for seven years. When he was released, he expressed his gratitude for his safe return home by giving 'the living'—the priest's position and income—of the church in Masham to St Peter's in York. But the Bishop of York was not prepared to make the long and arduous journey to Masham, with the strong possibility of being attacked by footpads. He released Masham from 'all the customs and claims of his archdeacons and officials' and set up the Peculier Court of Masham to deal with church and local law. Peculier is an old Norman-French word meaning particular, not odd, and indicated a parish outside the control of a bishop. The chairman of the court had a great seal made to mark his power. The seal shows the kneeling figure of Sir Roger de Mowbray and is still in use as the brewery's logo. The court, made up of 24 'good men from the parish' and chaired by the vicar, still sits to adjudicate on parish matters.

The beer that carries this heavy weight of history on its shoulders is probably the best-known old ale in the world, as it is widely exported, to the US in particular. It is brewed with pale and crystal malts, with some cane sugar, maize and caramel (95 colour units). The hops are Challenger, Fuggles and Goldings, which create 29 units of bitterness. Brewed in traditional vessels, including high-sided wooden fermenters, the beer has a big vinous fruit bouquet balanced by peppery hops and nutty malt. Raisin and sultana fruit, roasted grain and gentle hop bitterness fill the mouth, with a finish that is bitter-sweet and dominated by roasted and nutty malt and vinous fruit with a lingering touch of hop resins.

TASTING NOTES
Appearance
Aroma
Taste
Overall score

Traquair House Ale

Source: Traquair House Brewery, Innerleithen, Peebles-shire, Scotland
Strength: 7.2%
Website: www.traquair.co.uk

TASTING NOTES
Appearance
Aroma
Taste
Overall score

Parts of the mellow stone buildings that make up the Traquair estate date from 1107, though the main house was extended in the 17th century. It is Scotland's oldest inhabited stately home and was visited by Mary Stuart, Queen of Scots, and Prince Charles Edward Stuart—Bonnie Prince Charlie—who came to the house to seek support for the Jacobite cause.

Ale has been brewed at Traquair for centuries in an old brewhouse in outbuildings alongside the stream that flows into the River Tweed, the boundary between Scotland and England. The estate is owned by a branch of the Stuart clan, the Maxwell Stuarts, and they keep the main Bear Gates locked until a Stuart returns to the British throne.

In 1965, the 20th Laird, or Lord, of Traquair, David Maxwell Stuart, discovered the disused brewhouse. It had a four-barrel capacity, since extended, and an open copper or kettle installed in 1738—there is a receipt for it in the house archives. With advice from the Belhaven brewery, Maxwell Stuart started to brew again. House Ale quickly became a cult brew and is exported to Japan and the US. Lady Catherine Maxwell Stuart, who gave up a career in the theatre to administer the house and brewery, took over when her father died.

Brewing water comes from a spring in the valley of the Tweed, and the main grain is pale malt with just 1% black malt. The hops are exclusively East Kent Goldings, sourced from the farm of Tony Redsell near Faversham, renowned for the quality of his hops. The beer has 34 units of bitterness, a tawny colour and a ripe aroma of marmalade fruit, chocolate and peppery hops. Rich orange, lemon and lime fruits fill the mouth, with nuts, chocolate and hop resins. The finish has warming alcohol, tart fruit, nuts and a lingering peppery hop note.

Woodforde's Norfolk Nip

Source: Woodforde's Norfolk Ales, Broadland Brewery, Woodbastwick, Norfolk, England
Strength: 8.5%
Website: www.woodfordes.co.uk

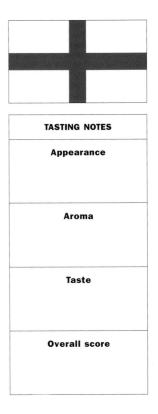

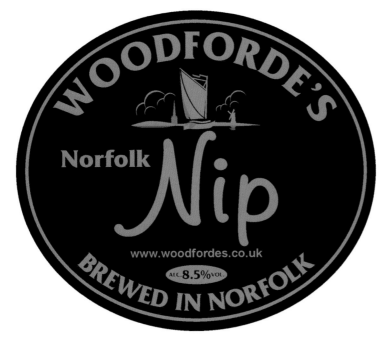

TASTING NOTES
Appearance
Aroma
Taste
Overall score

Woodforde's, founded in 1981, is one of England's longest-surviving craft breweries and today has reached the status of a small regional. It has led a peripatetic existence and is now at its third home, close to the chain of reed-fringed, ancient inland waterways known as the Norfolk Broads. The site was expanded at the turn of the new century to double production and now includes a shop, visitor centre and on-site pub, the Fur & Feather. Woodforde's has twice won CAMRA's Champion Beer of Britain competition with Wherry Best Bitter and Norfolk Nog. Most of its regular draught beers are now also available in bottle-fermented form.

Norfolk Nip revives a beer brewed from the late 1920s by the large Norwich brewery Steward & Patteson. S&P had the great misfortune to fall into the clutches of the infamous London brewer Watneys, which ran rampage in Norfolk in the 1960s, buying and closing Norwich's three breweries and axing hundreds of pubs in the county. Woodforde's restored the beer in 1992 to mark the 10th anniversary of the local CAMRA newsletter, *Norfolk Nips*. Brewing now takes place annually on St Valentine's Day, making it a true loving cup.

The beer is matured in cask in the brewery prior to bottling and will improve for at least two years. It is brewed from Maris Otter pale, crystal and chocolate malts and a touch of roasted barley. The hop is exclusively Goldings. The mahogany-coloured beer has a warm and embracing aroma of vine and citrus fruits, roasted grain and peppery hop resins. Fruits, ranging from pineapple to melon and cherry, coat the tongue, balanced by bitter chocolate and roast, with an underpinning of hop bitterness. The long and complex finish is ripe and fruity, with lingering roast and chocolate notes and a final tingle of bitter hops.

Porters & Stouts

It is a significant indication of the revival of interest in beer styles that the biggest section of this book is devoted to porter, which had once all but disappeared from the world's brewing scene, and stout, which to most people means Guinness in all its manifestations. Yet in my book *Classic Stout and Porter* (Prion, 1997), the index listed close to 100 porters and stouts in Britain and more than 250 in the United States. In the US, it was a style that had been wiped out in the 1920s by Prohibition and the subsequent domination of the market by bland national lager brands. But from the 1980s, the craft-brewing revolution in both countries spawned enormous interest in traditional styles, and no more so than in the case of porter and stout.

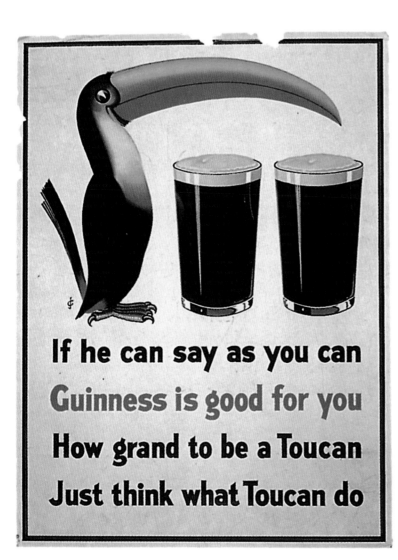

If he can say as you can
Guinness is good for you
How grand to be a Toucan
Just think what Toucan do

The domination of the stout market by Guinness has led many people to assume that stout and its offshoot porter are Irish types of beer. The origins, however, are in London. Early in the 18th century, as the capital was changing rapidly from a loose connection of small towns into a vibrant commercial and industrial hub, the new, burgeoning working class developed a taste for a beer known as three threads, or three thirds. It was a blend of three beers, twopenny pale ale, brown ale and 'stale', or well-matured old ale.

Specialist country brewers with the space to mature beer in large oak tuns supplied both twopenny—so-called because it was twice as dear as other beers—and stale to London. Brewers there, based chiefly in cramped taverns with small brewhouses attached, were anxious to break the power of the country suppliers and their expensive malts by making a beer that replicated the flavours of three threads without the need to blend beers in their cellars. They were aided by the development of an improved type of brown malt from the malting towns of Hertfordshire that supplied London via barges and canals. London brewers grasped the new malt to fashion a beer that came from one cask, or butt, that suited the demands of their customers. The brewers called the beer 'entire butt' but it quickly acquired the nickname of porter.

Much energy has gone into debating the origins of the name porter. I have heard such risible suggestions that it was a corruption of export or even the Latin *portare*, working-class Londoners at the time being fluent Latin speakers. It is always best to go to contemporary sources. A Swiss called César de Saussure wrote to his family: 'Another kind of beer [in London] is called porter... because the greater quantity of this beer is consumed by the working class.' A retired brewer who wrote under the pen name Obadiah Poundage noted that 'the labouring people, porters etc, experienced its wholesomeness and utility, they assumed to themselves the use thereof, from whence it was called Porter.' What is beyond dispute is that the early porters, or entires, were dark brown rather than black. And, following the fashion at the time to call the strongest beer in a brewery stout, the higher gravity versions of porter were dubbed stout porter, eventually shortened to just stout. In the early 19th century, around 100 years after porter and stout first appeared, the invention of roasting machines produced the black and chocolate malts that turned porter and stout into the jet-black beers we recognise today.

The clamour for porter and stout created a new breed of commercial brewers in London and other urban areas of Britain. Brewers such as Ben Truman and Sam Whitbread built their fame and fortune on porter. From 1760, Whitbread's brewery in London's Barbican had a system of vast underground cisterns, each containing the equivalent of 4,000 barrels of beer.

Porter and stout from London and Bristol were supplied to all parts of the United Kingdom, which then included the whole of Ireland. By 1787, Arthur Guinness was brewing porter and, in 1799, he took the momentous decision to phase out all other types of ale. In Cork, Beamish & Crawford also abandoned ale in favour of porter. The Murphy brothers, who moved from whiskey distilling to brewing, followed Beamish in Cork. At one stage in the 19th century, Beamish and Guinness were the two biggest brewers in the United Kingdom, such was the demand for porter and stout in Ireland.

The terrible famine in the 1850s devastated the Irish economy. Beamish never recovered its position but Guinness rebuilt its trade by using the canal system and then the railway to take porter—known as X or plain—and stout, branded XX, to all parts of Ireland. It was exported to Britain, to other parts of the Empire and also to the US. By the close of the 19th century, Guinness was the biggest brewer in Europe. By the end of World War One, it achieved the astonishing feat, in a country of just five million people, of becoming the biggest brewer in the world.

Guinness was aided by the decision of the British government during World War One to curb the use of dark malts, which used more energy. Coal, gas and electricity were needed by the munitions industry, and brewers had to switch to lighter beers for the duration. The British dared not impose such restrictions on the increasingly mutinous Irish with their demand for Home Rule. As a result, Guinness and other Irish brewers had the market in porter and stout to themselves.

Guinness had also refashioned porter and stout into a distinctive Irish style. Before changes were made in the 1880s, brewers paid tax not on the strength of their products but on the malt they used. Arthur Guinness II realised he would pay less tax to the British government if he used a small amount of unmalted—and therefore untaxed—roasted barley in his beer. The result was stout with a pronounced roasted and bitter flavour that became known as 'Dry Irish Stout'.

Pale ale and golden lagers eventually ate into sales of porter and stout. Even mighty Guinness eventually abandoned plain to concentrate on stout. But the styles never went away. Stout remains an iconic drink in Ireland, a symbol of its nationhood, while the British are the biggest consumers of stout in the world. And now today, thanks to the spirit and enterprise of craft brewers, we can revel in the many interpretations of the dark beers that changed the face of brewing 300 years ago.

Alaskan Smoked Porter

Source: Alaskan Brewing Company, Juneau, Alaska, USA
Strength: 5.5%
Website: www.alaskanbeer.com

TASTING NOTES
Appearance
Aroma
Taste
Overall score

By happy coincidence, the first beer in this section may give us a glimpse of what the early London porters tasted like, when malts cured over wood fires had a smoky tang. The inspiration for the beer came from the Bamberg region of Germany, where *rauch* beers are still made with smoked malts. But smoked porter is an ale, not a lager. It comes from a brewery, founded in 1988 by Geoff and Marcy Larson, which restored the brewing tradition to an isolated part of the US. During the 19th-century Gold Rush, Alaska at one time had 50 breweries, but many disappeared when the miners left and the breweries that remained closed during Prohibition. The Larsons built their business on the back of an Amber beer that was based on the German Alt style (see page 210). They were aware that over the road from the brewery, the Taku fish smokery produced fine-tasting smoked salmon. The Larsons asked the owner if they could use his smokery to lay dark malts on racks heated by an alderwood fire.

The result was a sensational beer made with two-row Klages pale, black, chocolate and crystal malts, and hopped with Chinook and Willamette varieties. Smoked porter has a smoky and woody aroma, with spicy hops, dark grain, coffee and chocolate. The dark, smoky malts dominate the palate, with a growing contribution from chocolate and coffee, but spicy hops come through strongly in the finish.

The porter has won more major awards at the Great American Beer Festival than any other beer. It is brewed once a year and vintage dated. The Larsons recommend it as a good companion for smoked fish or tangy cheeses.

Bridge of Allan Glencoe Wild Oat Stout

Source: Bridge of Allan Brewery, Bridge of Allan, Stirlingshire, Scotland
Strength: 4.5%
Website: www.bridgeofallan.co.uk

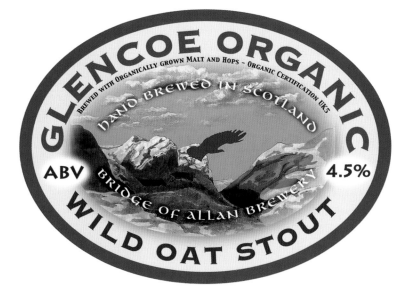

TASTING NOTES
Appearance
Aroma
Taste
Overall score

Scottish stouts have their own distinctive character, which is less bitter than the Irish style, not so hoppy as English versions and with a creamy note from the use of oats. Bridge of Allan's stout goes a step further: it is an organic beer and the oats used in its production grow wild in the Forth Valley.

The area where the brewery is based is of historic importance, with Stirling Castle, the Wallace Monument and the Trossachs close by. The Forth Valley is known as the Gateway to the Highlands, and invading armies marched through the area to do battle with the Scots. It was once an important brewing area, too, with 32 producers in the valley able to make use of the pure water from the Ochil Hills and high-quality malting barley from the fields. Douglas Ross restored the brewing tradition in 1997, when he opened Bridge of Allan in the spa town of the same name. He brews half a dozen regular cask beers and several seasonals, with many of them available in bottled form as well. His original five-barrel plant has been expanded and he has added a visitor centre.

Wild Oat Stout, suitable for vegetarians and vegans, is brewed with a rich and complex blend of Maris Otter pale, crystal, amber, dark roast and chocolate malts, with oats and wheat. The hop variety is Hallertauer Hersbrucker from Bavaria. The black beer with a ruby edge has a big aroma of burnt and roasted malt with hints of cappuccino coffee and raisins. Bitter dark fruit, creamy oats and spicy hops dominate the mouth, while the long finish has roasted grain, creamy oats, spicy hops and a late note of sour fruit.

Brooklyn Chocolate Stout

Source: Brooklyn Brewery, Brooklyn, New York City, USA
Strength: 8.7%
Website: www.brooklynbrewery.com

TASTING NOTES
Appearance
Aroma
Taste
Overall score

This is a big beer and it belongs to a style known as imperial stout, brewed in England in the 19th century for the Russian court. Such beers were brewed to high strengths and heavily hopped to withstand the long, often hazardous, sea journeys.

Garrett Oliver created the Brooklyn beer in 1994 while he brewed at the Manhattan Brewing Company in the SoHo district. Steve Hindy owned the Brooklyn Brewery but his beers were produced under licence in upstate New York. He wanted to open his own brewery and hoped to lure Garrett over the bridge to Brooklyn to become his brewmaster. Steve asked Garrett to develop a strong and memorable beer that would help put the new brewery on the map. Garrett recalls: 'Steve decided that this beer should be a strong stout. Within several days, I had written a recipe and brewed a seven-barrel batch at Manhattan Brewing Company. A few weeks later, I brought the beer to a meeting at Brooklyn Brewery. We originally thought we might actually add chocolate to the beer, but it turned out to be unnecessary— the blend of roasted malts gave the beer a flavour Steve and I had been looking for.' Garrett was hired and a few months later produced the first batch of Black Chocolate Stout.

It is brewed in the winter and has a long and complex mashing regime. The 'first runnings'— the concentrated wort extracted from the mash of grain before it is sparged or rinsed with water— is removed from the mash, which is discarded. The undiluted wort is then fermented into stout, which is aged for more than two months before it leaves the brewery. It has an intense aroma of Belgian chocolate with espresso coffee notes and bitter hops. In the mouth, rich, dark, roasted malts battle for supremacy with chocolate, spicy hops and a vinous fruitiness. The finish is long, with liquorice notes coming through to join vine fruits, bitter, spicy hops, chocolate and roasted grain. The malts used are American two-row pale, caramel, wheat, chocolate and black malts; the hops are American Fuggles and Willamette.

Broughton Scottish Oatmeal Stout

Source: Broughton Ales, Broughton, Peebles-shire, Scotland
Strength: 4.2%
Website: www.broughtonales.co.uk

Scotland has a cold climate and the people have developed grain-based food and drink to warm them. Whisky—the water of life—is a distillation of ale made without hops. Porridge is made from oats and the grain has been used for centuries in the country's distinctive strong, rich and lightly hopped ales. Oatmeal stout, a meal in itself, was a staple member of the portfolios of most Scottish breweries until 20th-century mergers created brewing giants that concentrated on light lagers and keg beers. The craft brewing revolution in Scotland—there are now more than 30 from the Borders to Orkney and Shetland—has restored pride and tradition to brewing and with it several versions of stout.

Broughton, founded in 1979, is one of the oldest independent breweries in Scotland and its Oatmeal Stout is considered to be the classic of the style, so much so that the bottled version is exported to the United States and several other countries. Hops were once brewed in the Borders, where Broughton is based—records show that home-grown hops were once used at the Traquair House brewery—but as the climate grew colder, the plant withered on the bine. As a result, Scottish brewers tend to be parsimonious with the use of the plant, imported from England. Lightly hopped stouts give free rein to the rich flavours of pale and dark malts and the creamy, nutty texture of oats or oatmeal.

The Broughton beer is brewed with Maris Otter pale malt, black malt, roasted barley and pinhead oats. It has 170 units of bitterness. The hops are

Fuggles and Goldings for aroma and Target for bitterness: 30 units of bitterness. It has a freshly ground roasted coffee beans and chocolate aroma with a gentle hint of spicy hops. Roasted and creamy grain, coffee and chocolate fill the mouth, while the finish has a silky smoothness with an underpinning of gentle hop spices, chocolate and bitter coffee.

TASTING NOTES	
Appearance	
Aroma	
Taste	
Overall score	

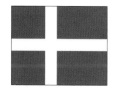

Carlsberg Carls Stout Porter

Source: Carlsberg Breweries, Copenhagen, Denmark
Strength: 7.8%
Website: www.carlsberg.com

TASTING NOTES
Appearance
Aroma
Taste
Overall score

Carlsberg is celebrated as the company that perfected the first pure strain of yeast that enabled brewers throughout the world to brew lager beers free from infection. It may seem curious to find Carlsberg listed in this section, but many brewers in Scandinavia in the 19th century produced porters and stouts. Some of the strong imperial stouts brewed in England and destined for Russia found their way en route to Scandinavia. The popularity of the beers encouraged domestic brewers to produce the style themselves. As they had switched their production methods to cold fermentation, they brewed, in effect, dark lagers but with the roasted grain and bitter hop character that are typical of porters and stouts produced by conventional warm fermentation.

The story of Carlsberg dates from the early 19th century when Christian Jacobsen opened a small brewery in Copenhagen. His son, Jacob Christian Jacobsen, the driving force of the company, went to Munich to study the new cold-fermented brown beers that had been developed there. He brought back a supply of Munich yeast and by 1847 had opened a new brewery on the outskirts of Copenhagen that produced, to popular acclaim, a brown lager. Once the technology existed, the company concentrated on golden lager beers in the Pilsner style. Jacobsen built a second brewery for his son Carl and, as the new plant stood on a hill, it was called Carlsberg.

The original brewery is now a museum, while Carl's plant remains one of the finest in the world with superb copper vessels in spacious tiled rooms. It was in the Carlsberg laboratories that the famous brewing scientist Emil Christian Hansen isolated the first pure strain of yeast that enabled both Carlsberg and eventually all other breweries to make consistent beers free from infection.

In spite of the success of pale lagers, Carlsberg continues to produce a wide range of beers, including the rather confusingly labelled Stout Porter that is in reality an imperial stout. It is brewed from pale and roasted malts, and hopped with German Hallertauer varieties. It has the clean flavours of a lager but with molasses and liquorice on the aroma, woody and bitter coffee character in the mouth, with a spicy hop note developing in the mouth and finish, and a final rich, warming deep roasted grain note.

Carnegie Stark Porter

Source: Pripps Brewery, Stockholm, Sweden
Strength: 3.5%/5.6%
Website: www.pripps.se

The Scandinavian love-hate relationship with alcohol has had a profound impact on this remarkable 'stark', or strong, beer. For a period, it was available only on doctor's prescription as a tonic, but in recent years it has been let out of the surgery and back into bars and is now available at a strength of 3.5% (which does not do the beer justice) and an annual vintage of 5.6% that places it firmly in the ranks of genuine porters.

The beer dates from 1803 when a Scot named David Carnegie opened a small brewery in Gothenburg. There had been strong trading links between Scotland and Sweden for centuries, and Carnegie, who also created a banking group in Scandinavia, launched his porter to meet the demand for the dark beer style among the Swedes. Eventually he sold the brewery to the giant Pripps group, which continued to brew at Gothenburg for a while before closing the plant. Pripps, a state-owned enterprise until the 1990s

that produces stunningly bland and uninteresting pale lagers, was expected to phase out Carnegie Porter, especially as it is brewed with a warm-fermenting ale yeast strain. But Pripps resurrected the beer in the 1990s, won the top prize for dark beers in the 1992 International Brewers' Exhibition, and introduced the annual vintage in a club-shaped bottle in 1995.

The beer is filtered and pasteurised but the brewers feel that it nevertheless does improve in bottle and eventually takes on a port wine note. When I visited the brewery and was able to sample several vintages, I was able to detect subtle differences between one brew and the next.

The beer is made from pale and roasted malts and hopped with German varieties. It has a roasted grain, cappuccino coffee and spicy hop aroma and palate, with a Dundee Cake fruitiness in the finish—appropriate given the founder's ethnic origins—and a hint of rich dark wine.

TASTING NOTES
Appearance
Aroma
Taste
Overall score

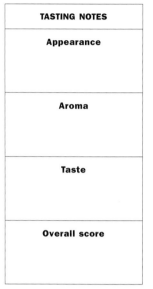

Castlemaine Carbine Stout

Source: Castlemaine Perkins Brewery, Brisbane, Queensland, Australia
Strength: 5.1%
Website: www.lion-nathan.com

TASTING NOTES
Appearance
Aroma
Taste
Overall score

It may come as a surprise to those who think Australians drink only pale, sweet lagers that the country has a rich tradition of dark stouts. Many have disappeared in recent decades as the country's brewing industry has fallen under the sway of two giant combines, Castlemaine and Foster's. Castlemaine was owned by the Bond Corporation but when that company collapsed as the result of financial skulduggery, it suffered the ultimate indignity of being taken over by the New Zealand drinks group Lion Nathan, which also owns Toohey's and Swan.

To many people's surprise, Lion Nathan has preserved a wide portfolio of beers, including the country's best-known dark beer, Carbine Stout. It was first brewed in 1925 by the Perkins Brewery before it merged with Castlemaine. The beer is named after a remarkable racehorse Carbine, which won the Melbourne Cup in 1890 and 32 other races, and was the sire of the Derby winner Spearmint. Carbine's bloodline can be traced to 70% of Australian thoroughbreds racing today.

The original recipe for the beer named in the horse's honour included pale, amber, crystal and black malts with cane sugar as an adjunct. It was fermented with an ale yeast culture. In the 1950s, the beer was dumbed down with a simplified malt blend and cold fermentation was introduced. More recently, however, dark malts, wheat and roasted barley have been introduced, though cold fermentation remains. The beer is hopped with Tasmanian and New Zealand varieties. It has a pleasing coffee, liquorice and roasted grain aroma, with spicy hops in the mouth and finish, and a bitter-sweet palate with hints of dried fruits.

Coopers Best Extra Stout

Source: Coopers Brewery, Adelaide, South Australia, Australia
Strength: 6.8%
Website: www.coopers.com.au

TASTING NOTES
Appearance
Aroma
Taste
Overall score

The brewery founded by Thomas Cooper in the 19th century and still run today by members of his family may be best known for its Sparkling Ale (see page 56) but it also produces a magnificent stout, a world classic. Like the pale ale, it is a sedimented beer in keg and bottle, maturing on its yeast. It is an uncompromising beer: the attitude at Coopers is that the company brews spectacular beers bursting with aroma and flavour, and any drinkers deterred by such characteristics should turn instead to the 'national blands' produced by bigger producers.

Extra Stout is made with pale, crystal and roasted malts, with an addition of cane sugar in the copper in the Australian fashion to encourage a full fermentation. The hops are Pride of Ringwood in pellet form. The colour rating is 175, bitterness 40. The beer has a full and tempting bouquet of roasted malt, with a pronounced oily, tarry note from the dark grain, balanced by coffee and bitter chocolate. The hops provide a firm underpinning of spicy and earthy resins in the mouth topped by coffee, chocolate and dark dried fruits. The big and complex finish is dry and bitter but balanced by rich malt and dark fruit flavours.

Nick Sterenberg of Coopers told me: 'The popularity of unfiltered bottled and keg-conditioned ales is increasing in Australia, the land of ice-cold, crystal-clear lager. We are now 2.5% of the national market and growing.'

Darwin Flag Porter

Source: Darwin Brewery, Sunderland, England
Strength: 5%
Website: www.darwinbrewery.com

TASTING NOTES
Appearance
Aroma
Taste
Overall score

The frequently asked question, 'What did the early porters really taste like?' is answered to some extent by this fascinating beer.

In 1988, deep-sea divers from the City of London Polytechnic were investigating the wreck of a ship that had sunk in the English Channel in 1825 and they brought to the surface several bottles of porter. They were handed over to Dr Keith Thomas who at the time ran the Brewers' Laboratory (Brewlab for short) at the same polytechnic.

The beer had been contaminated by sea water and was undrinkable, but Keith was able to isolate a few living yeast cells from one bottle. He cultured them in his laboratory and, with the help of Whitbread, was able to track down an 1850s porter recipe from the group's former brewery in Chiswell Street in London. The recipe that Keith Thomas then devised, which was based on the original Whitbread one, uses pale, brown, crystal and black malts and is hopped with just one variety, Fuggles. One of the many interesting facts discovered in the Whitbread archive was that the company was still using wood-kilned brown malt as late as 1850. The beer that Keith created had another surprise: it was not jet-black but dark ruby-red in colour; he suspects the original may have been even paler. This fits with the belief that as late as the mid-19th century there were two styles: brown porter and black porter. Flag Porter, as Keith called the beer, was first brewed by a London micro then moved to Elgood's in Wisbech, before finding its latest home at Darwin in Sunderland, where Brewlab is now also located at the university.

The beer has 34 units of bitterness: there is no direct comparison with Whitbread's Porter in 1850, as such measurements were not made. Fuggles did not exist as a variety at that time but, with a low bitterness, would not be dissimilar to mid-19th century hops. Keith Thomas, for the sake of historical accuracy, also points out that stewed crystal malt did not exist in 1850 and replaces a type called amber.

The beer is enormously complex. It has a dark tangy, slightly smoky and nutty aroma underpinned by spicy Fuggles. In the mouth there is a distinct fruitiness reminiscent of blood oranges, and the finish is rich in fruit, hops and bitter chocolate, becoming finally intensely dry with a herbal note. The beer is available in the United States: see the website legendslimited.com.

Foster's Sheaf Stout

Source: Tooth's Brewery, Sydney, New South Wales, Australia
Strength: 5.7%
Website: www.fosters.com.au

TASTING NOTES
Appearance
Aroma
Taste
Overall score

Who knows Foster's who only Foster's knows? The brewery famous for a global lager brand has a surprisingly large portfolio of beers in its own country as a result of mergers and takeovers. When it acquired Tooth's it found itself with a fine example of a genuine warm-fermented stout from a brewery founded by John Tooth. He came originally from Kent in South-east England and for many years he used the symbol of the White Horse of Kent, still embossed on hop sacks from the county. The white horse was the battle flag of Hengist and Horsa, the tribal leaders from Jutland who conquered Kent in the fifth century: their names mean Stallion and Horse.

When Tooth's was taken over by Carlton and United Breweries, since renamed Foster's, the beer's title has been shortened to Sheaf Stout, possibly on the grounds that Tooth's Sheaf was difficult to say when sober and impossible after a few pints. It has lost nothing else. Brewed from pale and crystal malts and roasted barley, with domestic hops, it has 200 units of colour and 35 units of bitterness. It is almost jet-black in colour with a woody, earthy aroma and a powerful punch of roasted grain, an oily and perfumy palate with strong hints of coffee and chocolate, and a long fruity finish with good spicy hop notes and continuing hints of chocolate, coffee and roasted grain.

Great Lakes The Edmund Fitzgerald Porter

Source: Great Lakes Brewing Co, Cleveland, Ohio, USA
Strength: 5.8%
Website: www.greatlakesbrewing.com

TASTING NOTES
Appearance
Aroma
Taste
Overall score

The Edmund Fitzgerald was a freighter that sank with all hands in Lake Superior in 1975. Several members of the crew came from Cleveland, once a mighty brewing city that lost its beery tradition as a result of Prohibition and subsequent takeovers and closures. The brothers Patrick and Daniel Conway, former teacher and banker respectively, have restored the tradition. They share a passion for European beer styles. In 1988 they pooled their resources to open Great Lakes in the heart of Cleveland's old brewing district and hired Thaine Johnson, who had been head brewer at the city's last major commercial brewery, Christian Schmidt.

The success of the enterprise led to the brothers moving into two former brewers' premises where they installed a 75-barrel plant capable of producing 70,000 barrels a year.

They have also kept open their original brew-pub in Market Avenue (see page 281).

The Edmund Fitzgerald Porter is brewed with two-row pale, crystal and chocolate malts and roasted barley, and is hopped with Cascade, Northern Brewer and Willamette varieties (60 bitterness units). The dark brown beer with a hefty collar of foam has a big chocolate and orange fruit bouquet, with hop bitterness, juicy malt, tart fruit and chocolate in the mouth, and a long, complex finish with roasted grain notes and a final burst of bitter hop resins and tangy fruit.

Guinness Foreign Extra Stout

Source: Guinness Brewing, Dublin, Ireland
Strength: 7.5%
Website: www.guinness.com

Guinness is a phenomenon. In a world dominated by golden lagers, it remains a global giant. Ten million pints of Guinness Stout are drunk every day. There are some 19 versions of the beer, and Foreign Extra Stout (FES) is sold in 55 countries and brewed under licence in a further 44. It is all a long way removed from the humble origins of Arthur Guinness, who opened a small brewery in Leixlip in 1756 with the help of a £100 gift from the local rector. Three years later, Guinness moved to Dublin, where he took a lease on a disused brewery in St James's Gate, an area packed with breweries as a result of the fine local water. By 1787 he was brewing porter as well as ale, and in 1799 he phased out ale in order to get a more lucrative share of the porter and stout market. His business expanded rapidly and he became the official supplier of porter to Dublin Castle, the seat of British power and authority. His son, also called Arthur, continued the expansion. As well as using roasted barley in the recipe (see introduction, page 137), he developed a strong beer for the export market called Foreign Extra Porter Stout, today's FES.

The beer today remains a palpable link with brewing practice in the 19th century. Tucked away in the vast Dublin brewery, which produces 2½ million pints of beer a day, are two wooden tuns that are more than 100 years old. Beer that will form part of FES is matured in the vats for up to three months. This is 'stale beer' that picks up some lactic sourness from the action of wild Brettanomyces yeast. Stale is then blended with fresh young stout, bottled and kept in the brewery for a further month before it is released.

FES is made from pale malt, 25% flaked barley and 10% roasted barley. The hops are a blend of several varieties, including Galena, Nugget and Target (60 bitterness units). The finished beer has the slightly sour and musty aroma that brewers call 'horse blanket' and which is the result of the action of wild yeasts in the wooden tuns. The bouquet is highly complex, with bitter roasted grain, a woody and vinous note and spicy hop resins. The palate is bitter from roast and hops, balanced by dark fruit, with a long, dry and bitter finish with hints of liquorice and dark mysterious fruits, including something akin to sour bananas.

FES is the base for the strong versions of Guinness produced for the Belgian market, brewed in Africa, where Guinness owns several plants, and under licence in other countries. For Africa, a dehydrated hopped wort is sent in cans to the Guinness breweries, where it is blended with a local beer made from barley malt and sorghum. Samples of all the beers brewed abroad are kept for analysis in Dublin and I once spent a happy hour there sampling beers from Nigeria and other African countries. It's dark and lonely work, but someone has to do it.

TASTING NOTES
Appearance
Aroma
Taste
Overall score

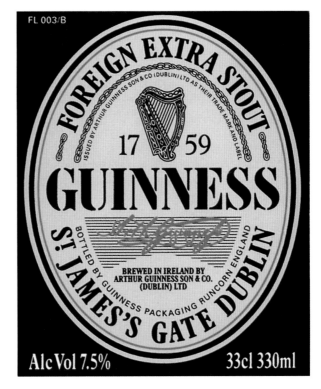

FL 003/B

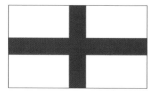

TASTING NOTES
Appearance
Aroma
Taste
Overall score

TASTING NOTES
Appearance
Aroma
Taste
Overall score

Hambleton Nightmare

Source: Nick Stafford Hambleton Ales, Holme-on-Swale, North Yorkshire, England
Strength: 5%
Website: www.hambletonales.co.uk

Hambleton was placed firmly on the map of British craft brewing when Nightmare won CAMRA's first-ever Champion Winter Beer of Britain award in 1996.

Nick Stafford's brewery on the banks of the River Swale in the picturesque Vale of York—with an ancient white horse carved in the chalk hillside—started life in outbuildings at the home of his wife Sally's parents. Capacity doubled to 100 barrels a week when new brewing equipment was installed in 2000 in a large barn in the village. Bottled beers can be bought direct from the brewery via the website.

Nightmare, with a dark ruby-red colour, is brewed with Halcyon pale malt, 8% crystal, 3% pale chocolate and 3% roasted barley. A single hop variety, Northdown, contributes 25 units of bitterness. The beer has a roasted grain and spicy hop bouquet with hints of chocolate and dried fruit. The palate is complex, with roast, bitter fruits, chocolate and earthy hop resins to the fore. The finish has great length and becomes finally dry, bitter and roasty, but there are continuing contributions from raisin fruit and smooth chocolate.

This flavoursome and refreshing beer was first called Nightmare Porter and is firmly in the 18th-century style of a well-hopped and quenching dark brown entire. Nick thinks it is a 'stout porter' but the alcoholic strength places it in the porter class.

Harveys Imperial Extra Double Stout

Source: Harvey & Son, Bridge Wharf Brewery, Lewes, East Sussex, England
Strength: 9%
Website: www.harveys.org.uk

This brilliant re-creation of a 19th-century beer restores a style lost to drinkers when Courage stopped brewing Imperial Russian Stout, a brand it had acquired from the great London brewer Barclay Perkins.

In mid-Victorian Britain, some 10 London brewers produced strong stouts for export to Russia and the Baltic states. The Thrale family owned the principal brewery on the banks of the Thames, which became Barclay Perkins. One consignment of Barclay's Imperial Russian Stout ended up on the seabed in 1869 when the Prussian ship *Oliva* was wrecked. In 1974, divers brought some bottles from the wreck to the surface bearing the mysterious name A Le Coq. Research showed that this was a Belgian called Albert Le Coq who had earned a living exporting imperial stout to Russia. He had been granted an imperial warrant from a grateful tsar for donating bottles of stout to Russian soldiers wounded in the Crimea. Early in the 20th century, Le Coq built a brewery in Tartu, now in modern Estonia, to increase the supply of stout, but the company was nationalised by the Bolshevik government in 1917. When Courage, by now part of the giant Scottish & Newcastle group, phased out its Imperial Stout in the 1990s, Harveys negotiated with descendants of Le Coq's family to acquire the original recipe for the beer.

It is brewed with Maris Otter pale, amber, brown and black malt, and hopped with East Kent Goldings and Fuggles. It is bottle fermented, has a cork stopper and is matured for 12 months before release to trade. It has a rich bouquet of vinous fruits, fresh leather, tobacco, smoky malt and peppery hops. Vinous fruits, hop resins, liquorice, roasted grain and bitter hops dominate the palate with a long and complex finish with warming alcohol, dark fruits, fresh tobacco, roasted grain and spicy hops to the fore. B United imports the beer to the US.

Hook Norton Double Stout

Source: Hook Norton Brewery, Hook Norton, Oxfordshire, England
Strength: 4.8%
Website: www.hook-norton-brewery.co.uk

This is such a brilliant example of a full-bodied, characterful English stout that it is a pity Hook Norton produces it only for the months of January and February every year.

The beer would have both refreshed and restored the farm labourers for whom the brewery was first built and then the army of navvies engaged in the back-breaking task of constructing a railway line that linked Hook Norton with Banbury and Oxford. The railway line has gone but the stout has been brewed since 1996 and has built up a legion of admirers as a result of its robust, punchy flavours produced by achingly traditional brewing methods, including fermentation in wood-jacketed hooped round vessels.

Double Stout is brewed with Maris Otter pale, mild ale, brown and black malts and brewing sugar. It has 110 units of colour. Challenger, Fuggles and Goldings whole hops produce 34 units of bitterness. The beer has a tempting aroma of dark, roasted grain, espresso coffee, liquorice and spicy and earthy hops. Coffee, liquorice, dark fruits, bitter grain and peppery hop resins fill the mouth, while the lingering finish is dominated by burnt fruit, roasted grain, bitter hops and a continuing coffee and bitter chocolate note.

'Double' in the title recalls the period in the 18th and 19th centuries when porters and stouts were labelled X and XX.

Koff Porter

Source: Sinebrychoff Brewery, Helsinki, Finland
Strength: 7.2%
Website: www.koff.fi

Koff Porter is not a cold cure—though it could bring pleasant relief—but a beer that is more in the imperial stout class. It is the strongest beer brewed in Finland and it comes from the country's oldest brewery. A Russian, Nikolai Synebrychoff, built the brewery in 1819. As a result of the distrust of the 'Big Bear' over the border, the Finns shortened the name to Koff and it stuck as the brand image. Synebrychoff, far from being Russian controlled, is now part of the Danish Carlsberg group. The brewery began life with warm-fermented porter and other ales, but as early as 1853 had switched to cold fermentation. In 1952, timed to coincide with the Helsinki Olympics, Synebrychoff revived Koff Porter, one of its founding beers. The brewers were keen to make it in true warm fermenting style but they lacked an ale yeast. They claim they saved the deposit from a bottle of Guinness and made a culture that is still going strong.

Koff Porter is brewed with four malts, including black and roast, and hopped with Northern Brewer and Hersbrucker varieties. The colour rating is 250 to 300, making it extremely dark; the bitterness units are 50. It is conditioned at a warm temperature for six weeks, bottled without filtration but then pasteurised. It has a roasty, vinous and bitter aroma, a big, slightly oily and perfumy body, and a long finish packed with dark fruit, roasted grain and intensely bitter, iron-like hops. The brewery now produces a vintage edition of the beer in an attractive club-shaped bottle.

The original brewery site still stands in Helsinki but a new brewery has been built in the suburbs. When I visited this computer-controlled stainless-steel factory geared to undistinguished pale lagers, I feared Koff Porter had been discontinued but, eventually, in a sampling room some bottles appeared to my great relief. A few years later, when I bumped into a director of Synebrychoff in St Petersburg, I suggested he should export Koff Porter to Russia. He shrugged and said: 'That's a beer for Finns.' Old prejudices die hard.

TASTING NOTES
Appearance
Aroma
Taste
Overall score

TASTING NOTES
Appearance
Aroma
Taste
Overall score

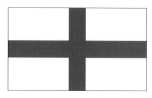

Larkins Porter

Source: Larkins Brewery, Larkins Farm, Chiddingstone, Kent, England
Strength: 5.2%
Website: None

TASTING NOTES
Appearance
Aroma
Taste
Overall score

When you consider the beer comes from a small craft brewery and is brewed only between November and April, Larkins Porter has established a remarkable national reputation as one of the finest of the revivalist members of the style. It helps when the owners grow their own hops, the classic Kentish Fuggles and Goldings.

Ted and Marjorie Dockerty come from a family that has been growing hops in Kent since Tudor times. In 1986, they bought the Royal Tunbridge Wells Brewery that, despite its grand title, was a micro based in lock-up garages. The Dockerty's son Bob, a keen home brewer, started to brew on the plant and moved it a year later to a converted oast house at his parents' farm. The brewery has been expanded to cope with the demand for the traditional ales and porter, which is delivered to some 70 pubs in the area.

Porter is brewed from Halcyon pale, crystal and chocolate malts. Fuggles and Goldings hops create a massive 59 units of bitterness. The beer has an intense aroma of roasted grain, pungent hop resins and bitter chocolate. Dark dried and vinous fruits coat the mouth, balanced by roasted grain and peppery hops. The punchy finish is long, dry and bitter but with balancing fruit and roast.

I enjoyed a glass of the beer in the Castle Inn in Chiddingstone, a beamed pub with lattice windows close to the Dockerty's farm. The castle in question was Hever, home of Anne Boleyn, who had the great misfortune to be one of Henry VIII's wives. The village has some fine examples of Tudor buildings.

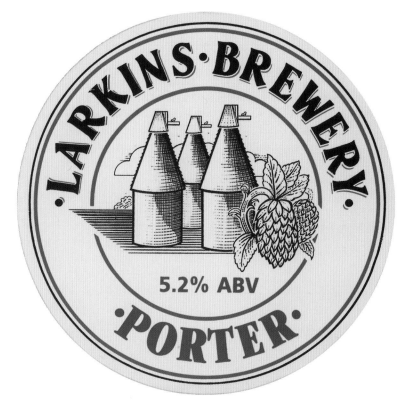

Le Coq Porter

Source: A Le Coq Tartu Oletehas Brewery, Tallinn, Estonia
Strength: 6.5%
Website: www.alecoq.ee

The Tartu brewery has had a roller-coaster history.
It was founded in 1823 and by the close of the
century had switched to cold fermentation and
lager beers. But, as explained in the entry
for Harveys (see page 148), Albert Le Coq, the
importer of Barclay's Imperial Russian Stout,
bought the brewery and started to brew porter
by 1910 to avoid paying import duties on beer.
His ownership of the brewery was short-lived.
In 1917, the Bolshevik government in Moscow
nationalised the plant and phased out porter.
In 1971, following years of legal wrangling over
compensation, the Soviet government paid
£240,000 to Le Coq's family. Following the
collapse of the Soviet Union, the brewery started
regular production of porter in the 1990s and
opened a London office to sell both lager
and porter in Britain, a neat reversal of history.

At 6.5%, Le Coq Porter is clearly in the imperial
Russian stout camp. It is brewed from pale,
black, chocolate and roasted grain, and hopped
with German varieties. It has a deep bouquet
of roasted grain, bitter chocolate, molasses
and liquorice, underpinned by spicy hops. Rich
flavours—roast, burnt fruit, chocolate and earthy
hop resins—fill the mouth. The finish is rich,
rewarding and warming, dominated by dark fruits,
bitter roasted grain, espresso coffee and a firm
hop bitterness.

TASTING NOTES
Appearance
Aroma
Taste
Overall score

Lion Dark

Source: Lion Brewery, Nuwara Eliya, Sri Lanka
Strength: 8%
Website: None

TASTING NOTES
Appearance
Aroma
Taste
Overall score

When English tea planters in Ceylon—the colonial name for Sri Lanka—needed more than tea to refresh them, they built a brewery high in the mountains, close to the holy city of Kandy. Brewing liquor comes from the nearby Lovers Leap waterfall, while Czech, Danish and English malts, along with Styrian hops from Slovenia and English ale yeast, are transported along precarious roads 1070m (3,500ft) above sea level. The journey from Colombo, the capital and main port, takes seven hours.

In Kandy and surrounding towns, Lion Dark is served in cask-conditioned form, while the rest of the world is supplied with the beer in bottles. It is a true warm fermented beer, with production taking place in wooden vessels. The malts are pale, chocolate and roasted barley, and the single hop is the Styrian Golding. It has an immense aroma of rich melting chocolate, cappuccino coffee, roasted grain and spicy hops. Coffee and hops build in the mouth with chocolate liqueur and hop resins. The finish is long and complex, offering warming alcohol alongside the liqueur, coffee, roasted grain and hop notes.

The beer used to be bottle-fermented but is now pasteurised, while the name has been changed from Lion Stout to Lion Dark, with a label that recommends it as a companion for curry dishes. I feel the brewery may be misreading the market for the beer. In Sri Lanka, fishermen like to blend the stout with arrack, distilled from coconut.

Mackeson Stout

Source: Interbrew UK, Luton, Bedfordshire, England
Strength: 3%
Website: www.inbev.co.uk

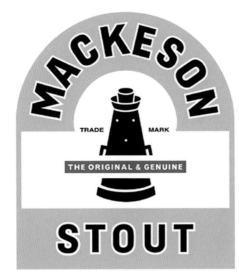

ABInBev, the world's biggest brewer, is sitting on a classic beer but does little with it. Mackeson is the only major survivor of a once widely produced type of dark beer known as 'milk stout'.

Mackeson was an ancient brewery that dated from 1669 and was based in the small Kentish port of Hythe. In 1907, it launched Mackeson Milk Stout with the help of a dietician and promoted it as a healthy beer. The first label had an image of a milk churn and the proclamation: 'Each pint contains the energising carbohydrates of 10 ounces of pure dairy milk.' In fact, the beer does not contain milk as such but lactose, or milk sugar. Lactose cannot be fermented by brewer's yeast and therefore gives a smooth, creamy and milky note to the beer. The beer was such a success that many other brewers rushed to produce their own versions of milk stout.

Mackeson was taken over several times and eventually became part of the national Whitbread group in the 1930s. The stout became a national brand and by the 1960s it accounted for half of the group's annual production. One of the earliest television commercials featured the voice of the actor Sir Bernard Miles, founder of London's Mermaid Theatre, who announced in a rich country burr: 'Mackeson—it looks good, it tastes good and, by golly, it does you good.' By this time, 'milk' had disappeared from the title, as the government frowned on the misleading labelling. The milk churn, however, remained.

Mackeson once rivalled Guinness in popularity but today sales are small. It is made from pale and chocolate malts, caramel and around 9% lactose. Lactose is added as powder in the copper. The lack of fermentability of the lactose can be seen by the fact that, while the stout has an original gravity (strength before fermentation) of 1042 degrees, the finished alcohol is a modest 3%. Target hops produce 26 units of bitterness, destroying the belief that milk stouts are sweet. The dark, almost jet-black beer, has a coffeeish aroma and palate with a gentle fruitiness and distinct hint of that ancient form f confectionery known as milk drops. An export version of the beer is 4.2% alcohol and has 34 units of bitterness. That is quite a beer—but you will have to go to Japan to drink it. InBev should not let Mackeson wither but should promote it as an English classic.

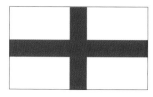

Meantime London Porter

Source: Meantime Brewing Co, Greenwich, London, England
Strength: 6.5%
Website: www.meantimebrewing.com

TASTING NOTES
Appearance
Aroma
Taste
Overall score

Brewmaster Alastair Hook, as we've seen from the section on IPA, is a stickler for historical accuracy. He emphasises the origins of porter with the use of the word London on the label and, in the manner of the first porter brewers early in the 18th century, he blends fresh and mature beers to make the finished, bottle-conditioned product. It's a handsome presentation in a 750ml bottled complete with a driven cork and a wire cradle. In the 1930s the Brewers' Society ran a campaign for beer with a simple, fetching slogan 'Drink the wine of the country'. Meantime picks up the gauntlet by presenting both IPA and Porter as the Champagnes of the beer world.

Alastair plans to dig even deeper into porter history. He will open in 2010 a second brewery on the site of the Old Royal Naval College in Greenwich. The college had its own in-house brewery in the 18th century where small batches of porter were produced for sick and dying sailors. Alastair will build a small brewing plant on the site and use it to produce small-batch reproductions of historic beer styles. The version of porter there will be fermented with a Brettanomyces yeast culture, the yeast famously used for the spontaneously-fermented lambic and gueuze beers in Belgium. He also plans a smoked porter aged in Islay whisky casks. Beer lovers who join the College Beer Club will be offered mail order supplies of specialist brews (see website).

London Porter is a highly complex beer, brewed with no fewer than seven malts: pale, pale crystal, smoked, Munich, brown, black and chocolate. Fuggles hops are used for bitterness, with Goldings added as a late hop for aroma (35 bitterness units). The beer is a deep brown/black in colour (colour rating 80) with a fluffy barley white head. Chocolate, espresso coffee, vanilla, smoked malt and liquorice vie for attention on the nose, underscored by roasted grain and bitter hops. Malt and fruit combine to give some sweetness on the palate, reminding us that porter was a beer brewed to replace the lost energy of street-market porters

in 18th-century London. But bitter hop resins and powerful coffee notes balance the sweetness. The finish is long and full, with continuing contributions from chocolate, coffee, liquorice, burnt fruit, roasted grain and bitter hops. It's finally dry.

Meantime will move its main brewery to new premises in the near future in order to keep pace with the growing demand for its beers, which can be enjoyed at its pub, the Greenwich Union, 56 Royal Hill, London SE10.

Mendocino Black Hawk Stout

Source: Mendocino Brewing Company, Hopland, California, USA
Strength: 5%
Website: www.mendobrew.com

Mendocino, alongside California's main artery Highway 101 South and in wine country 90 miles north of San Francisco, is based in attractive single-storey rustic buildings that include a restaurant as well as the brewery.

Mendocino's predecessor, the New Albion Brewery, has an important footnote in the history of brewing in the US. Its owner had to challenge Californian state law to permit a craft brewery to sell its products in its own bar rather than through distribution. New Albion was the first micro-brewery in California since Prohibition, and its success in changing the law helped dozens of other craft breweries to get off the ground. The law also annoyed the giant national brewers who tie up bars and restaurants through their distribution deals and lock smaller producers

out of the market. All in all, it's a small triumph worth toasting with a glass of Mendocino's Black Hawk Stout, named in the company style after an indigenous bird.

Black Hawk is brewed from two-row pale, crystal and black malts, and hopped with Cascade and Cluster varieties from the Pacific North-west: the hops are added three times during the kettle boil. This full-flavoured, rich beer has an entrancing aroma of old leather, fresh tobacco, dried fruits, coffee and tangy, bitter hop resins. Dark roasted malt fills the mouth with bitter dried fruit, liquorice and tangy hops. The big finish has creamy malt, burnt fruit, a further burst of leather and tobacco and a great punch of bitter hop resins. The brewery also produces an annual Yuletide Porter.

TASTING NOTES
Appearance
Aroma
Taste
Overall score

Nethergate Old Growler/Umbel Magna

Source: Nethergate Brewery, Pentlow, Essex, England
Strength: 5%/5.5%
Website: www.nethergate.co.uk

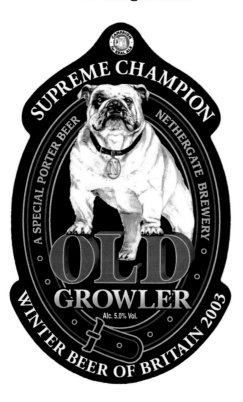

hops aroma, with bitter chocolate, liquorice and dried fruits. The palate is intensely fruity (raisins and sultanas) with a big spicy hop bitterness. The finish is hoppy with a rich chocolate note balanced by dark fruits and roasted grain. The beer was an instant success on draught and in bottle but Ian wasn't satisfied.

Other ingredients in the original recipe, which included coriander and bog myrtle, intrigued Ian. He was unable to find bog myrtle (though it does still grow) but he added ground coriander seeds to a batch of Old Growler. The result was a beer with all the character of the original but with a big herbal and spicy note. It was meant as a one-off brew but when I wrote a newspaper article about it, drinkers pleaded with the brewery to make it on a regular basis. The result is Umbel Magna, named after the shape of the coriander leaf. The Taylor Walker recipe shows that, even as late as the mid-18th century, brewers were still using other plants and herbs alongside hops in their beers.

Old Growler is based on the oldest-known porter recipe in England. Dr Ian Hornsey is a micro-biologist and former head brewer at Nethergate who has a fascination with brewing styles. His research unearthed the recipe for a porter brewed in the 1750s by the leading London company Taylor Walker.

Adapting the recipe to modern ingredients, he used Maris Otter pale malt (85%), wheat flour, crystal malt and black malt. Taylor Walker would have relied heavily on wood-cured brown malt. The colour of the beer is 70, while Challenger hops create 27 units of bitterness. Old Growler, named in honour of Ian's dog, has a peppery

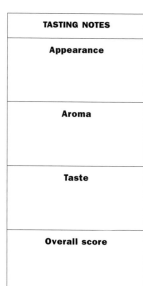

North Coast Brewing Old No 38 Stout/Old Rasputin Russian Imperial Stout

Source: North Coast Brewing Company, Fort Bragg, California, USA
Strength: 5.5%/8.9%
Website: www.northcoastbrewing.com

North Coast Brewing is a near neighbour of Mendocino Brewing and is based in Fort Bragg, once a fort in the mid-19th century and then a whaling port. Fine brewing water comes from the River Noyo that feeds the town. The brewery is sited in an old Presbyterian church and mortuary (no jokes, please, about live beer raising the dead).

Founder Mark Ruedrich acquired a taste for English ales as a result of his marriage to a British woman, and he opened his brewery, taproom and grill in 1987 to brew warm-fermented beers. He has two stouts in his range, though Old No 38 is described as 'Dublin Dry Stout' rather than an English style. It is named after a retired locomotive on a rail line known as the Skunk from the diesel fumes and which runs through the Californian redwoods, linking Fort Bragg with Willits.

Old No 38 is brewed with an English ale culture and uses pale, crystal and black malts with roasted barley. It is hopped with American Cluster and German Hallertauer varieties (50 units of bitterness). It has a wonderfully aromatic bouquet of bitter roasted grain, espresso coffee and tart hop resins. Hops, dried fruit, roasted grain and bitter chocolate build in the mouth, while the finish is deep with complex dark vine fruits, bitter grain and tangy hops, finally becoming dry.

Old Rasputin is firmly in the style of an English imperial stout and honours, if that is the word, Grigori Rasputin, the wild monk who had an unhealthy relationship with the Russian royal family and helped spark the Russian Revolution. To break his grip on the Tsarina and her children, Rasputin's enemies attempted to poison and shoot him. When he survived, they pushed him through a hole in the ice into the River Neva in St Petersburg.

The beer is brewed with a similar recipe to Old No 38, with the hops creating a whopping 75 units of bitterness. It has a tarry and oily aroma with massive earthy hop resins along with liquorice, bitter chocolate and fresh leather. Burnt grain, dark fruits, bitter roasted coffee beans and fruity hops fill the mouth, followed by an explosive finish packed with warming alcohol with a Cognac note, burnt grain and fruit, leather, tobacco and bitter hop resins.

TASTING NOTES
Appearance
Aroma
Taste
Overall score

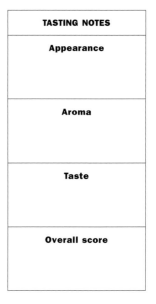

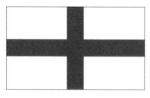

North Cotswold Arctic Global Warmer

Source: North Cotswold Brewery, Stretton-on-Fosse, Warwickshire, England
Strength: 15%
Website: www.northcotswoldbrewery.co.uk

TASTING NOTES
Appearance
Aroma
Taste
Overall score

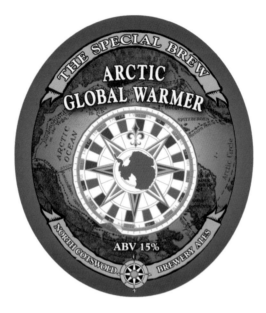

Jon Pilling doesn't do things by halves. He worked as a brewer at a number of small producers, including one of the home-brew Firkin pubs, the Phantom & Firkin in Loughborough, Leicestershire. When the opportunity to buy the 10-barrel brewing plant at Stretton-on-Fosse came up in 2005, Jon sold his house to raise the money, so keen was he to run his own operation.

He also brews strong beers, as the dauntingly powerful Arctic beer shows. He makes a regular porter called Hung, Drawn 'n' Portered but he wanted to recreate a Victorian stout and delved into the recipe books of the 19th century. He found that several English brewers had made astonishingly strong beers for Arctic expeditions. The level of alcohol not only kept out the cold but the beers were also a useful supply of protein while the large amounts of vitamin B combated that scourge of all lengthy expeditions: scurvy.

Allsopps and Bass, two of the great Burton brewers of Victorian times, brewed Arctic ales and Jon used a Bass recipe for his beer. The ingredients are Maris Otter pale, crystal, wheat and chocolate malts plus roasted barley. The hops are Challenger, Fuggles and Goldings. The yeast used for both primary and bottle conditioning is a secret culture but I suspect Jon has used either a wine or champagne yeast to finish the beer as conventional brewer's yeast cannot produce alcohol above 12%. See the Bock section and Eggenburg's Samichlaus for further information on how strong beers above 12% are made.

Arctic Global Warmer is dark brown/black with a massive aroma of bitter chocolate, espresso coffee, roasted grain and burnt fruit. The palate is rich and velvet smooth, with raisins and sultana fruit, chocolate, coffee and a solid underpinning of peppery hops. The finish starts sweet but dryness and hop bitterness develop with further notes of roasted grain, coffee and burnt malt.

The brewery has its own shop. Arctic Global Warmer, as a result of its strength and the lengthy production schedule, is only brewed occasionally so contact Jon Pilling to check availability: 01608 663947.

O'Hanlon Original Port Stout

Source: O'Hanlon's Brewing Company, Great Barton Farm, Whimple, Devon, England
Strength: 4.8%
Website: www.ohanlonsbeer.com

John O'Hanlon grew up in a pub in County Kerry and spent some time in Dublin playing rugby and doing the sort of social things associated with the game. So when he says his Port Stout is known in Ireland as a 'corpse reviver', we know we are listening to the voice of experience.

He uses top-quality Ferreira port at the rate of two bottles for every 36 gallons of stout. The wine raises the strength of the beer from 4.6% to 4.8%. When he owned a pub in London, John introduced this characterful version of stout to distinguish it from the Guinness he also sold. His point is that stout is more than just one brand.

The beer has done well for him. In 2001, it won the gold medal at Tucker's Maltings Bottled Beer Competition in Newton Abbot, Devon. The draught version took the top prize for stout in CAMRA's Champion Winter Beer of Britain awards in 2002, and the bottled version walked away with the national Champion Bottled Beer of Britain award in 2003. It is brewed with Optic pale malt, crystal malt and caramalt, with flaked barley and roasted barley. Phoenix hops are used for bitterness, Styrian Goldings for aroma. The beer has a superb fruity, vinous aroma with earthy hop resins and roasted grain. The delightful winy fruitiness continues through the palate and into the finish, accompanied by luscious tangy hops, roasted grain, coffee and chocolate. Hold the coffin!

Pitfield Shoreditch Stout/ 1850 London Porter/ 1792 Imperial Stout

Source: Pitfield Brewery, Epping, Essex, England
Strength: 4%/5%/9.3%
Website: www.pitfieldbeershop.co.uk

It's fitting that this range of porters and stouts were first brewed in a brewery in north London, for Sam Whitbread first brewed in the area before moving to the Barbican, while—according to legend—Ralph Harwood brewed his 'entire butt' nearby in Shoreditch and delivered it to the Old Blue Last in Great Eastern Street, a pub that survives to this day.

Pitfield, which is run by the energetic Martin Kemp, started life as the specialist Beer Shop in 1990 and the small brewery was added two years later. Pitfield converted its beers to organic ingredients in 2000 but has since added a range of 'historic beers' based on genuine recipes from the 18th, 19th and 20th centuries. In 2006 Martin moved his operation to an organic farm in Essex with 25 acres of organic barley for his use.

Shoreditch Stout, an organic beer, is brewed with Maris Otter pale malt, flaked barley and roasted barley, and hopped with Challenger, Fuggles and Target hops. The dark brown beer has a roasty and smoky bouquet balanced by spicy hop resins and a luscious malt note. Roast and dark fruits build in the mouth with a solid underpinning of floral and peppery hops. The finish has more smoked and roast malt notes, with dried fruits and tangy hops.

TASTING NOTES
Appearance
Aroma
Taste
Overall score

TASTING NOTES
Appearance
Aroma
Taste
Overall score

TASTING NOTES
Appearance
Aroma
Taste
Overall score

TASTING NOTES
Appearance
Aroma
Taste
Overall score

1850 London Porter is based on a Whitbread recipe and is brewed with Maris Otter pale and brown malt with roasted barley. Goldings are the single hop variety. The beer is deep ruby-red in colour, and the aroma is full of nutty malt, coffee and roasted grain notes, with a big waft of peppery hops. Pungent dark fruits build in the mouth with continuing roasted grain and bitter hops notes. The finish is lingering, quenching—as a good porter should be—with coffee, roast and nutty malt and peppery hops.

The 1792 Imperial Stout is another original London recipe, and is brewed with Maris Otter pale malt, wheat malt and roasted barley. Northdown is the single hop variety. This strong beer is jet-black in colour with a rich liquorice and dark fruits aroma, tangy hop resins and hints of leather and tobacco. Oily, tarry notes develop in the mouth as the dark fruits and tobacco build. The finish has enormous length with raisin fruit to the fore, backed by roasted grain, liquorice, oily and tarry notes, bitter coffee and earthy hops.

The beers are available by mail order within Britain: see website.

RCH Old Slug Porter

Source: RCH Brewery, West Huish, Weston-super-Mare, Somerset, England
Strength: 4.5%
Website: www.rchbrewery.com

If a brewery paid a slick marketing company to devise a name for a beer, I don't think Old Slug would be well received. But the name hasn't inhibited success of the RCH beer, which won a gold medal in the Tucker's Maltings Bottled Beer Competition in 1998. It is available in cask and bottle-fermented versions.

The brewery was once part of the Royal Clarence Hotel in Burnham-on-Sea but since the early 1990s has had a separate site near Weston. It was the slugs that thrived in the soil around the new brewery that encouraged the staff to give the curious name to the porter. The slugs have gone but the beer flourishes. It is brewed from pale, crystal and black malts, and hopped with Fuggles and Goldings. It is a dark ruby in colour and has a woody, grainy and fruity hop aroma. Cappuccino coffee notes break

through in the mouth, balanced by bitter, tangy dark fruit and earthy and spicy hop resins. The long, quenching finish offers an increasingly dry and bitter hop note, with burnt fruit and coffee notes. There is also a hint of sourness, which comes from the black malt and shows how the use of heavily roasted malts in the 19th century delivered the lactic sourness porter drinkers expected from the beer, a sourness previously supplied by long-matured stale, or old, ale.

TASTING NOTES
Appearance
Aroma
Taste
Overall score

Ridley's Witchfinder Porter

Source: Greene King, Bury St Edmunds, Suffolk, England
Strength: 4.3%
Website: www.greeneking.co.uk

The hunting of witches was a bleak and terrible period of English history. The Ridley family knows about religious persecution, as Bishop Nicholas Ridley was burnt at the stake by Mary Tudor for his Protestant beliefs. Many of the people harried, persecuted and hanged for witchcraft were religious dissenters. After the failure of the Gunpowder Plot in 1605, James I ruthlessly pursued so-called witches in Lancashire (see Moorhouse's Pendle Witches Brew, page 106) who were adherents to the 'old' Roman Catholic religion. The worst examples of witch-hunting were in eastern England, including Essex, between 1645 and 1647, when Matthew Hopkins adopted the title of Witchfinder General and caught and executed 200 or more 'witches'.

Perhaps it is fitting that a black beer commemorates this period of history. But let us be of good cheer, for this is a fine example of the style, available on draught in the autumn and winter but all year round in filtered bottle form. It is brewed from Maris Otter pale, crystal and chocolate malts, and hopped with Fuggles, Goldings and Styrian Goldings varieties. Colour units are 100, bitterness 44. It has a tempting aroma of roasted malts, dark fruit and peppery hop resins. Chocolate builds in the mouth with a solid base of spicy hops, burnt fruit and roast grain. The long finish becomes finally dry and bitter but with pleasing contributions from chocolate, dark fruits and rich roasted grain.

TASTING NOTES
Appearance
Aroma
Taste
Overall score

Rogue Shakespeare Stout/Imperial Stout

Source: Rogue Brewing Company, Newport, Oregon, USA
Strength: 6.1%/11%
Website: www.rogue.com

TASTING NOTES
Appearance
Aroma
Taste
Overall score

TASTING NOTES
Appearance
Aroma
Taste
Overall score

Brewmaster John Maier is so determined to create the correct English character for his dark beers that he imports specialist malts from the old country to get the required results. The use of hops from Oregon and Washington, however, give the two stouts a definable American quality.

Shakespeare Stout, a style of beer quite unknown to the Bard, is brewed with pale, crystal, English chocolate malt, rolled oats and roasted barley. The hops create a mighty 69 units of bitterness. The beer is unfiltered and throws a dense orange-brown foam and has a smooth chocolate aroma with a creamy note from the oats. Burnt currants, roasted grain, chocolate and bitter hops fill the mouth, while the deep and complex finish has tangy, tart hops, dark fruits, roasted grain and silky oats.

The Imperial Stout has a massive hop attack, with Cascade, Chinook and Willamette creating 87 units of bitterness. It is made from pale malt, Hugh Baird's crystal malt from England, chocolate malt also from England, black and Munich malts. It pours viscously into the glass like black Cognac, and the big, booming aroma conjures up dark and mysterious spices, espresso coffee, black chocolate and bitter oranges. It is chewy, oily and perfumy in the mouth followed by a long finish that has some surprisingly sweet glacé fruit notes balanced by dark grain and bitter hops, burnt fruit, smoky and roasted grain. This memorable mouthful is unfiltered and unfined and will improve in bottle. John Maier recommends letting it develop for a year before drinking.

Samuel Smith's Taddy Porter/Oatmeal Stout/ Imperial Stout

Source: Samuel Smith Old Brewery, Tadcaster, North Yorkshire, England
Strength: 5%/5%/7%
Website: www.samuelsmithbrewery.co.uk

Samuel Smith spearheaded the dark beer revival in the 1980s with three superb beers available only in bottle. They were originally designed for the American market, so much so that Charles Finkel, the founder of the Merchant du Vin import agency in Seattle, designed the label for Imperial Stout. In the late 1990s, however, Sam Smith's launched a special promotion for the beers in Britain complete with tasting notes and cooking recipes. The notoriously reclusive company does not release recipe information for its bottled products, though the brewery is known to favour the traditional English hop varieties Fuggles and Goldings. The beers are fermented in Yorkshire Square vessels described in the entry for the brewery's Pale Ale (see page 63).

Taddy is an affectionate diminutive for the small town of Tadcaster, where the brewery is based. Taddy Porter has the rich malty character that is typical of the brewery's beers. The aroma has a coffee and tart fruit nose, with more bitter fruit, roasted grain and hop spicy

TASTING NOTES
Appearance
Aroma
Taste
Overall score

TASTING NOTES
Appearance
Aroma
Taste
Overall score

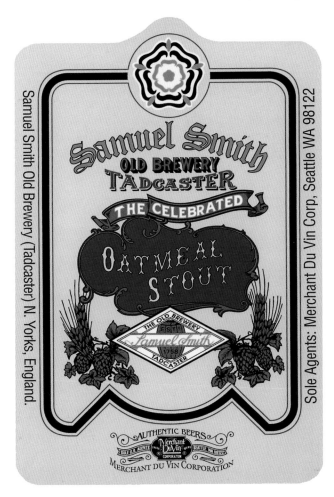

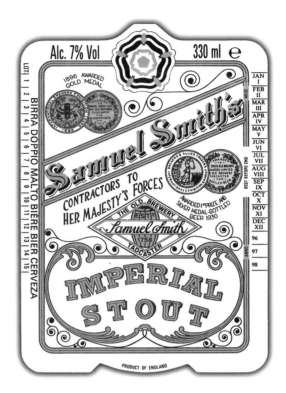

resins in the mouth. The finish is quenching, beautifully balanced between a luscious bitter-sweet dark malt character, dark fruits and tangy hops.

Oatmeal Stout recalls a style of beer popular early in the 20th century, when brewers were anxious to promote the healthiness of their products. Oats are a difficult grain to brew with, as they gelatinise during mashing and tend to clog up pipes and valves. They have to be used sparingly but add a delicious creamy and grainy note to beer. Sam Smith's Oatmeal Stout has a smooth and silky palate with hints of chocolate and espresso coffee on the nose, a full, rich palate dominated by rich and creamy dark grain, coffee and earthy hop resins. The finish has nutty dark malt, roasted grain, coffee, chocolate and bitter hop notes.

Samuel Smith's describes its Imperial Stout as the ideal digestif, the perfect replacement for Cognac. It even recommends serving it in a brandy balloon. Suggestions for companions at the dining table include Stilton and walnuts, baked sultana and lemon cheesecake, caviar, apricot-glazed bread and butter pudding, and chocolate trifle with roasted almonds. It has a complex roasted barley, burnt currants, cappuccino coffee and lactic sourness bouquet. Creamy malt, bitter and spicy hop resins and burnt fruit fill the mouth, while the finish bursts with sour fruit, roasted grain, bitter coffee and tangy hops.

Titanic Stout

Source: Titanic Brewery Co, Burslem, Stoke-on-Trent, Staffordshire, England
Strength: 4.5%
Website: www.titanicbrewery.co.uk

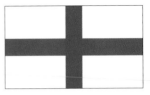

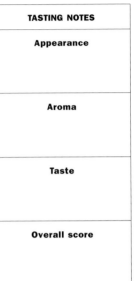

TASTING NOTES

Appearance
Aroma
Taste
Overall score

Titanic is one of the fastest-growing micro-breweries in England and has grown to small regional status. It was founded in 1985 and named in honour of the hapless Captain Smith of the Titanic, who was born in Stoke.

The brewery has uprooted three times to cope with demand for the beers and, in 2002, moved into former school premises with greatly expanded brewing and fermenting capacity. Owner Keith Bott is chairman of the Society of Independent Brewers, the umbrella organisation that looks after the interests of Britain's small producers. He also brews regularly at the ancient brewhouse at Shugborough Hall in Staffordshire, home of Lord Lichfield, the last country estate in England still to have a working house brewery.

Titanic Stout is available in both cask and bottle-fermented form. It is brewed with Maris Otter pale malt, wheat malt and roasted barley, and is hopped with Goldings, Northdown and Willamette varieties. This full-tasting and characterful beer has a big roasted grain, coffee, liquorice and tangy hop resins aroma, with dark dried fruits developing in the mouth alongside bitter hops and luscious dark malt. The finish is smoky, woody, hoppy, dry, fruity and quenching. Suggestions that Titanic beers go down well are not met with approval.

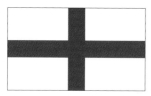

TASTING NOTES

Appearance

Aroma

Taste

Overall score

Wye Valley Brewery Dorothy Goodbody's Wholesome Stout

Source: Wye Valley Brewery, Stoke Lacey, Herefordshire, England
Strength: 4.6%
Website: www.wyevalleybrewery.co.uk

Dorothy Goodbody is not stout. With a complete disregard for political correctness, Wye Valley uses the image of a remarkably cantilevered blonde to adorn some of the specialist beers, the sort of image that used to appear on the fuselages of World War Two Spitfires.

The brewery had humble beginnings as a brew-pub, the Nags Head in Canon Pyon. It has moved twice and is now based in premises that enable 80 barrels a day to be produced. Wye Valley owns two pubs and supplies around 500 other outlets.

Stout is available both in cask and bottled fermented forms. The bottled version is filtered, kräusened and reseeded with fresh yeast to encourage continuing fermentation and maturation under glass. It is brewed with Maris Otter pale malt, flaked barley and roasted barley, and hopped with Northdowns. It is a deep nut-brown in colour with a big bouquet of roasted grain, tangy hops, chocolate and burnt currants. Chocolate, roast, bitter hop resins and rich fruit fill the mouth, while the long finish has smooth, silky malt, dried fruit, chocolate and earthy hop resins.

Miss Goodbody claims she found the recipe in her grandfather's brewing records, as he was once a brewer. The reality is that Wye Valley's founder Peter Amor once worked for a well-known Irish brewery whose stout was the inspiration for his beer, which was named Supreme Champion Winter Beer of Britain by CAMRA in 2002.

Young's Double Chocolate Stout

Source: Wells & Young's Brewing Co, Bedford, England
Strength: 5.2%
Website: www.wellsandyoungs.co.uk

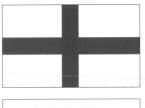

Young's, best known for its robust bitters, introduced Double Chocolate Stout in 1997 as a one-off brew but it found such favour that it is now a regular beer. It is principally a bottled beer in Britain, though it is occasionally on sale in Young's pubs on handpump and is also made available in cask form to CAMRA beer festivals. A draught version in the United States is filtered and pasteurised.

While most 'chocolate' stouts derive their flavour from the use of roasted malts, Young's head brewer Ken Don uses Cadbury's chocolate in both bar and essence form. Solid chocolate is added during the boil with hops, while essence is inserted as the beer is racked into casks. The grains used are Maris Otter pale, chocolate and crystal malts with roasted barley. The hops are Fuggles and Goldings. The beer is sweet by the standards of conventional stouts but not cloyingly so. The aroma has a creamy confectionery appeal, balanced by dark fruit and bitter hops. Rich chocolate fudge cake, tart hops and dark grains fill the mouth, while the long and complex finish offers intense chocolate flavours balanced by dark fruit and earthy hop resins. It is thought that this is the only stout in the world to use real chocolate as opposed to dark malt, and the bottle label pays homage to the chocolate's maker by using a similar design and typeface.

TASTING NOTES
Appearance
Aroma
Taste
Overall score

Zywiec Porter

Source: Zywiec Breweries, Cieszyn and Zywiec, Poland
Strength: 9.5%
Website: www.zywiec.com.pl

The Cieszyn brewery that stands fortress-proud above the small Polish town of the same name is home to one of the world's historic beer styles, Baltic Porter. Zywiec Porter is a redoubtable 9.5 per cent alcohol and, in common with Harvey's Imperial Russian Stout, is based on a recipe fashioned in London in the 19th century. The brewery in Cieszyn (pronounced 'Chetsin') was built on top of a hill in order that deep, cool cellars could be used to mature the beers following fermentation. It was opened in 1847 by Archduke Friedrich Habsburg, a member of the family that governed vast swathes of Europe until the First World War. The archduke's father told him: 'Own land and brew beer and you won't go wrong, my son.' At first the brewery produced wheat beer but Cieszyn is only a stone's throw from the Czech border and the impact of the brewing revolution in Pilsen in the 19th century was soon felt in Poland.

Cieszyn, aided by its deep cellars, switched to cold-fermented Pilsner-style beer. The brewery was a commercial success and the archduke built a second, larger brewery at Zywiec ('Ziv-ee-etch'), with a constant supply of pure water from the Tatra Mountains. It was here in 1881 that a brewer named Julius Wagner developed a recipe for porter based on the Baltic Porters and Stouts exported from England to Russia and the surrounding countries. Zywiec claims that Wagner was a Pole, which seems unlikely as his name is clearly Germanic. But whatever his ethnic origins, he launched a beer that is still popular in Poland and helps sustain the historic importance of the style.

The Zywiec breweries were bought by Heineken in 1994 and production of porter has been moved from the main brewery to Cieszyn. It accounts for 50 per cent of production in a plant that makes 60,000 barrels a year. With Baltic Porters and Imperial Stouts disappearing faster than snowdrops in spring, it's up to both beer lovers and beer writers to encourage Heineken to persevere with its fine interpretation of the style.

The beer enjoys a long and exhaustive brewing regime. In effect, it's now a lager, made by cold fermentation. But Alastair Hook, who brews his own interpretation of a strong London porter at Meantime brewery (page 155), says that when a beer is as strong as Zywiec Porter is makes no difference whether the yeast used is a lager or ale culture. The beer is brewed with Pilsner, caramalt, Munich and roasted malts. After a double decoction mash (see the feature on brewing on page 8) the wort is filtered in a lauter tun and is then pumped to the copper where it's boiled for four hours with Magnum, Nugget and Taurus hop varieties. The long boil—two or three times longer than the norm—is necessary because of the large quantity of malt used to make a beer of such strength.

Following 15 days primary fermentation in open vessels, the hopped wort is transferred to the lager cellars, 15 metres deep, which is kept at 2 degrees Celsius. The beer is matured for a minimum of 60 days. The beer that emerges from this long process has a deep coffee colour, an oily, tarry nose with powerful hints of espresso coffee, liquorice, molasses, burnt grain and dark fruit. Bitter hops, coffee, chocolate and dark grain fill the mouth, while the finish has coffee and liquorice to the fore with a good underpinning of hops, burnt grain and dark fruit. Seek it out, savour it and sustain it.

Golden Ales

Golden ales in both Belgium and Britain were created with one major aim in mind: to counter the growth of mass-advertised global lager brands. In Belgium, the first golden ale, Duvel, is the clear market leader and has spawned a legion of similar strong, warm-fermenting beers. It was the inexorable rise of Pilsner-style beers in Belgium that encouraged smaller brewers, who lacked the ability or capital investment to make lager, to add strong golden ales to their portfolios. The use of lighter varieties of malt allows hops to shine through, giving pulsating floral, piny, spicy and citrus aromas and flavours. The warming alcohol of beers such as Duvel, at 8.5%, along with deep malt, fruit and hop flavours, singles them out from Pilsner beers, whose only similarity is that of colour.

In Britain, consumers drink by the pint rather than sip reflectively from elegant, branded glassware, a habit that restricts the strength of beer. But more modest British golden ales have enabled craft brewers to set out their stall as producers of beers that are both pale in colour but packed with character. Many golden ales started life as summer refreshers. One of the best known of the breed, Hop Back's Summer Lightning, still suggests its seasonality in its name, though it is now brewed all year round.

The success of golden ales has enabled smaller British brewers to hang on to and even grow their market share at a time when giant global brewers exercise greater hegemony over the beer scene and flood both pubs and supermarkets with their bland and insipid interpretations of lager. There should be an International Court of Bibulous Rectitude that consigns to outer darkness some of the beers brewed in Britain that claim to have some tenuous connection to genuine European cold-fermented styles. Failing that, we should savour instead beers that manage to be both pale and interesting.

LEFT
Hop Back's Summer Lightning was one of the first of the new breed of Golden Ales in England and is now brewed all year round.

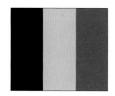

Achouffe La Chouffe

Source: Brasserie d'Achouffe, Achouffe, Belgium
Strength: 8%
Website: www.achouffe.be

TASTING NOTES
Appearance
Aroma
Taste
Overall score

Achouffe proves that brewing can be fun. The brewery and its products are based on the *Chouffe*, a bearded dwarf with a red hat, not dissimilar to a Smurf, who lives in the dense forest of the Ardennes in the Belgian province of Luxembourg and close to the Grand Duchy of the same name. In the late 1970s, the brothers-in-law Pierre Gobron and Chris Bauweraerts, keen home brewers, decided to launch a brewery and based their plant with borrowed farm and kitchen utensils in a small building in the then unknown village of Achouffe. Their strong, complex and bottle-fermented ales, with their striking labels depicting the dwarf, were sufficiently successful for the founders to give up their day jobs to brew full time and move into old farm buildings in 1986 with much improved equipment and a brew-length of 70 hectolitres (1,540 gallons). Sales improved dramatically when the company started to export to French Canada and they were able to open a new brewhouse and fermenting hall.

La Chouffe, the main product, is brewed with pure Ardennes water, Pilsner and crystal malts, white candy sugar and coriander. The hops are Czech Saaz and Styrian Goldings. The beer is deep gold with a rich sweet citrus fruit and coriander aroma. Vinous fruit builds in the mouth, balanced by juicy malt, herbal notes and gentle hop resins. The long finish is fruity and malty with light hop resins and a final powerful reminder of coriander. The beer is cold matured and then run into corked Champagne bottles, while a magnum version is called Big Chouffe. The beer will improve and develop greater fruit notes over time.

In 2006 the brewery was bought by the Moortgat group, brewers of Duvel (see page 174).

Castle Rock Nottingham Gold

Source: Castle Rock Brewery, Nottingham, England
Strength: 3.5%
Website: www.castlerockbrewery.co.uk

Castle Rock is the brewing division of the Tynemill pub group and both prove there is genuine demand for full-tasting beer. Tynemill was launched by Chris Holmes, a CAMRA pioneer and the campaign's energetic chairman in the formative years of the 1970s. His company owns 17 pubs in the East Midlands and all are based on a good range of cask beers from craft producers. While bigger pub groups concentrate on lager and keg beers, Tynemill sells more than 1,500 cask beers a year and is mightily successful as a result.

Castle Rock is a natural extension of the Tynemill philosophy and is equally successful. The brewery opened in 1996 and moved five years later to buildings alongside Tynemill's Vat & Fiddle pub, close to the local tax office and handily placed a few yards from Nottingham's main railway station. In 2003, in order to keep pace with demand, the brewery expanded from 30 barrels a week to 100. The brewing process can be viewed through windows in the pub wall.

Castle Rock produces a wide range of beers, but Nottingham Gold is a flagship beer, sold throughout the Tynemill estate and often under house names: Meadows Gold, for example, in the Vat & Fiddle. It is brewed from Maris Otter pale and crystal malts with a little torrefied wheat for a good head of foam. The hops are Goldings and Styrian Goldings. The beer has a rich and tempting aroma of peppery hops, tart citrus fruit and biscuity malt. Bitter hops resins, lemon jelly fruitiness and juicy malt fill the mouth while the lingering finish has tangy fruit, sappy malt and peppery hops.

TASTING NOTES
Appearance
Aroma
Taste
Overall score

Copper Dragon Golden Pippin

Source: Copper Dragon Brewery, Skipton, North Yorkshire, England
Strength: 3.9% draught/4.2% bottle
Website: www.copperdragon.uk.com

Copper Dragon is a phenomenon. It opened in 2002 and has been extended three times since that date, growing from a 10-barrel plant to a 120-barrel one.

Steve Taylor and Ruth Bennett opened Copper Dragon with a 10-barrel plant built by Bavarian Brewery Technologies, using mash mixer, lauter tun, brew kettle and conical fermenters. Within just six months the demand for the first beer, Best Bitter, forced Steve and Ruth to buy a new 30-barrel plant from the same company that ran alongside the original kit.

Then in November 2008 a new 'double 60 barrel' plant was opened at a cost of £4.5 million, complete with a visitor centre, shop, conference facilities and a bar and bistro. Beer is sold throughout northern England and the company owns 10 pubs, with plans to extend the range. Steve claims that Copper Dragon is the fastest-growing brewery in Britain and now enjoys the status of regional rather than small craft brewery.

Head Brewer Gordon Wilkinson is a passionate believer in Maris Otter, the finest variety of malting barley, but he looks further afield for his hops, using European and American varieties as well as English ones for his range of beers. Golden Pippen was launched as a seasonal cask beer but proved so popular that it's now a regular on draught and also in a stronger bottled version.

It's brewed with Maris Otter pale malt and American Cascade hops. The beer has a luscious gold/pale bronze colour with an equally luscious bouquet that is reminiscent of that old-style confectionary known as fruit gums: there's lemon, pears and apples—there has be an apple character in a beer called Golden Pippin.

Bitter hops burst through in the mouth, balanced by tart citrus fruit and slightly toasted grain. The finish is long and complex, wonderfully quenching, with a big tangy fruit note, biscuity malt and bitter hops.

Crouch Vale Brewers Gold

Source: Crouch Vale Brewery, South Woodham Ferrers, Essex, England
Strength: 4%
Website: www.crouch-vale.co.uk

Golden ales challenge the domination of lager beers in Britain, and Brewers Gold does so in a fascinating fashion, as the only grain used is lager malt and the single hop variety—and hence the name of the beer—is the German Brewers Gold.

The beer is one of a portfolio developed over 20 years by one of the longest-running and most successful micros. Run by Colin Bocking and Ollie Graham, Crouch Vale has built its success on the quality of its beers and also by acting as a wholesaler for other craft brewers, whose products they supply to some 250 pubs as well as beer festivals.

Crouch Vale owns one pub, the Queen's Head in Chelmsford, which is a fine watering hole for visitors to the Essex cricket ground. Brewers Gold boosted the fortunes of the brewery in 2003, when it won the Best Bitter class in CAMRA's Champion Beer of Britain competition: the success of golden ales in the competition prompted CAMRA to add a new and separate class for such beers in 2005.

Brewers Gold has a pungent aroma of cornflour and vanilla from the use of lager malt, balanced by a massive punch of citrus fruit and hop resins from the hops. Grapefruit bursts on the tongue, balanced by juicy malt and hop bitterness. The finish is intensely bitter with a further citrus fruit tang and rich, sappy malt. It is a beautifully balanced and wonderfully refreshing beer.

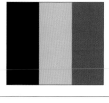

De Dolle Arabier

Source: De Dolle Brouwers, Esen, Belgium
Strength: 7%
Website: www.dedollebrouwers.be

There cannot be a style called 'mad beer' but the De Dolle Brouwers, the Mad Brewers, have carved out their own distinctive and eccentric niche in the world of brewing. The Herteleer family and friends may be eccentric but their madness is more akin to passion and enthusiasm than lunacy. The brewery is in Esen, near Diksmuide, not far from Ostend, and is on the site of a brewery that dates from the 1840s and seemed destined to close in 1980, when the owner was taken ill. But a group of keen home brewers, who started out with a kit from Boots the Chemist bought on a visit to England, took over the site and started to brew at weekends.

The driving force is Kris Herteleer, an architect by trade but now also a brewer of some experience. The brewery is open to visitors on Sundays with occasional group visits on other days. On my first visit I was shown round by Kris's mother, who shared her son's passion for beer and announced: 'Water is medicine, malt is medicine, hops are medicine, therefore beer is medicine', though her warning against 'savage yeasts' chilled the blood. I think she meant wild yeasts. The brewhouse is tiny and filled with antique equipment: a pre-World War One mash tun, a copper fired by direct flame, and an open wort cooler.

Arabier started life as a summer beer but is now brewed all year round. The name is a Flemish joke about parrots that's impossible to translate. The beer is brewed with pale, amber and Munich malts, and hopped with the Nugget variety from Poperinge in Belgium. It is dry hopped using Kentish Goldings. It is a hazy gold/bronze colour with a damson jam and spicy hops aroma, rich fruit, juicy malt and peppery hops in the mouth, and a big finish that ends peppery and bitter but along the way offers further tart fruit and sappy malt notes.

The brewery ran into problems at the turn of the century when Rodenbach stopped supplying yeast to De Dolle but Kris has since managed to get a different supply and has cultured it to suit the character of his beers.

TASTING NOTES
Appearance
Aroma
Taste
Overall score

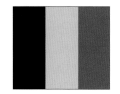

Duvel

Source: Brouwerij Moortgat, Breendonk, Belgium
Strength: 8.5%
Website: www.duvel.com

TASTING NOTES
Appearance
Aroma
Taste
Overall score

A sign in Flemish outside the Moortgat brewery says 'Ssh… Duvel is ripening'. This strong, infinitely complex and superbly aromatic beer is conditioned, refermented and matured by a long, slow and painstaking process. When I was allowed to sit in on a sampling of the beer by the brewing staff, I was amazed by the way the beer developed over weeks and months, moving from yeasty and estery when young, taking on malt, fruit and hop notes before finally blossoming into ripe and full-bodied maturity with its famous Poire William signature. In spite of its extreme pallor, Duvel (pronounced Doo-v'l, with the emphasis on the first syllable) is a warm-fermented ale.

The brewery, founded by Jan-Léonard Moortgat in 1871, has always been a specialist ale producer. Between the World Wars, when Scotch Ales were popular in Belgium, Moortgat asked the renowned brewing scientist Jean De Clerck from the brewing faculty at Leuven University to analyse a bottle of McEwan's Export. McEwan's in those days was bottle fermented, and De Clerck was able to isolate the yeast in the sediment and culture it for use at Moortgat. De Clerck discovered it had up to 15 different strains. The result was an amber-brown beer that, according to legend, was greeted by one brewery worker with the cry 'This is a devil of a beer'. Devil is duvel in Flemish. The name stuck and was used when Moortgat decided to add a golden beer to its portfolio in 1970, again with the help of De Clerck, who recultured the original yeast down to two strains.

Two-row summer French and Belgian barleys are specially malted for Moortgat. Duvel has a colour rating of seven to nine, only fractionally higher than a Pilsner's. The beer is infusion mashed and has an original gravity of 1056. Czech Saaz and Styrian Goldings hops are added to the copper boil in three stages and create between 29 to 31 units of bitterness. Dextrose is added before primary fermentation to boost the level of alcohol and encourage a full attenuation by the yeast. This lifts the gravity to 1066.

The two strains of yeast are used for primary fermentation, and the hopped wort is split into two batches in order to be attacked by the different strains. Primary fermentation lasts for six days followed by three days' secondary fermentation at cold temperature. The beer is then cold conditioned for a month, filtered, given an addition of dextrose and a dosage of one of the original yeasts. The gravity is once again boosted, this time to around 1073 degrees. The beer is bottled and held for two weeks, during which time it undergoes its third fermentation. The end result is a beer of 8.5% alcohol.

Duvel has a full, rich bouquet of hop resins, pear fruit and lightly toasted, biscuity malt. Fruit and hops dominate the mouth before the immensely long, warming finish develops an astonishing array of perfumy hops, rich pear fruit and juicy malt characteristics. The beer is poured into a special glass like an oversized brandy balloon in order to contain the vast head of foam. Some bars keep the glass in the refrigerator along with the beer. You may prefer Duvel chilled but I think its sublime character is best appreciated if served at an ale temperature.

The devil is a lucky man: not only does he have all the best tunes but one of the world's classic beers as well.

Exmoor Gold

Source: Exmoor Ales, Golden Hill Brewery, Wiveliscombe, Somerset, England
Strength: 4.5%
Website: www.exmoorales.co.uk

Exmoor Gold was the first of the new wave of golden ales in Britain but it wasn't meant to be a permanent beer. The brewery produced it in the early 1990s to mark its 1,000th brew. The enormous interest aroused by a beer that was as pale as lager and was a single malt ale with an intensely hoppy aroma and flavour led to it becoming a regular member of the company's portfolio. It has gone on to win some 30 awards for its quality.

Exmoor Ales was founded in 1980 in part of the old Hancock's Brewery that had closed in 1959. The omens were not good. The founders moved into a building in the depths of winter and found snow blowing in through an open wall. But the 13th brew of Exmoor Ale, to the astonishment of the brewing industry,

won CAMRA's Champion Beer of Britain competition that year. Since then the brewery has changed hands, and energetic new owners have expanded the site and now supply beer to 250 pubs in South-west England and nationally through wholesalers.

Exmoor Gold is brewed with 100% pale malt from the West Country and hopped with Challenger, Fuggles and Goldings. Colour units are 10, bitterness a resounding 40. The beer has a powerful punch of earthy hop resins, lemon fruit, juicy malt and a hint of butterscotch. Hops and fruit burst across the tongue, underscored by sappy malt and butterscotch. The finish lingers, becomes dry and intensely bitter but juicy malt continues to make its mark on a memorable and refreshing beer.

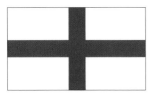

Freeminer Gold Miner

Source: Freeminer Brewery, Cinderford, Gloucestershire, England
Strength: 5%
Website: www.freeminer.com

TASTING NOTES
Appearance
Aroma
Taste
Overall score

Gold Miner was launched in 2003 as a bottle-fermented beer exclusively for the Co-op supermarket group. The beer had existed in cask form previously as Gold Standard and won the 1998 Beauty of Hops competition, where the judges praised the 'orange and apricot' character contributed by the hops. Beauty of Hops is an annual competition sponsored by growers who have increased public knowledge and appreciation of hops by describing the aromas and flavours of individual varieties. The growers encourage brewers to experiment with different blends of hops or to make 'single varietal' beers with just one variety.

Gold Miner is a single varietal beer, brewed with First Gold, the most successful of the new breed of hedgerow hops that grow to only half the height of conventional varieties. They are easier to pick and less prone to attack by pests and disease. Gold Miner is brewed with Optic pale malt and a touch of pale crystal malt. It has a tart and tangy bouquet of fresh orange peel, earthy hop resins and lightly toasted grain. Tart fruit, bitter hops and juicy malt fill the mouth, followed by a finish of great length that becomes hoppy and bitter but is balanced by a continuing tangy citrus fruit element and a rich malt note.

The Co-op was founded in the 19th century to provide goods and services—including funerals—at affordable prices for working people. In recent years, it has pioneered information for its customers with detailed labelling. The back labels of beer bottles include useful dietary information and even have a Braille section.

Hesket Newmarket Helvellyn Gold

Source: Hesket Newmarket Brewery, Hesket Newmarket, Wigton, Cumbria, England

Strength: 4%

Website: www.hesketbrewery.co.uk

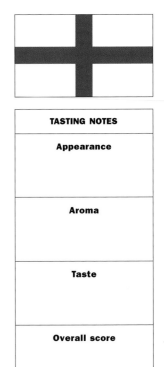

TASTING NOTES
Appearance
Aroma
Taste
Overall score

Hesket Newmarket Brewery was saved from closure in 1999, when both local people and drinkers from further afield formed a co-operative to run it. The brewery hadn't failed, but the couple that had run it since 1988 wanted to retire.

The tiny brewery supplies beer to the Old Crown Inn, which is also owned by a co-operative that includes locals and people from as far away as the United States and South Africa who have visited the area and fallen in love with the old inn, the beer and the surrounding fells and mountains. Both pub and brewery have featured in the national press and on television. They were visited in 2004 by the Prince of Wales who heads the Pub is the Hub campaign that seeks to maintain rural pubs as vital centres of their communities. The publicity has encouraged the brewery to expand. Mike Parker, a former brewer with Bass, is now in charge and has increased production to 120 barrels a week and added a temperature-controlled beer store. As well as supplying the Old Crown and other pubs in the

area, the brewery will sell beer to visitors who bring suitable containers (016974 78066). The beers are named after local mountains and fells, including Blencathra, Skiddaw and Old Carrock.

Helvellyn Gold is a recent addition to the range and is brewed with a skilful blend of ingredients. Maris Otter pale malt is the main grain with 3% malted oats to balance hop bitterness and 2% aromatic pale malt. Mike Parker described aromatic malt as similar to crystal malt, which means it is a stewed malt that doesn't need mashing. He says aromatic pale is less cooked than crystal and has a bitter-sweet character. The hops are Cascade, Fuggles and Goldings, added twice during the copper boil, with Styrian Goldings put into the copper at the end of the boil. The beer has a rich and pungent aroma of lemon jelly fruit, biscuity malt and hop resins. Creamy malt, bitter hop resins and tart fruit fill the mouth, followed by a lingering finish with a delicate and delicious creamy maltiness balanced by tangy citrus fruit and bitter hops.

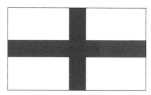

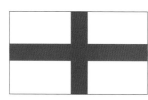

Hop Back Summer Lightning

Source: Hop Back Brewery, Downton, Salisbury, Wiltshire, England
Strength: 5%
Website: www.hopback.co.uk

Hop Back brews a wide range of beers but it is true to say that its success has been driven by Summer Lightning, a beer that has won a multitude of awards at CAMRA's Great British Beer Festival and other competitions. The brewery is yet another success story for British micros.

It started life in 1987, when John Gilbert added a tiny brewhouse to the Wyndham Arms pub in Salisbury. With support from the government's Business Expansion Scheme, the brewery moved to an industrial estate on the outskirts of Salisbury and now has a modern 20-barrel production line. It owns 11 pubs and supplies more than 200 other outlets. In the late 1980s, John decided to introduce a strong golden beer as an antidote to other beers of that strength, which, in his opinion, were both too dark and too sweet. The success of Summer Lightning, named after an obscure play of that title by P G Wodehouse, encouraged many other brewers, large and small, to add golden ales to their portfolios.

Now brewed all the year round, Summer Lightning is available in both cask and bottle fermented versions. It is brewed with 100% Maris Otter pale malt and has 14 units of colour. The cask version uses both Challenger and East Kent Goldings hops, while in bottle it is a single varietal beer with Goldings alone. Bitterness units are a powerful 38. The cask version has a massive aroma of peppery Goldings, tart citrus fruit and lightly toasted malt, with sappy malt, lemon and gooseberry fruit and earthy hop resins in the mouth. The big finish is intensely hoppy and bitter, balanced by tart fruit and juicy malt. The bottled version has a higher level of natural carbonation and a pronounced Goldings aroma and palate.

Kelham Island Pale Rider

Source: Kelham Island Brewery, Sheffield, South Yorkshire, England
Strength: 5.2%
Website: www.kelhambrewery.co.uk

Dave Wickett, an economics lecturer at Sheffield Hallam University and a long-standing member of CAMRA, launched Kelham Island in 1990. He wanted to restore Sheffield's proud brewing tradition that had disappeared when Bass and Whitbread closed their breweries in the city. He built his small brewery alongside the Fat Cat pub on an island formed by a mill race adjacent to the River Don. The success of the beers prompted a move a few yards away to new, purpose-built premises with a greatly increased capacity.

In 2004, Pale Rider was named Champion Beer of Britain by CAMRA, and Dave found his phone was red-hot with orders for the beers from as far away as Chicago. He was approached by Ridley's Brewery in Essex, and an agreement was swiftly reached whereby Ridley's would supplement Kelham Island's 25 barrels a week of Pale Rider with 60 additional barrels. Dave only gave the go-ahead to the deal when he was satisfied the Ridley's beer was a perfect match. I went to the brewery and found I could not detect the slightest difference between the two brews. However, as Dave is determined to counter any claims that he is passing off Ridley's version as his own, the beer from the Essex brewery is called Pale Island rather than Pale Rider.

Both versions are brewed with Maris Otter pale malt and a touch of wheat malt, and the only hop is the American Willamette. The beer has a pungent aroma of perfumy floral hops, tangy citrus fruit and biscuity malt. Hop resins, piny notes, tart fruit and sappy malt fill the mouth. Creamy and juicy malt builds in the long finish, balanced by a continuing citrus fruit note and bitter hop resins.

Oakham JHB

Source: Oakham Ales, Peterborough, Cambridgeshire, England
Strength: 3.8%
Website: www.oakham-ales.co.uk

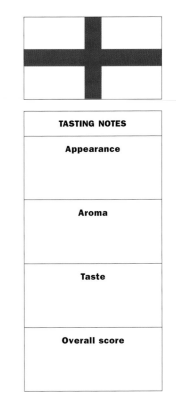

JHB has won five awards in CAMRA's Champion Beer of Britain competition, including Supreme Champion in 2001. It comes from the Brewery Tap (90 Westgate), the biggest brew-pub in Europe, based in central Peterborough and close to the railway station. The brewery can be seen behind the bar on the ground floor and there is a spectacular view from the mezzanine. The pub and brewery have been threatened for years by closure to make way for a road-widening scheme. But nothing has yet happened to spoil the pleasure of drinkers who come from far and wide to enjoy the home-brewed ales, a fine selection of Belgian beers and excellent Thai food.

JHB stands for Jeffery Hudson Bitter. Hudson was a midget from Peterborough who found favour at the court of Charles I. He was placed inside a large pie—but only after it was cooked—and he burst from it at the royal table, much to the amusement of the royal couple and their guests. Hudson was a staunch monarchist and supported the king during the English Civil War, which earned him a spell in the Tower of London when the parliamentary forces under Oliver Cromwell defeated the royalists.

The beer may be named in his honour but it is not short on aroma and flavour. It is brewed with Maris Otter pale malt with 5% wheat malt for clarity and head retention. The hops are Challenger for bitterness and American Mount Hood for aroma, and they create 33 units of bitterness. JHB has a profound citrus fruit, creamy malt and earthy hop resins bouquet with a big hop bitterness building in the mouth and almost overpowering the juicy malt and fruit notes. The finish is intensely dry and bitter but is balanced by sappy and creamy malt with a continuing tart fruit note. This is a big, full-bodied beer that drinks more than its strength would suggest and is for lovers of the hop.

TASTING NOTES
Appearance
Aroma
Taste
Overall score

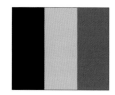

Silly Double Enghien Blonde

Source: Brasserie de Silly, Silly, Hainaut, Belgium

Strength: 7.5%

Website: www.silly-beer.com

TASTING NOTES
Appearance
Aroma
Taste
Overall score

Silly is a perfectly sensible name if you happen to be a Belgian from Wallonia, though it causes considerable mirth to English speakers. The village takes its name from the local river, the Sylle, in Hainaut province south of Brussels. In the 19th century, some of the bigger farms in the region not only grew barley and hops but also added small breweries to make beer for their families and workers. The Meynsbrughen family in Silly continued to farm until after World War Two but then decided to concentrate on brewing. The style of buildings and the cobbled yard still suggest a farm, and this type of brewing is known in Belgium as artisanal or rustic. In 1975, Silly bought the Tennstedt Decroes brewery in neighbouring Enghien and added its range of beers to its own. The main beers are all warm-fermented ales though the company—controlled by the fifth generation of the family—has recently added a Silly Pils: I have drunk a fair number of those over the years.

One of the Double Enghien beers is the mightily strong Blonde, brewed with pale malts from Belgium and France, and hopped with English Challenger and German Hallertauer. It has a stunning aroma of juicy malt, lemon jelly fruit and floral and spicy hops. Rich flavours of malt and fruit build in the mouth but are underpinned by a firm, spicy hop character. The finish has enormous length, with complex flavours of sappy malt, lemon fruit and a deep and intense spicy hop note. The beer for years was filtered but the brewery has bowed to demand and it is now bottle fermented and will improve and deepen its flavours over the months.

After a visit to the brewery, I enjoyed some of the brewery's beers and an excellent rustic lunch in the Café Titien in Bassilly, or Lower Silly. The bar has a version of bar billiards with the familiar mushroom-shaped guardians of the holes replaced by Champagne corks. I enjoyed a few silly games...

Unibroue Maudite

Source: Brasserie Unibroue, Chambly, Montréal, Québec, Canada
Strength: 8%
Website: www.unibroue.com

TASTING NOTES
Appearance
Aroma
Taste
Overall score

Some of the early French settlers in Canada came from Flanders and Normandy, and brought with them a beer rather than a wine culture. In the past 20 years, a number of craft breweries have sprung up to offer authentic French- and Belgian-style beers for the Francophone region, with Unibroue the clear market leader.

André Dion and Serge Racine founded the brewery and from its first tiny base moved to bigger premises in the Montréal suburb of Chambly. They worked at first in association with the Belgian brewing group Riva, which advised on the recipe of the first beer, Blanche de Chambly, a wheat, or white, beer launched in 1992. The brewery received a major injection of capital from the Canadian rock star Robert Charlebois and started to expand the range of products, which are exported to the United States and Europe.

The beers are bottle fermented and have eye-catching labels showing Canadian scenes and legends. *Maudite* means damned in French, and the name is taken from a fantastical French-Canadian story about a group of lumberjacks who sign a pact with the devil that allows them to fly their canoe home. But Satan reneges on the deal and leads them to their death.

Maudite is based on the Belgian golden ale style, and the brewers clearly had Duvel in mind when they devised their recipe, but they added coriander and spices to give their beer its distinctive bouquet and palate. American and European hops are used sparingly to allow full expression to the herbs and spices. Pale and Munich malts produce the deep red-gold colour. It has a rich and tempting nose of spices and nutty malt, with coriander and orange zest building strongly in the mouth. The complex finish is long, with nutty and juicy malt and a dry, herbal finale. The beer undergoes three fermentations and will improve in bottle for eight years.

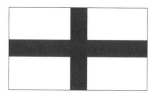

Young's Kew Gold

Source: Wells & Young's Brewing Co, Bedford, England
Strength: 4.8%
Website: www.wellsandyoungs.co.uk

TASTING NOTES
Appearance
Aroma
Taste
Overall score

This is not only a good beer but a beer that supports a good cause: the Royal Botanic Gardens at Kew in London. A royalty from the sale of each bottle goes to Kew Gardens to aid its vital work in helping to save species and habitats for the future—a noble cause at the best of times but essential as global warming threatens to kill many species and environments.

The bottle-conditioned beer contains some hops that were cultivated at Kew and which are now grown commercially. The variety is Styrian Goldings and it's a surprise to find them growing in England as its home is Slovenia, the small country just south of Austria and once part of the old Yugoslavia. But in a sense the hop is coming home: when Slovenia attempted to build a hop industry in the 19th century, farmers found that the only variety that would grow in their inhospitable soil was the hardy English Fuggle. They thought Fuggle was an odd name and called it Golding instead, after another famous English variety. So the hop created by an English farmer, Richard Fuggle, has come back with a different name from Europe to Kew Gardens.

Kew Gold was launched in 2008 and has been so popular that it's also available in cask-conditioned form in the summer. It's brewed at the Charles Wells brewery in Bedford and thereby hangs another tale. Young's was a much-loved London brewery, famous for its horse-drawn delivery drays and a menagerie of animals at the Wandsworth site. It was revered by beer lovers as one of the few companies that refused to go down the keg beer route in the 1970s and stayed loyal to real draught beer. But in 2006, Young's closed the Wandsworth site. It had to leave the area as a result of plans by the local council to flatten part of the town, including the brewery, which had become a 24-hour traffic jam. Young's couldn't find a suitable replacement site in London and merged with Charles Wells in Bedford.

As a departure from Young's usual practice, Kew Gold is brewed with lager malt rather than

Maris Otter. The single hop, as mentioned above, is Styrian Goldings. The beer is pale gold, with a pungent toasted malt and spicy hop resins aroma and a tart grapefruit note. The palate has tangy citrus fruit, toasted grain and bitter hop resins, followed by a dry finish in which bitter hops finally succumb to biscuity malt and citrus fruit. Drink it, enjoy it and do your bit for the environment.

Scottish Ales

As a result of temperament and temperature, the Scots have for centuries brewed ales that are distinctively different from those made south of the border. A cold climate requires beers that are hearty and warming; as a result Scottish ales tend to be dark, often brewed with the addition of heavily roasted malts, oats and other cereals, and rich with unfermented sugar.

The first brewers were Picts, not Celts. Their heather ale survived long after they were ethnically cleansed, and the style has recently been resurrected (see page 249). Ale brewed in a more conventional way had a poor reputation. In 1598, Fynes Morrison wrote that the local ale would 'distemper a strange body', while an 18th-century English traveller, Thomas Kirke, described it as 'sorry stuff, tunned up in a small vessel called a cogue [mash tun]; after it has stood a few hours, they drink it out of the cogue, yest and all'. Imports of ale from England reached such proportions that, in 1625, the Scottish Parliament passed an Act forbidding the 'Hamebringing of Foreyn Beir' but nobody paid any attention to the law. The probable reason for the superiority of English ale was the use of the hop, which gave it better keeping qualities. The Scottish climate was not conducive to the development of a hop industry and brewers used them sparingly or not at all.

Commercial brewing in Scotland took off almost by default. As a result of the Auld Alliance between Scotland and France, the Scots consumed substantial amounts of imported French claret and Burgundy. But supplies dwindled during the Napoleonic wars and entrepreneurial brewers, as distinct from brewers in inns and on farms, appeared to fill the gap. They also met a growing demand for beer from Scottish emigrants. The Highland Clearances had sent many landless and destitute Scots abroad to look for work, and their descendants in Australasia, the Caribbean and North America demanded ale from the old country. 'Export'—a darker and sweeter version of India Pale Ale—became a definitive brewing style. The best-known of the breed, McEwan's Export, remains a major brand for the Scottish & Newcastle group.

The brewing industry settled in the Lowlands around the cities of Alloa, Edinburgh and Glasgow, making use of the best-quality barley grown in the region. The names for beer are different from the English ones: mild in Scotland is called light, even when it is dark in colour; bitter and best bitter are known as heavy, while a wee heavy is a strong beer sold in nip bottles. Such beers are also known as 60, 70, 80 and 90 shilling ales from a 19th-century method of stating the wholesale price for beer per barrel. The names, however, should not detract from the more important fact that Scottish ales are brewed in a different way from English ones. The copper boil lasts for a shorter time. As fewer hops are used, it is important not to boil away the delicate aromas and flavours of the plant. Fermentation is at a lower temperature of 10˚C (50˚F), compared to 20˚C (70˚F) in England. As a result, the yeast works slowly, does not create a large head, does not need to be skimmed and eventually settles at the bottom of the fermenter. Fermentation lasts for around three weeks and the green beer is then stored for several more. The similarities with lager brewing are obvious. The system developed empirically before the Industrial Revolution, when brewing took place only in winter. It was the exceptionally cold weather in Scotland that created cold ferments and the system continued when refrigeration appeared. It is not difficult to understand why lager brewing took off so much earlier in Scotland than in England. Hugh Tennent's Wellpark Brewery, for example, started to brew lager beer in 1885.

As late as the 1960s, there were 16 breweries in Edinburgh alone. But Scottish brewing was devastated by mergers and takeovers even more effectively than in England. From the ashes of dozens of closures, two giants, Scottish & Newcastle and Tennent Caledonian, appeared and rapidly dominated the country with lager and keg beers. But choice and tradition have made a sturdy comeback. Today, Scotland, from the Borders to Orkney and Shetland, has around 36 craft breweries. Some concentrate on traditional 'Heavies', while newer arrivals have introduced Scottish drinkers to paler and hoppier brews.

Belhaven 80 Shilling/St Andrews Ale

Source: Belhaven Brewing Co, Dunbar, East Lothian, Scotland
Strength: 4.2%/4.9%
Website: www.belhaven.co.uk

TASTING NOTES
Appearance
Aroma
Taste
Overall score

TASTING NOTES
Appearance
Aroma
Taste
Overall score

Benedictine monks built a monastery with its own brewery in the 14th century on land close to the sea and the English border. The community that developed around the monastery became the small harbour town of Belhaven. Brewing on the same site restarted in 1719 and continues in mellow brownstone buildings that

once included a maltings. Belhaven's ales were exported widely and were prized in London and Vienna, where the Emperor praised them as 'the Burgundy of Scotland'. James Boswell, Dr Samuel Johnson's travelling companion and biographer, described the brewery's ale as 'the best small beer ever tasted'.

Today's Belhaven's 80 Shilling Ale is considered to be the classic of the style. It is brewed with Pipkin pale, black and crystal malts with liquid brewing sugar. The colour units are 33. Whitbread Goldings Variety hops are used for bitterness, Fuggles and Goldings for aroma. Bitterness units are 29. The beer is renowned for its luscious tart gooseberry fruit aroma and palate, balanced by toasted malt and spicy hops. Rich grain, tangy fruit and hop resins dominate the palate, with a finish that is dry, with good hop notes but dominated by nutty malt and a continuing presence of gooseberry fruit.

The original label of St Andrews Ale showed the Saltire, Scotland's flag. According to a legend, in 832AD, the Scottish army under King Angus mac Fergus was preparing for battle against the troops of Athelstane, King of Northumbria. On he eve of the battle, the Scots soldiers saw a cloud formation that resembled the cross of St Andrew, their patron saint. They duly went on to score a major victory the following day. The beer that commemorates this historic event is brewed with Pipkin pale, black and crystal malts, with liquid brewing sugar. The colour is 35. Fuggles, Goldings and WGV hops are used and create 36 units of bitterness. It is the only beer in the Belhaven range that is dry hopped in cask, and this gives it a big peppery note from aroma to finish. Toasted and nutty grain and tart fruit are also evident on aroma and palate, with a long, bitter-sweet finish packed with rich grain and fruit notes that finally becomes dry and bitter.

Bristol Laughing Lab

Source: Bristol Brewing Company, Colorado Springs, Colorado, USA
Strength: 5.3%
Website: www.bristolbrewing.com

Mike Bristol, who founded his brewery in 1994, doesn't mince his words. His mission, he says, 'is to make beer that brings three things to mind: quality, purity and sanity'. He built his brewery at the foot of Pikes Peak in Colorado to ensure a plentiful supply of fine brewing water. He sells fresh beer to bars, restaurants and liquor stores and he has a lounge at the brewery where visitors can sample his beers and meet the brewer.

Mike stages a party every year on April 7. That's the day Prohibition was repealed in the U.S. in 1933. Franklin D Roosevelt marked repeal by saying, 'Today would be a good day for a beer' but Mike uses stronger language: 'The aim of Prohibition was to eliminate crime, poverty and violence. Instead, for 13 years, we got the Mafia, the Great Depression and Bud Light. The origins of bad beer are rooted in the death of regional breweries.'

Now regional and craft breweries, numbering more than 1,200, are back on the map. Mike Bristol, who occasionally brews cask-conditioned beer, has won nine awards for Laughing Lab in both the World Beer Cup and Great American Beer Festival competitions in the Scottish Ale category. The beer is rich and complex due to the use of several malts in the grist: pale two row, two types of crystal, chocolate and carapils. The hops are Chinook and Willamette, which create 19 units of bitterness. Two-row barley is so-called because of the number of grains within each ear of barley: it's considered the finest type of barley for brewing. Many bigger breweries use six-row barley that produces an inferior, rougher-tasting beer.

The beer has a red-brown colour with a luscious roasted malt and burnt fruit—raisins and sultanas—aroma. The palate has a surprising dryness due to the dark malt, with rich fruit and gentle, spicy hops. This is a beer of continuing surprises as tart and peppery hops burst through in the finish, balanced by burnt fruit and roasted grain. The pronounced hop bitterness may not be quite true to style but this is a rich and rewarding beer.

Laughing Lab replaces Grant's Scottish Ale from the first edition. Bert Grant, Scottish-born, was one of the pioneers of the American craft brewing revolution and his Scottish ale was considered the finest interpretation of the style in the U.S. Sadly, Bert died between the two editions of this book. His brewery was bought by a wine company that rapidly proved that the grape and the grain don't mix and the brewery closed. Bert's famous remark, as one glass emptied, 'There's always time for one more beer', is now his epitaph. I salute his memory and his great contribution to the world of beer.

TASTING NOTES
Appearance
Aroma
Taste
Overall score

Harviestoun Bitter & Twisted

Source: Harviestoun Brewery, Alva, Clackmannanshire, Scotland
Strength: 3.8%
Website: www.harviestoun.com

TASTING NOTES
Appearance
Aroma
Taste
Overall score

Bitter & Twisted won CAMRA's title of Supreme Champion Beer of Britain in 2003, an award that turned the media spotlight on the advances made by small craft breweries in Scotland. Harviestoun has been brewing since 1985 and at first concentrated on beers that were firmly in the Scottish tradition. But Ken Brooker the founder, redefined his product range and reached out to a younger audience with beers that are paler and have a strong hop presence.

Ken is an Englishman—though he now wears a kilt on formal occasion—and came to Scotland from Dagenham to work as a representative of the Ford Motor Company. He had been a keen home brewer for years, and when he got bored with selling cars, he set up a small brewery in an old cow byre on a farm in Dollar. In 2004, the success of the company allowed Ken to move into custom-built premises in Alva, where there is a production line of 50 to 60 barrels. Ken has

a dry sense of humour—he uses Hersbrucker hops, for example, in his multi-award winning cask lager, Schiehallion—but he was not in a laughing mood when he named Bitter & Twisted. He had lost an appeal against a conviction for speeding and was feeling distinctly bitter and twisted—Essex man's version of angry—when he launched his new beer.

It is brewed with Pipkin pale and crystal malts, with 16% wheat and a small amount of oats: the recipe should satisfy Scottish traditionalists. The hops are Challenger and Hallertauer Hersbrucker for bitterness and Styrian Goldings for aroma. The colour rating is 10, bitterness 30. The beer has a rich creamy malt and spicy hop bouquet with underlying tangy citrus fruit. Hop resins and citrus fruit attack the tongue with a mellow but firm malt note. The long and deep finish is packed with fruity hop character and juicy malt. It is a splendidly refreshing beer.

Innis & Gunn Oak Aged Beer

Source: Innis & Gunn Brewing Co, Edinburgh, Scotland
Strength: 6.6%
Website: www.innisandgunn.com

This remarkable beer marries the techniques of both brewing and whisky distilling. Whisky, wine and Cognac are the drinks most closely associated with ageing in wood. It is now rare in the world of beer, though the lambic beers of Belgium (see page 240) are stored in wood for up to three years in casks bought from the port wine and Cognac makers. Innis & Gunn has restored the tradition.

Dougal Sharp is the former head brewer at the Caledonian Brewery, while his father, Russell, founded Caledonian and also worked for the whisky maker Chivas Regal, where he made a study of oak ageing. The Sharps developed their beer in association with the distiller William Grant & Sons. Grants aroused the interest of the brewing industry when the distiller bought beer to assist in developing its Cask Reserve Scotch Whisky. The beer was brewed solely to age the casks but Dougal Sharp was intrigued by the flavour and decided to make a commercial oak-aged beer. His beer enjoys a 77-day maturation process, 10 times the average for ale. This includes a 30-day rest period in lightly toasted American white oak casks, the preferred wood for maturing wine and spirits. After 30 days, the beer continues to age in a 'marrying tun', where the flavours infuse and mellow, and natural carbonation takes place.

The beer is brewed with Golden Promise pale and crystal malts, and is hopped with the Phoenix variety. It has a luscious amber colour, a dense and lasting collar of foam, and a tightly beaded, Champagne-style carbonation. The aroma is smoky and oaky, underscored by ripe malt, vanilla and tart

hops. There is more smoky malt on the palate with a blast of orange fruit and earthy hop resins, while the lingering finish is bitter-sweet, with an intriguing hint of Cognac. It is sold only in bottle, though a cask-conditioned version has been made available for CAMRA beer festivals. The beer, launched in 2003, made history by winning gold medals in two categories and the overall Supreme Champion prize at the 2004 International Beer Competition. In the same year the beer collected the Safeway Consumer Beer of the Year award.

TASTING NOTES
Appearance
Aroma
Taste
Overall score

Islay Saligo Ale

Source: Islay Ales, Islay, Scotland
Strength: 4.4%
Website: www.islayales.com

TASTING NOTES
Appearance
Aroma
Taste
Overall score

Islay is world-famous for its whiskies and the island has seven distilleries, including the sublime Laphroaig. When Paul Hathaway, Paul Capper and Walter Schobert came to settle on the island, they brought with them a love of beer and whisky, and they decided to use the famously peaty waters of the island to make beer. Walter is from Germany and he has written extensively about both beer and whisky. Islay Ales was launched in 2003 and, in such a romantic spot, is based on an extremely unromantic former tractor shed on a farm. Beers are produced in both cask and bottle-fermented versions for sale to visitors to the island and further afield. A visitor centre for the brewery is planned. The beers are named after landmarks and beauty spots on the island, such as Dun Hogs Head, Loch Finlaggan and Black Rock.

Saligo takes its name from Saligo Bay on the west coast of the island. It is brewed with pale, lager and wheat malts and hopped with Bramling Cross and Goldings. It has a pale bronze colour and a ripe pear and apricot aroma, balanced by juicy malt and peppery hops. Bitter, spicy hops burst across the tongue, balanced by sappy malt and tangy fruit. The finish is bitter but not dry, with a good balance of juicy malt, hop resins and fruit. And underpinning all the flavours there is a light but distinct hint of peat from the water.

TASTING NOTES
Appearance
Aroma
Taste
Overall score

Orkney Dark Island

Source: Orkney Brewery, Quoyloo, Sandwick, Orkney, Scotland
Strength: 4.6%
Website: www.orkneybrewery.co.uk

Roger White has won so many awards for his beers that it seems a pity he can't taste them, as he is teetotal. In all my travels, I have never come across another teetotal brewer. I look upon Roger as the Beethoven of the beer world, composing beautiful symphonies from malts and hops, but in common with the deaf maestro, unable to enjoy them to the full.

Roger is an engineer by trade and opened Orkney's first brewery for 50 years in 1988 in a former schoolhouse. At first he brewed only keg beers, as locals preferred cold, fizzy drinks. On one trip to the island I was told in no uncertain terms by sailors on the ferry: 'We don't drink that real ale!' But Roger built up good sales on the mainland and even across the border into England and, more for visitors than locals, now sells his beer properly cask conditioned in several Orkney bars and hotels. His success enabled him to expand in 1994 and can now brew 150 barrels at a time. The beers celebrate the island and its Viking past: the strong Skullsplitter, for example, is named after Thorfin Hausakliuuf, the seventh Viking earl of the island.

Dark Island is a true ruby-red Scottish 'Heavy' and is brewed with Maris Otter pale, chocolate and crystal malts, torrefied wheat and cane sugar: 100–120 units of colour. Omega hops for bitterness and Goldings for aroma contribute 20–24 units of bitterness. It has a fruity blackcurrant aroma with roasted grain and earthy hop resins. Dark roasted grain dominates the mouth along with peppery hop notes and tart fruit. The complex finish has vinous fruit, hop resins and rich dark grain, finally becoming dry but not overly bitter.

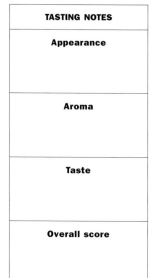

Wheat Beers

Munich & Bavaria

The Bavarians are famous not only as great consumers of beer but also as the people who have kept faith with the world's oldest beer law, the Reinheitsgebot. The 'Purity Pledge' of 1516 stipulates that only barley, water and yeast can be used in brewing. You will notice that wheat is missing. The reason is simple: it was the Bavarian royal family, the House of Wittelsbach, who drew up the terms of the Reinheitsgebot and their attitude was not altruistic.

The Bavarian royals drank wheat beer and they were determined that no one else should join them. The masses could make do with brown beers made from wood-cured malts but the princes and their families would enjoy the paler delights of wheat beer. The monarchy, in feudal fashion, held the monopoly to grow both barley and wheat, and refused to release wheat for brewing for the hoi polloi.

The Royal Court Brewery, the Hofbräuhaus, opened in Munich in 1589 to make wheat beer. At one stage there were 30 royal brewhouses in Bavaria dedicated to making the style for the aristocracy. Wheat beer only became available for general consumption in 1859, when the royal family licensed a Munich brewer named Georg Schneider to brew it: perhaps the royals were beginning to switch allegiance to the new lager beer brewed at Sedlmayr's Spaten brewery. Once wheat beer became available to the masses its sales soared. Schneider moved to new premises in the Tal (the Dale) close to Munich's Gothic town hall, the Rathaus, and demand forced him to open a second brewery at Kelheim in the heart of the Hallertau hop-growing region.

Many Bavarian brewers followed in Schneider's footsteps and added wheat beer to their range. But, by the late 20th century, the domination of the market by golden lager sent sales of wheat beer into steep and apparently terminal decline. In the 1970s, a German newspaper described it dismissively as a beer 'fit only for old ladies and those with nervous stomachs'. But a decade later, wheat beer enjoyed a remarkable revival. It was discovered by the young 'green generation', who believed that a beer sold mainly in bottle with natural yeast sediment and which was rich in protein was healthier than lager beer. Sales of wheat beer grew to such an extent that by the 1990s they accounted for 30% of the Bavarian beer market.

In spite of the name, wheat beer is made by a blend of wheat and barley malts. In Bavaria, wheat malt by law must make up at least half of the grain used in brewing wheat beer. Barley malt is essential, as it has a greater level of the enzymes that turn starch into fermentable sugar. Barley also has a husk that acts as a filter during mashing. Wheat is a huskless grain and is difficult to brew with, as it can become mushy and clog up the brewing vessels: the presence of barley malt in the mash prevents this happening. The main contribution wheat malt makes to beer is an appealing pale and hazy gold/yellow colour, and a characteristic aroma and flavour of spices and fruit: clove is the dominant spice, while apple and banana are typical fruit aromas.

Bavarian wheat beers also have a flavour characteristic that resembles bubblegum or Juicy Fruit. This is the result of the special yeast cultures used in its production. During fermentation, the yeast produces natural compounds called phenols and guaiacols that resemble the sap produced by tropical trees used in the manufacture of chewing gum. Hops are used sparingly, as bitterness and the floral and piny nature of hops do not blend well with the aromas and flavours produced by wheat and its special yeast cultures.

In Bavaria, the style is known either as Weizenbier—wheat beer—or Weisse, which means white and comes from the pale colour of the beer and its white collar of foam. In spite of the descriptor 'white', wheat beers come in dark—dunkel—versions as well as pale ones, and in varying strengths, including strong Weizenbocks. Most brewers produce two versions of wheat beers: Hefe or Mit Hefe, which means 'with yeast'; and Kristall or Ohne Hefe, which mean clear or without yeast. The unfiltered versions are by far the most popular and flavourful. Connoisseurs like to pour the beer slowly until the glass is almost full, then twirl the bottle and deposit the sediment of yeast in the glass. This is performed with great and even dramatic skill by experienced waiters.

*Visitors to Munich will find the original Hofbräuhaus at 9 Platzl. It is now owned by the government and no longer brews on the premises. Beer is supplied by a brewery on the outskirts of the city. The Schneider Weisshaus is at 10 Tal, close to the Marienplatz. The brewery was destroyed in World War Two and beer is now supplied by the Schneider brewery in Kelheim.

Berlin

When Napoleon's troops reached Berlin, they described the local wheat beers as the 'Champagne of the North'. It was a fitting and perceptive description, for the Chardonnay and Pinot grapes of the Champagne region produce such a tart wine that it becomes drinkable only as the result of a long, slow process in which a secondary fermentation in bottle involves some lactic activity and finally becomes sparkling. Berliner Weisse beers are so tart and lactic that drinkers add a dash of woodruff or raspberry syrup to cut the acidity. The style is traditionally low in alcohol, around 3%, is extremely pale in colour, has a light fruitiness and little hop aroma.

The origins of the style are unknown but one theory is that Huguenots fleeing persecution in the 16th and 17th centuries picked up the skill of brewing sour beer as they migrated north from France and Switzerland through Flanders, where they came across lambic and gueuze beers made by spontaneous fermentation.

Weisse was brewed by no fewer than 700 producers in the Berlin area at the height of its popularity. Today there are just two breweries left. The lactic cultures that work with a conventional warm-fermenting yeast to produce the style were isolated early in the 20th century by scientists who founded Berlin's university research and brewing school, the Versuchs und Lehranstadt für Brauerei, or VLB for short. The culture is named lactobacillus delbrücki after Professor Max Delbrück, the leading research scientist who studied the culture.

In Berlin bars, Weisse is served in a number of attractive glasses, some—most fittingly—shaped like a Champagne saucer. The beer is served with a Schuss, or shot of syrup, that, depending on the colour, will turn the beer red, green or amber: glasses of all three on the table will bring forth a joke among drinkers about traffic lights. Waiters will put a finger to the temple if you decline the syrup. My first-ever taste of Berliner Weisse was in a bar in Amsterdam, an equally cosmopolitan city to Berlin. I persuaded the waiter to serve it *au naturel*. It tasted like the health drink PLJ, or Pure Lemon Juice, and I was happy to add a shot of woodruff.

LEFT
The wheat beer from the Holy Stephen Brewery near Munich is highly regarded and comes from the oldest brewery in the world.

Berliner Kindl Weiss

Source: Berliner Kindl Brauerei, Neu Kölln, Berlin, Germany
Strength: 2.7%
Website: www.Berliner-kindl.de

The Kindl brewery dates from 1872 and is a magnificent example of the Bauhaus school of minimalist and functional architecture and design founded by Walter Gropius in 1919. Although the Nazis closed the Bauhaus school in 1933, the ideas live on in such masterpieces as Templehof airport and at Kindl. In fact, the copper vessels at the brewery were seized by the Russian Red Army and sent to the Soviet Union at the end of World War Two. But the plant was rebuilt along classic Bauhaus lines and copper was used rather than modern stainless steel.

Kindl uses well water, which is softened for brewing. The proportion of wheat malt is around 30%. Bitterness units measure a modest 10 from Northern Brewer hops, but the brewer is not looking for high bitterness. After mashing and boiling, the lactobacillus is added to start acidification, followed by a warm-fermenting yeast culture. Fermentation lasts for a week followed by several days of cold conditioning. The beer is then filtered, bottled with a fresh dosage of yeast and kräusened with partially fermented wort. The finished beer has a hazy pale gold colour with a complex and intriguing aroma of fresh lemons and rose petals. It is mouth-puckeringly acidic on the palate with a big lemon fruit bite and no discernible hop character. The finish is short, acidic and with a further blast of tart fruit.

The brewery is now part of the national Binding group but 'economies of scale' have not yet endangered weiss beer production.

TASTING NOTES
Appearance
Aroma
Taste
Overall score

Franziskaner Weissbier

Source: Gabriel Sedlmayr Spaten-Franziskaner-Bräu, Munich, Bavaria, Germany
Strength: 5%
Website: www.franziskaner.com

In Munich, the Spaten brewery has seen its world turned upside down. It is famous as the site where Gabriel Sedlmayr, a member of the ruling family, developed commercial lager brewing in the 19th century, but it now devotes half its capacity to wheat beer. They are sold under the Franziskaner label and have a separate website to avoid any confusion with Spaten's Pils and other lager brands.

The bottle labels for Franziskaner show a cheerful monk holding a mug of beer. The original wheat beer brewery was bought by Joseph Sedlmayr. The site dates from 1363 and was one of the oldest in Munich. It was next door to a Franciscan monastery, which gave its name and image to the beer. Joseph Sedlmayr eventually closed the site and merged with brother Gabriel's Spaten site. Production of wheat beer and lager are kept separate to avoid any cross fertilisation of yeast cultures.

Weissbier has a high wheat malt content of 75%. The brewers admit this can cause problems during mashing but they feel it gives a better flavour. The other Franziskaner beers, including Dunkel (dark) and Bock (strong) are made more conventionally from a 50:50 blend barley and wheat malts. A complex hop recipe is used of Orion, Perle, Spalt and Tettnang varieties. Fermentation takes place in conical vessels. The beer that emerges is centrifuged to remove the ale yeast and is re-seeded with a lager culture for bottle fermentation. Spaten is not alone in using a lager yeast in bottle, as brewers feel it gives greater stability and shelf life, though at some small cost to flavour. Still, the beer has a fruity aroma with hints of coriander. Creamy malt dominates the mouth but with powerful hints of spice and banana. The finish is long, quenching, spicy and fruity.

TASTING NOTES
Appearance
Aroma
Taste
Overall score

Hopf Export

Source: Hopf Weissbierbrauerei, Miesbach, Obberbayern, Bavaria, Germany
Strength: 5.3%
Website: www.hopsweisse.de

TASTING NOTES
Appearance
Aroma
Taste
Overall score

I have made many journeys in the quest for good beer but few have been more memorable than the trip from Munich to Miesbach in Obberbayern, or Upper Bavaria, a region of snow-capped mountains and deep, tree-fringed lakes. Hans Hopf, the owner of the family brewery, has a name marketing companies would drool over, for Hopf is almost identical to *Hopfen*, the German for hops. He even employs a brewmaster called Robert Weizbauer at a company that brews nothing but Weizenbier. And all this brilliant public relations comes free!

Hans's family started to brew in the Bavarian town of Garmish-Partenkirchen, where the arena for Hitler's Winter Olympics has been left as a grim reminder of that terrible period. The family moved to Miesbach in the 1930s. When I visited the brewery, production was running at 45,000 hectolitres (990,000 gallons) a year. Hans thinks that demand for his beers at home and abroad—they are available in the United States—will see volumes grow to 70,000 hectos (1½m gallons) but he would not want to go beyond that figure. He has a horror of getting too big and becoming prey to a bigger brewing combine. The brewhouse has already been extended to keep pace with demand, and old copper vessels nestle alongside modern stainless-steel ones.

Hans and Robert have access to the purest Alpine spring water and use French and German malts. Wheat malt accounts for 65% of the mash. Hops come from the Hallertau and are mainly the Spalt variety. The unusually shaped fermenting vessels look like a cross between Michelin men and the Daleks from the British TV science fiction series *Dr Who*. The stainless-steel vessels are closed save for openings like visors at the top, where the yeast can be seen vigorously at work. After primary fermentation, the beer in bottles and kegs is cooled to 10–15°C (50–59°F) to enable a second fermentation to start, encouraged by kräusening with wort from the brewhouse. The beer is kept at 12°C (54°F) for a week to purge diacetyl—

toffee flavours—and the temperature is then raised to 15°C (59°F) for three weeks. A blend of both top and bottom yeasts is used for secondary fermentation.

Hopf Export, the main brand, has 12 units of bitterness and a vast peppery and spicy aroma, overlain by banana and bubblegum. It is tart and spicy in the mouth, with rich and creamy malt, and has a long, quenching, fruity and spicy finish. Banana is very evident in the finish and is much relished in the bars in and round Miesbach.

Matilda Bay Redback

Source: Matilda Bay Brewing Company, North Fremantle, Western Australia, Australia

Strength: 4.8%

Website: www.matildabay.com.au

Matilda Bay was the creation of Philip Sexton, a former brewer with Swan. He installed a brewery in the Sail and Anchor pub in Fremantle in 1984 and created such demand for his beers that he opened the Matilda Bay micro-brewery in neighbouring Nedlands. In 1988, with Aus$4m of investment from the Carlton/Foster's group, a brand new brewery was added in Perth in a former Ford Motor Company building. The brewing equipment made a long journey, from the De Clerck brewery in northern France.

Matilda Bay was the first new brewery in Australia since World War Two and is thought to be the first to make wheat beer. Redback is named after a dangerous and extremely poisonous spider but the name did not deter drinkers. The refreshing nature of the beer in a hot country and its sharply different flavours from mainstream lagers created a large following. Redback is made from 65% malted wheat, grown in the Avon Valley with two-row barley malt (colour units eight). The hops are European Saaz and locally grown Pride of Ringwood (18 units of bitterness).

The beer has a fruity aroma with hints of spice and some gentle hop bitterness. Tart fruit and spices build in the mouth, with a rich creamy malt note. The finish is long with spices and tart fruit dominating, but there are some lingering light hop resins. In 1993, Redback was named Supreme Champion in the Australian International Beer Awards and it won a gold medal in the AIBA in 2003. The beer brewed in Western Australia is filtered but a new brewery in Melbourne produces a bottle-fermented version.

TASTING NOTES
Appearance
Aroma
Taste
Overall score

REDBACK & PRAWNS
~ AUSTRALIA'S CULINARY COAT OF ARMS ~

Schneider Weisse/Aventinus

Source: Privatbrauerei G Schneider & Sohn, Kelheim, Bavaria, Germany
Strength: 5.4%/8%
Website: www.Schneider-weisse.com

TASTING NOTES
Appearance
Aroma
Taste
Overall score

TASTING NOTES
Appearance
Aroma
Taste
Overall score

The Kelheim brewery is a curious but pleasing blend of Spanish and Gothic architecture. It was built in 1607 and is almost certainly the oldest continuous wheat beer brewery in the world. It is the tradition that the sons of the Schneider family are called Georg in order to maintain a link with the founder of the company. I met Georg V, his elegant wife Margareta who is in charge of public relations, and their son Georg VI, who, since my visit, has taken charge.

The brewery has open fermenters, a rare sight in Germany, where the fear of wild yeasts and contamination keeps most beers covered. Production is divided 90% for Weisse beer and 10% for Aventinus. Malts are blended in the proportion 60% wheat and 40% barley. Some Vienna and darks are added to give the Weisse its appealing bronze/copper colour. Hersbrucker hops from the neighbouring Hallertau are used in pellet form. Weisse has 14–15 units of bitterness. Water comes from local wells and is softened to remove some of the natural salts.

The modern brewhouse was installed in 1988 with stainless-steel mashing vessels and kettles standing on marble floors. In the fermenting hall, the atmosphere is ripe with fruity aromas as the yeast goes to work on the sugars. Banana is the most obvious of the Weisse aromas, with a powerful waft of apple as well. Fermentation lasts for between three and five days, after which the unfiltered beer is bottled at warm temperature. Yeast—the house culture, not a lager strain—and some unfermented wort are added. The beer is matured at 20°C (68°F) for a week. This produces a lively carbonation as secondary fermentation begins. The beer then has 14 days of cold conditioning at 8°C (46°F) to stabilise it. The beer that finally leaves the brewery has a pronounced banana,

cloves and nutmeg aroma with a tart, spicy and slightly acidic flavour in the mouth. The quenching finish has creamy malt, spices, fruit and gentle hop notes.

Aventinus is a Weizenbock, or strong wheat beer, with a label depicting Johannes Aventinus, the historian of Bavaria. The beer is bronze-red due to the use of caramalt (43 colour units) and has a rich spices, raisins and chocolate aroma and palate, with more spices, fruit and cloves in the finish. Schneider prefers its beers to be drunk within eight months but says they will remain in drinkable condition for eight years if they are kept cool in a dark place.

Georg Schneider VI told me Aventinus tastes like port wine after 25 years. He must have started drinking at an early age.

Schultheiss Berliner Weisse

Source: Schultheiss Brauerei, Hohenschönhausen, Berlin, Germany
Strength: 3%
Website: www.oetker.com

Since Berlin became one city again following the reunification of Germany, Schultheiss has closed two of its plants and moved production of its beers to a brewery dating from 1902 in the former eastern sector. The company became part of the national Brau und Brunnen group. In January 2004, the group's brewing interests, which includes a large brewery in Dortmund as well, was bought by the giant food and drinks combine Oetker. As Weisse accounts for a tiny proportion of Schultheiss's production, there is concern for the future of Berlin's second example of the style.

The beer is made by a blend of equal amounts of malted barley and wheat. Hallertau hop varieties create four to eight units of bitterness. Warm fermenting yeast and lactobacilli are blended together with a portion of wort that is between three and six months old. The blend encourages a lively fermentation that lasts for three or four days. The beer is warm conditioned for three to six months and is then kräusened and lactobacillus added for bottling. The result is an astonishingly complex, fruity, sour and quenching beer, with tart lemon fruit and floral notes on the aroma, stunning acidity and tangy fruit in the mouth and a dry, tart finish with more citrus fruit notes. As the beer is bottle fermented it will improve with age.

It would be tragedy if mergers in the German brewing industry were to rob drinkers of this classic beer. It would be advisable to lay in a stock and store it in a cellar.

Weihenstephaner Hefe Weissbier

Source: Weihenstephan Brauerei, Freising, Munich, Germany
Strength: 5.4%
Website: www.weihenstephaner.de

The 'Holy Stephen' brewery—the oldest brewery in the world—has already featured in this book with its superb Pilsener (see page 32). But it is primarily a wheat beer brewery and produces several versions of the style, including a Dunkel, or dark, beer and a filtered Kristall.

Its most revered beer is the unfiltered 'Hefe', or yeast beer. It is made from a blend of French and German barley and wheat malts, and is lightly hopped with varieties from the Hallertau region. The hazy orange/gold beer has a rich and tempting aroma of banana, cloves, nutmeg and gentle hop resins. Creamy malt fills the mouth, balanced by fruit and spices, with a long, refreshing, complex finish in which ripe malt competes with the growing influence of spices and fruit, with a late hint of hops.

The brewhouse is modern but the narrow windows with curved tops give an ecclesiastic touch that recalls the history of the complex of buildings that has been sacked, stripped of its religious roots, controlled by the Bavarian royal family and now by the state. One beer, Korbinian, recalls a legend about the founder of the monastery, an Irish Benedictine. He was en route to the Vatican when a bear ate his horse, which made the journey to Rome even more daunting. The monk, no doubt with some help from above, tamed the bear and made it carry his bags to the holy city. Today students make even longer journeys to the brewing faculty at Freising. It was encouraging to see young people from North America and the Far East attending classes and acquiring the skills to make good beer for future generations to enjoy.

TASTING NOTES
Appearance
Aroma
Taste
Overall score

TASTING NOTES
Appearance
Aroma
Taste
Overall score

Belgian-style Wheat Beers

While Bavarian wheat beers have enjoyed a remarkable recovery, their equivalents in Belgium have become cult drinks. The 'white beers' of the Brabant region—known as *bière blanche* or *wit bier*—were once a major beer style but it had all but disappeared until its fortunes were revived by Pierre Celis in the town of Hoegaarden.

Hoegaarden is a small town but in the 19th century it had no fewer than 30 breweries producing wheat beer. The town had its own brewers' guild and it exported its products to other parts of the Low Countries. Brabant has rich soil that produces an abundance of barley, oats and wheat, and farmers, peasants and monks took the products of the fields to fashion their beers. Monks were brewing in the region in the 15th century.

The beers took on a distinctive character when Dutch traders brought back spices from the east. The country known today as Belgium was part of the Netherlands at the height of Dutch seafaring, and spices and other exotic ingredients found their way into the cuisine of the Low Countries and its drinks. At a time when hops were used either sparingly or not at all in beer, coriander seeds and orange peel not only added spice but also countered the richness and inherent sweetness of malt. As in England, the habit of adding herbs and spices to beer continued for several centuries after the wide-scale adoption of the hop for bitterness.

The spices also balanced the sourness of the early white beers, which were made by spontaneous fermentation, allowing wild yeasts to turn malt sugars into alcohol. This style of natural fermentation survives in the lambic and gueuze beers of the Senne Valley area but it was once in wider use. White beers were also fermented in wood where they would have picked up additional sour notes from lactobacilli.

White beers today are brewed conventionally using warm-fermenting ale yeast cultures. The success of Hoegaarden has been a double-edged sword: it has brought the world's attention to the cloudy, quenching, spicy and complex beers of Belgium but, in an age of slick marketing and big brewers' insatiable quest for ever bigger volumes, it has also led to beers with less character in order to appeal to drinkers who find complexity too challenging.

As in Bavaria, the labelling of Belgian wheat beers can be confusing. As well as *bière blanche* or *wit bier*, they are also known as *bière de froment* or *tarwebier*, the French and the Flemish respectively for wheat beer.

LEFT
The symbol of a snail on the label suggests Troublette is slow brewed. It is an excellent example of the new breed of spicy Belgian wheat beers.

Abbaye des Rocs Blanche des Honnelles

Source: Brasserie de l'Abbaye des Rocs, Montignies-sur-Roc, Belgium
Strength: 6%
Website: www.abbaye-des-rocs.com

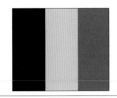

In spite of the impressive name, this is not a monastic brewery. It began life in the garage of the owner of a farm that, centuries ago, was a monastery: there are still a few ruins in the vicinity. The brewery is in a village in Hainaut province, close to Mons and the French border.

From tiny beginnings, the brewery has grown and for a time was run as a co-operative but has since been turned into a limited company. It is best known for its Abbaye des Rocs abbey beer, one of the better examples of beers that trade on the Trappist tradition.

All the beers are unfiltered and re-ferment in the bottle, and they also use pure local well water with no sugars or additives. Abbaye des Rocs has restored the tradition of using malted oats in its wheat beer, which adds a smooth, creamy and slightly oily note. It is strong for the style, is a hazy blond colour and has an appetising aroma of ripe or even overripe fruit, with orange and lemon to the fore. Hops give a pronounced peppery note to the aroma and palate, and the finish lingers, with delicious tangy fruit (orange-and-lemon slices) and juicy and creamy malt. The beer is named after two small local rivers called the Honnelles.

TASTING NOTES
Appearance
Aroma
Taste
Overall score

Caracole Troublette

Source: Brasserie la Caracole, Falmignoul, Belgium
Strength: 5%
Website: www.caracole.be

The snail (*caracole*) symbol used on the label of La Caracole's beers does not suggest that trouble is brewing, but troublette is a brewing term implying haze, or turbidity, in beer. Perhaps the snail—the symbol of the Namur region—was too slow to get the proteins out of the beer.

The brewery was founded by childhood friends Jean-Pierre Debras and François Tonglet in 1990 in Namur, but four years later they moved to Falmignoul in the Meuse Valley near Dinant. They found an ancient brewery dating from around 1776 that last brewed in 1971. The friends painstakingly restored the site and still use wood-fired mash tuns and coppers, with help from the plentiful supply of wood in the Ardennes forest. Wood, says Debras, a graduate of Leuven University's brewing faculty, has to be used with enormous care: if it flares, it will caramelise the brewing sugars and darken beers that are meant to be pale. La Troublette comes in two versions: regular and 'bio', or organic. The regular beer is brewed with pale malt and Saaz and Styrian hops varieties, while organic Spalt from Germany go into the bio version. Both beers are unfiltered and re-ferment in the bottle. They have a luscious tart and tangy lemon fruit aroma and palate, with a perfumy hop note that leads to some dryness in the finish. The Spalt hops give a spicier note to the bio beer. Both beers are wonderfully quenching.

TASTING NOTES
Appearance
Aroma
Taste
Overall score

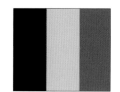

Du Bocq Blanche de Namur

Source: Brasserie du Bocq, Purnode, Belgium
Strength: 4.5%
Website: www.bocq.be

TASTING NOTES
Appearance
Aroma
Taste
Overall score

Blanche de Namur is named after a princess from the Namur province who became the Queen of Sweden. I think Greta Garbo once starred in a film about her.

The beer comes from a brewery that, in common with many in Belgium, started life as a farm. In 1858, Martin Belot decided to brew beer for his family and farm workers, using grains from the field and pure water from a spring. It is still family-owned and fiercely independent today. After World War One, sales grew when du Bocq (the name comes from the local river) launched a brown ale called La Gaulloise. Farming stopped in 1960 as the family concentrated on its brewing operations. Production currently runs at 60,000 hectolitres (1.3m gallons) a year.

Blanche de Namur is brewed with malted barley and wheat, and spiced with coriander and bitter orange peel, with Belgian and German hop varieties. It has just five units of colour and 12 units of bitterness. In common with all the beers, Blanche de Namur is cold conditioned in the brewery for three to five weeks following fermentation, then bottled and warm conditioned for a few more weeks. It has a pleasing bouquet of coriander, bitter oranges and spicy hops. Mellow malt builds in the mouth with spices and orange fruit, while the lingering finish is deeply refreshing, with creamy malt, tangy spice and tart fruit. The brewery is open to visitors: see website.

Hoegaarden

Source: Brouwerij Hoegaarden, Hoegaarden, Belgium
Strength: 5%
Website: www.InBev.com

The brand is so famous that it no longer needs to be called Wit: just Hoegaarden will do. This is the beer that rekindled the Belgian white beer phenomenon but, in so doing, a small craft brewery became part of a large Belgian group, Interbrew, that in turn became the world's biggest brewer, InBev.

In the 1960s, Pierre Celis, a milkman in Hoegaarden, who had done some part-time work as a child in the Tomsin brewery in the town, was musing over the loss of that brewery with friends in a bar and decided to start his own brewery. He opened on the site of a former farm and was scrupulous about using a true Brabant recipe: malted barley, unmalted wheat, oats, milled coriander seeds and dried Curaçao orange peel, with East Kent Goldings and Saaz hops. The beer quickly acquired cult status among students in nearby Leuven and then spread throughout Belgium and on to the Netherlands, France and Britain.

Following a fire at the site, Celis took financial help from Interbrew to rebuild it. It would be unfair on him to call the arrangement a Faustian pact, but Interbrew ended up controlling the company, while Celis left for Texas to launch a new brewery in the unlikely setting of Austin. As sales of Hoegaarden soared, Interbrew pumped money into the brewery. The artisan brewhouse on the ground floor, with attractive burnished copper vessels, has been joined by more modern and functional stainless-steel vessels on the first floor. Oats have been dropped from the grist, which is now comprised of 55% barley malt and 45% unmalted wheat. The hops create around 20

TASTING NOTES
Appearance
Aroma
Taste
Overall score

units of bitterness. Coriander seeds and orange peel are milled to coarse powders and added with the hops during the copper boil. Following fermentation, the green beer is warm conditioned for a month, primed with sugar and a dosage of fresh yeast, and then bottled or kegged. The beer has an appetising spicy nose with a clear hint of orange. It is tart and refreshing in the mouth, followed by a clean, bitter-sweet finish with hints of apple and orange zest.

Hoegaarden can be enjoyed in the smart Kouterhof bar and restaurant that is part of the brewery complex: for information on the restaurant and brewery visits, phone 016 769 811. The beer is undoubtedly less characterful than in the early days but at least InBev continues to brew it. InBev did close the brewery for a short time and moved production to one of its lager factories. This caused such outrage in Belgium that InBev quickly reopened the Hoegaarden brewery.

Unibroue Blanche de Chambly
Source: Brasserie Unibroue, Chambly, Montréal, Québec, Canada
Strength: 5%
Website: www.unibroue.com

TASTING NOTES
Appearance
Aroma
Taste
Overall score

The first beer brewed by Unibroue in 1992 was this interpretation of a Belgian white beer. The founders worked closely with the Riva group from Belgium, best known for its Liefman's brown ales (see page 45) but which also produces a widely available white beer called Dentergems. The end result of the consultation was Blanche de Chambly, the success of which enabled the company to move to bigger premises and an enlarged brewhouse and fermenting capacity.

The beer is brewed with pale barley malt and unmalted wheat from Québec. The beer is lightly hopped, and spices and other aromatics are added during the copper boil. The beer is unfiltered and ferments in bottle. It is a pale, hazy yellow-gold colour, throws a big fluffy head of foam and has a superb aroma of tart lemon fruit, rich malt and heady spices. Citrus fruit and spices build in the mouth, with some light floral hop notes. Creamy malt is evident in the long, quenching finish, with spices and aromatics balancing the dominant citrus lemon character.

On the back of the success of Blanche de Chambly and the subsequent beers, Unibroue has expanded aggressively and has set up distributors in France (Unibroue France) and the United States (Unibrew USA).

Belgian Sour Red Beer

Just as lambic and gueuze beers are confined to the region of the Senne Valley, the sour red beers are a speciality of West Flanders. They are beers with sharp and stunning flavours, the result of maturation in unlined oak vessels. They are also mysterious beers: nobody is certain where the style originated. While sour red beers are fermented with brewers' yeast cultures rather than wild yeasts, there are nevertheless similarities with lambic and gueuze. On the other hand, before the Industrial Revolution transformed brewing, the practice of storing beer in oak vessels was widespread and was certainly not confined to the Low Countries. It is an intriguing thought that it may have been a visit to England and its porter brewers that encouraged the development of the style.

Rodenbach Grand Cru

Source: Brouwerij Rodenbach, Roeselare, Belgium
Strength: 6%
Website: www.rodenbach.be

My first-ever taste of Rodenbach Grand Cru was in a restaurant in Ostend. A fellow Brit warned me: 'You may not like it—it's very sour'. But it was a case of love at first sip. Ever since, in bars and restaurants in several countries, I will call for a Rodenbach if it is available, for I delight in its tart and refreshing character.

The brewery is in the canalside town of Roeselare (Roulers in French) and the beer is the result of long maturation in unlined oak tuns. Here is yet another link with brewing's past: this is a beer that is deliberately allowed to stale from the action of wild yeasts and other micro-organisms.

The Rodenbachs are German in origin, from near Koblenz. Ferdinand Rodenbach was stationed in the Low Countries as a military surgeon when the region was under Austrian rule and he decided to settle there. The Rodenbachs threw themselves with great energy into all aspects of Belgian life, including the struggle for independence.

In 1820, Alexander Rodenbach, who was blind, bought a small brewery in Roeselare. In the 1870s, another member of the family, Eugene, went to England to study brewing techniques and his experience encouraged him to develop the stale, aged beer that is the company's hallmark.

There has been considerable speculation about which breweries Rodenbach visited. It has been suggested that he might have gone to Greene King in Suffolk, where the soured Strong Suffolk Ale is brewed (see page 127).

On one visit to Rodenbach, I took some bottles of Strong Suffolk with me for a comparative tasting. As a result, the two breweries have struck up friendly links but Rodenbach says there is nothing in the archives to suggest Eugene Rodenbach visited Greene King. The company believes he may instead have gone to the Tyneside region of North-east England. My research suggests that he probably went to the large brewery owned by John Barras, founded in Gateshead in 1770 and which moved to Newcastle in 1860 and later became part of Newcastle Breweries. Barras produced a renowned Porter that was stored for a full 12 months in wooden tuns. As the early porters were tawny or brown rather than black, I feel there is a strong possibility that the inspiration for Rodenbach's beer was the historic English style.

Rodenbach's St George's Brewery is a handsome complex on Spanjestraat. The grounds are dominated by an old malt kiln, which has been turned into a museum. Well water comes

TASTING NOTES
Appearance
Aroma
Taste
Overall score

from underground springs beneath a lake on the other side of the road, where the brewer lives in some style in a chateau provided by the company.

The beer is made from a blend of pale malts from both spring and winter varieties, and slightly darker Vienna malt that gives the beer its reddish hue. Malts make up 80% of the grist, the rest comes from corn grits. German Brewers Gold and Kent Goldings hops are used: both are low in bitterness and high in aroma. Rodenbach uses them chiefly for their preservative qualities, as it does not want too high a level of bitterness, which would not marry well with the tartness of the beer. A multi-strain warm-fermenting yeast culture carries out primary fermentation over seven days, after which the beer has a second fermentation in metal tanks.

The beer for ageing that becomes Grand Cru is then stored in ceiling-high oak tuns for at least 18 months and often as long as two years. There are more than 10 halls of giant, red-hooped tuns that stand on raised brick bases. The staves of each tun are numbered and a small army of coopers is kept busy repairing the vessels. The insides of the tuns are scraped regularly to keep the correct balance of tannins and caramels present in the oak. During the long rest in wood, lactobacilli and acetobacters are busy adding a sour, lactic quality to the beer.

Two beers are produced. Rodenbach Klassiek (5%) is a blend of fresh young beer and stale. It has a sour, winey aroma, is tart and quenching in the mouth, with more sour fruit in the finish. Grand Cru (units of colour 60, bitterness 14–18) is bottled straight from the oak tuns. The beer is bigger in all respects: oaky, woody, tannic and fruity with hints of vanilla. It is flash pasteurised. I have argued without success for an unpasteurised, bottle-fermented version. The beer is not only a superb companion for food but makes a formidable contribution to cooking.

In 1999, the Rodenbach family sold the company to the big ale brewery of Palm. This created fears about the future of the brands and, for a while, quality and consistency dipped. But more recently Grand Cru is back to its best and, with sales to the rest of Europe, the United States and Japan, it seems unlikely that Palm will lose this treasured brewery and its classic, historic beer.

Bières de Garde

Most of the beer consumed in France comes in the form of the unremarkable lagers of the Strasbourg region, with its Germanic roots and disputed boundaries. But many French people have discovered that in the flat lands between Calais and Lille there is a different tradition of farmhouse ales called bières de garde.

Translated into English, 'beer to keep' is identical to the German lager, meaning 'store'. However, the stored beers of northern France, in the Nord-Pas de Calais (comprising Artois, Flanders and Picardy), have different roots that pre-date rather than chime with the Industrial Revolution of the 19th century. Like the saisons of neighbouring Wallonia (see page 208), they were beers brewed in February and March and stored in wooden casks for summer drinking by farmers, their families and workers. In both the Calais region and in French-speaking Wallonia, farm labourers were once paid in kind, with beer and potatoes.

The French take beer seriously in an area that not only shares a common border with the Belgians but also where Flemish names abound and Lille was once the capital of medieval Flanders. One of the best known of the bières de garde brewers, Duyck, stresses the Flemish roots. Every summer, the people of Douai take to the streets for a festival celebrated with beer, a choice of drink that no doubt causes disbelief in wine-growing areas. But this is a vast area, with its flat landscape, lowering skies, marshes and rivers, that provides the essential ingredients for beer, not wine: fields of barley and hop orchards that straddle the border with Belgium. Beer is the natural drink of the people. They eat with it, they cook with it, and they welcome such special seasonal brews as Bière de mars (March beer) and Bière de Noël (Christmas beer) as joyously as Beaujolais Nouveau is greeted further south.

Beer was brewed not only for farm labourers but also for coal miners. The Lille area was once the great mining region of France but all the pits have closed and the beers of the region almost disappeared along with them. Two world wars in the 20th century ravaged Flanders and Picardy. Fields and breweries were destroyed. Invading armies took away copper vessels for the 'war effort'. The fields and their produce recovered but many of the brewery owners could not afford the costs of repair and were wary of new methods of brewing. At the same time, the big lager brewers of Strasbourg broke free of the region and began to dominate the whole of France. Today, Kronenbourg (owned by Scottish & Newcastle of Britain), Heineken from the Netherlands and InBev from everywhere on the planet have a stranglehold on beer consumption in France.

The beers of the north revived as a result of the worldwide interest in Belgian beers, a rediscovery of pride in the Pas de Calais, its history and cuisine, and the cult status of the Jenlain beers from Duyck among students in Lille from the 1970s. A consumer movement, Les Amis de la Bière (the Friends of Beer), was formed in 1986 to promote the products of the region. Being French, les Amis firmly reject any suggestion that they were inspired by CAMRA in Britain, but I suspect some cross-channel inspiration took place. As a result, existing breweries found encouragement and new producers sprang up to meet a demand for genuine French beer at home and abroad.

Bières de Garde are no longer seasonal brews, though such specialities as March and Christmas beers are by definition. A true member of the style should be made by warm fermentation, though some brewers use lager cultures but ferment at ale temperatures, or they may use lager yeast for bottle conditioning: as with some Bavarian wheat beer brewers, they talk in modern marketing terms about 'stability' and 'shelf life'. It is difficult to keep track of who uses what, as brewers seem to recant from time to time and return to the true path of traditional methods and ale yeasts. The beers are rich, malt accented, often spicy but not especially bitter. They come in blonde (pale), ambrée (amber), brune (brown) and rousse (russet) forms. Most importantly, in a vast country ground between the two millstones of wine and German-style lager, bières de garde have survived and revived.

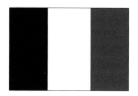

TASTING NOTES

Appearance	
Aroma	
Taste	
Overall score	

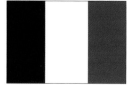

TASTING NOTES

Appearance	
Aroma	
Taste	
Overall score	

Annoeullin Pastor Ale

**Source: Brasserie d'Annoeullin,
Annouellin, France
Strength: 6.5%
Website: None**

To find this rustic brewery, you enter through a courtyard off the town's square named in honour of General de Gaulle, who was born in Lille. Typically of the area, the brewery, founded in 1905, was once a farm, and owner Bertrand Leper's wife Yolande comes from another farm brewery at Flers. When they married, they merged the two breweries, a sort of exchange of rings writ large.

In common with many farm breweries in both France and Belgium, the mash tun doubles as the boiling copper. After mashing, the wort is clarified in a separate vessel and then returns to the tun to be boiled with hops. Fermentation takes place in horizontal tanks in cellars that were once cattle byres. Primary fermentation lasts a week, followed by two weeks of cold conditioning—*la garde*. Only pale malt is used in Pastor Ale, with Flemish and Saaz hops.

The Lepers had to revive the fortunes of a brewery that had existed for years on brewing weak table beer for families and even weaker, 2% beer for schools. He said that when the school beer was discontinued, truancy increased. In the mid-1970s, he formulated a strong bière de garde that became popular and turned the brewery into a profitable concern. Pastor Ale has nothing to do with clerics but is a pun on pastorale and the country origins of the brewery. For a time the label carried the line '*C'est une symphonie*', with a bow towards Beethoven's Pastorale Symphony, but the delightful joke has been discontinued.

The beer is golden with pronounced orange fruit and earthy hops on the nose, more tangy fruit in the mouth balanced by juicy malt, and a complex finish that is dry, fruity, malty and quite hoppy and bitter for the style. The brewery also produces a superb wheat beer called L'Angelus. Cases of beer can be bought from the brewery shop. Smaller quantities, along with other beers from the region, can be obtained from Aux Caves d'Annoeullin in the town square.

Castelain Ch'ti Blonde

**Source: Brasserie Castelain,
Bénifontaine, near Lens, France
Strength: 6.4%
Website: www.www.chti.com**

The word ch'ti is Picardy dialect, a corruption of '*c'est toi*', which roughly translates as 'it suits you'. In common usage, it has come to mean anybody or anything from this part of northern France. The brewery, as is typical in the region, started life on a farm in 1926. The Castelain family bought it in 1966 and Roland handed it on to his children Yves and Annick in the mid-1970s. It was a difficult time for small breweries. Many were closing, unable to withstand the onslaught of Strasbourg lagers. The brewery produced a weak beer of around 2% for miners to down in vast amounts after a shift underground. The small museum has a poster for the beer showing a grinning miner grasping a foaming pint with a slogan announcing it is a beer made for the workers by the workers. But the mines and the workers' way of life were disappearing and Yves Castelain knew he had to find a new audience for his beer in order to survive. In 1978, he brewed a strong, pale Christmas beer called Ch'ti, matured for eight weeks. It was well received and a year later became a regular brew. All the old beers were unceremoniously dumped, though the miner in his helmet remained on the label of Ch'ti. Amber and brown versions of Ch'ti followed.

The brewery today has attractive copper vessels in tiled surrounds, visible from the road outside. Ironically, the road is called rue Pasteur: Yves makes a point of not pasteurising his beers. A wooden carving of Saint Arnold, the patron saint of brewers, guards the brewhouse. Yves marks the saint's importance by also producing a Belgian-style abbey beer named in his honour. Ch'ti Blonde accounts for 60% of the brewery's production. Water comes from a well on site that is 40 metres deep. It is brewed with four malts of the French Esterel and Scarlett varieties in pale, Munich, caramalt and torrefied forms. The hop varieties are Flemish and German Hallertauer varieties, used for aroma rather than bitterness. The beer is fermented with a lager yeast culture but at a relatively warm temperature of 14°C (57°F). Primary fermentation lasts for eight days, and *la garde* (cold conditioning) for a minimum of six weeks. It is then filtered and bottled in attractive containers with drawn corks and wire cradles. The blonde has a rich biscuity, perfumy hop and citrus fruit aroma, with fruit and malt dominating the palate, followed by a lingering finish that is bitter-sweet with notes of tart fruit, juicy malt and spicy hops.

The brewery has grown from 3,000 hectolitres (66,000 gallons) in 1978 to 35,000 today. Sadly, the miner on the label went from black to grey and has now disappeared altogether.

La Choulette Ambrée
Source: Brasserie la Choulette,
Hordain, France
Strength: 7.5%
Website: www.lachoulette.com

Alain Dhaussy has a passion not only for beer but also for the traditions of this part of France between Cambrai and Valenciennes. One of the traditions is a game called *la crosse en plain*, a type of golf in which a wooden ball, *la choulette*, is belted across the countryside. It was described in great detail by Zola in *Germinal* and inspired the French-Canadian game lacrosse. There are clubs and balls on display in the brewery's tasting room.

La Choulette is based in the former Bourgeois-Lecerf brewery, which dates from 1885. The owners made the disastrous decision to convert to lager production. They quickly discovered that the big lager brewers from Strasbourg could make it not necessarily better but cheaper, and they tied bars through loans and discounts. Alain, who had trained with a brewery in Douai, bought the redundant brewery in 1977, complete with attractive copper vessels in tiled surrounds.

His first beer was La Choulette Ambrée, launched in 1981 and still his biggest seller. Pale, Munich and caramalts are used, along with hops from Flanders and the German Hallertau. The russet-coloured beer throws a big fluffy head and has a spicy (coriander?), earthy hop resins and toffee-malt bouquet. Rich, slightly burnt grain and raisin fruit fill the mouth with a gentle hop balance. The finish is long and complex, bitter-sweet to begin but with a spicy dryness at the end, balanced by vinous fruits and chewy malt.

Alain is also a keen supporter of the French Revolution. He is equally famous for a golden Bière des Sans Culottes (6.5%), which honours the foot soldiers of the revolution, the urban poor who wore trousers, as they could not afford the culottes or silk breeches of the aristocracy. There is also an 8% Brassin Robespierre, which conjures forth jokes about not drinking too much of it in case you lose your head. In the fashion of the region, the beers are sold in attractive corked and cradled bottles.

TASTING NOTES
Appearance
Aroma
Taste
Overall score

Duyck Jenlain Ambrée

Source: Brasserie Duyck, Jenlain, France
Strength: 6.5%
Website: www.duyck.com

TASTING NOTES
Appearance
Aroma
Taste
Overall score

This is the beer that put bière de garde on the map as a classic style. It was known simply as Jenlain—the name of the village near Valenciennes—for many years but 'ambrée' was added when other Jenlain beers were added.

Four generations of the Duyck family have been involved in brewing. Léon Duyck was a farmer in Zeggers-Cappel in Flanders who added brewing to his other duties. He passed on his passion for beer to his son, Félix, who built a new brewery in farm buildings at Jenlain in 1922. He produced a bière de garde that eventually acquired the name Jenlain in the 1960s, when his son Robert took over. Robert was responsible for a considerable expansion of the site, which, now controlled by yet another son, Raymond, produces 90,000 hectolitres (2m gallons) a year. In spite of the size of the operation, every effort has been made to preserve the country farmhouse feel of the brewery, with production in traditional copper vessels.

Malts from Flanders, Champagne and Burgundy are used, along with four hop varieties from Belgium, France, Germany and Slovenia (25 units of bitterness). The russet-coloured beer has a spicy and fruity aroma, with biscuit malt, hints of vanilla and raisins in the mouth, and a long, complex finish that becomes dry with good spicy hops notes, tart fruit and sappy malt. For a time, Duyck experimented with lager yeast but has returned to the true path with an ale culture. The beer is filtered but not pasteurised and is sold throughout the world in attractive 75cl Champagne bottles with wired corks.

An abbey-style beer has joined the portfolio, along with Jenlain seasonal brands. In 2000, Duyck launched a Jenlain Blonde that was marketed in Britain as 'a lager-style beer'. After protests from myself and other beer writers, this affront to the noble heritage of classic French beer was withdrawn.

St Sylvestre 3 Monts

Source: Brasserie de St Sylvestre, St Sylvestre-Cappel, France
Strength: 8.5%
Website: www.brasserie-st-sylvestre.com

There is no doubting that we are in French Flanders, with *cappel* (chapel) in the name, in a village between Steenvorde and Hazebrouck, close to the border with Belgium. This is hop-growing country, and brewery owner Serge Ricour buys half the annual crop for his beers. Once again, we encounter the dry, ironic humour of the region. There are no mountains in this flat area. The 'three mountains' in the beer's name are no more than slight bumps but they are celebrated by the locals as if they were the Flemish version of the Alps. The hills are Monts des Cats, des Rocollets and Casel. Monts des Cats once had a Trappist monastery with its own brewery, so there is a rich tradition of beer in the area.

St Sylvestre is a fine example of an artisanal farm brewery that dates from 1860. It was inherited by Rémy Ricour from his uncle in 1920 and it has been handed down to his son,

Pierre, and then on to the next generation represented by Pierre's sons Christophe and Serge. They introduced 3 Monts in 1985 and it has become one of the biggest selling and best-known members of the bière de garde family.

It is made with extremely pale Pilsner malt and some brewing sugar, and hopped with local Brewers Gold and German Hallertauer varieties. It is gold coloured, with a fruity, winey aroma balanced by biscuity malt and spicy hop resins. Tart vinous fruit, juicy malt and spicy hops fill the mouth, while the big finish has great length, with an enormous fruity, vinous note balanced by earthy hop resins and creamy malt. The beer is filtered but not pasteurised and comes in the familiar corked and cradled Champagne-style bottle. The brewery also produces an abbey-style beer called Bière des Templiers, which is bottle fermented, and seasonal March and Christmas beers.

TASTING NOTES
Appearance
Aroma
Taste
Overall score

Saison

In French-speaking Wallonia they feel their beers, with the exception of Trappist ales, are overlooked and underrated. They complain that all the attention goes to the beers brewed in the Flemish-speaking areas. Neglect can lead to decline and it would be tragic if the beers of the region were to disappear, especially the style known as saison.

In recent years, there has been some recovery of interest, with small brewers starting to export to other countries and winning acclaim for products with a fascinating tradition. Saisons, by definition, are seasonal beers. They were originally brewed—and in some cases are still brewed—by farmers who made them in the winter months and stored them for summer drinking. The style, the breweries and the tradition have powerful links with the bières de garde across the nominal border with the Nord-Pas de Calais province of France, though saisons tend to have more hop character and occasionally use spices. Saisons are warm fermented, often incorporate dark malts, have generous hop rates and a big fruity character. The more commercially minded of the producers now make them on a regular basis.

I have stayed several times in the fine city of Tournai, with its awesome cathedral, as a base for visiting the local breweries, all of them tiny and artisanal. They are continung a tradition from the 19th and early 20th centuries, when saisons were brewed to meet a variety of needs: to refresh farm labourers and as drinks to accompany family meals. In common with the beers from French Flanders, there were even extremely weak beers made for schoolchildren, a habit that would cause outrage in education circles today.

A typical saison would be quenching and at the same time brewed to leave some unfermented sugars in the beer to help restore lost energy. Research indicates that some brewers would allow their worts to acetify to give the beer a lactic tang, which gives the style common cause with both the early white beers of the Flemish area, the lambics of the Senne Valley and, further afield, the early Porters in England.

RIGHT
Saison Dupont, from a farm brewery near Tournai, is regarded as arguably the best example of a Belgian saison, or seasonal, ale.

Saison Dupont

Source: Brasserie Dupont, Tourpes-Leuze, Belgium
Strength: 6.5%
Website: www.brasserie-dupont.com

Dupont is acclaimed as the classic brewer of saison. It dates from 1844 when it was a farm brewery known as Rimaux-Deridder. Louis Dupont bought the site in 1920 and gave it to his son to run to persuade him from emigrating to Canada. Today, Marc Rosier, the grandson of Louis, runs the business with his sisters and other members of the extended family. The brewery, set among buildings that surround a cobbled courtyard, still has the feel of a farm, though a statuette of Saint Arnold indicates there is beer to watch over. An on-site well provides good quality, hard water. The brewhouse is filled with steam when mashing is underway in an open vessel that also acts as the boiling copper, another Belgian farm-brewery tradition when space is limited.

With the exception of a Pils-type lager, all the Dupont beers are bottle conditioned and are stored for six to eight weeks at a warm temperature before they are released. 6,500 hectolitres (143,000 gallons) are produced a year, and the flagship brand is Saison Dupont, with the subsidiary name of Vieille Provision, or Old Provision, which recalls the time when the beer was part of the farm's nutrition and diet. It is brewed with Pilsner malt only and hopped with East Kent Goldings and Styrian Goldings. Before warm conditioning, it is re-seeded with fresh yeast and brewing sugar. The hazy orange-gold beer has a fluffy collar of foam and a big peppery Goldings bouquet balanced by toasted malt. Hops, tart fruit and juicy malt dominate the palate, followed by a long and complex finish with a big spicy hop note, sappy malt and light fruit notes.

The Duponts acquired the neighbouring Moinette farm, which produces cheese, pâté and bread, some with beer included. Moinette means little monk and the name comes from a monastery that once stood in the area. Marc has added Moinette Blonde and Brune to his portfolio. There are also organic ('bio') versions of the beers, including the Saison.

Saison de Pipaix

Source: Brasserie à Vapeur, Pipaix, Belgium
Strength: 6.5%
Website: www.vapeur.com

Pistons clank and pulleys heave in this amazing farm steam (*vapeur*) brewery in a village that is also home to Dubuisson. The site, which included a farm and a maltings, has been traced back to the late 18th century. Power for the mash mixer and rakes in the present brewery is provided by a steam engine installed in 1885. Other equipment dates from the early 20th century.

The brewery closed in the 1980s and was rescued by two schoolteachers, Jean-Louis Dits and his wife, Anne-Marie Lemaire. The couple eventually took over the Pipaix site and worked at weekends to restore the equipment, while they continued to teach. Their first commercial beer was a saison, based on a beer produced by the former owners. Tragedy struck the new concern when Anne-Marie was killed in an accident in the brewery. Jean-Louis struggled on with the help of his two daughters, one of whom is keen to take over as manager in due course. Jean-Louis has since remarried and his new wife, Vinciane Corbisier, runs an on-site shop selling ingredients to bakers, home brewers and cheese makers.

Jean-Louis has developed a passion for spices and herbs over the years. During one visit, I was taken through a range of beers in a building like a large garden shed. This included a quite remarkable beer brewed with the addition of ginger. Today his saison includes six 'botanicals', including anis, black pepper, orange peel and medicinal lichen. He uses two or three malts and East Kent Goldings. In the old Wallonian style, he allows his mash in an open tun to gain some lactic character before the copper boil. The beer is not filtered in bottle and will improve with age. I have tasted several vintages and noticed how, over the years, it gained in depth of character, with tart orange and lemon fruit, the 'horse blanket' aroma of wild yeasts, with surprising malty sweetness in the mouth, and a shatteringly dry finish with hops and spices balancing the tart, sour fruit and rich honey malt. A magnificent beer in memorable surroundings.

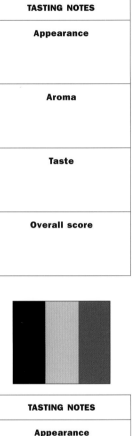

TASTING NOTES
Appearance
Aroma
Taste
Overall score

TASTING NOTES
Appearance
Aroma
Taste
Overall score

Alt & Amber Beers

Germany enjoys such renown and respect for its lagers that it comes as a shock to many people to discover other styles in that country. We have already seen how the wheat beers of Bavaria, members of the ale family, have enjoyed a major revival. Now, further north, beers made by warm fermentation are acquiring greater appreciation and are being reinterpreted abroad, in the United States in particular, where a substantial number of people are of German descent. The style is often called Amber in the US.

'Alt' means old in German. In the context of beer, it means a style that predates the introduction of lagering and cold fermentation on a commercial scale in the 19th century. While Alt—sometimes labelled Altbier—is brewed in small amounts in Hanover and Münster, its traditional home is the city of Düsseldorf in North Rhine-Westphalia. Close to both the Dutch and Belgian borders, Düsseldorf was once a major coal-mining area. This may explain some similarity between the Alt beers of the city and the saisons of Wallonia and the bières de garde of Northern France: they were fashioned to refresh people after a hard day's labour at the coal face or in the fields. With their copper colour, Alt beers are also similar to British bitter or pale ale, but the resemblance should not be exaggerated. This is a classic style in its own right and its growing popularity in its heartland and throughout Germany suggests that younger people do not consider Old beer to be fit only for wrinklies. (In the United States, the style is often represented by the name Amber, a reference to the colour of the beer, rather than the type of malt used.)

Just as English bitter or pale ale will vary from brewery to brewery, there is no such thing as a typical Alt beer. Pale malt, usually of the Pilsner type, may be blended with Munich or even a tiny proportion of black malt. Fermenters may be open or closed, and both infusion and decoction mashing are used. The aim is for a firm, rounded maltiness underscored by generous aromatic hoppiness. The beers will be stored for up to a month before being released to trade.

Of all my quests for good beer, few have been more pleasurable than my search for Alt beer in Düsseldorf with its charming cobbled town centre lit by gas lamps. It is known as the Altstadt, or Old Town, a fitting name for an area with several brew pubs that specialise in Alt. Im Füschen, the Little Fox, in Ratinger Street, is a vast, cavernous building with red-tiled floors, and wooden benches and tables, where pork dishes are served alongside small glasses of Alt that come straight from casks on the bar. The beer is served by its own natural gas and as soon as one cask is drained, another is delivered by a dumb waiter to the bar. Zum Schlüssel, the Key, is in Bolker Street, birthplace of the poet Heinrich Heine. The copper brewing vessels can be seen through a window at the back. A local at the bar raised his glass and confided in me: 'After the fifth one you start to taste it.' It is not just the British who underestimate their greatest achievements.

Alaskan Amber

Source: Alaskan Brewing Company, Juneau, Alaska, USA
Strength: 5%
Website: www.alaskanbeer.com

It's a long way from Düsseldorf to Alaska but German emigrants reached even the remotest parts of the United States. In the case of the most northerly state of the union, the German presence in Alaska was almost certainly due to the Gold Rush, where the prospectors' thirst for gold was matched by their thirst for beer. There were 50 breweries in the state at the time of the frantic search for gold, and Germans ran several of them.

When Geoff and Marcy Larson opened their brewery in 1988, they discovered a recipe for Alt beer left by a German brewer, who had used Saaz hops from Bohemia. The Larsons were brave people to launch their company with a warm-fermenting ale in a vast region where imported pale lagers are the norm. But they were determined to make a beer with flavour and character. Geoff, with a background in pharmaceuticals, did painstaking research into yeast before selecting a strain that would convert the main maltose sugars in the wort into alcohol but leave some other sugars behind for body and 'mouth feel'.

He uses pure, glacier-fed water and two-row pale and crystal malts (colour units 22). The hops are American Cascade and, true to tradition, Saaz from a country now known as the Czech Republic (bitterness units 18). The copper-coloured beer has a spicy hop aroma balanced by nutty and toasted malt, with hints of orange fruit. Smooth nutty malt, tangy fruit and hop resins dominate the mouth, followed by a lingering finish with spicy hops to the fore but with a good balance of rich malt and tart fruit.

Soon after its launch, Alaskan Amber won a major prize at the Great American Beer Festival and has gone on to win many more awards. The brewery has achieved fame abroad for its Smoked Porter (see page 138), but Amber is far and way the company's biggest-selling beer.

TASTING NOTES
Appearance
Aroma
Taste
Overall score

Diebels Alt

Source: Brauerei Diebels, Issum, near Düsseldorf, Germany
Strength: 4.8%
Website: www.diebels.de

TASTING NOTES
Appearance
Aroma
Taste
Overall score

Diebels, in the village of Issum, is the biggest producer of Alt beer in Germany. Josef Diebels, a proud Westphalian, founded the company in 1878 and it passed to four generations of the family. It remained independent until the turn of the 21st century, when the ever-expanding Interbrew group, now InBev, bought it. So far, there have been no attempts to downplay the importance of Alt, which accounts for 1.5m hectolitres (34.8m gallons) a year.

The modern Steinecker brewhouse has tiled walls with a mosaic showing the old brewery at the turn of the 20th century. Four mash kettles feed four wort kettles, where the hops are added in one addition. A decoction mashing system is used. The 50-year-old yeast strain is an ale culture that works at a warm temperature but it is cropped from the base of conical fermenters. It is noticeably less fruity than typical ale yeasts and fully attenuates the malt sugars. A brewer at Diebels earnestly wrote in my notebook that he used Saccharomyces cerevisiae 'unlike you British who use Brettanomyces', which is actually the wild yeast uses in lambic brewing. Primary fermentation is rapid, lasting just two days. The green beer has a short diacetyl rest to purge it of toffee and butterscotch flavours and is then cold conditioned for between 10 days and three weeks. It is still a shock to hear Germans say they lager their beer when they are referring to ale, but the term simply means 'store'.

Diebels Alt is copper coloured with a pronounced peppery hop aroma balanced by rich malt and a gentle hint of fruit. It has earthy hop resins in the mouth with toasted malt, followed by a dry and nutty finish, a hint of orange fruit and a solid base of gently bitter hops. The grist is made up of 98% pale Pils malt with—rare for the style—2% roasted malt. Hops are predominantly Northern Brewer for bitterness, with Perle for aroma: bitterness units are 32. Brewing liquor comes from on-site wells and calcium hydroxide (lime milk) is used to soften it. Diebels is the sixth biggest brewing company in Germany: the other five are all Pils brewers.

Duckstein

Source: Brauerei Feldschlössen, Brunswick, Germany
Strength: 4.9%
Website: www.duckstein.de

Is this the favourite beer of Count Duckula? In spite of the cartoon name, this is a beer with considerable history. Its name is a corruption of Tuffstein, a type of volcanic rock that formed around a famous spring, the Lufferquelle, in the town of Königslutter in the Elm Mountains near Brunswick (Braunschweig in German).

In the Middle Ages, some 73 small breweries were recorded in the town, using the calcium-rich water to help them make beer. In the German medieval fashion, they were probably small breweries based in houses and shared communal brewing equipment. Beer was also brewed at the local prince's court. It became fashionable and was the favourite brew of the Prussian king, Friedrich Wilhelm I. In 1987, the Feldschlössen brewery in Brunswick, part of the Carlsberg/Holsten group, revived the style with Duckstein. It soon achieved popularity and is now widely exported to other mainland European countries, Britain and the United States.

It is brewed with pale and darker Munich malts, and is hopped with Hallertau varieties. The brewery makes much of the fact that it is matured over beechwood chips. If this has a familiar ring, it is because the American brewer Anheuser-Busch makes a similar claim for its version of Budweiser. The use of beechwood is an ancient German tradition and has little to do with maturation: the wood attracts yeast and helped clarify the beer before modern filtration methods were introduced. The bronze-red beer has a fruity, raisin-like aroma with rich malt and spicy hops. The fruit notes dominate the mouth with earthy hop resins and biscuity malt. The finish is spicy, dry, slightly vinous, with bitter hops notes and is wonderfully refreshing.

While Brunswick is some distance from Düsseldorf, the Alt style clearly travelled, as the brewery also makes a Brunswick Alt.

TASTING NOTES
Appearance
Aroma
Taste
Overall score

Full Sail Amber Ale

Source: Full Sail Brewing, Hood River, Oregon, USA
Strength: 5.8%
Website: www.fullsailbrewing.com

Pinkus Müller Alt

Source: Brauerei Pinkus Müller, Münster, Nordrhein-Westfalen, Germany
Strength: 5%
Website: www.merchantduvin.com

TASTING NOTES
Appearance
Aroma
Taste
Overall score

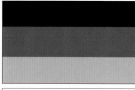

TASTING NOTES
Appearance
Aroma
Taste
Overall score

Full Sail is based in one of the most spectacular locations of any brewery in America. It is in an old cannery sited close to a deep gorge that is popular with windsurfers as a result of the powerful breezes that sweep along the meeting point of the Hood and Columbia rivers. The lush soil of the region produces grapes, apples, cherries and pears.

Jamie Emmerson and Irene Firmat founded the brewery in 1987 with a belief in craft beers made by hands-on methods. Even today, when the company produces 60,000 barrels a year, the production process is manual. The company is owned by its employees, who bought out the founders in 1998: the joke among the 54 staff, reworking the old Remington razor advertising gag, is 'We liked the beer so we bought the brewery'.

Amber Ale is one of the most successful and respected craft-brewed beers in the US and has won a gold medal no fewer than seven times in the World Beer Championships. It is brewed with two-row pale, crystal and chocolate malts, and is hopped with Cascade and Mount Hood varieties from the Pacific North-west. The amber-red beer has a big spicy hop, tart citrus fruit and creamy malt aroma, with sweet biscuity malt in the mouth balanced by hop resins and tangy fruit. The long, complex finish is quenching, dry and hoppy, but with good spicy, malty and fruity notes.

Full Sail also owns a brew pub of the same name in nearby Portland. I left a camera there and have been meaning ever since to go back and retrieve it.

The remarkable brewery and tavern started life in 1816 as a chocolatier and bakery as well as a brewery. Today the sixth generation of the Müller family runs the enterprise. Pinkus was a nickname given to Carl Müller, who controlled the company for many years after World War Two. Members of the family told me Pinkus is a nickname for 'the singing brewer', but I have since been told it means something saucier in the local dialect.

The tavern has four intimate wood-panelled dining rooms. The main room has a traditional Westphalian oven in a surround of blue and white tiles. Members of the family look after customers' needs for food and drink, led by Hans Müller and his son-in-law Friedhlem Langfeld, who is the brewmaster.

The brewery produces 20,000 hectolitres, or 12,000 barrels a year. Most of it is consumed in the city and surrounding area but bottled versions find their way to other mainland European countries, Britain, the US and Japan.

Since the 1990s, the family has used only organic malts and hops for all its beers. Their Alt is a classic, brewed with Bioland Pilsener malt and Tettnanger hops. After primary fermentation with an ale yeast culture, the beer is lagered for a remarkable five to seven months in horizontal tanks in the cellars. A carefully controlled lactic culture is added to give a hint of sourness and touch of vinous fruit. The beer is also kräusened with yeasty wort to encourage a strong second fermentation. The beer that emerges from this long maturation is pale with a hint of bronze and a thick and lively collar of foam. The aroma offers biscuity malt, tart fruit and gently spicy hops. Juicy malt, tangy fruit and bitter hops dominate the mouth, while the finish has enormous length with a touch of sourness, ripe fruit, toasted malt and pungent hops.

The brewery also produces a wheat beer and two cold-fermented beers, Pils and Special.

St Stan's Amber Alt/Dark Alt

Source: Stanislaus Brewing Company, Modesto, California, USA
Strength: 4.8%/6%
Website: www.st-stans.com

Modesto in central California has powerful German roots. Members of a strict German Baptist sect live in Stanislaus County and it is not surprising that the local brewery concentrates on Alt beer and is not shy of using the proper German name.

It is the biggest producer of Alt-style beer in the US. Garith Helm, an American, and his German wife, Romy Graf, launched the brewery in 1984. They brewed at first in converted dairy vessels on Garith's farm but later moved to a complex they designed that includes brewery, pub, restaurant and beer garden.

Amber Alt, with 28 units of bitterness, has a complex grain recipe that comprises pale, caramalt, carapils, chocolate malt and black malt. The hops are Cascade, Willamette and imported German Tettnanger. It has a massive punch of hops, citrus fruit and biscuity malt on the noise, with tart fruit, spicy hop resins and sappy malt in the mouth. The finish is deep and long, finally dry and bitter but punctuated by toasted grain and citrus fruit.

The strong Dark Alt has 31 bitterness units and is brewed with pale malt, caramalt, black malt and roasted malt. The hops are Bullion, Cascade and English Fuggles. There is a rich and pleasing chocolate note on the aroma and palate, with roasted grain, earthy hops and light fruit. The long finish is bitter-sweet, with more chocolate character balanced by toasted grain and spicy hops.

The pub section of the complex stages regular celebrations for such events as St Patrick's Day and Halloween. In June, the brewery produces a special Graffiti Wheat Beer to commemorate the George Lucas movie *American Graffiti* that was filmed in the area. What the strict German Baptists make of these shenanigans is anyone's guess.

TASTING NOTES
Appearance
Aroma
Taste
Overall score

TASTING NOTES
Appearance
Aroma
Taste
Overall score

Zum Uerige Alt

Source: Obergarige Hausbrauerei Zum Uerige, Düsseldorf, Germany
Strength: 4.6%
Website: www.uerige.de

TASTING NOTES
Appearance
Aroma
Taste
Overall score

The Alt beer from this wonderful tavern in Berger Strasse off the Altstadt is considered by many to be the classic of the style, though others have criticised it for being too hoppy, not a charge I would make against any beer.

If the beer is a mouthful, so is the name of the tavern: *Obergarige* means 'top fermenting', while *Hausbrauerei* is 'brew-pub'. *Zum Uerige* means 'the place of the cranky fellow', which refers to the curmudgeon who opened it in the 1830s. The tavern was bombed during World War Two but rebuilt in its original style. It is a maze of rooms, some with vaulted ceilings. Others have cartoons, graffiti and photos of old Düsseldorf. The centrepiece is the spacious main bar called the Brewhouse, with copper brewing vessels forming a backdrop.

I met the energetic and enthusiastic owner Josef Schnitzler, who managed to serve beer to me and many other customers at great speed, at the same time extolling the virtues of craft brewing, the finest ingredients and that all-important element: passion.

His beer is brewed with pale malt, caramalt and a touch of black malt, and hopped with the Spalt variety. It has a big spicy hop, toasted malt and light fruit aroma, with earthy hop resins, rich malt and orange fruit in the mouth. The finish is complex and long, with toasted malt, tart fruit and bitter hops. Great beer in a brilliant setting.

Kölsch

Brewing has been a major occupation in Cologne (Köln), the capital of the Rhineland, since Roman times. The German name Köln refers to the city's colonial role during the period of the Roman Empire. Monasteries dominated production for centuries following the Roman withdrawal. When the power of the church was broken at the time of the Reformation, brewing passed into the hands of small-scale commercial producers, mainly based in taverns. A Guild of Brewers was established in 1396 and is the oldest trade association in the city.

Today, Cologne and its surrounding districts still have some 20 breweries all dedicated to the one style of pale, perfumy, warm-fermented beer. In terms of numbers, Cologne is the greatest brewing city in the world. The style is often referred to as 'wiess', which is the local rendition of white, spelt 'weiss' in other regions. This is a reference to its pale colour and heavy collar of foam, though the beer may well have been darker in previous times.

The name also suggests, as it does in Bavaria, that wheat is used, though this is not the case with all brewers. In the 20th century, Kölsch came under pressure from the spread of pale Pils-style beers. As a result, the style was tweaked: pale malts were used and beers were matured and served at lower temperatures, but warm fermentation was retained. The Cologne Association of Brewers organised the changes to the style and then, in the 1960s, took steps to protect the city's brewing tradition. They were troubled by the fact that brewers in other parts of Germany were producing beers called Kölsch. Several court cases were initiated to stop the use of the name outside its city of origin. Then, in 1985, as a result of protracted negotiations between the association and the government, the beer style was given a decree, similar to a French appellation. The brewers are rightly proud of the Kölsch Convention, printed on parchment, which guarantees the sanctity of the style and restricts it to brewers in Cologne and to a handful of other towns and cities, including Bonn. The Convention carries the signatures and seals of each of the brewers.

In common with Alt and the beers of Wallonia and northern France, Kölsch developed as beer to refresh people engaged in hard manual labour. Today it has found a new and encouragingly young audience, to such an extent that new breweries have sprung up to produce the style. A modern Kölsch is around 5% with a malty aroma, some light fruit, soft in the mouth from the local water and with delicate, perfumy hop notes. Bittering units are normally in the high 20s, but extreme bitterness is avoided. Hallertauer and Tettnanger are the preferred hop varieties. The yeast cultures attenuate the malt sugars and the beers tend to be dry in the finish.

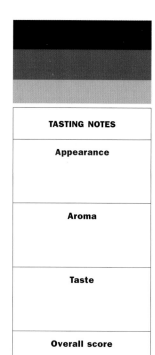

Früh Kölsch

Source: Kölner Hofbräu P J Früh, Cologne, Germany
Strength: 4.8%
Website: www.frueh.de

TASTING NOTES
Appearance
Aroma
Taste
Overall score

P J Früh is the best-known tavern in which to relish the city's classic beer style. Service is rapid and carried out by waiters known as *Kobes*. They wear high-buttoned blue uniforms over leather jackets and carry circular trays with central tall handles that hold half a dozen or more glasses of beer. *Kobes* is a diminutive of Jakob and it assumes that all the waiters have the same name. It is a habit that reminds me of my East End upbringing in London where, if you didn't know a man's name, you called him John, as in 'Got a new motor then, John?'

The main area of the tavern is known affectionately as the *Schwemme*, which means the swimming bath. This is a standing area where tall glasses of beer are both dispensed by the *Kobes* and sunk at a rapid pace by the customers. You can escape from the *Schwemme* into the many other rooms of the tavern where beer is served at a more leisurely pace, along with snacks or full meals, based on many varieties of pork. The tavern on the Am Hof near the twin-towered cathedral used to brew on the premises but a new brewery was built just outside the city centre. The company dates from 1904 when Peter Josef Früh opened the brewhouse and it passed on to successive members of the family.

The beer is brewed only with pale malt and Hallertauer and Tettnanger hop pellets. It is a dangerously drinkable beer with a lilting aroma of biscuity malt, perfumy hops and gentle citrus fruit. Juicy malt dominates the palate but with a good balance of hop resins, while the finish is dry, full of soft malt and light fruit and hops. The beer is so popular that there is a tradition in the tavern of a male drinker telling his female companion: '*Liebling, das ist mein Lieblingsbier*', which means, roughly, 'Darling, this is my darling beer', but it may lose something in translation and could prompt divorce proceedings on the grounds that 'You love your beer more than me.'

Hellers Kölsch/Ur-Weiss

Source: Brauhaus Heller, Cologne, Germany
Strength: 4.5%
Website: www.hellers-brauhaus.de

Heller is proof of the enduring popularity of Kölsch, as the brew-pub at 33 Roon Strasse dates only from the 1990s.

Hubert Heller is a qualified engineer who developed a passion for brew-pubs as a student in Berlin in the 1960s. In the 1980s, he was at last able to turn his love into a commercial enterprise when he bought a former distillery in his home city of Cologne. In 1991, he added brewing equipment and started to produce his distinctive interpretations of the city's beer. The brewery is modern but has a fine traditional feel, with copper vessels inside wood jackets.

Two versions of the main beer are produced: a naturally-conditioned, sedimented Ur-Weiss (Original White) and a filtered version called Kölsch. Barley malt from the Rhineland and Herbrucker and Spalt hops are used in full flower form. The unfiltered version has a yeasty, fruity, creamy malt and floral hop aroma, with firm malt and earthy hop resins in the mouth. The finish is smooth and ends dry with good bitter hops notes balanced by toasted malt and tangy fruit.

The filtered Kölsch has greater malt character, is sweeter in the mouth with a more restrained hop character, but is wonderfully refreshing with some late citrus fruit notes.

The tavern has striking architecture, with a vaulted brick cellar, stained-glass windows, and gargoyles commissioned by Herr Heller and carved from basalt rock from the Eifel lakes. The coppers that can be seen behind the bar date from the 1920s and came from a former brewery in the city.

The tavern opens at 4am but closes for lunch, after which it reopens until one in the morning.

TASTING NOTES
Appearance
Aroma
Taste
Overall score

TASTING NOTES
Appearance
Aroma
Taste
Overall score

Trappist Beers

Belgium is a rich storehouse of beer but it is the ales produced by Trappist monks that have drawn the most attention in recent years. The calm and cloistered atmospheres of the abbeys are first and foremost places of worship and retreat.

Beer was brewed originally to aid the monks' work and contemplation. Small amounts were sold commercially to help renovate buildings, enable the monks to develop their missionary work far from home, and establish new communities. In a cynical world, the Trappists are frequently accused of bowing to the forces of commercialism by selling increasing amounts of beer to the outside market, of handing over production to lay workers, installing modern brewing plants, and cutting corners by using inferior raw materials.

In fact, the development of commercial sales after World War Two was on a 'survive or die' basis. The monks' breweries had been stripped of copper and other metals by the invading Nazi forces to help make bullets and tanks. Many of the abbeys had been damaged or destroyed. Income was desperately needed. Lay workers have always been involved in the brewing process: they are essential in abbeys where the monks are called to prayer, often on an hourly basis. The Orval brewery, for example, was at first run solely by workers from outside the abbey, though this is no longer the case. Where modernisation is concerned, even monastic breweries get old, start to fall apart and need to be replaced. The monks vigorously deny the charge they are using cheaper materials in their beers, and some are willing to reveal the grains, hops and sugars they permit.

The most powerful counter-argument to the cynics is the awesome dedication of the monks. They have united across the linguistic divide to defend their traditions against the flood of imitation 'abbey' beers. And they acted speedily to withdraw the Trappist credentials from the La Trappe brands produced at the Koningshoeven abbey in the Netherlands when it was bought by a commercial brewery.

St Benedict in the sixth century, at the abbey of Monte Cassino in Italy, drew up the guidelines for how monks should carry out their duties. The Benedictine philosophy was reinterpreted in the 12th century by

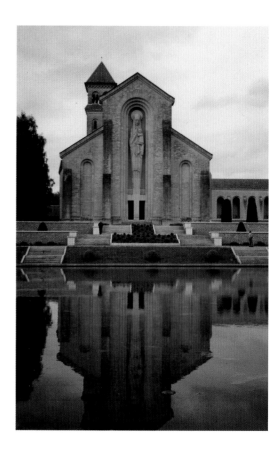

new ideas of stricter observance developed by St Bernard of Clairvaux at the monastery of Cîteaux near Dijon in France. The Latin name for Cîteaux is Cistercium and the monks who followed this new tradition were known as Cistercians. The monks of the Abbey of La Trappe, founded in Normandy in 1664, were Cistercians who argued for even stricter observance of monastic rules. They became the Cistercian Order of the Strict Observance, better known as Trappists.

At the time of the French Revolution, the Trappists were driven from their monasteries as their abbeys were sacked. They found refuge in the Low Countries, where they founded new abbeys, lived off the produce of the fields, and set up small breweries to offer beer to guests and pilgrims, to drink with their simple meals, and sustain them during Lent. The Trappists became famous as the 'silent monks'. In fact, they not only speak but also would find it difficult to carry out their missionary work if they were mute. They prefer an atmosphere of silence in their abbeys, but they can exchange views and discuss ideas, although prayer is considered more important than speech.

The nature of the Trappists' life, working in isolated communities, and divided in Belgium between French and Flemish speakers, means there is little communication between the houses, save for occasional religious gatherings. Brewing remains unique to each abbey: the monks are at pains to stress there is no such thing as a 'Trappist style' of beer. The only similarity is that their beers are all warm-fermented, members of the ale family, but each house style has evolved in a different way.

It was remarkable, therefore, that representatives of all five Trappist breweries in Belgium convened meetings in 1997 to discuss ways of protecting their brewing tradition. They were forced to act as a result of the confusion caused by the growing number of Abbey beers coming onto the market. These are beers brewed commercially, some under licence from non-brewing abbeys, but many with no religious connections at all. Abbey beers, in the view of the Trappists, not only confuse the public but also dilute the importance of the monks' contribution and dedication to good brewing practice.

The result was the formation, with Koningshoeven of the Netherlands, of the International Trappist Association. The association places a common seal, 'Authentic Trappist Product', on their beers. This is not an indication of a common style but something more profound. Koningshoeven lost the use of the logo in 1999 as a result of the brewery's association with the commercial Bavaria brewing group. However, the decision was rescinded in 2005 and the monastery can now use the Trappist logo once more (see page 224).

Achelse Blond 5/Achelse Brune 5
Source: Brouwerij St Benedictus, Abdij de Achelse, Kluis, Hamont-Achel, Belgium
Strength: 5%
Website: www.achelsekluis.org

The five Trappist breweries in Belgium became six in 1998 when the monks at Achel decided to restore brewing. The abbey is on the border with the Netherlands, and the nearest major conurbation is the Dutch city of Eindhoven. Cistercian monks settled in the area from the 12th century and cultivated the land. Trappists founded their abbey in 1845 and, somewhat confusingly, dedicated it to St Benedict. Their brewery was wrecked during World War One when the Germans dismantled the mash tuns and coppers to help build their armaments. Since then, the monks concentrated on their farm, where they grew vegetables and raised cows and pigs. In the 1990s, the brothers confronted a problem common to all monasteries today. They were getting older, farm work was demanding, and attracting new recruits to the order was difficult. They decided it would be easier to restore brewing and raise funds for the abbey by selling beer. Some of the monks were also keen to brew, as they were unimpressed by the commercial beers available to them, mass market lagers in particular. To raise the funds for the brewery, the monks sold off a parcel of land worth £300,000. The brewing equipment was installed in a former dairy, its stainless-steel vessels in sharp contrast to the burnished copper of some of the other Trappist plants.

Unlike the other monasteries, where the beers are sold at nearby cafés and taverns, Achel has built a café in the main buildings of the abbey, restoring the traditions of centuries ago, though today's 'pilgrims' are more likely to wear shell suits and trainers than pilgrims' habits. The abbey promotes itself as the only Trappist brew-pub in

TASTING NOTES
Appearance
Aroma
Taste
Overall score

TASTING NOTES
Appearance
Aroma
Taste
Overall score

the world. The café draws large crowds, who not only enjoy the beers but are also fascinated by the view of the brewhouse. At first the beers were available only on draught at the abbey but the monks started to bottle them for commercial sale in 2004. The installation of the brewery was masterminded by one of the most revered figures in Trappist brewing. Father Thomas, the former head brewer at the Westmalle Abbey, came out of retirement to oversee the fitting of the brewing equipment. The yeast culture at Achel came from Westmalle. When Father Thomas was taken ill, another retired head brewer, this time Brother Antoine from Rochefort, took his place.

Day-to-day brewing is carried out by Tom Poncelet, who brews every 10 days and produces around 10,000 hectolitres (220,000 gallons) a year. Achelse Blond 5 is brewed with Pilsner malt, East Kent Goldings, Hallertauer-Hersbrucker and Czech Saaz hops. It is a golden beer with a pungent, spicy hop aroma balanced by clean biscuity malt, with quenching malt and floral hops in the mouth, and a long, dry finish dominated by spicy hop notes.

Achelse Brune 5 has the same ingredients, with the addition of caramalt. It is a russet-coloured beer with a toasted malt and peppery hops aroma, followed by a firm, malty palate with pronounced touches of malted loaf, and a big finish dominated by dark, roasted grain and spicy hops.

For café opening times, phone 011 800 760.

Chimay Rouge/Blanche/Bleue
Source: Abbaye de Notre-Dame de Scourmont, Forges-les-Chimay, Hainaut, Belgium
Strength: 7%/8%/9%
Website: www.chimay.com

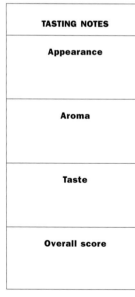

TASTING NOTES
Appearance
Aroma
Taste
Overall score

Chimay is the biggest of the Trappist breweries and the best known internationally. In 1850, 17 monks at the Westvleteren abbey were given permission by their abbot to leave the community and build a new one on land donated by the Prince of Chimay. The monastery was built 10 miles from the villages of Forges-les-Chimay in the Ardennes. Building work was completed in 1864, but a small brewery had been constructed two years earlier to provide sustenance for the monks and raise funds. The importance of brewing to the monks was underscored by the fact that abbey and brewery were built on the site of a well that provided copious amounts of pure water. The beer was made available in bottled form in 1885, and in 1925 the prior allowed wider commercial distribution. Labels bore the image of the abbey and the enigmatic letters ADS, which stand for Abbaye de Scourmont. It was the first time that Trappist brewers sold beer to the outside world.

German troops occupied the abbey and its brewery during World War Two, and vital brewing equipment was removed for the Nazi war effort. After the war, the monks sold their beers more vigorously to help pay for rebuilding work. The renowned brewing scientist Jean De Clerck, from Leuven University's faculty of brewing, was invited by Chimay's head brewer, Father Théodore, to advise on the design of new brewing vessels. Crucially, De Clerck took the house yeast and isolated a pure culture that developed the fruity character of their beers, with their powerful blackcurrant note.

The monks, rightly, treat their beers as seriously as wine. On my first visit, the head brewer, Father Thomas, led me to a sampling room where we tasted several vintages. He expounded on the need to allow the Grand Cru versions—sold in Bordeaux-shaped bottles with corks and wire cradles—to breathe when opened, in order to vent off some of the natural carbon dioxide produced during bottle fermentation. All three beers can be laid down to improve, but Father Thomas (who died in 2000) said that after five years the two darker ones would develop a 'port wine' character.

In 1989, the brewhouse designed by Jean De Clerck, with glowing copper vessels, was replaced by a new one based on stainless steel, with many vessels hidden from view behind tiled walls. Production is in the region of 110,000 hectolitres (2.4m gallons) a year. The local water, still drawn from the abbey well, is soft and remarkably free from agricultural and urban impurities. The beers are known by the colours of their caps: red, white and blue, and all three are also available in Grand Cru bottles. In true Trappist fashion, the monks are reluctant to say too much about the raw materials they use, but I was able to discover, over lunch in an inn in Forges-les-Chimay with lay employees from the brewery, that barley comes from the Champagne region of France, and is malted to the monks' specification in Belgium. Aroma hops come from the German Hallertau and the American North-west, with the American Galena preferred for its robust bitterness. The beers are given a dosage of yeast and sugar to encourage a strong fermentation in bottle. The monks also make soft cheese for sale, including one made with their own beer.

Red (Première in Grand Cru bottles) is brewed with pale Pilsner malt, caramalt and German Hallertauer and American Galena hops. The beer is copper coloured with blackcurrant fruit on the aroma and palate and nutmeg spice and tart hops. The finish is vinous, spicy but with a good underlying hop bitterness. White (Cinq Cents in Grand Cru bottles) is brewed with pale Pilsner malt, caramalt, and Hallertauer and Galena hops. The colour is orange/peach with a big citrus fruit aroma and palate, a hint of spice in the mouth, and a big, dry finish balanced between tart fruit and bitter hops. Blue (Grande Réserve in Grand Cru bottles) is made with pale Pilsner malt, Hallertauer and Galena hops. It has a deep copper colour, with an enormous vinous fruitiness on the aroma and palate: the brewers describe the vinous note as being similar to Zinfandel. There is also a spiciness from hops and the house yeast, and the big rich and fruity finish finally becomes dry with a good underpinning of spicy hops. The beers should be served at room temperature, not chilled.

TASTING NOTES
Appearance
Aroma
Taste
Overall score

TASTING NOTES
Appearance
Aroma
Taste
Overall score

Koningshoeven La Trappe Blond/Dubbel/Tripel

Source: Bierbrouwerij De Koningshoeven BV, Berkel-Enschot, Tilburg, Netherlands
Strength: 6.5%/6.5%/8%
Website: www.latrappe.nl

TASTING NOTES
Appearance
Aroma
Taste
Overall score

TASTING NOTES
Appearance
Aroma
Taste
Overall score

Koningshoeven is back in the fold—or more accurately back in the Sheepsfold (see below). In 1999 the brewery in the grounds of the brooding abbey of Koningshoeven was expelled from the International Trappist Association when it was bought by the Bavaria group, a large Dutch company that specialises in own-label beers for supermarkets. The brewery continued to call its beer La Trappe and lobbied quietly to be allowed back in to the association. When I visited the abbey in 2006, the abbot, Brother Bernardus, made it clear that he was in overall charge of the brewery and that Bavaria and its employees worked to the guidelines laid down by the monks. The brewery has been restored to ITA membership.

Koningshoeven means King's Gardens, and the land was given to the monks by the monarch when they moved north from La Trappe in Normandy to escape the French Revolution. The rustic-sounding Schaapskoi (Sheepfold) brewery was built in the 1880s to raise funds for the restoration of the abbey. Following World War Two, the brewery was bought by Stella Artois of Belgium, which wanted to establish a bridgehead in the Netherlands. It produced an unlikely Trappist Pils and installed a small lager plant. The beer

was not a success and the monks raised funds to buy back the brewery. Perhaps it was this brush with Mammon that led the brothers down the path of unrighteousness, allowing commercial brewers to make some of their beers and signing a deal with the British supermarket group Sainsbury's to sell an own-label Trappist beer.

A new, modern brewhouse, with stainless-steel vessels, was installed in 1986; the original traditional brewhouse is depicted on the tiles of the walls. The flexibility of the site, as well as the renown of the La Trappe brands, attracted the Bavaria group, and now production of other beers, including a Pils, has been moved to Koningshoeven. Critics of the sell-out (myself included) expected the quality of the ales to decline but they are consistently good.

La Trappe Blond is a recent addition to the range and is brewed with pale malt and German Northern Brewer hops. It has a tart lemon fruit, juicy malt and spicy hop aroma, with tangy fruit, sappy malt and perfumy hops in the mouth. The finish is quenching, finally dry and hoppy but with balancing notes of malt and lemon fruit.

Dubbel is made with pale, Munich and other coloured malts and, again, the hop variety is

Northern Brewer. It has a tawny colour, a powerful orange Muscat aroma and palate, overlain by peppery hops.

The copper-coloured Tripel has ripe sultana and raisin fruit on nose and palate, the fruitiness balanced by rich malt and a powerful blast of peppery Goldings hops that leads to a dry and bitter finish.

In January 2006 Koningshoeven was restored fully to the Trappist fold. It can now use the Authentic Trappist Product logo on its beers once more. This follows assurances givien to the International Trappist Association that monks, while working with Bavaria, are in charge of all decisions concerning brewing and marketing.

Orval

Source: Brasserie de l'Abbaye Notre-Dame d'Orval, Villers-devant-Orval, Belgium
Strength: 6%
Website: www.orval.be

The Abbey of Our Lady of Orval stands in densely wooded countryside in the Ardennes, on a sharp bend in the old Roman road that runs from Trier in Germany to Rheims in France, one of the important salt routes of earlier times. The abbey and grounds are places of great beauty and serenity that belie a turbulent past that has seen the site destroyed by fire, rebuilt, and then destroyed again during the French Revolution. The present complex surrounds the ruins of the former abbey.

The abbey uses the symbol of a trout with a ring in its mouth to emphasise a legend connected to the origins of the site. Orval is a reworking of 'Val d'Or', or Golden Valley. The overlord of the region, Countess Matilda, the Duchess of Tuscany, came to the valley in 1076 to visit a small group of Benedictine monks who had made the arduous journey from Calabria in Italy to build an abbey. Matilda was in mourning for her late husband. As she sat by the side of a small lake, her wedding ring slipped from her finger into the water. Overcome with grief, she prayed that the ring would be restored to her. At that moment a trout broke the surface of the water with the ring in its mouth. 'This is truly a golden valley!' the duchess exclaimed, and she gave a generous endowment to the monks, who used it to extend the size of the abbey.

The monastery was rebuilt in the 12th century by Cistercian monks from the Champagne region of France. It burnt down soon afterwards and was rebuilt. For centuries it played an important role in the political and spiritual life of the region. Then it was sacked following an artillery barrage in 1793 by French revolutionaries who came over the border in the mistaken belief that the deposed Louis XV was hiding there.

The present buildings were constructed over a long period between 1926 and 1948. Trappist monks came from as far away as Brazil to answer the call to settle at Orval, and help re-create a place dedicated to prayer and charitable work in the community. The modern abbey was designed by the architect Henri Vaes, a great admirer of Cistercian buildings. His impressive creation, with the main buildings reflected in an ornamental lake, is a stunning blend of Romanesque and Burgundian styles, with some startling 1920s Art Deco touches. Vaes even designed the brewery's pre-Raphaelite beer goblet and skittle-shaped bottle.

A brewery was added in 1931 to provide sustenance for the monks, and to generate finance for the construction and maintenance of the abbey. The brewhouse is in a chapel-like room with a crucifix on the wall, an obligatory icon in all the Trappist breweries. The walls are half decorated with mustard-coloured tiles, and the brewing vessels stand on bases made from the same material. The formula for the beer was devised by a German brewer named Pappenheimer, who worked to the monks' specification that includes the English method of 'dry hopping'. This entails adding a handful of hops to the finished beer for aroma and bitterness.

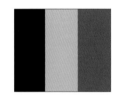

The brewery is unique among the Trappist establishments in producing just one beer, called, simply, Orval. Enormous care and dedication go into every stage of production, starting with the selection of four or five spring barleys from England, France, Germany and the Netherlands. A small amount of English crystal malt is added to the pale varieties to give the beer its distinctive orange-peach colour. Pure white candy sugar is added during the copper boil to encourage a powerful fermentation. The hops used for the copper boil are German Hallertauer varieties and Styrian Goldings from Slovenia. East Kent Goldings are used for dry hopping, and are chosen for their piny, resiny aromas. Brewing liquor is still drawn from the well that gave rise to the legend of Orval. The beer has three fermentations. Primary fermentation is with a conventional ale yeast. The beer is pumped to conditioning tanks, where four or five more yeast strains are added. One of these is a wild yeast, a member of the Brettanomyces family used in making the 'spontaneous fermentation' lambic beers in the Brussels area. The yeast's signature is an aroma known as 'horse blanket'. The yeast strain, now carefully cultured in the brewery's laboratory, can attack dextrins as well as maltose sugars in the wort.

The result is a beer with a high level of attenuation, strong in alcohol, and with virtually no sugars left. The beer is bottled with a dosage of the first yeast and some candy sugar, which encourages a third fermentation. It is then stored for six weeks before being released for sale. Although it is declared at 6.2% alcohol, it will reach close to 7% as a result of bottle fermentation. The acidity of the beer, especially when it is aged for months or a few years, makes it the perfect aperitif. It should be stored upright at a cellar temperature of 12°C (54°F). The monks produce some 38,000 hectolitres (836,000 gallons) of beer a year, of which around 10% is exported.

The abbey shop sells the beer as well as bread and cheese made by the monks. A rustic restaurant known as L'Ange Guardien (Guardian Angel) is just a few minutes' walk from the abbey on the main road. It sells dishes cooked in Orval, while the entrance bears the symbol of the trout with a ring in its mouth. The beer has an orange/peach colour, an aroma of peppery hops and tart fruit, followed by a palate dominated by gooseberry fruit, with a long and intensely bitter finish with hints of herbs and a touch of lactic sourness from the action of the wild yeast.

Rochefort 6/8/10
Source: Brasserie de Rochefort, Abbaye de Notre-Dame de St-Rémy, Rochefort, Belgium
Strength: 7.5%/9.2%/11.3%
Website: None

Rochefort is one of the most secluded of the Trappist monasteries. It is another settlement in the Ardennes but, unlike Orval, the abbey doesn't stand prominently on a major road but is reached along a narrow, wooded road. Perhaps in an attempt to deter visitors, the beer is labelled simply Rochefort rather than using the full name of the abbey. Rochefort is a small town near the abbey and has many shops offering bread, locally raised and made meats and chocolate, with cafés serving the local beer.

The abbey has a history almost as turbulent as Orval's. It was founded as a convent in 1230 by Gilles de Walcourt, the Count of Rochefort. The hard climate and grinding poverty proved too much for the nuns, and monks replaced them in 1464. Documents show that a small brewery existed from around 1595 to provide beer for the community, using barley and hops grown in the grounds. The monks were forced to abandon the abbey during the French Revolution, when scant attention was paid to the border between France and the Low Countries. The abbey was rebuilt in 1887 by Trappists from Achel, and a brewery was opened two years later.

The present brewhouse dates mainly from the 1960s, with some additions in the 1970s. It produces around 15,000 hectolitres (330,000 gallons) a year. Blessed by the customary crucifix on the wall and the image of St Arnold, the patron saint of brewers, the brewhouse has burnished copper vessels set amid tiled walls, with the sunlight pouring through stained-glass windows and glinting on the mashing vessels and coppers. One tun carries the warning: 'Ne pas toucher les cuivres avec les mains!'—'Don't touch the vessels with the hands!'

Under the long regime of head brewer Brother Antoine, the perfect blend of barleys was assembled, using Pilsner and darker Munich malts grown from grain in Belgium, France and the Netherlands. Dark candy sugar is used in the copper, along with hops from the German Hallertau and Styrian Goldings. To make the point that there is no uniform Trappist style, the beers from Rochefort are dark and malty, unlike the pale and intensely bitter beer from Orval. Brother Antoine maintained that the character of his ales was determined by their original use as 'liquid bread' during periods of fasting.

Two strains of yeast are used for primary and bottle fermentation. The beer is given a dosage of white sugar to encourage the bottle ferment. The three beers have red, green and black crown caps and are labelled 6, 8 and 10 from an old and now defunct Belgian method of indicating strength.

Six is brewed from Pilsner and Munich malt, and hopped with German Hallertauer varieties and Styrian Goldings. It has a reddish-brown colour, with a fruity and slightly herbal aroma and palate, and a finish dominated by rich malt with gentle hop notes.

Eight has identical ingredients, is copper-brown, with a rich fruity aroma and palate reminiscent of raisins and sultanas, and a long, complex finish dominated by the dark grain and a yeasty/bread-like note.

Ten, again, has the same ingredients, is red-brown in colour, with a vast aroma and palate of toasted grain, soft, vinous fruits, nuts and chocolate. The finish is dominated by warming alcohol, with more chocolate, ripe fruit and gentle hop notes.

Westmalle Dubbel/Tripel

Source: Brouwerij Westmalle, Abdij der Trappisten van Westmalle, Malle, Belgium
Strength: 7%/9.5%
Website: www.trappistwestmalle.be

The Abbey of Our Lady of the Sacred Heart, better known as the Trappist Abbey of Westmalle, finds it more difficult to find seclusion than the monasteries further south in the Ardennes. It stands in flat, wind-swept countryside close to Antwerp. Over the centuries, tall elms and walls have grown and been built to offer some protection from both the elements and possible attack. The monks have every reason to be protective, given the stormy origins of their settlement. During the French Revolution, three Trappist monks escaped from France to Switzerland, and planned to go to Amsterdam and from there sail to Canada. But revolutionaries were active in the Low Countries, and their close links with fellow revolutionaries in America meant that a sea journey to Canada would be hazardous. Abandoning their plans, the monks accepted an invitation from the Bishop of Antwerp to establish a religious community in his bishopric. In 1794, a farmer at Westmalle donated some of his land to the brothers. They were joined by other refugee Trappists, and a dozen monks set to work to build an abbey in the hard, unyielding countryside. The mellow stone complex was completed in 1804.

A brewery was added in 1836 and for some time supplied only the monks' daily needs. In 1865, a brewing monk of Prussian origin, Ignatius Van Ham, extended the brewery in order to sell beer commercially and help finance a Trappist community in the Belgian Congo. Sales were restricted to the immediate area around Westmalle and were not sold more widely until the 1920s. In 1932, the Abbot of Westmalle, Edmond Ooms, gave his beers the appellation 'Trappistenbeer', and thus announced to the outside world, rather more emphatically than Chimay, the presence of monks and brewing in the Low Countries. Two years later Abbot Ooms commissioned a secular architect to design a

TASTING NOTES
Appearance
Aroma
Taste
Overall score

TASTING NOTES
Appearance
Aroma
Taste
Overall score

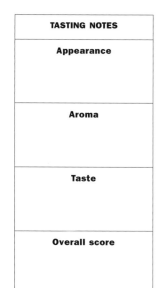

new, bigger brewhouse. Classic copper vessels are set on tiled floors in a powerful 1930s design with Art Deco influences. The brew kettle is fired by direct flame, a method that gives a defining toasted malt and toffeeish character to the beers, as some of the malt sugars are caramelised during the boil with hops. The brewing liquor is hard, which suits brewers in a region where such classic pale ales as De Koninck in Antwerp are produced. The monks use Bavarian and French summer barleys that are kilned at low temperatures to produce extremely pale Pilsner malts. Whole hop flowers are used: the monks are rather reticent about naming all the varieties but will admit to putting Bavarian Tettnanger, Czech Saaz and Styrian Goldings in the kettle in three stages. Candy sugar is also added during the boil. The two beers enjoy slow secondary fermentations in tanks before being bottled with priming sugar and re-seeded with yeast.

Westmalle is the second biggest of the Trappist breweries, producing more than 100,000 hectolitres (2.2m gallons) a year. Its contribution to Belgian brewing has been profound. The monks introduced the designations Dubbel and Tripel for their two beers and the terms are now widely used. They are not so much indications of strength, though a Triple is stronger than a Double, but are taken to mean that a Double is darkish and malty, while the Triple, introduced after World War Two, is pale, hoppy and fruity. Westmalle Trippel, with just 13 units of colour, has become a world classic, the benchmark beer for strong, pale and hoppy ales.

Dubbel is brewed with Pilsner malt, highly-kilned dark malt, dark candy sugar, with Tettnanger, Saaz and Styrian Goldings hops. It is russet coloured, with a chocolaty, fruity spicy aroma and palate. The fruitiness is complex with hints of guava and other tropical products. The finish is dry and malty, with chocolate notes from the dark malt and rich fruit.

Tripel is brewed with Pilsner malt only. The hops are Tettnanger, Saaz and Styrian Goldings. It is orange coloured, with a floral Saaz-inspired aroma and orange citrus fruit, followed by a tangy, fruity palate with big spicy hop notes, and a long, lingering finish with warming alcohol, resiny hops and a tantalising herbal character.

Westvleteren Blond/Extra/Abt
**Source: Abdij Sint Sixtus, Westvleteren, Belgium
Strength: 5.8%/8%/11%
Website: www.sintsixtus.be**

The Abbey of Sint Sixtus is the smallest of the Trappist breweries and the most reclusive. It sells only limited amounts of its beer commercially, though they are available for collection at the abbey. Visitors, save for pilgrims, are not welcome. Nevertheless, the abbey has been a force for good and for change. It was monks from Westvleteren who founded Chimay. And, in 1997, the abbot set in train events that led to all the monastic breweries in Belgium identifying their beers as coming from the Trappist tradition. The abbot held talks with the management of the St Bernardus Brewery in neighbouring Watou and made a simple request: 'Please remove the image of a monk from your labels.' In 1946, the monastery had entered into an arrangement with St Bernardus whereby the monks restricted their production to personal consumption and for sale in a café across the road from the abbey, while the commercial brewery could sell the beers, brewed to the same specification, more widely. Confusion reigned, especially as the commercial beers carried the word 'Sixtus' on the label. When the licence to brew the Westvleteren beer expired in 1992, St Bernardus dropped the word Sixtus, but five years later the monks requested an end to any suggestion that the commercial beers came from the Trappist tradition.

The abbey was founded in 1831 in the village of Westvleteren in flat Flanders countryside near Ypres and overlooking the hop fields centred on Poperinge. A small brewery was added in 1838 solely to provide beer for the monks. In the 1920s, the abbot, Dom Bonaventure De Groote, renovated the brewery in local Flemish artisanal style, with brewing vessels set in tiled surrounds. In the early 1990s, this brewhouse was replaced with a modern one using stainless-steel vessels. Production is restricted to around 3,500 hectolitres (77,000 gallons) a year. Brewing does not take place on a daily basis. When a new batch is ready, a message on the brewery's answerphone draws queues of drivers in cars, vans and even on bikes who wait patiently to buy their maximum allowance of 10 cases each. Only one beer is available at a time. The beer bottles carry no labels and are identified by the colours of the caps: green, blue and yellow, though the green is also known as Blond, the blue as Extra, and the yellow as Abt, which means Abbot.

While the brewhouse has changed, brewing practice has not. Only pale malt is used, and the beers achieve their colours as a result of white or dark candy sugar. The hops are Northern Brewer and the yeast strain comes from Westmalle. The beers are not filtered. Protein and yeast are allowed to drop out naturally during maturation, and the beer is then reseeded with yeast when bottled. The green cap beer is a recent addition to the range. It is extremely pale and is a sign that even the monks of Wetvleteren are aware of the demand for pale-coloured ales in Belgium, though they emphasise that the beer was introduced primarily as a lower-strength beer for their own consumption.

On my first visit to the abbey, on a rainy and blustery autumn day, cowled monks hurried out and emphatically pulled the main gates closed. I was able to speak at a side gate to an amiable monk called Brother Mathias, and then tasted the beer range in the Café Vrede on the other side of the road from the abbey gates. A sign in the cafe says: 'The Good Lord has changed water into wine, so how can drinking beer be a sin?'

Blond (with a green cap) is brewed with pale malt, pale candy sugar and Northern Brewer hops. It has a pale gold colour. A big herbal, hoppy aroma leads to a firm malty body balanced by tart hops, followed by a hoppy, lightly fruity and finally dry finish.

Extra (with a blue cap) is brewed with pale malt, dark candy sugar and Northern Brewer hops. It has a deep russet colour with a vast aroma of tart, plummy fruit, mouth-filling malt, fruit and hops, and a complex finish of rich malt, tart hops and bitter fruit.

Abt (with a yellow cap) is made with pale malt, dark candy sugar and Northern Brewer hops. It is a dark brown beer, with a massive attack of vinous fruit, toffee and roasted grain on the nose, chewy malt, dark fruit and hops in the mouth, and a warming alcohol, toasted grain and hops finish.

*Sales from the abbey, when available, are between 10am and 12 noon and 2pm and 5pm. No sales on Friday, Sunday or public holidays, 1–14 January or the week after the third Sunday in September. Phone 057 400 376.

TASTING NOTES
Appearance
Aroma
Taste
Overall score

TASTING NOTES
Appearance
Aroma
Taste
Overall score

Abbey Beers

Abbey beers fall into two categories. In the first, an abbey that no longer brews licenses a commercial brewery to make beer for it. The monks may exercise some control over ingredients and recipes, and derive income in the form of royalties they use to further their religious work. The second category involves modern commercial breweries that produce beers with monastic-sounding names and often religious artefacts on their labels but which have little or no connection with any religious houses.

As a result, confusion reigns and many drinkers, even those with more than a passing knowledge of the world of beer, often mistake abbey beers for Trappist ales. The problem was sufficiently serious for the brewers of true Trappist ale to give their products a seal of origin (see page 220).

The abbey beers that fall into the first category have some history on their side. Many abbeys and their breweries were destroyed during the Napoleonic wars that raged over the Low Countries. Some were attacked as late as World War One. In order to raise funds to rebuild their abbeys, the monks decided to abandon brewing and to seek commercial brewers who would make beers to the monks' specifications and pay them royalties. Many of the commercial breweries were small and close to the abbeys. Unfortunately, the late 20th-century's rampant commercialism and the quest among big brewers for mergers and centralisation of production put an end to the old tradition of a close link between abbey and local brewer.

The Leffe beers are the best known and most widely marketed of abbey brands. I visited the Mont St Guibert brewery near Brussels in the early 1990s, where all but one of the Leffe beers were brewed. It was a charming, rustic brewery and, although part of the Interbrew group, seemed to enjoy a considerable degree of independence. But a few years later, Interbrew closed the site and moved production to its vast beer factory at Leuven. The beers that carry the name of the Abbey of Grimbergen have had an even more tortuous history. At one stage they were brewed by the Alken-Maes group when it was controlled by Grand Metropolitan of Britain, best known for the infamous Watney beers of the 1970s. The group passed into the hands of the French biscuit and yoghurt maker Danone, which at the turn of the 21st century sold its brewing interests to Scottish & Newcastle. When S & N unveiled the Grimbergen range at a lavish event in Edinburgh, Norbertine monks in flowing white robes from the abbey were in attendance, giving the beers a holy blessing they did not altogether deserve.

The 'second wave' of abbey beers has a more direct link to Mammon. There are no royalties to monks, only the income from commercial sales. No criticism can be levied at breweries in the United States, which is too young a country to have a monastic tradition but where several producers with a passion for Belgian beers make beers in the abbey style.

I am aware that this is the only section of the book hedged around with concerns about confusing labelling. Some labels may mislead consumers into thinking they are getting beers brewed in abbeys when they come instead from commercial companies. My concerns should in no way be taken to mean that the beers that follow are anything less than of the highest quality. If they did not meet the criteria set by the book, they would not be included. The Trappists, given their traditions and belief in quietude, have taken a bold step in setting the seal of authenticity on their products. It is high time for the rest of the Belgian brewing industry to make it clear to consumers that abbey beers are commercial products with little or no connection with religious houses. A clearer and less ambiguous labelling for these beers would be in the best interests of their owners, enabling them to be judged in their own right and not as imitations of Trappist ales.

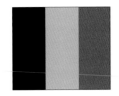

Abbaye des Rocs

Source: Brasserie de l'Abbaye des Rocs, Montignies-sur-Roc, Belgium
Strength: 9%
Website: www.abbaye-des-rocs.com

TASTING NOTES
Appearance
Aroma
Taste
Overall score

Jean-Pierre Eloir launched his brewery at his home in 1979 as a part-time venture in a garden shed, producing 50 litres (11 gallons) of beer every other week. The first beer, and still the main product, is called simply Abbaye des Rocs. As explained in the section on Belgian-style wheat beer (see page 196), the religious connection amounts to a few stones from a monastery that became a farm.

Jean-Pierre, a former tax inspector, has a great passion for Belgian Trappist and abbey beers, and has painstakingly created his ale with due reverence. It is brewed with pale malt, several varieties of darker grains and malted oats. Jean-Pierre was one of the first craft brewers in Belgium to experiment with malted oats, a difficult grain to brew with but which gives a smooth and creamy note to the beer. The beer is hopped with Belgian, Czech and German varieties and spiced with coriander. No sugars or adjuncts are used. Abbaye des Rocs is unpasteurised and improves in bottle. It has a rich claret colour that leads to a big vinous fruit aroma with spices and dark malt notes. Ripe fruit, coriander, chewy grain and hop resins fill the mouth, followed by a big, complex finish that is sweet at first, then becomes fruity and spicy but with a solid underpinning of hops. The brewery has moved and developed over the years and now produces 2,000 hectolitres (44,000 gallons) a year. The abbey beer is exported to Italy and the United States.

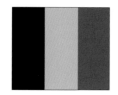

Affligem Blond

Source: Affligem Brouwerij BDS, Opwijk, Belgium
Strength: 6.7%
Website: www.heinekeninternational/affligem_blond.jsp

TASTING NOTES
Appearance
Aroma
Taste
Overall score

Affligem is a Benedictine abbey in the hop-growing region of Aalst, where the monks once cultivated their own hop garden. The original abbey, now in ruins, dates from 1074, and a new site was built in the 1920s. The monks reached an agreement with the nearby brewery of De Smedt to produce beers for commercial sale. De Smedt is not as old as the original abbey but it has a history that dates from 1790 and enjoyed a good reputation for the quality of its ales, the pale Op-Ale in particular.

The success of the Affligem beers encouraged De Smedt to rename itself after the brand name. This, in turn, caught the attention of global giant Heineken, which took a 50% stake in 1999 and increased it to 95% two years later. The abbey has retained control of the Affligem brand name and has an assurance that the beers must be brewed in Belgium for the next 30 years. Will this be honoured more in the breach than the observance? Already a large proportion of draught Affligem Blond is taken in tankers to France, where it is kegged by Heineken in Lille.

There are brown and triple versions of Affligem but the Blond is far and away the biggest of the brands and, in true Heineken style, is now widely exported. It is brewed with pale malt and has a colour of 12. The hop varieties are not revealed but are thought to be local ones. Bitterness units are 24. The beer has a honey-gold colour, a juicy malt, lemon fruit and hop resins aroma, with tart fruit, sappy malt and a solid bitter hop note in the mouth. The finish is quenching, bitter-sweet, with tangy lemon, creamy malt and spicy hops. An up-rated seasonal version of the beer at 7% is called Paters Vat (the fathers' brew). Affligem/Heineken has filled its boots with abbey beers, also producing ales for the Saint Feuillien and Postel abbeys.

Bosteels Tripel Karmeliet

Source: Brouwerij Bosteels, Buggenhout, Belgium
Strength: 8%
Website: www.karmeliet.be

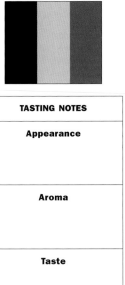

The name and label commemorate the Carmelites of Dendermonde who had a reputation for brewing fine ales, including one made from three grains. The Bosteels brewery was keen to brew a similar beer and happily came across detailed information about the monks' version from a recipe dated 1679. The grains in question are barley, wheat and oats, while Styrian Goldings are the chosen single variety of hop. Bosteels has enjoyed such success with the beer that it is now best known as the Karmeliet brewery, even though it had much earlier gained a reputation for its strong Pauwel Kwak ale served in its distinctive wooden 'shoe' (see page 107).

Karmeliet is one of the finest new beers I have tasted in recent years. It is accompanied by an elegant serving glass with a fleur-de-lys motif. The glass was designed by Antoine Bosteels who, with his father Ivo, represents the sixth generation to run the family brewery. The three grains are used in both malted and unmalted form and the result, not surprisingly, is a highly complex bronze-gold beer with a profound aroma of biscuit grain, vanilla and banana, and spicy hop resins. Ripe fruit, creamy malt, vanilla and hop resins fill the mouth, while the finish is long, complex, rich, fruity, malty and with a final tart, quinine-like bitterness from the hops. The vanilla and banana character comes from the house yeast culture. The beer is used as both an ingredient and a companion for meals in a restaurant also called Karmeliet in Bruges.

TASTING NOTES
Appearance
Aroma
Taste
Overall score

Leffe Triple

Source: Brouwerij Hoegaarden (Interbrew), Hoegaarden, Belgium
Strength: 8.1%
Website: www.leffe.be

TASTING NOTES
Appearance
Aroma
Taste
Overall score

Triple is the only beer in the Leffe range that is bottle fermented. It is brewed at the Hoegaarden brewery, controlled by Interbrew, which is famous for its spiced white beer and where there is expertise in the delicate area of reseeding beer with yeast in bottle.

While Interbrew busily turns Leffe Blonde and Brune into international brands, the Triple is the only beer in the range that is true to the monastic tradition and may bear some resemblance to the type of beer once brewed by the Norbertine brothers in the Abbey de Notre-Dame de Leffe.

The abbey's origins lie in the 12th century and it stands at the confluence of the Leffe and Meuse rivers near Dinant. The present buildings date from the 18th century. The abbey has enjoyed a tumultuous history: it has been ravaged by fire and then partially destroyed during the Napoleonic wars. In the 1950s, the monks reached an agreement with a local brewer to make beers for them under licence. It is thought to be the first such agreement between representatives of the church and the outside commercial world. The original commercial brewery was eventually taken over and the Leffe beers were transferred to the Mont St-Guibert plant, best known for Vieux Temps ales. The house yeast culture was used to ferment the Leffe brands and is still used for primary fermentation of Triple. The Hoegaarden strain is used for bottle fermentation.

It is a deceptively pale, golden beer with a fruity, vinous aroma and palate, balanced by spicy hops and juicy malt. The finish is warming, rich and packed with sappy malt, spices, bitter hops and ripe fruit.

Maredsous 8/10

Source: Brouwerij Moortgat, Breendonk, Belgium
Strength: 8%/10%
Website: www.duvel.be

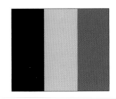

Maredsous is an ancient religious community based at Denée, south of Namur. It graduated from a humble community of Bavarian monks to a full-blown abbey in 1878, with striking buildings in the neo-Gothic style of the 19th century. At some time, the monks stopped brewing and, in 1963, they approached Moortgat with a view to the brewery making beer for them. Were the monks aware that Moortgat was best known for a beer called Duvel, which means devil? The beer had not then achieved world fame, as it was still a dark beer and only became golden in colour six years later. But this was still a remarkable coming together of the representatives of paradise and perdition.

The Maredsous beers produced by Moortgat are generally considered to be among the finest of the abbey beers brewed in Belgium, which is perhaps not surprising given the quality of the brewery's other products. The monks control the recipes and monitor the quality of the beers. Their intervention may account for the fact that little information is available about the grains and hops used, which is frustrating for those who revel in the aromas and flavours of the beers.

Maredsous 8 is russet coloured with a rich aroma and palate of chocolate and cappuccino coffee: colour and flavour suggest the use of well-roasted malts. The finish is sweet with more chocolate notes, with rich fruit and a gentle but firm hop bitterness.

Maredsous 10 is a burnished golden ale with massive ripe fruit notes—oranges and pears—on the aroma and palate, with good earthy and spicy hops and a long, complex finish that interweaves between rich fruit, juicy malt and earthy hops.

These bottle-fermented beers are left to ripen for two months in the brewery and will improve in bottle for three years, developing an even more profound fruit character.

TASTING NOTES
Appearance
Aroma
Taste
Overall score

TASTING NOTES
Appearance
Aroma
Taste
Overall score

Ommegang Abbey Ale

Source: Brewery Ommegang, Cooperstown, New York, USA
Strength: 8.5%
Website: www.ommegang.com

TASTING NOTES
Appearance
Aroma
Taste
Overall score

Don Feinberg and Wendy Littlefield have had a long love affair with Belgium and its beers. They were inspired by a visit to the country in 1980 and began to import Belgian beers into the US. In 1997, with the active support and advice of the Belgian brewers Affligem, Dubuisson and Moortgat, they opened their Ommegang Brewery in Cooperstown, upper New York State, world famous as the home of the Baseball Hall of Fame.

The custom-built brewery is on the site of a former hop farm: this region of New York was once a major hop-growing area but the industry was ruined by Prohibition. The brewery is designed along the lines of a Belgian abbey-cum-farmhouse and is named after the Ommegang, or walkabout, held every year in July in the Grand' Place in Brussels, where the Belgian Brewers' headquarters are based.

The Cooperstown brewery has been a great success from opening day. Don and Wendy refuse to compromise on quality, despite pressure to increase production. Their beers are matured slowly and lovingly on site before being bottled on their yeast. The Abbey Ale is in the style of a Belgian Dubbel. It is brewed with pale, Munich and caramalt grains, and hopped with American and Belgian varieties. It is a Burgundy-coloured ale with a deep collar of foam, a complex aroma of fruit, hops and spices, a palate rich in caramel, liquorice, toffee, chocolate and earthy hops, and a dry finish in which vine fruits, peppery hops and ripe grain dominate.

Stoudt's Triple

Source: Stoudt's Brewing, Adamstown, Pennsylvania, USA
Strength: 9%
Website: www.stoudtsbrewing.com

TASTING NOTES
Appearance
Aroma
Taste
Overall score

Carol Stoudt got tired of the joke that 'Stoudt's don't brew a stout', so she added a warm-fermented black ale to her portfolio. But since the brewery opened in 1987, it has built its reputation on the quality of its Belgian and German-style beers. Carol is married to Ed Stoudt. His German family came to the US as early as 1733. Ed went into the restaurant business while Carol toured Bavarian breweries and then took a university course in brewing before setting up shop in Adamstown. The area is known as 'Pennsylvania Dutch', but there is no Dutch influence: the word is a corruption of Deutsch, for a German community developed there.

Stoudt's has won many prizes and plaudits, including gold awards at the Great American Beer Festival. Carol not only brews a stout but has also added an IPA, but one of her outstanding beers is her Belgian-style abbey Triple. It is made with two-row Pilsner pale malt and Munich malt, and is hopped with four varieties from the German Hallertau. It is orange coloured with a big spicy hop and rich biscuity malt aroma, a warming malt palate rich in alcohol, fruit and spicy hops, and a long, lingering finish with earthy hop resins, ripe sappy malt and tart fruit. It is fermented with a Belgian yeast culture and is not filtered.

The Stoudt complex includes a shopping mall with a bakery and restaurant.

Tongerlo Double Brown/Triple Blond

Source: Browerij Haacht NV, Bortmeerbeek, Belgium
Strength: 6%/8%
Website: www.primus.be

The Abbey of Tongerlo is one of the most striking in Belgium, its imposing buildings rising out of the flat lands known as the Kempen close to the Dutch border. It is a Norbertine abbey, named after the followers of the migrant preacher Norbert of Gennep who became St Norbert. He founded a community at Prémontré in France in 1121. His followers built a monastery at Tongerlo in 1133 where the River Grote Nette waters the fields and meadows. From this lush countryside the monks were able to grow barley and hops to make their own beer. The abbey that grew out of the community became a major centre of religion and culture and has a replica of Leonardo da Vinci's *Last Supper*.

World War One put an end to brewing at Tongerlo, when the invading German troops dismantled the brewhouse and confiscated the copper vessels for the war effort. In 1989, the monks approached the Haacht brewery and asked them to produce beers for them. Haacht is best known for its Jan Primus beers named after the famously bibulous 13th-century Duke of Brabant whose name, corrupted to Gambrinus, became an inspiration for brewers in the Low Countries and further afield. The Tongerlo beers are carefully controlled by the monks and are refermented in the bottle and will improve with age.

The Double Brown has a deep copper colour, a spicy aroma with raisin and sultana fruit and spicy hops. The firm, full palate has powerful hints of coffee and liquorice with rich malt and earthy hops, followed by a long finish that is bitter-sweet, vinously fruity and ends with peppery hops.

The Triple Blond has a glowing amber colour, tart lemon fruit, juicy malt and spicy hops on the nose, and warming alcohol, citrus fruit, biscuity malt and spicy hop resins in the mouth. The finish is big, complex, with citrus fruit, rich malt and spicy hop resins.

The beers are accompanied by attractive glasses that show the image of the abbey. Several rustic restaurants in the neighbourhood of the abbey serve rustic meals with the beers.

TASTING NOTES
Appearance
Aroma
Taste
Overall score

TASTING NOTES
Appearance
Aroma
Taste
Overall score

Steam Beer

Many people assume that steam beer is a reference to the steam-driven engines that transformed brewing during the Industrial Revolution. There are a few breweries that use the word steam in this context. But in San Francisco it has a more precise meaning. It refers to a style, now confined to a single brewery, where both ale and lager techniques combine to produce a beer with the richness and fruitiness of an ale with the quenching character of a lager. It was a style created during the California Gold Rush and which survives and flourishes today due to the passion of a man who saved his local brewery and, in so doing, helped launch the American beer revolution.

Anchor Steam Beer
Source: Anchor Brewing Co, San Francisco, California, USA
Strength: 5%
Website: www.anchorbrewing.com

TASTING NOTES
Appearance
Aroma
Taste
Overall score

Fritz Maytag was a student at Stanford University in the 1960s and enjoyed a San Francisco speciality known as 'steam beer'. In 1965, he ordered a glass in his local bar and was told it would be the last because the producer, the Anchor Steam Brewery, was about to close. As a result, Fritz wrote his chapter of the American Dream. He cashed in some of his shares in the family's washing machine business, bought the brewery and created a legend.

Steam beer is unique to San Francisco. It is a style that dates from the California Gold Rush of the 1890s. When prospectors poured into the small town, they found a mainly Mexican population drinking wine or tequila. The gold diggers wanted beer and, in particular, they wanted the lager beers they enjoyed back east. Brewers in the area were desperate to meet the demand but refrigeration had not yet arrived, and the Californian coast, unlike Bavaria, does not have icy caves in which beer can be stored. The brewers tackled the problem with remarkable ingenuity by fermenting their beers with lager yeasts but at ale temperatures. They developed shallow vessels that exposed more of the beer to the atmosphere and encouraged it to cool rapidly. The beer continued a lively fermentation in casks in the bars, producing a high level of natural carbonation. As a result, when a cask was tapped, it let off such a hiss of escaping gas that drinkers said it sounded like steam.

The brewery Fritz inherited in the 1960s was on its last legs, and so strapped for cash that it used baker's yeast for fermentation and had just one employee. Fritz nursed it back to success, though it took 10 years for the Anchor Brewery to show a profit. Eventually he was able to move from a run-down site under a freeway to an impressive 1930s Art Deco building that had previously been the offices of a coffee-roasting company. Over the years, Fritz has immersed himself in the history, the culture and craft of brewing. He has re-created a beer from the Old World, using a recipe translated from cuneiform writing on stone tablets, and toured the great brewing nations. He has also built a brewery that is a shrine to the art of brewing. The reception area is like a comfortable club, with deep leather chairs, prints of old San Francisco and its brewing history, and a bar where all the Anchor beers are tapped. Plate glass windows allow visitors to view the brewhouse, with copper vessels standing on a tiled floor, handcrafted for Fritz by a German company. Anchor Steam has played a pivotal role in the American craft brewing revolution. Its success encouraged many others to fire mash tuns and kettles, revive old beer styles and develop new ones.

Fermentation for Anchor Steam takes place in open vessels just 60cm (2ft) deep, using a lager yeast culture but a warm temperature of between 16 to 21°C (60 to 70°F). The grist is a blend of pale and crystal malts with no added sugars. Hops are Northern Brewer, which are added three times during the copper boil (units of bitterness 30–35). Following fermentation, the green beer is warm conditioned for three weeks and then kräusened by adding some partially fermented wort to encourage a strong secondary fermentation.

The beer that emerges from this exhaustive process is bronze coloured, with a rich malty-nutty aroma, tart fruit and a spicy, earthy hop resins note. The firm, full palate has juicy malt, citrus fruit and tangy hops, followed by a long finish at first dominated by sappy malt and tart fruit but with a late burst of bitter hops. It is a complex and quenching beer, a world classic.

Lambic & Gueuze

Lambic and gueuze are potent symbols of brewing's past. Their vinous and cidery palate stresses the absurdity of building barriers between beer and fruit-based alcohols. Their long ageing process helps destroy the myth that beer is a rough and ready drink. And even though the act of turning sweet wort into alcohol is left to nature, the production of lambic demands the highest skill.

Lambic beers have been made for 400 years—possibly much longer. The method stretches back to 3000BC, when the first beers were made in the Old World by yeasts in the atmosphere. Today, there is only a handful of producers left, grouped in the valley of the River Senne that runs through Brussels in a region known as Payottenland. This is Breughel country, and the stolid peasant folk carousing in the paintings of Pieter the Elder are drinking lambic, not wine, from their earthenware pots.

The term 'lambic' is lost in history and has many interpretations. One theory is that the name was taken from the town of Lembeek, which has had a guild of brewers since the 15th century and an annual pilgrimage to the shrine of the patron saint of lambic brewers, Saint Veronus. One of the principal lambic producers, Frank Boon, is based in the town. Another theory is that the conquering Spanish in the 16th and 17th centuries called the farm-house breweries in the Senne Valley *alembics*, or distilleries.

What is beyond dispute is that lambic is the oldest beer style in existence. It is an agricultural beer that was once the only type drunk in Brussels and its environs. It declined in step with rural life and the spread of industry. Lambic's cause was not helped when a type of prohibition in Belgium at the turn of the 20th century prevented gin and other spirits being sold in cafés and bars. Drinkers turned to strong ales rather than the weaker lambics. The rapid spread of Pilsner-type beers did little to help lambic, either. Lambic and gueuze have been protected by Belgian law since 1965 and by a European Union ordinance of 1992. But such backing will keep the beers in production only if they are supported by consumers.

The method of production remains slow, ruminative and bucolic. Brewing does not take place in summer. In centuries past, farmers would not have brewed in the summer months, as they needed to devote all their energies to the harvest. And even spontaneous fermentation is too unpredictable and uncontrollable in hot weather.

Lambic is a type of wheat beer. Its protective laws and ordinances lay down that at least 30% wheat must be used in the mash. The wheat is not malted. The reasons are probably empirical: farmer-brewers had limited time at their disposal and knew that sufficient extract and enzymes could be provided by barley malt. Wheat also gave a tart, quenching and spicy character to the beer. The malt used in lambic breweries is exceptionally pale. As a result of the presence of wheat, the wort produced is turbid and milky white. A lambic will usually have an original gravity of around 1050 degrees and a finished alcohol of 4.5 to 5%. This can rise to 6% when fruit is added during maturation. The copper boil is a long one, often lasting for three hours. The wort is heavily hopped, using Belgian, English or German varieties. But the hops are four years old, have lost much of their aromatics and have a cheesy smell. They are used solely for their preservative qualities, as hop aroma and bitterness do not marry well with the characteristics imparted by wheat, wild yeasts and storage in oak vessels.

Following the boil, the hopped wort is pumped to the brewery attic. This is common to all lambic producers, for it is under the roof that alcohol starts to be made. The wort is run into a shallow open fermenter known as the cool ship, made either of copper or stainless steel. The room fills with steam as the wort runs into the fermenter and begins to cool. The louvred windows are left open and during the night wild yeasts enter and attack the sugars in the wort once the temperature has fallen to below 18°C (66°F). To encourage the yeasts, brewers even remove a few tiles to leave gaps in the roofs.

Research at the brewing faculty of Leuven University has identified two main types of *Brettanomyces* yeast, *bruxellensis* and *lambicus*. But when all the yeast strains in the atmosphere, the cellars and inside the casks are added together, they number as many as 35. When the beer reaches the maturation halls and is stored in oak casks, it is attacked by both microflora in the wood and the atmosphere. The wild organisms create a flor on top of the maturing beer similar to the flor in sherry casks that prevents oxidation.

The oak casks are bought from Portuguese port makers, Spanish sherry producers or Cognac distillers in France. The beer will stay in cask for several years: some are more than six years old. In the now closed Belle-Vue brewery I once walked down the dimly lit, cool avenues between the casks, each one chalked to indicate the year and month it was filled, and every so often tasting a small glass that had been tapped for me. A month-old lambic had a yeasty aroma and a bready taste. A year-old beer was sour on the nose, sweet and sour in the mouth and had a cheesy finish from the hops. At 18 months, the beer had taken on a delightful sherry colour, a musty Brettanomyces nose, a vinous palate and a dry finish with still a hint of cheesy hops. At 6½ years, the beer was much paler, had a sour, winey aroma, a sharp tangy palate with a pronounced sherry character and a sour, lactic finish. The cheese note had disappeared. It takes some time for Brettanomyces yeasts to dominate the other wild strains.

A straight lambic, tart, cidery and served flat, is usually on draught. The most popular form of the beer is gueuze (also spelt gueze), a blend of young and old lambics in bottle. The young lambic causes a fresh fermentation in the bottle. The result is a spritzy, foaming beer served from a bottle that has been corked with a wire cage like Champagne. The blending requires enormous skill. The blender must decide how much young lambic to marry with old: usually 60% young, but the beer will have more character if as much old lambic as possible is used. The bottles will be stored on their sides in cellars for between six and 18 months. Gueuze beers tend to be around 5.5% alcohol and are dry, tart and wonderfully refreshing. Again, no one is certain about the origin of the name but it is possible that it is a nickname derived from geyser, as the beer tends to rush and foam when released from the bottle. The Bruxellois certainly pronounce it with great force: gur-zer. On the Channel Islands, I discovered that, in Norman-French, gueuze is an old name for wheat, which may possibly provide a link to the beer style at a time when spontaneous fermentation extended beyond Payottenland.

The most exotic versions of lambic are those in which a further fermentation is caused by the addition of fruit. The two basic fruits used are cherry and raspberry. The use of these fruits is similar to the addition of juniper at a time when hops were not part of brewing. The fruit increases fermentability and adds tartness to the finished beer that blends well with the malt. And fruit seems to fuse especially well with beers in which wheat, with its fruity, apple-like flavour, is used. Small, hard cherries grow in abundance in the Brussels area. The preferred variety is the Schaarbeek, though the Gorsem is also used. The cherries are picked late so the fermentable sugars are concentrated. It is similar to the 'noble rot' grapes used in wine. As soon as the cherries are harvested they are added to casks, usually at the rate of 1kg (2¼lbs) of fruit to 5 litres (9 pints) of beer, with the addition of some young lambic. The sugars in the fruit and the young beer create a new fermentation. The tannins on the skins add to the dryness of the finished beer, while the pips impart further dryness and an almond-like note. A cherry lambic is called kriek from the Flemish word for the fruit: the French term is never used. A raspberry beer, on the other hand, is known by both Flemish and French words: frambozen or frambois.

The way in which lambic is made and blended means that aromas and flavours and even alcoholic strength will vary from one batch to another. The tasting notes are my most recent ones but expect variation. Go, drink and marvel.

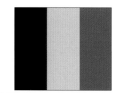

Boon Geuze/Mariage Parfait Kriek

Source: Brouwerij Frank Boon, Lembeek, Belgium
Strength: 6%/6%
Website: www.boon.be

TASTING NOTES
Appearance
Aroma
Taste
Overall score

TASTING NOTES
Appearance
Aroma
Taste
Overall score

Frank Boon (pronounced 'bone') has the perfect address: Fonteinstraat (Fountain Street) in Lembeek, the historic centre of lambic brewing. Frank came into the industry from running a student bar at college, then wholesaling beer, blending other producers' lambics and finally making the beer itself. He took over the De Vits brewery in Lembeek in 1975 when the owner retired. It is a site with considerable history: the present buildings date from 1810 but there had been a farm brewery and distillery since the late 17th century.

During the past 30 years, Frank's reputation has covered all the bases: eccentric, maverick, traditionalist, revivalist, innovator and, inevitably, compromiser as a result of making some filtered, sweetened and commercial lambics. Without doubt, he also makes some of the finest and most characterful traditional lambics. Blended lambics are sold under the Mariage Parfait label: perfect marriage.

Visitors are welcomed by wooden casks at the entrance, and the brewery inside is achingly traditional, down to the open cool ship in the attic, where fermentation begins when the wort is impregnated with wild yeasts. The beers have a softness and delicacy that makes them highly drinkable with less of the assertive acidity in other lambics. The Geuze (Frank's interpretation of the spelling) is a bottled blend of old and young lambics. It is spritzy and tart, with a lemon and ginger aroma, tart fruit in the mouth and a dry finish with hints of oak and fruit.

Mariage Parfait Kriek is superb, an annual vintage that is a blend of the year's young lambic and matured versions that have been in wood for between 18 months and two years. The blend enjoys a further maturation with the addition of cherries and is then held in bottle for up to two years. The beer that emerges is tart and has the toasted note that is also the signature of dry Champagne. The aroma is heady with tangy, sour cherries, and the fruit note continues through the palate into the long, quenching finish.

Cantillon Rosé de Gambrinus/Gueuze-Lambic/ Kriek/Foufoune

Source: Brasserie Cantillon, Anderlecht, Brussels, Belgium
Strength: All 5%
Website: www.cantillon.be

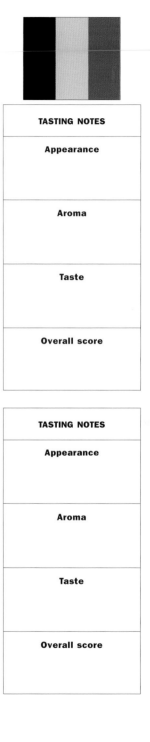

Cantillon dates from 1900. The present owner, Jean-Pierre Van Roy, married into the Cantillon family, took charge in 1978 and built the brewery's reputation. He is passionate about lambic to a degree that often upsets other producers of the style. 'Industrial gueuze' is not a phrase that endears Jean-Pierre to his competitors but, as he nears retirement and hands over to his son Jean, he is concerned that breweries that shorten maturation periods and use syrups rather than whole fruit will lower the standing of the lambic family. In recent years, Jean-Pierre has switched to organic production as his contribution to saving the planet. He brews from the end of October to the end of March. 'We used to brew in May, but we've lost a whole month as a result of global warming,' he says.

Cantillon calls itself the Museum of Gueuze and maintains strict traditional brewing methods. On the ground floor, a mash of barley malt and wheat is made in a small mash tun, and the turbid wort is pumped to the copper, where it is boiled for an extraordinary four or even five hours. The hopped wort then goes to the cool ship in the attic to invite inoculation by wild yeasts. Once fermentation is under way, the liquid is transferred to oak or chestnut casks bought from wine and Cognac makers.

Rosé de Gambrinus is a remarkable beer, a blend of raspberry lambic with a small amount of kriek. It has a superb aroma and palate of tart fruit and a bone dry and spritzy finish packed with more tart fruit, with raspberry to the fore.

The Gueuze-Lambic is sour with an almond-like nuttiness, lemon and bitter apple fruit and a deliciously mellow finish.

The Kriek has a glowing red colour, a sour fruit aroma, fresh tart fruit in the mouth and a dry and lingeringly fruity finish.

Foufoune is a recent addition to the range, a lambic made with the addition of apricots.

TASTING NOTES
Appearance
Aroma
Taste
Overall score

TASTING NOTES
Appearance
Aroma
Taste
Overall score

TASTING NOTES
Appearance
Aroma
Taste
Overall score

TASTING NOTES
Appearance
Aroma
Taste
Overall score

It is extremely pale, dry, acidic, tart and bone dry in the finish. Jean-Pierre, with a wolfish grin, explained that *foufone* in the Brussels dialect means pussy. When you consider the shape of an apricot, you know he is not referring to the brewery cat.

Cantillon is five minutes from Brussels Midi, the Eurostar terminus. It is open to visitors at any time during working hours. For a fee of €3.50, you can visit the brewery and enjoy a beer. Groups must book: tel: 0032 2521 4928; email: info@cantillon.be. Closed Sunday and public holidays.

Drie Fonteinen Oude Gueuze/Framboos/Oude Kriek

Source: Brouwerij Drie Fonteinen, Beersel, Belgium
Strength: 6%/5%
Website: www.3fonteinen.be

Someone in Rome must have thrown three coins in the Trevi fountain for, lo and behold, a new lambic brewer of that name appeared and has helped breathe life back into the sector.

The Debelder family has run an acclaimed restaurant in Beersel for many years and also acted as lambic blenders, taking beer from the likes of Boon, Girardin and Lindeman, and bringing them to fruition in oak casks. Then, in 1999, the brothers Armand and Guido took the giant step of opening the first new lambic brewery for 80 years. They continue to buy in lambic from Girardin and Lindeman until their own beers have reached an acceptable maturity and are ready for blending.

As well as the beers featured here, they have made the almost-lost style of Faro, a sweetened lambic, and have also made lambics with the addition of Chardonnay and Pinot Noir grapes. The bottled beers will improve with age.

Oude Gueuze has a shockingly dry, musty, tart lemon bouquet and palate, with a long, fruity, sour, acidic finish. Framboos is a true raspberry beer, made with whole fruit, not syrup. It has a luscious pink colour, a delightfully fruity but dry aroma and palate, with tart, slightly sour fruit in the lingering finish. Anybody who thinks fruit lambics are too challenging should sample this beer and let it cast aside any preconceptions. A bottled version is 6% and has more depth of fruit flavours.

Oude Kriek has a superb aroma of bitter cherry fruit and 'horse blanket' yeast mustiness. The fruit, with an almond-like underpinning from the pips, dominates the palate, while the finish is dry, sour, fruity and nutty. Again, the bottled version is 6% and is a revelation, with enormous sour fruit, yeast bite and almonds dominating from nose to finish.

The Drie Fonteinen restaurant is round the corner from the brewery at 3 Herman Teirlinckplein (closed Tuesday and Wednesday; tel: 02 331 0652). It serves top-class food and draught gueuze and lambic.

TASTING NOTES
Appearance
Aroma
Taste
Overall score

TASTING NOTES
Appearance
Aroma
Taste
Overall score

LEFT
Drie Fonteinen brewery cellar and Armand (right) and Guido, the first new Lambic Brewery owners for 80 years.

TASTING NOTES
Appearance
Aroma
Taste
Overall score

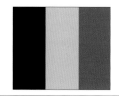

TASTING NOTES
Appearance
Aroma
Taste
Overall score

Girardin Gueuze Black Label 1882

Source: Brouwerij Girardin, Sint Ulriks Kapelle, Belgium
Strength: 5%
Website: None

This is one of the few remaining genuine farm brewers in the Senne Valley still making lambic. The brewery was launched in 1882 by Francis Girardin and today Paul is the fourth generation of the family to run the company. The farm still grows the wheat that is blended with barley malt to make beer. The small complex is fronted by oak casks and, inside, mashing and boiling take place in attractive, burnished copper vessels, watched over by an effigy of St Arnold, the patron saint of brewers.

Fermentation begins in a cool ship and continues in oak casks. Girardin produces framboise and kriek, but the Black Label is considered to be not only the best product but also one of the finest examples of a blended gueuze. It is full-bodied, with rich and creamy malt on the nose and palate, spritzy from natural carbonation and with a tongue-tingling sour lemon fruit note that dominates from start to finish, all overlain by a musty, 'horse blanket' character from the attack by Brettanomyces yeasts.

Do not confuse Black Label with Girardin's White Label 1882, which is a filtered version, perfectly acceptable and pleasant but a shadow of the unfiltered beer with its great depth of flavours that will improve in bottle for years, if not decades.

Beers made with Fruit, Spices, Herbs & Seeds

In 1588, Jacob Theodor von Bergzabern, describing contemporary brewing practice in Europe, noted that hops were increasingly being used but added: 'The English sometimes add to the brewed beer, to make it more pleasant, sugar, cinnamon, cloves and other good spices in a small bag. The Flemings mix it with honey or sugar and precious spices and so make a drink like claret or hippocras [spiced wine]. Others mix in honey, sugar and syrup, which not only makes the beer pleasant to drink, but also gives it a fine brown colour.' He added that brewers had learned from 'the Flemings and the Netherlanders' that adding laurel, ivy or Dutch myrtle to beer strengthens it, preserves it and stops it going sour.

As late as 1750, London brewers were still using bog myrtle and coriander to flavour their beers. As we have seen, Belgian brewers continue to add spices and orange peel to white, or wheat, beers, as well as hops. The addition of sugars, herbs and spices to beer is far older than the 16th century. We know from research and the translation of hieroglyphics on clay tablets that the Ancient Egyptians used dates, honey and even mandrake—a plant that, alarmingly, is a member of the nightshade family—in beer making.

From 3000BC to modern times, brewers have grappled with the problem of how to balance the biscuity nature of malt with ingredients that add a welcome bitterness and spiciness. When European brewers discovered the hop plant, they started to use it in brewing more for commercial reasons than for those of taste.

In his *Perfite Platforme for a Hoppe Garden*, first published in 1574 in England, Reynold Scot's arguments in favour of the plant were principally commercial: 'Whereas you cannot make above 8–9 gallons of indifferent ale from 1 bushel of malt, you may draw 18–20 gallons of good beer. If your ale may endure a fortnight, your beer through the benefit of the hop shall continue a month.' In other words, hops gave beer better 'shelf life', to use an ugly modern expression, and less malt had to be used.

The cost of raw materials was an important consideration as brewing moved from being a church-based pastime to a business activity. At a royal banquet in Windsor Park in 1528, 15 gallons of ale and 15 gallons of beer were ordered. The beer cost 20 pence, the ale two shillings and sixpence. The difference in price is significant and is caused almost completely by the greater quantity of malt used in ale.

The ability of the oils, acids and tannins in the hop plant protected beer against bacterial infection, which was a major problem in a period when it was almost impossible to control fermentation temperatures. Scot, whose book ran to several editions and was highly influential, did add that one of the advantages of hopped beer was 'the grace it yieldeth to the taste all men may judge that have sense in their mouths'.

But hopped beer, as opposed to unhopped and flavoured ale, did not please all drinkers. A debate raged for several centuries in England over the benefits of ale and beer. Hops were banned in Norwich, even though many Flemish weavers, who had introduced the plant to England, had settled there. In 1519, the use of the 'wicked and pernicious weed' was prohibited in Shrewsbury. Henry VIII instructed his royal court brewer to use neither brimstone nor hops in his ale. Drinkers, from the humble to the mighty, preferred the old flavours of spices, honey, flowers, plants and herbs. Their use lingered on for several centuries. They persist in a handful of styles. And, to add to both the pleasure and a greater understanding and appreciation of beer, their use has been revived in a number of countries by craftspeople who have given us another fascinating glimpse of brewing's past.

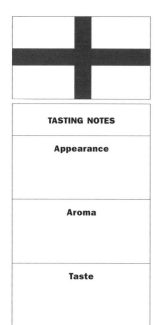

Daleside Morocco Ale

Source: Daleside Brewery, Harrogate, North Yorkshire, England
Strength: 5.5%
Website: www.dalesidebrewery.co.uk/morocco.htm

TASTING NOTES
Appearance
Aroma
Taste
Overall score

Morocco Ale is brewed to a secret recipe held at Levens Hall, a moated Elizabethan complex, famous for its topiary, near Kendal in Cumbria. The beer is thought to date from the time of Elizabeth I and was given its name by Colonel James Grahme, a courtier of Charles II. Charles's queen, Catherine of Braganza, brought Tangiers as part of her dowry, and Grahme may have associated the Moors of the region with the dark beer consumed at Levens.

The recipe for the beer had been buried in the garden of the hall under evergreens during the English Civil War. Following the restoration of the monarchy, the beer was brewed every May until 1877. Each batch was matured for 21 years and was served at feasts held in the gardens of the hall. At one stage, meat was part of the recipe in order to give the yeast nutrition to sustain it over such an extraordinary period of maturation. New guests were required to stand on one leg and empty, in a single draught, a tall 'constable' glass of the beer.

The beer was resurrected in the 1990s by the Daleside Brewery for Levens Hall and has since been made available commercially. Brewery and hall are tight-lipped about the ingredients, though they confirm meat is no longer used. It will rapidly become clear when the beer is sniffed and sipped that ginger is a major ingredient. The other spicy notes suggest nutmeg, while the rich marmalade fruit and roasted and toasted notes will come from the malts and hops used: Daleside uses Challenger and Goldings in its regular beers.

The beer is available from Levens Hall (015395 60321) and from Booths supermarkets in the north of England.

Fraoch Heather Ale/Kelpie Ale

Source: Williams Brothers Brewing Company, Alloa, Scotland
Strength: 4.1%/4.1%
Website: www.fraoch.com

The earliest brewers in Scotland were not Celts but Picts, the cave-dwelling race that raided Roman Britain but which was exterminated in a series of pogroms in the fourth century by marauders from Ireland. According to legend, the last Pict threw himself from the cliffs into the sea rather than pass on the secret of heather ale to the invading forces of the king of Ireland.

But heather ale lingered on in remote parts of the Highlands and Islands. A visitor to Islay in 1744 noted that beer there was made from malt, hops and 'heath'. Ancient Pictish kilns have been discovered in the Galloway region where heather ale was once made. In his 19th-century book *Curiosities of Ale and Beer*, John Bickerdyke described the way in which heather was used

to brew: 'The blossoms of the heather are carefully gathered and cleansed, then placed in the bottom of the vessels. Wort of the ordinary kind is allowed to drain through the blossoms and gains in its passage a peculiar and agreeable flavour known to all familiar with heather honey.'

In 1993, Bruce Williams in Glasgow obtained a translation from the Gaelic of a recipe for heather ale that was in the possession of a woman in the Western Isles. Bruce's Fraoch Ale aroused enormous interest. The beer was produced under licence for him at several Scottish breweries until he and his brother were able to acquire the Forth Brewery site in Alloa.

Fraoch (pronounced 'frook', the Gaelic for heather) is available on draught and bottle. It is brewed with pale malt, carapils, flowering heather and bog myrtle, and hopped with First Gold, which produce 19 units of bitterness. The hopped wort is infused with fresh heather flowers for an hour before fermentation. The beer has a delicate flowery, fruity bouquet with flowery and minty flavours in the mouth, balanced by gentle hop resins and juicy malt. The finish is dry, earthy, minty, floral and quenching.

Kelpie is Gaelic for seaweed. The beer recalls the time 400 years ago when coastal and island farmers used seaweed beds to grow cereal crops. Bladderwrack seaweed is used with organic pale malt and First Gold hops to produce a pale beer with an iron-like aroma and palate, balanced by juicy malt and spicy hops. The finish is lingering, tart, tangy, with a herbal and fruity intensity. The bottled beers are available in Canada and the US.

TASTING NOTES
Appearance
Aroma
Taste
Overall score

TASTING NOTES
Appearance
Aroma
Taste
Overall score

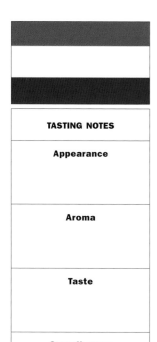

Jopen Koyt

Source: Jopen BV, Haarlem, Netherlands
Strength: 8.5%
Website: www.jopen.nl

TASTING NOTES
Appearance
Aroma
Taste
Overall score

For centuries, European and Scandinavian brewers added gruit, a type of bouquet garni of herbs and spices, to beer. Gruit was big business and it was controlled by the church, which fought a powerful rearguard action against the use of hops in brewing. In Cologne, the archbishop cornered the gruit market through a decree called the Grutrecht and he attempted to outlaw the use of hops. In the Low Countries, from the 14th century, the religious controllers of the gruit market placed punitive taxes on hopped beer imported from Bremen and Hamburg. But the march of history and drinkers' preference prevailed and eventually the gruit market was abandoned, though the church did well out of the deal,

accepting rents or royalties in return for giving up their rights to supply gruit to brewers.

The great Dutch trading city of Haarlem was once a major brewing centre. Water from the canals was used until pollution made the supply unsafe. Pure brewing liquid was then brought to Haarlem by a new canal: it still exists today as Brewers Canal. In the 17th century, Haarlem was home to around 100 brewers. The number had fallen to seven by the 19th century and the last brewery closed in 1916. In 1995, a group of beer enthusiasts led by Michel Ordeman launched a range of beers based on medieval recipes that used gruit. The flagship regular beer is Koyt, an old Dutch word for gruit, while jopen is another old term for a beer cask.

Koyt is brewed for Jopen by the Van Steenberge brewery in Belgium (Jopen does not brew Koyt itself). Michel and his friends wanted to brew Koyt without hops but the Dutch authorities will not permit any beer to be made without hops—a fussy, bureaucratic attitude that rather misses the point of the endeavour. So Koyt has hops but also uses sweet gale, coriander and other herbs and spices. In the medieval fashion, the grains are malted barley, wheat and oats, with a darker barley malt that gives the beer a luscious russet colour. It has a rich spicy aroma of coriander with a woody, grassy note, along with nutty and creamy malt and light hops. Spices and rich malt fill the mouth while the finish is long and complex, with spices and creamy malt dominating.

Meantime Coffee Beer/Red Beer

Source: Meantime Brewing Co, Greenwich, London, England
Strength: 4%/4.5%
Website: www.meantimebrewing.com

Meantime was created in 2000 by master brewer Alastair Hook to produce handcrafted European beers. Alastair is a graduate of both Heriot Watt brewing and distilling school in Edinburgh and of the brewing faculty at Weihenstephan in Freising near Munich, widely regarded as the finest brewing school in the world. His mission has been to brew small-batch beers to exacting standards, producing lagers with character and flavour rather than gas and gaiters, and ales that snap and crackle with hop aroma. He brews beers for the Sainsbury's supermarket group under the Taste the Difference label. Meantime owns the Greenwich Union pub (56 Royal Hill, London SE10) where draught and bottled beers can be tasted.

The Coffee Beer is brewed with the addition of Fairtrade Rwanda Maraba Bourbon coffee to East Anglian pale and dark barley malts and Fuggles hops. The coffee, like the beer, is hand-crafted, roasted by Union Coffee Roasters. It has a superb aroma of freshly roasted beans, vanilla and dark malt, with a good spicy undertow of hops. Coffee, vanilla, grain and hops pack the mouth, followed by a long, complex finish that is dry, roasty and hoppy.

Alastair's interpretation of a Belgian-style fruit beer uses fresh raspberry juice added to a beer base. It has a luscious red colour and a rich raspberry aroma balanced by sappy malt and gentle hops. The palate is spritzy, with lush and tart fruit, juicy malt and spicy hops, followed by a lingering finish packed with tangy raspberries, biscuity malt and earthy hop resins.

TASTING NOTES
Appearance
Aroma
Taste
Overall score

TASTING NOTES
Appearance
Aroma
Taste
Overall score

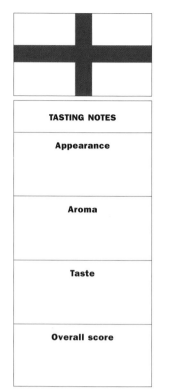

Nethergate Augustinian Ale

Source: Nethergate Brewery Co, Pentlow, Essex, England
Strength: 5.2%
Website: www.nethergate.co.uk

TASTING NOTES
Appearance
Aroma
Taste
Overall score

Nethergate moved to Essex in 2004. Its first base was in the attractive market town of Clare in Suffolk, where there is an Augustinian priory and a small group of monks. The brewery reached an agreement with the prior to produce what in Belgium would be called an abbey beer, using images of the church and St Augustine, one of the most influential saints. There are religious houses throughout the world where Augustinians faithfully follow his doctrines. A royalty on sales of the beer is paid to the prior in Clare.

Augustinian Ale is brewed with Maris Otter pale and crystal malts, is hopped with Fuggles and spiced with coriander. It is a rich, deep bronze in colour with a spicy aroma from the coriander, and a piny and earthy note from the Fuggles, with a solid base of biscuity malt. Citrus fruit enters on the palate with continuing notes of spice, juicy malt and hop resins. The lingering finish is spicy, with nutty and biscuity malt, bitter hops and tangy fruit. The beer is filtered and then reseeded with fresh yeast prior to bottling. It is produced principally for sale in the United States but it can be bought by mail order direct from the brewery: 01787 277244. The beer should not be confused with Nethergate's beer of the same name, which is a draught 4.5% cask-conditioned beer and is not spiced.

RCH Ale Mary

Source: RCH Brewery, West Hewish, Weston-super-Mare, Somerset, England
Strength: 6%
Website: www.rchbrewery.com

Ale Mary is a bottle-fermented version of the brewery's regular draught cask beer Firebox with the addition of spices. And what spices! Ginger, cloves, cinnamon, coriander, nutmeg and pimento join pale and chocolate malts and Progress and Target hops to produce a beer that stunned the judges—myself included—in CAMRA's 2001 Champion Bottled Beer of Britain competition, which it duly won.

Firebox has a tart and tangy orange fruit character and this comes through powerfully in the bottled version. But the fruit is fighting for attention with the spicy, peppery and almost sneeze-inducing aromatics. What a wonderful companion for Indian cuisine the beer would make instead of the insipid mock lagers most restaurants serve. Ginger and coriander in particular blast the tongue but are balanced by raisin and sultana fruit and earthy hops. The finish is warming, ripe with alcohol and lingering spices, with a dry and finally bitter end but with a solid underpinning of juicy malt and vine fruit.

The brewery firmly denies any suggestion the beer is named in honour of Lady Mary Archer, wife of the disgraced peer and novelist Lord Jeffrey Archer of Weston-super-Mare. In a famous court case, the judge described Lady Archer as 'fragrant' but probably didn't have nutmeg or pimento in mind.

TASTING NOTES
Appearance
Aroma
Taste
Overall score

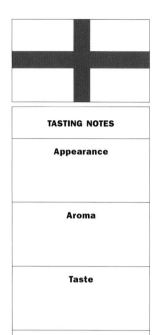

St Austell Clouded Yellow

Source: St Austell Brewery Co, St Austell, Cornwall, England
Strength: 4.8%
Website: www.staustellbrewery.co.uk

When Roger Ryman, the head brewer at St Austell, decided to brew a German-style wheat beer for the brewery's annual Celtic Beer Festival in 1999, he called it Hagar the Horrible. In spite of this less than mellifluous name, the beer was well received and in 2003 Roger entered it for the Beer Challenge staged by the giant supermarket group Tesco. It won, gained shelf space with Tesco nationally and achieved wide praise and appreciation under the gentler name of Clouded Yellow, a rare butterfly that visits Britain during the summer in common with several German wheat beers.

Roger's aim was to create his interpretation of a German Weissbier but he was anxious not to introduce an imported yeast strain in case it cross-fertilised with his prized house culture.

In order to create the true flavour of a German weiss, with its banana and bubblegum character, he used vanilla pods, cloves, coriander and maple syrup alongside Maris Otter pale malt, wheat malt and spicy American Willamette hops. The spices are added in a vessel known as the hop back that receives the hopped wort after the copper boil. Maple syrup is blended with sugar and used as a priming to encourage fermentation in bottle. The burnished gold beer has a full and tempting aroma of spices, banana and vanilla with creamy malt and light hop resins. Spices and vanilla fill the mouth but there is a continuing rich malt note. The finish is quenching, lingering, rich with banana, vanilla, spices, rich malt and light earthy hops. A complex, intriguing and refreshing beer.

Wells Banana Bread Beer

Source: Wells & Young's Brewery, Bedford, England
Strength: 4.5% cask/5.2% bottle
Website: www.wellsandyoungs.co.uk

TASTING NOTES
Appearance
Aroma
Taste
Overall score

Wells & Young's is England's biggest family-owned, independent regional brewery. Not satisfied with the success and growth of its premium cask beer Bombardier (see page 100), it has added to the range a beer that not only offers the ripe aroma and flavour of banana—the most popular fruit in the country—but actually uses real fruit during the production process.

The Campaign for Real Ale, ever anxious to win new supporters to the cause of cask ale, organised a tasting for women-only visitors to the Great British Beer Festival in London and found that Banana Bread Beer met with great acclaim and appreciation. Hop bitterness is one frequent reason given by women for not drinking real ale, and the lush smoothness and creaminess of banana clearly helped make the beer more acceptable.

The cask version is a seasonal beer, the stronger bottled one is available all year round. It is brewed with pale and crystal malts and hopped with Challenger and Goldings varieties. Banana pulp is added during the copper boil stage. The pale bronze beer has a rich banana aroma, while the palate has both banana and pear drop flavours, allied to juicy malt and a light tingle of hops. The finish is fruity, creamy but finishes dry with a late crackle of spicy hops and smooth, creamy malt.

Pale Lagers

Brewing in continental Europe was transformed by the development of golden lager beer in Pilsen, Bohemia, in the mid-19th century. But it was in neighbouring Bavaria that brewers grasped the potential of cold fermentation to produce a wider portfolio of beers made with the use of ice-making machines, better-quality malt and hops, and purer strains of yeast.

Such was the impact of the new beers from Munich and the surrounding region that brewers elsewhere in Europe and Scandinavia referred to 'Bavarian beer' as both a style and one they wished to emulate. It was the fame of Bavarian beers that sent J C Jacobsen, the founder of the Carlsberg brewery in Copenhagen, on a long and arduous coach journey to Munich in order to get a supply of yeast from Spaten in order to make beer by cold fermentation.

The first commercial Bavarian beers were dark in colour, a luscious, transluscent red/brown as a result of using malts kilned over wood fires. The Bavarians, more stolid and conservative than the famously unconventional Bohemians, remained loyal to dark beers they called 'dunkel'. But the success of Pilsner beer and the introduction of modern methods of kilning malt to make lighter varieties encouraged the Munich brewers to introduce paler versions of lager beer. They made their own interpretations of Pilsner beer—usually shortened to Pils to avoid legal action from Pilsen. But, just as British brewers introduced a weaker, everyday version of India Pale Ale called simply pale ale, the Bavarians developed a pale lager that was fractionally lower in alcohol than a Pils but noticeably less hoppy, perhaps 22 units of bitterness compared to the 38 of a Pils. The style is known as Helles or Hell and means pale.

This is the style of quaffing beer that is downed in beer gardens, bars and restaurants in Bavaria. Pils is seen as a beer for a special occasion or perhaps as the fitting end to a drinking session. Helles is a style that has been widely copied. Brewers throughout the world may call their golden lagers Pils or Pilsner but few have the aggressive hop bitterness of the original. Helles has even made its impact felt across the border in the modern Czech Republic, for the classic Budweiser Budvar has more in common with a Munich Helles than with a beer from Pilsen.

With the exception of the Japanese and Russian beers, the lagers listed below are brewed in accordance with the German Purity Law, the Reinheitsgebot, that stipulates that only malt, hops, water and yeast can be used in the brewing process. Sugars and cheaper grains are outlawed. Czech brewers, such as Budvar, produce 12 degree or premium beers in accordance with the Reinheitsgebot in order to sell them in Germany.

ABOVE LEFT
Baltika is a fine-tasting lager from Russia's major brewing group owned by Carlsberg.

LEFT
An early 20th-century promotion by Budvar for its classic golden lager was aimed at women.

Augustiner Hell

Source: Brauerei Augustiner, Munich, Bavaria, Germany
Strength: 5.2%
Website: www.augustiner-braeu.de

Munich is München in German, a corruption of Mönchen, meaning the Monks' Place. The city was founded in 1158 when a Bavarian duke built a bridge across the River Isar, enabling it to become an important trading post on the salt route from Austria to the north German ports. Benedictines and Franciscans were among the orders that built monasteries in the town but it was the Augustinians who developed a community there in 1294 and added a brewery in 1328. Augustiner can therefore lay claim to being the oldest brewery in Munich, though it has long since moved from its original site to a modern brewery in the city centre.

In common with most of the old breweries in Munich, Augustiner has had a turbulent history: secularised in 1803, taken over first by the Bavarian royal family and then by the state when the monarchy lost power after World War One, and bought by the Wagner family. Today it is a public company. While it is less known outside Bavaria than some of the other big Munich breweries, Augustiner is the most popular beer in the city and is consumed with relish in such beer gardens and bars as the Augustiner Keller on Arnulf Strasse, the brewery tap on Neuhauser Strasse and the large Hirschgarten near the Nymphenburg Palace. I have even enjoyed a glass in the pavilion of the MCC, the Munich Cricket Club, run by ex-pats in the Englischer Garten.

The beer is a burnished gold colour, is brewed with pale malt (around eight units of colour) and Hallertau hop varieties that produce 22 units of bitterness and has a rich toasted malt, light citrus fruit and floral hop aroma. Ripe, juicy malt and hop resins fill the mouth, followed by a long finish with some dryness at the end but dominated by sweet, soft malt, light but punchy hops and a delicious hint of lemon fruit.

Baltika Classic No 3

Source: Baltika Brewery, St Petersburg, Russia
Strength: 4.8%
Website: www.baltika.ru

There is a certain irony in the fact that the number of breweries in Russia has fallen by almost half since the collapse of the Soviet Union. Whisper it quietly, but there was more choice under communism than capitalism. The Russian tradition of brewing dark beers, including porters and imperial stouts, is under threat as global brewers dominate the market, centralise production and concentrate on pale lagers. As this book was being completed, the Baltika group announced it was brewing Foster's under licence. Oh, you lucky Russians! When I visited the Vena brewery in St Petersburg, a subsidiary of Baltika, and asked to taste its porter I was told it was no longer produced.

The main Baltika plant was built in 1978 on a greenfield site outside Leningrad, now St Petersburg. The state enterprise was privatised in 1992 and is now owned by Baltic Beverages Holding, a group jointly owned by Carlsberg and Scottish & Newcastle, which includes Sinebrychoff in Finland. Baltika is now the biggest brewing group in Russia with close to a quarter of the market. As well as St Petersburg, it has plants in Rostov on Don and other major urban centres. In the Russian tradition, the beers are labelled simply 1 to 7, the last one being a porter.

The pale lagers tend to be rather bland, mass market beers devoid of much aroma or taste. The exception is Classic, also branded as No 3. Vena has a similar beer called Original at 5%. Baltika uses pale malt and a touch of dark malt for colour and flavour. Hops, in the form of pellets, are imported from Germany, as the Russian hop industry is currently too small to supply sufficient quantities. The beer is exceptionally pale with a rich cornflour, vanilla and juicy malt aroma and a touch of lemon fruit. The fruit note builds in the mouth with a toasted malt note and light floral hops. The finish is dry with developing bitter hop notes balancing the tangy fruit and sappy malt.

TASTING NOTES

Appearance

Aroma

Taste

Overall score

TASTING NOTES

Appearance

Aroma

Taste

Overall score

Budweiser Budvar 12°
Source: Budějovicky Budvar, České Budějovice, Czech Republic
Strength: 5%
Website: www.budvar.cz

TASTING NOTES
Appearance
Aroma
Taste
Overall score

Controversy surrounds one of the world's classic lager beers. Budweiser Budvar is seldom out of the headlines. It is constantly involved in court battles and trade mark disputes with the giant American brewer, Anheuser-Busch, owner of the world's biggest beer brand, also called Budweiser.

The Americans claim their beer is the original, but history is not on their side. The South Bohemian town of České Budějovice has been a major brewing centre for centuries. It had 44 breweries in the 15th century and, under the town's old German name of Budweis, the beers were known generically as Budweiser, just as beers from Pilsen are called Pilsner. The royal court brewery was based in Budweis, enabling the products to be called 'the beer of kings'. In the 19th century, a major, German-owned brewery, Budweiser Burgerbrau, made and widely exported beer under the Budweiser name. It still exists but is now known as Samson.

In 1875, two German-born emigrants called Anheuser and Busch opened a brewery in St Louis, Missouri, and among its beers it had one called Budweiser, based on the Czech style, which it subsequently tagged 'the king of beers'.

Sound familiar? Twenty years later, Czech speakers in Budweis opened a new brewery, the Budějovicky Pivovar, which means the Budweis Brewery. For convenience, the name is shortened to Budvar. When the Czechs attempted to export their beer to the United States, sparks flew and litigation involving the two brewers of Budweiser has rumbled on ever since.

Today, the two beers could not be more different. The American beer lists rice before barley malt on the label, and the minute amount of hops used in production create no more than 12 units of bitterness. Budvar, on the other hand, is a pure malt beer that adheres to the German purity law. It is made in a magnificent brewhouse, with large copper mashing and brew kettles set on tiled floors. A double decoction mash is used. Primary fermentation is in small conicals, ripening or lagering in classic horizontal tanks. Lagering lasts for 90 days, one of the longest periods of cold conditioning in the world. Only pale Moravian malt and Žatec hops are used (20 units of bitterness). Soft brewing water comes from a deep underground natural reservoir that dates back several thousand years. Budvar has a rich malt and vanilla aroma, it is quenching in the mouth with a floral hop character, and the finish has a fine balance of juicy malt, tangy hop resins and a delicate hint of apple fruit. It is unquestionably one of the world's finest lager beers, sold in the United States under the name of Czechvar.

Kirin Ichiban

Source: Kirin Brewery Co, Tokyo, Japan
Strength: 5%
Website: www.kirin.com

Ichiban means 'Number One' or, literally, the best. Kirin Lager enjoys a reputation as the best Pils-style beer in Japan, but it added to the pleasure of beer drinking in 1990 with the introduction of Ichiban, fractionally stronger than the lager. It is made from the 'first running', or first pressing, of the wort in the mash tun. Instead of leaving the mash of malt and water to stand and then sparging, or sprinkling, it with more fresh water to squeeze out as much malt sugar as possible, the Kirin brewers run off the first, biscuity wort from the mashing vessels and discard the grain. The wort is clarified in a lauter tun, boiled with hops, fermented and then ripened or lagered, in this case for two months. Pale barley malt and Czech Saaz and German Hallertauer hops are used.

The delicious and refreshing beer that emerges, on draught and in bottle, has a lilting lemon grass, toasted malt and light floral hop aroma, with juicy malt, hop resins and delicate fruit in the mouth, and a lingering finish with biscuity malt, tangy fruit and spicy hops.

The beer has been so successful that it is now brewed under licence in both Britain and the US.

TASTING NOTES
Appearance
Aroma
Taste
Overall score

Spaten Münchner Hell

Source: Spaten-Franziskaner-Bräu, Munich, Bavaria, Germany
Strength: 4.8%
Website: www.spatenbraeu.com

Spaten traces its brewing roots back to 1397, with commercial rather than monastic production dating from 1522. In 1807, Gabriel Sedlmayr the Elder, master brewer at the Royal Court Brewery, bought the company, whose Spaten name means 'spade': the logo shows a maltster's shovel, used for turning grain in a maltings. In 1839, his son Gabriel the Younger took over and began energetically to transform production of beer to make use of the new technologies of the Industrial Revolution. Together with the Viennese brewer Anton Dreher, he visited Britain to see how the new pale ales were made. He built a new brewery in 1851 on the site of deep cellars and, with the aid of ice-making machines, turned his earlier experiments into full-blown commercial production of beers by the method of cold fermentation.

As I explained in the introduction to this section, the first lager beers in Munich were brown in colour but, in 1893, Sedlmayr launched the first pale or Helles beer in the city. It would be hyperbolic to suggest it marked a transformation of brewing. Most of the other Munich brewers did not begin to brew pale lagers until the 1920s, such was the consumer devotion to dark, or Dunkel, beers. But Spaten had produced the benchmark beer and that style today is the major one alongside wheat beers.

Spaten's Hell, lagered for two months, brewed from pale malt and Hallertauer hop varieties (22 units of bitterness) has a lightly toasted malt, gentle hop resins and delicate lemon fruit aroma and palate, with a quenching finish that is bitter-sweet to start and ends dry with delicate hop notes, juicy malt and tangy fruit.

TASTING NOTES
Appearance
Aroma
Taste
Overall score

Žatec 12°
Source: Žatec Brewery, Žatec, Czech Republic
Strength: 5%
Website: www.zatec-brewery.com

TASTING NOTES
Appearance
Aroma
Taste
Overall score

On my first visit to the brewery, it was semi-derelict, with a reception area recently vacated by the Young Communist League. Two years later, the brewery had been transformed, sparkling with fresh paint. Previously leaking lagering cellars with rusting pipework were now spick and span. The transformation is due to the energetic ownership of Anglo-Swedish businessman Rolf Munding. The town of Žatec, in the former German-speaking Sudetenland, gives its name to the surrounding hop-growing region, famous for producing some of the finest and most aromatic varieties in the world, known outside the Czech Republic by their German name of Saaz. The dark red soil, rich in ferrous oxide, is ideal for hop growing. The brewery is based in a former castle with a commanding position over the town and river. The castle cellars, 24m (80ft) below ground, proved ideal for storing beer when the site became a brewery in the 19th century, modelled on the Pilsner Urquell plant in Pilsen, where the first golden lager had been made. Žatec has a capacity of 160,000 hectolitres a year and produces 10, 11 and 12 degree beers: the 11 degree is available in selected bars and restaurants in Britain where Rolf Munding has interests, but I have chosen the 12 degree as the best of the three.

It is stored or lagered for 45 days and brewed with pale Moravian malt and local hops: the hops are added to the kettle three times, after 30 minutes, one hour and 1½ hours. Primary fermentation is in open vessels, lagering in horizontal tanks. For a Czech lager, the beer has a surprising hint of banana fruit on the nose from the house yeast culture, with massive hop resins, juicy malt and citrus lemon. Floral hops dominate the palate, and the long, dry hoppy finish has more juicy malt and lemon fruit.

A sign in the brewer's office announces: 'Where beer is brewed there is a good life' and the good life has certainly returned to a brewery that, in the early 1990s, seemed destined to close.

Black & Dark Lagers

Dark lager, in common with dark mild in England, is enjoying a renaissance. Both are beer styles that developed at the time of the Industrial Revolution and refreshed the new urban working class. They also reflect an earlier period of brewing, when all beers were brown in colour as a result of the way in which malt was prepared: cured or kilned over wood fires.

Wood fires are difficult to control. They often flare and scorch the grain, giving a smoky character to the finished beer. When coke and, later, gas replaced wood as the fuels for curing malt, brewers were able to make beers from pale malt with its far higher level of the natural enzymes that transform starch into fermentable sugar. Even dark beers started to be made from pale malt with the addition of darker grains for colouring and flavour. Dark lager—known in Bavaria as dunkel or dunkles—was different in one important respect from dark mild. It was the first beer to be made by the new system of cold fermentation. Cold conditioning took place in deep cellars cooled by ice. The wooden casks in which the beer was stored were lined with pitch and the result was a beer with a brown or russet colour and a luscious flavour reminiscent of vine fruits, nuts, liquorice and coffee. It was 'Bavarian beer' that started to transform European brewing practice and paved the way for the Pilsner revolution of the mid-19th century.

In Bavaria, home of the first dark lagers, most brewers kept a dunkel beer as part of their portfolios. But dunkel was a minority taste for older drinkers: what the English call a 'cloth cap'

beer. The style was rejuvenated by one man: Crown Prince Luitpold in his castle at Kaltenberg near Munich (see page 263). As a result of his endeavours, dunkel now enjoys a much higher profile and is brewed with some enthusiasm.

Across the border in Czechoslovakia, dark lager remained an important part of the brewing scene, partly because heavy industry lingered on for much longer than on the other side of the Iron Curtain and also as a result of the extreme conservatism of the communist regime. It was the lack of funds to invest in new brewing methods that enabled both genuine Pilsners and dark lagers to survive. We have seen that the arrival of the 'free market' in the new Czech Republic has done little to improve the quality of pale lagers but so far dark versions have survived intact and even been given a small amount of support and promotion.

Dark lager has been boosted further in the United States. A new generation of brewers, many of them of German descent, are brewing beers with enormous devotion to the original styles, including dunkel, which has brought dark lager to a new and appreciative audience.

TASTING NOTES

Appearance
Aroma
Taste
Overall score

TASTING NOTES

Appearance
Aroma
Taste
Overall score

Gordon Biersch Dunkles

**Source: Gordon Biersch Brewery,
Palo Alto, California, USA**
Strength: 5%
Website: www.gordonbiersch.com

The American Dream is alive and well in California. Dan Gordon graduated from a five-year course at the Weihenstephan faculty of brewing near Munich, the first American to do so for 40 years. When he returned to California, he met Dean Biersch, a restaurateur and beer lover, and they planned a brew-restaurant in Palo Alto that would offer first-class food, backed by Dan's faithful re-creations of German beers.

Palo Alto opened in 1988 and such has been the success of the venture that, backed by investment from a Las Vegas-based entertainment group, Dan and Dean have built a brewery with a capacity of 85,000 barrels a year in San José and opened new restaurants in Hawaii, Nevada and Washington State. Hops from the Bavarian Hallertau and a yeast strain from Weihenstephan are imported to brew and ferment the beers.

Dunkles has a rich and tempting russet-brown colour, a ripe bouquet of liquorice, coffee, dark grain and vine fruits, and a full palate dominated by raisin fruit, coffee, burnt malt and light hop resins. The lingering, complex finish is packed with rich, dark fruit, caramel, bitter-sweet grain and earthy hops.

Kaltenberg König Ludwig Dunkel

**Source: Schlossbrauerei Kaltenberg,
Geltendorf, Bavaria, Germany**
Strength: 5.6%
Website: www.kaltenberg.de

His Royal Highness Crown Prince Luitpold of Kaltenberg is an unlikely brewer. But, despite the title, he has no power and with a large castle to run he decided to turn the small family brewery into a commercial enterprise that would help pay for the upkeep of the estate. He took charge of the castle and brewery in 1976 when he was in his mid-20s and is still in control today.

A castle was built on the site in the 13th century by Duke Rudolph of Bavaria and was attacked, ransacked, destroyed and rebuilt in medieval times. The current castle dates from 1670 but was redesigned in neo-Gothic style in the 1840s. Thirty years later the castle brewery spread its wings and began to supply local taverns as well as the royal household with beer. When Prince Luitpold took charge he decided to turn the local speciality, a dark lager, into the main brand to restore dunkel beer to its rightful position as a proud Bavarian style. It is named in honour of King Ludwig, one of his ancestors. The brewery at first could make just 25,000 hectolitres (550,000 gallons) a year but capacity has grown to more than 100,000 hectos (2.2m gallons).

Prince Luitpold uses Bavarian pale, dark and roasted Bavarian malts, and he hops the beer three times with Hersbrucker and Tettnanger varieties from the Hallertau (colour 40, units of bitterness 26). The mash is a long triple decoction one. After the copper boil, the beer has a primary fermentation in small conical vessels, followed by a long ripening in steel tanks in the cellars of the castle. The original wooden lagering tanks are for display only. The beer is kräusened with partially fermented wort to encourage a strong second fermentation during lagering. To avoid the sweetness associated with some dunkel beers, Prince Luitpold attenuates the beer more than most brewers, turning 80% of the malt sugars into alcohol: the Bavarian norm is around 70%.

He also adds a lactic delbrücki culture (see page 190) to help counteract sweetness. Most unusually—as the practice is frowned on by German brewers—he dry hops the beer in the British manner for additional aroma and flavour before it leaves the brewery. The beer that emerges is chestnut coloured, with a pronounced roasted malt, coffee, figs and floral hops aroma. Dark grain and fruit flavours crowd the palate, followed by a long, spritzy, quenching finish dominated by vine fruits, coffee and gently bitter hops.

The Munich brewers refuse to allow Prince Luitpold to have a beer tent at the annual Oktoberfest and he has hit back by organising a remarkable jousting tournament every July, held over three weekends. It is like taking a step back in time. At night, torch flares light the sky. Ancient crafts are practised in the many tents. Troubadours, falconers and tumblers entertain the large crowds, while the jousting is full-blooded, with no quarter given by professional stuntmen. There is a pervading aroma of earth, straw and horse sweat, overlain by the richer smells of cooking. And the event is toasted by endless exquisite draughts of King Ludwig Dark Lager.

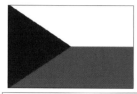

TASTING NOTES

Appearance
Aroma
Taste
Overall score

TASTING NOTES

Appearance
Aroma
Taste
Overall score

Klasterni St Norbert Dark

Source: Klasterni Pivovar St Norbert, Strahov, Prague, Czech Republic
Strength: 5.5%
Website: www.klasterni-pivovar.cz

Klasterni Pivovar means 'cloister brewery' and it stands in the grounds of the white-walled monastery of St Norbert in Strahov, an outlying district of Prague. My first visit was in the winter, and as I arrived snow was falling and the monks were singing their plain song inside the church. The centuries, unlike the snow, melted away, and for a moment I thought I was back in a time before war, religious oppression, occupation and dictatorship ravaged central Europe.

The brewery and restaurant match the monastery, its whitewashed and red-roofed buildings set round a small courtyard used as an outside drinking area in good weather. The monastery dates from 1140 when King Vladislav II donated land to followers of St Norbert. A brewery was built at some time between the 13th and 14th centuries. In 1629, Abbot Kaspar Questenberg built a new brewery on the spot where the present restaurant is located.

Following the Velvet Revolution, monks revived their community at Strahov and leased the buildings for the restaurant complex to a commercial company. The main bar includes the burnished copper vessels used for mashing, filtering and boiling. Fermentation and maturation take place in separate rooms at the rear of the complex. Brewer Martin Matuska previously worked at the famous Prague brew-pub U Fleků and therefore has considerable experience at producing a tmavé, or dark beer. He uses four malts, Pilsner, Munich, crystal and black, and hops the beer with Žatec varieties that create 37 units of bitterness. The beer is ruby/black with an aroma bursting with bitter chocolate, figs, burnt grain and floral hops. The mouth fills with rich flavours of dark fruit and grain with a solid underpinning of earthy hops. The long and complex finish is fruity, with chocolate and earthy hop notes. The beer can be taken away in attractive black bottles with gold embossed lettering and swing-top closures. The restaurant, brewery and monastery are at 302 Strahovské nádvoří.

Köstritzer Schwarzbier

Source: Köstritzer Schwarzbierbrauerei, Bad Köstritz, Thuringia, Germany
Strength: 4.6%
Website: www.koestritzer.de

On my first visit to the Bitburger brewery in Germany, I was intrigued to find, in a plant dedicated to pale Pilsner lager, some bottles of black beer in the brewer's office. I was told it was a speciality known as Schwarzbier, or black beer, from the Erfurt region of Saxony that had just emerged from the former German Democratic Republic beyond the wall. The beer style had been made in local castles in the area in the 16th and 17th centuries, and later

became a commercial beer that had refreshed, among others, the German writer and poet Goethe when he visited the spa town of Bad Köstritz to recover from illness.

In its earliest form, the beer would have been warm fermented but it had become a black lager. It survived during the communist period with a low strength and was recommended for nursing mothers with the addition of egg or milk. The current chairman of Bitburger, Dr Axel Simon, remembered the beer from his childhood and he bought the brewery when it came up for sale following the collapse of the communist regime. I visited the brewery, a red-brick complex built in 1907 but in urgent need of investment. Bitburger spent a small fortune bringing the brewery up to date and making the beer available in other parts of Germany and then in export markets. The strength was increased dramatically from 3.5% to 4.6% and production was brought within the strict terms of the Reinheitsgebot purity law, which had been ignored during the communist period.

The beer is made with pale malt, Munich malt and roasted malt, and is hopped with Hüller and Hallertau Mittelfrüh varieties. The colour rating is 900—an indication of how dark it is—and the bitterness units are 35. It has an aroma of dark fruit, malt loaf and bitter chocolate, followed by a creamy palate with roasted grain, coffee, chocolate and a hint of figs and a gentle hop note. The finish is smooth, creamy, with strong notes of burnt grain, bitter chocolate, dark fruit and spicy hops.

Třeboň Dark Regent

Source: Pivovar Regent, Třeboň, Czech Republic
Strength: 4.4%
Website: www.pivovar-regent.cz

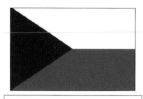

TASTING NOTES
Appearance
Aroma
Taste
Overall score

My most recent visit to the Regent brewery began with an oompah band and a singer greeting me with a vivacious rendition of 'Roll Out the Barrel'. I discovered the song is of Bohemian origin and was brought to Britain by Czech fighter pilots in World War Two. It was a jolly way to start a brewery tour and was in stark contrast to my first visit in the late 1980s. I was accompanied then by a suspicious guide from the government tourist agency Čedok and I was confronted by a brewery that managed to produce excellent beer from a site in urgent need of investment.

But Regent has had a long and dramatic history. Augustinian monks brewed in Třeboň from 1367. The local aristocrats, the Rosenbergs, built a castle on the site of the monastery and, in 1482, dug new cellars for the brewery. In 1706, the brewery was moved to the castle armoury, where it stands today, though the site was rebuilt in 1888 to take account of the developments in Budweis and Pilsen that enabled cold-fermented beers to be produced. Between the two World Wars of the 20th century, the brewery was owned by another aristocratic family, the Schwarzenbergs, but they lost control when Regent became a state enterprise during the communist period. The brewery was privatised in 1992 and got the investment it needed to install new equipment. It brews golden lagers but its speciality is Dark Regent, also known as Bohemia Regent in some markets.

It is brewed from pale, caramalt and dark malts, and hopped with Saaz varieties. It has a rich garnet colour with an appealing aroma of floral, spicy hops, bitter chocolate and dark grain. Chocolate, earthy hops and burnt grain fill the mouth, while the finish is hoppy and malty with a powerful hint of cappuccino coffee.

The town of Třeboň in southern Bohemia is famous for its lakes packed with carp, and Dark Regent is traditionally drunk during the winter, at Christmas in particular, with fish.

TASTING NOTES
Appearance
Aroma
Taste
Overall score

TASTING NOTES
Appearance
Aroma
Taste
Overall score

U Fleků Flekovský Dark
Source: U Fleků Brewery and Restaurant, Prague, Czech Republic
Strength: 4.5%
Website: www.ufleku.cz

The most celebrated beer in Prague comes from the world's oldest brew-pub, U Fleků, at 11 Kremencova in the New Town, where the entrance is marked by a large hanging clock. Beer has been brewed on the premises since at least 1499, and isotopic measurements of the remains of paintings on the wooden ceiling of the brewhouse date them back to 1360.

The present name of the establishment stems from 1762 when Jakub Flekovský and his wife bought it. In the Czech fashion, the tavern was known as U Flekovskych, which was shortened over time to U Fleků: in Czech *U* serves the same purpose as *chez* in French.

The tiny brewhouse, with a capacity of 6,000 hectolitres (132,000 gallons), is the smallest in the country. With its open cool ship fermenter, it is reminiscent of a Belgian lambic brewery but no wild yeasts are encouraged here. New brewing vessels are made of copper and date from 1980. The single beer made on the premises uses Pilsner pale malt, Munich malt, caramalt and roasted malt. A double decoction mash is used and Žatec hops are added in three stages. The beer has a chocolate, coffee and liquorice aroma with floral hops. Creamy malt, roasted grain, earthy hops and coffee notes fill the mouth, while the finish is bitter-sweet at first but becomes dry with good hop notes, balanced by coffee, chocolate and liquorice.

One wall in the brewhouse has a portrait of the present brewer and the inscription 'God bless the mother who gave birth to a brewer', a statement of such profound good sense that it survived the communist period. The six rooms in the tavern have dark wood-panelled walls, benches and alcoves. Simple, filling Czech fare of the pork and dumplings variety is served. There are regular burlesque shows and occasional oompah bands dressed in military uniforms that recall the heady days of the first independent Czechoslovak republic in the early 20th century.

Xingu Black Beer
Source: Cervejarias Kaiser, Brazil
Strength: 4.6%
Website: www.kaiser.com.br

If a beer can be controversial, Xingu fits the bill. It's the work of American anthropologist and beer writer Alan D Eames, who died in 2007. Eames was known as the Indiana Jones of Beer as a result of his researches into the origins of the world's favourite drink.

He discovered black beer as a result of an especially hazardous trip through the Amazon jungle. He found that 16th century Amazon tribes treated black beer with reverence. It was brewed by women and the brewing process was started by young virgins who started fermentation with their pure saliva.

When Eames wrote and lectured about his discovery in the United States, he was encouraged by a group of women beer lovers in Vermont in 1986 to recreate black beer. As a result, Eames worked with the Kaiser brewery in Brazil and in 1988 Xingu—named after a region of the Amazon delta—went on sale in the U.S. and Latin America.

Critics of Eames—and there's no shortage of them—pointed out that Xingu is far removed from any type of beer brewed in the Amazon jungle in the 16th century. It's a black lager, brewed by a company founded by Germans, and uses hops, which were unknown in Brazil 400 years ago.

But let's put disputes behind us and treat the beer at face value. It's brewed with pale, coloured and roasted malts and hopped with German Hallertau varieties. It has 200 colour units and 22 bitterness units. It has a spicy and liquorice aroma with roasted grain notes. The palate has a rich malty sweetness, balanced by roasted notes and light hops, while the bittersweet finish has liquorice, roasted grain and gentle spicy hops.

I wonder how Alan Eames would have felt about the final twist in the story. The Kaiser brewery was bought by the American-Canadian giant MolsonCoors who announced in 2008 they planned to close the Brazil plant. Xingu will continue to be made—it's a popular brand throughout the Americas and also on sale in Britain. Perhaps when it moves to a new plant, MolsonCoors will invite some Amazonian virgins to start the first brew with their saliva.

Bocks

Bavarians will assure you that Bock is a style of beer indissolubly linked to their country. But its origins lie in Lower Saxony, some distance from Bavaria. The historical fact is stressed by the legend above the Einbecker Brewery in Einbeck: '*Ohne Einbeck gäb's kein Bockbier*'—'Without Einbeck there would be no Bock beer.' To emphasise the point, all the brewery's products are labelled Ur-Bock, meaning Original Bock, while the entrance to Einbeck has a sign saying 'Beer City'.

Einbeck was an important member of the Hanseatic League, the community of trading towns and cities of the 14th and 15th centuries in Germany, the Low Countries and Scandinavia. Each member of the league offered a special contribution, and Einbeck was famed as a brewing centre. Its citizens had been granted brewing rights from the 14th century. They spread malt and hops in the lofts of their houses to dry, while a communal brewing vessel toured the city for them to use in turn. The high arches of the houses, designed to allow the vessel to pass through, are still visible today.

The beers of Einbeck achieved fame and notoriety in the 16th century when supplies were sent to Martin Luther, an Augustinian friar, to sustain him between sessions of the Diet of Worms in 1521, where he was excommunicated for attacking the excesses of the Papal court in Rome and the sale of indulgences. Luther, the leader of the Protestant Reformation in Europe, had cause to thank the brewers of Einbeck for their nourishing beer at a trial that amounted to a witch-hunt and during which he made his defiant statement: 'Here I stand— I can do no other'.

The beer of Einbeck was called in the German fashion 'Einbecker', meaning 'of Einbeck'. The people of Munich and Bavaria first came across Einbecker beer in the 17th century when the Duke of Brunswick in Lower Saxony married the daughter of a Bavarian aristocrat. The wedding was held in Munich and the duke brought a master brewer with him to make beer for the celebration. The Bavarians took to the strong, rich style and, over the course of time, their powerful southern dialect turned Einbecker into 'Oanbocker'. By the 18th century, the Munich Hofbräuhaus, the Royal Court Brewery, was producing an Oanbock beer. This, in turn, was shortened to the simple and explosive 'Bock'. The new name was a pun. *Bock* in the Bavarian dialect means billy goat and, as a symbol of virility and strength, was the ideal name for the beer style. Many producers of Bock use the image of the goat on their labels.

The benchmark version of strong Bock beer was developed by monks at the Paulaner Brewery (see page 273). Bock beer became so engrained in the Bavarian way of life that a special version, Maibock, is brewed to herald the arrival of spring, with an even stronger version, called Doppelbock, or Double Bock, for Lent. Under Bavarian law, a Bock beer must be at least 6.4% alcohol, a Double Bock 6.9%. Monks called Bock beer 'liquid bread', as it helped sustain them during the Lenten fast. The Bock style was picked up in other European countries and eventually made its way to the United States, where it is brewed with enthusiasm and dedication by German-style brewers.

Ayinger Celebrator

Source: Brauerei Aying Franz Inselkammer, Aying, Bavaria, Germany
Strength: 6.7%
Website: www.aying-bier.de

TASTING NOTES
Appearance
Aroma
Taste
Overall score

Celebrator is a Double Bock and the point is emphasised on a label that shows two goats holding a glass of the dark chestnut-coloured beer.

Aying has built a fine reputation for its wheat beers as well as lagers, and is typical of the many small country breweries in Bavaria that first and foremost serve their local communities. In the case of Aying, founded in 1878 by the Inselkammer farming family, the community is no more than a tiny huddle of houses and a church, with a maypole on the village green, all standing at the foot of the Alps. The village of Aying is too small to sustain a brewery in the modern world and so owner Franz Inselkammer exports widely to North America, Italy, France and Scandinavia.

His powerful Celebrator is the most successful beer in export markets and is an outstanding example of the Double Bock style. It is brewed with four malts, including pale, Munich, caramalt and roast, and hopped with Hallertauer varieties. Pure water comes from the Alps. The beer enjoys a double decoction mash and then between four and six months' cold maturation in the lager cellars. The beer throws a lively and dense collar of foam that leads to an entrancing aroma of creamy and roasted grain, coffee, figs and gentle hop resins. Ripe malt, dark fruit and spicy hops fill the mouth, while the long finish has a delicious bitter-sweet character with notes of figs, coffee and dry, gently bitter hops.

The brewery complex includes a restaurant serving hearty Bavarian food, and a hotel. Herr Inselkammer organises many beer events and festivals during the course of the year.

Eggenberg Samichlaus

Source: Schlossbrauerei Eggenberg, Vorchdorf, Austria
Strength: 14%
Website: www.schlosseggenberg.at

TASTING NOTES
Appearance
Aroma
Taste
Overall score

In the Swiss-German dialect, *Samichlaus* means Santa Claus. The name is given to a powerful Swiss interpretation of Bock. The beer is called Santa Claus because it is brewed every year on 6 December, St Nicholas's Day, and lagered for nine or 10 months before being bottled and released for the following year's celebration.

Samichlaus was first made by the Hürlimann brewery in Zürich and, at 14% alcohol, is listed as the world's strongest regularly brewed beer. It was not a title sought by the brewery, which made the beer as part of scientific research into yeast. The brewery was founded in 1865 at a time when beer making was being transformed as a result of the lager revolution in Munich, Pilsen and Vienna. The dedicated research by Hürlimann's scientists into the temperatures at which yeast will turn malt sugars into alcohol complemented the work of other lager pioneers.

Unlike a wine or Champagne yeast, which can produce high levels of alcohol, brewer's yeast 'goes to sleep' at around 12%, overwhelmed by the alcohol it has produced. The researchers at Hürlimann worked for several decades to culture a strain of yeast that would continue to work above 12%. In 1979, they used a new culture to make an experimental Christmas beer and the interest created encouraged the brewery to make it on an annual basis. During the long ripening process, the beer is roused from time to time by pumping it from one tank to another to prevent the yeast from slumbering. A double decoction mash is involved and hops are added three times during the copper boil.

In the late 1990s, Hürlimann was bought by the Swiss brewing giant Feldschlössen, which said it would discontinue Samichlaus. A year later, the Austrian brewer Schloss Eggenberg announced it had won agreement to brew the beer again and the first vintage appeared, fittingly, in time for Christmas 2000. The castle (*Schloss*) brewery at Eggenberg dates from the 12th century and stands in an area of great natural beauty, with

deep lakes, high mountains and dense forests. The russet-coloured Samichlaus is made from pale malt and three darker ones. It is hopped with Hallertauer, Hersbrucker and Styrian Goldings (30 units of bitterness). It has a complex aroma of port wine, dried fruit, toasted malt and peppery hops. The palate offers coffee, bitter chocolate, nuts and malts, while the finish is long, lingering, bursting with rich malt, vinous fruit and spicy hops, with a hint of Cognac. The beer is pasteurised but it will develop in bottle.

Einbecker Ur-Bock

Source: Einbecker Brauhaus, Einbeck, Lower Saxony, Germany
Strength: 6.9%
Website: www.einbecker.com

TASTING NOTES
Appearance
Aroma
Taste
Overall score

Beer has been brewed in the small town of Einbeck, near Brunswick and Hanover, since at least 1351. Einbecker beers were sold as far afield as Amsterdam and Stockholm, and they were made strong to help them withstand long journeys by road and water. The early brews would have been dark and warm fermented, probably made from a blend of barley and wheat malts. At a time when most brewing was carried out in monasteries and castles, the citizens of Einbeck brewed themselves. Every May Day, lots were drawn in the town square to decide the order in which the official brewmaster would visit more than 700 houses with the public brewing pan to help them make beer for domestic use and for public sale.

A commercial brewery was built in Einbeck in 1794 and has been rebuilt on several occasions. Three versions of Bock are produced, all with alcoholic strengths of 6.9% and all labelled, quite reasonably, Ur-Bock: Original Bock. Soft water comes from deep springs, malt from the Brunswick area, and hops—Northern Brewer, Perle and Hersbruck—from the Bavarian Hallertau. The beers are hoppier and drier than a Bavarian Bock but the main characteristic is a rich and rounded maltiness that avoids a cloying sweetness. The pale Hell (colour 15, bitterness units 38) has an appealing biscuity malt aroma and palate with a late burst of spicy hops in the finish. The dark, or Dunkel, version has 40 units of colour and the same bitterness rating. Dark grains give hints of roasted malt, figs and coffee on aroma and palate, with malt and fruit balanced in the finish by the hops. A Maibock produced for the spring has a tempting bronze colour (25 colour units, 36 bitterness), a dry and crisp aroma and palate with juicy malt, light fruit and floral hops, followed by a quenching malty and gently hoppy finish. The Hell and Dunkel are lagered for eight to 10 weeks, the Maibock for six.

The brewery houses a small museum and good beer and food are served in its tavern on the market square.

EKU Kulminator/28

Source: Erste Kulmbacher Unionbraurei, Kulmbach, Germany
Strength: 7.5%/13.5%
Website: www.eku.de

To most drinkers outside Germany, the beers from EKU are the best-known interpretations of Bock. For many years, the branded glass that accompanies 28 declared it was the 'strongest beer in the world' but as it is very slightly weaker than Samichlaus, the bottle label more modestly claims it to be one of the strongest. The name of the brewery indicates it was the first (*erste*) united brewery in the famous brewing town of Kulmbach, formed by a merger of two companies in 1872.

EKU brews a fine Pils but is best known for its two Double Bock beers. They are made with water from the surrounding mountains and local barley malt. Hops, which are added four times during the copper boil, are Hersbruck, Perle and Tettnang. Darker malts are blended with pale to produce Kulminator, which has a deep cherry red colour (65 units) and a ripe fruit, rich malt and spicy hop resins aroma. Warming alcohol fills the mouth, underscored by earthy hops and rich fruit, while the finish is fruity, malty with a gentle spicy hop note (24 bitterness units).

The even stronger 28 is known as Kulminator 28 in domestic markets but EKU 28 abroad. It is brewed from pale malt only but the sheer volume of malt and some caramelisation of the sugars in the copper give the finished beer an orange/amber glow. The alcohol produces quite a glow, too, backed by rich malt on the aroma,

some citrus fruitiness on the palate, and a long, deep, intense, rich and warming finish. The colour rating is 35, bitterness units 30.

The number 28 comes from an old method of expressing the strength of beer. The beer is lagered for nine months and towards the end of the storage period ice crystals form in the tank. The brewery does not claim the beer is an 'Ice Bock', a speciality of the region, as the beer already has sufficient alcohol without adding more from the concentration of beer and ice.

Some drinkers claim EKU is a cure for the common cold. It would certainly take your mind off the sniffles.

TASTING NOTES
Appearance
Aroma
Taste
Overall score

TASTING NOTES
Appearance
Aroma
Taste
Overall score

Hübsch Doppelbock

Source: Sudwerk Privatbrauerei Hübsch, Davis, California, USA
Strength: 7.1%
Website: www.sudwerk.com

TASTING NOTES
Appearance
Aroma
Taste
Overall score

The inspiration is clear from the name: this is a strictly German brewery based in California. *Sudwerk* is the German name for a brewhouse, and the impact of German brewing names and techniques can be measured by the fact that a widespread slang word for beer in the US is 'suds'.

Founder Ron Broward named his brewery after his German mother's maiden name: she had regaled him with stories of the wonderful beer halls in her native country. His first venture was a brew-pub in Davis in 1990. He has since opened a 20,000-barrel brewery in Sacramento, the state capital.

Ron is a stickler for detail. He brews to the German *Reinheitsgebot*, imports malts and hops from Bavaria, and uses a yeast culture from the Weinhenstephan brewing faculty near Munich. His Doppelbock is made with pale and chocolate malts, and Hallertauer and Tettnanger hop varieties. It has a deep copper colour with a massive aroma of roasted malt and chocolate that carries through to the palate, followed by a chewy malt, chocolate and light hop finish that finally becomes dry.

Ron also produces a 6.5% Maibock for the spring. It has a deep bronze colour with nutty malt and spicy hops.

Paulaner Salvator Doppelbock

Source: Paulaner-Salvator-Thomasbräu, Munich, Bavaria, Germany
Strength: 7.5%
Website: www.paulaner.de

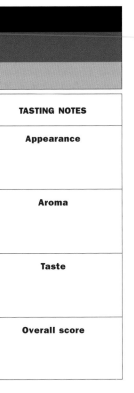

Paulaner produces the classic Munich Bock, the benchmark for the style. The beer is so famous that its name, Salvator, is incorporated in the company name, along with the title of a long-extinct brewery, Thomas, taken over in 1923.

The Paulaner brewery was founded in 1634 by monks who were followers of St Francis of Paula in Calabria in Italy. They were Pauline monks, not Franciscans, who are followers of another St Francis, the better-known patron saint of animals from Assisi. The monks built their Paulaner monastery on a hill on the outskirts of Munich, and added a small brewery. The hillside helped the monks defend themselves from attack: it later proved invaluable in allowing maturation cellars to be dug where beers were stored at low temperatures.

The monks made, among others, a strong beer for the Lent period called *Salvator*, which means Saviour or Holy Father. The beer was sold commercially from the late 18th century to help raise funds for the monastery. When, a century later, the monastery was secularised, the new owner, Franz-Xaver Zacherl, vigorously promoted sales of Salvator, with such success that other Munich brewers launched their own brands under the same name. Zacherl took them to court in 1894. The result was that his competitors dropped the name but gave their brands new titles ending in –or, such as Triumphator or Kulminator. Every year, three weeks before Easter, a cask of the year's first batch of Salvator is tapped by a local dignitary, such as the Mayor of Munich, in the brewery's beer garden. This heralds the 'Starkbierzeit', or strong beer period, when people, weather permitting, invade the city's many beer gardens to sup Salvator and other rich brews that help shrug off the memories

of a long Alpine winter and usher in the spring. Drinking Doppelbock is known as the *Frühlingskur*—the 'spring cure'.

Salvator is brewed with pale lager malt, caramalt and Munich malt and Hallertauer hop varieties. It has a russet-brown colour with a rich malt loaf aroma, a yeasty, bready palate, and a complex finish rich in sultana-like fruit, malt and hops. The beer is lagered for at least three months.

TASTING NOTES
Appearance
Aroma
Taste
Overall score

Vienna Red, Märzen & Oktoberfest Beers

It is a curiosity of brewing that a beer called Märzen should be identified with the world's most celebrated drinking festival, the Munich Oktoberfest. Märzenbier means March beer. The beers at the modern Oktoberfest are cold-fermented lagers but before cold storage developed in the 19th century, March was the last month in which beer could be safely brewed in Bavaria, with its long, hot summers.

The Munich tradition was to brew a strong beer in March and store it in Alpine caves, protected by the cold from the heat and wild yeast infections. Brewers noticed that the low ambient temperatures in the caves produced a long, slow second fermentation in cask. The yeast settled at the bottom of the vessels, while maturation created a lively, natural carbonation. The lagering, or cold storage, of beer was under way.

Casks of March beers were broached in late September or early October. The ceremony took on added significance in 1810 when a festival was held in a large open space in Munich to celebrate the marriage of the Crown Prince of Bavaria. The meadow was dubbed the *Theresienweise*, or Theresa's Meadow, after the royal bride. Every year since 1810 there has been an annual jamboree on the site, lasting for 16 days from late September but dubbed the Oktoberfest as the festival concludes in that month. The festival is launched by a horse-drawn parade by Munich's brewers, who sell vast amounts of Oktoberfest beer in their great tents decorated like baronial halls, with central stands for oompah bands.

The Märzen beers took on a more central role in Bavarian life as commercial lagering of beer gathered pace. March beer became a special treat, launched every year at the Oktoberfest. At first the beers were dark brown but the innovative Munich brewers Gabriel and Josef Sedlmayr worked closely with the Viennese brewer Anton Dreher, who was developing his own style of cold-fermented beer. While lagers were dark in Munich and golden in Pilsen, Dreher at his brewery in the Schwechat district of Vienna used malt kilned to a slightly higher temperature than pale lager malt to produce a beer that was dubbed 'Vienna Red'. The colour was probably amber or orange, rather than red, and not dissimilar to English pale ale. But pale ale was unknown to Austrian drinkers and Dreher's 'red beer' had such an impact that he was invited to open breweries in Bohemia, Hungary and Trieste to reproduce the style. When Mexico was briefly part of the Austrian empire, breweries there also produced Vienna Red lagers that survive today in the shape of Dos Equis and Negra Modelo.

Sedlmayr's brother Josef, who ran his own Franziskaner Brewery in Munich, studied Dreher's technique and produced a March beer for the Oktoberfest with a polished amber colour that became the benchmark for the style. The beer was brewed in March then lagered in the brewery's ice-packed cellars until the autumn. The Sedlmayr breweries merged in the 1920s and today it is Spaten that makes the benchmark version of a Märzen.

True March beers are now hard to find. Austrian brewers shrug their shoulders at the mention of Vienna Red and churn out beers in the Pilsner style. The beers sold at the Oktoberfest are also golden rather than amber. But the flag is being flown across the Atlantic by American brewers who have a passionate devotion to brewing beers strictly to style.

RIGHT
The Oktoberfest is the world's oldest and biggest beer festival. The beers brewed for the event are rich and strong.

Boston Samuel Adams Lager

Source: Boston Beer Company, Boston, Massachusetts, USA
Strength: 5%
Website: www.samueladams.com

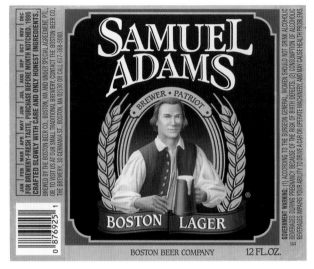

TASTING NOTES
Appearance
Aroma
Taste
Overall score

Samuel Adams Lager was the beer that put the Boston Beer Company on the map. As the first national brand that was not produced by a brewing giant, it gave a kick-start to the craft brewing revival in the United States. The founder and owner Jim Koch is a charming, quietly spoken man, but behind the urbane exterior lurks a tough, no-nonsense entrepreneur. He has raised hackles by his aggressive selling techniques and his style—now widely copied—of having his beer brewed under licence in different centres. Waiting for planes, I have enjoyed his beers at both Dallas and St Louis airports, brewed a long distance from Boston. To have the franchise for beer at St Louis airport, the hometown of mighty Anheuser-Busch, brewer of Budweiser, takes a fair degree of chutzpah.

Koch, whose name is pronounced 'Cook' to avoid bringing a blush to the cheek of Americans who prefer rooster to cock, comes from a family of German origin who arrived in America in the 19th century. Five generations of the family ran breweries. There was a Koch brewery in St Louis that was taken over and closed down by Anheuser-Busch, which explains why Jim wanted

a franchise there. Jim won a degree in management at Harvard University, and his father, who left the brewing industry as the like of A-B tightened its noose on sales and distribution, was not best pleased when his son said he wanted to make beer. Jim didn't have a brewery and he had Boston Lager, bearing the image of patriot Sam Adams, made for him by the Pittsburgh Brewing Company. Jim launched the beer in 1985 and he sold it door to door. It was a sensation: drinkers starved of choice and used to the bland 'suds' of the nationals, suddenly discovered that lager beer could have rich aroma and flavour. Jim eventually opened his own brewery in Boston but that is used mainly to produce Boston Ale (see page 54).

His lager, based on the Bavarian March style, is still contract brewed around the country. It uses two-row American pale malt and caramalt, and is hopped with German Hallertauer 'noble' varieties, including Mittelfrüh. The amber beer has a floral hop bouquet balanced by biscuity malt. Spicy hops build in the mouth with delicious juicy malt. The lengthy finish has a superb balance of spicy, bitter hops and sappy malt but finally becomes dry with firm hop bitterness.

Brooklyn Lager

Source: Brooklyn Brewery, Brooklyn, New York City, USA
Strength: 5%
Website: www.brooklynbrewery.com

TASTING NOTES
Appearance
Aroma
Taste
Overall score

My first-ever taste of Brooklyn Lager was in a bar in Manhattan. The amber colour and the rich malt and peppery hops character of the beer entranced me. I thought it was one of the finest beers I had ever tasted and nothing since made me change my mind. At the time, the beer was brewed under licence by the F X Matt Brewery in Uttica, New York State. The beer was the brainchild of journalist Steve Hindy and banker Tom Potter who wanted to restore Brooklyn's great brewing tradition that had been wiped out by Prohibition and the Great Depression. At one time, Brooklyn had 48 breweries and they were responsible for one of every 10 barrels of beer brewed in the United States. Steve and Tom commissioned a retired German-American brewer, Bill Moeller, to develop a recipe for Brooklyn Lager. Bill's grandfather had brewed in Brooklyn and bequeathed his recipe books to his grandson. Using the old brewing books, Bill fashioned a beer that is a true Vienna Red. Its classy label was designed by Milton Glaser, best known for his I ♥ NY logo.

The Brooklyn Brewery now has its own plant, where brewmaster Garrett Oliver fashions the lager from two-row Pilsner malt, caramel malt and Munich malt. He hops the beer with Cascade, Hallertauer Mittelfrüh and Vanguard varieties. The beer has 14 units of colour and 30 bitterness units. It has a floral and piny hop aroma balanced by biscuity malt. The mouth is filled with juicy malt and caramel flavours and a big punch of spicy hops. The finish is a superb balance of sweet malt, a hint of tangy citrus fruit, and crisp, bitter hops. Unusually for a lager, the beer is dry hopped in the English style for additional aroma.

Hofbräu Märzen

Source: Staatliches Hofbräuhaus, Munich, Bavaria, Germany
Strength: 5.7%
Website: www.hofbraehaus.de

It's not often that drinking beer sends a chill down my spine but it happened during one of many visits to the Hofbräuhaus. I was sitting in a side room on a comfortable wooden settle when a companion asked: 'Do you know who used to sit there?' I shook my head but I had a horrible feeling I could guess the answer: Adolf Hitler. The Nazi leader's first attempt to grab political power, the *Kapp Putsch*, was planned in that very room in the tavern. Don't be put off. This remarkable, sprawling beer hall on a small square called the Platzl, with vaulted roofs, brass bands, men in lederhosen and Alpine hats supplied by Central Casting, and a delightful beer garden shaded by chestnut trees provide one of the great drinking experiences.

The Hofbräuhaus, or Royal Court Brewery, was built in the 16th century by Duke Wilhelm V of Bavaria to supply the royal family with beer. It maintained the monopoly for more than 300 years. When the royal family lost power after World War One, the tavern and its brewery were taken over by the state. Brewing no longer takes place on the premises: a new, modern plant has been built on a greenfield site out of town. It supplies beer in large wooden casks that are tapped in the beer hall. The Hofbräu started life as a wheat beer brewery, added Bock beer along the way, and bolted on a March beer when cold fermentation held sway in Munich.

The amber beer is made from pale and Munich malts, and is hopped with Hallertauer varieties. It has a rich bready, biscuity, nutty and spicy hop aroma and palate, followed by a complex finish dominated by ripe, vinous fruit, creamy malt and piny hops.

Don't miss the beer hall, decorated in the blue and white flags of Bavaria, or the succulent beer.

Negra Modelo

Source: Cerveceria Modelo, Mexico City, Mexico
Strength: 5.3%
Website: www.gmodelo.com

It's one of the oddities of Latin America that the language and culture owe a great deal to the Portuguese and Spanish invaders yet the modern brewing traditions are Germanic. The Austrians were empire builders in the 18th and 19th century and left deep beery footprints in their wake. The Habsburg dynasty ruled Mexico for three disastrous years between 1864 and 1867: the Emperor Maximilian thought the Mexicans would welcome him with open arms but he was executed by nationalist forces and sent home in a box.

The Austrian rule may have been brief but it found time for brewers from Europe to establish plants there and to model their beers on the Vienna Red style developed by Anton Dreher. Today most Mexican beers are pale lagers, of which Corona and Sol are the best known: thin, bland beers made with large amounts of rice.

A visit to Mexico proves there are far better beers than these. Negra Modelo dates from the 1920s but follows the developments in brewing technique from the previous century. The name means Black Modelo but this is a misnomer as it's amber coloured, though perhaps a little too dark to be a true representative of the style.

The colour of Negra Modelo derives from the use of amber malt, blended with pale malt. It gives the beer a delicious aroma and flavour that has nutty, juicy and toffee notes. It's the biggest-selling Vienna-style beer in Mexico. German hops contribute 19 units of bitterness. There's a touch of chocolate and dark malt in the mouth, and a finish that is bittersweet with hints of spices, chocolate and roasted grain. Mexicans enjoy the beer with chicken mole but I became addicted to guacamole and found the beer to be the perfect companion for the avocado-based dish.

The rival Moctezuma group produces a Vienna Red beer called Dos Equis—Two Crosses—a fine, 4.8 per cent version of the style. So the beer lives on in Mexico and is rather more revered than the hapless Emperor Maximilian.

TASTING NOTES
Appearance
Aroma
Taste
Overall score

TASTING NOTES
Appearance
Aroma
Taste
Overall score

Spaten Ur-Märzen

Source: Gabriel Sedlmayr Spaten-Franziskaner-Bräu, Munich, Bavaria, Germany
Strength: 5.6%
Website: www.spaten.de

TASTING NOTES

Appearance

Aroma

Taste

Overall score

Ur- in the title is short for *Urtyp*, which means 'original'. Spaten should perhaps blow its trumpet rather louder, for this is the classic Munich March beer: a rich and transluscent amber/bronze/red-tinged beer, the first to be fashioned in the city by Josef Sedlmayr in collaboration with Anton Dreher.

It became a Spaten brand when the two Sedlmayr breweries merged in the 1920s. Spaten can trace its origins back to the 14th century. Its current name is a play on word: it means spade, but stems from George Spaeth, who became the owner of the brewery in 1622. Ownership passed to Gabriel Sedlmayr the Elder, the Royal Court brewer, in 1807. It was his son, also called Gabriel, who pioneered cold fermentation in Munich. The company is now a public one but members of the Sedlmayr family retain an interest. It has merged with another famous Munich brewer, Löwenbräu [Lion Brew] but they have separate brewhouses to ensure the integrity of the beers.

The Spaten March beer is brewed with pale and Munich malts, and hopped with Hallertauer varieties. It has 32 units of colour and 21 bitterness units. It has a toasted malt, nutty, slightly vinous aroma with a gentle floral and grassy hop note. Rich biscuity malt, vinous fruit and hop resins fill the mouth, while the long and lingering finish is bitter-sweet in the start but becomes dry with good balancing juicy malt and earthy hop notes.

In a belt-and-braces style, Spaten also brews a paler Oktoberfest beer. Let us hope the March beer does not disappear. Many other Munich March beers have been replaced by golden Oktoberfest beers. Spaten's version, the benchmark, the classic, deserves to survive.

Dortmunder Export

Export is a rather over-blown description for a style of beer that is largely restricted to Dortmund and a few other towns and cities in the Ruhr and Westphalia. It crept over the border into the Netherlands and, in that narrow respect, it was exported. Dortmund has had a brewing tradition since the 13th century, specialising in dark wheat beers, often flavoured with herbs and spices.

In the 19th century, Dortmund, sited at the confluence of the small river Dort and the mighty Ruhr, grew rapidly as a major industrial city based on mining and steel industries. It had a large army of thirsty workers to satisfy, and brewing rushed to satisfy them. At one time, Dortmund had more breweries than any other German city. The Kronen Brewery switched to cold fermentation as early as the mid-1840s. Other breweries followed, and by the 1870s, the city had its signature style, Export.

The aim of Export beer was a simple one: to quench the prodigious thirsts of industrial workers and to restore energy lost after long stints digging coal or making steel. The beer style played a similar role to mild ale in England but the similarities should not be exaggerated. Export is not only a lager beer but it is also high in alcohol, slightly stronger than a Pilsner. It has a deep burnished gold colour as a result of slightly darker Munich malt being blended with pale. Brewing water is rich in calcium carbonate and sulphate, and the salts draw more flavour from the malt. The beer is not 'fully attenuated', which means some malt sugars are left to give richness and fullness to the flavour. Hop bitterness is restrained, in the mid-20s.

The Dortmund breweries in recent decades have given little support to their Export brands. They prefer to promote their Pils and seem reluctant, in some cases, to even mention they still make Export. It is true that heavy industry in the region has declined massively but that is surely no reason for downplaying a flavoursome beer with the type of tradition that other German cities, such as Cologne and Düsseldorf, cherish. The process has not been helped by considerable rationalisation of brewing in Dortmund. For most of the 20th century, the city was dominated by two fiercely independent and competitive companies, Dortmunder Actien Brauerei and Dortmunder Union Brauerei, known for short as

DAB and DUB. Actien indicates a company listed on the stock market, while Union stands for a merger of several breweries.

DUB was famous for its plant in the centre of Dortmund, where the single neon-lit letter U blazed out at night from a central tower. In 1988, DUB and another local brewery, Ritter, became part of Brau und Brunnen that owns other breweries and mineral water manufacturers. The DUB site closed in 1994 and production was concentrated at the Ritter brewery, which has enjoyed considerable investment. In the meantime, the Oetker food and drinks group bought DAB. The final indignity came in 2004, when Oetker took over Brau und Brunnen and now owns both DAB and DUB. Further rationalisation can be expected.

As a result of its penetration of the Dutch market, some brewers in the Netherlands make a similar style of beer they have shortened to Dort, to avoid any suggestion the beer originates in Dortmund. And, once again, the style has crossed the Atlantic where it is brewed with an enthusiasm sadly lacking in its city of origin.

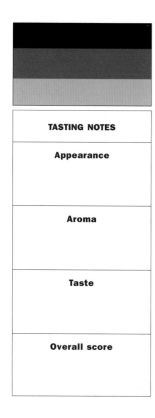

Alfa Super Dortmunder

Source: Alfa Brouwerij, Schinnen, Limburg, Netherlands
Strength: 7.5%
Website: www.alfa-bier.nl

TASTING NOTES
Appearance
Aroma
Taste
Overall score

Limburg once had scores of breweries, meeting the demand for refreshing beer from the legion of industrial workers there. It's not surprising that, in common, with Dortmund, just over the Dutch-German border, rich and malty beers were brewed to slake the thirsts of miners and others engaged in hard manual labour.

The breweries have declined in step with industry and Alfa, along with Gulpen, (page 282) are the last major producers in Limburg.

Alfa was founded in 1870 by Joseph Meens and the brewery is still owned by his family and is fiercely independent. It has the only underground spring in the Dutch brewing industry and is checked every six months by the Ministry of Health and Welfare.

The beers are produced by traditional lager methods: mash mixer, lauter tun and brew kettle.

Czech and German hops are used and there's a late addition of the Tettnang variety, which gives a delightful woody/resin note. A well-kilned pale malt produces a beer with a rich bronze/gold colour. It's lagered for two months and emerges with a rich buttery/creamy aroma, a firm body with a grainy/bready character balanced by light citrus fruit and grassy hops. The finish is bittersweet with a creamy malt, light fruit and tangy hop character.

Alfa makes a range of lagers and produces 12,000,000 litres a year. In 1995 the company was granted a royal warrant from Queen Beatrix, a fitting tribute to a brewery that has stayed loyal to the Dortmunder style.

DAB Export

Source: Dortmunder Actien Brauerei, Dortmund, Germany
Strength: 5%
Website: www.dab.de

TASTING NOTES
Appearance
Aroma
Taste
Overall score

DAB was founded in 1868 by the Fischer family but it became a public company just four years later. It was a proud brewer of the Export style and won a gold medal for the beer at the World Fair in Paris in 1900. After World War Two, DAB began to concentrate on Pilsner and downplayed the importance of Export. In the late 1970s, DAB merged with another local brewer, Hansa, and a decade later they closed both their town-centre breweries and moved to a new combined plant in the suburbs. More recently, DAB has taken over Dortmunder Kronen, which developed cold fermentation and the Export style in the 19th century.

The spate of mergers, takeovers and closures in Dortmund, once dubbed 'the Burton of Germany', is doing little to maintain confidence in the local style of beer as more and more effort goes into marketing Pilsners. The Pils-type beers brewed in Dortmund are perfectly acceptable, but they rather miss the point. If the Kronen version of Export is still brewed, the company keeps remarkably quiet about it.

DAB Export is pale for the style, with nine units of colour. It is made from a blend of pale and Munich malt and hopped with Hallertau varieties (25 bitterness units). It has a rich toasted malt aroma with light hop resins and a touch of citrus fruit. It is smooth, creamy and malty in the mouth with a gentle touch of spicy hops. The finish is sweet to start but develops a late flourish of hop and a hint of lemon fruit.

Great Lakes Dortmunder Gold

Source: Great Lakes Brewing Co, Cleveland, Ohio, USA
Strength: 5.8%
Website: www.greatlakesbrewing.com

TASTING NOTES
Appearance
Aroma
Taste
Overall score

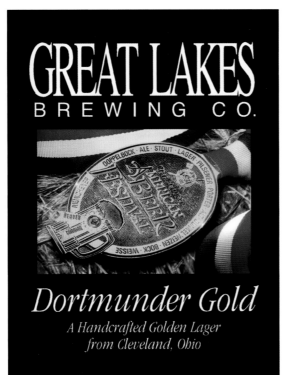

When Patrick and Daniel Conway opened their brew-pub at 2516 Market Avenue, Cleveland, in 1988, their first beer was named after a local football star but was eventually relabelled Dortmunder Gold. It was the beer that made their reputation and is still the flagship brand, brewed in the brothers' new, adjacent plant based in one of the city's last commercial breweries that were wiped out during Prohibition and subsequent bouts of merger mania. The Conways employed Thaine Johnson, who had worked at the last brewery in Cleveland, Christian Schmidt, to close its doors. Between them, they fashioned a big, full-bodied interpretation of Dortmunder Export that is recognised as the benchmark version of the style brewed in the US. It has won five gold medals in the annual World Beer Championships.

It is brewed from pale and Munich malt, and hopped with Hallertauer and Tettnanger varieties that create a robust 30 bitterness units. It is a shade darker than a German original, orange to light bronze, with a new-mown grass aroma, rich biscuity malt, tangy and spicy hops and some citrus fruit in the mouth, and a big finish with a great whack of bitter, herbal, spicy hop notes balancing the biscuity malt and gentle fruit.

It can be enjoyed in the brew-pub in several rooms on different levels, including the Rockefeller Room where John D of that ilk had his humble legal offices before branching out into the oil business.

Gulpener Dort

Source: Gulpener Bierbrouwerij BV, Gulpen, Netherlands
Strength: 6.5%
Website: www.gulpener.nl

TASTING NOTES
Appearance
Aroma
Taste
Overall score

Gulpen is a village near Maastricht in the Limburg region of the Netherlands, the narrow neck of the country that has Belgium and Germany in close proximity. The brewery was founded by the Rutten family in 1825 and over the years has built a solid reputation for both the quality and eclectic nature of its beer range. It brews ales and lagers, and they include a Dutch interpretation of a Belgian 'sour red', a spiced wheat beer, an abbey beer, a barley wine and two Pilsners. It has recently experimented with fruit beers. It must be good fun being a brewer at Gulpen: 'I'm off to work, dear. I think I may try a Pils today or, hang about, perhaps I'll have a go at a raspberry beer.' In 1995 Grolsch arrived and took a major holding in the company. The relationship has proved benign: Gulpen is free to develop its beer range, while the national company sells them far and wide.

The brewery's interpretation of a Dortmunder is fascinating. It is considerably stronger than the German template and is made with pale malt, maize and caramel, which indicates that Dortmunder Export may have crossed the border but left the Reinheitsgebot purity law behind. It is hopped with Hallertau varieties that create 20 units of bitterness. The beer is lagered for 10 weeks. The beer that emerges from the lager cellar has a bright bronze/orange colour, a heavy collar of foam, a spritzy, sappy, biscuity and creamy aroma with a delightful fresh, floral hop note. Rich juicy malt, a faint hint of liquorice and spicy hop resins fill the mouth, followed by a lingering and complex finish dominated by malt and fruit but with a good hop resin balance.

Pinkus Special

Source: Brauerei Pinkus Müller, Münster, Nordrhein-Westfalen, Germany
Strength: 5.4%
Website: www.merchantduvin.com

The Dortmunder Export style made the short journey to Münster, where it is brewed with verve and gusto at the renowned tavern and brewery of Pinkus Müller. Brewmaster Friedhelm Langfeld is a great believer in the proper lagering of beer. His beers are stored in horizontal steel tanks in his lager *Keller*. Unlike modern vertical tanks that encourage a fast second fermentation, the beer ripens more slowly in horizontal tanks, some unfermented malt sugars are left to give the beer body, and a good natural carbonation is achieved. Special is brewed with organic Bioland Pilsner malt and organic Tettnanger hops from Bavaria. As a result of the cramped conditions in the brewhouse, the mash tun also acts as the boiling copper. From the tun, the sugary extract is filtered in a lauter tun, then returns to the first vessel for the boil with hops. Following primary fermentation, Special enjoys three months in the lager *Keller*.

The pale bronze beer that emerges from this long process has a slight haze, as it is not filtered. It has a massive fruity aroma reminiscent of ripe pears, with toasted malt and floral hops. Bitter hop resins dominate the palate, balanced by juicy malt and fruit, while the long finish has tart fruit, sweet malt and bitter hops. It is a wonderfully refreshing beer, best enjoyed in the convivial atmosphere of the tavern, with its swift service and generous portions of Westphalian food. Neither the tavern nor the beer should be missed.

TASTING NOTES
Appearance
Aroma
Taste
Overall score

Sapporo Yebisu

Source: Sapporo Breweries, Hokkaido, Japan
Strength: 5%
Website: www.sapporo.jp

TASTING NOTES
Appearance
Aroma
Taste
Overall score

Japan, with its four brewing giants Asahi, Kirin, Sapporo and Suntory, is a major force in world brewing, and it has achieved this status in a remarkably short time. Beer was unknown in the country until 1853, when an American trade mission went to Japan accompanied by ships of the US Navy under the control of Commodore Matthew Perry. When Japanese dignitaries went on board one of Perry's ships, they were offered beer. One of the visitors was sufficiently intrigued by the taste to search out a handbook on brewing, translate it from Dutch into Japanese and start brewing at home.

Following the reforms of Emperor Mutsuhito in 1868, which encouraged westernisation and industrialisation, a commercial brewing industry started to develop. The first brewery was established with American help and finance, but the Japanese looked to Europe for inspiration. As a result 'Bavarian beers' started to appear, followed by other German styles.

Sapporo, formed in 1876, is one of the oldest breweries in Japan and is named after the northern town of the same name where it started in business. It now owns five breweries in the country and many consider that Yebisu, named after a Shinto god and also a district in Tokyo, is its best beer.

Yebisu is promoted as an all-malt product and is firmly in the Dortmunder style. It is hopped with Hallertauer Mittelfrüh and Hersbrucker varieties. It is a pale gold colour, with a malty aroma balanced by floral hops and a hint of lemon fruit. Creamy and biscuity malt dominate the palate but there is a growing hop resin presence and light fruit. The finish is bitter-sweet, firmly malty but with a good hoppy and fruity finish.

Sapporo's beer can be enjoyed in the Beer Station grouping of bars and restaurants at the Yebisu site.

Švyturys Ekstra

Source: Švyturys Utenos Alus, Klaipeda, Lithuania
Strength: 5.2%
Website: www.svyturys.lt

Lithuania, one of the first republics to break away from the former Soviet Union, has a long brewing history that dates back to the Middle Ages.

Commercial brewing started to develop in the 17th and 18th centuries. Švyturys was founded in 1784 and is now the oldest brewery in the country and the last remaining beer producer in Klaipeda, once a major brewing town. Following privatisation, the company has come under the wing of Carlsberg, which has a 20% share. In 1999, the European Bank for Reconstruction and Development took a similar stake and invested heavily in the brewery, which produces 350,000 hectolitres (7.7m gallons)

a year. The Ekstra brand is its flagship beer and is widely distributed in the United States, where it won a gold medal in the Dortmunder Export class in the 2001 World Beer Championship.

The beer is brewed with local malt and imported German hop varieties. It is a burnished gold in colour with a grainy, malty, biscuity aroma, backed by spicy hops. The full-bodied palate is dominated by ripe, juicy grain, earthy hop resins and a touch of citrus fruit, while the lingering finish is quenching, bitter-sweet, with delicious juicy malt notes and a final attack by bitter and spicy hops.

TASTING NOTES
Appearance
Aroma
Taste
Overall score

Smoked Beer

The smoked, or Rauch, beers of the Bamberg region of German Franconia are a powerful link with brewing's past, when malt was kilned over wood-fuelled fires and beer had a smoky character as a result. Bamberg is famous for its stunning medieval architecture, a Benedictine abbey and Romanesque-Gothic cathedral. The abbey's former brewery, which dates from the 11th century, is now a brewing museum that underscores the important role the small city and its surrounding area have played in the history and development of beer. Malt is also made in Bamberg. Beechwood is collected from the surrounding forests to supply fuel for the malt kilns. As well as the main producer of Rauch beer listed here, also sample the smoked beers of the Christian Merz brew pub at 10 Obere König Strasse, and the beers of the Kaiserdom brewery.

BELOW LEFT
Rauchbier, or smoked beer, is a style confined to the Bamberg region of Germany.

BELOW RIGHT
The Schlenkerla beers are available in the handsome tavern in Bamberg.

Aecht Schlenkerla Rauchbier

Source: Brauerei Heller-Trum, Bamberg, Franconia, Germany
Strength: 5.1%
Website: www.schlenkerla.de

Brewing began in the Schlenkerla tavern in the city (junction of Dominikaner Strasse and Sand Strasse, beneath the cathedral) in 1678, when the beer was stored in caves in the nearby hill of Stephansberg. The need for more space in the tavern and a growing demand for the beer forced the Trum family to move to new premises nearby.

The sixth generation of the family still runs the business. The brewery yard is packed with beechwood logs. Inside, there is a smokehouse where the barley malt lies on a mesh above a beechwood oven that throws up wonderful aromas reminiscent of garden fires in autumn.

The copper brewhouse uses a double-decoction mashing regime. The extract is filtered in a lauter tun, then pumped to a copper brew kettle in a tiled surround where it is boiled with hops

from the Hallertauer (29–32 units of bitterness). Following seven days' primary fermentation, the beer is stored for six to eight weeks.

The finished beer is dark chestnut in colour with an intense smoked malt aroma and palate, with dry malt in the mouth and a long and lingering finish, with herbal and smoky notes and a gentle underpinning of spicy hops. The word Aecht in the name of the beer means 'original'.

The brewery also produces an autumn smoky Bock and a Helles, or pale, lager. The beers can be enjoyed with hearty local dishes in the Schlenkerla tavern (9.30am–11.30pm, closed Tuesdays). The name comes from the nickname given to a former brewer who walked in a slightly odd fashion that suggested he might have over-indulged in his product.

TASTING NOTES
Appearance
Aroma
Taste
Overall score

Glossary

ABV (Alcohol by Volume): international method for measuring and declaring for tax purposes the strength of beer. In the US, a system known as Alcohol by Weight is used: 5% ABV is 4% ABW. Many American brewers now also declare the strength of beer in ABV.

Abbey beer: commercial beers—produced principally in Belgium—that may be brewed under licence from monasteries, though some have no monastic links whatsoever. Not to be confused with Trappist beers (qv). Abbey beers are labelled Abbaye (French) or Abdij (Flemish).

Adjuncts: cereals and sugars added to beer, often as a cheap substitute, but sometimes used by craft brewers for special flavours. Producers of mass-market lagers may often dilute the barley mash with corn [maize] or rice. On the other hands, Belgian brewers use candy sugar for palate, while British brewers often use caramel and invert sugar. Adjuncts are not permitted in Germany where the Reinheitsgebot (qv) allows only malted grain.

Ale: the world's oldest beer style, produced by warm or top fermentation. The term covers such styles as (in Britain, Ireland and the US) mild, bitter, porter, stout, old ale and barley wine, and in the Low Countries, Abbey and Trappist ales, and some types of Bock, or Bok.

Alpha acid: the natural acid in the cone of the hop plant that gives bitterness to beer. Some international brewers use only 'high alpha' or 'super alpha' hops that give a high level of bitterness but little aroma.

Alt & Amber: an 'old' style of warm-fermented beer from the Dusseldorf region of Germany, often known as Amber in the US.

Aroma: the 'nose' of a beer that gives an indication of the malty, hoppy and possibly fruity characteristics to be found in the mouth.

Attenuation: If a beer is 'fully attenuated', most or all of the malt sugars will have turned to alcohol. In some styles, such as English mild or Dortmunder Export, some malt sugars are left in the beer for fullness of palate and some sweetness. Such beers are not 'brewed out' or fully attenuated.

Barley: the preferred grain used by all brewers as the main ingredient in beer and source of fermentable sugar.

Beer: generic term for an alcoholic drink made from grain. It includes ale, lager and Belgian lambic/gueuze.

Bière de Garde: French 'keeping beer', a style associated with French Flanders, first brewed by farmer/brewers in spring and stored to refresh their labourers during the summer months, but now produced all year round.

Bitter: A draught English pale ale that may range in colour from gold through amber to copper. The name indicates a generous amount of hop bitterness.

Blond/blonde: term used in mainland Europe to indicate a light-coloured beer. The term is often used when a brewery produces brown and pale versions of the same or similar beers, as in the case of Leffe Blonde and Brune.

Bock: German term for a strong beer, which can be pale or dark, usually stored or lagered for several months. The term is associated with the 'liquid bread' beers brewed by monks to sustain them during Lent. In the Netherlands, the term is sometimes spelt Bok, and beers there may be warm fermented.

Bottle conditioned/bottle fermented: a beer bottled with live yeast that allows the beer to mature, gain condition ('sparkle') and extra alcohol in its glass container.

Bragget: an ancient beer style associated with the Celtic regions of the British Isles, usually brewed without hops but often with the addition of herbs and spices. A Bragget beer is occasionally brewed at the Blue Anchor brew-pub in Cornwall.

Brew-pub: a pub that brews beer on the premises.

Brune: a brown beer. See blond.

Burtonise/Burtonisation: addition of such salts as gypsum and magnesium to replicate the hard brewing waters found in Burton-on-Trent.

Campaign for Real Ale (CAMRA): Beer drinkers' organisation founded in 1971 to protect cask-conditioned beer—dubbed 'real ale'. CAMRA now has 83,000 members.

Carbon dioxide (CO$_2$): a gas naturally produced by fermentation. When beers are said to be 'naturally conditioned', as in cask-conditioned ale or bottle-conditioned beer, the gas is natural. When beers are filtered in the brewery, CO$_2$ may added either in the brewery or as part of the dispense system in a bar or pub. This can make beer too gassy.

Cask ale: also known as cask beer or real ale. A draught beer that undergoes a secondary fermentation in the cask in the pub cellar, reaching maturity as a result of natural processes. The style is mainly confined to Britain.

Condition: the level of carbon dioxide (CO$_2$) present in beer, which gives beer its sparkle.

Copper: vessel used to boil the sugary wort (qv) with hops. Traditionally made of copper but more often today of stainless steel. Known as a brew kettle in the US.

Decoction mashing: a system used mainly in lager brewing or German wheat beer production, in which portions of the mash are removed from the mashing vessel, heated to a higher temperature and then returned to the first vessel. Improves enzymic activity and the conversion of starch to sugar.

Doppelbock (double bock): extra strong type of Bock, usually around 7.5% ABV or more, but not—despite the name—twice the strength of an ordinary Bock.

Draught: beer served from a bulk container and drawn to the bar. Spelt 'draft' in the US.

Dry hopping: the addition of a small amount of hops to a cask of beer to improve bitterness and aroma. Usually associated with cask-conditioned beer in Britain.

Dubbel: Flemish word for double, first coined by the Westmalle Trappist brewery, to indicate a strong dark ale of around 6.5% ABV.

Dunkel: German for 'dark', indicating a lager beer in which colour is derived from well-roasted malts.

Enkel: Dutch word for single, used to indicate a beer of modest strength, as in La Trappe Enkel.

Esters: Flavour compounds produced by the action of yeast turning sugars into alcohol and carbon dioxide (CO$_2$). Esters are often similar to fruits, and fruitiness is associated with members of the ale family.

Fermentation: turning malt sugars into alcohol and carbon dioxide (CO$_2$) by the action of yeast. Ale is made by warm fermentation, lager by cold fermentation. These are often called top and bottom fermentation but the terms are misleading, as yeast works at all levels of the liquid.

Fining: Clarifying beer with the addition of finings, usually isinglass made from fish bladders. Caragheen [Irish Moss] can also be used and is preferred by vegetarians and vegans.

Finish: the aftertaste of a beer; the impression left at the back of the tongue and the throat.

Grand Cru: a term given to the finest beer of a brewery, one thought to typify the house style. Often used by Belgian brewers.

Grist: brewers' term for the milled grains to be used in a brew. The term comes from the word 'grind' and is still used in the expression 'all grist to the mill'.

Gruit: medieval method of adding a blend of herbs and spices to beer.

Gueuze: see Lambic.

Hefe: German for yeast. Beers 'mit hefe' are naturally conditioned and not filtered. Usually applies to wheat beers.

Helles: German for light, indicating a pale beer, either lager or wheat beer.

Hops: climbing plant with cones containing acids, resins and tannins that gives aroma and bitterness to beer, and helps prevent bacterial infection.

IBU: International Units of Bitterness, a scale for measuring the bitterness of beer.

Infusion: method of mashing beer, mainly associated with British ale brewing. The grain is left to soak with pure hot water in a mash tun at a constant temperature; enzymes in the malt convert starch to sugar.

IPA: short for India Pale Ale, the first pale beer in the world, associated with Burton-on-Trent in the English Midlands in the 19th century. First brewed for soldiers and civil servants based in India, it spawned pale ale and bitter in England, and even inspired the first lager brewers of Austria and Germany.

Kräusen: The addition of some partially fermented wort (qv) to beer in the lager cellar to encourage a strong secondary fermentation.

Lager: from the German meaning store or storage place, similar to the English word larder. Following primary fermentation, beer is 'cold conditioned' in tanks where the temperature is held just above freezing. As the yeast settles at the bottom of the tanks, a slow secondary fermentation takes place, carbonation increases, and a clean, quenching, spritzy beer results, usually lacking the fruity esters associated with ale.

Lambic: Belgian beer made by 'spontaneous fermentation', using wild yeasts in the atmosphere. True lambics are confined to the area of the Senne Valley centred on Brussels. A blended lambic, using young and aged beers, is known as gueuze. When cherries or raspberries are added, the beers are known as kriek and framboise, or frambozen.

Lauter: vessel used to run off and filter the wort from the grain after mashing. The word comes from the German for clarify, and the vessels were once associated with lager or wheat beer brewing. But many ale brewers with modern equipment now employ lauter tuns, as the mash tun (qv) can be used to start a new brew once the mash has been pumped to the lauter.

Liquor: Brewers' term for the pure water used in the mashing and boiling process.

Maibock: in Germany, a strong, usually pale, lager brewed to herald the arrival of spring.

Malt: grain—usually barley— that has been partially germinated, dried and cured or toasted in a kiln. The grain contains starches that will be converted by natural enzymes into fermentable sugar during the mashing period in the brewery. The colour of malt is determined by the degree of heat in the kiln. All beers are made primarily from pale malt, which has the highest level of natural enzymes. Colour and flavour are derived from darker malts, such as amber, brown or chocolate.

Märzen: Traditional Bavarian lager brewed in March and stored until the autumn, when it is tapped at the Oktoberfest.

Mash: the mixture of malted grain and pure hot water, the first stage of the brewing process, when sugars are extracted from the malt. Mashing can be either by decoction or infusion (qv).

Mash tun: vessel in which malted grain is mixed with 'liquor' to start the brewing process.

Micro-brewery: a small brewery with a small staff, often just a couple of people, brewing batches of beer for local distribution. 'Micros' in Britain and the US have been at the forefront of the craft beer revival in the past 20–30 years. Many micros have re-created old beer styles and designed new ones. In the US, micros may be big by European standards, but are considered small when compared to giant American producers.

Mouth-feel: the sensation that beer and its constituent parts—malt, hops and fruity esters—make in the mouth. The tongue is a highly sensitive organ and can detect sweetness, sourness, saltiness and bitterness as the beer passes over it.

Oktoberfest beers: medium-strength lager beer brewed in Munich for consumption at the famous autumn beer festival.

Original Gravity (OG): system once used in Britain for measuring the level of 'fermentable material'—malt, other grains and sugars—in a beer. Tax was levied on the OG until the system was replaced by Alcohol By Volume (ABV—qv). However, many brewers still list the OG and the ABV of their beers.

Parti-gyle: making more than one beer from a brew with the addition of brewing liquor to water the wort (qv) down to the required strengths.

Pasteurisation: heating process developed by Louis Pasteur that kills bacteria and stabilises the beer. It can be done quickly by flash pasteurisation as the beer passes through a pipe or more slowly by tunnel pasteurisation when the beer comes into contact with heat. If pasteurisation is clumsy, the beer can take on unpleasant cardboard or cabbage-like aromas and flavours. Many brewers now prefer to sterile filter beer. One leading opponent of pasteurisation was Pasteur himself, who developed the method to protect wine, and said beer was too delicate to withstand it.

Pilsner/Pilsener/Pils: originally a golden, hoppy lager brewed in the city of Pilsen in Bohemia, now part of the Czech Republic. A true Pilsner is usually around 4.5–5% ABV. In Germany, many brewers either spell the word Pilsener or shorten it to Pils, to avoid any suggestion their beers come from Pilsen. In the Czech Republic, Pilsner is an 'appellation': only beers from Pilsen can use the term.

Porter: a brown (later black) beer first brewed in London early in the 18th century. Called 'entire butt' by brewers, it acquired the name of porter due to its popularity with street-market porters. The success of porter created the modern commercial brewing industry in England and later in Ireland. The strongest porters were known as stout (qv).

Priming: the addition of priming sugar to encourage a strong secondary fermentation.

Quadrupel: a Belgian beer of exceptional strength but rarely four times as strong as other beers.

Racking: running beer from a conditioning tank into a cask or keg.

Real Ale: term coined by CAMRA (qv) in Britain to denote a beer that is neither filtered nor pasteurised, which undergoes a secondary fermentation in its container and is not served by applied gas pressure.

Reinheitsgebot: The Bavarian 'Pure Beer Law' dating from 1516 that lays down that only malted barley and/or wheat, hops, yeast and water can be used in brewing. Cheaper cereals, such as corn or rice, and sugar are not permitted. The law now covers the whole of Germany, but export beers may not necessarily adhere to it.

Sparge: to rinse the grain after mashing to flush out any remaining malt sugars (from the French *esperger*, meaning to sprinkle).

Stout: Once a generic English term for the strongest or 'stoutest' beer produced in a brewery. With the rise of porter (qv) in the 18th century, strong porters were known as stout porters. Over time, the term was shortened to just stout, indicating a strong, jet-black beer, made with highly roasted malts and roasted barley, and generously hopped. The style is most closely associated today with Ireland.

Trappist: beers of the ale family made in breweries controlled by Trappist monks in Belgium.

Tripel: strong, usually pale beer, associated with the Westmalle Trappist brewery in Belgium, but now widely used throughout the Low Countries.

Tun: a large vessel once used to store beer. The term today is confined to the mash tun, the vessel in which malt and water are blended at the start of the brewing process (qv).

Vienna Red: term for the first successful commercial lager beer brewed in Austria in the 19th century. It was a halfway house between the dark lagers of Munich and the golden lagers of Bohemia. Vienna Red inspired the Munich Märzen beers (qv).

Wheat beer: known as weizen (wheat) or weiss (white) in Germany, blanche in French or wit in Dutch and Flemish. Beer made from a blend of wheat and barley malt. Wheat beers are members of the ale family and may be unfiltered and cloudy, or filtered bright.

Wort: the sweet, sugary extract produced by mashing malt and water. Wort is boiled with hops, then cooled prior to fermentation.

Yeast: a natural fungus that attacks sweet liquids such as wort, turning malt sugars into alcohol and carbon dioxide (CO_2). Brewers' yeasts are either warm or top fermenting cultures for ale brewing, or cold or bottom fermenting cultures for lager brewing. Belgian lambic brewers (qv) use wild yeasts from the atmosphere.

Index

By beer name

- [ ] Shepherd Neame Master Brew Bitter (England) 76
- [ ] Shipyard Fuggles IPA (USA) 19
- [ ] Shipyard Longfellow Winter Ale (USA) 110
- [ ] Sierra Nevada Bigfoot (USA) 132
- [ ] Sierra Nevada Pale Ale (USA) 64
- [ ] Silly Double Enghien Blonde (Belgium) 180
- [ ] Spaten Münchner Hell (Germany) 259
- [ ] Spaten Ur-Märzen (Germany) 278
- [ ] Spendrup's Old Gold (Sweden) 31
- [ ] Stoudt's Triple (USA) 236
- [ ] Švyturys Ekstra (Lithuania) 285

- [ ] Theakston's Old Peculier (England) 133
- [ ] Thornbridge Jaipur IPA (England) 20
- [ ] Timothy Taylor's Landlord (England) 96
- [ ] Titanic Stout (England) 165
- [ ] Tongerlo Double Brown (Belgium) 237
- [ ] Tongerlo Triple Blond (Belgium) 237
- [ ] Traquair House Ale (Scotland) 134
- [ ] Třeboň Dark Regent (Czech Republic) 265
- [ ] Triple fff Alton's Pride (England) 77
- [ ] Trumer Pils (Austria) 32

- [ ] U Fleků Flekovský Dark (Czech Republic) 266
- [ ] Uley Bitter (England) 78
- [ ] Unibroue Blanche de Chambly (Canada) 200
- [ ] Unibroue Maudite (Canada) 181
- [ ] Upper Canada Dark Ale (Canada) 97

- [ ] Wadworth 6X (England) 98
- [ ] Weihenstephaner Hefe Weissbier (Germany) 195
- [ ] Weihenstephaner Pilsner (Germany) 32
- [ ] Wellington Arkell Best Bitter (Canada) 99
- [ ] Wells Banana Bread Beer (England) 255
- [ ] Wells Bombardier (England) 100
- [ ] Welton's Pridenjoy (England) 79
- [ ] Westmalle Dubbel (Belgium) 227
- [ ] Westmalle Tripel (Belgium) 227
- [ ] Westvleteren Abt (Belgium) 228
- [ ] Westvleteren Blond (Belgium) 228
- [ ] Westvleteren Extra (Belgium) 228
- [ ] Wild River Extra Special Bitter (USA) 110
- [ ] Wolf Granny Wouldn't Like It (England) 101
- [ ] Woodforde's Norfolk Nip (England) 135
- [ ] Woodforde's Wherry (England) 80

- [ ] Worthington's White Shield (England) 21
- [ ] Wychwood Hobgoblin (England) 111
- [ ] Wye Valley Brewery Dorothy Goodbody's Wholesome Stout (England) 166

- [ ] Xingu Black Beer (Brazil) 266

- [ ] Young's Double Chocolate Stout (England) 167
- [ ] Young's Kew Gold (England) 182
- [ ] Younger's Special Bitter (USA) 65

- [ ] Žatec 12° (Czech Republic) 260
- [ ] Zum Uerige Alt (Germany) 216
- [ ] Zywiec Porter (Poland) 168

Index

By beer style

India Pale Ales

Pilsners

Brown & Mild Ales

Pale Ales

Bitters

Best Bitters

Books for Beer Lovers

CAMRA Books, the publishing arm of the Campaign for Real Ale,
is the leading publisher of books on beer and pubs. Key titles include:

Good Beer Guide 2013

Editor: Roger Protz

The *Good Beer Guide* is the only guide you will ever need to find the right pint, in the right place, every time. It's the original and best-selling guide to around 4,500 pubs throughout the UK. In its 40th anniversary year, this annual publication is a comprehensive and informative guide to the best real ale pubs in the UK, researched and written exclusively by CAMRA members and fully updated every year.

£15.99 ISBN 978-1-85249-290-8

Great British Pubs

Adrian Tierney-Jones

Great British Pubs is a celebration of the British pub. This fully illustrated and practical book presents the pub as an ultimate destination—featuring pubs everyone should seek out and make a visit to. It recommends a selection of the very best pubs in various different categories, as chosen by leading beer writer Adrian Tierney-Jones. Every kind of pub is represented, with full-colour photography helping to showcase a host of excellent pubs from the seaside to the city and from the historic to the ultra-modern.

£14.99 ISBN 978-1-85249-265-6

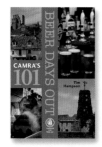

101 Beer Days Out

Tim Hampson

101 Beer Days Out is the perfect handbook for the beer tourist wanting to explore beer and brewing culture in their local area and around the UK. From historic city pubs to beer festivals; idyllic country pub walks to rail ale trails—Britain has beer and brewing experiences to rival any in the world. *101 Beer Days Out* brings together for the first time the best of these experiences—perfect for any beer tourist.

£12.99 ISBN 978-1-85249-288-5

London's Best Beer, Pubs & Bars

Des de Moor

London's Best Beer, Pubs & Bars is the essential guide to beer drinking in London. This practical book is packed with detailed maps and easy-to-use listings to help you find the best places to enjoy perfect pints in the capital. Laid out by area, find the best pubs serving the best British and international beers wherever you are. Features tell you more about London's rich history of brewing and the city's vibrant modern brewing scene, where well-known brands rub shoulders with tiny micro-breweries.

£12.99 ISBN 978-1-85249-262-5

Good Bottled Beer Guide

Jeff Evans

A pocket-sized guide for discerning drinkers looking to buy bottled real ales and enjoy a fresh glass of their favourite beers at home. The 7th edition of the *Good Bottled Beer Guide* is completely revised, updated and redesigned to showcase the very best bottled British real ales now being produced, and detail where they can be bought. Everything you need to know about bottled beers; tasting notes, ingredients, brewery details, and a glossary to help the reader understand more about them.

£12.99 ISBN 978-1-85249-262-5

Good Beer Guide Belgium

Tim Webb

The completely revised and updated 6th edition of the guide so impressive that it is acknowledged as the standard work for Belgian beer lovers, even in Belgium itself. The Good Beer Guide Belguim includes comprehensive advice on getting there, being there, what to eat, where to stay and how to bring beers back home. Its outline of breweries, beers and bars makes this book indispensible for both leisure and business travellers a well as for armchair drinkers looking to enjoy a selection of Belgian brews from their local beer store.

£14.99 ISBN 978-1-85249-261-8

Good Beer Guide West Coast USA

Ben McFarland & Tom Sandham

Taking in the whole western seaboard of the USA, as well as Las Vegas, Alaska and Hawaii, this is a lively, comprehensive and entertaining tour that unveils some of the most exhilarating beers, breweries and bars on the planet. It is the definitive, totally independent guide to understanding and discovering the heart of America's thriving craft beer scene, and an essential companion for any beer drinker visiting West Coast America or seeking out American beer in the UK, Written with verve and insight by two respected young beer journalists, Good Beer Guide West Coast USA is a must—not just for those who find themselves on the West Coast, but for all discerning beer enthusiasts and barflies everywhere.

£14.99 ISBN 978-1-85249-244-1

Order these and other CAMRA books online at ***www.camra.org.uk/books***, ask at your local bookstore, or contact: CAMRA, 230 Hatfield Road, S Albans, AL1 4LW. Telephone 01727 867201

A Campaign of Two Halves

Campaigning for Pub Goers & Beer Drinkers

CAMRA, the Campaign for Real Ale, is an independent not-for-profit, volunteer-led consumer group. We campaign tirelessly for good-quality real ale and pubs, as well as lobbying government to champion drinkers' rights and promote local pubs as centres of community life. As a CAMRA member you will have the opportunity to campaign to save pubs under threat of closure, for pubs to be free to serve a range of real ales at fair prices and for a reduction in beer duty that will help Britain's brewing industry survive.

Enjoying Real Ale & Pubs

CAMRA has over 140,000 members from all ages and backgrounds, brought together by a common belief in the issues that CAMRA deals with and their love of good quality British beer. From just £23 a year—that's less than a pint a month—you can join CAMRA and enjoy the following benefits:

Subscription to *What's Brewing*, our monthly colour newspaper, and *Beer*, our quarterly magazine, informing you about beer and pub news and detailing events and beer festivals around the country.

Free or reduced entry to over 160 national, regional and local beer festivals.

Money off many of our publications including the *Good Beer Guide*, the *Good Bottled Beer Guide* and *CAMRA's Great British Pubs*.

Access to a members-only section of our national website, **www.camra.org.uk**, which gives up-to-the-minute news stories and includes a special offer section with regular features.

Special discounts with numerous partner organisations and money off real ale in your participating local pubs as part of our Pubs Discount Scheme.

Log onto **www.camra.org.uk/joinus** for CAMRA membership information.

CAMPAIGN
FOR
REAL ALE

Praise for

Once Upon a Dream

"Four of America's most beloved romance authors present what is sure to be a popular collection of magical stories."
—*Publishers Weekly*

"Nora Roberts launches a phenomenal new anthology. . . . This collection is a complete and utter delight. These extremely talented authors deliver a truly magical performance."
—*Romantic Times*

"Excellent stories with intriguing characters and fantasy elements."
—*Rendezvous*

Titles in the Once Upon series

Once Upon A Rose

NORA ROBERTS
JILL GREGORY
RUTH RYAN LANGAN
MARIANNE WILLMAN

JOVE BOOKS, NEW YORK

ONCE UPON A ROSE

A Jove Book / published by arrangement with the authors

PRINTING HISTORY
Jove edition / October 2001

Collection copyright © 2001 by Penguin Putnam Inc.
"Winter Rose" copyright © 2001 by Nora Roberts.
"The Rose and the Sword" copyright © 2001 by Jan Greenberg.
"The Roses of Glenross" copyright © 2001 by Ruth Ryan Langan.
"The Fairest Rose" copyright © 2001 by Marianne Willman.
Cover art and design by Tony Greco.

Visit our website at
www.penguinputnam.com

ISBN: 0-515-13166-0

A JOVE BOOK®
Jove Books are published by The Berkley Publishing Group, a division of Penguin Putnam Inc., 375 Hudson Street, New York, New York 10014.
JOVE and the "J" design are trademarks belonging to Penguin Putnam Inc.

PRINTED IN THE UNITED STATES OF AMERICA

10 9 8 7 6 5

CONTENTS

WINTER ROSE

Nora Roberts

For the three roses,
Ruth, Marianne and Jan,
who've made this so much fun

1

THE WORLD WAS white. And bitter, bitter cold. Exhausted, he drooped in the saddle, unable to do more than trust his horse to continue to trudge forward. Always forward. He knew that to stop, even for moments, in this cruel and keening wind would mean death.

The pain in his side was a freezing burn, and the only thing that kept him from sliding into oblivion.

He was lost in that white globe, blinded by the endless miles of it that covered hill and tree and sky, trapped in the frigid hell of vicious snow gone to icy shards in the whip of the gale. Though even the slow, monotonous movements of his horse brought him agony, he did not yield.

At first the cold had been a relief from the scorching yellow sun. It had, he thought, cooled the fever the wound had sent raging through him. The unblemished stretch of white had numbed his mind so that he'd no longer seen the blood staining the battleground. Or smelled the stench of death.

For a time, when the strength had drained out of him along with his blood, he'd thought he heard voices in the rising wind. Voices that had murmured his name, had whispered another.

Delirium, he'd told himself. For he didn't believe the air could speak.

He'd lost track of how long he'd been traveling. Hours, days, weeks. His first hope had been to come across a cottage, a village where he could rest and have his wound treated. Now he simply wanted to find a decent place to die.

Perhaps he was dead already and hell was endless winter.

He no longer hungered, though the last time he'd eaten had been before the battle. The battle, he thought dimly, where he'd emerged victorious and unscathed. It had been foolish, carelessly foolish, of him to ride for home alone.

The trio of enemy soldiers had, he was sure, been trying to reach their own homes when they met him on that path in the forest. His first instinct was to let them go. The battle had been won and the invasion crushed. But war and death were still in their eyes, and when they charged him his sword was in his hand.

They would never see home now. Nor, he feared, would he.

As his mount plodded onward, he fought to remain conscious. And now he was in another forest, he thought dully as he struggled to focus. Though how he had come to it, how he had gotten lost when he knew his kingdom as intimately as a man knew a lover's face, was a mystery to him.

He had never traveled here before. The trees looked dead to him, brittle and gray. He heard no bird, no brook, just the steady swish of his horse's hooves in the snow.

Surely this was the land of the dead, or the dying.

When he saw the deer, it took several moments to register. It was the first living thing he'd seen since the flakes had begun to fall, and it watched him without fear.

Why not? he mused with a weak laugh. He hadn't the strength to notch an arrow. When the stag bounded away, Kylar of Mrydon, prince and warrior, slumped over the neck of his horse.

When he came to again, the forest was at his back, and he faced a white, white sea. Or so it seemed. Just as it seemed, in the center of that sea, a silver island glittered. Through his hazy vision, he made out turrets and towers. On the topmost a flag flew in the wild wind. A red rose blooming full against a field of white.

He prayed for strength. Surely where there was a flag flying there were people. There was warmth. He would have given half a kingdom to spend the last hour of his life by a fire's light and heat.

But his vision began to go dark at the edges and his head swam. Through the waves of fatigue and weakness he thought he saw the rose, red as blood, moving over that white sea toward him. Gritting his teeth, he urged his horse forward. If he couldn't have the fire, he wanted the sweet scent of the rose before he died.

He lacked even the strength to curse fate as he slid once more into unconsciousness and tumbled from the saddle into the snow.

The fall shot pain through him, pushed him back to the surface, where he clung as if under a thin veil of ice. Through it, he saw a face leaning close to his. Lovely long-lidded eyes, green as the moss in the forests of his home, smooth skin of rose and cream. A soft, full mouth. He saw those pretty lips move, but couldn't hear the words she spoke through the buzzing in his head.

The hood of her red cloak covered her hair, and he reached up to touch the cloth. "You're not a flower after all."

"No, my lord. Only a woman."

"Well, it's better to die warmed by a kiss than a fire." He tugged on the hood, felt that soft, full mouth meet his—one sweet taste—before he passed out.

Men, Deirdre thought as she eased back, were such odd creatures. To steal a kiss at such a time was surely beyond folly. Shaking her head, she got to her feet and took in hand the horn that hung from the sash at her waist. She blew the signal for help, then removed her cloak to spread over him. Sitting again, she cradled him as best she could in her arms and waited for stronger hands to carry the unexpected guest into the castle.

The cold had saved his life, but the fever might snatch it back again. On his side of the battle were his youth and his strength. And, Deirdre thought, herself. She would do all in her power to heal him. Twice, he'd regained consciousness during his transport to the bedchamber. And both times he'd struggled, weakly to be sure, but enough to start the blood flowing from his wound again once he was warm.

In her brisk, somewhat ruthless way, she'd ordered two of her men to hold him down while she doused him with a sleeping draught. The cleaning and closing of the wound would be painful for him if he should wake again. Deirdre was a woman who brooked no nonsense, but she disliked seeing anyone in pain.

She gathered her medicines and herbs, pushed up the sleeves of the rough tunic she wore. He lay naked on the bed, in the thin light of the pale gold sun that filtered through the narrow windows. She'd seen unclothed men before, just as she'd seen what a sword could do to flesh.

"He's so handsome." Cordelia, the servant Deirdre had ordered to assist her, nearly sighed.

"What he is, is dying." Deirdre's voice was sharp with command. "Put more pressure on that cloth. I'll not have him bleed to death under my roof."

She selected her medicines and, moving to the bed, concentrated only on the wound in his side. It ranged from an inch under his armpit down to his hip in one long, vicious slice. Sweat dewed on her brow as she focused, putting her mind into his body to search for damage. Her cheeks paled as she worked, but her hands were steady and quick.

So much blood, she thought as her breath came thick and ragged. So much pain. How could he have lived with this? Even with the cold slowing the flow of blood, he should have been long dead.

She paused once to rinse the blood from her hands in a bowl, to dry them. But when she picked up the needle, Cordelia blanched. "My lady . . ."

Absently, Deirdre glanced over. She'd nearly forgotten the girl was there. "You may go. You did well enough."

Cordelia fled the room so quickly, Deirdre might have smiled. The girl never moved so fast when there was work to be done. Deirdre turned back to her patient and began carefully, skillfully, to sew the wound closed.

It would scar, she thought, but he had others. His was a warrior's body, tough and hard and bearing the marks of battle. What was it, she wondered, that made men so eager to fight, to kill? What was it that lived inside them that they could find pride in both?

This one did, she was sure of it. It had taken strength and will, and pride, to keep him mounted and alive all the miles he'd traveled to her island. But how had he come, this dark warrior? And why?

She coated the stitched wound with a balm of her own making and bandaged it with her own hands. Then with the worse tended, she examined his body thoroughly for any lesser wounds.

She found a few nicks and cuts, and one more serious slice on the back of his shoulder. It had closed on its own and was already scabbed over. Whatever battle he'd fought, she calculated, had been two days ago, perhaps three.

To survive so long with such grievous hurts, to have traveled through the Forgotten to reach help, showed a strong will to live. That was good. He would need it.

When she was satisfied, she took a clean cloth and began to wash and cool the fever sweat from his skin.

He was handsome. She let herself study him now. He was tall, leanly muscled. His hair, black as midnight, spilled over the bed linens, away from a face that might have been carved from stone. It suited the warrior, she thought, that narrow face with the sharp jut of cheekbones over hollowed cheeks. His nose was long and straight, his mouth full and somewhat hard. His beard had begun to grow in, a shadow of stubble that made him appear wicked and dangerous even unconscious.

His brows were black slashes. She remembered his eyes were blue. Even dazed with pain, fever, fatigue, they had been bold and brilliantly blue.

If the gods willed it, they would open again.

She tucked him up warm, laid another log on the fire. Then she sat down to watch over him.

For two days and two nights the fever raged in him. At times he was delirious and had to be restrained lest his thrashing break open his wound again. At times he slept like a man dead, and she feared he would never rouse. Even her gifts couldn't beat back the fire that burned in him.

She slept when she could in the chair beside his bed. And once, when the chills racked him, she crawled under the bedclothes with him to soothe him with her own body.

His eyes did open again, but they were blind and wild. The pity she tried to hold back when healing stirred inside her. Once when the night was dark and the cold rattled its bones against the windows, she held his hand and grieved for him.

Life was the most precious gift, and it seemed cruel that he should come so far from home only to lose his.

To busy her mind she sewed or she sang. When she trusted him to be quiet for a time, she left him in the care of one of her women and tended to the business of her home and her people.

On the last night of his fever, despair nearly broke her.

Exhausted, she mourned for his wife, for his mother, for those he'd left behind who would never know of his fate. There in the quiet of the bedchamber, she used the last of her strength and her skill. She laid hands on him.

"The first and most vital of rules is not to harm. I have not harmed you. What I do now will end this, one way or another. Kill or cure. If I knew your name"—she brushed a hand gently over his burning brow—"or your mind, or your heart, this would be easier for both of us. Be strong." She climbed onto the bed to kneel beside him. "And fight."

With one hand over the wound that she'd unbandaged, the other over his heart, she let what she was rush through her, race through her blood, her bone. Into him.

He moaned. She ignored it. It would hurt, hurt both of them. His body arched up, and hers back. There was a rush of images that stole her breath. A grand castle, blurring colors, a jeweled crown.

She felt strength—his. And kindness. A light flickered inside her, nearly made her break away. But it drew her in, deeper, and the light grew soft, warm.

For Deirdre, it was the first time, even in healing that she had looked into another's heart and felt it brush and call her own.

Then she saw, very clearly, a woman's face, her deep-blue eyes full of pride, and perhaps fear.

Come back, my son. Come home safe.

There was music—drumbeats—the laughter and shouts of men. Then a flash that was sun striking off steel, and the smell of blood and battle choked her.

She muffled a cry as she caught a glimpse in her mind. Swords clashing, the stench of sweat and death and fear.

He fought her, thrashing, striking out as she bore down with her mind. Later, she would tend the bruises they gave each other in this final pitched battle for life.

Her muscles trembled, and part of her screamed to pull back, pull away. He was nothing to her. Still, as her muscles trembled, she pit her fire against the fever, just as the enemy sword in his mind slashed against them both.

She felt the bite of it in her side, steel into flesh. The agony ripped a scream from her throat. On its heels, she tasted death.

His heart galloped under her hand, and the wound on his side was like a flame against her palm. But she'd seen into his mind now, and she fought to rise above the pain and use what she'd been given, what she'd taken, to save him.

His eyes were open, glassy with shock in a face white as death.

"Kylar of Mrydon." She spoke clearly, though each breath she took was a misery. "Take what you need. Fire of healing. And live."

The tension went out of his body. His eyes blurred, then fluttered shut. She felt the sigh shudder through him as he slid into sleep.

But the light within her continued to glow. "What is this?" she murmured, rubbing an unsteady hand over her own heart. "No matter. No matter now. I can do no more to help. Live," she said again, then leaned down to brush her lips over his brow. "Or die gently."

She started to climb down from the bed, but her head spun. When she fainted, her head came to rest, quite naturally, on his heart.

2

HE DRIFTED IN and out. There were times when he thought himself back in battle, shouting commands to his men while his horse wheeled under him and his sword hacked through those who would dare invade his lands.

Then he was back in that strange and icy forest, so cold he feared his bones would shatter. Then the cold turned to fire, and the part of him that was still sane prayed to die.

Something cool and sweet would slide down his throat, and somehow he would sleep again.

He dreamed he was home, drifting toward morning with a willing woman in his bed. Soft and warm and smelling of summer roses.

He thought he heard music, harpsong, with a voice, low and smooth, matching pretty words to those plucked notes.

Sometimes he saw a face. Moss-green eyes, a lovely,

wide mouth. Hair the color of dark, rich honey that tumbled around a face both unbearably beautiful and unbearably sad. Each time the pain or the heat or the cold would become intolerable, that face, those eyes, would be there.

Once, he dreamed she had called him by name, in a voice that rang with command. And those eyes had been dark and full of pain and power. Her hair had spilled over his chest like silk, and he'd slept once more—deeply, peacefully—with the scent of her surrounding him.

He woke again to that scent, drifted into it as a man might drift into a cool stream on a hot day. There was a velvet canopy of deep purple over his head. He stared at it as he tried to clear his mind. One thought came through.

This was not home.

Then another.

He was alive.

Morning, he decided. The light through the windows was thin and very dull. Not long past dawn. He tried to sit up, and the movement made his side throb. Even as he hissed out a breath, she was there.

"Carefully." Deirdre slid a hand behind his head to lift it gently as she brought a cup to his lips. "Drink now."

She gave him no choice but to swallow before he managed to bring his hand to hers and nudge the cup aside. "What . . ." His voice felt rusty, as if it would scrape his throat. "What is this place?"

"Drink your broth, Prince Kylar. You're very weak."

He would have argued, but to his frustration he was as weak as she said. And she was not. Her hands were strong, hard from labor. He studied her as she urged more broth on him.

That honey hair fell straight as rain to the waist of a simple gray dress. She wore no jewels, no ribbons, and still managed to look beautiful and wonderfully female.

A servant, he assumed, with some skill in healing. He would find a way to repay her, and her master.

"Your name, sweetheart?"

Odd creatures indeed, she thought as she arched a brow.

A man would flirt the moment he regained what passed for his senses. "I am Deirdre."

"I'm grateful, Deirdre. Would you help me up?"

"No, my lord. Tomorrow, perhaps." She set the cup aside. "But you could sit up for a time while I tend your wound."

"I dreamed of you." Weak, yes, he thought. But he was feeling considerably better. Well enough to put some effort into flirting with a beautiful housemaid. "Did you sing to me?"

"I sang to pass the time. You've been here three days."

"Three—" He gritted his teeth as she helped him to sit up. "I've no memory of it."

"That's natural. Be still now."

He frowned at her bent head as she removed the bandage. Though a generous man by nature, he wasn't accustomed to taking orders. Certainly not from housemaids. "I would like to thank your master for his hospitality."

"There is no master here. It heals clean," she murmured, and probed gently with her fingers. "And is cool. You'll have a fine scar to add to your collection." With quick competence, she smeared on a balm. "There's pain yet, I know. But if you can tolerate it for now, I'd prefer not to give you another sleeping draught."

"Apparently I've slept enough."

She began to bandage him again, her body moving into his as she wrapped the wound. Fetching little thing, he mused, relieved that he was well enough to feel a tug of interest. He skimmed a hand through her hair as she worked, twined a lock around his finger. "I've never had a prettier physician."

"Save your strength, my lord." Her voice was cool, dismissive, and made him frown again. "I won't see my work undone because you've a yen for a snuggle."

She stepped back, eyeing him calmly. "But if you've that much energy, you may be able to take some more broth, and a bit of bread."

"I'd rather meat."

"I'm sure. But you won't get it. Do you read, Kylar of Mrydon?"

"Yes, of course I . . . You call me by name," he said cautiously. "How do you know it?"

She thought of that dip she'd taken into his mind. What she'd seen. What she'd felt. Neither of them, she was sure, was prepared to discuss it. "You told me a great many things during the fever," she said. And that was true enough. "I'll see you have books. Bed rest is tedious. Reading will help."

She picked up the empty cup of broth and started across the chamber to the door.

"Wait. What is this place?"

She turned back. "This is Rose Castle, on the Isle of Winter in the Sea of Ice."

His heart stuttered in his chest, but he kept his gaze direct on hers. "That's a fairy tale. A myth."

"It's as real as life, and as death. You, my lord Kylar, are the first to pass this way in more than twenty years. When you're rested and well, we'll discuss how you came here."

"Wait." He lifted a hand as she opened the thick carved door. "You're not a servant." He wondered how he could ever have mistaken her for one. The simple dress, the lack of jewels, the undressed hair did nothing to detract from her bearing. Her breeding.

"I serve," she countered. "And have all my life. I am Deirdre, queen of the Sea of Ice."

When she closed the door behind her, he continued to stare. He'd heard of Rose Castle, the legend of it, in boyhood. The palace that stood on an island in what had once been a calm and pretty lake, edged by lush forests and rich fields. Betrayal, jealousy, vengeance, and witchcraft had doomed it all to an eternity of winter.

There was something about a rose trapped in a pillar of ice. He couldn't quite remember how it all went.

Such things were nonsense, of course. Entertaining stories to be told to a child at bedtime.

And yet . . . yet he'd traveled through that world of white and bitter cold. He'd fought and won a battle, in high summer, then somehow had become lost in winter.

Because he, in his delirium, had traveled far north. Perhaps into the Lost Mountains or even beyond them, where the wild tribes hunted giant white bear and dragons still guarded caves.

He'd talked with men who claimed to have been there, who spoke of dark blue water crowded with islands of ice, and of warriors tall as trees.

But none had ever spoken of a castle.

How much had he imagined, or dreamed? Determined to see for himself, he tossed back the bedcovers. Sweat slicked his skin, and his muscles trembled, appalling him—scoring his pride—as the simple task of shifting to sit on the side of the bed sapped his strength. He sat for several moments more, gathering it back.

When he managed to stand, his vision wavered, as if he was looking through water. He felt his knees buckle but managed to grip the bedpost and stay on his feet.

While he waited to steady, he studied the room. It was simply appointed, he noted. Tasteful, certainly, even elegant in its way unless you looked closely enough to see that the fabrics were fraying with age. Still, the chests and the chairs gleamed with polish. While the rug was faded with time, its workmanship was lovely. The candlesticks were gleaming silver, and the fire burned quietly in a hearth carved from lapis.

As creakily, as carefully, as an aged grandfather, he walked across the room to the window.

Through it, as far as he could see, the world was white. The sun was a dim haze behind the white curtain that draped the sky, but it managed to sparkle a bit on the ice that surrounded the castle. In the distance, he saw the shadows of the forest, hints of black and gray smothered in snow. In the north, far north, mountains speared up. White against white.

Closer in, at the feet of the castle, the snow spread in sheets and blankets. He saw no movement, no tracks. No life.

Were they alone here? he wondered. He and the woman who called herself a queen?

Then he saw her, a regal flash of red against the white. She walked with a long, quick stride—as a woman might, he thought, bustle off to the market. As if she sensed him there, she stopped, turned. Looked up at his window.

He couldn't see her expression clearly, but the way her chin angled told him she was displeased with him. Then she turned away again, her fiery cloak swirling, as she continued over that sea toward the forest.

He wanted to go after her, to demand answers, explanations. But he could barely make it back to the bed before he collapsed. Trembling from the effort, he buried himself under the blankets again and slept the day away.

"My lady, he's demanding to see you again."

Deirdre continued to work in the precious dirt under the wide dome. Her back ached, but she didn't mind it. In this, what she called her garden, she grew herbs and vegetables and a few precious flowers in the false spring generated by the sun through the glass.

"I have no time for him, Orna." She hoed a trench. It was a constant cycle, replenishing, tending, harvesting. The garden was life to her world. And one of her few true pleasures. "Between you and Cordelia he's tended well enough."

Orna pursed her lips. She had nursed Deirdre as a babe, had tutored her, tended her, and since the death of Queen Fiona, had stood when she could as mother. She was one of the few in Rose Castle who dared to question the young queen.

"It's been three days since he woke. The man is restless."

Deirdre straightened, rested her weight on the hoe. "Is he in pain?"

Orna's weathered face creased with what might have been impatience. "He says not, but he's a man, after all. He has pain. Despite it, and his weakness, he won't be kept to his chamber much longer. The man is a prince, my lady, and used to being obeyed."

"I rule here." Deirdre scanned her garden. The earlier plantings were satisfactory. She couldn't have the lush, but she could have the necessary. Even, she thought as she looked at her spindly, sun-starved daisies, the occasional indulgence.

"One of the kitchen boys should gather cabbages for dinner," she began. "Have the cook choose two of the hens. Our guest needs meat."

"Why do you refuse to see him?"

"I don't refuse." Annoyed, Deirdre went back to her work. She was avoiding the next meeting, and she knew it. Something had come into her during the healing, something she was unable to identify. It left her uneasy and unsettled.

"I stayed with him three days, three nights," she reminded Orna. "It's put me behind in my duties."

"He's very handsome."

"So is his horse," Deirdre said lightly. "And the horse is of more interest to me."

"And strong," Orna continued, stepping closer. "A prince from outside our world. He could be the one."

"There is no one." Deirdre tossed her head. Hope put no fuel in the fire nor food in the pot. It was a luxury she, above all, could ill afford. "I want no man, Orna. I will depend on no one but myself. It's woman's foolishness, woman's need, and man's deceit that have cursed us."

"Woman's pride as much as foolishness." Orna laid a hand on the staff of the hoe. "Will you let yours stop you from taking a chance for freedom?"

"I will provide for my people. When the time comes I

will lie with a man until I conceive. I will make the next ruler, train the child as I was trained."

"Love the child," Orna murmured.

"My heart is so cold." Tired, Deirdre closed her eyes. "I fear there is no love in me. How can I give what isn't mine?"

"You're wrong." Gently Orna touched her cheek. "Your heart isn't cold. It's only trapped, as the rose is trapped in ice."

"Should I free it, Orna, so it could be broken as my mother's was?" She shook her head. "That solves nothing. Food must be put on the table, fuel must be gathered. Go now, tell our guest that I'll visit him in his chambers when time permits."

"This seems like a fine time." So saying, Kylar strode into the dome.

3

HE'D NEVER SEEN anything like the garden before. But then, Kylar had seen a great deal of the unexpected in Rose Castle in a short time. Such as a queen dressed in men's clothing—trousers and a ragged tunic. The result was odd, and strangely alluring. Her hair was tied back, but not with anything so female as a ribbon. She'd knotted it with a thin leather strap, such as he did himself when doing some quick spot of manual labor.

Her face was flushed from her work and as lovely as the flower he'd first taken her for. She did not look pleased to see him. Even as he watched, her eyes chilled.

Behold the ice queen, he thought. A man would risk freezing off important parts of his body should he try to thaw her.

"I see you're feeling better, my lord."

"If you'd spared me five minutes of your time, you'd have seen so before."

"Will you pardon us, Orna." She knelt and began to plant the long eyes of potatoes harvested earlier in the year. It was a distraction, one she needed. Seeing him again stirred her, in dangerous ways. "You'll excuse me, my lord, if I continue with my task."

"Are there no servants to do such things?"

"There are fifty-two of us in Rose Castle. We all have our places and our duties."

He squatted beside her, though it caused his side to weep. Taking her hand, he turned it over and examined the ridge of callus. "Then I would say, my lady, you have too many duties."

"It's not for you to question me."

"You don't give answers, so I must continue to question. You healed me. Why do you resent me?"

"I don't know. But I do know that I require both hands for this task." When he released her, she continued to plant. "I'm unused to strangers," she began. Surely that was it. She had never seen, much less healed, a stranger before. Wouldn't that explain why, after looking into his mind, into his heart, she felt so drawn to him?

And afraid of him.

"Perhaps my manners are unpolished, so I will beg your pardon for any slight."

"They're polished diamond-bright," he corrected. "And stab at a man."

She smiled a little. "Some men, I imagine, are used to softer females. I thought Cordelia would suit your needs."

"She's biddable enough, and pretty enough, which is why you have the dragon guarding her."

Her smile warmed fractionally. "Of course."

"I wonder why I prefer you to either of them."

"I couldn't say." She moved down the row, and when he started to move with her, he gasped. She cursed. "Stubborn." She rose, reached down, and to his surprise, wrapped her arms around him. "Hold on to me. I'll help you inside."

He simply buried his face in her hair. "Your scent," he told her. "It haunts me."

"Stop it."

"I can't get your face out of my head, even when I sleep."

Her stomach fluttered, alarming her. "Sir, I will not be trifled with."

"I'm too damn weak to trifle with you." Hating the unsteadiness, he leaned heavily against her. "But you're beautiful, and I'm not dead." When he caught his breath, he eased away. "I should be. I've had time to think that through." He stared hard into her eyes. "I've seen enough battle to know when a wound is mortal. Mine was. How did I cheat death, Deirdre? Are you a witch?"

"Some would say." Because his color concerned her, she unbent enough to put an arm around his waist. "You need to sit before you fall. Come back inside."

"Not to bed. I'll go mad."

She'd tended enough of the sick and injured to know the truth of that. "To a chair. We'll have tea."

"God spare me. Brandy?"

She supposed he was entitled. She led him through a doorway, down a dim corridor away from the kitchen. She skirted the main hallway and moved down yet another corridor. The room where she took him was small, chilly, and lined floor to ceiling with books.

She eased him into a chair in front of the cold fireplace, then went over to open the shutters and let in the light.

"The days are still long," she said conversationally as she walked to the fireplace. This one was framed in smooth green marble. "Planting needs to be finished while the sun can warm the seeds."

She crouched in front of the fire, set the logs to light. "Is there grass in your world? Fields of it?"

"Yes."

She closed her eyes a moment. "And trees that go green in spring?"

He felt a wrench in his gut. For home—and for her. "Yes."

"It must be like a miracle." Then she stood, and her voice was brisk again. "I must wash, and see to your brandy. You'll be warm by the fire. I won't be long."

"My lady, have you never seen a field of grass?"

"In books. In dreams." She opened her mouth again, nearly asked him to tell her what it smelled like. But she wasn't sure she could bear to know. "I won't keep you waiting long, my lord."

She was true to her word. In ten minutes she was back, her hair loose again over the shoulders of a dark green dress. She carried the brandy herself.

"Our wine cellars were well stocked once. My grandfather, I'm told, was shrewd in that area. And in this one," she added, gesturing toward the books. "He enjoyed a glass of good wine and a good book."

"And you?"

"The books often, the wine rarely."

When she glanced toward the door, he saw her smile, fully, warmly, for the first time. He could only stare at her as his throat went dry and his heart shuddered.

"Thank you, Magda. I would have come for it."

"You've enough to do, my lady, without carting trays." The woman seemed ancient to Kylar. Her face as withered as a winter apple, her body bowed as if she carried bricks on her back. But she set the tea tray on the sideboard and curtseyed with some grace. "Should I pour for you, my lady?"

"I'll see to it. How are your hands?"

"They don't trouble me overmuch."

Deirdre took them in her own. They were knotted and swollen at the joints. "You're using the ointment I gave you?"

"Yes, my lady, twice daily. It helps considerable."

Keeping her eyes on Magda's, Deirdre rubbed her thumbs rhythmically over the gnarled knuckles. "I have a tea that will help. I'll show you how to make it, and you'll drink a cup three times a day."

"Thank you, my lady." Magda curtseyed again before she left the room.

Kylar saw Deirdre rub her own hands as if to ease a pain before she reached for the teapot. "I'll answer your questions, Prince Kylar, and hope that you'll answer some of mine in turn." She brought him a small tray of cheese and biscuits, then settled into a chair with her tea.

"How do you survive?"

To the point, she thought. "We have the garden. Some chickens and goats for eggs and milk, and meat when meat is needed. There's the forest for fuel and, if we're lucky, for game. The young are trained in necessary skills. We live simply," she said, sipping her tea. "And well enough."

"Why do you stay?"

"Because this is my home. You risked your life in battle to protect yours."

"How do you know I didn't risk it to take what belonged to someone else?"

She watched him over the rim of her cup. Yes, he was handsome. His looks were only more striking now that he'd regained some of his strength. One of the servants had shaved him, and without the stubble of beard he looked younger. But little less dangerous. "Did you?"

"You know I didn't." His gaze narrowed on her face. "You know. How is that, Deirdre of the Ice?" He reached out, clamped a hand on her arm. "What did you do to me during the fever?"

"Healed you."

"With witchcraft?"

"I have a gift for healing," she said evenly. "Should I have used it, or let you die? There was no dark in it, and you are not bound to me for payment."

"Then why do I feel bound to you?"

Her pulse jumped. His hand wasn't gripping her arm now. It caressed. "I did nothing to tie you. I have neither desire nor the skill for it." Cautiously, she moved out of reach. "You have my word. When you're well enough to travel, you're free to go."

"How?" It was bitter. "Where?"

Pity stirred in her, swam into her eyes. She remembered the face of the woman in his mind, the love she'd felt flow between them. His mother, she thought. Even now watching for his return home.

"It won't be simple, nor without risk. But you have a horse, and we'll give you provisions. One of my men will travel with you as far as possible. I can do no more than that."

He put it aside for now. When the time came, he would find his way home. "Tell me how this came to be. This place. I've heard stories—betrayal and witchcraft and cold spells over a land that was once fruitful and at peace."

"So I am told." She rose again to stir the fire. "When my grandfather was king, there were farms and fields. The land was green and rich, the lake blue and thick with fish. Have you ever seen blue water?"

"I have, yes."

"How can it be blue?" she asked as she turned. There was puzzlement on her face, and more, he thought. An eagerness he hadn't seen before. It made her look very young.

"I haven't thought about it," he admitted. "It seems to be blue, or green, or gray. It changes, as the sky changes."

"My sky never changes." The eagerness vanished as she walked to the window. "Well," she said, and straightened her shoulders. "Well. My grandfather had two daughters, twin-born. His wife died giving them life, and it's said he grieved for her the rest of his days. The babes were named Ernia, who was my aunt, and Fiona, who was my mother, and on them he doted. Most parents dote on their children, don't they, my lord?"

"Most," he agreed.

"So he did. Like their mother, they were beautiful, and like their mother, they were gifted. Ernia could call the sun, the rain, the wind. Fiona could speak to the beasts and the birds. They were, I'm told, competitive, each vying for their father's favor though he loved them both. Do you have siblings, my lord?"

"A brother and a sister, both younger."

She glanced back. He had his mother's eyes, she thought. But her hair had been light. Perhaps his father had that ink-black hair that looked so silky.

"Do you love them, your brother and your sister?"

"Very much."

"That is as it should be. But Ernia and Fiona could not love each other. Perhaps it was because they shared the same face, and each wanted her own. Who can say? They grew from girl to woman, and my grandfather grew old and ill. He wanted them married and settled before his death. Ernia he betrothed to a king in a land beyond the Elf Hills, and my mother he promised to a king whose lands marched with ours to the east. Rose Castle was to be my mother's, and the Palace of Sighs, on the border of the Elf Hills, my aunt's. In this way he divided his wealth and lands equally between them, for he was, I'm told, a wise and fair ruler and a loving father."

She came back to sit and sip at tea gone cold. "In the weeks before the weddings, a traveler came and was welcome here as all were in those days. He was handsome and clever, quick of tongue and smooth with charm. A minstrel by trade, it's said he sang like an angel. But fair looks are no mirror of the heart, are they?"

"A pleasant face is only a face." Kylar lifted a shoulder. "Deeds make a man."

"Or woman," she added. "So I have always believed, and so, in this case, it was. In secret, this handsome man courted and seduced both twins, and both fell blindly in love with him. He came to my mother's bed, and to her sister's, bearing a single red rose and promises never meant to be kept. Why do men lie when women love?"

The question took him aback. "My lady . . . not all men are deceivers."

"Perhaps not." Though she was far from convinced. "But he was. One evening the sisters, of the same mind, wandered to the rose garden. Each wanted to pluck a red rose for her lover. It was there the lies were discovered. Instead of comforting each other, instead of raging against the man who had deceived them both, they fought over him. She-wolves over an unworthy badger. Ernia's temper called the wind and the hail, and Fiona's had the beasts stalking out of the forest to snarl and howl."

"Jealousy is both a flawed and a lethal weapon."

She angled her head. Nodded. "Well said. My grandfather heard the clamor and roused himself from his sickbed. Neither marriage could take place now, as both his daughters were disgraced. The minstrel, who had not slipped away quickly enough, was locked in the dungeon until his punishment could be decided. There was weeping and wailing from the sisters, as that punishment would surely be banishment, if not death. But he was spared when it came to be known that my mother was with child. His child, for she had lain with no other."

"You were the child."

"Yes. So, by becoming, I saved my father's life. The grief of this, the shame of this, ended my grandfather's. Before he died, he ordered Ernia to the Palace of Sighs. Because of the child, he decreed that my mother would marry the minstrel. It was this that drove Ernia mad, and on the day the marriage took place, the day her own father died in despair, she cast her spell.

"Winter, endless years of it. A sea of ice to lock Rose Castle away from the world. The rosebush where flowers had been plucked from lies would not bear bud. The child her sister carried would never feel the warmth of summer sun on her face, or walk in a meadow or see a tree bear fruit. One faithless man, three selfish hearts, destroyed a world. And so became the Isle of Winter in the Sea of Ice."

"My lady." He laid a hand on hers. Her life, he thought, the whole of it had been spent without the simple comfort of sunlight. "A spell cast can be broken. You have power."

"My gift is of healing. I cannot heal the land." Because she wanted to turn her hand over in his, link fingers, feel that connection, she drew away. "My father left my mother before I was born. Escaped. Later, as she watched her people starve, my mother sent messengers to the Palace of Sighs to ask for a truce. To beg for one. But they never came back. Perhaps they died, or lost their way. Or simply rode on into the warmth and the sun. No one who has left here has ever come back. Why would they?"

"Ernia the Witch-Queen is dead."

"Dead?" Deirdre stared into the fire. "You're sure of this?"

"She was feared, and loathed. There was great celebration when she died. It was on the Winter Solstice, and I remember it well. She's been dead for nearly ten years."

Deirdre closed her eyes. "As her sister has. So they died together. How odd, and how apt." She rose again to walk to the window. "Ten years dead, and her spell holds like a clenched fist. How bitter her heart must have been."

And the faint and secret hope she'd kept flickering inside that upon her aunt's death the spell would break, winked out. She drew herself up. "What we can't change, we learn to be content with." She stared out at the endless world of white. "There is beauty here."

"Yes." It was Deirdre that Kylar watched. "Yes. There is beauty here."

4

HE WANTED TO help her. More, Kylar thought, he wanted to save her. If there had been something tangible to fight—a man, a beast, an army—he would have drawn his sword and plunged into battle for her.

She moved him, attracted him, fascinated him. Her steady composure in the face of her fate stirred in him both admiration and frustration. This was not a woman to weep on a man's shoulder. It annoyed him to find himself wishing that she would, as long as the shoulder was his.

She was an extraordinary creature. He wanted to fight for her. But how did a man wage war on magic?

He'd never had any real experience with it. He was a soldier, and though he believed in luck, even in fate, he believed more in wile and skill and muscle.

He was a prince, would one day be a king. He believed in justice, in ruling with a firm touch on one hand and a merciful one on the other.

There was no justice here, where a woman who had done no wrong should be imprisoned for the crimes and follies and wickedness of those who had come before.

She was too beautiful to be shut away from the rest of the world. Too small, he mused, too fragile to work her hands raw. She should be draped in silks and ermine rather than homespun.

Already after less than a week on the Isle of Winter, he felt a restlessness, a need for color and heat. How had she stayed sane never knowing a single summer?

He wanted to bring her the sun.

She should laugh. It troubled him that he had not once heard her laugh. A smile, surprisingly warm when it was real enough to reach her eyes. That he had seen. He would find a way to see it again.

He waded through the snow across what he supposed had once been a courtyard. Though his wound had troubled him on waking, he was feeling stronger now. He needed to be doing, to find some work or activity to keep his blood moving and his mind sharp. Surely there was some task, some bit of work he could undertake for her here. It would repay her in some small way, and serve to keep his mind and hands busy while his body healed.

He recalled the stag he'd seen in the forest. He would hunt, then, and bring her meat. The wind that had thrashed ceaselessly for days had finally quieted. Though the utter stillness that followed it played havoc with the nerves, it would make tracking through the forest possible.

He moved through a wide archway on the other side of the courtyard. And stopped to stare.

This, he realized with wonder, had been the rose garden. Gnarled and blackened stalks tangled out of the snow. Once, he imagined, it would have been magnificent, full of color and scent and humming bees.

Now it was a great field of snow cased in ice.

Bisecting that field were graceful paths of silver stone, and someone kept them clear. There were hundreds of bushes, all brittle with death, the stalks spearing out of their cold graves like blackened bones.

Benches, these, too, cleared of snow and ice, stood in graceful curves of deep jewel colors. Ruby, sapphire, emerald, they gleamed in the midst of the stark and merciless white. There was a small pond in the shape of an open rose, and its flower held a rippled sheet of ice. Dead branches with vicious thorns strangled iron arbors. More spindly corpses climbed up the silver stone of the walls as if they'd sought to escape before winter murdered them.

In the center, where all paths led, was a towering column of ice. Under the glassy sheen, he could see the arch of blackened branches studded with thorns, and hundreds of withered flowers trapped forever in their moment of death.

The rosebush, he thought, where the flowers of lies had been plucked. No, he corrected as he moved toward it. More a tree, for it was taller than he was and spread wider than the span of both his arms. He ran his fingertips over the ice, found it smooth. Experimentally, he took the dagger from his belt, dragged its tip over the ice. It left no mark.

"It cannot be reached with force."

Kylar turned and saw Orna standing in the archway. "What of the rest? Why haven't the dead branches been cleared and used for fire?" he asked her.

"To do so would be to give up hope." She had hope still, and more when she looked into Kylar's eyes.

She saw what she needed there. Truth, strength, and courage.

"She walks here."

"Why would she punish herself in such a way?" he demanded.

"It reminds her, I think, of what was. And what is." But not, Orna feared, of what might be. "Once, when my lady was but eight, and the last of the dogs died, breaking her heart, she took her grandfather's sword. In her grief and temper, she tried to hack through that ice into the bush. For nearly an hour she stabbed and sliced and beat at it, and could not so much as scratch the surface. In the end, she went to her knees there where you stand now and wept as if she'd die from it. Something in her did die that day, along with the last of the dogs. I have not heard her weep since. I wish she would."

"Why do you wish for your lady's tears?"

"For then she would know her heart is not dead but, like the rose, only waiting."

He sheathed his dagger. "If force can't reach it, what can?"

She smiled, for she knew he spoke of the heart as much as the rose. "You will make a good king in your time, Kylar of Mrydon, for you listen to what isn't said. What can't be vanquished with sword or might can be won with truth, with love, with selflessness. She is in the stables, what is left of them. She wouldn't ask for your company, but would enjoy it."

The stables lined three sides of another courtyard, but this one was crisscrossed with crooked paths dug through or trampled into the snow. Kylar saw the reason for it in the small troop of children waging a lively snow battle at the far end. Even in such a world, he thought, children found a way to be children.

As he drew closer to the stables, he heard the low cackle of hens. There were men on the roof, working on a chimney. They tipped their caps to him as he passed under the eaves and into the stables.

It was warmer, thanks to carefully banked fires, and clean as a parlor. The queen, he thought, tended her goats and chickens well. Iron kettles heated over the fires. Water for the stock, he concluded, made from melted snow. He noted barrows of manure. For use in her garden, he decided. A wise and practical woman, Queen Deirdre.

Then he saw the wise and practical woman, with her

red hood tossed back, her gold hair raining down as she cooed up at his warhorse.

When the horse shook its great head and blew, she laughed. The rich female sound warmed his blood more thoroughly than the fires.

"His name is Cathmor."

Startled, embarrassed, Deirdre dropped the hands she'd lifted to stroke the horse's muzzle. She knew she shouldn't have lingered, that he would come check on his horse as it had been reported he did twice daily. But she'd so wanted to see the creature herself.

"You have a light step."

"You were distracted." He walked up beside her, and to her surprise and delight, the horse bumped his shoulder in greeting.

"Does that mean he's glad to see you?"

"It means he's hoping I have an apple."

Deirdre fingered the small carrot from her garden she'd tucked in her pocket. "Perhaps this will do." She pulled it out, started to offer it to Kylar.

"He would enjoy being fed by a lady. No, not like that." He took her hand and, opening it, laid the carrot on her palm. "Have you never fed a horse?"

"I've never seen one." She caught her breath as Cathmor dipped his head and nibbled the carrot out of her palm. "He's bigger than I imagined, and more handsome. And softer." Unable to resist, she stroked her hand down the horse's nose. "Some of the children have been keeping him company. They'd make a pet of him if they could."

"Would you like to ride him?"

"Ride?"

"He needs the exercise, and so do I. I thought I would hunt this morning. Come with me."

To ride a horse? Just the idea of it was thrilling. "I have duties."

"I might get lost alone." He brought her hand back up, ran it under his along Cathmor's silky neck. "I don't know your forest. And I'm still a bit weak."

Her lips twitched. "Your wits are strong enough. I could send a man with you."

"I prefer your company."

To ride a horse, she thought again. How could she resist? Why should she? She was no fluttery girl who would fall into stutters and blushes by being alone with a man. Even this man.

"All right. What do I do first?"

"You wait until I saddle him."

She shook her head. "No, show me how to do it."

When it was done, she sent one of the boys scurrying off to tell Orna she was riding out with the prince. She needn't have bothered, for as they walked the horse out of the stables, her people began to gather at the windows, in the courtyard.

When he vaulted into the saddle, they cheered him like a hero.

"It's been a long time since they've seen anyone ride," she explained as Cathmor pranced in place. "Some of them, like me, never have." She let out a breath. "It's a long way up."

"Give me your hand." He reached down to her. "Trust me."

She would have to if she wanted this amazing treat. She offered her hand, then yelped in shock when he simply hauled her up in the saddle in front of him.

"You might have warned me you intended to drag me up like a sack of turnips. If you've opened your wound again—"

"Quiet," he whispered, entirely too close to her ear for comfort, and with her people cheering, he kicked Cathmor into a trot.

"Oh." Her eyes popped wide as her bottom bounced. "It's not what I expected." And hardly dignified.

With shouts and whoops, children raced after them as they trotted out of the castle.

"Match the rhythm of your body to the gait of the horse," he told her.

"Yes, I'm trying. Must you be so close?"

He grinned. "Yes. And I'm enjoying it. You shouldn't be uneasy with a man, Deirdre, when you've seen him naked."

"Seeing you naked hardly gives me cause to relax around you," she shot back.

With a rolling laugh, he urged the horse to a gallop.

Her breath caught, but with delight rather than fear. Wind rushed by her cheeks, and snow flew up into the air like tattered lace. She closed her eyes for an instant to absorb the sensation, and the wild thrill made her dizzy.

So fast, she thought. So strong. When they charged up a hill she wanted to throw her arms in the air and shout for the sheer joy of it.

Her heart raced along with the horse, continued to pound even when they slowed at the verge of the forest that had been known as the Forgotten for the whole of her lifetime.

"It's like flying," she mused. "Oh, thank you." She leaned down to press her cheek to the horse's neck. "I'll never forget it. He's a grand horse, isn't he?"

Flushed with pleasure, she turned. His face was too close, so close she felt the warmth of his breath on her cheek. Close enough that she saw a kind of heat kindling in his eyes.

"No." He caught her chin with his hand before she could turn away again. "Don't. I kissed you before, when I thought I was dying." His lips hovered a breath from hers. "I lived."

He had to taste her again; it seemed his sanity depended on it. But because he saw her fear, he took her mouth gently, skimming his lips over ones that trembled. Soothing as well as seducing. He watched her eyes go soft before her lashes fluttered down.

"Kiss me back, Deirdre." His hand slid down until his arm could band her waist and draw her closer. "This time kiss me back."

"I don't know how." But she already was.

Her limbs went weak, wonderfully weak, even as her pulse danced madly. Warmth enveloped her, reaching places inside that had never known its comfort.

The light that had sparked inside her when their hearts had brushed in healing spread.

On the Isle of Winter in the snowy rose garden, beneath a shield of ice, a tiny bud—tender green—formed on a blackened branch.

He nibbled at her lips until she parted them. And when he deepened the kiss she felt, for the first time in her life, a true lance of heat in her belly.

Yearning for more, she eased back, then indulged herself by letting her head rest briefly on his shoulder. "So it's this," she whispered. "It's this that makes the women sing in the kitchen in the morning."

He stroked her hair, rubbed his cheek against it. "It's a bit more than that." Sweet, he thought. Strong. She was everything a man could want. Everything, he realized, that he wanted.

"Yes, of course." She sighed once. "More than that, but it starts like this. It can't for me."

"It has." He held her close when she would have drawn away. "It did, the minute I saw you."

"If I could love, it would be you. Though I'm not sure why, it would be you. If I were free, I would choose you." She turned away again. "We came to hunt. My people need meat."

He fought the urge to yank her around, to plunder that lovely mouth until she yielded. Force wasn't the answer. So he'd been told. There were better ways to win a woman.

5

SHE SPOTTED THE tracks first. They moved soundlessly through the trees, and she was grateful for the need for silence.

How could she explain or ask him to understand, when she couldn't understand herself? Her heart was frozen, chilled to death by pride and duty, and the fear that she might do her people more harm.

Her father had made her in lies, then had run away from his obligation. Her mother had done her duty, and she had been kind. But her heart had been broken into so many pieces there had been none left for her child.

And what sort of child was it who could grieve more truly for a dead dog than for her own dead mother?

She had nothing emotionally to give a man, and wanted nothing from one. In that way she would survive, and keep her people alive.

Life, she reminded herself, mattered most. And what

she felt for him was surely no more than a churning in the blood.

But how could she have known what it was like to be held by him? To feel his heart beat so strong and fast against hers? None of the books she'd read had captured with their clever words the true thrill of lips meeting.

Now that she understood, it would be just another precious memory, like a ride on horseback, to tuck away for the endless lonely nights.

She would decide later, she thought, if the nights were longer, lonelier, with the memory than they were without it.

But today she couldn't allow herself to think like a woman softened by a man's touch. She must think like a queen with people to provide for.

She caught the scent of the stag even before the horse did, and held up a hand. "We should walk from here," she said under her breath.

He didn't question her, but dismounted, then reached up to lift her down. Then his arms were around her again, her hands on his shoulders, and her face tilted up to his. Even as she shook her head, he brushed his lips over her brow.

"Deirdre the fair," he said softly. "Such a pretty armful."

The male scent of him blurred the scent of the stag. "This is not the time."

Because the catch in her voice was enough to satisfy him, for now, he reached over for his bow and quiver. But when she held out her hands for them, he lifted his eyebrows.

"The bow is too heavy a draw for you." When she continued to stare, hands outstretched, he shrugged and gave them to her.

So, he thought, he would indulge her. They'd make do with more cabbage tonight.

Then he was left blinking as she tossed aside her cloak and streaked through the trees in her men's clothes like a wraith—soundless and swift. Before he could tether his horse, she'd vanished and he could do no more than follow in her tracks.

He stopped when he caught sight of her. She stood in the gloomy light, nearly hip-deep in snow. With a gesture smooth and polished as a warrior, she notched the arrow, drew back the heavy bow. The sharp *ping* of the arrow flying free echoed. Then she lowered the bow, and her head.

"Everyone misses sometimes," he said as he started toward her.

Her head came up, her face cold and set. "I did not miss. I find no pleasure in the kill. My people need meat."

She handed the bow and quiver back to him, then trudged through the snow to where the stag lay.

Kylar saw she'd taken it down, fast, mercifully fast, with a single shot.

"Deirdre," he called out. "Do you ask yourself how game, even so sparse, come to be here where there is no food for them?"

She continued walking. "My mother did what she could, leaving a call that would draw them to the forest. She hoped to teach me to do the same, but it's not my gift."

"You have more than one," he said. "I'll get the horse."

Once the deer was strapped onto the horse, Kylar cupped his hands to help Deirdre mount. "Put your right foot in my hands, swing your left leg over the saddle."

"There isn't room for both of us now. You ride, I'll walk."

"No, I'll walk."

"It's too far when you've yet to fully recover. Mount your horse." She started to move past him, but he blocked her path. Her shoulders straightened like an iron bar. "I said, mount. I am a queen, and you merely a prince. You will do as I bid."

"I'm a man, and you merely a woman." He shocked

her speechless by picking her up and tossing her into the saddle. "You'll do what you're told."

However much she labored side by side with her people, no one had ever disobeyed a command. And no man had ever laid hands on her. "You . . . *dare*."

"I'm not one of your people." He gathered the reins and began to walk the horse through the forest. "Whatever our ranks, I'm as royal as you. Though that doesn't mean a damn at the moment. It's difficult to think of you as a queen when you're garbed like a man and I've seen you handle a bow that my own squire can barely manage. It's difficult to think of you as a queen, Deirdre," he added with a glance back at her furious face, "when I've held you in my arms."

"Then you'd best remember what that felt like, for you won't be allowed to do so again."

He stopped, and turning, ran his hand deliberately up her leg. When she kicked out at him, he caught her boot and laughed. "Ah, so there's a temper in there after all. Good. I prefer bedding a woman with fire in her."

Quick as a snake the dagger was out of her belt and in her hand. And its killing point at his throat. "Remove your hand."

He never flinched, but realized to his own shock that this wasn't merely a woman he could want. It was a woman he could love. "Would you do it, I wonder? I think you might while the temper's on you, but then you'd regret it." He brought his hand up slowly, gripped her knife hand by the wrist. "We'd both regret it. I tell you I want to bed you. I give you the truth. Do you want lies?"

"You can bed Cordelia, if she's willing."

"I don't want Cordelia, willing or not." He took the knife from her hand, then brushed a kiss over her palm. "But I want you, Deirdre. And I want you willing." He handed her back the dagger, hilt first. "Can you handle a sword as well as you do a dagger?"

"I can."

"You're a woman of marvels, Deirdre the fair." He began to walk again. "I understand developing skill with the bow, but what need have you for sword or dagger?"

"Ignoring training in defense is careless and lazy. The training itself is good for the body and the mind. If my people are expected to learn how to handle a blade, then so should I be."

"Agreed."

When he paused a second time, her eyes narrowed in warning. "I'm going to shorten the stirrups so you can ride properly. What happened to your horses?"

"Those who left the first year took them." She ordered herself to relax and pleased herself by stroking Cathmor's neck again. "There were cattle, too, and sheep. Those that didn't die of the cold were used as food. There were cottages and farmhouses, but people came to the castle for shelter, for food. Or wandered off hoping to find spring. Now they're under the snow and ice. Why do you want to bed me?"

"Because you're beautiful."

She frowned down at him. "Are men so simple, really?"

He laughed, shook his head, and her fingers itched to tangle in his silky black mane rather than the horse's. "Simple enough about certain matters. But I hadn't finished the answer. Your beauty would be enough to make me want you for a night. Try this now, heels down. That's fine."

He gave her foot a friendly pat, then walked back to the horse's head. "Your strength and your courage add layers to beauty. They appeal to me. Your mind's sharp and cleaves clean. That's a challenge. And a woman who can plant potatoes like a farmwife and draw a dagger like an assassin is a fascinating creature."

"I thought when a man wanted to pleasure himself with a woman, he softened her with pretty words and poetry and long looks full of pain and longing."

What a woman, Kylar mused. He'd never seen the like of her. "Would you like that?"

She considered it, and was relaxed again. It was easier

to discuss the whole business as a practical matter. "I don't know."

"You wouldn't trust them."

She smiled before she could stop it. "I wouldn't, no. Have you bedded many women?"

He cleared his throat and began to walk a bit faster. "That, sweetheart, isn't a question I'm comfortable answering."

"Why not?"

"Because it's . . . it's a delicate matter," he decided.

"Would you be more comfortable telling me if you've killed many men?"

"I don't kill for sport, or for pleasure," he said, and his voice turned as frigid as the air. "Taking a man's life is no triumph, my lady. Battle is an ugly business."

"I wondered. I meant no offense."

"I would have let them go." He spoke so softly that she had to lean forward to hear clearly.

"Who?"

"The three who set upon me after the battle had been won. When I was for home. I would have let them pass in peace. What purpose was there in more blood?"

She'd already seen this inside him, and knew it for truth. He had not killed in hate nor in some fever of dark excitement. He had killed to live. "They wouldn't let you pass in peace."

"They were tired, and one already wounded. If I'd had an escort as I should, they would have surrendered. In the end, it was their own fear and my carelessness that killed them. I'm sorry for it."

More for the waste of their lives, she realized, than for his own wounds. Understanding this, she felt something sigh inside her. "Kylar."

It was the first time she'd spoken his name, as she might to a friend. And she leaned down to touch his cheek with her fingertips, as she might touch a lover's.

"You'll rule well."

• • •

She invited him to sup with her that night. Another first. He dressed in the fresh doublet Cordelia brought him, one of soft linen that smelled lightly of lavender and rosemary. He wondered from what chest it had been unearthed for his use, but as it fit well enough, he had no cause to complain.

But when he followed the servant into the dining hall, he wished for his court clothes.

She wore green again, but no simple dress of home-spun. The velvet gown poured down her body, dipping low at the creamy rise of her breasts and sweeping out from her waist in soft, deep folds. Her hair was long and loose, but over it sparkled a crown glinting with jewels. More draped in shimmering ropes around her throat.

She stood in the glow of candlelight, beautiful as a vision, and every inch a queen.

When she offered a hand, he crossed to her, bowed deeply before touching his lips to her knuckles. "Your Majesty."

"Your Highness. The room," she said with a gesture she hoped hid the nerves and pleasure she felt upon seeing the open approval on his face, "is overlarge for two. I hope you'll be comfortable."

"I see nothing but you."

She titled her head. Curious, this flirting, she decided. And entertaining. "Are these the pretty words and poetry?"

"They're the truth."

"They fall pleasantly on the ear. It's an indulgence to have a fire in here," she began as she let him escort her to the table. "But tonight there is wine, and venison, and a welcome guest."

At the head of the long table were two settings. Silver and crystal and linen white as the snow outside the windows. Behind them, the mammoth fire roared.

Servants slipped in to serve wine and the soup course. If he'd been able to tear his gaze away from Deirdre, he might have seen the glint in their eyes, the exchanged winks and quick grins.

She missed them as well, as she concentrated on the experience of her first formal meal with someone from outside her world. "The fare is simple," she began.

"As good as a bounty. And the company feeds me."

She studied him thoughtfully. "I do think I like pretty words, but I have no skill in holding a conversation with them."

He took her hand. "Why don't we practice?"

Her laugh bubbled out, but she shook her head. "Tell me of your home, your family. Your sister," she remembered. "Is she lovely?"

"She is. Her name is Gwenyth. She married two years ago."

"Is there love?"

"Yes. He was friend and neighbor, and they had a sweetness for each other since childhood. When I last saw her she was great with her second babe." The faintest cloud passed over his face. "I'd hoped to make my way home for the birthing."

"And your brother?"

"Riddock is young, headstrong. He can ride like the devil."

"You're proud of him."

"I am. He'd give you poetry." Kylar lifted his goblet. "He has a knack for it, and loves nothing more than luring pretty maids out to the garden in the moonlight."

She asked questions casually so he would talk. She was unsure of her conversational skills in this arena, and it was such a pleasure to just sit and listen to him speak so easily of things that were, to her, a miracle.

Summer and gardens, swimming in a pond, riding through a village where people went to market. Carts of glossy red apples—what would they taste like? Baskets of flowers whose scent she could only dream of.

She had a picture of his home now, as she had pictures in books.

She had a picture of him, and it was more than anything she'd ever found in a book.

Willing to pay whatever it cost her later, she lost herself in him, in the way his voice rose and fell, in his laugh. She thought she could sit this way for days, to talk like this with no purpose in it, no niggling worries. Just to be with him by the warmth of the fire, with wine sweet on her tongue and his eyes so intimately on hers.

She didn't object when he took her hand, when his fingers toyed with hers. If this was flirtation, it was such a lovely way to pass the time.

They spoke of faraway lands and cultures. Of paintings and of plays.

"You've put your library to good use," he commented. "I've known few scholars as well read."

"I can see the world through books, and lives through the stories. Once a year, on Midsummer, we put on a pageant. We have music and games. I choose a story, and everyone takes a part as if it were a play. Surviving isn't enough. There must be life and color."

There were times, secretly, when she pined near weeping for true color.

"All the children are taught to read," she continued, "and to do sums. If you have only a window on the world, you must look out of it. One of my men—well, he's just a boy really—he makes stories. They're quite wonderful."

She caught herself, surprised at the sound of her own voice rambling. "I've kept you long enough."

"No." His hand tightened on hers. He was beginning to realize it would never be long enough. "Tell me more. You play music, don't you? A harp. I heard you playing, singing. It was like a dream."

"You were feverish. I play a little. Some skill inherited from my father, I suppose."

"I'd like to hear you play again. Will you play for me, Deirdre?"

"If you like."

But as she started to rise, one of the men who'd helped

serve rushed in. "My lady, my lady, it's young Phelan!"

"What's happened?"

"He was playing with some of the boys on the stairs, and fell. We can't wake him. My lady, we fear he's dying."

6

AFRAID TO MOVE him, they'd left the boy covered with a blanket at the base of the stairs. At first glance, Kylar thought the child, for he was hardly more, was already dead. He'd seen enough of death to recognize its face.

He judged the boy to be about ten, with fair hair and cheeks still round with youth. But those cheeks were gray, and the hair was matted with blood.

Those who circled and knelt around the boy made way when Deirdre hurried through.

"Get back now," she ordered. "Give him room."

Before Deirdre could kneel, a weeping woman broke free to fall at her feet and clutch at her skirts with blood-stained hands. "My baby. Oh, please, my lady! Help my little boy."

"I will, Ailish. Of course I will." Knowing that time was precious, Deirdre bent down and firmly loosened the terrified woman's hold on her. "You must be strong for him, and trust. Let me see to him now."

"He slipped, my lady." Another youth came forward with a jerky step. His eyes were dry, but huge, and there were tracks of tears still drying on his cheeks. "We were playing horse and rider on the stairs, and he slipped."

"All right." Too much grief, she thought, feeling waves of it pressing over her. Too much fear. "It's all right now. I'll tend to him."

"Deirdre." Kylar kept his voice low, so only she could hear over the mother's weeping. "There's nothing you can do here. I can smell death on him."

As could she, and so she knew she had little time. "What is the smell of death but the smell of fear?" She ran her hands gently over the crumpled body, feeling the hurts, finding so much broken in the little boy that her heart ached from it. Medicines would do no good here, but still her face was composed as she looked up.

"Cordelia, fetch my healing bag. Make haste. The rest, please, leave us now. Leave me with him. Ailish, go now."

"Oh, no, please, my lady. Please, I must stay with my boy."

"Do you trust me?"

"My lady." She gripped Deirdre's hand, wept on it. "I do."

"Then do as I bid you. Go now and pray."

"His neck," Kylar began, then broke off when Deirdre whipped her head around and stared at him.

"Be silent! Help me or go, but don't question me."

When Ailish was all but carried away, and the two of them were alone with the bleeding boy, Deirdre closed her eyes. "This will hurt him. I'm sorry for it. Hold him down, hold him as still as you can, and do nothing to interfere. Nothing, do you understand?"

"No." But Kylar shifted until he could clamp the boy's arms.

"Block thoughts of death from your mind," she ordered. "And fear, and doubt. Block them out as you would in battle. There's too much dark here already. Can you do this?"

"I can." And because she asked it of him, Kylar let the cold come into him, the cold that steeled the mind to face combat.

"Phelan," she said. "Young Phelan, the bard." Her voice was soft, almost a crooning as she traced her hands over him again. "Be strong for me."

She knew him already, had watched him grow and learn and be. She knew the sound of his voice, the quick flash of his grin, the lively turn of his mind. He had been hers, as all in Rose Castle were hers, from the moment of his first breath.

And so she merged easily with him.

While her hands worked, stroking, kneading, she slid into his mind. She felt his laughter inside her as he pranced and raced with his friends up and down the narrow stone steps. Felt his heart leap inside her own as his feet slipped. Then the fear, oh, the terror, an instant only before the horrible pain.

The snap of bone made her cry out softly, had her head rearing back. Something inside her crushed like thin clay under a stone hammer, and the sensation was beyond torment.

Her eyes were open now, Kylar saw. A deep and too brilliant green. Her breath came fast and hard, sweat pearled on her brow. And the boy screamed thinly, straining under his grip.

Both made a sound of agony as she slid a hand under the boy to cup his neck, laid her other on his heart. Both shuddered. Both went pale as death.

Kylar started to call out to her, to reach for her as she swayed. But he felt the heat, a ferocious fist of it that seemed to pump out of her, into the boy until the arms he held were like sticks of fire.

And the boy's eyes opened, stared up blindly.

"Take, young Phelan." Her voice was thick now, echoed richly off the stone. "Take what you need. Fire of healing." She leaned down, laid her lips gently on his. "Live. Stay with us. Your mother needs you."

As Kylar watched, thunderstruck, color seeped back into the boy's face. He would have sworn he felt death skitter back into the shadows.

"My lady," the boy said, almost dreamily. "I fell."

"Yes, I know. Sleep now." She brushed her hand over his eyes, and they closed on a sigh. "And heal. Let his mother in, if you will," she said to Kylar. "And Cordelia."

"Deirdre—"

"Please." The weakness threatened to drag her under, and she wanted to be away, in her own chamber before she lost herself to it. "Let them in so I can tell them what must be done for him."

She stayed kneeling when Kylar rose. The sounds of her people were like the dull roar of the ocean in her head. Even as Ailish collapsed next to her son, to gather him close to kiss Deirdre's now trembling hand, Deirdre gave clear, careful instructions for his care.

"Enough!" Alarmed by her pallor, Kylar swept her off the floor and into his arms. "Tend the boy."

"I'm not finished," Deirdre managed.

"Yes, by the blood, you are." The single glance he swept over those gathered challenged any to contradict him. "Where is your chamber?"

"This way, my lord prince." Orna led him through a doorway, down a corridor to another set of stairs. "I know what to do for her, my lord."

"Then you'll do it." He glanced down at Deirdre as he carried her up the stairs. She had swooned after all, he noted. Her skin was like glass, her eyes closed. The boy's blood was on her hands. "What did she risk by snatching the boy from death?"

"I cannot say, my lord." She opened a door, hurried across a chamber to the bed. "I will care for her now."

"I stay."

Orna pressed her lips together as he laid Deirdre on the bed. "I must undress her. Wash her."

Struggling with temper, he turned to stalk to the window. "Then do so. Is this what she did for me?"

"I cannot say." Orna met his eyes directly when he turned back. "She did not speak of it to me. She does not speak of it with anyone. Prince Kylar, I will ask you to turn your back until my lady is suitably attired in her night garb."

"Woman, her modesty is not an issue with me." But he turned, stared out the window.

He had heard of those who could heal with the mind. But he had not believed it, not truly believed, before tonight. Nor had he considered what price the healer paid to heal.

"She will sleep," Orna said some time later.

"I won't disturb her." He came to the bed now, gazed down. There was still no color in her cheeks, but it seemed to him her breathing was steadier. "Nor will I leave her."

"My lady is strong, as valiant as ten warriors."

"If I had ten as valiant, there would never be another battle to fight."

Pleased with his response, Orna inclined her head. "And my lady has, despite what she believes, a tender heart." Orna set a bottle and goblet on the table near the bed. "See that you don't bruise it. When she wakes, give her some of this tonic. I will not be far, should you need me."

Alone, Kylar drew a chair near the bed and watched Deirdre sleep. For an hour, and then two. She was motionless and pale as marble in the firelight, and he feared she would never wake but would sleep like the beauty in another legend, for a hundred years.

Even days before he would have deemed such things foolishness, stories for children. But now, after what he'd seen, what he'd felt, anything seemed possible.

Still, side by side with the worry inside him, anger

bloomed. She had risked her life. He had seen death slide
its cold fingers over her. She had bargained her life for
the child's.

And, he was sure now, for his own.

When she stirred, just the slightest flutter of her lashes,
he poured the tonic Orna had left into the cup.

"Drink this." He lifted her head from the pillow. "Don't
speak. Just drink now."

She sipped, and sighed. The hand she lifted to his wrist
slid limply away again. "Phelan?" she whispered.

"I don't know." He brought the cup to her lips a second
time. "Drink more."

She obeyed, then turned her head. "Ask. Ask how
young Phelan fares. Please. I must be sure."

"Drink first. Drink it all."

She did as he bade, and kept her eyes open and on his
now. If she'd had the strength, she would have gone to
find out herself. But the weakness was still dragging at
her, and she could only trust Kylar to the task. "Please. I
won't be easy until I know his condition."

Kylar set the empty cup aside, then crossed the chamber
to the door. Orna sat on a chair in the corridor, sewing
by candlelight. She glanced up when she saw him. "Tell
my lady not to fret. Young Phelan is resting. Healing."
She got to her feet. "If you would like to retire, my lord,
I will sit with my lady."

"Go to your bed," he said shortly. "I stay with her tonight."

Orna bowed her head and hid a smile. "As you wish."

He stepped back inside, closed the door. And turning
saw that Deirdre was sitting up in bed, with her hair spilling like honey over the white lawn of her nightdress.

"Your boy is resting, and well."

At his words, he saw color return to her face, watched
the dullness clear from her eyes. He came to the foot of
the bed, which was draped in deep red velvet. "You recover quickly, madam."

"The tonic is potent." Indeed she now felt clear of

mind, and even the echoes of pain were fading from her body. "Thank you for your help. His mother and father would have been too distraught to assist. Their worry could have distracted me. More, fear feeds death."

She glanced around the room, a little warily. Orna hadn't laid out her nightrobe. "If you'd excuse me now, I'll go see for myself."

"Not tonight."

To her shock he sat on the side of the bed near her. Only pride kept her from shifting over, or tugging up the blankets.

"I have questions."

"I've answered several of your questions already."

He lifted his brows. "Now I have more. The boy was dying. His skull crushed, his neck damaged if not broken. His left arm was shattered."

"Yes," she said calmly. "And inside his body, more was harmed. He bled inside himself. So much blood for such a little boy. But he has a strong heart, our Phelan. He is particularly precious to me."

"He would have been dead in minutes."

"He is not dead."

"Why?"

"I can't answer." Restlessly, she pushed at her hair. "I can't explain it to you."

"Won't."

"Can't."

When she would have turned her face away, he caught her chin, held it firmly. "Try."

"You overstep," she said stiffly. "Continually."

"Then you should be growing accustomed to it. I held the boy," he reminded her. "I watched, and I felt life come back into him. Tell me what you did."

She wanted to dismiss him, but he had helped her when she'd needed his help. So she would try. "It's a kind of search, and a merging. An opening of both." She lifted a hand, let it fall. "It is a kind of faith, if you will."

"It caused you pain."

"Do you think fighting death is painless? You know better. To heal, I must feel what he feels, and bring him up. . . ." She shook her head, frustrated with words. "Take him back to the pain. Then we ride it together, so that I see, feel, know."

"You rode more than pain. You rode death. I saw you."

"We were stronger."

"And if you hadn't been?"

"Then death would have won," she said simply. "And a mother would be grieving her firstborn tonight."

"And you? Deirdre of the Ice, would your people be grieving you?"

"There is a risk. Do you turn from battle, Kylar? Or do you face it knowing your life might be the price paid at end of day? Would you not stand for any one of your people if they had need? Would you expect me to do less for one of mine?"

"I was not one of yours." He took her hand before she could look away. "You rode death with me, Deirdre. I remember. I thought it a dream, but I remember. The pain, as if the sword cut into me fresh. That same pain mirrored in your eyes as you looked down at me. The heat of your body, the heat of your life pouring into me. I was nothing to you."

"You were a man. You were hurt." She reached out now, laying her hand on his cheek. "Why are you angry? Should I have let you die because my medicines weren't enough to save you? Should I have stepped back from you and my own gift because it would cause me a moment's pain to save you? Does your pride bleed now because a woman fought for your life?"

"Perhaps it does." He closed his hand over her wrist. "When I carried you in here I thought you would die, and I was helpless."

"You stayed with me. That was kind."

He made some sound, then pushed himself off the bed to pace. "When a man goes into battle, Deirdre, it's sword to sword, lance to lance, fist to fist. These are tangible things. What you've done, magic or miracle, is so much more. And you were right. I can't understand it."

"It changes how you think of me."

"Yes."

She lowered her lashes, hid the fresh pain. "There is no shame in it. Most men would not have stayed to help, certainly not have stayed to speak with me. I'm grateful. Now if you'd excuse me, I'd like to be alone."

Slowly, he turned back to her. "You misunderstand me. Before I thought of you as a woman—beautiful, strong, intelligent. Sad. Now I think of you as all of that, and so much more. You humble me. You expect me to step away from you, because of all you are. I can't. I want to be with you, and I have no right."

With her heart unsteady, she looked at him again. "Is it gratitude that draws you to me?"

"I am grateful. I owe you for every breath I take. But it isn't gratitude I feel when I look at you."

She slid out of bed to stand on her own feet. "Is it desire?"

"I desire you."

"I've never had a man's arms around me in love. I want them to be yours."

"What right do I have when I can't stay with you? I should already be gone. Both my family and my people wait."

"You give me truth, and truth means more than pretty words and empty promises. I wondered about this, and now I know. When I healed you I felt something I've never felt before. Mixed with the pain and the cold that comes into me so bitter there was . . . light."

Watching him, she spread her hands. "I said I did nothing to bind you to me, and that is truth. But something happened in me when I was part of you. It angered me, and it frightened me. But now, just now . . ." She drew a breath and spoke without a blush. "It excites me. I've been so cold. Give me one night of warmth. You said you wanted me willing." She reached up, tugged the ribbons loose from the bodice of the nightdress. "And I am," she said as the white gown slid down to pool at her feet.

7

SHE WAS A vision. More than he could have dreamed. Slim and small, she stood in the glow of candle and firelight.

"Will you give me a night?" she asked him.

"Deirdre. My love. I would give you a lifetime."

"I want no pledges that can't be kept, no words but truth. Only give me what can be, and it will be enough," she replied somberly.

"My lady." He felt, somehow, that the step toward her was the most momentous of his life. And when he took her hands, that he was taking the world. "It is the truth. Why or how I don't know. But never have I spoken cleaner truth."

She believed he meant it, in this time. In this place. "Kylar, lifetimes are for those who are free."

So she would be, he promised himself. Whatever had to be done. But now wasn't for plans and battles. "If you won't accept that pledge, let me pledge this. That I have loved no other as I love you tonight."

"I can give that vow back to you. I thought it would be for duty." She lifted her hands to his face, traced the shape of it with her fingers. "And I thought the first time, it would be with fear." She laughed a little. "My heart jumps. Can you feel it?"

He laid a hand on her breast, felt the shiver. Felt the leap. "I won't hurt you."

"Oh, no." She laid a hand on his heart in turn. They had brushed once before, she thought. Heart to heart. Nothing had been the same for her since. Nothing would be the same for her ever again. "You won't hurt me. Warm me, Kylar, as a man warms his woman."

He drew her into his arms. Gently, gently. Laid his lips on hers. Tenderly. There once more, she thought. There. That miracle of mouth against mouth. Sighing out his name, she let herself melt into the kiss.

"The first time you kissed me, I thought you were foolish."

His lips curved on hers. "Did you?"

"Half frozen and bleeding, and you would waste your last breath flirting with a woman. Such is a man."

"Not a waste," he corrected. "But I can do better now." With a flourish that pleased them both, he swept her into his arms. "Come to bed, my lady."

As she had once longed to do, she toyed with his silky black hair. "You must teach me what to do."

His muscles tightened, nerves and thrills, at the thought of her innocence. Tonight she would give him what she had given no other. In the candle glow he saw her face, saw that she gave him this treasure without fear, without shame.

No, he would not hurt her, but would do all in his power to bring her joy.

He laid her on the bed, rubbed his cheek against hers. "It will be my pleasure to instruct you."

"I've seen the goats mate."

His burst of laughter was muffled in her hair. "This, I can promise, will be somewhat different than the mating of goats. So pay attention," he said, grinning now as he lifted his head, "while I give you your first lesson."

He was a patient teacher, and surely, she thought as her skin began to shiver and sing under his hands, a skilled one. His mouth drank from hers, deep, then deeper until it was how she imagined it might be to slide bonelessly into a warm river.

Surrounded, floating, then submerged.

His hands roamed over her breasts, then cupped them as if he could hold her heartbeat in his palms. The sensation of those strong, hard hands on her flesh shimmered straight down to her belly. His mouth skimmed the side of her throat, nibbling.

"How lovely." She murmured it, arching a little to invite more. "How clever for breasts to give pleasure as well as milk."

"Indeed." His thumbs brushed over her nipples, and made her gasp. "I've often thought the same."

"Oh . . . but what do I . . ." Her words, her thoughts trailed off into a rainbow when that nibbling mouth found her breast.

She made a sound in her throat, half cry, half moan. It thrilled him, that sound of shocked pleasure, the sudden shudder of her body, the quick jolt of her heart under his lips. As she arched again, her fingers combed through his hair, gripped there and pressed him closer. The sweet taste of her filled him like warmed wine.

He rose over her to tug his doublet aside, but before he could satisfy himself with that glorious slide of his flesh to her flesh, she lifted her hands, ran them experimentally over his chest.

"Wait." She needed to catch her breath. It was all running through her so quickly that it nearly blurred. She wanted everything, but clearly, so that she might remember each stroke, each taste, each moment.

"I touched you when you were hurt. But this is differ-

ent. I looked at your body, but didn't see it as I do now."
Carefully she traced her finger along the scar running up
his side. "Does this trouble you?"

He felt the line of heat, took her hand quickly. "No."
Even now, he thought, she would try to heal. "There will
be no pain tonight, for either of us."

He lowered to her, took her mouth again. There was a
hint of urgency now, a taste of need. So much to feel, she
mused dreamily. So much to know. And with the warmth
of him coursing through her, she enfolded him. There was
a freedom here, she discovered, in being about to touch
him, stroke, explore, with no purpose other than pleasure.
The hard muscles, the pucker in his smooth skin that was
a scar of battle.

The strength of him excited her, challenged her own so
that her hands, her mouth, her movements under him became more demanding.

This was fire, she realized. The first true licks of flame
that brought nothing but delight and a bright, blinding
need for more.

"I'm not fragile." Indeed she felt alive with power,
nearly frantic with a kind of raging hunger. "Show me
more. Show me all."

No matter how his blood swam, he would be careful
with her. But he could show her more. His hands roamed
down her body, over her thighs. As if she knew what they
both needed, she opened to him. Her breath came short,
shivering out with quick little moans. Her nails bit into
his back as she began to writhe under him.

He lifted his head and watched her fly over that first
peak of pleasure.

Heat, such heat. She had never known such fire outside
of healing magic. And this, somehow, this went deeper,
spread wider. Her body was like a single wild flame. She
cried out, the wanton sound of her own voice another
shock to her system. Beyond control, beyond reason, she
gripped his hips and called out his name.

When he plunged into her, the glory of it was like a

shaft of lightning, bright and brilliant. There was a storm of those glorious and violent shocks as he thrust inside her. She locked herself around him, her face pressed against his neck and repeated his name as that miraculous heat consumed her.

"Sweetheart." When he could speak again, he did so lazily, with his head nuzzled between her breasts. "You are the most clever of students."

She felt golden, beautiful, and for the first time in her memory, more woman than queen. For one night, she told herself, one miraculous night, she would be a woman.

"I'm sure I could do better, my lord, with a few more lessons."

She was flushed, all but glowing, and her hair was a tangle of honeyed ropes over the white linen. "I believe you're right." He grinned and nibbled his way up her throat, lingered over her lips, then shifted so that she lay curled beside him.

"I'm so warm," she told him. "I never knew what it was like to be so warm. Tell me, Kylar, what's it like to have the sun on your face, full and bright?"

"It can burn."

"Truly?"

"Truly." He began to toy with her hair. "And the skin reddens or browns from it." He ran a fingertip down her arm. Pale as milk, soft as satin. "It can dazzle the eyes." He turned so he could look down at her. "You dazzle mine."

"There was an old man who was my tutor when I was a child. He'd been all over the world. He told me of great tombs in a desert where the sun beat like fury, of green hills where flowers bloomed wild and the rain came warm. Of wide oceans where great fish swam that could swallow a boat whole and dragons with silver wings flew. He taught me so many marvelous things, but he never taught me the wonders that you have tonight."

"There's never been another. Not like you. Not like this."

Because she read the truth in his eyes, she drew him closer. "Show me more."

As they loved, inside a case of ice, the first green bud on a blackened stalk unfurled to a single tender leaf. And a second began to form.

When he woke, she was gone. At first he was baffled, for he slept like a soldier, and a soldier slept light as a cat. But he could see she had stirred the fire for him and had left his clothes folded neatly on the chest at the foot of the bed.

It occurred to him that he'd slept only an hour or two, but obviously like the dead. The woman was tireless—bless her—and had demanded a heroic number of lessons through the night.

A pity, he mused, she hadn't lingered in bed a bit longer that morning. He believed he might have managed another.

He rose to draw back the hangings on the windows. He judged it to be well into the morning, as her people were about their chores. He couldn't tell the time by the light here, for it varied so little from dawn to dusk. It was always soft and dull, with that veil of white over sky and sun. Even now a thin snow was falling.

How did she bear it? Day after day of cold and gloom. How did she stay sane, and more—content? Why should so good and loving a queen be cursed to live her life without warmth?

He turned, studied the chamber. He'd paid little attention to it the night before. He'd seen only her. Now he noted that she lived simply. The fabrics were rich indeed, but old and growing thin.

There had been silver and crystal in the dining hall, he recalled, but here her candlestands were of simple metal, the bowl for her washing a crude clay. The bed, the chest, the wardrobe were all beautifully worked with carved roses. But there was only a single chair and table.

He saw no pretty bottles, no silks, no trinket boxes.

She'd seen to it that the appointments in his guest chamber were suited to his rank, but for herself, she lived nearly as spartanly as a peasant.

His mother's ladies had more fuss and fancy in their chambers than this queen. Then he glanced at the fire and with a clutching in his belly realized she would have used much of the furniture for fuel, and fabric for clothes for her people.

She'd worn jewels when they dined. Even now he could see how they gleamed and sparkled over her. But what good were diamonds and pearls to her? They couldn't be sold or bartered, they put no food on the table.

A diamond's fire brought no warmth to chilled bones.

He washed in the bowl of water she'd left for him, and dressed.

There on the wall he saw the single tapestry, faded with age. Her rose garden, in full bloom, and as magnificent in silk thread as he'd imagined it. Alive with color and shape, it was a lush paradise caught in a lush moment of summer.

There was a figure of a woman seated on the jeweled bench beneath the spreading branches of the great bush that bloomed wild and free. And a man knelt at her feet, offering a single red rose.

He trailed his fingers over the threads and thought he would give his life and more to be able to offer her one red rose.

He was directed by a servant to Phelan's room, where the young bard had his quarters with a gaggle of other boys. The other boys gone, Phelan was sitting up in the bed with Deirdre for company. The chamber was small, Kylar noted, simple, but warmer by far than the queen's own.

She was urging a bowl of broth on Phelan and laughing in delight at the faces he made.

"A toad!"

"No, my lady. A monkey. Like the one in the book you lent me." He bared his teeth and made her laugh again.

"Even a monkey must eat."

"They eat the long yellow fruit."

"Then you'll pretend this is the long yellow fruit." She snuck a spoonful in his mouth.

He grimaced. "I don't like the taste."

"I know, the medicine spoils it a bit. But my favorite monkey needs to regain his strength. Eat it for me, won't you?"

"For you, my lady." On a heavy sigh, the boy took the bowl and spoon himself. "Then can I get up and play?"

"Tomorrow, you may get up for a short while."

"My lady." There was a wealth of horror and grief in the tone. Kylar could only sympathize. He'd once been a small boy and knew the tedium of being forced to stay idle in bed.

"A wounded soldier must recover to fight another day," Kylar said as he crossed to the bed. "Were you not a soldier when you rode the horse on the stairs?"

Phelan nodded, staring up at Kylar as if fascinated. To him the prince was as magnificent and foreign as every hero in every story he'd ever heard or read. "I was, my lord."

"Well, then. Do you know your lady kept me abed three full days when I came to her wounded?" He sat on the edge of the bed, leaned over and sniffed at the bowl. "And forced the same broth on me. It's a cruelty, but a soldier bears such hardships."

"Phelan will not be a soldier," Deirdre said firmly. "He is a bard."

"Ah." Kylar inclined his head in a bow. "There is no man of more import than a bard."

"More than a soldier?" Phelan asked, with eyes wide.

"A bard tells the tales and sings the songs. Without him, we would know nothing."

"I'm making a story about you, my lord." Excited now, Phelan spooned up his broth. "About how you came from beyond, traveled the Forgotten wounded and near death, and how my lady healed you."

"I'd like to hear the story when you've finished it."

"You can make the story while you rest and recover." Pleased that the bowl was empty, Deirdre took it as she stood, then leaned over to kiss Phelan's brow.

"Will you come back, my lady?"

"I will. But now you rest, and dream your story. Later, I'll bring you a new book."

"Be well, young bard." Kylar took Deirdre's hand to lead her out.

"You rose early," he commented.

"There's much to be done."

"I find myself jealous of a ten-year-old boy."

"Nearly twelve is Phelan. He's small for his age."

"Regardless, you didn't sit and feed me broth or kiss my brow when I was well enough to sit up on my own."

"You were not so sweet-natured a patient."

"I would be now." He kissed her, surprised that she didn't flush and flutter as females were wont to do. Instead she answered his lips with a reckless passion that stirred his appetite. "Put me to bed, and I'll show you."

She laughed and nudged him back. "That will have to wait. I have duties."

"I'll help you."

Her face softened. "You have helped me already. But come. I'll give you work."

8

THERE WAS NO lack of work. The prince of Mrydon found himself tending goats and chickens. Shoveling manure, hauling endless buckets of snow to a low fire, carting precious wood to a communal pile.

The first day he labored he tired so quickly that it scored his pride. On the second, muscles that had gone unused during his recovery ached continually.

But the discomfort had the benefit of Deirdre rubbing him everywhere with one of her balms. And made the ensuing loving both merry and slippery.

She was a joy in bed, and he saw none of the sadness in her eyes there. Her laughter, the sound he'd longed to hear, came often.

He grew to know her people and was surprised and impressed by the lack of bitterness in them. He thought them more like a family, and though some were lazy, some grim, they shouldered together. They knew, he realized, that the survival of the whole depended on each.

That, he thought, was another of Deirdre's gifts. Her people held the will to go on, day after day, because their lady did. He couldn't imagine his own soldiers bearing the hardships and the tedium with half as much courage.

He came upon her in her garden. Though the planting and maintenance there was divided, as all chores were in Rose Castle, he knew she often chose to work or walk there alone.

She did so now, carefully watering her plantings with snowmelt.

"Your goat herd has increased by one." He glanced down at his stained tunic. "It's the first such birthing I've attended."

Deirdre straightened, eased her back. "The kid and the she-goat are well?"

"Well and fine, yes."

"Why wasn't I called?"

"There was no need. Here, let me." He took the spouted bucket from her. "Your people work hard, Deirdre, but none as hard as their queen."

"The garden is a pleasure to me."

"So I've seen." He glanced up at the wide dome. "A clever device."

"My grandfather's doing." Since he was watering, she knelt and began to harvest turnips. "He inherited a love for gardening from his mother, I'm told. It was she who designed and planted the rose garden. I'm named for her. When he was a young man, he traveled, and he studied with engineers and scientists and learned much. I think he was a great man."

"I've heard of him, though I thought it all legend." Kylar looked back at her as she placed turnips in a sack. "It's said he was a sorcerer."

Her lips curved a little. "Perhaps. Magic may come through the blood. I don't know. I do know he gathered many of the books in the library, and built this dome for his mother when she was very old. Here she could start seedlings before the planting time and grow the flowers she loved, even in the cold. It must have given her great pleasure to work here when her roses and other flowers were dormant with winter."

She sat back on her heels, looked over her rows and beyond to the sad and spindly daisies she prized like rubies. "I wonder if somehow he knew that his gift to his mother would one day save his people from starvation."

"You run low on fuel."

"Yes. The men will cut another tree in a few days." It always pained her to order it. For each tree cut meant one fewer left. Though the forest was thick and vast, without new growth there would someday be no more.

"Deirdre, how long can you go on this way?"

"As long as we must."

"It's not enough." Temper that he hadn't realized was building inside him burst out. He cast the bucket aside and grabbed her hands.

She'd been waiting for this. Through the joy, through the sweetness, she'd known the storm would come. The storm that would end the time out of time. He was healed now, and a warrior prince, so healed, could not abide monotony.

"It's enough," she said calmly, "because it's what we have."

"For how much longer?" he demanded. "Ten years? Fifty?"

"For as long as there is."

Though she tried to pull away, he turned her hands over. "You work them raw, haul buckets like a milkmaid."

"Should I sit on my throne with soft white hands folded and let my people work?"

"There are other choices."

"Not for me."

"Come with me." He gripped her arms now, tight, firm, as if he held his own life.

Oh, she'd dreamed of it, in her most secret heart. Riding off with him, flying through the forest and away to beyond. Toward the sun, the green, the flowers.

Into summer.

"I can't. You know I can't."

"We'll find the way out. When we're home, I'll gather men, horses, provisions. I'll come back for your people. I swear it to you."

"You'll find the way out." She laid her hands on his chest, over the thunder of his heart. "I believe it. If I didn't I would have you chained before I'd allow you to leave. I won't risk your death. But the way back . . ." She shook her head, turned away from him when his grip relaxed.

"You don't believe I'll come back."

She closed her eyes because she didn't believe it, not fully. How could he turn his back on the sun and risk everything to travel here again for what he'd known for only a few weeks? "Even if you tried, there's no certainty you'd find us again. Your coming was a miracle. Your safe passage home will be another. I don't ask for three in one lifetime."

She drew herself up. "I won't ask for your life, nor will I accept it. I will send a man with you—my best, my strongest—if you will take him. If you will give him good horses, and provisions, I will send others if the gods show him the way back again."

"But you won't leave."

"I'm bound to stay, as you are bound to go." She turned back, and though tears stung her throat, her eyes were dry. "It's said that if I leave here while winter holds this place, Rose Castle will vanish from sight, and all within will be trapped for eternity."

"That's nonsense."

"Can you say that?" She gestured to the white sky above the dome. "Can you be sure of it? I am queen of this world, and I am prisoner."

"Then bid me stay. You've only to ask it of me."

"I won't. And you can't. First, you're destined to be king. It is your fate, and I have seen the crown you'll wear inside your own mind and heart. And more, your family would grieve and your people mourn. With that on your conscience, the gift we found together would be forever tainted. One day you would go in any case."

"So little faith in me. I ask you this: Do you love me?"

Her eyes filled, sheened, but the tears did not fall. "I care for you. You brought light inside me."

" 'Care' is a weak word. Do you love me?"

"My heart is frozen. I have no love to give."

"That is the first lie you've told me. I've seen you cuddle a fretful babe in your arms, risk your life to save a small boy."

"That is a different matter."

"I've been inside you." Frustrated fury ran over his face. "I've seen your eyes as you opened to me."

She began to tremble. "Passion is not love. Surely my father had passion for my mother, for her sister. But love he had for neither. I care for you. I desire you. That is all I have to give. The gift of a heart, woman to man, has doomed me."

"So because your father was feckless, your mother foolish, and your aunt vindictive, you close yourself off from the only true warmth there is?"

"I can't give what I don't have."

"Then take this, Deirdre of the Sea of Ice. I love you, and I will never love another. I leave tomorrow. I ask you again, come with me."

"I can't. I can't," she repeated, taking his arm. "I beg you. Our time is so short, let us not have this chill between us. I've given you more than ever I gave a man. I pledge to you now there will never be another. Let it be enough."

"It isn't enough. If you loved, you'd know that." One hand gripped the hilt of his sword as if he would draw it and fight what stood between them. Instead, he stepped back from her. "You make your own prison, my lady," he said, and left her.

Alone, Deirdre nearly sank to her knees. But despair, she thought, would solve no more than Kylar's bright sword would. So she picked up the pail.

"Why didn't you tell him?"

Deirdre jolted, nearly splashing water over the rim. "You have no right to listen to private words, Orna."

Ignoring the stiff tone, Orna came forward to heft the bag of turnips. "Hasn't he the right to know what may break the spell?"

"No." She said it fiercely. "His choices, his actions must be his own. He is entitled to that. He won't be influenced by a sense of honor, for his honor runs through him like his blood. I am no damsel who needs rescuing by a man."

"You are a woman who is loved by one."

"Men love many women."

"By the blood, child! Will you let those who made you ruin you?"

"Should I give my heart, take his, at the risk of sacrificing all who depend on me?"

"It doesn't have to be that way. The curse—"

"I don't know love." When she whirled around, her face was bright with temper. "How can I trust what I don't know? She who bore me couldn't love me. He who made me never even looked on my face. I know duty, and I know the tenderness I feel for you and my people. I know joy and sadness. And I know fear."

"It's fear that traps you."

"Haven't I the right to fear?" Deirdre demanded. "When I hold lives in my hands, day and night? I cannot leave here."

"No, you cannot leave here." The undeniable truth of that broke Orna's heart. "But you can love."

"And loving, risk trapping him in this place. This cold place. Harsh payment for what he's given me. No, he leaves on the morrow, and what will be will be."

"And if you're with child?"

"I pray I am, for it is my duty." Her shoulders slumped. "I fear I am, for then I will have imprisoned his child, our child, here." She pressed a hand to her stomach. "I dreamed of a child, Orna, nursing at my breast and watching me with my lover's eyes, and what moved through me was so fierce and strong. The woman I am would ride away with him to save what grows inside me. The queen cannot. You will not speak of this to him, or anyone."

"No, my lady."

Deirdre nodded. "Send Dilys to me, and see that provisions are set aside for two men. They will have a long and difficult journey. I await Dilys in the parlor."

She set the bucket aside and walked quickly away.

Before going inside, Orna hurried through the archway and into the rose garden.

When she saw that the tiny leaf she'd watched unfurl from a single green bud was withering, she wept.

9

Even pride couldn't stop her from going to him. When time was so short there was no room for pride in her world. She brought him gifts she hoped he would accept.

And she brought him herself.

"Kylar." She waited at his chamber door until he turned from the window where he stared out at the dark night. So handsome, she thought, her dark prince. "Would you speak with me?"

"I'm trying to understand you."

That alone, that he would try, lightened her heart. "I wish you could." She came forward and laid what she carried on the chest by his bed. "I've brought you a cloak, since yours was ruined. It was my grandfather's, and with its lining of fur is warmer than what you had. It befits a prince. And this brooch that was his. Will you take it?"

He crossed to her, picked up the gold brooch with its carved rose. "Why do you give it to me?"

"Because I treasure it." She lifted a hand, closed it over his on the brooch. "You think I don't cherish what you've given me, what you've been to me. I can't let you leave believing that. I can't bear the thought of you going when there's anger and hard words between us."

There was a storm in his eyes as they met hers. "I could take you from here, whether you're willing or not. No one could stop me."

"I would not allow it, nor would my people."

He stepped closer, and circled her throat with his hand with just enough force that the pulse against his palm fluttered with fear. "No one could stop me." His free hand clamped over hers before she could draw her dagger. "Not even you."

"I would never forgive you for it. Nor lie willingly with you again. Anger makes you think of using force as an answer. You know it's not."

"How can you be so calm, and so sure, Deirdre?"

"I'm sure of nothing. And I am not calm. I want to go with you. I want to run and never look back, to live with you in the sunlight. To once smell the grass, to breathe the summer. Once," she said in a fierce whisper. "And what would that make me?"

"My wife."

The hand under his trembled, then steadied before she drew it away. "You honor me, but I will never marry."

"Because of who made you, how you were made?" He took her by the shoulders now so that their gazes locked. "Can you be so wise, so warm, Deirdre, and at the same time so cold and closed?"

"I will never marry because my most sacred trust is to do no harm. If I were to take a husband, he would be king. I would share the welfare of all my people with him. This is a heavy burden."

"Do you think I would shirk it?"

"I don't, no. I've been inside your mind and heart. You keep your promises, Kylar, even if they harm you."

"So you spurn me to save me?"

"Spurn you? I have lain with you. I have shared with you my body, my mind, as I have never shared with another. Will never share again in my lifetime. If I take your vow and keep you here, if you keep your vow and stay, how many will be harmed? What destinies would we alter if you did not take your place as king in your own land? And if I went with you, my people would lose hope. They would have no one to look to for guidance. No one to heal them. There is no one here to take my place."

She thought of the child she knew grew inside her.

"I accept that you must go, and honor you for it," she said. "Why can't you accept that I must stay?"

"You see only black and white."

"I *know* only black and white." Her voice turned desperate now, with a pleading he'd never heard from her. "My life, the whole of it, has been here. And one single purpose was taught to me. To keep my people alive and well. I've done this as best I can."

"No one could have done better."

"But it isn't finished. You want to understand me?" Now she moved to the window, pulled the hangings over the black glass to shut out the dark and the cold. "When I was a babe, my mother gave me to Orna. I never remember my mother's arms around me. She was kind, but she couldn't love me. I have my father's eyes, and looking at me caused her pain. I felt that pain."

She pressed her hands to her heart. "I felt it inside me, the hurt and the longing and the despair. So I closed myself off from it. Hadn't I the right?"

There was no room for anger in him now. "She had no right to turn from you."

"She did turn from me, and that can't be changed. I was tended well, and taught. I had duties, and I had playmates. And once, when I was very young there were dogs. They died off, one by one. When the last . . . his name was Griffen—a foolish name for a dog, I suppose. He was very old, and I couldn't heal him. When he died, it broke something in me. That's foolish, too, isn't it, to be shattered by the death of a dog."

"No. You loved him."

"Oh, I did." She sat now, with a weary sigh. "So much love I had for that old hound. And so much fury when I lost him. I was mad with grief and tried to destroy the ice rose. I thought if I could chop it down, hack it to bits, all this would end. Somehow it would end, for even death could never be so bleak. But a sword is nothing against magic. My mother sent for me. There would be loss, she told me. I had to accept it. I had duties, and the most vital was to care for my people. To put their well-being above my own. She was right."

"As a queen," Kylar agreed. "But not as a mother."

"How could she give what she didn't have? I realize now, with her bond with the animals, she must have felt grief as I did for the loss. She *was* grief, my mother. I watched her pine and yearn for the man who'd ruined her. Even as she died, she wept for him. His deceit, his self-ishness stole the color and warmth from her life, and doomed her and her people to eternal winter. Yet she died loving him, and I vowed that nothing and no one would ever rule my heart. It is trapped inside me, as frozen as the rose in the tower of ice outside this window. If it were free, Kylar, I would give it to you."

"You trap yourself. It's not a sword that will cut through the ice. It's love."

"What I have is yours. I wish it could be more. If I were not queen, I would go with you on the morrow. I would trust you to take me to beyond, or would die fighting to get there with you. But I can't go, and you can't stay. Kylar, I saw your mother's face."

"My mother?"

"In your mind, your heart, when I healed you. I would have given anything, anything, to have seen such love and pride for me in the eyes of the one who bore me. You can't let her grieve for a son who still lives."

Guilt clawed at him. "She would want me happy."

"I believe she would. But if you stay, she will never know what became of you. Whatever you want for yourself, you have too much inside you for her to leave her not knowing. And too much honor to turn away from your duties to your family and your own land."

His fists clenched. She had, with the skill of a soldier, outflanked him. "Does it always come to duty?"

"We're born what we're born, Kylar. Neither you nor I could live well or happy if we cast off our duty."

"I would rather face a battle without sword or shield than leave you."

"We've been given these weeks. If I ask you for one more night, will you turn me away?"

"No." He reached for her hand. "I won't turn you away."

He loved her tenderly, then fiercely. And at last, when dawn trembled to life, he loved her desperately. When the night was over, she didn't cling, nor did she weep. A part of him wished she would do both. But the woman he loved was strong, and helped him prepare for his journey without tears.

"There are rations for two weeks." She prayed it would be enough. "Take whatever you need from the forest." As he cinched the saddle on his horse, Deirdre slipped a hand under his cloak, laid it on his side.

And he moved away. "No." More than once during the night, she'd tried to explore his healing wound. "If I have pain, it's mine. I won't have it be yours. Not again."

"You're stubborn."

"I bow before you, my lady. The queen of willful."

She managed a smile and laid a hand on the arm of the man she'd chosen to guide the prince. "Dilys. You are Prince Kylar's man now."

He was young, tall as a tree and broad of shoulder. "My lady, I am the queen's man."

This time she touched his face. They had grown up together, and once had romped as children. "Your queen asks that you pledge now your loyalty, your fealty, and your life to Prince Kylar."

He knelt in the deep and crusted snow. "If it is your wish, my queen, I so pledge."

She drew a ring from her finger, pressed it into his hand. "Live." She bent to kiss both his cheeks. "And if you cannot return—"

"My lady."

"If you cannot," she continued, lifting his head so their gazes met, "know you have my blessing, and my wish for your happiness. Keep the prince safe," she whispered. "Do not leave him until he's safe. It is the last I will ever ask of you."

She stepped back. "Kylar, prince of Mrydon, we wish you safe journey."

He took the hand she offered. "Deirdre, queen of the Sea of Ice, my thanks for your hospitality, and my good wishes to you and your people." But he didn't release her hand. Instead, he took a ring of his own and slid it onto her finger. "I pledge to you my heart."

"Kylar—"

"I pledge to you my life." And before the people gathered in the courtyard, he pulled her into his arms and kissed her, long and deep. "Ask me now, one thing. Anything."

"I will ask you this. When you're safe again, when you find summer, pluck the first rose you see. And think of me. I will know, and be content."

Even now, he thought, she would not ask him to come back for her. He touched a hand to the brooch pinned to his cloak. "Every rose I see is you." He vaulted onto his horse. "I will come back."

He spurred his horse toward the archway with Dilys trotting beside him. The crowd rushed after them, calling, cheering. Unable to resist, Deirdre climbed to the battlements, stood in the slow drift of snow and watched him ride away from her.

His mount's hooves rang on the ice, and his black cloak snapped in the frigid wind. Then he whirled his horse, and reared high.

"I will come back!" he shouted.

When his voice echoed back to her, over her, she nearly believed it. She stood, her red cloak drawn tight, until he disappeared into the forest.

Alone, her legs trembling, she made her way down to the rose garden. There was a burning inside her chest, and an ache deep, deep within her belly. When her vision blurred, she stopped to catch her breath. With a kind of dull surprise she reached up to touch her cheeks and found them wet.

Tears, she thought. After so many years. The burning inside her chest became a throbbing. So. She closed her eyes and stumbled forward. So, the frozen chamber that trapped her heart could melt after all. And, melting, bring tears.

Bring a pain that was like what came with healing.

She collapsed at the foot of the great ice rose, buried her face in her hands.

"I love." She sobbed now, rocking herself for comfort. "I love him with all I am or will ever be. And it hurts. How cruel to show me this, to bring me this. How bitter your heart must have been to drape cold over what should be warmth. But you did not love. I know that now."

Steadying as best she could, she turned her face up to the dull sky. "Even my mother did not love, for she willed him back with every breath. I love, and I wish the one who has my heart safe, and whole and warm. For I would not wish this barren life on him. I'll know when he feels the sun and plucks the rose. And I will be content."

She laid a hand on her heart, on her belly. "Your cold magic can't touch what's inside me now."

And drawing herself up, turning away, she didn't see the delicate leaf struggling to live on a tiny green bud.

• • •

The world was wild, and the air itself roared like wolves. The storm sprang up like a demon, hurling ice and snow like frozen arrows. Night fell so fast that there was barely time to gather branches for fuel.

Wrapped in his cloak, Kylar brooded into the fire. The trees were thick here, tall as giants, dead as stones. They had gone beyond where Deirdre harvested trees and into what was called the Forgotten.

"When the storm passes, can you find your way back from here?" Kylar demanded. Though they sat close to warm each other, he was forced to shout to be heard over the screaming storm.

Dilys's eyes, all that showed beneath the cloak and hood, blinked once. "Yes, my lord."

"Then when travel is possible again, you'll go back to Rose Castle."

"No, my lord."

It took Kylar a moment. "You will do as I bid. You have pledged your obedience to me."

"My queen charged me to see you safe. It was the last she said to me. I will see you safe, my lord."

"I'll travel more quickly without you."

"I don't think this is so," Dilys said in his slow and thoughtful way. "I will see you home, my lord. You cannot go back to her until you have reached home. My lady needs you to come back to her."

"She doesn't believe I will. Why do you?"

"Because you are meant to. You must sleep now. The road ahead is longer than the road behind."

The storm raged for hours. It was still dark, still brutal when Kylar awoke. Snow covered him, turning his hair and cloak white, and even the fur did little to fight the canny cold.

He moved silently to his horse. It would take, he knew, minutes only to move far enough from camp that his trail would be lost. In such a hellish world, you could stand all but shoulder to shoulder with another and not see him beside you.

The man Dilys would have no choice but to return home when he woke and found himself alone.

But though he walked his horse soundlessly through the deep snow, he'd gone no more than fifty yards when Dilys was once more trudging beside him.

Brave of heart and loyal to the bone, Kylar thought. Deirdre had chosen her man well.

"You have ears like a bat," Kylar said, resigned now.

Dilys grinned. "I do."

Kylar stopped, jumped down from the horse. "Mount," he ordered. "If we're traveling through hell together, we'll take turns riding." When Dilys only stood and stared, Kylar swore. "Will you argue with me over everything or do as your lady commanded and I now bid?"

"I would not argue, my lord. But I don't know how to mount the horse."

Kylar stood in the swirling snow, cold to the marrow of his bones, and laughed until he thought he would burst from it.

10

On the fourth day of the journey, the wind rose so fierce that they walked in blindness. Hoods, cloaks, even Cathmor's dark hide were white now. Snow coated Dilys's eyebrows and the stubble of his beard, making him look like an old man rather than a youth not yet twenty.

Color, Kylar thought, was a stranger to this terrible world. Warmth was only a dim memory in the Forgotten.

When Dilys rode, Kylar waded through snow that reached his waist. At times he wondered if it would soon simply bury them both.

Fatigue stole through him and with it a driving urge just to lie down, to sleep his way to a quiet death. But each time he stumbled, he pulled himself upright again.

He had given her a pledge, and he would keep it. She had willed him to live, through pain and through magic. So he would live. And he would go back to her.

Walking or riding, he slipped into dreams. In dreams

he sat with Deirdre on a jeweled bench in a garden alive with roses, brilliant with sunlight.

Her hands were warm in his.

So they traveled a full week, step by painful step, through ice and wind, through cold and dark.

"Do you have a sweetheart, Dilys?"

"Sir?"

"A sweetheart?" Taking his turn in the saddle, Kylar rode on a tiring Cathmor with his chin on his chest. "A girl you love."

"I do. Her name is Wynne. She works in the kitchens. We'll wed when I return."

Kylar smiled, drifted. The man never lost hope, he thought, nor wavered in his steady faith. "I will give you a hundred gold coins as a marriage gift."

"My thanks, my lord. What is gold coins?"

Kylar managed a weak chuckle. "As useless just now as a bull with teats. And what is a bull, you'd ask," Kylar continued, anticipating his man. "For surely you've seen a teat in your day."

"I have, my lord, and a wonder of nature they are to a man. A bull I have heard of. It is a beast, is it not? I read a story once—" Dilys broke off, raising his head sharply at the sound overhead. With a shout, he snagged the horse's reins, dragged at them roughly. Cathmor screamed and stumbled. Only instinct and a spurt of will kept Kylar in the saddle as the great tree fell inches from Cathmor's rearing hooves.

"Ears like a bat," Kylar said a second time while his heart thundered in his ears. The tree was fully six feet across, more than a hundred in length. One more step in its path and they would have been crushed.

"It is a sign."

The shock roused Kylar enough to clear his mind. "It is a dead tree broken by the weight of snow and ice."

"It is a sign," Dilys said stubbornly. "Its branches point there." He gestured, and still holding the reins, he began to lead the horse to the left.

"You would follow the branches of a dead tree?" Kylar shook his head, shrugged. "Very well, then. How could it matter?"

He dozed and dreamed for an hour. Walked blind and stiff for another. But when they stopped for midday rations from their dwindling supply, Dilys held up a hand.

"What is that sound?"

"The bloody wind. Is it never silent?"

"No, my lord. Beneath the wind. Listen." He closed his eyes. "It is like . . . music."

"I hear nothing, and certainly no music."

"There."

When Dilys went off at a stumbling run, Kylar shouted after him. Furious that the man would lose himself without food or horse, he mounted as quickly as he could manage and hurried after.

He found Dilys standing knee-deep in snow, one hand lifted, and trembling. "What is it? My lord, what is this thing?"

"It's only a stream." Concerned that the man's mind had snapped, Kylar leaped down from the horse. "It's just a . . . a stream," he whispered as the import raced through him. "Running water. Not ice, but running water. The snow." He turned a quick circle. "It's not so deep here. And the air. Is it warmer?"

"It's beautiful." Dilys was hypnotized by the clear water rushing and bubbling over rock. "It sings."

"Yes, by the blood, it is, and it does. Come. Quick now. We follow the stream."

The wind still blew, but the snow was thinning. He could see clearly now, the shape of the trees, and tracks from game. He had only to find the strength to draw his bow, and they would have meat.

There was life here.

Rocks, stumps, brambles began to show themselves beneath the snow. The first call of a bird had Dilys falling to his knees in shock.

Snow had melted from their hair, their cloaks, but now it was Dilys's face that was white as ice.

"It's a magpie," Kylar told him, both amused and touched when his stalwart man trembled at the sound. "A song of summer. Rise now. We've left winter behind us."

Soon Cathmor's hooves hit ground, solid and springy, and a single beam of light streamed through trees that were thick with leaves.

"What magic is this?"

"Sun." Kylar closed his hand over the rose brooch. "We found the sun." He dismounted and on legs weak and weary walked slowly to a brilliant splash of color. Here, at the edge of the Forgotten, grew wild roses, red as blood.

He plucked one, breathed in its sweet scent, and said: "Deirdre."

And she, carrying a bucket of melted snow to her garden, swayed. She pressed a hand to her heart as it leaped with joy. "He is home."

She moved through her days now with an easy contentment. Her lover was safe, and the child they'd made warm inside her. The child would be loved, would be cherished. Her heart would never be cold again.

If there was yearning in her, it was natural. But she would rather yearn than have him trapped in her world.

On the night she knew he was safe, she gave a celebration with wine and music and dancing. The story would be told, she decreed, of Kylar of Mrydon. Kylar the brave. And of the faithful Dilys. And all of her people, all who came after, would know of it.

On a silver chain around her neck, she wore his ring.

She hummed as she cleared the paths in her rose garden.

"You sent men out to scout for Dilys," Orna said.

"It is probably too early. But I know he'll start for home as soon as he's able."

"And Prince Kylar. You don't look for him?"

"He doesn't belong here. He has family in his world,

and one day a throne. I found love with him, and it blooms in me—heart and womb. So I wish for him health and happiness. And one day, when these memories have faded from his mind, a woman who loves him as I do."

Orna glanced toward the ice rose, but said nothing of it. "Do you doubt his love for you?"

"No." Her smile was warm and sweet as she said it. "But I've learned, Orna. I believe he was sent to me to teach me what I never knew. Love can't come from cold. If it does, it's selfish, and is not love but simply desire. It gives me such joy to think of him in the sunlight. I don't wish for him as my mother wished for my father, or curse him as my aunt cursed us all. I no longer see my life here as prison or duty. Without it, I would never have known him."

"You're wiser than those who made you."

"I'm luckier," Deirdre corrected, then leaned on her shovel as Phelan rushed into the garden.

"My lady, I've finished my story. Will you hear it?"

"I will. Fetch that shovel by the wall. You can tell me while we work."

"It's a grand story." He ran for the shovel and began heaving snow with great enthusiasm. "The best I've done. And it begins like this: Once, a brave and handsome prince from a far-off land fought a great battle against men who would plunder his kingdom and kill his people. His name was Kylar, and his land was Mrydon."

"It is a good beginning, Phelan the bard."

"Yes, my lady. But it gets better. Kylar the brave defeated the invaders, but, sorely wounded, became lost in the great forest known as the Forgotten."

Deirdre continued to work, smiling as the boy's words brought her memories back so clearly. She remembered her first glimpse of those bold blue eyes, that first foolish brush of lips.

She would give Phelan precious paper and ink to scribe the story. She would bind it herself in leather tanned from deer hide. In this way, she thought with pride, her love would live forever.

One day, their child would read the story, and know what a man his father was.

She cleared the path past jeweled benches, toward the great frozen rose while the boy told his tale and labored tirelessly beside her.

"And the beautiful queen gave him a rose carved on a brooch that he wore pinned over his heart. For days and nights, with his faithful horse, Cathmor, and the valiant and true Dilys, he fought the wild storms, crossed the iced shadows of the Forgotten. It was his lady's love that sustained him."

"You have a romantic heart, young bard."

"It is a *true* story, my lady. I saw it in my head." He continued on, entertaining and delighting her with words of Dilys's stubborn loyalty, of black nights and white days, of a giant tree crashing and leading them toward a stream where water ran over rock like music.

"Sunlight struck the water and made it sparkle like diamonds."

A bit surprised by the description, she glanced toward him. "Do you think sun on water makes diamonds?"

"It makes tiny bright lights, my lady. It dazzles the eye."

Something inside her heart trembled. "Dazzles the eye," she repeated on a whisper. "Yes, I have heard of this."

"And at the edge of the Forgotten grew wild roses, fire-red. The handsome prince plucked one, as he had promised, and when its sweetness surrounded him, he said his lady's name."

"It's a lovely story."

"It is not the end." He all but danced with excitement.

"Tell me the rest, then." She started to smile, to rest on her shovel. Then there came the sound of wild cheering and shouts from without the garden.

"This is the end!" The boy threw his shovel carelessly aside and raced to the archway. "He is come!"

"Who?" she began, but couldn't hear her own voice over the shouts, over the pounding of her blood.

Suddenly the light went brilliant, searing into her eyes so that with a little cry of shock, she threw a hand up to shield them. Wild wind turned to breeze soft as silk. And she heard her name spoken.

Her hand trembled as she lowered it, and her eyes blinked against a light she'd never known. She saw him in the archway of the garden, surrounded by a kind of shimmering halo that gleamed like melted gold.

"Kylar." Her heart, every chamber filled with joy, bounded in her breast. Her shovel clattered on the path as she ran to him.

He caught her up, spinning her in circles as she clung to him. "Oh, my love, my heart. How can this be?" Her tears fell on his neck, her kisses on his face. "You should not be here. You should never have come back. How can I let you go again?"

"Look at me. Sweetheart, look at me." He tipped up her chin. "So there are tears now. I'd hoped there would be. I ask you again. Do you love me, Deirdre?"

"So much I could live on nothing else my whole life. I would not have had to risk yours to come back." She laid her palms on his cheeks. Then her lips trembled open, her fingers shook. "You came back," she whispered.

"I would have crossed hell for you. Perhaps I did."

She closed her eyes. "That light. What is that light?"

"It is the sun. Unveiled. Here, take off your cloak. Feel the sun, Deirdre."

"I'm not cold."

"You'll never be cold again. Open your eyes, my love, and look. Winter is over."

Gripping his hand, she turned to watch the snow melting away, vanishing before her staring eyes. Blackened stalks began to crackle, break out green and at their feet soft, tender blades of grass spread in a shimmering carpet.

"The sky." Dazed, she reached up as if she could touch

it. "It's blue. Like your eyes. Feel it, feel the sun." She held her hands out to cup the warmth.

On a cry of wonder, she knelt, ran her hands over the soft grass, brought her hands to her face to breathe in the scent. Though tears continued to fall, she laughed and held those hands out to him. "Is it grass?"

"It is."

"Oh." She covered her face with her hands again, as if she could drink it. "Such perfume."

He knelt with her, and would remember, he knew, the rapture on her face the first time she touched a simple blade of grass. "Your roses are blooming, my lady."

Speechless, she watched buds spear, blooms unfold. Yellows, pinks, reds, whites in petals that flowed from bud to flower, and flowers so heavy they bent the graceful green branches. The fragrance all but made her drunk.

"Roses." Her voice quivered as she reached out to touch, felt the silky texture. "Flowers." And buried her face in blooms.

She squealed like a girl when a butterfly fluttered by her face and landed on a tender bud to drink.

"Oh!" There was so much, almost too much, and she was dizzy from it. "See how it moves! It's so beautiful."

In turn, she tipped her face back and drank in the sunlight.

"What is that across the blue of the sky? That curve of colors?"

"It's a rainbow." Watching her was like watching something be born. And once again, he thought, she humbled him. "Your first rainbow, my love."

"It's lovelier than in the books. In them it seemed false and impossible. But it's soft and it's real."

"I brought you a gift."

"You brought me summer," she murmured.

"And this." He snapped his fingers, and through the arch, down the path raced a fat brown puppy. Barking cheerfully, it leaped into Deirdre's lap. "His name is Griffen."

Drowned in emotion, she cradled the pup as she might a child, pressed her face into its warm fur. She felt its heartbeat, and the quick, wet lash of its tongue on her cheek.

"I'm sorry," she managed, and broke down and sobbed.

"Weep, then." Kylar bent to touch his lips to her hair. "As long as it's for joy."

"How can this be? How can you bring me so much? I turned you away, without love."

"No, you let me go, with love. It took me time to understand that—and you. To understand what it cost you. There would have been no summer if I hadn't left you, and returned."

He lifted her damp face now, and the puppy wiggled free and began to race joyfully through the garden. "Is that not so?"

"It is so. Only the greatest and truest love, freely given, could break the spell and turn away winter."

"I knew. When I plucked the rose, I understood. I watched summer bloom. It came with me through the forest. As I rode, the trees behind me went into leaf, brooks and streams sprang free of ice. With every mile I put behind me, every mile I came closer to you, the world awoke. Others will come tomorrow. I couldn't wait."

"But how? How did you come back so quickly?"

"My land is only a day's journey from here. It was magic that kept you hidden. It's love that frees you."

"It's more." Phelan wiggled his way through the crowd of people who gathered in the archway. He gave a cry of delight as the pup leaped at him. "It is truth," he began, "and sacrifice and honor. All these tied by love are stronger than a shield of ice and break the spell of the winter rose. When summer comes to Rose Castle, the Isle of Winter becomes the Isle of Flowers and the Sea of Ice becomes the Sea of Hope. And here, the good queen gives hand and heart to her valiant prince."

"It is a good ending," Kylar commented. "But perhaps

you would wait until I ask the good queen for her hand and her heart."

She dashed tears from her cheeks. Her people, her love, would not see her weep at such a time. "You have my heart already."

"Then give me your hand. Be my wife."

She put her hand in his, but because she must be a queen, turned first to her people. "You are witness. I pledge myself in love and in marriage, for a lifetime, to Kylar, prince of Mrydon. He will be your king, and to him you will give your service, your respect, and your loyalty. From this day, his people will be your brothers and your sisters. In time, our lands will be one land."

She let them cheer, let his name ring out along with hers into the wondrous blue bowl of sky. And her hand was warm in Kylar's.

"Prepare a feast of celebration and thanks, and make ourselves ready to welcome the guests that come on the morrow. Leave us now, for I need a moment with my betrothed. Take the pup to the kitchen, Phelan, and see that he is well fed. Keep him for me."

"Yes, my lady."

"His name is Griffen." Her gaze met Orna's, and smiled as her people left her alone with her prince. "There is one last thing to be done."

She walked with him down the path to where the reddest roses bloomed on the tallest bush under thinning ice. Without a thought, she plunged her hand through it, and the shield shattered like glass. She picked the first rose of her life, offered it to him.

"I've accepted you as queen. That is duty. Now I give myself to you as a woman. This is for love. You brought light to my world. You freed my heart. Now and forever, that heart is yours."

She started to kneel, and he stopped her. "You won't kneel to me."

Her brows lifted, and command once again cloaked her. "I am queen of this place. I do as I wish." She knelt. "I am yours, queen and woman. From this hour, this day will be known and celebrated as Prince Kylar's Return."

With a gleam in his eye, he knelt as well, and made her lips twitch. "You will be a willful wife."

"This is truth."

"I would not have it otherwise. Kiss me, Deirdre the fair."

She put a hand on his chest. "First, I have a gift for you."

"It can wait. I lived on dreams of your kisses for days in the cold."

"This gift can't wait. Kylar, I have your child in me. A child made from love and warmth."

The hand that had touched her face slid bonelessly to her shoulder. "A child?"

"We've made life between us. A miracle, beyond magic."

"Our child." His palm spread over her belly, rested there as his lips took hers.

"It pleases you?"

For an answer he leaped up, hoisted her high until her laughter rang out. She threw her arms toward the sky, toward the sun, the sky, the rainbow.

And the roses grew and bloomed until branches and flowers reached over the garden wall, tumbled down, and filled the air with the promise of summer.

The Rose and the Sword

❧

Jill Gregory

*To my dear and extraordinary friend Karen Katz,
with love and friendship always*

1

"You sent for me, Your Highness?"

Smiling, Brittany curtseyed before Queen Elysia and waited quietly in the queen's drafty bedchamber for the snowy-haired woman wrapped in ermine robes to reply.

Outside the castle walls, in the small kingdom of Strathbury, fat snowflakes tumbled from a leaden winter sky, and the fields and hills were wrapped in gauzy layers of snow every bit as thick and white as the ermine of the queen's robes. Inside, the flickering candles illuminated the chamber's velvet bed hangings, the rich tapestries, the heavy, gilt-trimmed furnishings as Brittany shivered in her green wool gown and awaited the queen's bidding.

It was strange the way Elysia was staring at her, almost as if she had never seen her before—which was ridiculous, since Brittany had been her ward ever since she could remember. But Queen Elysia's kindly old eyes were fixed on her unblinkingly, intensely, as if she was memorizing the face of the girl she had known for nearly twenty years.

"Your Highness, are you well?" Brittany asked uncertainly, as the woman suddenly lifted a hand to her brow and closed her eyes as if she were in pain. "How can I help you?" Without waiting for a formal invitation, Brittany hurried forward.

Queen Elysia took a deep, shuddering breath and clasped the hand of the girl who sank down upon the edge of her bed. "Ah, child, do not fear for me. I am in pain, yes, but it is not a physical ailment. My heart grieves because the time has come for me to tell you something, something that will change our lives forever. Something that will take you away from me."

"Take me away from you? Oh, Your Highness, no! Please, no. Whatever I have done, I will fix. If I have offended, please allow me to—"

"Child, child, you have done nothing—nothing but earn my love and respect, my admiration." The queen smiled at her through a glimmer of tears that made her faded blue eyes appear the color of the winter sky. "You have been an exceptional ward. A handful, perhaps, but a lovely handful. I care for you, child, as if you were my own daughter. If it were up to me, I would have you with me always, safe and by my side. But that is impossible. I waited as long as I could to tell you the truth, but now your twentieth birthday will arrive in only a few days, and I fear I may have delayed too long. There isn't much time."

Brittany stared at her in complete confusion. It was unlike her to be lacking in either words or comprehension. The petite, dainty young woman with the smooth, honey-colored hair, delicate features, and wide-set green eyes that were flecked with gold had the spirit of an imp and the courage of a soldier. She had been raised at the queen's side as a lady, but from the time she was a girl she had been taught to ride, to shoot an arrow, and to wield a sword with the skill of a man. Brittany had never understood why the queen had allowed her man-at-arms to train her in these things, but she hadn't questioned it because she'd craved the challenge. She was a girl who loved to run, loved to race her horse through the wood and jump the streams that meandered behind the castle. There was no tree in the kingdom she hadn't climbed, no flower she hadn't gathered, and no person, high- or low-born, in the land whom she did not know by name and who did not bow or curtsey before her, out of respect for the beautiful girl whose laughter made even the sourest old man smile.

But now the young woman who was loved throughout the tiny kingdom felt her heart breaking into a thousand pieces. She was to be sent away! *Why?* a voice shrieked in her head.

"I don't understand." Brittany moistened her lips. The sad words and grave expression upon her guardian's face filled her with foreboding. "I don't wish to leave. Not you, not Strathbury. If I haven't displeased you, then why must I go? I wish . . . I wish to stay with you always!"

"If only you could, my child." Queen Elysia shook her head. "But this castle will hold no safety for you, not after your twentieth birthday has passed. The danger draws near. Every moment only brings it closer. To escape, you must go, you must find your betrothed and—"

"My betrothed!"

Shocked, Brittany stared at the queen, wondering if she had lost her senses. Then, suddenly, she understood, and she laughed aloud with relief.

"I don't have a betrothed, Your Highness." She couldn't contain a smile. "As you well know. Is that what this is all about? You wish to send me away so that I can find a husband?"

"Not just any husband, child. The one who is pledged to you. The one to whom *you* are pledged, have been pledged for all these past years. Oh, dear." Elysia's thin lips trembled. "I never should have delayed this long. But I . . . I wanted to keep you here with me for as long as possible. I didn't want this day, this moment, ever to come."

The ground seemed to shift beneath Brittany's feet. Nothing the queen was saying to her made any sense. But it filled her with dismay. If she was pledged to some man—had been pledged all her life—why was she only just learning of it? Why had she been allowed to dance at court festivities with handsome knights and dashing noblemen? Why had she been allowed to fall in and out of love half a dozen times, allowed to hope and to dream of one day finding her one true forever love?

Why hadn't anyone ever told her she'd been promised—and to *whom*? she wondered in mounting horror. A vision of a stout, ugly toad of a duke suddenly filled her mind, and she choked back panic.

It dawned on her that everything she knew about her life and her past now seemed to be unraveling. From the time she was a little girl, she'd been told that her parents had been well born, that her mother had died giving birth to a babe when Brittany was not yet two years old, that her father shortly after had died of a fever and she'd been sent to live with Queen Elysia because the queen was a cousin to Brittany's mother, and childless, and kind as could be.

No one had told her about any danger, about ever having to leave this castle—or about any "betrothed."

"I am trying to understand," she told the queen in a voice that trembled a little, though she strove for calm. "But your words are a riddle to me, Your Highness. I beg you, if you love me, explain what all this means. And tell me why I have never before heard a word about this man to whom I am supposedly betrothed."

"It was a secret, child. A secret I have kept for eighteen long years, in order to protect you. You could not know the truth. But now it is time. I must tell you all of it, so that you are prepared. The time is short, because I delayed, dreading this day of telling you what lies ahead." The queen's hands trembled upon the bedcoverings. "But you have a right to know, child. A right to the life that was stolen from you—and a right to be warned about the danger that will come. And once you know, you must leave. In the morning, at first light."

"So soon?" Brittany gasped. "I think . . . you had best tell me, Your Highness. Why must I go, and what is this danger?"

"You are more than what you know, my dear child. More even than the beautiful and brave young woman we have all come to love. You are royal, Brittany, every bit as royal as I, and more than that, you are powerful. Very powerful. Have you never felt it? Have you never felt the power deep inside your blood?"

Power? Brittany sat very still. Was that what it was? Power? Sometimes, at odd moments, there would come a chill. A chill that pervaded her skin and made her shiver, yet at the same time her blood would seem to heat and tingle. She would sense something, something in herself that was not quite of herself. She would feel that there was something she must do, something she would do, but then . . . the feeling would fade as quickly as it had come. Was that it—was that the power?

"I don't know," she said quietly, while her thoughts raced. She was royal and she had power. How could this be?

"Your Highness, perhaps it would be best if you tell me more, tell me all of it. For example, this power—what does it do?"

"Would that I could tell you, child." The queen sighed. "I only know that it is in you, and that it must be very strong, very potent. Otherwise, Darius would not have tried to kill you along with the other members of your family."

"Darius!" Now confusion and the first inkling of fear settled over her. Darius was a wizard, the most powerful wizard of the times, and he ruled the land of Palladrin, a vast kingdom far greater and wealthier than Strathbury. Stories of Darius's cruelty and his seemingly limitless powers terrorized citizens of every land, and his name was mentioned to children as the source of ultimate evil.

"Darius . . . killed my family? Are you saying that my mother did not die in childbirth and my father of a fever?"

Brittany jumped up, no longer able to sit calmly upon the bed. She paced back and forth around the chamber, turmoil churning within her, and questions swirling through her brain, even though she tried to subdue the panic inside her. If she was going to have an enemy, why did it have to be Darius? Why not merely a dragon, or a troll, or some wild outlaw scoundrel? Why did it have to be Darius the Wizard, who was rumored to be able to turn an oak tree into an acorn with the flick of a finger?

"Your Highness, I beg you—tell me all of it. Tell me at once. I must know the entire truth or I shall go mad."

With sorrow and quiet understanding the queen studied the distraught girl pacing her chamber. "Come, my child. Seat yourself upon my gilded chair as befits a princess, and I will tell you. Listen carefully, though, Brittany, for there is not much time. Though what I am going to say will shock you, you must gather your wits and your resolve. My men will escort you upon your journey at first light—every moment of every day will be vital if you are to succeed. And," she added, her voice breaking, "if you are to survive."

The girl slipped into the golden chair facing the bed, her heart pounding. "I'm ready," she whispered, grateful that her voice sounded steadier than she felt.

The queen told her then, told her that even her name was not her own. Her real name was Britta, and she was the princess of Palladrin.

She was the youngest daughter of the royal family, all of whom had been murdered on Darius's orders when he came to power: her mother, Queen Alvina, her father, King Raulf, and her brother, Dugal, seven years old when he was slain.

"And you, child, were a babe of not yet two winters. But your mother somehow managed to save you and you were smuggled to safety. Another child, one from the village who had died of the fever, was substituted and shown to Darius with a blade through its heart."

Brittany gasped, all the color fading from her face. The tale seemed wild, impossible, but somehow, deep inside, she felt that it was all too true.

"That is why," the queen continued heavily, "all the world believes that the last of your royal line is dead. That there is no longer any threat to Darius. That, and the spell that your mother cast upon you, to shield you."

"What . . . kind of spell?" Brittany asked, her throat dry.

"One that hid you in a fairy mist, protected from Darius's Sight. A spell that would not allow his evil eye to see or to sense your presence in the land of the living." A smile trembled across Elysia's lips. "And it has worked. If it had not, Darius and his soldiers would have found you. And killed you," she added with a shudder.

"How is it that my mother came by such power? It must be very great to deceive a wizard of Darius's skill."

The queen nodded. "Indeed, yes. You and your mother are descended from the great sorcerer Zared."

"Zared!" All the world knew of Zared the Powerful, the greatest sorcerer since Merlin himself. His powers were said to have surpassed even those of Darius.

"He is your grandsire, child—your mother's father. And he created the Rose Scepter for your mother and for you, and for all future generations of women in his line. There is a power in it that can be used only by the women descended from Zared. A power that you must claim now and use to unleash your own magic. Your mother used the Rose Scepter to save you—to conjure up a spell powerful enough to protect you from Darius's Sight for all these many years. But the spell was conjured with only enough magic to last until your twentieth birthday—on that day, the fairy mist will fade as suddenly as morning dew, and Darius will be able to sense your presence. He will know that you live."

She hesitated, her face turning pale, but before she

could say the final words, Brittany said them for her.

"And he will try to destroy me."

A silence fell, a silence so complete that Brittany was sure she could hear the snowfakes falling outside the window.

"Yes, dear child," the queen replied at last. "But he will not succeed—not if you can do two things. These two things will enable you to fight Darius—and win."

"I'm listening." The girl swallowed, trying to take in everything she'd been told, to comprehend that her true past and her true identity were far different from what she'd always believed, that she was someone whom the wizard Darius, with all his power and might, would want to seek out and destroy. "What must I do?"

"There is a legend, child, an ancient legend of Palladrin that foretold all of the events I have related to you. Even that of Darius coming to power, slaughtering your family, and taking the kingdom that was theirs—and that is now rightfully yours. According to the legend, the Rose and the Sword, raised together, can defeat Darius, or any evil that threatens the land of Palladrin."

"The Rose and the Sword? What does that mean?" Brittany cried, desperate for a solution, for something she could do to stop the series of events that she felt even now spinning into motion.

"The Rose Scepter—it is yours. You must find it. No one knows where it is, probably not even Darius—it was hidden at the same time you were smuggled out of your castle. But the scepter alone will not defeat him. For that you need your betrothed."

Her betrothed again. "Why do I need him? And who *is* he?"

She tried to banish the image of the old toad of a duke from her mind, and failed. "I think I would prefer to take my chances with Darius myself, rather than align myself with some stranger. I have no desire to marry a man I don't even know and who—"

"You are pledged to him, child, and he to you. Because of the legend of the Rose and the Sword."

"Well, it is up to me to find the Rose, but what is this Sword, Your Highness? Many men have swords, and I don't see why it makes any difference—"

"If you are going to defeat Darius and rule your people, child, you need to learn patience and you need to listen," the queen said, meeting the girl's gaze with a quelling glance. "I know this is all a shock to you, but you must let me finish and then you will see. Contain your impatience, and your ideals. They are well and good, and they become you, Brittany—I mean Britta," she corrected herself grimly—"but you would also do well to learn to subdue your temper, your youthful impatience, and learn to think like the ruler you will become. If you find the Rose Scepter, great power will be yours. You must learn to wield it wisely and well—with a cool head, not a hot one."

Chastened, Brittany took a deep breath. What she wanted to do was to scream, to run out of the castle and race through the woods, losing herself in the darkness and the deep, drifting snow and the cold of the night. To leave behind this wretched tale, this frightening truth about who she was and what she must do.

But she couldn't. She had to face it, accept it. And deal with it. She forced herself to remain still, to keep a calm facade, and to heed the words of Elysia, remembering that there was little time.

"The Sword in the legend is that of the family of Marric. It is a jeweled sword from the time of Arthur, a sword blessed by Merlin himself, that is endowed with keen powers when it is raised against that which is evil. It was foretold that when the Rose and the Sword are raised together against evil, their magic will be powerful indeed—powerful enough to defeat the enemies of Palladrin. Such a joining of forces was foreseen long ago as the only way to defeat Darius, and that is why, long before the threat became real, you were pledged to the young prince of

Marric and he to you. You were only a child in swaddling clothes at the time, and he was a boy of six. But the promise made then that you would be joined in marriage, is binding as long as you both shall live. You are bound by honor to marry him—not only to fulfill the pledge between your families but to save yourself and your kingdom."

Kingdom. I have a kingdom. Brittany swallowed as the enormity of what lay ahead of her began to sink in.

"This prince of Marric, does he have a name?" she asked.

"His name is Lucius of Marric. I sent Sir Richmond in search of him more than a fortnight ago, and he has returned after searching near and far. Prince Lucius is in Gullvantium—two days' journey from here. You will leave at dawn, and you must find him, my child. Find him and call upon him to fulfill his pledge, to aid you and protect you as you try to find the Rose Scepter—and in the battle that will come between you and Darius."

Brittany closed her eyes. *The battle that will come between you and Darius.* Something shook her at these words—that feeling came over her again, sharper than ever before. A burning, icy feeling, and for a moment she heard wind whooshing through her ears. A faraway wind. For an instant she couldn't breathe; the wind seemed to be eating all of the air in her lungs.

The moment passed. Her head ached, but nothing else remained.

"What is it, child?" The queen's face was filled with concern. "You are whiter than my robes. Are you faint?"

"No, no, Your Highness, only . . . stunned by all you have told me." But Brittany knew, just as she knew that the queen's words were the truth, that what she had just felt was a taste of the magic and the power and the evil before her. She didn't know what it meant, or where it would lead. She knew only that never before had she experienced such a sensation.

Of course, never before had she been so near to her twentieth birthday.

This might be only the beginning of the changes that would come, of what she must face, learn, use. Brittany took a deep breath. A short time ago, she had been sewing in her own candlelit chamber, enjoying conversation with the queen's ladies-in-waiting, sipping spiced wine. Now her entire life had been turned upside down, and she was contemplating a journey, a quest, a marriage.

And a battle.

"How will I convince him—Prince Lucius—that I am who I say I am? He thinks I'm dead, does he not?"

The queen beckoned her forward, and Brittany returned to kneel at the bedside of the old woman who had been her gentle guardian and the closest to a mother that she could remember. "The birthmark," the queen said. She touched a spindly finger to Brittany's shoulder. "Here, I believe?"

Mute with wonder, the girl nodded. Never before had it occurred to her—the birthmark in the shape of a rose upon her right shoulder. She'd never seen any significance in it before. But now . . .

"That is your proof. Your heritage. The mark of the Rose. Lucius will believe. And he will help you, child." She clasped the girl's slender fingers in her own and clung to them a moment, gazing into Brittany's face as if she was indeed memorizing every lovely, delicate feature.

"May the angels keep you safe," she whispered. "May you win all that is yours."

She was trembling all over, and Brittany saw with a surge of worry that Elysia looked wearier and older and more fragile than she had ever looked before.

"Sleep now, Your Highness. I will ready myself for the journey and come to you in the morning before I leave."

The woman nodded. "You are brave, Britta. Brave and beautiful and good. You will meet this challenge. With Prince Lucius's help, you will conquer Darius."

With Prince Lucius's help. Those words echoed in Brittany's ears as she hurried along the chilly stone corridor toward her own chamber.

Her heart was heavy. Her throat was dry. How she wished that this was only a dream, that she could remain here in Strathbury forever, wait for her one true love to find her, and live in peace among the good people she had always known.

But it was not to be. Her real family had been slaughtered. Slaughtered by a great wizard—who would be hunting for her soon. And she would need all her wits if she was going to survive.

Not only to survive, she told herself with determination and a sudden sharp flick of anger, but to take back what Darius had stolen. The kingdom for which her family had been murdered.

I'll need more than my wits, she thought, as she descended a narrow stair lit by torches and then rounded the corner to her own chamber. *And more than mere courage and determination. I'll need the help of that man. My betrothed.*

She drew a ragged breath. She had always thought she would marry for love. A forever love. The kind Queen Elysia had had with her husband, Coll, all the years they were wed, until he died, a year before Brittany had come to Strathbury.

Brittany had grown up on stories of how they'd met, courted, wed. Stories of the strength of their love and the gentle passion that flared between them always.

She had wanted the same kind of love for herself, a love that was true and deep and lasting. But now her dreams would have to be put aside.

Toad or no, it seemed she would need Prince Lucius's help. *Prince Lucius of Marric.* Her betrothed.

She shook her head as she entered her chamber and hastily began to gather what she would need for the journey.

If the Rose and the Sword together could save Palladrin

from Darius's rule, then together they would be.

Tomorrow she would set out for Gullvantium and find her betrothed.

And marry him—even if he was a toad.

2

"ANOTHER JUG OF wine, Ula!" Lucius of Marric called to the lushly endowed serving wench bestowing kisses upon all the men at the Bones and Blood Inn as she made her way through the room.

"Make that two jugs," he added, laughing, and returned his attention to Drusy, sprawled in his lap, then forgot about his thirst as he drank in the redheaded serving girl's lusty kisses.

"Let's go upstairs, me lord," she suggested, her hands sliding all over him despite the crowded room. Of course, the air was so thick with woodsmoke, chances were no one could see, but Lucius only chuckled, yanked her closer, and kissed her some more. He would bed her before the night was through, but he wasn't drunk enough yet. Not nearly enough. He needed more wine, more merriment, maybe even a good fight—and then the girl. Then perhaps, when it was done with and his brain and body were sated, perhaps he would sleep . . .

And know a few hours of peace.

Ula brought the wine, and he shared the jug with Drusy while she brazenly jiggled her wares at him, teasing him into going up the stairs to the room with the rough hay mattress that smelled of a goat. Lucius never even noticed the inn door swing open, never saw the girl who slipped inside, bundled up to her neck in a blue woolen cloak, her cheeks flushed from the cold. He did glance up in time to see the gruff, bowlegged old soldier who stepped in after her, though, and his eyes narrowed in the firelight from the roaring hearth.

That the man was a soldier he had no doubt. Despite his plain dark cloak and filthy boots, Lucius would have wagered a chest of coins that there was chain mail beneath the deceptively simple garments. He hadn't been away from battle so long that he didn't recognize a trained soldier when he saw one. And seeing one here, in an inn as coarse and disreputable as the Bones and Blood, not exactly known for its high company, was almost as startling as seeing . . . well, as seeing a girl like the one who stood talking earnestly with the soldier in a place as low as this.

She was small and lovely. He could almost hear the soft murmur of her voice, but not her words. She didn't belong here, in this wild, smoky place amid the din of drunken men and the shrieking laughter of the serving women and the stench of sweat and ale and burnt meat.

What the devil were the two of them doing here? Lucius wondered sharply, then realized that he must not yet have consumed enough wine, if he was puzzling over such things. They didn't concern him. Nothing concerned him. Not anymore.

He wrapped a muscular arm around Drusy and laughed as he reached for the second jug of wine, while the girl squealed and giggled and squirmed on his lap.

In the corner of the inn near the door, Brittany spoke

forcefully to Sir Richmond, Queen Elysia's man-at-arms.

"Go. Leave me now. Your duty is done."

"I will not leave you in a place like this, my lady. With men like this . . ." The old soldier glared at the noise and commotion all around, at the men arguing loudly, cursing, shoving against one another at the far end of the room, perilously close to the roaring hearthfire, while others tipped ale tankards or jugs of wine and sang at the top of their lungs, and brazen serving women bustled to and fro, waggling their hips. Richmond's glance included the tall, dark-haired man with a day's growth of beard upon his swarthy face, the man seated on the bench in the center of the room, practically undressing the red-haired wench in his lap.

"Your men confirmed that that is indeed Prince Lucius, did they not?" Brittany asked, trying to sound calm, though she was praying that there was some terrible mistake. That man, that giant handsome man who was practically swallowing the serving maid whole, he could not . . . could not be her betrothed. *Could he?*

Please, she prayed silently as she stared at that starkly handsome face, *I would so much rather have a toad.*

The man across the room was the opposite of a toad. He looked tough and dangerous and entirely unsuitable to be anybody's husband. He looked like an outlaw, she thought with a shock. And not a very pleasant one. And the way he was fondling that woman . . .

Her stomach felt queasy. It had been hours since she'd eaten even a morsel of food, and she and the small troop of soldiers Elysia had sent with her had been traveling for nearly two days. She was sore, stiff, and exhausted, and her stomach had been growling in a most unladylike manner.

Worst of all, the day after tomorrow was her birthday and after that—well, she didn't know what would happen after that, but it seemed likely that Darius might well get some inkling that she was alive. And then—

Then she would need a protector. Someone to help her

find the Rose Scepter, someone to lift the Sword of Marric on her behalf.

But not him, she thought desperately. *Oh, please, don't let it be him.*

Yet even as she tore her gaze away from the black-haired man in the dark tunic and fixed it once more upon Sir Richmond's grim face, her heart sank. She saw the truth in the soldier's eyes even before he answered her.

"They did confirm it, my lady. That is Prince Lucius. May the heavens help you."

May they indeed, Brittany thought with a gulp as her stomach roiled again. Yet she spoke with firm resolve. "Then all will be well. He is pledged to me, and I have every confidence that he will keep that pledge. Please leave me so that I may . . . approach him," she finished.

"I prefer to stay and ensure your safety, my lady. I know that Queen Elysia would wish—"

"She would wish you to obey me." Brittany spoke quietly, but there was steel beneath the gentle tone. The knight stared down into those flashing green-gold eyes for a moment, saw the determination tightening the delicate features, then slowly nodded with respect.

"As you wish," he sighed.

"You and your men may break your camp and return to Strathbury at first light."

"Not before I have spoken with you again and assured myself that you're under the prince's protection," he countered swiftly.

Despite her determination, Brittany nodded. She was grateful for his concern. But she was concerned enough for both of them.

She wasn't at all convinced that the man on the bench kissing that woman and drinking wine as if his life depended upon it would actually agree to help her.

Or be *able* to help her. Why, he could be intoxicated for days. And they didn't have much time before Darius might be swooping down upon them like a great bloody-fanged dragon.

"I will see you on the morrow, Sir Richmond. Have you obtained lodging for me in this . . . place?"

"Yes, my lady. Such as it is."

"Then leave me now. The hour is growing late and I must speak with my betro—, I mean, with Prince Lucius. Now. Alone."

Gravely, the knight took her gloved hand, kissed it, then turned and marched out of the inn. A great gust of wintry wind swept in as the door banged shut behind him, and the firelight flickered eerily across the walls and the earthen floor.

It glowed on the dark face of the man on the bench and made him look as forbidding and dangerous as the devil himself.

But there was no time to waste, Brittany reminded herself, and taking a deep breath, she started toward him. Just as she did so, he swept the woman on his lap into his arms and arose from the bench with a great roar of laughter.

"Come along, then, wench, up the stairs with you. It is time for bed," he said with a wide, drunken grin.

"Prince Lucius," Brittany murmured quickly, stepping directly into his path. "Please wait . . . I must speak with you."

He halted, the serving girl clamped easily in his arms, her mouth dropping as she gaped at Brittany, who had planted herself between them and the stairway. The tall man with the close-cropped black hair and the sharply handsome features didn't gape, but he did frown at her as if her intrusion was most unwelcome, his dark gray eyes, the color of a stormy sea, piercing her.

"Do I know you?" he asked curtly.

"No . . . not exactly. That is, we have met before . . . but it was long ago. Very long ago . . . much too long for you to, er, remember," she finished lamely.

By the heavens, she was babbling. She never babbled. Not a good beginning, not at all.

Why couldn't he be a toad? Brittany thought. Then she

straightened her spine, remembering her family whom she'd never known, how they'd been slaughtered by Darius. Remembering the quest for the Rose Scepter and the great danger ahead.

"My business with you is urgent," she told him, her chin lifting in a gesture of stubbornness and pride. "We must speak privately—at once."

"I'm busy."

The serving wench in his arms threw back her head and laughed.

"This is more important." Brittany drew herself up to her full height, which fell just short of his powerful shoulders. She ignored the woman and fastened her gaze on the man looming before her.

Lucius of Marric stared at her, a good, long stare of the sort that had been known to shake the confidence of seasoned warriors. The woman blocking his path was a petite beauty wrapped up to her long, lovely neck in a blue woolen cloak. The hood was thrown back, however, revealing masses of hair the color of wild honey, hair that tumbled down in a cascade of curls around a delicate face of astonishing beauty. Fiery green-gold eyes regarded him from beneath winged brows. Her features were exquisitely chiseled, her mouth looked soft and full and eminently kissable. But it was not any of that which made his stomach tighten, made his senses suddenly come alert, despite the effects of the wine heating his blood. It was something in her bearing—a tension, a determination—and something even more in those brilliant eyes. Intelligence, spirit, and purpose glowed in them. Along with just a trace of fear.

Perhaps it was the glimmer of fear that he perceived in their depths that decided him. He set Drusy down, ignoring her loud protests, and gave the honey-haired girl his full attention.

"Urgent, you say? Somehow I doubt it. But come, be seated, and tell me your tale. If it's a champion you seek, however, you've come to the wrong place—and the wrong man. We who favor the Bones and Blood serve only ourselves."

Brittany peered swiftly around the dark, noisy room, taking in the drunken, brutish men who filled the place, then returned her gaze to the tall, midnight-haired man regarding her through those shrewd gray eyes, eyes that held no softness, only an icy calm. And something more— a deep, long-held sorrow that even the wine could not dull, she realized suddenly.

If he thought to convince her that he was just like the others here, aimless and coarse and indifferent, he had failed. He was not like them—she could see that much at once. She wondered suddenly if his words to the contrary were meant to convince her—or himself.

"Don't listen to her now. Come upstairs with me!" the serving wench shrieked, hanging on to his powerful arm.

He flicked her off with no more than a glance. "Leave us."

"But—"

"Leave us." The ice in his tone stilled her shrill protests, and she dropped his arm, stepped back, and whirled on Brittany. For a moment Brittany thought the woman would strike her, but even as the serving girl clenched her hand into a fist and let out a hissing oath, Lucius of Marric gave her a swat on the bottom that sent her staggering for several paces.

"Bring more wine, Drusy," he said lazily, his gaze still fixed on Brittany's drawn face. "And don't fret. I'll be finished with her soon enough, and then you and I will have our pleasure."

"Ah, fine, then." The woman tossed her head and planted her hands on her hips. "I'll hold you to that, don't think I won't." With one last glare in Brittany's direction, she flounced off.

Lucius gazed into Brittany's face for one more moment, then seized her arm and began steering her toward a low

bench and table in the darkest corner of the inn, far from
the fire, far from the center of the noise and the other
patrons.

"This way."

3

No one paid any attention to them as they made their way through the thick smoke, the games of dice, and shouting matches. A man with a full black beard yelled something and shoved another man, who would have barreled right into Brittany, but Lucius thrust himself in front of her and grabbed hold of the man first, sending him reeling in the opposite direction.

"Thank you," she said quietly as she hurried past the fracas, but Lucius only clenched his jaw and made no reply.

By the time they reached the bench, Brittany was more than happy to sink down on it. Her stomach was rumbling in earnest now, and she was grateful that the din in the inn would prevent her companion from hearing it. But she was beginning to feel weak from lack of food, and as Drusy stalked over and banged a jug of wine onto the table, she quickly said, "Kindly bring bread and meat as well."

"All we have is boiled mutton," the girl retorted, but Brittany nodded.

"That will do."

There was no mistaking the soft elegance of her speech, nor the subtle air of command, which Drusy obviously resented, but felt compelled to obey.

As Drusy moved away, Lucius gave his companion a hard, curious look.

"You're going to have to sup alone, my lady," he told her shortly. "I won't be staying long enough to join you. I have business to attend to—upstairs." The drunken grin returned. It was clear he meant his business with Drusy. "Say what is so urgent and be done with it."

"I fear it won't be that easy to rid yourself of me, Prince Lucius."

His eyes narrowed. "Lucius will do." He took a swig of the wine, without inquiring if she wanted any. "How do you know who I am?" he asked with a scowl.

"Perhaps you ought to ask who I am," she countered.

His gaze swept over her once more, then returned to the jug of wine. "It doesn't matter," he said with a shrug. "Whatever you want, I'm not interested and I can't help you." He took another long, noisy gulp of the wine.

"I am your betrothed," Brittany said softly.

At that, Lucius of Marric choked on his mouthful of wine. Great coughs wracked him. He set the jug on the table with a thump as he bent over, gasping.

Brittany couldn't sit idly by and watch this. Without even thinking she jumped up and began pounding him on the back. "I probably should have broken it to you more gently. It's most awkward, I know. And highly unusual. I wish you would stop choking," she said sharply, in growing concern, as his coughs grew more violent. Her blows upon that broad, strong back became more rapid and fierce. "This usually helps. Samu the juggler did this for me once when I sneaked into the kitchen in the dead of night and choked on a sip of warm mead. I couldn't sleep, you see, because . . . ooooh!"

She gasped as his hand closed tightly around her arm and he yanked her around and onto the bench beside him so roughly that she cried out. Though she tried to pull free, she couldn't. His grip was like iron. Seated this close to him, so close she could see the dangerous-looking black flecks in his intense gray eyes, a strange dizziness washed over her.

At least he's stopped coughing, she thought as she tried to keep breathing herself. Being so close to him was unsettling, to say the least. A powerful jolt of heat ran through her, locking her breath in her chest. She couldn't tear her gaze from that darkly handsome and oh-so-furious face.

"What . . . did you say?" he managed to choke out, his voice low and raw, his grip on her wrist so tight she had to fight to keep from wincing.

"I said that I am your betrothed. And kindly let go of my wrist before you break it. Oooh, *thank you*."

He released her abruptly, and she jerked her arm away and began to rub her bruised flesh. From the expression in his eyes, she could see that he hadn't realized how tightly he was holding her. He looked like a man in shock, a man who had just jumped into an icy river and could barely stay afloat in the shock of the cold.

He gave his head a shake and leaned toward her so that their noses were almost touching. "No," he said forcefully, his eyes like flint. "You're lying."

"I do not lie. I wish I were. I mean, I wish it was not true. I wish none of it was true." Brittany took a deep breath. She was babbling again. She never babbled. What cruel joke was this that this man whom she was bound to marry should have this effect on her, to make her chatter like a magpie.

"My name is Britta. Britta of Palladrin," she continued in a low whisper, glancing around uneasily. To her relief, no one appeared to be listening. No one except Lucius, who was frozen before her, an expression of utmost horror upon his face.

"When you were six years old and I was not yet two, our families pledged us to one anoth—"

"I know what my family did when I was six," he hissed, his hands shooting out and grasping her by the shoulders. "But you're dead. That is . . . *she's* dead. You're no more Princess Britta than I'm Arthur of Britain!"

"Everyone thinks I'm dead—but they'll know the truth soon enough if you don't keep your voice down," Brittany retorted, her heart thudding. This wasn't going well. Lucius of Marric wasn't exactly getting down on one knee and promising to serve her, protect her, and marry her. He looked like he wanted to strangle her.

"I am alive, but perhaps not for long unless you help me. Which you will do, I trust," she added hastily, her tone brisk as she tried to sound expectant and far more confident than she felt. "We must be married at once and you must help me to defeat Dar—"

"Hold on. Don't say another word. I know how to settle this."

He stood up, seized her arm, and dragged her away from the bench, even as Drusy appeared with a tray of food.

"Wait! Where are you—aaarrgggh!" The serving wench's shriek echoed as Lucius hauled Brittany up the stairs of the inn, ignoring her protests and futile attempts to pull free.

"What are you *doing*? I am not going upstairs with you. Let me go at once! I wish to eat my boiled mutton and . . . and this is most uncalled for. Not to mention improper. We . . . we are not married . . . not yet, and . . ."

Goodness, Brittany thought in panic as Lucius didn't even slow his pace. *He doesn't intend to claim his husbandly rights, does he? We have not yet been wed. Only pledged.* Apprehension rushed through her, and she tried again to get him to release her. But no matter how im-

peratively she flung orders at him, he paid no heed and
continued to pull her helplessly up the stairs as if she
hadn't spoken. Her strength was no match for his, and she
could do nothing but be borne along, down a dingy corridor lit by a single candle. The hallway smelled repulsive,
of spilled ale and rotting wood, but at last they reached a
tiny chamber at the end of it.

Lucius dragged her inside and kicked the door shut.

Several candles illuminated a dank little room, with few
furnishings aside from a lumpy bed covered by a moth-
eaten woolen blanket and a plain wooden chest against
the wall. The single window was shuttered against the
cold.

There was no fire, no hearth, and the room was nearly
as cold as a barn. Brittany shivered, not only from the
cold but from the ruthless expression in Lucius's eyes as
he surveyed her.

"Take off your cloak."

"I will not!"

"The hell you will not." He spoke between clenched
teeth, and before Brittany could do more than gasp, he
had his hands on her again and had ripped the cloak from
her shoulders.

"You're a madman! How dare you!"

"Now your gown."

"I am *not* taking off my gown and if you try—"

"Slip it down off your shoulder," he ordered tersely.
"Or I will do it for you."

Understanding came to her in a flash.

The rose birthmark.

"It's there. The birthmark. It's on my right shoulder.
Everything I told you is the truth."

"Show me. *Now*."

Her vivid green-gold eyes met his glittering gray ones.
A silent battle ensued in that tiny, dim room while the
clamor of the inn roared below.

Brittany, gazing defiantly at those hard, commanding
features, knew that he meant what he said. He would re-

move her gown to see the birthmark—or lack of one—for himself if she didn't obey his request. What sort of man was he, what sort of past did he have, that his distrust ran so deep? That he was so cynical, so careful?

So hostile.

"Very well," she said at length, with all the dignity she could summon. "Once I prove it to you, may I trust that you will honor your pledge and help me?"

"I'll make no bargain with you. Not before you've shown me the birthmark. But if you're lying, I promise you this: I'll make you sorry you ever set foot in this inn. That's one pledge I *will* honor."

Brittany said nothing more. With her eyes locked on his, she began unfastening the bodice of her dark green gown, only enough to allow her to slide the fabric off her right shoulder. In the flickering candlelight, she watched Lucius's eyes. Her heart began to race as he took in the tiny birthmark in the shape of a rose. He stepped closer, stared harder, then swung his gaze back to her face.

"Satisfied?" she asked coolly, but an odd fluttering had sprung up deep inside her. She yanked her gown back up on her shoulder with hands that shook a little, all too aware of the intensity of his scrutiny. Quickly she began refastening it, but his hand shot out and stopped her, his fingers warm on hers.

"Just what the hell do you want from me?" he rasped.

"Only that you honor your pledge."

"Marry you, you mean?" He gave a jeering laugh, his mouth twisting unpleasantly, and the warm little flutter inside her went still.

"Are you that desperate for a husband, a comely wench like you?" He stepped closer, his fingers still clamped around hers, and Brittany felt the heat and energy of him searing her. She couldn't breathe for a moment, could only stare up into that angry, dangerous face. Then she reminded herself that it would not do to let Lucius of Marric intimidate or belittle her, that she was no longer merely the ward of a queen, she was royal herself.

"I'm not a wench, Lucius. I'm a princess, as royal as you, and you would do well to remember that."

Even as she eyed him haughtily, a tiny part of her again tingled with warmth. He thought she was comely.

Why should that matter? she asked herself. He probably thinks every hag within a hundred miles is comely. At least, comely enough for his purposes. She continued quickly. "I am desperate—yes. I won't deny it. I'm desperate for a protector. And since you were pledged to me by your family—by *our* families—then I expect you to fulfill that responsiblity. I am about to find myself in very great danger and—"

"What sort of danger?" Suddenly, understanding lit his eyes.

"Darius." He spat out the word. "Of course. Ruler of all Palladrin. Don't tell me you want me to fight Darius for you?" He gave a great crack of laughter. "I wouldn't even fight Darius for *me*," he said, shaking his head.

"Are you afraid?"

"Let me tell you something, *Princess*," he told her with thinly veiled contempt. His hand tightened, but Brittany didn't even protest, so caught up was she in the bitterness reflected in his face. "I fought Lothbin the Giant and poked out both his eyes. I killed two dragons before my fifteenth winter, and I have fought in one war after another for almost half my life. I'm not afraid—not of anything— not of death, and by all the demons in hell, surely not of Darius."

"Then why—"

"I don't care. Understand? *I don't care.* I just want to enjoy some decent food, some good ale, and savor the company of whatever comely wenches cross my path. I'm nobody's champion, nobody's hero, nobody's fighting man—not anymore. And I'm certainly nobody's prince. So find yourself another champion. I'm out of the dragon- and wizard-slaying business."

"You don't care about your family's honor?"

He gritted his teeth, and she saw a shadow cross those

deep-gray eyes. But when he spoke his voice was like a whiplash. "I don't care about anything—or anyone. So don't bother me again. I won't be so patient with you next time."

He turned on his heel and left her there. For a moment Brittany stood in shock. Then, trembling, she sank down upon the cot and covered her face with her hands.

Lucius wouldn't help her. Now what would she do?

Despair and the first twinges of terror began to creep through her. Soon Darius would be able to sense her presence in the world of the living—and she had no doubt that he would seek her out and try to destroy her. There had to be another way—besides the Sword of Marric— to gain her powers and claim her kingdom.

There had to be!

What that way might be, she had no idea, but she knew one thing. She couldn't waste time here at this inn. Not another moment.

Besides, after seeing the manner of men who frequented the place—including the prince of Marric—she felt it was clearly too dangerous for a woman to stay here alone, with no protector. She had to get her horse from the stable and find the camp of Sir Richmond and his men. Sir Richmond was a seasoned warrior, experienced in battle and strategy. Perhaps he could help her to devise another plan, a way to hide herself from Darius as she searched for the Rose Scepter. Or he might suggest another ally, someone who, unlike Lucius of Marric, *did* care about someone other than himself.

Blindly, she finished fastening up her gown, flung on her cloak, and made her way downstairs and through the crowded inn. She was too distraught to heed anyone around her, and she refused even to peer about for Lucius of Marric. She never saw him glance up from his efforts to soothe Drusy's ruffled feathers in a warm, dark corner of the room, never saw him drop his hands from the serving girl's waist to stare piercingly after her, a scowl upon his face as she tore down the stairway and hurried toward the door of the inn. She'd been wrong about him, that's all she knew. He *was* a toad—for all his handsome face and powerful muscles and keen eyes, he was nothing but a selfish, lowly toad who cared only for himself.

She gasped as she threw open the door and a blast of wintry air struck her. Shivering, she plunged out into the night and with head bent, veered toward the stables as snow swirled around her and the wind bit into her flesh. But as she reached the stable doors, two men emerged from the murky depths of the structure and blocked her path.

"Whoa, what's this?" The first one grabbed her as the wind nearly knocked her over.

The second one paused, fingering his dark beard, which was encrusted with bits of snow and ice. His eyes were red-rimmed and bloodshot, and an evil scar stretched across his left cheek.

"What's a lovely thing like you doing out here in this ugly night?" he bellowed in a voice as thick as congealed gravy.

"Let me pass." Brittany spoke firmly and tried to step around them, but the first man, whose sharp, narrow eyes were the color of horse dung, refused to release her. Instead he swung her up against his chest.

"Not so fast, my pretty. Come with us into the inn. We'll buy you some ale to warm you and—"

"Let go of me and be on your way!" Brittany kicked out at him and tried with all her might to pull free of his grasping hands. She suddenly wished she'd never sent Sir Richmond away from the Bones and Blood, that she'd had him wait here for the outcome of her meeting with Lucius. She'd been so certain that her betrothed would help her. So certain that she wouldn't need Sir Richmond's aid once she'd found Lucius of Marric.

"I'm warning you—" she began desperately, but the two men both threw back their heads and laughed. Panic bubbled inside her as she struggled in vain to break away.

Suddenly the man who held her yanked her closer and

pressed his mouth against hers. Wet, cruel lips crushed hers, and Brittany nearly retched at the sour taste of him. Frantically, she kicked, clawed, struck out, but he only tightened his hold on her and bent her backward with the force of the kiss.

"Gangrin," the scar-faced man hissed, as wind roared all around them and snow whirled in a fury, "take her into the stable! We'll both have her, then get to our ale. Quick, before someone sees!"

But even as he glanced over his shoulder toward the inn door to make sure no one was there to witness what they were about, a fist struck his jaw and sent him flying back into the snow. Brittany felt herself flung aside, and she stumbled to her knees as the man who had held her was thrown hard against the wall of the stables.

She heard the rasp of a sword being drawn, peered up dazedly as terror burst through her—and saw a towering man facing the two who had accosted her. He held a sword, a sword whose jeweled hilt glittered fiercely in the night, hurting her eyes with the brilliance of it. The man's feet were spread apart, planted on the ground, his face grim and deadly as the two who'd accosted her sprang upright and drew their swords as well.

"Defend yourselves as best you can. Then prepare to die," warned Lucius of Marric.

4

Gangrin gave a great bellowing yell and charged toward Lucius even as the scar-faced man raised his own sword over his head. Brittany screamed, but Lucius moved faster than either of the attackers and the scream died in her throat as he sliced his blade into Gangrin's heart, yanked it free in the blink of an eye, and spun about in time to slam it against the scar-faced man's head. Before the man could do more than grunt and stagger, Lucius killed him, plunging the sword into his throat.

It was over—over so quickly that Brittany's scream was still echoing in her chest. She gasped, fought the bile that rose in her at the gruesome sight of the dead men, and closed her eyes. "Are you hurt?" Lucius knelt beside her. His voice was rough, but his hands were gentle as he touched her. She forced her eyes open and stared at him, unable to speak.

"Are you hurt?" he repeated with a tinge of impatience.

She shook her head.

"Where's that damned soldier who entered the inn with you? Why were you out here alone?"

"Sir Richmond. I . . . sent him away."

"Brilliant."

"Those men—"

"Forget about them. They're dead." He scowled. "I'd best get you back inside before you freeze."

"Why . . . did you . . . help me?"

"I'll be damned if I know." He lifted her into his arms as if she weighed no more than one of the snowflakes melting on her lashes, and stomped toward the door of the inn.

Brittany had no strength to argue or to question him. A faintness had stolen over her, and she fought against slipping away into the warm blackness that loomed near. Only dimly was she aware of Lucius carrying her through the inn and up the stairs, then to the door of the very same room where he'd taken her before.

But this time the door was shut fast.

Lucius kicked it in, and there upon the cot Drusy was rolling about with a burly man who had wild straggly hair the color of straw. They both gasped in astonishment as Lucius stepped into the dim chamber with Brittany in his arms.

"Out," Lucius ordered between clenched teeth.

"Aucchh! *You* get out!" Drusy screeched, and the man surged to his feet.

"We got here first—" he growled, but Lucius cut him off.

"*Out.*" The single word held so much menace that Brittany was stunned out of her half-fainting state. She saw the man look into Lucius's eyes, and whatever he saw there made him blanch.

He gulped, backed up a step, then grabbed Drusy's hand and tugged her behind him as he all but scurried from the room.

Lucius kicked the door shut behind them, still scowling, and lowered Brittany's feet to the floor.

Supporting her, he slid his cloak off and draped it over the rough mattress. Then he eased her down upon the bed.

"Sleep."

She shook her head. "Too c-c-cold."

He swore, a litany of words that she'd heard only when she had hidden once in the stable loft and heard the grooms talking roughly among themselves. With a grimace he pushed her back against the mattress and folded his cloak around her, as if swaddling a child.

He turned on his heel and would have strode to the door, but Brittany snatched his hand and held on to it for dear life.

"You're very kind. You don't want anyone to know it, do you? But you are—kind."

"You're as mad as Ejax the Gnome, Princess."

He would have yanked his hand away, but she gripped it still. Lucius stared down at the slender fingers entwining his larger, stronger ones, and his scowl deepened.

"What do you want from me?" he rasped.

"I want you to help me. Fight—not for me—but *with* me."

"Fight? Do you know what those cutthroats almost did to you back there? And they'd have killed you—slit your throat and left you to die in a horse stall—when they were finished with what they had in mind. So what do you think Darius, ruler of all Palladrin, will do to you?"

"If you help me, I can find my powers. I'm supposed to have powers," she said, as if trying to convince herself. "They'll help me once I find the Rose Scepter and you raise the Sword of Marric—"

"Fairy tales," he growled. "Stories of the past. Myths and legends that end well but reflect nothing of life in this world we know."

"And what kind of a world might that be?" she asked.

"A world of savagery. Of war and cold and hunger and death. A world where good men die and bad ones flourish—" He broke off and clamped his lips together.

"Go to sleep, Princess," he sighed.

But still Brittany clutched his hand. Her eyes held his, searching, but she knew not what she sought. "I need you," she whispered at last. In the feeble light, she saw the harshness of his gaze and wondered how she could breach the wall he'd built around himself. "Please. Whatever you've lost, whatever you've known or suffered that has brought you to this place, at this time, with such hardness in your heart, perhaps . . . we can heal it together. I need you. My . . . my kingdom needs you. The people are suffering under Darius's rule. Won't you help them? Help *me* to help them?"

Lucius stared down into her pale face, so lovely, so delicate. In the shadows of the dim room, her cheeks looked sunken, her eyes desperate. Afraid. She must have ridden far today, a grueling ride in biting cold and drifting snow. At the end of that ride, he'd rejected her, and she'd been accosted by cutthroats of the lowest order. And she would soon have Darius after her. Not a pretty prospect. Yet . . . in her eyes there was hope. Trust. A sweet, heart-rending appeal that touched something deep within him, something he had thought was dead to all touch, to all life.

She was either incredibly foolish—or incredibly brave.

"By the devil's tail, why not?" he muttered. A harsh smile curled his lips. "Fighting Darius is as good a way to die as any." He shrugged those great shoulders. "So why the hell not?"

He stalked out of the room without another word and slammed the door behind him. Exhausted, and relieved beyond words, Brittany stared after her betrothed for a moment, then curled up in his cloak. Her pounding heart slowed, her limbs melted wearily into the mattress, and she allowed her heavy lids to drift shut.

To her own surprise, despite her worries and her troubles—chief among them the knowledge that in little more

than a day an evil wizard would know of her existence
and come after her—she felt strangely at peace.

She nestled within Lucius's heavy woolen cloak—and
slept.

5

LUCIUS GROANED AND came awake with the first stirrings in the inn's kitchen below. The aroma of gruel and hot bread drifted up to him, and his stomach growled its hunger. Even his muscles grumbled a protest as he sat up in the inn's still darkened hall.

The pallet he had thrown down upon the hard floor directly before the doorway of the chamber where Princess Britta slept was not much softer than the floor itself, where a cold draft had flowed like a river all through the night. He still didn't understand why he hadn't availed himself of Drusy's bed—or Ula's—where he would have had warmth and comfort and pleasure. What odd notion of chivalry had compelled him to spend the night guarding the chamber where a honey-haired girl slept?

No doubt the same idiotic notion that had urged him to accept her plea for help.

Damn. He'd committed himself—to her, to the fight ahead of her, to . . . marriage.

For a moment Lucius had to choke back the urge to howl with laughter. He, Lucius of Marric, whose poor judgment had lost him a kingdom, whose idiocy had gotten his most loyal friend killed, whose so-called skill with a sword had brought nothing but disaster, was about to take responsibility for an innocent and helpless princess on an impossible quest.

He scrambled to his feet, raked a hand through his hair, and scowled at the closed door behind which the princess slept.

For a moment he wondered if she indeed had already acquired her magic powers and cast a spell on him. There was no other explanation for it.

Even after he had donned armor and dressed himself in a black tunic of thick wool, had partaken of thin gruel and mutton and coarse bread, had seen Sir Richmond slip into the inn and settle himself in a chair in the corner near the door, no doubt awaiting a final word with the princess—even then there was no sound of stirring from the room where she slept.

Lucius pushed open the door and entered, his booted feet moving with remarkable quiet for so large and powerful a man. He stood over the bed, gazing down at the girl. She was curled on her side, her hair spread like lace across the pillow. One slender hand nestled beneath her cheek, and his cloak was still bundled around her. Her breathing was deep, even, and the long eyelashes that lay against her cheek did not so much as flutter.

Something tightened deep inside him as he gazed at her. She was utterly defenseless, utterly innocent of the evils of the world she was about to enter. If he had been an enemy, he could have killed her in an instant. If he were Darius . . .

"Awaken, Princess. We must ride far this day." He spoke harshly, shattering the calm of the little room, shattering whatever dreams held her. She jerked upright, a gasp in her throat, and her eyes widened upon him with terror.

"Oh, it's *you*." Relief filled her lovely face, and there was even the hint of a smile, which only made Lucius's muscles tense. By all that was holy, she thought he was a hero, her hero. Little did she know that he could well bring her to ruin, as he'd brought everything else.

"Dress and break your fast quickly. Your Sir Richmond awaits you belowstairs. If you wish to go with him, tell me now—if not, ready yourself for a hard journey. I won't hear any complaint."

"Are you always this grumpy in the morning?" Brittany asked, swinging her legs over the side of the bed. She scooped up his cloak and handed it to him.

"If we reach Dag Omer, you'll find out."

"Dag Omer? Where is that?"

"That is where the holy man lives who will marry us tonight. If you still want to marry me, that is. Then for certain you will know what I am like in the morning," he added.

She swallowed, staring into that dark, sardonic face so full of hardness and a bitterness she couldn't understand. Her heart trembled at the idea that she was surrendering herself, her life, her fate to this stranger. That by this evening, they would share not only danger but, if he chose, a bed.

"You are my pledged betrothed," she answered quietly. "An alliance between us is our only hope. Tomorrow . . ."

She took a deep breath. "Tomorrow is my twentieth birthday. After that, Darius will know that I am alive and that I am a threat to him." She shuddered suddenly as a thought occurred to her. "You should know that he could kill me before I ever find the Rose Scepter, before we have a chance to fight. He could kill you, too."

For the first time she realized the depth of the danger she was thrusting upon him. "Are you sure you want to go ahead with all this?"

"A fine time you've chosen to ask me that." Eyes glinting, Lucius wheeled away from her toward the door. "As it happens, Princess, I don't have anything better to do. Life's been dull lately—ever since I lost my own kingdom," he added carelessly. "So why not take a stab at yours? It's my duty, as you reminded me. But don't keep me waiting. I've no patience for dawdlers."

And he was gone, the door slamming behind him.

Her thoughts in a whirl, Brittany soon found herself sitting down before a platter of mutton and thick bread in the inn's main room, after dismissing a reluctant Sir Richmond.

By the time she ventured out into the blowing snow beneath the dull gray sky, the hood of her cloak tumbling back in the wind that ripped through naked trees, she was wondering at her own audacity in challenging the great Darius.

Not even the sight of Lucius of Marric standing beside a black destrier of impressive height and muscularity reassured her. Beside the great steed, her own pretty brown mare with the snowy feet looked small and dainty as a toy. But she was sturdy and had a great heart, Brittany reminded herself, remembering how the mare had carried her through the woods of Strathbury on her daily explorations.

They rode throughout the day—long, cold, grueling hours with the snow biting into her cheeks, the wind whipping her cloak, the cold seeping into her bones. Stealing sideways glances at Lucius, she thought that none of it seemed to disturb him at all. He was all soldier, all warrior, riding tall and straight in the saddle, his keen eyes always fixed straight ahead.

What was it that he'd said? He'd lost his own kingdom. Questions fluttered through her. She guessed the answers would reveal something of the dark emptiness that tormented him. And though she knew she ought to keep her mind focused on the challenges besetting her, she couldn't help but wonder what those answers might be.

They rode through thick forests and through low brown

hills, along the winding, frozen River of Moons, and finally they crossed into the rougher, wilder country of Llachdrum, a land Brittany had never seen before, which bordered the southern tip of Palladrin.

As the afternoon waned, so did the snow, but the wind rose, howling around them as the horses galloped through a forest knotted with huge trees and ancient twisted roots, where carrion birds wheeled overhead, screeching, and where there seemed to be no path to follow. Each time she began to panic that they were hopelessly lost, that they would wander in the dark depths of the forest forever, she would glance at Lucius and see him riding placidly along, intent on some unseen destination, stalwart as always.

And then at last the trees widened, not much, but enough, and she saw a series of dips and vales ahead. At the bottom of one of these, in a place where the sky now showed the blue shadows of night descending and the final glimmers of a rose-orange setting sun, there stood a hut made of bark and logs and mud.

Dark smoke puffed out of the chimney, and behind the dwelling, Brittany saw as they approached and the horses slowed, was a rough stable.

Her legs were so stiff from riding that they trembled and gave out when Lucius helped her down. He caught her around the waist and saved her from falling.

"Sore, are you? Not used to long rides? There will be more of the same on the morrow."

"I made no complaint," Brittany said quietly, mindful of his earlier warnings and all too aware of his strong arm around her waist and of his nearness. In the gloom his face was more handsome and more dangerously aloof than ever—yet his presence was warm, vigorous, giving off a vibrant heat that spoke of strength and vitality and raw male energy. He smelled faintly of leather and of pine, and of clean sea breezes—or was that the scent of the air wafting around them?

She knew only that while they stood like this, she no longer felt the bite of the cold.

Odd, when in the saddle only a moment ago, she had felt quite frozen.

"Inside," he told her, with a jerk of his head toward the hut. Clearly an order. "His servant will tend to the horses."

She allowed herself to be led toward the hut, suddenly wondering what kind of a holy man lived in a dwelling such as this.

The door opened as they approached and a diminutive figure in a pale-gray robe and a high crimson ruff peered up at the pair of them. He had no hair and no eyebrows, and his wrinkled layers of skin were pasty white above the ruff—whiter than the snow. His eyes were sunk deep within his lined face, yet they were not faded and dim with age. They were more like the eyes of a far younger man, bright and keen and the color of polished coal.

"Lucius!" The pasty face broke into a wide grin, showing small, rounded teeth every bit as white as his flesh. "I saw you coming in the light, but could not see your companion. Let me make you welcome, both of you—"

He broke off as he shifted his glance toward Brittany. For a moment he stared transfixed at the girl shivering before him in the blue cloak, her radiant face flushed with cold, a few strands of hair escaping her hood to tumble down around her cheeks.

"Come in," he said swiftly, opening the door wider. "Come in at once."

As they obeyed, he peered outside at the deepening shadows of the moonless night, looked furtively all around, and then closed the door with a thud.

"Casso will see to your horses. Come, sit. I have soup and venison and cheese. And wine. Yes, wine. It is good wine, the only thing in this humble dwelling truly fit for a princess."

Brittany froze where she stood and stared at him, fear surging through her. "You know who I am?" she gasped.

"Of course. How would I not know? I foresaw this day long ago—not clearly, you understand, but enough to know that it would come. I never saw your face, not until now, except for when you were a wee babe and—"

He broke off as suddenly as he had begun and shook his head.

"Forgive me, Your Highness, and you, too, my prince. There will be time for talk. Come and make yourselves comfortable."

"There's not much time," Lucius interrupted, frowning as the man led Brittany forward to a low couch set beneath flickering lanterns.

"I know that."

"And you know why we have come?"

"To be married. As agreed upon years ago. Who should know that better than I?"

"And who . . . are you?" Brittany managed to utter.

Lucius and their host exchanged glances.

The holy man stepped forward, his hands clasped before him. A ruby ring upon his right hand glinted in the lantern light. The brightness of its glow made Brittany blink and sent crimson shadows dancing through every corner of the hut.

"I am known now as Melistern, a simple holy man who serves the Visions of Right. Once, in another day, another time, I was known as Melvail, and I was a minor magician and counselor to Prince Lucius's father, King Raz. I was there, Princess, when the young prince was ushered into the castle of Palladrin, and when you, a wisp of a child cradled in your mother's arms, were pledged to him and he to you in a solemn ceremony that had been ordained years earlier by your grandfather, the great wizard Zared—"

"So it was my grandfather's wish that we be betrothed," Brittany murmured and threw a quick glance at Lucius. There was no reading his expression. He stood near the fire, his arms folded across his chest, apparently no more intrigued by Melistern's tale than by the howling of the wind.

"It was more than a wish. Zared ordered it," Melistern

corrected her. "As he grew older and his own powers waned, he foresaw the rise of Darius's might. Darius had been his student, and at one time was both brilliant and good—but the dark side touched him and wormed its poison through him, pulling him away from the Visions of Right. As he came into his full powers, your grandfather's began to wane and he could not stop Darius. Your grandfather foresaw the fall of Palladrin, and the Rule of Darius tyrannizing your people, Princess. And he foresaw the deaths of your family. But he also saw that in you the power would be strong. That with the Rose Scepter in your hand, and the Sword of Marric by your side"—the holy man flicked a glance at Lucius, whose face tightened even more—"you could defeat Darius. You and you alone. Thus," he finished, "the alliance with the prince of Marric."

"You knew all along, then—that she was alive?" Lucius swung away from the fire, his eyes glinting with anger. "I have visited you over the years, but you never once told me—"

"You did not need to know. Not then."

"But how did you know?" Brittany broke in. "That I was alive, I mean. I've been told my mother cast a spell to hide me from Darius, so that he would not sense my presence among the living."

"Indeed she did. I taught her that spell. I helped her to perform it," Melistern said gently.

A silence fell as Brittany stared into that wise old face, at the shining black eyes. The ruby ring winked and burned like fire.

"You see, in my early days, I also was a student of your grandfather." The holy man's voice was soft. "My gift of power was never so great as his, or Darius's. I could do charms and spells, and my visions were true. But that was all. There was never greatness in me," he told her calmly. "Only goodness. That is what Zared often told me. When Darius stormed Palladrin and danger surrounded your family, I was on my way from Marric with a message from King Raz. Dragons and great beasts surrounded the castle, servants of Darius, but I found a way in—and your mother, who refused to leave your father and your brother, entrusted you to me in the precious seconds that were left before her death. With my aid, she performed the spell, and you were shrouded from Darius's sight. It was I who brought you to Queen Elysia. I, who have waited for this day. But," he said, directing a piercing look at her, "as Lucius has said, there is little time. You and the prince must be married at once. For on the morrow—"

He broke off.

"What? What will happen on the morrow?" Brittany asked, her hands at her throat.

"Have you foreseen something?" Lucius asked sharply.

"No. Not yet. What is to come has remained hidden from me. My powers, too, alas, now have weakened with the onslaught of years. But I know that the spell that was cast will be broken at midnight. From that moment on, you will be known to Darius. He will sense you, see you, know that you live. So you must marry the prince and make plans to retrieve the Rose Scepter at once—for when the morn arrives, there will be little time. And the greatest danger."

"Then let's get it over with," Lucius growled. He came forward and took Brittany's arm, raising her from the couch.

But as he looked into her face, he suddenly frowned.

"What's wrong?"

She looked alarmingly pale, her cheeks drawn, and there were shadows beneath her eyes.

"It's nothing. Let's get on with the ceremony."

"But you—"

"She needs food, my prince." Melistern regarded him with mild reproval. "Not everyone on earth is as strong as you, able to go days without food or rest. You have no doubt forced her to ride all day, haven't you? I think you have something to learn about the care of women."

"I know plenty about women," Lucius retorted, his eyes narrowing, and Melistern laughed.

"Some women," the holy man agreed smoothly. "But not this one."

Lucius looked down at Brittany, and she felt herself flushing under that dark scrutiny.

"I'm not *that* hungry," she muttered. "We can have the ceremony first and then—"

"We sup first and wed afterward." His tone was firm. "Then," the prince of Marric added, his gaze burning into hers, "if my bride is still weary, I shall gladly permit her to spend the rest of the night—" He smiled, an enigmatic smile that never reached his eyes. "Abed."

6

BRITTANY SCARCELY REMEMBERED anything of the
meal that Melistern's servant, Casso, served them in the
tiny hut. She remembered roasted venison and morsels of
cheese, and light flickering from the lanterns. She remembered quiet talk and periods of silence.

She began to feel stronger after the food and the wine,
which Melistern poured into thin silver goblets. Yet when
Lucius led her away from the table, and they knelt before
Melistern to be blessed in marriage, the room seemed to
sway and blur.

She murmured the words Melistern instructed her to
say, she gave her hand to Lucius. And she looked into the
prince's narrowed eyes, as he held her slender fingers in
his and promised to cherish and protect her always.

The aroma of incense filled her nostrils, the smoke from
the fire stung her eyes, and a dreamlike aura overtook her.

Until the moment when Melistern raised them, when

he placed his hands upon their heads and blessed them, and gave Lucius of Marric leave to kiss his bride.

Then her heart began to pound, and the sense of unreality faded like mist. The small room with the couch and the lanterns and the silk tasseled hangings upon the wall came flashing back, and so did the solid, handsome form of her new husband, still holding tight to her hand.

Lucius pulled her toward him, and his arm slid around her waist. His other hand came up to cradle her chin. She stared deep into his eyes and suddenly realized that she'd been married in naught but a plain midnight-blue gown of unadorned wool, without so much as a whisper of embroidery or satin, and her hair hung anyhow about her face. Surely this was no way for a princess to wed a prince?

Then Lucius's mouth touched her lips and she forgot about her gown, her hair. She forgot her weariness and the danger that would soon be upon her. She even forgot about Melistern, watching them through the golden candlelight. She forgot everything but the sweet roughness of a kiss that brought flames of heat alive inside her. A kiss that swept her into a churning sea that was strangely peaceful in its center. A kiss that made her toes tingle and her heart race and had her swaying in Lucius's arms. That only made him drag her closer, hold her tighter, and kiss her even more thoroughly, leaving her breathless and afire and dizzy when he let her go and stepped back.

He looked shaken. But not nearly as shaken as she felt, Brittany thought dazedly.

For a moment they stared at each other, their gazes locked, searching . . . searching.

"Melistern, where are we to slee—" But Lucius broke off as he glanced at the spot where the holy man had stood.

Melistern was gone.

Only the candlelight and the goblets of wine and the wind wailing at the door remained.

"Where did he go?" Brittany asked in wonder.

"No doubt to spend the night in the stable with the horses and his servant so that we may share our wedding night together. Alone."

Alone.

"How kind of him," Brittany managed, and Lucius shot her an amused look.

"Fear not, Princess. I don't bite. Not usually," he added, grinning as she froze.

He's teasing you. Trying to . . . to frighten you. Or, she thought, suddenly realizing the truth, *trying to put you at your ease.*

Lucius found a straw pallet in a tiny rear chamber, tossed it down before the hearthfire, and then threw down a sheepskin he had dug out of a carved chest, creating a thick nest.

Brittany came slowly forward and seated herself upon the soft bed he'd made for them.

They would sleep here together now—as husband and wife. There would perhaps be more kisses, she thought hopefully.

And what else?

A whisper of panic as well as a strange eagerness fluttered inside her.

She was breathless looking at him—frightened, and yet not frightened, and when he came to sit beside her, her heart leaped into her throat.

"You're afraid." He was studying her trembling lips.

"I am not."

His brows lifted, and he hunched closer to her. "You look afraid."

"I do not." Her chin angled up, and Lucius was struck by the magnificence of those green-gold eyes blazing into his.

"At a time like this, Princess Britta, every woman is afraid. It's nothing to be ashamed of."

"I am not ashamed. And not afraid. Not really." She hesitated only a moment. "You see, I could never be afraid of you."

"Oh?" Amusement, and more than a little skepticism, flickered in the gray depths of his eyes. "And why is that?"

"Because there is kindness in you." She couldn't hold back a smile even as the words spilled out. "I told you that last night," she reminded him. "There's a kindness that you try to hide. But I can see it."

For a long moment he stared at her, speechless. Then she did something impulsive, something she could never afterward explain. She reached out and covered his hand with hers.

A trembling heat passed between them. Lucius's skin burned. Her touch, the gentle gesture, and the simple trust he saw in her lovely face, as well as the saucy sweetness that emanated from her very soul suddenly made his blood roar. And sent a river of conflicting emotions coursing violently through him.

She thought he was a champion, *her* champion. She thought him someone she could count on, could trust. He, who didn't trust or count on anyone.

He wanted to laugh at the absurdity of it, but the laughter died in his throat. He wanted to hit someone, fight someone, but the only one there was this lovely, gallant girl who wanted to fight a wizard and liberate a kingdom.

Every muscle in his body tensed. Fury lashed him like a whip.

"You think you know everything," he snarled, and seized her by the shoulders so suddenly that she jumped. When she tried to pull away, he yanked her closer, right up against his chest.

"But you know nothing, Princess. Do you understand? *Nothing.* Nothing of what really awaits you on the morrow, nothing of true darkness, true evil—and nothing about me." It was a growl, wolflike, from deep in his throat. He saw the alarm in her face, saw the quick panic as she tried to struggle free, and felt a surge of bitter satisfaction.

She was scared at last. Good. She should be scared. Of

him, of the world. But her fear, and his own role in it, only intensified his anger. But it was directed as much at himself as at her.

"You're so damned innocent!" he shouted and saw her eyes widen, then flash.

"So why don't you tell me—tell me about you?" Brittany gasped. She was finally afraid. Not much, but a little. He looked not the least bit kind now. Only dangerous and strong and unpredictable, like a wild wolf prowling beneath the moon.

"About me? You want to hear about me?" He gave a short, hard laugh. "What do you want to know?"

"You . . . you said you lost a kingdom. Your kingdom. H-how?"

He was hurting her. His fingers were strong, pressing into her flesh, but she refused to tell him. Yet he seemed to sense it in the breathless way she bit out her words, and his glance suddenly shifted to where his fingers gripped her.

They went slack at once and he released her suddenly. He scowled at her, then sprang up from the floor and began to pace with long, restless strides, sending the lantern light dancing.

"My father had two sons," he rasped at last. He had paused not far from the fire and was staring into the flames, his face a harsh mask. "I was the younger by a little over a year. For as long as I can remember, there was rivalry between Sedgewick and me. He hated me— because I happened to ride better than he, because my aim with an arrow was straighter, mostly perhaps because our father favored me. I tried when I was small to be a brother to him, to follow and admire him, but he would kick me and shout at me, and once he paid the village boys with gold to thrash me down near the bank of the river."

He ignored her gasp of horror and continued as if she hadn't made a sound.

"I never told our father, though he demanded to know

the cause of my bruises, the reason I could scarcely walk for a week."

"Why didn't you tell?" Brittany burst out, gripping her hands together as she watched his face.

Lucius's big shoulders lifted in a shrug. "He was my brother," he said simply, "and I knew what my father would do to him if he learned the truth."

Silence fell but for the hiss of the logs in the fire, the scream of the wind. Brittany shivered and drew the sheepskin closer around her.

"What happened . . . to your brother?" she asked at length.

Lucius swung toward her. In the golden light, his eyes looked dark as thunderclouds. "He became king of Marric when our father died."

"But that was his right, wasn't it? He was the elder. How can you say you lost a kingdom when as the first-born, he—"

"Listen," Lucius hissed, stepping toward her, seeming to loom like a dark giant in the tiny hut. "My father grew ill, feeble. But his mind was still strong. He knew that Sedgewick was weak and that he was a bully. By the time I was grown past the age of eight, I knew it, too." His voice lowered. "I came to fear for the kingdom because of it. I feared that the people would suffer—" He broke off and wheeled away from the wavering flames to stand before her.

"My father wanted me to succeed him—he told me so. But he couldn't order it outright, so he devised a way." His lip curled. "With the help of Melvail the Counselor, he came up with a challenge for the two of us. A test of sorts. I had already defeated my brother in a contest that won me the Sword of Marric. In every generation of my family it has always gone to the strongest son. But this contest would be for the kingdom. Sedgewick was furious. He argued that by all rights the kingdom should be his—and he was right. I didn't want the kingdom, didn't want the contest—not at first. I wanted only to lead our army, because it was clear that a great war was coming with Darius to the south. But Sedgewick told me that if he was king, he would never let me lead his army, that he didn't trust me, that I wasn't good enough—"

"It was an ugly quarrel," he continued softly. "And at the end of it we came to blows. Afterward, I went to my father and told him I agreed to the contest."

"You were right to do so." Brittany jumped up, still clutching the sheepskin around her. "Your brother wasn't fit to be king. Obviously, your father was very wise and knew that you were twice the man Sedgewick would ever be and—"

"Don't be so quick to spring to my defense, Princess. You don't know the rest."

"Tell me." She stood before him, small and lovely and shivering, and it was suddenly all Lucius could do not to take her in his arms, bury his face in her hair, let her softness and her beauty drown out the memories.

"We were supposed to hunt wild boar in the forest for a day. Whoever returned with either the most carcasses or the largest, if there should be only one apiece, would win the throne of Marric. Each of us was allowed to take one companion along on the hunt. I chose Connor, who had been my groom and my loyal friend since I was a boy."

"And how old were you at the time of this contest?" she whispered.

"Seventeen. Sedgewick was nearly nineteen. He chose Sir Geoffrey, one of the knights. I wish to heaven I'd chosen one of the knights as well."

Brittany's flesh prickled. There was a haunted look to his eyes, a grim bitterness that made dread knot inside her.

"What happened?" she asked in a soft tone, stepping closer to him without even realizing it.

"We rode through the forest all morning, following signs of the boar but unable to spot him. Finally, in the early hours of the afternoon, we found him—and I killed him. We staked out the spot for those who would come to retrieve the beast's carcass, and we continued deeper into the wood, for I was determined to kill at least two more. But then," he said, drawing a deep breath, "something happened that changed everything. We heard a scream, faintly, in the distance. A woman's scream."

Brittany went perfectly still. Lucius continued speaking, his eyes grim and hard as rock. "The scream came from the opposite direction of the tracks we were following. I hesitated, then heard it again. A woman's scream, again and again, filled with pain or with terror, I couldn't tell which." His mouth twisted.

"I couldn't ignore those screams," he said. "So I turned my horse toward the sound. Connor cautioned me, reminding me that an entire kingdom was at stake, a kingdom consisting of many people, and that all together, they were more important than a single inhabitant of Marric. We couldn't afford to turn aside from the hunt, the day was already waning . . ."

Lucius shook his head. "Such were his entreaties," he said in a bitter tone. "But I wouldn't listen. I told him I would find the woman and discover what had befallen her while he continued to follow the boar tracks. I told him that I'd catch up to him soon enough. But he begged me to let him accompany me instead. No doubt he felt compelled to act as a guard of sorts, though I was no longer a child and needed no escort. Still, I let him come. I suppose I felt I might need his help with the woman and that together we could dispose of whatever trouble afflicted her much more quickly. At any rate, Connor and I both veered from the path of the boar and followed the sounds of her screams."

"You found her?" It was a whisper.

"Oh, yes, we found her. Her screams had stopped by then, but we were close enough to complete the search. It was Eynneth, a girl from the village. She was in a clearing at the bottom of a gully—lying facedown upon the earth."

"Dead?" A quick chill of horror ran through her.

"Alive. Very much alive. The moment we reached her and I leaped off my horse, she sprang up. And at the same time we heard a great noise in the brush. In less time than *that*"—he suddenly snapped his fingers—"we were surrounded. Seven, eight, nine men," he said grimly. "I can't recall now exactly how many there were. All I know is that they were a filthy bunch of cutthroats, part troll, by the looks of them. Eynneth slipped away, right through their ranks, and they let her pass without shifting their gazes from us. By then, of course, I knew. It was a trap. Sedgewick had set a trap for me, and fool that I was, I'd ridden straight into it."

Brittany couldn't speak. She watched his face, reading the tortured shadows there, the darkness that haunted his gray eyes, and she shivered again beneath the sheepskin. In the silence a log popped and she jumped, gasped, but Lucius merely lifted his gaze from the fire to regard her bleakly.

"We fought them, Connor and I. But we were surrounded and outnumbered. And I, even with the Sword of Marric, even with the so-called skills with a sword for which I was so renowned," his voice grew thick with sarcasm, "could not slash quickly enough to kill them all. And Connor, he had only a short sword, and his bow and arrows. They had swords, knives, and cudgels. They killed him first, before I could stop it, and his blood ran slippery beneath my feet as I fought. He was the best man I'd ever known, the best friend to me of anyone, far more like a brother than my own brother ever had been—and then he was dead—murdered—in service to me."

"It wasn't your fault, Lucius—"

"Whose, then? *Whose?*" He spun on her, his face savage, and grasped her arms. "I chose to follow the screams, rather than the tracks of the boar. I allowed him to accompany me. And I watched them cut him down—watched three of them hack at him as if he was naught but a block of wood."

"You couldn't stop them, there were too many."

"Damn right there were too many. I allowed myself to be tricked and trapped. Now is that the judgment of a king, I ask you? I lost my kingdom and I lost my friend. This is the man you've wed, Princess, the man you think can help you defeat Darius."

He gave a rough bark of a laugh, full of pain and rancor, and released her arms, wheeling away. He stalked to the table where the wine and goblets were set, poured himself some, and tossed it back. As he began to refill the goblet, splashing some of the wine like blood across the fine silver-embroidered cloth Melistern had laid for them, Brittany went to him quickly and laid her hand on his arm.

"Tell me the rest. What did they do to you?"

"It doesn't matter. As you see, they didn't kill me. They kept me busy, fighting, hacking, slashing—while Connor bled to death. I managed to kill three of them and wounded a fourth, but it didn't matter. They left as suddenly as they'd appeared. And there I was, nary a scratch on me, but the day of the hunt had waned and was gone, Connor lay dead, and my brother . . ." His lips twisted. "My brother returned to the castle having killed two boars. Besting me. Marric was his."

"And you had lost your friend," Brittany murmured, her heart heavy for him. "I suspect that was worse for you than losing your kingdom."

He said nothing, only stared at her, then slowly nodded.

She reached up, touched his face, then quickly let her hand drop to her side.

"My father knew, of course, as well as I did, that Sedgewick had hired those bastards, as well as Eynneth, to thwart me. But it couldn't be proved, for they were never found—alive, that is. And as for Eynneth, she was never seen again, so she could not be made to speak the truth. My father had already dared to offer the contest, he couldn't then refuse to grant the kingdom to the winner, his firstborn. So I left Marric, joined the army of Duke

Valmoor, and from that time on spent my days fighting in one battle after another, in whichever army would pay the most for my services. I've traveled the six lands and across two seas, returning to Marric only once, to attend my father's funeral. I was glad he didn't live to see the day when Sedgewick joined forces with Darius in an unholy alliance that has bled Marric dry of all its former riches."

"So you have punished yourself by fighting all these years. Yet it brought you no peace."

Peace. Lucius's lips thinned. "What is peace?" he asked contemptuously. "It is something for fools and dreamers. The world is fraught with war."

"And you were between these wars when I found you in the inn," she murmured.

"You could say that. I chose at last to leave the battlefield for a time, to seek my pleasure in inns, with whores and dice and tankards of ale."

He shrugged, choosing not to tell her how hard he worked at fighting and at whoring to try to forget. "I'd thought to go back—but not as soon as this," he added with a hard smile.

"And not with a woman depending on you. On you—who doesn't trust your own judgment." Her voice was a whisper, but she was gazing at him steadily through the flickering lantern light. "Or is it your heart you don't trust, Lucius?" she asked softly. "The heart that led you to help someone you thought was in need?"

"My heart has nothing to do with this, or with anything," he said sharply, frowning at her. "And I do trust my judgment—now. Because I learned not to trust anyone else—no one. Not woman nor man. I learned to stay my own course and not be swayed by anyone else. I learned to do what's best for me. Only me. And to keep others at a distance."

"Yet you helped me at the inn." Though his frown deepened, she continued resolutely. "You killed those men who would have hurt me—and you brought me here, to shelter and safety. You wed me and took on this danger that we'll face any hour now."

"Another lapse in judgment," he said carelessly. "And here I thought I was cured." He lifted the wine to his lips, but Brittany closed her hands over the goblet and gently tugged it away.

"You're a much better man—and a much better prince—than you ever thought, Lucius of Marric," she said impatiently. "You were seventeen when you made that mistake—if it *was* a mistake. I happen to think it was brave and good of you to choose to help a woman in need."

He groaned and would have argued with her, but she cut him off. "And now you've done it again. You're not nearly as callous and cold as you'd have the world believe."

"The devil save me from foolish women who see the world as they wish it to be!" He pulled the goblet from her grasp, slammed it down on the table, and seized her roughly in his arms.

"I told you once—I'm no hero. No noble knight ready to sacrifice himself for the sake of chivalry." His eyes were gray marble slits, and as his fingers tightened on her arms, he gave her a shake. "I'll help you—but do you know why? Because you're my last tie, my last obligation to who and what I once was, to the House of Marric. When this is over, I'm done. I thought you were dead, and that I had no more obligation to that stupid pledge made when I was a child, but now you've shown up, and heaven help me, I'm saddled with you. Well, so be it. I'll damn well live up to my duty so that I can be finished with the past once and for—"

He broke off at the flash of pain that crossed her face and cursed his own temper and his tongue. "Never mind," he muttered. His fingers slackened on her arms. "I didn't mean it that way. Now that we're in the thick of it, it isn't so bad. I have nothing better to do and—"

"Kindly let me *go*," Brittany ordered with all the dignity she could muster. She tried to twist free, but he still held her too firmly for that. His touch didn't hurt her, though. Only his words did. Words that repeated themselves in her mind, searing her in some intimately painful way.

I'm saddled with you.

Of course, that's how he sees it, she told herself angrily. *He didn't ask for this fight. Or for this marriage. I'm a burden to him, an obligation, nothing more.* Why had she thought, hoped, that there would be something more? She was furious with her own foolishness. And when had she started to think that way? Was it after their vows, when he kissed her? Because of the way she'd *felt* when he kissed her?

A tremor of dismay ran through her. He was right. She was nothing but a dreamer, a fool.

"Let me go," she ordered again between clenched teeth.

His jaw tightened, and instead of releasing her, he hauled her closer. So close she could feel the iron hardness of his chest pressing against her breasts, so close that his breath feathered her eyelashes.

"Maybe now you see why you should be afraid. I can hurt you. I *did* hurt you."

"Don't be . . . silly. It isn't as if I didn't know that our marriage is . . . is only a matter of duty and need, that it has nothing to do with love—"

"Love?" He looked startled. Then he laughed. "Another word, Princess, like peace, that has no meaning."

"You've never loved anyone?"

A heavy silence fell. "My father," he said at last. "And my friend. But that's different from what you mean. I've never loved a woman. Bedded many, but loved—never."

Her gaze dropped from his. He reached out his hand and cupped her chin, forcing it up until she had no choice but to meet his eyes.

"I think, though," Lucius said softly, carefully, "that if ever I *would* love a woman, there's a good chance she would be . . . someone like you."

Now why in hell did I say that? Horror filled him. What devilish sprite had jumped inside his mouth and brought forth those words? He didn't know where they came from, but he saw the light fill her eyes. Light and wonder.

"She . . . would?"

The princess sounded dazed. Almost as dazed as he felt. Yet, as he stood there with her in his arms, gazing into that lovely face full of hope and beauty, he felt something quiver inside his heart. He'd told her more of his story than he'd ever told another soul. She now knew more than any human being except Melistern about Prince Lucius of Marric. And she hadn't turned away from him, or pitied him, or looked askance at him.

There was sympathy in her gaze, yes, but also something else—understanding, perhaps. Admiration, even.

"And if I were ever to love a man," she said softly, her eyes searching his, "I think he would be someone like you."

He wanted to laugh, but no sound emerged. He wanted to speak, but couldn't think what to say.

He was lost in her eyes, those soft, brilliant eyes that shone so intoxicatingly in the firelight.

He would be someone like you.

She lifted a hand, touched his face. The gentleness of it stunned him. The women he'd bedded, whores and serving maids like Drusy and Ula, touched his body with coarse lust, never with this exquisite tenderness, like the lightest flutter of a feather.

He'd never experienced anything like the storm of emotions that swept him then. Every muscle in his body clenched, his loins heated, his blood roared.

He tightened the circle of his arms around her and brought his lips down to hers. It was a light kiss, lighter than any he'd ever known. As tender as her touch.

When it was over, they stared at one another.

Then it was she who rose on tiptoe and once again swept her lips to his.

This time the fire exploded in him. All of the tenderness

fled as he kissed her deeply, single-mindedly, plundering the soft, pliable mouth that she offered to him with such innocent joy.

Damn, she was delicious. Sweet, so sweet. Like a peach fresh from a sunlit garden. He wanted her, *needed* her—needed her then and there with a fierceness that annihilated everything else. She was kissing him still—kissing him with a passion hot as flame. With a growl, Lucius swept her off her feet, crushing her to his chest. As she gasped and then moaned, his mouth laid savage claim to hers. A surging heat enveloped them as their tongues brushed and circled, battling softly as he bore her to the pallet near the fire, lowered her upon it, and covered her body with his own. She was his wife, after all. *His.* She was soft beneath him, soft and willing, and her hair was rich with the scent of wild roses, like those that grew in the north of Palladrin.

Lucius's blood surged. He captured her mouth again, tasted it, savoring her honeyed flavor and the rich musk of passion that clung to her. This girl, this Princess Britta, his *wife*, was kissing him as though she was starving, her hands raking through his hair, and her hunger and need intensified his a thousandfold until he was wild with it and fighting all his basest instincts to take care with her.

Go slow, go careful, he told himself desperately even as her arms wound around his neck and pulled him eagerly down to her.

He began to touch her—her skin, her breasts—and he was lost. He never stopped kissing her as somehow he got her free of her gown, and then his hands were exploring, stroking that lush, smooth body that shimmered golden in the firelight, the curves that seemed to fit so perfectly against his own hard frame. His mouth lingered at her shoulder, where the delicate rose birthmark was nearly lost in the satin smoothness of pale skin.

The birthmark, her heritage—the link between Palladrin and Marric, between princess and prince.

And between this man and this woman.

The hut was no more, and the wine was forgotten. Melistern might have been nothing but a memory, a ghost of another lifetime. There was only the lantern light and the firelight, the rush of the wind and the roughness of the pallet, the honey-haired woman and the dark, taut-muscled man. Heat and magic and want enveloped them.

They needed nothing more.

Brittany knew only that he was raining kisses upon her, stroking her, making love to her with such exquisite tenderness that her senses whirled. When Lucius touched her breasts, kneading them until she moaned aloud, he took her to a world like none she'd ever known. Sensations coursed through her and heat devoured her as Lucius licked her ear until she was awash in shivers. And then he whispered hoarsely that he would try not to hurt her.

"I trust you," she breathed, and her eyes shone into his as he kissed her until her body shook and glistened. He circled her nipples with his tongue, loving each in turn, igniting her with a torturous pleasure.

The night and the fire and the passion swirled around them as their touches grew more urgent, their kisses more frenzied. When at last he kissed her mouth, her throat, her hair, and plunged inside her, there was fleeting pain, sharp as starlight, and then wonder and joy, and a wild thrusting, deep and filling, as he surged deep inside her and she rocked with him in a sweet, primal dance. Her hands stroked his hard, corded muscles, and she breathed in the sweat and the power of him, even as her body welcomed him, clung to him. Their hearts and souls, their breath and their bodies joined, fused, linked by lightning and by passion and by sweet, sweet fire.

And after the dizzying fulfillment, the flood tide of passion, after the fire dwindled and the lanterns burned low, she lay in his arms beneath the sheepskin, weak with pleasure, half dreaming as their two hearts beat together, solid and strong, beating as one.

7

SHE AWAKENED ALONE, to absolute silence.

Opening her eyes, Brittany saw that Lucius no longer lay beneath the sheepskin with her. She jerked upright, pushed her hair out of her eyes, and cast a glance about the hut. There was no sign of Lucius, no sign of Melistern. Or of the servant, Casso.

A strange stillness hung in the air.

She heard nothing from outside the hut, no birdsong, no trace of wind. She sprang up and hastily dressed, donning a clean gown from her pack, smoothing her hair with her fingers, and growing increasingly uneasy as the moments passed and Lucius and Melistern didn't return.

Had last night been only a dream? The sweet kisses, the fiery lovemaking, the warmth and strength of Lucius's body locked with her own?

No, no. Her skin still felt warm from his touch, her lips scorched from the heat of his kisses. The memories were too vivid—it was no dream. They were wed, husband and wife, and they had lain together in this bed, in each other's arms. All of it was real. Blessedly real.

But today was her twentieth birthday, Brittany recalled with a stab of apprehension. Perhaps even now, at this moment, Darius *knew* that she lived. What would he do? How much time did she have?

She fastened her cloak with trembling fingers and hurried to the door of the hut.

"Lucius! Melistern!" Her voice echoed in the eerie silence.

"Lucius!" she called again, stepping out into pale sunshine. The sky had never looked so blue, the bare winter trees etched sharply against it. She turned toward the tiny stable behind the cottage, and that was when she saw them.

Two men lying on the ground. The metallic glint of blood. One of the men on his belly . . . crawling . . .

"Lucius!" Her heart in her throat, she darted forward, only to see that it was Melistern crawling toward her, blood streaming from his face and arms, a hunting knife gripped in his fingers. Behind him lay the still, bloodied form of Casso, the servant.

"By the angels, what happened?" She dropped down on her knees beside Melistern as he gazed up at her, his mouth working, but no words coming out. "What can I do?" she asked desperately. "Where's Lucius?"

"H-hunting. D-deer . . . and berries for your breakfast." His words were so low, so weak that she had to lean down, straining to hear. Terror filled her as she gazed into his black eyes, the life already draining from them.

"He left before . . . before . . . they came . . . you must get inside . . . they'll be back . . ."

"I'm not going anywhere without you." Brittany slipped her arm beneath him, trying to lift him, but he grew more agitated and the knife slid from his fingers to thud against the ground.

"Run, Princess . . . it's you they're after. They'll carry . . . you off . . . you must . . ."

She saw his eyes widen then, staring past her, and she swiftly whipped her head in the same direction. Her breath caught in her throat, and icy fear rose within her.

Half a dozen giant carrion birds, black crows as big as young stags, perched upon the branches of the trees, where before there had been nothing but scrawny limbs. Now those limbs sagged beneath the weight of the huge birds, all of whom were watching Brittany through dark, wickedly gleaming eyes.

"Leave me," Melistern begged. "Get . . . inside, while you still may . . ."

Brittany swallowed. "Not without you," she whispered back, and with desperate strength, tried to help him to his feet.

All the while she watched the great crows, whose gleaming eyes were fixed unblinkingly upon her.

The holy man leaned heavily upon her as they inched forward, toward the hut. One step. Two.

The largest of the birds, on the lowest branch, jutted his great beak forward, and a rough squawk came from his throat. Some kind of command, Brittany realized with a gasp as all six of the birds swooped as one to the ground, blocking the doorway of the hut.

"Princess . . . I beg you . . . run . . . into the wood—"

To Brittany's horror, Melistern slumped to the ground despite her efforts to hold him up. She bent over him, tears filling her eyes, then she straightened and stared at the leader of the crows. "Begone with you," she commanded. "Return to your master."

With a great rush the birds all flapped their wings and soared upward, then zoomed straight toward her and Melistern, their claws outstretched.

Brittany screamed and whirled, lunging for the knife Melistern had dropped. The leader of the crows swooped in upon her, and she stabbed upward with the blade, but missed as the creature veered out of reach. Two more plunged at her, screeching, and she slashed out in terror.

"Britta, get down! *Down!*" Suddenly there was a rush of hooves, a violent blur of motion, and she saw Lucius charging toward her on his destrier, the Sword of Marric swinging at the great birds as they dove and screeched and tried to soar above the danger.

Quick as a bolt of lightning, the glittering blade cut a deadly swath through the air. Two birds tumbled, the others screeched even louder, and the leader screamed to the heavens and dove at Lucius in a blinding rush of wings and claws.

The destrier reared, the sword arced, and Lucius sliced off the head of the great carrion bird. The creature crashed to earth, and the other crows cried out, circling, dipping, and then with a great rush of wings they flapped off over the treetops toward the distant hills of Palladrin.

"Are you hurt?" Lucius was already swinging down from the destrier, running toward her, but Brittany shook her head.

"No, but Melistern is greatly injured! And Casso is dead." She spun back toward the holy man, who lay slumped and bleeding, his eyes glazed now with pain. "Oh, Lucius, I fear he's dying. We must get him into the hut!"

His face grave, Lucius lifted Melistern in his arms. By the time they had the holy man settled upon his bed, he could barely summon the strength to speak. Yet somehow, as they began to clean and stanch and bandage his wounds, he whispered to them to fetch certain herbs from a golden pouch within a carved chest, and told them how to prepare a broth using the herbs.

"It will kill the poison," the holy man whispered, his voice as dry as dead leaves, and Brittany realized then that the poison in the punctures he had sustained from the crows' beaks was far more serious than the wounds themselves.

Within moments of consuming the brew, Melistern's eyes were clearer, and his speech held more strength.

From his bed, he lifted a hand to beckon Brittany closer, and the ruby ring winked on his finger.

"Princess—now you must go. You and Lucius. Tarry no more."

"We won't leave you until you're better."

"You must!" His glance shifted to Lucius, standing in grim silence behind Brittany. "Even now the potion is working. The effects of the poison are fading. By sunset, my strength will return."

"But until then you're weak, Melistern. And vulnerable." Lucius studied him intently. "And they may come back."

"They will indeed come back. Perhaps with other servants of Darius, servants even more deadly, more difficult to defeat. But they won't come here, not unless the princess is still here. Do you wish to bring them down upon my simple hut again?" he asked Brittany.

She turned pale. "You know I don't!"

He nodded, and offered a feeble smile. "Go, then. Now. They will follow you, for Darius will direct them. Your only hope is to find the Rose Scepter. The powers it will grant will be your best protection. Lucius and the Sword of Marric alone cannot withstand the full force of Darius's magic. Those creatures were only a hint of the evil he can send against you."

"But where do I look for the Rose Scepter? I don't even know where to begin."

"I know."

The whispered words stunned her. She stared at Melistern's face, remarkably tranquil for a man who had just been nearly killed, a man still fighting for his life.

"I have always known. For I am the one who hid it."

"Where?" Brittany and Lucius spoke the question at the same time, and the holy man permitted himself another wan smile.

"It is in Palladrin—in the Valley of Ice. I have frozen it deep within the heart of the Devil's Cave."

"Frozen it?" Lucius asked sharply.

"Within the walls of the cave. It is encased in ice, hidden by rock. Here."

He suddenly tugged the ruby ring off his finger and pressed it into Brittany's hand. The stone seemed to burn into her palm.

"The rose carved into the scepter has a ruby dewdrop atop it," Melistern said. "That ruby is the sister of this one. They will speak to one another when you draw near."

"Speak to one another?" she asked, baffled.

"You will see. Take the ring, Princess. And leave me. *Now.*"

Lucius came forward and grasped Brittany's arm. "You heard him."

"But he's ill. Shouldn't we wait until—"

"Until you bring some other beasts or perhaps a demon or two down on him? Is that what you want, Princess?"

She stared into his eyes, shocked by the sharpness of his tone, the impatience underlying it. She was still trembling from the encounter with the crows, from the horror of the attack upon Casso and Melistern. And now Lucius was regarding her with coldness, as if she were a silly, wayward child—not his bride, not the woman whom he'd kissed and stroked and made love to last night.

That gentle lover was nowhere to be found in the hardened soldier who gazed back at her.

She felt a staggering sense of loss, and her heart seemed to sink to the pit of her stomach. But even so, she suddenly saw that he was right. The danger would follow her. She must lead it away from here, away from Melistern.

And above all, she had to retrieve the only weapon that would be of use against Darius. The Rose Scepter.

Suddenly another thought occurred to her. Lucius was every bit as much at risk as she—until she had the scepter, and thereby her powers. For his sake, as well as her own, she had to find it.

And quickly.

"How far from here to the Valley of Ice?"

"A day's ride. We could reach it by tonight."

She nodded and turned away from the coolness in his eyes. "Then let us get started."

They rode without speaking, the only sound the clattering of their horses' hooves upon the rock path. Lucius sat the destrier with apparent ease, but she noticed the way he looked from side to side, up at the surrounding hills, back down the trail from which they'd come, even scanning the sky.

She knew he was watching for the next attack. His outward calm was reassuring—but she sensed his keen alertness, a wariness in the set of those powerful shoulders. Yet she couldn't read his face at all. Did he even remember all that had passed between them in the night, the fire and the storm of their lovemaking, the blinding pleasure of kisses that she'd wanted never to end?

She knew that he was riding with her to help her and protect her in the most dangerous battle of his life, but only because of his obligation to his family honor—his *last* obligation, he'd said. She felt lost and adrift. And more alone than she'd ever felt before.

"Do you want to stop for a while? To rest?"

"No." Though he'd slowed his mount, Brittany kept hers at the same hard pace. She shook her head as she rode past him. "I want to get to the Valley of Ice—the sooner the better."

She spurred her horse forward, leaving him in a cloud of flying snow, determined not only to get to the scepter as quickly as possible but to hide from him the hurt festering inside her.

Hurt over a man she'd only just met? How could he have this effect on her so quickly, so powerfully?

Grimly, Lucius followed, staying close. She was angry with him. Which was just as well, he reflected. Better if she kept her distance and he kept his. Last night . . .

Last night had brought them too close. Not only physically, but in some other way he couldn't explain. When he'd returned to the hut this morning and seen the crows attacking her, he'd gone cold with fear. Fear for her—for the honey-haired princess with a spine of iron and skin as soft as the petals of a rose.

For the woman who had lit a fire in his blood last night. Who'd planted herself in front of Melistern and faced the crows with knife in hand, like some ancient warrior goddess. The woman who was now riding straight into danger.

He'd been casting about in his mind for some way to spare her, some way that he could go alone into the Valley of Ice and find the scepter for her—instead of escorting her right into Palladrin virtually under Darius's nose.

But it was futile, he realized. The danger would follow her. He dared not leave her alone, unprotected, for it was as certain as the imminent rising of the moon that Darius would attack her once more.

His mouth tightened with resolve. His horse quickened its pace. He had to protect her—somehow.

Throughout the ride, he maintained strict vigilance, constantly expecting the attack to come. When they reached Palladrin and began to cross the plain that would lead them to the cliffs and the Valley of Ice, he saw that her shoulders were beginning to slump with weariness and her face looked flushed from the cold.

"We stop here and sup," he ordered, riding up alongside her. "You'll be of no use to me or your people if you collapse from hunger."

Brittany was only too glad to rein in and join him in a meal of berries, bread, and cheese. The light was beginning to fade, and night would fall fast.

"How long before we reach the Valley of Ice?" she asked as they broke their camp and he came to help her into the saddle.

"No more than a few hours. The moon is full and will light the path—that'll make it easier."

She nodded, but as he took her hand to help her, she

suddenly clasped her fingers around his. "Lucius, I'm sorry."

"For what?"

"For entangling you in this. It isn't that I didn't know the danger when I began. Queen Elysia made it clear and I . . . I was afraid. But . . . it was something I had to do. Darius killed my family. My parents, my b-brother. A brother I never even knew I had. He has enslaved my people. I'm their only hope."

"Then what are you sorry for, Princess?"

"For dragging you into it. If I didn't need your help, if I didn't know that I can't succeed without the Sword of Marric, I would release you from your pledge right now. This isn't your fight, and I . . . I don't want anything to happen to you."

He stared at her. Her words rang in his head. *I don't want anything to happen to you.* It had been a long while since anyone—other than Melistern—had cared at all about what happened to him.

"I've fought in plenty of tough battles before, Princess. Don't worry about me."

"I can't help it." Her eyes were troubled as they searched his. "You didn't ask for this fight."

He boosted her into the saddle before he could give in to the temptation to pull her into his arms. To taste just one more kiss.

"Neither did you," he said roughly, fighting the urges she stirred in him, trying to focus his mind only on keeping her alive.

Britta of Palladrin stared at him for a moment, then clamped those lush lips together. She urged the horse forward without another word, and Lucius vaulted upon his destrier and followed. He had the feeling that he'd lost something, something precious, more precious even than the kingdom that had been taken from him when he was a youth. But he didn't know for certain what it was.

Lavender shadows deepened to a heavy purple darkness as they rode across open fields and through a forest gilded by moonlight, at last nearing the cliffs and the sea and the Valley of Ice.

8

THE VALLEY OF Ice was the coldest place in Palladrin—cold even at the height of summer. Now, in the winter, ice layered the dead brush and trees and slicked the pathways, and they could hear the frosty roar of the sea in the distance. By the time Brittany and Lucius entered the valley and picked their way, shivering, to the base of the towering cliffs, Brittany felt as though she herself was about to freeze into a block of ice. She huddled in her cloak and gazed up toward the top of the cliffs, and there at last she saw it.

The castle of Palladrin. Her onetime home.

It rose against the sky, beautiful and strong, shining silver in the moonlight. But to her eyes, a shadow, like a low-hanging cloud, seemed to hover over the parapets.

Something evil, she thought, and a chill went through her.

Was Darius at one of the windows or parapets, even now? Was he watching her?

Her throat tightened with fear.

"Quick," she said with a certainty she didn't understand. "I think there isn't much time. The Devil's Cave—where is it?"

"Here. This way."

She followed him, suddenly feeling that her powers were starting to awaken, that her senses were sharper and clearer. The Rose Scepter—it must be near. Reaching out to her.

Warning her. Darius was coming.

They rode beneath the overhanging ledge of a yawning cave entrance that opened into thick darkness.

"Wait here," Lucius told her in a low tone. She heard him dismount, his boots scraping softly against the rocky floor of the cave.

Then he lit the end of a stick at the cave entrance, and the makeshift torch glowed, revealing the long, tunnel-like depths of the cave.

They left the horses near the entrance and, side by side, made their way along the glimmering rock wall, moving carefully over the uneven floor of the cave.

Brittany stuffed her gloves into her cloak pocket and held up her hand in the torchlight. The burning of the ruby ring nearly hurt her eyes.

"It's glowing stronger. We must be near the scepter." She moved closer to the wall and saw the brightness of the ring flicker. When she moved to the opposite side, it began to burn brightly once more.

"It's on this side. We're close to it—I'm certain!"

Even as the words left her lips, a huge chunk of rock ripped away from the roof of the cave and crashed down straight at her. Lucius pushed her aside just in time, but an instant later more rocks dislodged and began raining down upon them.

"This is Darius's doing!" Lucius shouted over the crash of the rocks splintering all around them. He extinguished the torch and shoved Brittany flat up against the wall, then closed in behind her, shielding her body with his. They were now in utter darkness, and she trembled against him as the rocks continued to slam down. But suddenly she saw a glimmer of red light.

The ruby ring. It was sending off a stream of light, glowing red light, which burned like fire right into the wall of the cave. Snatching it off, she pressed it against the wall and saw the light begin to burn even hotter. Suddenly, as she stared at the wall, her heart pounding, even the sounds of the falling and crashing rocks faded. She saw the Rose Scepter, clearly outlined within a block of ice, set at arm's length within the wall of the cave. It was wrought of silver bright as stars, and gracefully made. Its tip was shaped like an exquisite rose and upon the delicately sculpted petals a ruby dewdrop sparkled with a fiery radiance.

"Lucius—the scepter! It's here! We have to get it out!"

He looked at the wall. "Where?" he demanded as a rock smashed behind him.

"Here. Right here," she gasped. "Don't you see?"

But he could see nothing, though she pointed, still clenching the ring, directly at the rock wall.

Even as a rock struck his shoulder with a glancing blow, Lucius dragged out his sword. He began to hack at the wall, though the rocks flew faster.

As he gouged out an opening, Brittany saw the ruby dewdrop begin to glow brighter, and the scepter shimmered with silver fire.

"Wait! I think I can reach it . . ."

She shoved her hand into the opening as far as she could, but she still couldn't touch the block of ice that encased the scepter. But as she stretched her fingertips toward it, straining to touch the gleaming silver, the ice began to crumble. The scepter shone brighter, the ice broke apart, and suddenly the scepter shot toward her outstretched hand.

A tingling jolt shuddered up her arm, then a burst of

heat, followed by a burst of cold. Her head swam wildly. But only for a moment. It cleared abruptly and she knew a cool serenity as her fingers closed tightly around the scepter's hilt.

"Lucius, I have it!" She slid the scepter out of the wall just as a rock slammed into his back. She felt him tense, heard his grunt, but he never shifted from his protective stance.

Suddenly a calm voice reached their ears.

"Give that to me."

Brittany and Lucius both became aware that the rocks had ceased to fall—that a deathly stillness had come over the cave. Lucius turned, and Brittany, clutching the scepter and the ring, moved away from the wall of the cavern and confronted the figure who stood blocking the passageway that would lead out of the cave.

The man who stood there was tall and gaunt, and his face was kind. The face of a benevolent grandsire. Snowy white hair glistened atop his head, and he wore robes of black edged with gold. A wavery gray light surrounded him, dim as mist yet strong enough to light the cavern so that Brittany could see every crevice in the walls, every rat scurrying in the corners. His voice was soft and cool as a running river.

"The scepter. Give it to me."

She felt the scepter slipping out of her grasp and sought frantically to hold on to it, even as it strained to escape her. She stared at it, and at the ring she held, Melistern's ring.

"Stay," she whispered and felt a jolt through her veins.

Then with a whoosh, the ring flew from her grasp and sailed across the dim cavern, as Darius held up his hand. The ring flew onto his finger.

And the scepter began to follow.

"No!" She squeezed her hand more tightly around it and managed to keep it within her grasp.

"It's . . . mine." Her eyes blazed at the wizard standing calmly before her. "The royal blood of Palladrin flows through my veins. You have no right to this scepter. You are an interloper."

"Foolish girl." Darius chided her as if she were a petulant child. "You have no knowledge of what you speak. You cannot wield the power of the scepter—it will destroy you. Just as those rocks might have destroyed you if I had allowed them to do so. I wanted only to show you a taste of true power, so that you may realize how unfit you are even to attempt to wield it."

Suddenly the scepter burned her fingers like a lighted torch. With a cry of pain, Brittany dropped it and sank to her knees. Lucius knelt beside her, his face taut.

"What did you do to her?" he demanded, throwing Darius a look of fury.

The wizard shrugged, but the smile curling his lips now held a hint of malice. Yet his voice remained gentle, almost regretful.

"I merely showed her how trying to wield great power can harm someone who is not trained to do so, who is not fit to use it for the right purposes. The scepter burned her hand. If she tries to touch it again, it could prove deadly."

"Let me show you something else that's deadly." Lucius straightened and strode forward, straight and tall, his sword drawn. It glittered even in the dimness, but the wizard didn't shrink from the dark, broad-shouldered warrior advancing upon him.

He lifted a hand in a circular motion, and immediately three specters appeared. As Brittany watched, their indistinct forms became solid and turned into large, rough men wielding swords and cudgels.

Lucius froze, and she saw the blood drain from his face.

"How can this be?" he croaked in a hoarse tone.

"Lucius!" She scrambled up and ran to his side.

"It's . . . them. The same men. The ones who killed Connor the day of the hunt. But . . . they're dead. I killed them . . . I know I killed them . . ."

"What magic is this?" she cried, spinning toward Darius.

"The kind of magic you cannot even fathom," the wizard replied slyly.

"They are visions, Lucius." She gripped his arm as he stood motionless. "Men, perhaps they might be, but he has given them the appearance of the men who attacked you that day. To make you remember, to hurt you—"

"They will indeed hurt him. They will kill him."

Suddenly Darius laughed, and the facade of kindness fell away, like a mask removed. His eyes were thin, gleaming, cruel, his skin drawn tight, his lips curling with malevolence.

The men advanced. Still Lucius didn't move, only stared at them, frozen in shock. It's some kind of spell, Brittany realized in despair.

How could she break it?

"Lucius . . . please, please, my love." She jumped before him as the men closed in. "No, I won't let you touch him."

Behind her, Lucius felt his head clearing. It had been filled with sickly greenish light and with memories—memories of that day when Connor's blood had run beneath his feet.

He hadn't even been able to see the wizard—only the men, with the faces of his old enemies.

But now . . . now something had penetrated the greenish haze.

Please, please, my love. My love.

It all became clear, crystal clear.

Brittany stood before him, her slender form braced as if she could somehow ward off the men circling, closing in. She had no weapon, no magic—only courage.

And love?

My love.

Did she love him? Had it been love in her voice? Was that what had yanked him from the mire of the spell?

He grabbed her, thrust her behind him, and sprang forward, his sword slashing out.

Brittany's heart leaped into her throat as the three men attacked and Lucius fought them, all three at once. His strength was powerful, his skill superior. There was naught but single-minded determination in his face, and the same deadly ruthlessness that she'd glimpsed the night outside the inn when she'd been accosted. He fought with a dazzling ferocity that soon cut down one of his enemies and left the other two sweating and pressing forward much more cautiously.

Before she could think how she might help him, there was a burst of light and Darius appeared directly before her in a puff of smoke.

He extended his hand, on which Melistern's ruby ring now glimmered, and reached down toward the Rose Scepter on the floor of the cave. It flew up, fairly leaping into his grasp, and as his fingers closed around it a smile of triumph lit his face.

"No!" Brittany cried, trembling.

"Yes, you foolish child. It is mine, clearly. See how it came to me. When you tried to hold it, it scorched your flesh. That should tell you that you're not meant to have it."

All around her clanged the sounds of the battle between Lucius and the specter men. Grunts and hisses, the clatter of swords, the thump of feet on stone. She smelled sweat, fear, death in the cavern, and she saw the smug, cruel smile on the wizard's face.

In his hand the Rose Scepter gleamed, the ruby dewdrop afire.

And her hand stung and burned. The scepter had scorched her, turned against her. Perhaps Darius was right . . .

Then came the voice of Queen Elysia. *You are more than what you know, my dear child. . . . You are royal, Brittany, every bit as royal as I, and more than that, you are powerful. Very powerful. Have you never felt it? Have you never felt the power deep inside your blood?*

"In the name of the people of Palladrin and of my slain

family, the rightful, royal rulers of this land, I order you to hand over the scepter, to leave this place, this land— and never again to darken its borders with your evil."

Her voice rang out pure and clear, echoing in the cavern even as she heard a scream of pain from the men fighting. She spun around and saw that Lucius had killed a second man—she could smell the acrid odor of spilled blood— and she glimpsed the harsh weariness of her husband's face.

Fear clawed at her as Darius began to laugh. How she yearned for power, the power to help Lucius, to vanquish Darius. She felt no different than before. What powers was she supposed to have?

There was only one way to know. She had to have the scepter—hold it, wield it. She had to get it back.

"For the last time, give it to me!" she said, aware that her voice shook with desperation and that Darius could see how close she was to despair.

"Come and take it." Taunting her, he held the scepter aloft. "But if you touch it again, it will burn you alive."

Her hand stung. His eyes mocked. Fear filled her, even as the Sword of Marric rang and clashed in the murky gray light.

She fixed her gaze on the scepter.

My grandsire fashioned you for the women of my family. Not for this evil interloper. Come to me.

It seemed to her that the scepter glowed brighter, the silver nearly blinding.

"Come to me," Brittany whispered.

Darius frowned, lifted a hand, and a gust of wind hurtled through the cavern, and blew Brittany straight back against the wall.

"Come to me!" she called over the raging gusts that blasted her. "You are mine—you were fashioned for good, not evil. Hear me, for I am Britta of Palladrin!"

She thrust her hand forward, and watched as the Rose Scepter jerked free of Darius's grasp and flew across the cavern straight into her palm.

She braced herself for the fiery pain as the silver touched her skin, but there was none. Now the scepter felt cool and smooth, the rose atop it glistened, and the dew-drop alone burst with ruby fire.

The wind blew and whistled, pressing her back. She lifted the scepter, waved it from side to side, and the wind died as swiftly as it had begun.

Power.

She saw Darius's lips move, knew he was trying to cast another spell upon the scepter, to turn it against her. She quickly pointed it at him.

"Let this evil one speak no more."

The wizard's mouth froze, and his face contorted as he tried to break the spell. Yet no words would emerge from his throat.

Brittany whirled toward Lucius in time to see him run the third man through. He yanked the Sword of Marric free as the man crumpled to the ground beside his fallen companions. Immediately, their bodies vanished, leaving no trace, not even a speck of blood.

But as Lucius turned toward Brittany, fear coursed through him, stronger than any he'd ever known. Darius had grown to thrice his size—he was now a veritable giant—and he loomed over the unsuspecting girl whose gaze was fastened upon Lucius.

In his hand he held a spear of fire, brilliant flames bursting from it as he arced it over his head and slammed it down toward the princess.

"Britta!" Lucius's roar sent her spinning around just in time to see the spear coming at her, the wizard towering over her, his face suffused with hate. At the same moment, Lucius sprang forward with a desperate slash of his sword and Brittany instinctively brought the scepter up to intercept the wizard's blow.

The Rose Scepter and the Sword of Marric crossed and rang together just as the spear came down. The blow struck them, and so did the fire—yet they were untouched, strong and whole and solid. Instead the flames of the spear jumped back onto themselves, leaping up the base of the spear and in an instant bounding onto the sleeve of Darius's black-and-gold robes.

He couldn't scream—the magic of the Rose Scepter still held his lips frozen—but his eyes shrieked his rage and his agony as the fire consumed him. Snapping blue flames spread in a blink and a roar, and in a moment the wizard was swallowed up in them. Black smoke exploded, then dissolved into a hissing shower of sooty dust.

When the dust settled, there was nothing left of Darius, nothing but a faint odor of rotting leaves and the ruby ring of Melistern glinting upon the ground.

Darkness filled the cave once more. Brittany lowered the scepter, her arm shaking. Lucius let fall his sword and pulled her to him.

"Are you hurt?"

"N-no." She clutched at him, trying to peer through the darkness into his face, but all she could see was the faint gleam of his eyes. "Are *you*?" she asked tremblingly.

"Nary a scratch." She heard him grin in the darkness. "Come on, Princess, let's get out of here."

He scooped up his sword and the ruby ring, and together they made their way to the horses at the mouth of the cave and led them out of the darkness.

The night was clear, cold, bathed in ice and moonlight. Brittany carefully tucked the Rose Scepter deep into the pocket of her cloak and lifted her gaze to the castle of Palladrin. The shadow that had hovered over the castle's parapets was gone.

"Lucius," she breathed, turning to him, lifting wondering eyes to his face. "We did it. And we're *alive*."

"Barely."

She laughed, and his arms went around her, pulling her close. His eyes bored into her lovely upturned face, glowing softly in the light of the moon.

"When I saw that spear coming at you, I couldn't breathe," he said, his voice thick.

"When I saw those three men coming at you, while you

stood frozen, my heart stopped," she whispered.

She lifted a hand, touched his face. "Lucius."

"Princess?"

"Nothing," she murmured, her eyes shining at him. "Just *Lucius*."

Gazing at her, he felt as if someone had just whacked him in the stomach with a battering ram. Did she really have to look so beautiful? So . . . wonderful? So full of life and hope and happiness? All the things he'd decided years ago to abandon—all the things he'd banished from his warrior's existence.

And she was looking at him as if he were some perfect knight, some hero from the legends.

He scowled at her as ferociously as he could. "If you keep looking at me that way—"

"Yes?"

"I'll—" He stopped, sucked in his breath.

"You'll what?"

"You don't want to know, Princess."

Her lips curved upward in an enchanting smile that made his chest ache. Suddenly she flung her arms around his neck. "Yes. I do."

The tension of the night must have been affecting him, he told himself, because instead of pushing her away, he drew her even closer. She was trembling from the cold, and instinctively he wrapped his arms tight around her to protect her from the biting night air.

The Valley of Ice. Strange, here in this frozen place, everything he'd been holding frozen inside of himself seemed to be melting.

Especially with her arms around his neck, her vivid eyes gazing searchingly into his.

"What are you going to do, my prince?" Her voice was softer than the velvet collar of her cloak. Teasing, daring. Enticing. "I assure you I'm not afraid."

"That much I know. After tonight I doubt you're afraid of anything."

Her eyes danced. "Certainly not of you."

"Maybe you should be," he muttered, and his eyes glinted a warning at her.

"Why? Because you slew those crows for me, you married me, you faced an evil wizard for me and fought the demons of your past? You raised the Sword of Marric and helped me to defeat Darius? For all these things I should fear you?" It was she who pulled him closer, she who tightened her arms around his neck and nestled her body even more snugly against his as the white stars beamed down and the moon sailed through a jet sky, and the Valley of Ice glittered like diamonds.

"If you want to know what I think, Prince Lucius, I think you're the one who's afraid. You're afraid of what you feel, afraid to trust your instincts, afraid to imagine that you could be on the brink of getting everything you want."

"And just what do you imagine I want?"

"Your kingdom back. A chance to rule it as wisely and well as your father knew you could. A chance to cease fighting and begin leading. And . . ." She hesitated only briefly. "A chance to put the past behind you, to come to peace with it—and with yourself."

Her words shook him. His jaw clenched. "You talk too much, Princess," he told her, but his voice held a trace of amusement and of awe. *Were all women so wise?* he wondered. *Or just this one?*

She stretched up on tiptoe so that her lips were only a breath away from his. "I know I do. But you haven't seemed inclined to silence me."

His hand caught her chin, tilting it up even as his head lowered, dipping toward hers. "Let's remedy that," he said as he captured her mouth with his and kissed her long and deep and hard.

Brittany clung to him throughout that dazzling, heart-stopping kiss. She had no choice but to cling to him because her bones seemed to melt and she lost all trace of reason and sanity and will.

There was only Lucius and the frozen night, joy and heat and splendor.

When he finally pulled back, her eyes were radiant, her cheeks flushed. He scooped her up into his arms and spun her around and around until her laughter grew breathless. Then still holding her, he kissed her again, gently this time, as if she were a precious, fragile treasure.

"I love you, Britta of Palladrin. Whether you knew it or not, you had magic even before you found the Rose Scepter. You enchanted my heart almost from the first moment I set eyes on you. The spell has only deepened since then, and now I'm hopelessly in your power."

Her eyes softened on his, and he lost himself in their gold-flecked depths. "Then I command you, my prince— kiss me again. Because I love you, too." Her lips brushed his mouth, slid across his jaw, gently nibbled his ear. "And if you even think about kissing anyone else ever again, I'll simply have to turn you into a toad."

His laughter joined hers, as their lips met tenderly. By moonlight and starlight, in the shadow of the castle, they celebrated victory, hope, and the wonder of love.

Epilogue

OF COURSE THERE was a feast.

Torchlight shimmered and the long tables in the great hall of Palladrin groaned beneath the overflowing platters of roasted venison and capons and pheasants, and dishes of sweetmeats, jellied eggs, and tarts. There were golden goblets filled with spiced wine, sweet music of harp and flute, jugglers and minstrels, much dancing and laughing and cheering. The castle was alive and vibrant with merrymaking as noble and villager alike celebrated the return of Britta of Palladrin—and the demise of Darius.

A week had passed since the night the Rose Scepter and the Sword of Marric had been raised together, ending the wizard's cruel reign. During the intervening days, Lucius had spent his time organizing and deploying an army of men loyal to the princess, unearthing those who had served Darius, and making the borders of the kingdom secure. Brittany had met with counselors and nobles and villagers, learning much about the land and the people from whom she'd been exiled since her childhood.

From far and wide people had come for the feast, to catch a glimpse of the beautiful princess with the honey-colored hair and gold-flecked eyes, the princess whom all had believed dead for so long, and who had in the end recovered the legendary Rose Scepter and rescued all of Palladrin from tyranny.

Queen Elysia had traveled from Strathbury, accompanied by her ladies-in-waiting and a company of nobles and knights led by Sir Richmond. Melistern, fully recovered from his injuries, sat beside Lucius on the dais and, preceding the first of the many toasts and songs, had made an announcement to the hushed crowd: upon learning of Darius's defeat, the neighboring people of Marric had risen up against King Sedgewick. Sedgewick had fled and was being hunted by his subjects—and Prince Lucius was to be crowned king in his stead. A formal treaty had been drawn up that very day, joining the kingdoms of Palladrin and Marric, uniting them in peace and freedom from this time forward under the joint reign of the soon-to-be-crowned Britta and her husband, King Lucius.

But the best part of the feast, in Britta's royal opinion, came when Lucius absconded with her as the midnight hour neared and swept her away from a most boring conversation with the minister of Palladrian taxes, bundling her out of the hall and down a corridor, up a flight of winding, torchlit stairs, and finally into her bedchamber. He shoved the massive door shut behind them, surveyed her in her low-necked gown of ruby velvet, her braided hair bound with jeweled ribbons, and grinned the wolf-ishly appealing grin that made her heart turn over.

"You look most beautiful in that gown, my love, but I think I'm ready to see you out of it."

"Lucius!" Laughter bubbled in her throat. "You *did* see me out of it—you saw me out of *everything* every evening and every morning all this week. And have you forgotten this afternoon, in *your* bedchamber—just as poor Cook was searching for me high and low to ask if thirty pheasants would be enough—"

"Of course I remember this afternoon," he chuckled. His eyes gleamed at her in the candlelight, and Brittany thought she had never seen him look so handsome. In his dark tunic trimmed in gold, he was sleek and tall and powerful, and her heart skittered happily merely at the sight of him. "I enjoyed it so much I've scarce been able to think of anything else," he continued, coming toward her, his lips curving. "Except a continuation of all our frolic."

"Frolic?" Brittany laughed softly and her cheeks flushed a delciate pink as he took her in his arms. "Is *that* what you call it, my husband?"

"What would you call it, my wife?" His hands cupped her face, then slid down her arms and came to rest at her slender waist.

"I would call it wonderful. Intoxicating. And most gratifying," she whispered, reaching up to brush her lips against his.

"Then let us delay no longer." He was chuckling deep in his throat as he began to kiss her, long, deep, delicious kisses that nearly distracted her from realizing that he already had her halfway out of her gown.

"But, Lucius, our guests—"

Her words were lost as he rained kisses upon her eyelids, her cheeks, her mouth—gentle, exquisite kisses that made her forget everything but this man and the love she felt for him. A lasting, forever love, just as she'd once dreamed about. Breathless and dizzy, she clutched him, her fingers raking through his hair, her mouth sipping eagerly from his. When his hands found her breasts, she gave a desperate moan of pleasure.

"What was that about guests?" he whispered, nuzzling her throat.

"They . . . won't . . . miss us," she murmured, opening her lips and, as always, her heart to him, as he chuckled again and backed her toward the bed.

As he gently lowered her to the silken coverings, the Rose Scepter suddenly twitched upon its crystal shelf and a shower of rose petals drifted over them, rich with sweet fragrance.

They were only dimly aware of it, for they were lost in each other, lost in joy and in passion.

As the guests drank and danced and laughed far below in the great hall, Brittany and Lucius lay in each other's arms upon the rose-strewn bed and practiced a brand of magic that was all their own.

THE ROSES OF GLENROSS

Ruth Ryan Langan

For Nora, Jill, and Marianne,
who share my belief in the healing power
of love and friendship

And for Tom, my partner in magic

1

"Not yet, lads. We'll wait until they're closer." Jamie Morgan stood with his comrades, hoping to calm their fears as wave after wave of invaders marched out of the mist, swords poised for battle.

" 'Tis said they violated the women, and even children, before burning Penrodshire to the ground, Jamie. They left not a soul alive. And what livestock they couldn't take with them, they slaughtered." Duncan MacKay was Jamie's oldest and closest friend. The two had trained as warriors together from the time they were lads. And though Jamie was descended from the royal house of Moray, and Duncan's father had been stablemaster to the laird, the two were closer than brothers.

"This isn't Penrodshire, Duncan. I swear on my father's grave that these barbarians will not take Ballycrue. This day we will drive them back to the sea from whence they came."

"What if we can't, Jamie?" Duncan shivered in the cold, driving rain.

Jamie pressed a hand to his friend's shoulder. "Then we'll die like warriors." He turned to the men who huddled under the thin protection of their plaids. "They've not seen us yet. That gives us our only advantage, since we're badly outnumbered. Keep yourselves concealed as long as possible. Once they spot us, we fight to the death, lads. Is that understood?"

The warriors nodded, united not only by love of their country but also by their devotion to their leader.

As the invaders drew near, the men clutched their swords and dirks and tensed, awaiting Jamie's command. When it came, they ran forward, screaming like banshees, catching the barbarians by surprise. Soon the air was filled with the clash of steel and the cries of the wounded. And though the ground beneath them ran red with blood, one man continued calling encouragement to his men as he leapt from skirmish to skirmish, determined to drive back the invaders.

The battle had been raging for hours. And though Jamie Morgan and his warriors fought valiantly, the barbarians had relentlessly inched their way through the tiny village, and beyond, to the forest, where the old men had taken refuge along with the women and children.

Alexa MacCallum huddled in the shadows with her family. Besides her frail mother she had two sisters, one with a babe at her breast, and her father, who had to stop every few steps as a fit of coughing overtook him.

Hearing the crunch of booted feet behind them, Angus MacCallum motioned his family to take cover. Then he stood, sword lifted, ready to protect his loved ones from these barbarians.

There were half a dozen of them, their nakedness covered only by pelts of fur, their eyes hot with blood lust. Though Angus fought with a courage born of desperation, he was no match for these giants, who laughed as they easily dispatched him.

Seeing her father fall, Alexa raced out of her place of concealment and took up his sword, determined to protect the rest of her family. For a moment the invaders were caught by such surprise that they merely stared and laughed at the lass holding a sword as big as she.

Finally one of them stepped forward to engage her. He wasn't prepared for her courage or her skill with a weapon. As he advanced, she refused to retreat, choosing instead to stand and fight. The first swipe of her sword caught his arm, and he choked back a cry of rage before calling to his comrades to join him. Within minutes they had driven the lass back against a tree, where they easily disarmed her. Though she could no longer defend herself, she lifted her head high in a final act of defiance as she awaited death.

Instead, one of them held her while the others plunged into the thicket, easily driving the rest of her family out from their places of concealment.

With tears streaming down her face, Alexa was forced to watch as they brutalized her mother and her sisters, as well as the infant, before finally killing them.

Then the barbarians turned back to Alexa. And though she couldn't understand their words, she was well aware of their intentions. Her blood turned to ice. She crossed herself and whispered a prayer for courage, then closed her eyes, helpless against what was to come. She was resigned to whatever sort of horror would be hers at the hands of these barbarians before they snuffed out her life.

Suddenly she heard a strangled cry and opened her eyes to see her enemy falling to the ground and a magnificent Scots warrior standing over him, brandishing a sword. Blood streamed from the brave warrior's wounds, completely soaking his plaid, but he took no notice.

Jamie Morgan took one look at the lass and felt his heart swell with admiration for her courage. She was as brave and proud as any of his warriors. And so beautiful that she had his breath catching in his throat.

He swept her behind him for protection, while he turned to face the others. And though he was badly outnumbered by his enemy, he drove them back with each lunge of his sword, easily disposing of one after another, until all lay dead.

Weeping uncontrollably, Alexa dropped to her knees, too weak to stand. Jamie longed to take her in his arms and comfort her. But before he could utter a word he heard the cries of his comrades. With a last lingering glance at the lass with the fiery curls and green eyes swimming with tears, he was gone—leaving Alexa alone in the forest, surrounded by unspeakable carnage.

She stared around as though in a daze. All she saw was death and destruction. All those she'd once loved were gone, their lifeblood slowly seeping into the soil that had once nurtured them.

Numb beyond belief, she remained with the dead as darkness overtook the land.

"How does our patient fare, Sister Fiona?" Mother Superior stepped into the room and paused at the bedside.

"His wounds would have killed a lesser man." A brown-robed nun pressed a cool cloth to the forehead of a still, silent figure swathed in coarse linens. "He must fight for every breath, Reverend Mother." She shook her head sadly and began to weep. "I fear he will never awaken."

"Here now." The older nun touched a hand to her shoulder. "We must have faith, Sister Fiona. After all, this is no ordinary man. Were it not for the laird, we would already be enslaved by our enemies."

"Aye, I know, Reverend Mother." The younger sister wiped at her tears. "That's why it grieves me that there's so little we can do for him."

"You're wrong, Sister Fiona. There is much we can do. Besides the herbs and balms, there is our faith. I believe that we are all part of a great, eternal plan. Laird Jamie

Morgan was brought here to us for a reason. Now we must do what we can and put the rest in the hands of the Almighty." She turned away. At the door she added, "I shall gather the rest of the sisters in chapel now. If we must, we will storm heaven on our laird's behalf."

"Have you seen him?" The young novice, in her stiff white gown and apron, stood in the midst of a huddle of brown-robed nuns. Though she kept her voice to a whisper, it was obvious that she was nearly bursting with news of their patient. "He's so noble, his face so bonnie, it fair breaks my heart."

"Aye." A hunched old sister limped forward to join in. "I heard Mother Superior telling Father Lazarus that the young laird must indeed be blessed with very special gifts from heaven, for, despite his wounds, he is with us still."

The novice, eyes as big as the covered dishes on her tray, leaned closer. "All of Scotland is rejoicing, and singing the praises of our laird. They are calling Laird Jamie Morgan the laird of lairds, the hero of Ballycrue. While all around him men fell, he stood alone, displaying uncommon valor as he took punishing blows and continued beating back the barbarians until they were forced to flee for their lives. This day our land is free once more, because of him. They are even saying—" She looked up and caught sight of Mother Superior swooping down on them, her face as dark as a thundercloud.

"Gossiping, young Mordrund? When there is work to be done? If your chores are finished for the day, Sisters, I expect you to be on your knees in chapel, praying for those in need."

Properly chastised, the cluster of women scattered. But all along the hallways they whispered among themselves about the heroic warrior who had been brought to their abbey, and who even now lay on his pallet, fighting for his life.

• • •

Mother Mary of the Cross stood at the window, watching the slight figure at work in the garden.

She marveled as the lass patiently tended the fragile flowers. When she'd first arrived here, the lovely walled garden had been nearly destroyed by the invaders. One wall had been smashed, the graceful old stone benches overturned. There had been deep grooves in the earth from the booted feet of the barbarians. But as soon as she was physically able, like someone driven by an inner frenzy, the lass had begun single-handedly restoring the garden to its former beauty. Though she never spoke and rarely acknowledged those around her, the work in the fresh air had brought color to her pale cheeks and had begun restoring her strength.

The transformation in her had been amazing to watch. For weeks after she'd been brought to them, she'd done nothing more than lie on her pallet, staring silently at the good nuns who had patiently bathed her, fed her, and forced her to live when she'd wanted nothing more than to die. Yet she had lived. Against all the odds, she had lived.

It would be the same for the laird, Reverend Mother thought. In time his health would be fully restored. She believed fervently that he had been brought to their care because he was meant to live. There was, she believed, a purpose for everything, even the simplest of events.

She turned away from the window and hurried out to the corridor to relieve Sister Fiona, who had sent a request that she be allowed to go to the chapel.

"How does our patient fare this day?"

"It is the same, Reverend Mother." Poor Sister Fiona seemed always on the verge of tears these days. "I can think of nothing more now except prayer."

"Then go, and I'll stay here with the laird. Send the little novice, Mordrund, with more of the healing balm."

The old nun knelt beside the pallet and bowed her head in prayer. Suddenly she heard a whisper, low and raspy, as though spoken with great effort.

"So. I'm dead, then?"

"My laird." Her head came up sharply. "Nay. You're very much alive, my laird." She touched a hand to his forehead and was relieved to see that the fever that had burned for days was now gone. "Praise heaven."

"You praise heaven? A robed angel?" His words were slurred as he struggled to focus. "What is this place, then? Heaven or hell?" He thought, by the fire that raged through him, that it couldn't possibly be heaven.

"Neither heaven nor hell, my laird. I am Mother Mary of the Cross. You're at the Abbey of Glenross."

"The abbey?" He could vaguely recall the great stone structure with its tall spires and the bells summoning the villagers to take refuge inside its walls when the battle had begun. "It wasn't destroyed, then?"

"Nay, my laird. Though it was badly damaged, it survived, thanks to you."

"The invaders?" He started to sit up.

"Gone, my laird. Again, because of you." She pressed him gently back against the fur throw. "You were gravely wounded. Now you must rest so that your health can be restored to you."

"My comrades-at-arms?"

She shook her head, wishing to avoid the question. "We'll not speak of that now, my laird."

Despite the gravity of his wounds, his fingers gripped her wrist like claws. "You will tell me of my fellow clansmen. What has been their fate?"

"It is said that . . . they did not survive."

She saw the light go out of his eyes, to be replaced with something dark and dangerous. A whisper of fear clutched her heart. "You must rest now, my laird, and regain your strength."

His handsome face was dark with fury. "Why must I?"

She sighed. "Because the work of rebuilding the land will fall on the shoulders of the young and strong. And because your people will look to you for guidance."

He could feel the room beginning to spin. He closed

his eyes, cursing this weakness. Though the physical pain had lessened considerably, there was an even more intolerable pain around his heart that was almost crippling in its intensity as the knowledge began to seep into his consciousness. Duncan. His comrades. The men who had been family to him. All gone.

He gave himself up to the darkness, embracing it as it took him down and down until he was at the bottom of a great, bottomless pit of misery. A pit from which there seemed no way out.

It was just as well, he thought. He deserved no hope, no light of day. He'd led his friends into the viper's den. Now they were all gone. And he alone had survived.

That knowledge shamed him to the core.

2

"I HATE THIS weakness. I'm as useless as a bairn." Jamie fell back against the bed pillows, exhausted from the effort of walking across the room.

"Aye, my laird. It's to be expected at first." Sister Fiona caught his hand and easily hauled him to his feet before draping his arm around her sturdy shoulders.

"Where are we going?" He moved weakly by her side, allowing her to steer him only because he had no choice. Her strength was matched only by her determination.

"Outside. 'Tis a lovely day, and a bit of sun will be good for you." She helped him through an arched doorway and into a walled courtyard, where a chaise had been set in a patch of sunlight.

"You should have seen this just scant weeks ago, my laird." She pointed to the wall, where new stones now replaced the ones that had been battered and smashed by the invaders. "When the barbarians came, they destroyed everything in their path. The flowers, the trees, the beautiful old stone benches."

After easing him into a comfortable position, she wrapped him in fur.

He gave a hiss of annoyance. "You needn't treat me like a frail old man, Sister."

"Not frail, my laird. Merely weak. But it'll pass soon enough, you'll see. Now enjoy the sunshine, and I'll be back in a bit with some broth."

"Broth." He sighed as she bustled away. If he were home in his own castle, he would order a servant to fetch him ale strong enough to curl a man's beard.

He stroked his chin and felt the smooth skin where the beard had recently been removed. The ever-efficient Sister Fiona had even shaved him.

He frowned at the thought of being shaved by a nun. But, as she'd explained to him, before joining the convent Fiona MacGillivray had raised seven younger brothers, giants all. And, according to her, full of the devil all. There was nothing she didn't know about caring for the male of the species. Her brothers had tormented her unmercifully, so the rigors of convent life had seemed like play. She was, she boasted, perfectly suited to the life of a healer here at the abbey.

Still, as competent as his nurse was, and as peaceful this setting, there was no peace within him. Only torment. The knowledge that he had survived when those he loved had died ate at his heart and lay festering within his soul.

He longed for his home and his people. And yet the thought of sending a messenger to the Highlands informing his clan that he had survived, when all others had not, was repugnant to him.

As Jamie sat hunched in his furs, he caught a blur of movement in a sheltered corner of the yard. A hooded figure was kneeling in the dirt, painstakingly turning the earth with a small hand tool. Each time the tip of the tool encountered a rock or stone buried in the earth, it would be dug up and piled atop a broken section of the wall, where stone steps led to the top.

There was a time, he thought, when such work would have seemed like child's play to him. Now it tired him just to watch. He leaned his head back and closed his eyes. But instead of enjoying the warmth of sunlight on his face, he was plunged once more into the horrors of the battle, seeing the faces of his comrades as they sustained mortal wounds. In his mind he could hear their cries and the low moaning of those who lay dying all around him.

He had hoped by now to be back in the Highlands, celebrating their deliverance from the barbarians. Instead, he found himself alone with strangers who wanted to hail him a hero.

A hero. He experienced a flash of pain. It was an empty victory to learn that, though the barbarians had fled, the cost had been the lives of all those he'd held dear. And yet he couldn't regret his life as a warrior. It was all he knew. All he'd been trained to do. As his beloved father had explained to him so many years ago, it was not a life a man would choose. But because of that choice, other men would be free to make their own choices.

Jamie had always thought that a noble truth. Now it was hard to see nobility in the death and destruction left by war.

He closed his eyes. The peace and silence of this place mocked him as he heard again in his mind the echoing cries of the dead and wounded.

Alexa set another stone in place along the top of the wall, then stood back to admire her handiwork. It felt good to be out in the sunlight doing hard physical work. She'd lost track of how long she'd been toiling in this place. At first she had taken on this task as her punishment for living when those she'd loved had been less fortunate. Then, as the work progressed, she had embraced this as her payment to the good sisters, who had nursed so many tormented souls through the suffering caused by this terrible war. Now she had taken a vow, which she'd written on parchment. It had been witnessed by old Father Lazarus. She would remain here, tilling, planting, trimming, until the garden had been completely restored to its former beauty.

The first plot she'd restored was an herb garden, since the sisters had need of herbs for the treatment of so many ills. She tugged at the weeds and loosened the soil around the shallow rows of agrimony, aloe, wood anemone, and angelica. A second flower bed held lady's mantle, lavender, and myrtle.

She worked slowly, methodically, weeding and working the soil as the sun climbed high overhead.

There was something magical about this place. When she worked here, the fears that plagued her throughout the night were dispelled. The sounds of her loved ones' voices, calling to her to come to their aid, were silenced. The pain of her loss seemed to melt away. If she could, she would work here day and night, just to avoid the demons that stalked her in sleep.

She paused a moment to catch her breath. As she did she realized she wasn't alone. She turned to see a hunched figure wrapped all in fur, seated on a chaise.

A warrior. She'd heard the whispers. It was impossible not to hear all the things being said about the one they called the laird of all lairds. But Alexa had no curiosity about this Highlander. To her he was just another warrior, trained to kill.

She felt the trembling begin in her legs, and knew that just thinking about war had brought back the fears. She slumped down in the dirt and waited until the weakness subsided. Then she returned her attention to the task at hand, blotting out every other distraction.

"Here's your broth, my laird." Sister Fiona was trailed by the little novice, Mordrund, who was carrying a small wooden table.

After the table was placed beside the chaise, Sister Fiona uncovered a bowl, releasing fragrant steam.

"This will not only warm you, but also give you strength." She could see the sudden frown line between Jamie's dark brows. "Are you feeling ill, my laird?"

He shook his head. "Nay. Just . . . weary."

"Well, then." Sister Fiona looked up as the noon Angelus bells were rung. "I'm needed in the refectory now. If there's anything you want, you're to ask Mordrund. I've directed her to stay with you until I return, my laird." She sent the little novice a warning look before hurrying away.

Mordrund, honored at the prospect of caring for the laird, dipped a spoon into the broth and held it to his lips.

Annoyed, Jamie waved her away. "I can feed myself."

"Aye, my laird." Flustered, the little novice ran damp hands down her stiff skirts before handing him the bowl. She stood back, watching as he ate listlessly. "Are you enjoying the broth?"

"Not particularly." After only a few sips he placed the bowl on the table and leaned back, feeling utterly exhausted.

Deflated, Mordrund looked around for something that might interest the laird. "Isn't the lass doing a fine job restoring our garden?"

"Lass?" He looked over and saw the figure kneeling in the dirt. "I thought it was a lad from the village."

"Oh, nay, my laird." Mordrund gave a laugh, delighted to have found something she could discuss with this important man. "The lass was found in the forest, more dead than alive. From her garments it was determined that she was of the same clan as the dead lying around her. She appeared to have been there without food or water or shelter for days."

"Has she not spoken of it?"

"She hasn't spoken at all, my laird. She seems incapable of speech, though it is unclear whether she was born mute or has been rendered that way by her injuries. The sisters here at the abbey have begun calling her Eve, not only because she was the first woman found alive after the battle but because of her love for our garden."

"Why does she hide away out here? Has she been maimed?"

"Not that we can tell. But Reverend Mother says that not all injuries are visible to the eye. Many who survive war must endure grave pain to the heart, and sometimes to the very soul. As healers we must treat these with the same compassion that we treat the body's wounds." She barely paused for breath. "I hope one day to be a healer, as fine as the sisters here at the abbey. It was my reason for joining their number. But Reverend Mother has told me that I must first learn to curb my tongue. She says—" The little novice stopped and clapped a hand to her mouth. "Here now, I've done it again, saying far more than I ought. I . . . hope you won't mention to Sister Fiona that I discussed the lass. For it wasn't my place to do so. In fact, Reverend Mother has said that our first duty is to our patients. We must always respect their privacy."

He shook his head, his gaze narrowed on the figure near the wall. "You need have no fear. I've no intention of repeating what was said here. It will be our secret, Mordrund."

"Thank you, my laird." Delighted, she turned away suddenly, taking the wooden table under one arm and the bowl of broth in the other hand when she caught sight of the nun returning to her patient. "I'll go now and visit the chapel. Perhaps, if I pray hard enough, I'll remember to think before I speak again."

Sister Fiona studied the flushed face of the novice as she dashed past her. "Did our Mordrund pester you with her silly gossip, my laird?"

When he merely lifted a hand in dismissal, the nun gave a sigh of relief. There was no telling what the foolish child would say. "Do you wish to return to your room now, my laird?"

He surprised her by saying, "I believe I'll sit here in the sun a while longer, Sister."

"Do you need anything, my laird?"

"Nay."

"Then I shall return in an hour or so to fetch you back to your pallet."

He made no response. But she noted that this time, instead of closing his eyes, he seemed to focus on the lovely flowers in the garden.

Perhaps, she thought as she walked away, Reverend Mother had been right to suggest this place. There was magic in a garden. Magic that could begin to heal the wounds that were outside the realm of their experience.

Jamie sat for almost an hour, but the diligent gardener never once looked his way. She painstakingly hoed, shoveled, and removed stones and rocks from the soil. She pressed seeds into tiny rows and tended delicate seedlings that had just broken ground.

He found himself mystified by her. Despite the heat of the afternoon, she was completely covered by a hooded cloak. Why did she hide herself so? Mordrund had assured him that the woman wasn't maimed. Yet her actions said otherwise. How could anyone keep up this pace for hours on end without stopping for food or drink? She worked like one driven by demons. She was so intent on it, in fact, that she seemed to have slipped away to another world.

When Sister Fiona came for him, he was actually reluctant to leave. Yet he felt foolish admitting such a thing to the nun, and so he allowed her to help him to his feet. At once he was surprised by his weakness. For the brief time he'd spent here in the garden, he'd been able to forget about his wounds and their lingering effects.

"I'm afraid I'll have to lean on you, Sister."

She smiled. "That's why I'm here, my laird." She gathered the fur throw around him, then put a strong arm around his waist, helping him across the short span to the arched doorway.

As they stepped inside, she saw him glance over his

shoulder and felt a rush of pleasure. "You enjoyed the flowers, my laird?"

"Aye. They were . . . most pleasant."

"You see?" She helped him along the silent corridor until they came to his room. Like all the other rooms in the abbey, it was nothing more than a cell, with a pallet, a washbasin, a fireplace, and in his case a wooden chaise draped with furs pulled up before the fire.

"Reverend Mother thinks you're still too weak to take your meals in the refectory, my laird. So I've asked young Mordrund to bring you some food."

"Thank you, Sister." He was grateful when she eased him onto the chaise and left with a rustle of skirts.

He leaned his head back and closed his eyes. Soon now he would have to send word to his clan to come and fetch him home.

Home. That word should have brought such pleasure. Instead, the very thought of returning without his friends left him utterly bereft.

He leaned forward, pressing his hands to his face in a gesture of weariness.

By the time the young novice arrived with his meal, the black mood had descended upon him once more. He refused the food, choosing instead to crawl onto his pallet, where he closed his eyes and sank into deep despair.

3

MISTY MORNINGS GAVE way to gentle summer after-
noons. As the flowers began bursting into bloom, more
and more of the sisters of the Abbey of Glenross found
excuses to spend time in the walled garden. There, walking the narrow paths or sitting on the carefully restored
stone benches, they would recite their formal prayers or
occasionally lift their voices in songs of praise.

They had learned to avoid the laird, who had also taken
to sitting in the sunlight. Though he often remained there
for hours, he spoke to no one unless it was necessary, and
then only replied to questions in a monotone.

Sister Fiona walked to the window in Mother Superior's office and glanced out the window with a sigh. "It
isn't the laird's physical wounds that worry me, Reverend
Mother. Those are healing nicely. In no time he'll be able
to wield a sword with the best of men. 'Tis the wounds
to his heart that have me concerned. Look at him. How

can anyone sit in that garden and not be moved by its beauty?"

"He cannot yet see the beauty, Sister. His eyes are clouded by the horrors he saw on the field of battle. He witnessed too much death. It is with him still, keeping him from the light."

"But we call ourselves healers, Reverend Mother. How can we consider our patient healed if the life he has been restored to only brings him pain?"

The older woman smiled gently. "We do what we can, but some things are completely beyond our control. For now, you must give the laird time. Time often proves to be a great healer. As does faith."

The younger nun gave a weary nod of her head. "If only I knew how to reach out to the laird."

"Perhaps it is now up to the laird to reach out to others."

Sister Fiona walked away, shaking her head. She hoped Mother Superior was right. But she'd come to know Laird Jamie Morgan during these long days and nights of his recovery. He was a proud man, perhaps too proud to ever reach out to anyone for help.

The voices of the sisters singing evening vespers drifted from the chapel window. Alexa sat back on her heels to listen. She'd been so absorbed in her work she'd been unaware of the passing of so many hours. Could it possibly be evening already?

Pressing a hand to the small of her back she got slowly to her feet. As she did, she realized she wasn't alone. She whirled to find the warrior standing directly behind her. There was no chance to see his face. Just the sight of that tall, muscled body sent terror rippling through her. She seemed to shrink back into her hooded robe, as if to escape.

Jamie had long ago discarded the fur in favor of his plaid. He wore it in the manner of a warrior, tossed over one shoulder, leaving the other bare to the sunlight. His legs, too, were bare and bronzed from the sun.

"You can hear." He saw her back up a step and turn away from him so quickly that she nearly fell over the hoe at her feet.

At once he closed a hand over her upper arm to keep her from falling. Though it was no more than a touch of her through the heavy woolen cloak, he felt the sizzle of heat through his veins. It shocked him to the core. As soon as she was steady on her feet, he drew his hand away as though burned.

She kept her back to him, refusing to look at him.

He struggled to keep his voice soft so as not to frighten her more. "Forgive me for startling you. It wasn't my intention. I do admit that I've been watching you. The little novice told me that you don't speak. But I saw you listening to the singing."

She bent and picked up the hoe, then started walking away from him.

His voice, so close behind her, warned her that he was following. "I'm told you're called Eve. My name is Jamie. Jamie Morgan."

She opened a small door in the wall of the garden and set the hoe inside, then reached into the pocket of her cloak and removed a hand tool, which she set on a shelf. Closing the door, she latched it, then started toward the arched doorway.

"Wait." Again Jamie touched a hand to her arm. Just a touch, but the heat was there again, burning a trail of fire through his veins. He knew now that he hadn't imagined that first time. "I grow weary of doing nothing more strenuous than lifting a spoon to my mouth. I thought I might help you. Now that my wounds have begun to heal, I could till the soil while you plant. And I could prune the branches of those trees too tall for you to reach."

She shivered and drew the cloak around her, before walking through the doorway without a backward glance.

He stood watching as she hurried along the dim corridor until she'd disappeared around a corner. Then he turned in the opposite direction, along a moonlit path, deep in thought.

She had heard him. Of that he was certain. But she'd chosen to ignore him. Was she frightened of him? Repulsed by him? That thought brought him up short, and he crossed his arms over his chest to consider. As a son of privilege, he had seen many maidens glance his way. And later, as a warrior, there had been too many to count. He'd taken his looks, as he'd taken his life of privilege, for granted. But here was a lass who refused even to look at him.

What a strange creature was this Eve. She both puzzled and intrigued him. Though he didn't wish to cause her alarm, he knew there was no way he could turn away from her now that he had taken this first step.

But how to win her over?

He stood very still, thinking.

When he'd been a lad of no more than six or seven, his father had taken him hunting. In the middle of the forest his father had taken aim at a great stag. Just as he'd drawn back his bow, a doe had stepped in front of him, taking the arrow meant for the stag. While his father regretted the mistake, he had no choice but to skin the doe and carry it home with the rest of their game. While he bent to his chore, young Jamie saw a fawn step out of the forest, in search of its mother.

Seeing his young son trying to coax the animal to him, his father had said, "Nay, Jamie. That's the wrong way to deal with a frightened creature. Be very still, and let it come to you."

"But it's afraid."

"Aye, lad. But there's something stronger than fear. And that's need. The fawn needs its mother, and now she's gone, it must turn to another for help. You see? Even now it starts toward you, eager to see if you are friend or foe."

Jamie found himself remembering that summer when he and the young deer had become inseparable. And by summer's end, when the deer, now grown, had disappeared into the forest, Jamie had been bereft, until his father comforted him with the thought that his animal friend was now with creatures like itself.

The mere thought of those idyllic days had him smiling.

The smile froze on his lips when he caught sight of a shimmering image taking shape before him. While he stood, unable to look away, a beautiful woman came toward him. She didn't so much walk as float. Her hair was as golden as the moonlight that seemed to glimmer around her in a halo of light. Her gown was a lovely column of gold and silver cloth that skimmed over her body as though it had been spun by angels.

She hurried past him without even a glance. As she climbed the stone steps to stare out over the wall, she wore the eager look of a maiden awaiting her lover.

Transfixed, Jamie stood watching for more than an hour while the woman waited patiently, hands clasped at her waist, a smile on her lips. When a bank of clouds blotted out the moon, she suddenly shivered and descended the steps, weeping softly. On her face was a look of such sadness and despair, Jamie instinctively reached out a hand to comfort her.

"What is it, my lady? Is there something I can do to . . . ?" Shock rippled through him when he realized that his hand had passed completely through her. Though she continued on, his hand was as cold as if it had been dipped into a frigid Highland stream.

He stood perfectly still, eyes narrowed in concentration, as he watched the woman pause by the far wall before dissolving into a shimmer of light. In the blink of an eye there were only shadows where the light had been.

Though he was a practical man, Jamie knew what he'd just seen. And what he'd touched. Or almost touched.

Still wearing a frown, he went in search of Mother Superior.

* * * *

"So. You've seen her." Mother Mary of the Cross listened to Jamie's description of the woman before nodding. "She is Lady Anne, our benefactor. It was she who gave us this fine castle to be used as an abbey more than one hundred years ago."

"You've seen her?"

The old nun shook her head. "I've not been so fortunate. There are, in fact, few who've actually seen Lady Anne. But over the years there have been enough to know that she is still here, waiting."

"Waiting for what?" Jamie walked to the window, unable to keep from scanning the garden in search of another glimpse of the famous ghost.

The Mother Superior folded her hands atop the desk. "Lady Anne was the daughter of a Scots mother and an English nobleman. She was raised gently here in this magnificent palace, where she was tutored in music and art by French and Italian teachers. It is said that she spent many happy hours in the lovely walled garden, painting the flowers on canvas. There were many visitors to her father's home, and one of them was a bold, handsome warrior, who was so taken by the beautiful young maiden, it's said he lost his heart in an instant. The same was true for her. They became lovers in that very garden. He enjoyed watching her paint, and could have happily spent the rest of his life with her here. But when the country was plunged into war, he had no choice but to go off to do battle. Before he left, he begged her to marry him and come with him. According to legend, though she loved him more than life itself, she couldn't bear the thought of leaving the comfort of her home and garden to follow him into battle. And so she refused, saying on the day he returned, they would wed."

Jamie nodded, already anticipating the end of the tale. "And so she waits to this very day for a warrior who will never return."

Mother Mary of the Cross turned to him. "Aye. But there's more. She never married. And when her melancholy became more than she could bear, she invited our sisters to her castle to care for her until her death. In payment, she offered the castle and grounds to us for all time. We've been here ever since, using our simple skills to care for others."

Jamie turned away from the window and studied the profile of the old nun. "You say she died. Why can she not simply"—he nodded toward the heavens—"go the way of the dead?"

Mother Superior shrugged. "It's said there is something she must do before she can join those who have gone before her."

"Do?" Jamie crossed to her desk. "What can a ghost possibly do?"

The old woman steepled her hands. "I know not, my laird. But it's said that it was her selfish desire for ease and comfort that kept her from going with her lover. Perhaps she must find a way to make amends before she can finally take her leave of this place. Until then . . ." She smiled. "You must consider yourself most fortunate, my laird. There are few whom the lady deems worthy to visit."

"Aye. Thank you, Reverend Mother. Though I doubt you could call our brief moments in the garden a visit." Deep in thought, Jamie let himself out of the office and made his way to his room.

As he lay on his pallet, he found himself thinking about the sad tale of Lady Anne. She had chosen comfort over love and was now paying the price for all eternity.

Lady Anne. So beautiful. So heartbreakingly sad.

He'd actually had a better look at a ghost than he had at the mysterious Eve. The hooded cloak made it impossible to see her. In that one moment when she'd turned to him, he'd had a quick impression of eyes wide with fear and a mouth rounded in silent protest. But there had been no time to see more before she'd turned away.

"Why are you hiding from the world, little Eve?" he

wondered aloud. "What secrets do you carry in your heart?"

It occurred to him that this was the first night since he'd arrived at the abbey that he hadn't once been plunged into the depths of despair with thoughts of the battles and the comrades who'd fallen. Instead his thoughts were of two very intriguing women, one dead, one hiding.

As a lad, Jamie had always loved a mystery. How could he possibly resist this one?

4

"Look, Reverend Mother." Sister Fiona, slightly out of breath, bustled into the office and pointed out the window. "At first I couldn't believe what I was seeing. But young Mordrund tells me the laird has been in the garden since early this morning."

Mother Superior pushed away from her desk to stand beside the younger nun. What she saw had her smiling. "It would seem that Laird Jamie Morgan has begun to heal."

"Aye. See how easily he wields a shovel? His leg, which once caused him to limp painfully, now presses the blade into the soil without hesitation. And his arm, which recently couldn't even lift a sword, now lifts the damp earth as though it weighs nothing at all."

The older sister smiled indulgently. "I wasn't speaking of his physical healing, Sister Fiona. It would seem that the laird is finally able to look beyond himself."

"Oh. Aye." The younger sister shot her superior a brilliant smile. "I hadn't thought of that. It's just so grand to see him standing tall and becoming involved. Even though it is merely with the mundane work here at the abbey."

"It is indeed grand." Mother Superior continued watching. "What of our Eve? How does she accept his help?"

Sister Fiona sighed. "Grudgingly, I fear. When he first began to dig beside her, we all expected to see her run and hide. But though she shuns the laird, at least she remains in the garden."

"A very big step for our Eve as well, wouldn't you say, Sister Fiona?"

The younger nun looked startled. It hadn't occurred to her until this very moment that the healing of one patient might affect the other. She gave a weak smile. "Aye. I would indeed, Reverend Mother. Is there anything you would like me to do?"

"Do?" The old sister shook her head. "I think we should leave the laird and the lass alone, to work things out as they will."

"Very well, Reverend Mother."

As the younger nun hurried away, the older one remained at the window watching for long minutes. Finally, looking pleased, she turned away and returned her attention to the work at hand.

The healing had taken a turn none of them had anticipated. But a turn for the better all the same.

Jamie stopped to mop his face with the edge of his plaid. "The sun's hot this day."

The lass said nothing as she tugged at a weed.

He stared down at the hooded figure kneeling in the dirt. She had to be maimed. Aye, that was it. It was the only reason he could think of for staying hidden in that infernal cloak during the warmest part of the day.

"Sister Fiona has brought us a jug of water." He thrust the shovel into the earth and started toward a stone bench. "Shall I bring you some?"

The lass moved away to another patch of soil, where she began methodically pulling weeds.

Annoyed, Jamie took a long drink, then splashed some of the water over his head. He stood for a moment watching her, then picked up his shovel and stepped up beside her, turning the earth in smooth, easy strokes.

"Ah." He gave an exclamation of delight as he stooped beside her to touch a hand to the plant at his feet. "Yarrow. Now this is a plant I know well. In our home in the Highlands, my mother used to make an ointment of this and apply it to our wounds. And as we were a family of warriors, there were many wounds that needed healing." Seeing no reaction, he added, "Did you know that this is also used to find one's true love?"

He was pleased to see that she actually looked at the plant for a moment before returning her attention to the weeds.

Warming to his subject, he said, "It's well known that a lass should sew an ounce of yarrow into a small pouch and place it under her pillow before going to bed. Then she must repeat this verse twice. 'Thou pretty herb of Venus's tree, thy true name it is yarrow. Now who my bosom love must be, pray reveal it on the morrow.' "

Her hands had gone very still. Because of the hood, he couldn't tell where she was looking. But at least he knew that he had her attention.

His voice lowered. " 'The wise lass will wait for a knock on her door on the morrow. When it comes, the enchantment of true love will begin.' "

He thought he heard a hiss of annoyance. The sound brought a smile to his lips.

The lass could hear. He was now more certain of it than ever.

So why did she not speak? Was it because she couldn't? Or wouldn't?

The intriguing question fueled his energy and kept him going until dusk. And though he might have continued working longer, he made no protest when the lass suddenly walked to the small door in the wall and began to store her tools. He followed her, carefully putting away the hoe and shovel. When he turned, she was already walking through the archway. All that could be seen of her was the hem of her cloak swirling around her ankles. It wasn't the sight of those shapely ankles that had him sweating, he told himself. It was merely that he had become unaccustomed to the rigors of hard work.

It had been good to work. He'd missed it. Missed the pleasant ache of straining muscles and the good feeling that came after a day of honest sweat.

He took himself off to his room to bathe away the grime of the day and to eat the food he knew would be waiting on his table. He had no doubt his muscles would protest the hard work he'd undertaken this day. He hoped it would help him sleep through the night without waking in a cold sweat, something he hadn't accomplished since first arriving at the abbey.

Mother Mary of the Cross looked up as the shadow of the man fell over the doorway. "My laird. You are up late tonight. I would have thought all that work in the garden would persuade you to sleep."

"So did I, Reverend Mother." He crossed to her desk, a frown upon his handsome face. "I'm here with a request."

"Anything, my laird." She sat back, folding her hands on the desktop.

"What can you tell me about the lass you call Eve?"

The old woman arched a brow. "It is not our way to speak of one patient to another, my laird. If the lass were to ask about you, I would tell her the same."

He gave a sigh of impatience. "I understand. I have no wish to violate her privacy, but I wonder about her devotion to the garden. What fuels it?"

"I know not, my laird. She seems driven in her determination to restore it. In fact, she has taken a vow to remain here until the garden is exactly as it once was."

At that his frown deepened. "How would she know the way it once was? I was given to understand that, like me, she is only recently arrived at the abbey since the battle."

"That's true, my laird." Mother Superior paused, as though considering how much to tell him. Getting to her feet, she beckoned him to follow. "Come. I wish to show you something."

She led him up the stairs to a gallery that ran the length of the upper abbey. It was lined with ancient portraits. "This is Lady Anne's mother, and this is her father."

Though he wondered what this had to do with the lass called Eve, Jamie studied the lovely flaxen-haired woman and could see that her beauty had been passed on to the ghostly maiden he'd seen in the garden. As for the handsome man, he seemed both aristocratic and haughty, characteristics that had also been passed on to his daughter.

"I don't have to tell you who this is." Mother Mary of the Cross paused beneath a portrait of the woman Jamie had seen in that single encounter.

He nodded. "She looks exactly the same. Even down to the gown she wore when I saw her." He glanced around. "But what has this to do with Eve?"

The old nun led him further along the gallery until they came to several framed watercolors of colorful flowers and graceful trees.

"These are some of Lady Anne's paintings of the garden as it looked when she was a young lass."

Studying them, Jamie nodded. "Her talent is most impressive. It's easy to see that she had a special gift." Suddenly he muttered a word of surprise. "But how can this be? They look the same now as they did in these pictures."

"Aye." Reverend Mother gave him a measured look.

"Then Eve has been up here to see these? She used these as her guide?"

The nun shook her head. "Not that I know of. In fact, I don't believe our Eve has ever been anywhere in the abbey except in her room and in the garden. Almost from the day she was strong enough to leave her pallet she began working the soil, and it was as if she knew exactly where everything should be. Where to plant the herbs, and the flowers and climbing vines. No one has coached her. At least no one here in the abbey."

"Are you saying that Lady Anne may have befriended her?"

The old nun gave an expressive shrug of her shoulders. "I cannot say, my laird. Since the lass has never spoken, we have no way of knowing what she has experienced. But since Lady Anne showed herself to you, it isn't so difficult to imagine that she may have visited the lass as well. Though for what purpose, I cannot imagine."

He saw at once that the old nun had given him the route he would take to break through that wall of silence Eve had built around herself. He felt a sense of growing excitement. "You believe the lass has seen Lady Anne?"

"It seems a reasonable assumption."

"Thank you, Reverend Mother."

As he walked away, the old nun's sharp eyes suddenly danced with undisguised merriment. It would seem the laird was taking an inordinate interest in someone other than himself. It was another step away from the illness that plagued his soul. Now if only he might persuade the lass to do the same.

It was only a step, she reminded herself. But then, each journey had to begin in just such a manner.

Jamie knew that after the day he had put in he ought to be asleep. But he couldn't stay away from the garden this night. Not after what Mother Mary of the Cross had hinted in the upper gallery. He was eager to see Lady Anne again. Now, knowing her story, he wouldn't find himself awed in her presence, as he'd been that first time.

He drew the plaid around his shoulders and walked the length of the wall, then back again. For more than two hours he remained there, occasionally sitting on a stone bench before resuming his pacing.

Just as he was about to give up and return to his room,

the clouds that had been rolling across the heavens suddenly drifted off, leaving the land awash in moonlight. It was at that moment he saw her.

At first there was just a shimmer of light. Then it grew brighter and seemed to take shape as the woman drifted toward him. He waited until she climbed the stone steps to stare out over the wall. Then he walked up beside her.

"I know you wait for your warrior."

She turned her gaze fully on him, and he could actually feel her sadness. "It is my punishment. I must spend eternity waiting for my Malcolm."

"Why are you being punished, my lady?"

"Because I was given the gift of true love and squandered it."

"You were a gentle lady, reared in this lovely setting. Many would understand why you would be reluctant to leave it for the discomfort and danger of a field of battle."

She gave him a sad smile. "It is obvious that you have never truly loved."

"Why do you say that?"

"When you love, with all your heart and soul, you cannot bear to be separated from your lover for even a moment. That's how it was for my Malcolm. And so I sent him not only into battle alone but with a heavy heart. As a warrior, you must know the advantage that gave to his enemies."

"Are you saying that you feel responsible for his death?"

She gave no answer before turning to stare out over the land.

Jamie took a deep breath, hoping he wouldn't drive her away with his questions, for they needed to be asked.

"Do you know of the lass Eve, who toils here each day in your garden?"

"Why do you call her Eve?"

"It is the name the sisters have given her. Do you know her?"

"I do. She has taken a vow to restore the gardens to

their former beauty." She continued staring into the distance.

"Do you tell her where you want the soil tilled and the seeds planted?"

"I do."

"Then she can hear you." He paused a beat before asking, "Does she answer you?"

"Sometimes."

The sigh of relief rose up from deep inside his chest. "I'd hoped it was so. Can you tell me why she chooses not to speak?"

"Perhaps she shall, when she has something to say." She turned and descended the steps, then began drifting slowly away.

As before, there was a bright glimmer of light, and then she was gone, leaving only shadows where the light had been.

Jamie stayed where he was, thinking over what Lady Anne had said. Of all the things she'd told him, the only thing that mattered was the fact that the lass could speak.

Now he must find a way to get her to speak to him.

He would begin his assault on her defenses first thing in the morning.

5

JAMIE STOOD JUST inside the arched doorway, staring sullenly at the rain that had been falling all morning. He'd been awake since dawn, planning the many cunning ways he would trick Eve into talking while they worked together in the garden. Now the rain had spoiled everything. Eve had remained closed in her room. Not a single soul dared to venture outside.

By the time the bells tolled the noon Angelus, the rain had slowed to a trickle. Though he feared the soil was too wet to work, Jamie dutifully opened the door in the wall and removed a hoe and shovel. He worked alone for more than an hour, and had begun to realize that the day was slipping away, when suddenly he saw the cloaked figure step through the arch. He felt a sizzle of anticipation and tried not to stare as she retrieved her tools and began working alongside him in silence. Suddenly the sun burst

219

through an opening in the clouds, bathing the land in brilliant light.

All his well-made plans were gone in the blink of an eye. Without thinking, he stopped work and leaned on the hoe, staring down at the hooded figure as she knelt in the dirt.

"Lady Anne appeared to me in just such a manner. One minute I was alone in the darkness. The next she was there, in a blaze of light, walking toward me."

"Truly? The lady showed herself to you?" Then instantly, realizing what she had done, she clapped a hand to her mouth.

He bent down and caught her by the upper arms, lifting her to her feet. On his face was a look of absolute delight.

"I knew you could talk. And now you have."

The hand trowel slipped from her nerveless fingers as she looked at him for the first time and caught sight of his eyes. Though she'd seen them for only a moment one other time, they were eyes that had been indelibly imprinted in her mind when a brave warrior had leapt to her defense, sweeping her behind him for protection while he fought off her attackers.

These were his eyes. The warrior's eyes.

Blue they were. Not the blue of the sky in summer, but a deep midnight blue, the pupils ringed with gold. There had been such kindness in them. And such fierce determination. Minutes later, with a slight bow of his head, he'd been gone, rushing headlong into yet another battle, leaving her the lone survivor of her clan.

"It's you." Her voice was little more than a hushed whisper. "The bold warrior who saved me."

"I saved you? Where? When?"

"In the forest of Ballycrue. You came to me in my hour of need and slew my enemies."

The story of her family's flight, and their fate at the hands of the barbarians, tumbled from her lips. Like a stream that had long been dammed up and had finally been set free, the words spilled one after the other until finally she was forced to pause for breath.

As she did she lifted a hand to the hood, slipping it aside to reveal a mass of fiery hair that tumbled down her back in a riot of curls. "I've never forgotten you, my brave warrior."

His breath caught in his throat when he recognized the lass who had so tugged at his heart that day in the forest. "Nor I you. Had I but seen those eyes as green as a Highland loch, or this hair like autumn leaves, I'd have known you long before this, lass." He touched a hand to her cheek. Only a touch, but the heat spread through his veins like liquid fire. "Tell me your name. For on that fateful day, there was no time."

"Alexa. Alexa of the clan MacCallum, my laird."

"Alexa." He couldn't tear himself away from the fathomless depths of her eyes, which seemed to glow with some inner light. "My name is Jamie, of the clan Morgan. You've never been far from my mind, Alexa MacCallum. So often I wondered what had happened to you. In my despair, I feared that your fate had been the same as that of so many others who had come to mean something to me."

"Are you saying you lost loved ones as well?"

"All my friends and clansmen who fought beside me are gone, I'm told. And there was no time to bid them farewell. When I awoke, I found myself here at the abbey."

She lay a hand gently over his. "I know how you have suffered, for it was the same for me. The worst was wondering why my life should have been spared when there were so many more worthy."

"Aye. That's it exactly." He looked down at her small hand touching his and felt such a rush of tenderness it almost overwhelmed him.

He kept his eyes steady on hers as he framed her face with his big hands. "But now, suddenly, seeing you, hearing your voice, I feel as though I've just awakened from a long, deep sleep and have been given back my reason for living."

Though she could feel the heat flooding her cheeks, she couldn't look away. "It's the same for me."

"Is that why you stopped speaking? Because it was too painful?"

"Aye, my laird. The pain was so great that at times I felt as though my heart must surely break from it. Each morning when I awoke and realized I was still here, I was sad, knowing that I would have to suffer through another day alone."

He shook his head and touched a finger to her lips. "You're not alone, Alexa MacCallum. Nor will you be ever again."

Her eyes widened. "What are you saying?"

"Shhh." He lowered his face and brushed her lips with his. It was the merest touch of mouth to mouth, but both of them took a step back as though jolted.

Then, because he couldn't seem to help himself, he drew her close and pressed his lips to her temple. "Oh, Alexa. My beautiful, wonderful Alexa. We're alive. We're here in this lovely place. And we've just been given a reason to be grateful for the strange twist of fate that brought us both here."

At a burst of voices in the doorway they looked up and stepped apart as a group of novices walked out to enjoy the late-afternoon sunshine.

As they smiled and nodded and walked on, Jamie leaned close to whisper, "I suppose we must find some task in the garden or invite their gossip."

Alexa nodded and bent down to retrieve her hand tool. As she did, Jamie knelt beside her and gave her a smile that had her heart doing strange things in her chest.

"I wish it were nighttime."

"Why, my laird?"

He couldn't help laughing at her innocence. "If you don't know, my sweet Alexa, perhaps you'd consent to meet me here tonight. I'd be happy to show you all the things I'd like to do when no one is around to watch."

"My laird!" She turned her face away to hide the blush that bloomed on her cheeks.

He cupped a hand under her chin and lifted it for his inspection. "Oh, Alexa. Your sweetness is such that I do believe I have to kiss you right this minute."

"You mustn't." She got to her feet and shook down her skirts. When she looked up, he was laughing. Her heart took another quick tumble in her chest before returning to its natural rhythm.

For the rest of the time she spent in the garden, tilling the soil, pruning, weeding, she was achingly aware of the handsome young man who worked alongside her. Whenever she glanced his way, he would pause in his work to smile or wink, causing the most delicious flutter deep inside her.

Though she blushed often, and quickly turned away to hide it, there was no denying the fact that this day something strange and wonderful had occurred. Her heart felt lighter than she'd ever known before. All the darkness that had so often clouded her vision seemed to have lifted.

She felt as if she'd been reborn.

It was all because of the bold and handsome warrior Jamie Morgan.

Jamie mopped the sweat from his brow and looked up in surprise to see that the sun was already setting in a glorious display of color. Where had the day gone? He hadn't wanted it to end. Not when he had just discovered sweet, beautiful Alexa MacCallum.

He liked working beside her while they talked and talked. She told him about her childhood with her parents and sisters. Told him about growing up in the Lowlands, always fearful of attack by the barbarians who came from across the sea. He told her about growing up in the Highlands, and his training as a warrior with his friend Duncan. After so many days and weeks of silence, they couldn't seem to get enough of the sound of one another's voice.

She loved the deep timbre of his, and the rumble of easy laughter. He loved the way her words seemed to whisper over his senses, causing a prickly feeling inside. He even loved the fact that they could go for long stretches of time without saying a thing, yet feel completely comfortable in each other's company.

Not exactly comfortable, he thought, glancing over to catch sight of her shapely backside. Now that she'd shed the heavy cloak, he could see the lithe, slender body that she'd kept hidden from view. Even the coarse gown the sisters had provided her couldn't hide the softly rounded breasts, the waist so tiny that his hands could surely span it with room to spare, the gentle slope of her hips. At the sight of her his throat went dry and the heat rushed to his loins. He found himself spending a great deal of time thinking about the way her lips parted when she smiled.

He wanted to taste them again.

At once he felt that quick rush of heat, the sudden jolt to his heart. What was he going to do about these wild, reckless feelings that stirred inside him?

Without taking the time to think his intentions through, he ambled across the garden to where she stood putting away her tools.

As he set the hoe and shovel inside, he leaned close to whisper, "Meet me out here tonight when the others have retired to their pallets."

She gave him no answer as she turned away and started through the arched doorway.

He watched the sway of her hips and felt a hunger building inside him.

He glanced at the gathering shadows and found himself eager for the darkness.

Alexa stripped off her coarse robe and gown and stood beside the basin of water in her room. The tray of food on her night table lay forgotten. She was too nervous to think about eating. Instead she began to wash away the grime of the garden. As she did, she studied her body.

What did Jamie Morgan see when he looked at her? Surely a Highland laird would have had many women eager to please him. He could choose from the most beautiful maidens in the land.

Though she'd had scant opportunities in her young life to be kissed, there had been a time or two. But they'd been mere lads. Jamie Morgan was a man who'd kissed her the way a man kissed a woman. When he'd brushed his lips over hers, she'd felt the flash of heat all the way to her toes. And with the heat, something more. A strange, hungry yearning, unlike anything she'd ever known before.

Oh, what was she to do about these feelings?

She tossed aside the square of linen and began to wring her hands. What sort of woman would even consider meeting a man in the garden, under cover of darkness? Worse, what would he think of her if she did?

She slipped into the coarse gown and began to pace the length of her room. Then she resolutely climbed between the covers of her sleeping pallet, determined to put such foolishness out of her mind for good.

Jamie had been in the garden for hours, walking the paths, counting off the number of paces from one side of the wall to the other. He'd watched the candles in the abbey windows slowly being extinguished, until finally the one in Mother Superior's office went out and the structure was in total darkness.

Still the arched door remained closed.

Where was Alexa? Why hadn't she come to him as he'd asked? Was it fear that kept her from him? Or was it simply that she had no wish to be with him?

That thought had him sighing as he once again turned and made his way along the wall. Suddenly he caught sight of the shimmering light that told him of the arrival of Lady Anne. He stood perfectly still, fascinated as always at the way the light took on the shape of a young woman standing before him, the hem of her silvery gown billowing around her ankles.

"Like me"—her voice was a mere whisper on the wind—"you await the arrival of your love."

"Aye." He couldn't keep the sadness from his tone. "I fear that like you, I may be waiting in vain."

"Then we shall wait together." She began to climb the stone steps, and Jamie found himself following her to the top of the wall.

She looked out over the countryside, bathed in pale moonlight. "He comes for me soon now. I can feel it."

"What will you do if he doesn't appear?"

She shook her head, sending golden waves tumbling around her hauntingly beautiful face. "What I've done for all these years. I shall wait. For I know that one day I'll be given a chance to make amends for having squandered his love. And when that day comes, I'll be free to leave the bonds that hold me here and join my beloved in that other life for all eternity."

Jamie thought of the green-eyed maiden who stirred his soul as no other had. What if she never came to him? What if he had to spend a lifetime thinking about what might have been? Would he return to his Highlands and mourn his loss? Or would he give his heart to another?

A scant day ago he'd have scoffed at the idea of mourning the loss of the love of a lass he hardly knew. And yet there was something about Alexa MacCallum that was like no other.

Lady Anne turned soulful eyes to him, eyes brimming with unshed tears. "Beware, my laird. True love is a rare and precious gift. Once you have tasted it, nothing else can satisfy the cravings of your heart."

"Are you warning me to walk away now before it's too late?"

She gave him a sad smile before descending the steps. Over her shoulder she called, "For some, love is a slow-growing flower that takes many seasons to bring to bloom.

But for some, all it takes is one look, one touch of the pretty petals, to seal a fate for a lifetime."

As she stepped into the shadows, her light began to shimmer and fade. When she was gone, Jamie stood perfectly still, allowing her words to play through his mind.

It was true, he realized. It had taken but one look from Alexa MacCallum to touch his heart and to unlock all its secrets.

If she didn't come to him, he was doomed to wait, as did the lovely ghost of the abbey.

6

JAMIE DRAPED HIS plaid about his shoulders to ward off the midnight chill. Though he knew he was behaving like a foolish, lovestruck lad, he couldn't bring himself to give up and return to his room. It wasn't sleep he craved. It was Alexa.

The thought of holding her, kissing her, had him alternately pacing, then dropping onto a bench, his head in his hands. What was he going to do about this wanting? Sweet heaven, he wanted her with his heart, his soul, his entire being.

"You look so sad." At the sound of that whispered voice, his head came up sharply. There was a flood of warmth where a hand was touching his shoulder. "Do I dare hope that at least some of that sadness is because of me?"

"Alexa." He was on his feet, his hands at her shoulders. "You came to me."

"I tried not to. I couldn't stay away. I couldn't sleep. And I fear I've worn a path in the floor of my room from all my pacing."

"Oh, my love." He couldn't stop staring at her. He wondered if she had any idea how truly beautiful she was. "I'd given up hoping that . . ."

She stopped his words with a finger to his lips. "You, my laird? Now I know you jest. 'Tis said of you that you never give up."

"I don't?"

"Nay, my laird. No matter how many of the enemy you faced on the field of battle, you continued fighting even when all around you had fallen. It was you, and you alone, who drove the barbarians from our land."

He closed a hand over hers and absorbed the familiar rush of heat through his system. "Now where did you hear all that?"

"The sisters and the novices." She gave a soft laugh that wrapped itself around his heart and gently tugged. "They talked easily around me, since they thought I could not hear."

"You little vixen. What else did you hear?"

"That you are called the laird of lairds. The one most loved in your Highlands." She looked up at him. "Is this true?"

He shrugged. "I don't wish to speak of me. I'd rather speak of you, Alexa. Tell me why you came to me."

"How could I not?" She slid her hands along his arms and lifted her face to his. In the moonlight her eyes gleamed like emeralds.

"Oh, my beautiful Alexa." The touch of her, the look of her, had his heartbeat thundering. He drew her close and covered her mouth with his, drinking in her sweetness like a man starved for the taste of her. He couldn't seem to get enough of her. Even when she tried to pull back, he took the kiss deeper, until they were both breathless.

He felt her tremble and thrilled to it, gathering her even closer, until he could feel the pounding of her heartbeat inside his own chest. Still he continued kissing her, taking them both higher, then higher still.

In her entire life, Alexa had never felt like this. Icy needles seemed to be racing up and down her spine. Yet she was hot. So hot she could hardly breathe. The strong, work-worn hands moving along her back were causing the most amazing sensations to curl through her veins. Somewhere deep inside a fist seemed to tighten. She had to clutch at his waist for fear of falling, for surely her legs would soon fail her.

She could feel herself quivering, her breath coming harder and faster as he continued assaulting her senses. His mouth was so warm. So firm. When his hands moved slowly up her sides and his thumbs encountered her breasts, she gasped and pulled a little away. Moments later, her fear was forgotten as he kissed her eyes, her cheeks, the tip of her nose.

She seemed to hold her breath, waiting for his mouth to find hers once more. When it did she sank into the kiss with a sigh that sounded very much like the purring of a cat.

This time when his hands found her breasts, she had no will to resist. Instead she sighed again and lifted her arms to his neck, needing to anchor herself to keep from falling.

"You know I want you, Alexa." He spoke the words inside her mouth.

"Aye, my laird."

"Not 'my laird.' " He lifted his head, his eyes hot and fierce. "The one who would love you is not the laird of lairds. It is the man, Jamie Morgan. Do you understand?"

He could see that she didn't comprehend. He felt a quick twist of frustration. "Why did you come to me, Alexa? I need to know."

"Because you asked." She offered her lips for another kiss. "And because I owe you my life."

"You owe me . . ." He went very still before drawing away.

All that he'd felt, all that he'd wanted, all that he'd hoped, was shattered by those simple words.

As he withdrew from her, she felt the cold seep into her, where only seconds earlier she'd been so hot.

With his arms crossed over his chest, he said simply, "Go to bed now, Alexa."

"To . . . bed?" She studied the taught, rigid line of his jaw. The haughty lift of his head. The angry flare of nostrils. "I thought you wanted me."

"I thought so, too. I was wrong. Now leave me."

She touched a hand to his arm and felt him stiffen and pull back. "Tell me what I've done wrong, my laird."

His voice seemed more sad than angry as he turned away from her. "You've done nothing wrong, Alexa. I was the one who was wrong. So very wrong." His tone was the harsh command he'd used with his comrades when he needed to be obeyed. "Go now. Quickly."

For long minutes Alexa continued watching him, seeing the rigid, unyielding line of his back. He didn't move, standing as still as a statue, his gaze on a distant star. It was as though he had already cut her out of his life. Out of his heart.

Oh, if only she knew how to make things right between them. Something she had said or done had changed everything in the blink of an eye. One minute he'd been kissing her as though he would never stop. The next he'd behaved like a stranger, ordering her to go.

Was it her inexperience? Was that what had changed everything between them? She felt like such a fool. It was all she could do to keep from weeping.

Gathering her cloak around her, she turned away and started across the garden. Though tears welled up in her eyes, she blinked them away. She was not going to shed tears over Jamie Morgan. The laird of lairds indeed.

His words began playing through her mind, taunting her.

The one who would love you is not the laird of lairds.

It is the man, Jamie Morgan. Do you understand?

How could she understand when he made no sense? How was it possible to separate the man from the title? Was not the king the king? Why would one so far above all others also desire to be a mere man?

She stopped in her tracks as the answer came to her in a flash of understanding.

When he was in love.

He was, in fact, a mere man. It wasn't her gratitude he wanted; it was her love. Not the love of a grateful subject, but the pure, simple love of a woman for a man.

She clapped her hands to her mouth to keep from crying out.

How could she have been so blind?

Now, if only she could find a way to make him listen.

She had to find the way. For unless she made him understand now, this very moment, all would be lost.

Alexa hurried back along the path she'd just traveled, then came to a sudden halt. For a moment she almost lost her nerve. Jamie looked so distant and untouchable. Then she thought about the man who had held her and kissed her until her bones had melted. This was the man to whom she would pour out the secrets of her heart.

"I've hurt you, my lair—" She caught herself in time and moistened her lips with her tongue. "I've hurt you, Jamie, though it was not my intention to do so."

Even though he was caught unawares, he didn't bother to turn around. "I told you to leave me."

"Aye. In truth, you commanded it, as the laird might order one of his underlings." She took a deep breath and forced herself to lay a hand on his arm, feeling him flinch as she did. Though his reaction momentarily stopped her, she was determined to see this through, no matter what the outcome. "But you are not my laird, and I am not your subject. I come to you as a woman would come to a man." Her voice faltered. "A man she loves."

He turned, his flesh still burning where she'd touched

him. It took all his willpower to keep from dragging her into his arms. Instead he merely looked at her with such intensity that she almost lost her nerve.

Though she was trembling, she lifted her chin. "Do you doubt that I love you, Jamie?"

"You confuse love with gratitude, my lady."

"Nay." She lay a hand on his cheek and saw his eyes narrow fractionally.

So. He was not as unmoved by her touch as he pretended. That knowledge gave her the courage to continue. "On that point I have never been confused. I confess that I spoke myself badly. I was . . . overwhelmed. I've had little experience speaking of love. You are my first."

His fingers curled around her wrist as he held it a little away from him. "You want me to believe that in these last few minutes you've come to the conclusion that you love me, Alexa?"

"Is that what you think? I have loved you from the first moment I saw you, Jamie Morgan. That day, on that bloody field of battle, you were the most magnificent man I had ever beheld. But so much happened on that day that I was forced to lock those feelings in a tiny room in my mind, where they stayed until today. Today, when I looked at you, I remembered, and the door to that room opened, even though I tried desperately to keep it closed. Now, having seen you again, there is no going back. I know, as surely as I know my name, that I love you, Jamie. Only you. And I believe that you love me, too." She stared deeply into his eyes. "Can you deny it?"

He continued holding her away, his eyes as hot and fierce as they'd been in battle. She feared for a moment that he would turn away from her once more and order her to leave.

If he did, her heart would surely shatter beyond repair.

She held her breath, afraid to breathe. Even her heart forgot to beat as she waited.

He shook his head slowly. His voice was little more

than a whisper. "I can't deny it, Alexa. I love you. Only you."

"Then kiss me, Jamie. Before I die from the wanting." She started to reach for him, but he stopped her.

"I cannot."

"And why not?"

"Because if I kissed you again, I would never be able to stop."

"And why should you stop?"

"You're a maiden, Alexa. You said yourself that I'm the first."

"Aye." This time she did reach for him and felt him flinch. "My first. My last. My only."

Still he held back, as if unable to believe what he was hearing. "I'll not settle for mere kisses this time. I'm a man, Alexa. With a man's hunger. I want you. All of you. The way a man desires a woman. Do you understand?"

She gave a slight nod of her head. "I understand, Jamie."

"This is what you want? Truly?"

"Truly." Though she felt a moment of pure terror, she managed a quick smile. "Please, Jamie. Kiss me now."

At her words he knew there would be no holding back.

"Oh, my darling." He dragged her roughly into his arms, and his mouth covered hers with a savageness that had them both gasping. "I'm not certain I can be gentle. The wanting is so fierce."

She felt her heart nearly overflow with relief. With love. With wild, exuberant joy. "Aye. I know, Jamie, for it's the same for me."

7

ALEXA WRAPPED HER arms around Jamie's neck and returned his kisses with head-spinning fervor. She loved the rough texture of his cheeks and chin, which just this morning had been clean-shaven. She delighted in the quick, fluttery thrills each time his tongue mated with hers.

She could feel herself melting into him. Becoming aware of so many things she'd never felt before. The way the backs of her hands tingled where his hair brushed them. The way her skin warmed and heated at his touch. The way his warm breath tickled the hair at her temple as he pressed soft, moist kisses to her face.

Just as quickly the kiss softened, gentled, as he lingered over her mouth, drawing out all the sweet, fresh flavor that was uniquely hers. There was a sweetness, a freshness about her that put him in mind of a Highland meadow when the heather was in bloom.

He lowered his mouth to the sensitive skin of her throat, running nibbling kisses lower, to her collarbone, then lower still to her breast, until she gasped and clutched at him.

He lifted his head. His voice was gruff. "Would you like me to stop, Alexa?"

"Nay." The word came out in a long drawn-out sigh.

"Ah. Praise heaven." He nibbled the spot between her neck and shoulder until she shivered and clutched at his waist. "For I'm not sure I can."

He slipped the cloak from her shoulders and let it drop to the ground, then reached for the buttons of her gown. When the bodice parted, he untied the ribbons of her chemise until it, too, was parted. At the sight of all that soft, lovely flesh he gave a sigh of pleasure. "You're even more beautiful than I'd dreamed, Alexa."

When he bent to her and took her breast into his mouth she thought she would surely die. Waves of unbelievable pleasure seemed to wash over her at her very core. Her skin was damp, her breathing labored as she reached for his plaid and tugged it free.

Now at last they were standing flesh to flesh in the moonlight. She wrapped her arms around him, greedy for another kiss. He dragged her close, his mouth feasting on hers while his clever hands drove her higher and higher until she thought she would go mad with the need.

"Jamie." Her voice was a desperate plea. Heeding it, he took her hands, and together they dropped to their knees on the cloak.

He couldn't get enough of that soft, soft skin and those luscious lips as he lingered over them, savoring each taste, each touch.

Needing more, he lay with her on the cloak in the cool grass of the garden. He moved over her, his hands and mouth taking her higher, then higher still. She writhed beneath him, her hands and mouth as eager, as avid as his.

With each kiss, each touch, they drew ever closer to

the edge of a high, steep cliff. One step, and they would surely soar. Still he held back, wanting, needing, to take them both higher.

He loved the way she looked, steeped in pleasure. Lips moist and swollen from his kisses. Eyes heavy-lidded with passion. Her body taut as a bowstring, desperate for release.

"Alexa. My beautiful Alexa." He kissed her long and slow and deep, drawing out the moment until she gave a low moan, wrapping her arms around his neck, her body rising up to meet his.

Despite the coolness of the air and the dampness of the grass beneath them, heat rose up, clogging their throats, threatening to choke them.

He'd never known a need this powerful. A desire so overwhelming, it seemed to take over his will. He knew he had to have her. Now. This moment. Or go mad. For there was a demon inside, struggling to be free.

As he entered her he heard her little gasp of shock.

"Dear heaven, I've hurt you." At once he started to pull back.

"Nay, my love." She pulled him close and wrapped herself around him, drawing him even deeper. Then she began to move with him, climb with him, and whatever protest he was about to make was lost.

Now, he knew, there was no turning back. Though in truth he'd known it as soon as she'd returned to him in the garden. From that very first moment he'd been lost.

"I love you, Alexa. Only you," he whispered as they began moving faster, climbing higher.

"And I love you, my brave, handsome warrior. Only you, Jamie."

The words were torn from her lips as she felt herself hurtling out of control.

Wrapped around each other, they took that final leap and found themselves soaring through space. It was the most amazing, breathless journey of their lives.

Moments later they shattered into millions of glittering stars before drifting slowly to earth.

"I didn't mean to be so rough." His face was buried in her throat.

They lay, still joined, their breathing ragged, their bodies slick with sheen.

"You weren't." She gave a weak laugh. "Well, not much."

"Am I too heavy?" .

"Nay." She thought she could lie just so for the rest of her life. The feel of his heartbeat, as unsteady as her own, was oddly comforting. The press of his lips against her throat more wonderful than anything she'd ever known. She felt deliciously sated and happily content.

"Alexa. My Alexa." He shifted, rolling to one side and drawing her gently into the circle of his arms. "Isn't that better?"

"Aye."

"Are you cold?"

"Not a bit." It occurred to her that she ought to be, for they were naked, with nothing but a cloak to shield them from the chill night air. But the warmth of his body was enough to warm her the way nothing else ever could. "Are you cold, Jamie?"

"How could I be cold when I'm holding you, my love?"

My love. She thought she'd never heard two more beautiful words. She traced a finger over the dark hair that matted his chest until she encountered a long, raised scar.

"What is this?"

"Nothing." He closed a hand over hers to still her movements. "Just an old wound."

"I hate knowing you've been so hurt."

"It doesn't matter now, love. Now that I have you here in my arms, all my wounds are forgotten. They no longer have the power to cause me pain."

It was true, he realized. He felt healed. Reborn. He framed her face with his hands. "We've all been scarred by wars, Alexa. But we've survived, you and I. Until now I hated that I had survived when others had died. Now, because of you, I realize that we've been given much more than the gift of life."

"And what is that?"

"The gift of love," he whispered against her lips.

He held her a little away, then drew her close and kissed her again, this time lingering over her lips before taking the kiss deeper.

"My lovely Alexa. You're so incredible. And I love you so very much."

Love. She hugged the word to her heart, knowing there was nothing he could have said that would mean as much.

"You're cold." He began to draw the cloak around her. "I felt you shiver."

"It wasn't from the cold, Jamie." She wrapped her arms around his neck and pressed her body to his, thrilling to the fact that he was once again fully aroused. "It was from this. Only this."

Growing bolder, she pressed moist little kisses along his throat, then lower, to his chest. When he gave a groan of pleasure she grew bolder still, until he caught her by the upper arms to still her movements. "Woman, do you have any idea what you're doing to me?"

"I do indeed, my laird." She chuckled and brushed the damp hair from his eyes, loving the look of love she could see there. "Do you object?"

"I'll object only if you stop, my lady."

As he lost himself in her, he realized that he felt as if he'd been waiting for this woman, this moment, and this unexpected gift of love all his life.

"Jamie. What have you done?" Alexa awoke to find Jamie sitting cross-legged beside her in the grass. On his face was a look of smug confidence as he began removing items hidden beneath his plaid.

"I've brought us food. And some fine wine as well."

She looked up to see that it was barely dawn. The two

lovers had spent the night in the garden, huddled together in her warm cloak. And though they'd managed a little sleep, most of their time had been spent loving.

At times they'd felt as if the very earth shook with the enormity of their love. At other times their loving had been as easy, as gentle, as if they'd always been together.

It was how she felt, Alexa realized. As though this man had been her lover from the very beginning of time.

She sat up, shoving fiery curls from her eyes. "Are the sisters awake already?"

"Nay. There was no one in the refectory, so I helped myself to whatever I wanted. And as I was rummaging around I discovered a jug of church wine." He filled a goblet and offered it to her. "I'm sure old Father Lazarus won't mind if we enjoy a bit."

"Church wine?" With the goblet halfway to her lips she paused and shot him an incredulous look. "You stole church wine?"

"I didn't steal it, love. In fact, I'll be more than happy to replace whatever we drink." With a roguish smile he broke off a hunk of cheese. "You have to admit that we're in need of sustenance, Alexa, love."

"Aye." She returned his smile and sipped the wine, feeling the warmth flow through her veins.

When he offered her a bite of bread and cheese, she accepted it gratefully.

"Of course—" His smile grew as he sipped from the goblet before passing it back to her. "I had a selfish reason for fetching all this food and drink."

"And what would that be?"

He leaned close to brush his mouth over hers. At once they both absorbed the quick rush of heat.

"I want you refreshed and renewed, my love, so that we can take advantage of these last precious moments before the sisters awaken for the day."

"I should have known your motives weren't entirely noble, my laird."

He took the goblet from her hands and set it aside before framing her face with his hands and covering her mouth with his.

Against her lips he murmured, "You must admit that my idea was a fine one."

"A fine idea indeed." With a purr of delight she wrapped her arms around his waist and gave herself up to the pleasure.

"Reverend Mother, something is amiss."

The older nun looked up from her desk. "What is it, Sister Fiona?"

"When young Mordrund took a tray to the lass's chamber, she found it empty. She said that the bed linens don't appear to have been slept in, for they were cold to the touch."

"Perhaps she went to chapel with the novices."

"She didn't. I already looked there. But there is more, Reverend Mother." The nun worried the skirt of her coarse gown. "When I checked the laird's chamber, it was also empty."

Mother Superior pushed away from the desk and began to pace. As she did, she glanced out the window and stopped in her tracks. Then she stepped closer to the window and gave a long, deep sigh.

"What is it, Reverend Mother?" The younger nun hurried to her side, then let out an exclamation of surprise at the sight of Alexa and Jamie seated side by side on a stone bench, their shoulders brushing as they carried on an animated conversation.

"The lass is without her cloak, Reverend Mother."

"Aye. I noticed."

"I've never seen her with her head uncovered. Look how her hair blazes in the sunlight."

"I see it."

"And she appears to be . . . laughing."

"She does indeed."

"It's nothing short of a miracle." The younger nun

turned to her superior with a look of amazement. "Wouldn't you agree, Reverend Mother?"

"Aye, Sister Fiona. It would appear that both the lass and the laird have finally come out of the darkness."

"I must go and share this good news with the others. Perhaps Father Lazarus will offer up a prayer of thanksgiving."

"A fine idea." Mother Mary of the Cross waited until the door to her office closed behind the eager young nun. Then she returned her attention to the couple in the garden.

She had been praying for a miracle, and at first glance it would seem that one had been granted. Still, though she had taken a vow to turn away from the things of the world, she considered herself a practical woman. Practical enough to know that love alone was sometimes not enough to cure the ills of body, heart, and soul.

She hoped and prayed that she was wrong. She desperately wanted a happy ending for these two wounded people.

She saw the laird touch a hand to the lass's shoulder before leaning close to say something that made her smile.

Mother Superior turned away, feeling very much like an intruder.

8

"LOOK AT THEM, Reverend Mother." Sister Fiona paused in the arched doorway to stare at the young couple working side by side in the garden. "It does my heart good to see them so happy." She sighed. "And so in love."

"Aye." The older nun nodded.

There was no denying it. The transformation in Alexa and Jamie was amazing to all who saw them. The sound of their laughter couldn't help but lift every heart at the abbey. The sight of them, shyly holding hands as they walked the garden path after their evening meal, had the nuns and novices openly smiling. Especially when they recalled how wounded these two had been such a short time ago. Now that they had heard the tale of the lass's painful loss of family, they were even more amazed that she had emerged into the light.

Mother Mary of the Cross glanced around approvingly. The gardens had never looked better. There were dahlias as large as serving platters, in every color imaginable, and behind them, in stately rows, snapdragons as tall as a man. Some beds were overflowing with bright yellow and orange nasturtiums, while others boasted pale pink verbena and deep purple foxglove.

Even the walls were abloom with color. Pink and white sweet peas and vibrant purple wisteria snaked along the stones and spilled over the top, filling every available space with fragrant blossoms.

It was as though the flowers, like the people who resided in the abbey, were basking in the luminous glow that emanated from these two lovers.

While he worked beside her, Jamie paused and tried to keep the excitement from his voice. "Do you know what I love best about this garden?"

"What?" Alexa looked up.

"The knowledge that it brought us together. First as a refuge from the world, and later as proof that there can still be peace and beauty in a world torn apart by battle."

She smiled. "It's true. This is our world now, Jamie."

Something about the way she said it had him shaking his head. " 'Tis only a brief respite, my love. Our world still awaits us, out there." He pointed toward the distant forest. "There in the Highlands is my home. My people. Now that I'm well and strong again, I long to be with them. I want you to go with me and accept them as your people, too, Alexa."

She went very still. Seeing it, Jamie dropped to his knees beside her. "Forgive me, love. I'd meant to set a more solemn tone when I asked you. But you must admit that we've been here long enough to heal our bodies and souls. Now it's time to return to the real world. I've already sent a message to my people, letting them know that I'm alive and well and strong enough to return to lead them. I want you to return with me, Alexa, as my bride. I hope I'm not too bold to ask that you marry me, my love, and return with me to the Highlands where we'll make our home together."

"Make a home in the Highlands?" The hand tool dropped from Alexa's fingers. She seemed unaware as she got to her feet. "I thought this was our home now, Jamie."

He stood beside her, too happy to note her little frown. "This is an abbey, love. It was a fine refuge while we recovered from our wounds. Now we must get on with our lives. Since you no longer have a clan of your own, I offer you mine. My people will love you as I do."

As he gathered her close he heard her sudden sigh of distress and held her a little away from him. "What is it, Alexa?"

"I thought you understood. I can't possibly leave here."

"Why not?"

"Because I took a vow. Because"—she looked around wildly, her mind awhirl with sudden fear—"my task here is not yet complete." At his puzzled look she knelt and retrieved something from the ground. "You see? How can I leave when this has happened again?"

"What has happened?"

"This." She opened her hand to reveal several shriveled rosebuds. "There's a blight. No matter what I do, they refuse to open. Instead the buds fall off and die."

He laughed. "Then we'll pull out the roses and replace them with something else. Something that will fill the garden with glorious blooms."

"Nay." She shook her head vigorously. "The roses must be here, in the center of the garden."

He tried to rein in his impatience. "Why must they?"

"Because." She lowered her head, avoiding his eyes. "What is a garden, after all, without roses?"

He lifted her chin. "Such a simple problem as this shouldn't upset you so. What is it you're not telling me, love?"

She pulled away, again avoiding his eyes. "There must be roses here. Without them the garden isn't complete."

He spread his hands. "Look around you, Alexa. See what you've accomplished. Without you, this would still be barren earth and tumbled stones. Thanks to you, the abbey's garden is once more a place of beauty and serenity. Why can't you simply enjoy what you've done and replace the roses with something that will thrive?"

"You don't understand." She looked up, and her eyes glittered with unshed tears. "I see the garden as it once was."

"You see it?"

She nodded, afraid he would think her mad, yet needing to admit the truth. "Each time I close my eyes, I see the garden as it was a hundred years ago. It . . . haunts my dreams. As do Lady Anne and her sadness."

"I see." Jamie drew her close and felt her shiver. "No wonder you were so withdrawn from the world, love. By day you were back on the field of battle, and by night you were thrust into the distant past. But what about the present, Alexa? And the future? Our future, together?"

She took a deep breath. "I know not, Jamie. I know only that I have given my word to Lady Anne that I will restore the gardens to their former beauty. That way, she will have a measure of comfort while she is confined to this earthly prison. Furthermore, I took a vow before Father Lazarus." She gave a deep sigh. "So you see, I cannot leave here until the roses are brought to bloom, or I would be breaking my vow."

"And if my men come for me and the roses have not yet bloomed? What then, Alexa? Will you send me away alone?"

She swallowed. "If I must."

Jamie's eyes narrowed. "Are you saying that you love this garden more than you love me?"

"Nay." She clenched her hands at her sides, to keep from reaching out to him. "I will never love anyone or anything as much as I love you, Jamie Morgan. But I made a vow."

"Vows can be broken."

She shook her head. "Nay. I gave my word to Lady Anne."

"Your word to a ghost is more important than your love for me?"

"You don't understand."

"I understand this: You feel safe here, Alexa. This place offers you peace, and beauty, and a refuge from the reality of life beyond these walls. The life I offer you is one of hard work and strife, and yes, possibly war. But I also offer you undying love. Can there be anything more important in life than that?"

When she remained silent, he said, "Heed my word, Alexa. The women here, both those alive and the one whose spirit walks the garden, can never love you as I do. Nor can these flowers."

"You sound as though"—she blinked furiously to hold back the tears that burned her lids—"you intend to leave with or without me."

"My people look to me to lead, Alexa. When my men come for me, I must leave with them. Though my heart will be heavy, I will abide by your decision."

She lifted her chin, as determined as he not to back down. "I love you, Jamie. Only you. I would be proud to make your people my people, but only if my task here is complete. I gave my word to Lady Anne, to restore her gardens exactly as they were when she first walked them."

His tone rang with challenge. "If the roses bloom, will you take that as a sign that your task here is complete? Or will you find another excuse to hide from the world?"

"Is that what you think? That I'm using my vow to keep me here?"

His voice lowered. "I ask again, Alexa. If the roses bloom, will you go with me?"

She nodded.

"And if they should not?"

She shook her head and turned away, unwilling to let him see the tears she could no longer hold back.

For long minutes he stood watching. Then he turned away and strode through the arched doorway, his booted feet echoing in the silence of the abbey.

• • •

Word of the lovers' disagreement swept through the halls of the abbey, casting a pall over everyone's joy. Throughout the days that followed, the nuns and novices watched as the roses continued to shrivel and die.

Each day Jamie walked to the garden with eager expectancy. Each day, as Alexa knelt in the soil to retrieve the latest fallen rosebuds, he turned away with a look of such sadness, it tore at the hearts of all who saw him.

Too soon, word of a procession of Highland warriors approaching their village swept through the abbey. As always, it was the novice, Mordrund, who first heard the news and carried it to the others.

"Giants they are," she reported to her superior. "And so fair of face that all the maidens are weeping with joy."

Mother Mary of the Cross shoved away from her desk and started toward the door, saying dryly, "I'm sure we'll be able to maintain our composure at the sight of them, Mordrund. Go and inform the laird that his clansmen approach."

"Aye, Reverend Mother."

By the time the line of warriors arrived at the gates, the nuns and novices had assembled in the courtyard, along with Alexa. Jamie rushed forward to welcome his kinsmen. When he caught sight of their leader he gave a shout of delight.

"Duncan. By all that is holy, is it truly you?"

The two men fell together in a fierce embrace before laughing and stepping apart.

"I'd feared that you were lost to me, Duncan."

"Aye, Jamie lad. I'd feared the same, for my wounds were grave, but a kind family took me in and nursed me back to health. I made my way back to the Highlands only a fortnight ago. When we got your missive that you were alive, there was great rejoicing, for we'd feared the worst."

Jamie turned to Alexa. "This is my oldest and dearest

friend, Duncan MacKay." His tone softened. "Duncan, this lovely creature is Alexa MacCallum."

Duncan bowed before her and saw the way she shrank back from him. "I realize I look a bit wild, my lady. We all do." He swept a hand to include the other warriors, who still sat astride their mounts. "We've come a long way to fetch our laird home."

To smooth over the awkward moment, the head of the abbey stepped forward. "I am Mother Mary of the Cross, the superior here. You and your men are most welcome to refresh yourselves for as long as you please before you return to the Highlands. We have a meal ready in the refectory, and Father Lazarus has added pallets on the floor of the chapel for your nightly comfort."

"My men and I thank you for your kindness, Reverend Mother." Duncan threw an arm around his old friend. "Will you join us in the refectory?"

"Aye."

As Jamie was surrounded by his clansmen, he tried to draw Alexa into their circle. She backed away from him and fled to the garden.

He kept his smile in place as he greeted his old friends and walked with them into the abbey, but his thoughts were on the lass who, like a motherless fawn, was trying to find her way in a frightening new world.

Supper was a grand affair, with much shouting and laughter as the men washed away the grime of the journey with ale provided by Father Lazarus.

Jamie sat at a table with his men, while Alexa sat with the women in a small alcove to one side, since it wasn't considered proper for the nuns to be seated in the company of raucous warriors.

"Will we leave on the morrow?" Duncan asked.

Jamie glanced toward the table where Alexa was seated. "I . . . would think you would desire some rest before you undertake the return to the Highlands."

"There's no time to be wasted, Jamie. There is much

disarray among our people." Duncan emptied his goblet, more than a little surprised at the quality of ale at the abbey. He was even more surprised when the elderly priest produced a second jug as soon as the first one was emptied.

Duncan refilled his goblet and drank deeply. "There are some who claim that you aren't really alive. They claim that your friends are trying to hide your death from them in order to keep the clans together. There are even a few who whisper among themselves that it is time to appoint a new laird from among the remaining warriors. I would advise you to leave at first light, Jamie, in order to stop the rumors and assure peace in our Highlands."

Jamie digested this news before giving a grudging nod of his head. "I hadn't realized the seriousness of the situation. You're right, of course, my friend. We'll leave at first light."

He saw Alexa excuse herself and knew that she was going to the garden. Though he still felt a small measure of hope, there was a heaviness in his heart, for he'd seen that same look on her face before, and he knew that she intended to keep her promise to Lady Anne. No matter what the cost.

All the lights of the abbey had been extinguished. From the chapel came the rumble of snoring as the Highland warriors slept.

Jamie stepped through the arched doorway. The garden was bathed in moonlight, giving the flowers, the trees, even the stone benches, a luminous quality. The air was sweet with the perfume of hundreds of flowers.

He took no notice of the beauty of the place, however. Instead he crossed directly to where Alexa stood studying the roses in the middle of the garden. Seeing the look on her face, he felt a hard, quick tug at his heart.

"They continue to die?"

She nodded and held out her hand. "The latest buds have already begun to shrivel." She couldn't keep the pain from her voice. "By morning they'll be littering the ground like all the others."

He absorbed the blow at the knowledge that he would be returning to the Highlands alone. His heart lay like a stone in his chest as he gathered her into the circle of his arms.

Against his throat she whispered, "I can't bear the thought of your leaving, Jamie."

Heat pulsed through his veins at the warmth of her breath against his skin. "Then come with me, Alexa. It's the only thing I'll ever ask of you."

"Don't do this, my love. You know I can't do as you ask. A solemn vow once made cannot be broken on a whim."

"You call our love a whim?" His voice was made deep with pain. "You were a gift to me, Alexa. A very special gift. Because of you I'm healed in body and mind. Now, because of a vow made to a lost, tormented soul, you would condemn us both to a life of loneliness." He couldn't hide the bitterness in his tone. "Could this be why she remains here? To see that other lovers are denied the happiness she denied herself?"

"Is that what you think? That she somehow extracted a promise from me in order to bind me to her?"

"Can you think of another reason?"

Alexa lifted brimming eyes to his. "I'm so weary of thinking, Jamie. So weary." She touched a fingertip to his mouth and saw the blaze of desire flare in his eyes. "If we can't have a lifetime, at least we can have tonight."

"It will only make the parting that much more painful on the morrow."

She shook her head. "I care not about tomorrow. I need you now. This night."

He framed her face with his hands and covered her mouth with his. Against her lips he muttered, "How could I refuse you, my love?"

He kissed her long and slow and deep, until they nearly wept with need. Then lifting her into his arms he strode across the garden and carried her to his room.

As the couple disappeared through the arched doorway, a shimmering figure appeared in the garden.

As always, she climbed the stone steps to the top of the wall, where, as she had for a hundred years, she stared off into the distance, her expression a mixture of hope and despair.

9

THIN RIBBONS OF dawn light streaked the sky as the Highland warriors trooped out of the chapel and began the preparations for the journey home. The courtyard of the abbey rang with shouts as horses were saddled and provisions were loaded in wagons.

Alexa choked back tears as Jamie wound the plaid about his shoulders and reached for his sword and dirk.

All night there had been such urgency, such passion to their lovemaking. A passion born of desperation. The knowledge that this was to be their last time had them clinging to one another as though to life itself.

His face was devoid of emotion as he turned to her. "Will you walk with me to the courtyard?"

"Aye." Though she dreaded the thought of the entire assembly witnessing their good-bye, she knew it would be cowardly to hide here in his room. He deserved the same courage from her that he'd shown on the field of battle. And so she reached for his outstretched hand and moved woodenly along beside him.

"Will we stop first in the garden?"

She glanced at the still-darkened sky before reluctantly shaking her head. "It will only add to the pain of our farewell."

"I suppose." He walked with her into the courtyard.

The Highlanders stood beside their horses, awaiting their laird. When they caught sight of him, their voices grew hushed, for they had heard of his painful dilemma. The love between him and the lass, and the vow that would now separate them, was all that was being discussed in the abbey. Even the old priest had spoken of it.

The sisters, too, fell silent at the sight of Jamie and Alexa, heads high, staring straight ahead as they made their way among the waiting men.

Duncan was holding the reins of two horses. As Jamie approached, his friend handed him the reins to a magnificent black stallion. It occurred to Alexa that the animal suited the man. Both looked a bit untamed, and more than prepared for whatever task lay before them.

She touched a hand to Jamie's arm, determined to get through this with as much dignity as she could. "Goodbye, Jamie Morgan. Godspeed."

He didn't touch her. Couldn't. For he knew if he did, he would surely take her in his arms and force her to accompany him, and to hell with her solemn vow. But now, as he had with the fawn of his childhood, he must let go and take comfort in the knowledge that she would be with her own kind.

"Farewell, Alexa MacCallum. I'll never forget you."

He pulled himself into the saddle and stared straight ahead as Mother Superior stepped to the head of the column of Highlanders and lifted her hand in a blessing.

Before she could speak the words, there was a shout. Everyone turned as the young novice, Mordrund, came rushing into the courtyard, her skirts hiked up in a most unladylike fashion, her chest heaving from the exertion of her run.

Reverend Mother's eyes flashed in a rare display of anger. "You will take yourself to the chapel, Mordrund, and pray for the humility befitting a servant of the Lord."

"Aye, Reverend Mother. I shall. As soon as I tell you . . ."

"Now." Mother Mary of the Cross could feel her patience snap. "Can you not see how difficult this moment is for all of us? I'll not have it made worse by your impertinence. Now leave us."

"I will, Reverend Mother. But first . . ." The poor novice looked from her superior to the laird seated upon his steed, and then to the lass, who was close to tears. "I must tell you that a miracle has occurred in the garden."

"A miracle?" Reverend Mother's head came up sharply. "What are you saying, Mordrund?"

"The roses are abloom! Not just a few, but dozens of them."

For the space of a heartbeat there was complete silence at her announcement. Then, as her words sank in, there seemed to be complete chaos. While the sisters ran ahead, Jamie scooped Alexa into his arms and turned his mount toward an opening in the wall, with the Highlanders following on their steeds.

"Oh, my sweet heaven." Alexa clapped a hand to her mouth as she stared at the rosebushes, bathed in streams of morning sunlight in the middle of the garden.

Where only last night there had been shriveled buds, there were now dozens, perhaps hundreds of perfect blooms.

"Do you know what this means, my love?" Jamie brought his lips to her temple.

"Aye. It is as young Mordrund said. A miracle. A sign that my work here is finished."

"You're prepared to come with me to my Highland fortress, my love? Now? This very hour?"

"I will. Oh, Jamie. I know now that what you said was

true. I've been hiding out here, lost and afraid. Now, though I'm still afraid of the world beyond these walls, I'm even more afraid of life without you. I need you, Jamie. Only you. And I love you so." She wound her arms around his neck and hugged him fiercely. "I feel so useless. I have nothing to bring with me, for I came here with nothing."

"You'll bring everything that matters, Alexa. Your sweetness, your goodness, your love." He lifted his voice. "Reverend Mother, give us your blessing, for we must leave you now and return to our home."

"Home." At the sound of that word Alexa began to weep. Softly at first, and then more openly, as she realized the enormity of what had just occurred. "I had no home to return to, Jamie. No clan to call my own. And now I will have both."

"Aye. And I'll have the woman I love beside me always."

As silence settled over the crowd, Reverend Mother's voice rose above the sigh of the wind. "Go with God, Laird Jamie Morgan and Alexa MacCallum. We hope you will think of us from time to time. And when you do, we hope you will whisper a prayer. For the two of you will be in our hearts and our prayers forever. Each time we walk our beautiful garden, we will think of you and remember the time you spent here."

Mordrund came bounding forward. "Shall I pick you a bouquet of roses for your journey, Alexa?"

Before she could reply Duncan shouted, "There's no time, my laird. We must leave now."

Alexa smiled at the little novice. "I thank you, Mordrund. But the memory of all those lovely roses will be enough for me. I leave the blooms for all of you to enjoy in my stead."

Jamie wheeled his mount, and a great shout went up from his men as they followed their laird through the courtyard and up the grassy meadow beyond.

Atop a hill Jamie reined in his mount for a final look

at the place that had brought them both healing and love. Then, with matching smiles, they turned toward home.

As the Highlanders disappeared into the mist, the sisters hurried to chapel to pray for a safe journey.

Reverend Mother was just turning away to follow when Mordrund called to her. "Reverend Mother, you must come at once."

The old sister gave a sigh. "What is it now, Mordrund?"

"Look, Reverend Mother." The young novice pointed to the rosebushes, where a breeze was causing the blossoms to blow about. She lifted her hand and caught hold of one.

"It's perfect," Mother Mary of the Cross said.

"Aye, Reverend Mother. But feel it."

As the novice pressed the blossom into her hand, the old nun gave a gasp of surprise. "What is this?"

"Parchment, Reverend Mother."

"What are you saying?" She held it up to the sunlight and could see that it was indeed made of parchment. She reached for another, and yet another. Some were made of parchment, others of cloth. Each had been perfectly painted to resemble a rose. "But how can this be? Who . . . ?"

Mordrund pointed, and Reverend Mother looked up to see Lady Anne on the top step of the wall, holding out her arms. As they watched in wonder, they saw a warrior coming for her on a golden cloud. With a shout of triumph he gathered her close, and as they embraced, they shimmered with a blinding light before disappearing from sight.

The old nun and the young novice stood transfixed, watching until the vision dissolved.

Mother Superior's voice was hushed. "What we have witnessed this day is truly a miracle. Lady Anne has finally learned the truth. When her gifts were used for purely unselfish reasons, she was set free of the bonds of this world. Free at last to be with her warrior for eternity."

"What of Alexa and the laird?" The little novice

seemed genuinely concerned. "Should we not send word of the truth?"

"What is the truth, Mordrund? Did not the roses bloom, thus freeing our Alexa from her vow?"

"Aye, Reverend Mother."

The old woman's eyes burned with inner fire. "The love we saw between a wounded laird and lass was quite extraordinary. Such a love is rarely found. When it is, nothing should be allowed to stand in the way of love's special healing. We are, after all, healers, are we not?"

"Aye, Reverend Mother."

"Come, then, Mordrund. Let us join the others at chapel and praise heaven for the miracle of healing granted this day."

The little novice dutifully followed her superior to chapel. Though she prayed that she would one day learn to curb her tongue, it wasn't to be. Only two women witnessed Lady Anne flying into the heavens with her warrior, and from the lips of one, the story was passed from village to town until it became a legend.

In the Highlands, the laird of lairds wed his beloved before his entire clan. It is said they raised up many fair sons and daughters. Though all were trained as warriors, their true task on earth was to preserve the peace among all clans in the Highlands.

All who knew them said that their love blazed so brightly even death could not extinguish it. To this day, each time the roses bloom in the garden of the Abbey of Glenross, it is seen as proof that the love of Jamie and Alexa, like the love of Lady Anne and her warrior, Malcolm, endures for all time.

THE FAIREST ROSE

Marianne Willman

To Nora, Ruth and Jan,
the fairest roses of them all

Prologue

"TODAY MY TRUE love returns home to my arms!"

Deirdre smiled before the small looking glass on her cottage wall. She'd dressed her dark hair with wild pink roses that she'd plucked from the riverbank, still fresh with morning dew, and a length of silver ribbon the same shade as her clear gray eyes. Her lover had bought it for her at the Beltane fair.

A ring of hammered gold circled her finger, gleaming in the warm morning light. He'd placed it there at midnight, to symbolize their vows to one another: In the midst of war, there had been no time for priests and marriage bans. They had pledged their love in the ways of old, by clasping hands and leaping together over the sacred Beltane fire. Afterward, they had lain together in the sweet scented grass and whispered their undying love while the stars danced overhead.

She smoothed the blue fabric she'd woven herself over

her swollen belly. Nine long months had passed since that magical night. Soon she would bear the fruit of their love. The precious babe within her womb would be born before the moon came full.

Ah, Gilmore! What a happy surprise you'll have when you learn of it.

He had answered the call to arms and ridden into battle with his loyal followers, not knowing that he had fathered a child. Those had been lonely and terrible times for her. Months of fear, endless rumors of defeat and banishment. Or worse.

She shivered, remembering. Indeed, for the last month she'd fought dark despair. The news from the war had been bad, and she'd feared for Gilmore's life. Then, as she stood by the beckoning river seven nights ago, she'd seen something blaze across the night: a shimmering golden bird that left glittering trails of jeweled light against the midnight sky.

She had recognized it at once: the mystical phoenix, symbol of eternal life and beauty. Legend said the magical bird lived in the high reaches of the Misted Mountains, an enchanted no-man's-land between Airan and the borders of the Eastern Lands. Some debated whether the creature existed at all. The occasional sightings, they claimed, were of falling stars, such as could be seen on any summer night.

But she had seen it, soaring and shining brighter than the stars. She'd taken it as an omen, for the phoenix was Gilmore's emblem. She'd known then that he would return to her in triumph.

Her instincts had proved right. The very next day the countryside had rung with the news of his victory. He'd rallied the troops and won the day with his fierce courage, and had been rewarded for it with the highest honor. Where before he had been a landless knight, Gilmore was now king of Airan.

Her lover had always been ambitious, and she had championed his dreams of uniting the country—but she had never imagined it would come to this! Some even whispered that he would be named High King of All the Western Lands when the clans met again. He'd been crowned upon the battlefield, with all the nobles and their allies pledging support. Only the stubborn men of Far Islandia had refused to bend their knees and take the oath of allegiance.

As Deirdre was tucking the last of the fragrant roses into the silver ribbon, she heard it: the song of golden-throated bugles announcing the arrival of the new king.

Her heart gave a leap of joy. She raced out of the cottage, her lovely face radiant. Nothing could be seen of Gilmore and his soldiers yet, except the cloud of dust churned up by the approaching cavalcade.

Movement closer by caught her eye. It was Elva, the wisewoman who made simples and remedies for the village. She came out of the deep woods, thin as a birch stick in her light gray gown. There was a basket of fresh-gathered herbs and medicinal plants over her arm, smelling of green forest and damp summer earth.

She turned to greet Deirdre, a slight frown between large eyes as dark as peat. For a moment a shadow seemed to sweep across Deirdre, as if a great black bird had flown between her and the sun.

"You should not run so near your term, mistress. You must save your strength for what is to come."

"Indeed, my feet have wings today. Gilmore has returned to Airan," Deirdre said. "He has come for me. For *us*."

She looked dreamily across the river, to Castle Airan. It rose above the rushing water, all white towers and turrets and crumbled stone walls. Soon Gilmore's phoenix pennant would fly there. And they would live out their lives together in happiness, with this child she carried, and all their children to come.

It seemed like a fairy tale, too astonishing, too good to be true.

She turned and smiled down the road. Already she

could see Gilmore's banner topping the rise: a golden phoenix on a ground of royal blue. Deirdre's heart was so full the joy spilled over in tears of happiness.

A moment later the colorful cavalcade poured through the dark gap in the rolling hills and down into the river valley. The breeze carried faint sounds to them: the jingle of harness, the rumble of hooves, and the creaking moan of treasure-burdened wagons. Down the dusty road the villagers were hurrying out of their cottages to greet the victors, but Deirdre waited patiently at her gate for her lover.

First came the outriders, with their festive banners, then Gilmore's private guard in their dark blue tabards, his phoenix insignia embroidered with gold thread upon them. Then he was there, Gilmore himself, on a prancing white steed with a golden bridle. He was so splendid she hardly recognized him. A cloak of crimson velvet hung from his wide shoulders, and his tunic was woven of cloth of gold. The glinting coronet upon his thick red hair was centered with a sapphire that was no bluer than his eyes. Deirdre's heart stood still with love for him.

"Your father," she whispered to the child within her womb.

He reined in as he reached the curve before the cottage and slowed his horse to a walk, frowning slightly. *He is looking for me among the throng,* she thought. What a surprise he will get!

"Gilmore!" Her face shone, and she lifted her arms in greeting as he pulled abreast of her.

But the young king kept his handsome head high and his gaze straight ahead as he rode past in his newfound glory. Not so much as a single glance did he cast her way.

Deirdre was stunned. Why hadn't he stopped? Why hadn't he acknowledged her? She was hand-fasted to him, as much his wife as if they'd exchanged vows before the high altar.

Then Deirdre saw what she hadn't noticed before: A woman rode beside him. She was gowned in cloth of gold, with a cloak of emerald satin, and a thin gold circlet rested low on her brow. Her skin was white as milk, her hair and eyes as gold as coins; but her beautiful face was hard with arrogance, and her red mouth a disdainful slash.

As she passed Deirdre her golden eyes narrowed as if in recognition. Her gaze was cold and dagger-sharp. Deirdre staggered back in pain, as if she had been impaled on a poisoned blade. Although the sun was hot, she felt a darkness filling her chest, congealing her blood. It thickened and slowed in her veins.

While she stood frozen to the spot, the line of soldiers and wagons rumbled by. Elva stepped out to accost one of the men-at-arms who was her kinsman. He pulled over at the roadside.

"God save you, cousin. Who is the woman riding at Gilmore's side?" she asked.

"Why, that is Bryn, daughter of wily Monfort."

"But Monfort is our sworn enemy," Elva said.

"No longer," her kinsman said. "They have signed an accord and sealed it in blood." He made a grimace of distaste. "The Lady Bryn is now queen of this land. She and Gilmore were wed in high ceremony, before all."

Deirdre heard, and the words slammed into her, almost knocking her off her feet. The man rode on to join the rest, but it seemed to her that it happened in total silence. Her ears went deaf to the glad shouts, her eyes blind to the bright summer sky and the green hills spilling down to the winding river. She stumbled back toward the cottage.

Elva saw. She caught Deirdre's arm and guided her inside. "Lie down upon your bed beneath the warm blankets. Your skin is like ice!"

Deirdre stared at her blankly. "He did not stop. He did not so much as acknowledge me!"

Elva's black eyes filled with anger. And fear. "Gilmore has not abandoned you—he has forgotten you."

"How could he do so? We grew up together in this

valley, playing beneath the castle walls. He has had my heart since I was a mere child, and I, his."

"Do not judge him too harshly. His new queen has cast a spell upon him. I know a wicked sorceress when I see one!"

"There must be some way to break the spell." Deirdre's eyes welled up with tears. "You know the ancient arts. Can you not find a way to free Gilmore from the enchantment of this sorceress?"

The wisewoman shook her head. "I know the healing ways, and the charms to draw love, or make crops bloom with abundance. But I have never studied evil. She has, and her power is too great for such as me."

Suddenly Deirdre doubled over. The birth pang caught her by surprise, and her silver-blue eyes glazed with pain. With fear. "Ah, no! Not yet."

But the babe within her was eager to be born. It would not be denied.

Elva helped her to the bed and prepared for the confinement. It was not long at all before the child came, a girl, small and vulnerable, born into a world that was hostile to her. Exhausted, Deirdre lay back against her pillow. She sipped the wild cherry cordial that Elva held to her lips, but it gave her no strength or warmth. Her thoughts were only for her newborn daughter, nestled in her arms. She smoothed the soft, dark auburn curls, caressed the velvet cheek, and marveled at the tiny fingers wrapped around her own.

But even as she felt the heat of that small body nestled against hers, her own grew increasingly colder. She saw the sorrow in Elva's eyes. Knowledge of what was to come burdened her gentle soul.

"Elva, I know I am beyond your help—I knew my fate the moment that woman looked at me with such hatred. She has cast a curse upon me, and my hours on earth are numbered. But what of my daughter? Can you save her, at least?"

Elva hesitated, remembering. "Once upon a time, when

I was very young, I was told the Spell of Forgetting. Perhaps I can use it against Bryn's curse, turn it inside out upon itself to suit our purpose. If only I can recall it now."

She struggled to dredge it up from the depths of memory. But true to its name, the spell kept sliding away from her, as if it were mist. A bit here, another there. Shifting, shifting. She began to fear it was beyond her reach.

Elva threw herself back in time, past her memory and her mother's memory, into the realm of long ago. Her dark eyes went flat and opaque. Then her breath came out in a sigh of relief, and the corners of her wide mouth turned up in triumph.

"I have it now! I know what I must do."

If only she could bring it all together. The old woman who had been her mentor had passed on before she could share all her accumulated wisdom.

She smoothed the damp hair back from Deirdre's cold cheeks. "Rest for a while," Elva told her. "I must fashion an amulet."

"Keep her safe for me," Deirdre whispered. She felt the cold and dark closing in with every beat of her heart.

"I shall," Elva said fiercely. "I swear it."

She hurried from the cottage. Time was running out. The distant hills shimmered with misty rain, but the river still lay in dappled sunlight. The water shone gold and brown and silver, singing softly as it rushed down to the sea. She plucked green moss from the rocks along the verge.

The wisewoman's fingers moved in a blur of speed while she murmured ancient words in a low, sweet voice. She wove the strands of dark moss into a slender chain. It changed to gleaming silver in her hands.

Next, she reached into the rippling stream and brought a quartz pebble from among the water weeds. It was oval and clear as glass. "Ah! Perfect!"

Elva held the pebble high, toward the rainbow that now arced across the far hills, and murmured another phrase in the language that few mortals remembered. The rainbow vanished from the sky and reappeared as shifting planes of dancing color within the stone's transparent heart.

The crystal grew warm in her hand. Her spirits soared. Yet she must not grow overconfident. There was more she must do to bind the spell.

Back in the cottage, she saw that both mother and child were asleep. It was better so. Her skills might fail them yet. Elva pushed the thought away.

Taking one of the wild roses discarded from Deirdre's hair, she pulled the petals loose and wrapped them around the shining stone with trembling fingers. She smoothed each one carefully in place. Then she caught the single tear that trembled on Deirdre's dark lashes and the tiny tear that lingered at the side of the infant's closed eye.

As the tears mingled and fell upon the petal-wrapped stone, it was instantly transformed. The crumpled petals turned smooth and glossy. Their color deepened until they were red as heart's blood.

Elva closed her eyes and lifted her head, then threw off the protective barriers of self, became open and defenseless, naked to the universe. "I command the Power of Good and summon it to this place. Hear me!"

For a moment she seemed to be tumbling head over heels through the air. Then she felt it stirring around her, like a summer breeze through the trees. The power grew and shook her as if she were a leaf in a storm.

Sweat broke out on her forehead and her breathing grew labored. Taking the silver chain with its amulet, she wrapped it around the wrists of mother and child so it bound them together.

"By the Power of Heaven and the Power of Good, by the magic of earth and water, wind and fire, I weave the Spell of Forgetting. May this amulet protect against all who would do you harm. May only those who wish you well remember you. May you be kept safe until one day a hero comes, a man with a noble heart that beats to the rhythm of yours, and a soul as true and passionate as your own. Then, and only then shall this spell I have woven, unravel."

Something jolted through her, like a lightning blast. A torrent of sunbeams poured through the small cottage windows, bathing the room in a powerful crystalline light. It haloed the sleeping mother and child in the bed. Then the air blazed a rich, vibrant gold. Elva had to blink her eyes and turn away from what was an almost painful radiance. Her heart hammered with excitement.

The brightness vanished as suddenly as it had come, but she was so dazzled it took a moment before her vision cleared. When it did, the sun had sunk behind the hills, plunging the room into twilight.

Nothing else seemed to have changed at all.

Elva leaned back in the chair, completely drained.

Had the phenomenon been a true response to her summons, or merely a trick of the eye, caused by the angle of the setting sun? Only time would tell.

While the baby slept and Elva watched, Deirdre dreamed. Of Beltane, and a red-haired man who smiled down at her with love in his eyes. Of a glittering golden bird that streaked like a comet across the dark night sky, aflame with light.

She took wing and followed it, soaring up among the stars.

1

Tor reined in his mount beneath an ancient oak and waited for his companion to catch up with him. The twisted silver torque around his throat gleamed in the half-light of the grove, and his eyes—as jet-black as his long, thick hair—shone with bold resolve.

The light breeze sighed through the oak leaves and brushed like tasseled silk against his sun-bronzed cheek. The cool green dimness was welcome after his hard ride, but rest was not his goal. That lay on the far side of the river.

Castle Airan.

There it rose, beyond the river's green verge, like a sorcerer's illusion. Soaring white towers and crenellated battlements burned bright against the deep-blue summer sky. For a moment Tor was dazzled by it.

He'd journeyed long and far to reach this place. He

only hoped it would prove worth his while. His gloved hands gripped the reins tightly.

He would make it so.

Dismounting lightly, he tied his horse by the little stream that flowed down to the river, and rubbed it down. Once his mount was settled, Tor removed a cloak from his saddlepack. It was of wool, finely woven and as dark as the heart of a forest. He fastened it in place with a simple bronze ornament, set with polished agate.

Another rider entered the oak grove and reined in beside him. He was a grizzled warrior, with hard blue eyes and leathered skin. A third horse was tied behind his, a noble creature with a restive manner.

"Why do you stop?" the man said. "The castle is across the river."

"We'll leave our horses here, Broch, and go afoot."

"And likely come back to find them gone," his companion said darkly. "I don't like this place. There might be thieves lurking about. Or trolls. They steal travelers' horses. Airan is said to be thick with them."

Tor laughed. "I don't believe in trolls. No one I know—including you—has ever seen one."

"Well, I've seen enough thieves in my time." Broch eyed the grove as if one thief might be lurking behind each massive trunk.

"Enough of your grumbling," Tor told him. "The beasts will be safe enough here in the grove. Look how their dark coats blend into the shadows."

He rubbed the nose of the third horse, and it whickered softly. "As for the thieves and cutpurses who prey on crowds, they will be too busy fleecing the fine lords and ladies to bother with us."

Broch shot him a mistrustful look. "You're a deep one. I wish I knew what deviltry you are up to."

Tor turned away hiding his smile. "If I told you, you'd throw me into the river!"

"I may do it anyway."

"Don't worry, old friend. You'll know soon enough."

Tor's laughter died away and his face grew sober. He stood with arms akimbo, eyes on the bright banners flying from the castle ramparts. Each blue pennant was emblazoned with the insignia of a golden bird.

It was a familiar symbol in the Western Lands: the rising phoenix was the emblem of Gilmore of Glendon, a man who had risked all in a desperate battle—and had won himself a kingdom by his wits and skill. Although there were some who felt another warrior had had more right to Airan's crown.

"Airan is a place where dreams can come true," Tor said, "if a man only dares to risk enough!"

Broch swung down beside him. He patted his mount and went to the other horse they'd brought with them, grumbling the whole time.

"I'm a highlander. I've no use for Airan. The mountains are too low, and the sky is too far above to suit my tastes."

Tor shook his head. "By the gods! I swear you'd find fault with heaven." Taking down the worn leather case that held his harp, he slung it over his shoulder.

The other man eyed it suspiciously. "Can you even play that harp?"

"Aye, you sorry doubter! And sing like an angel, too." Tor's wide grin was back. "Come, Broch. Destiny awaits us!"

"Or the dungeon."

"Not if I succeed, my friend. Try and have a little faith in me."

"You have enough for both of us. I pray it's not misplaced."

"You, pray?" Tor slapped the old warrior on the shoulder. "I'd give half my purse of coins to see it."

With the horses hidden deep inside the ancient grove, they crossed the meadows and the stone bridge that spanned the river, joining the others thronging in through the castle gates.

The great outer courtyard had been cleared of its usual

hucksters and clutter, but it was crowded with people. There were minor dignitaries, wealthy merchants, and their wives at the back.

Nearer the wide stone steps to the inner court, Tor saw, were ranks of princes and lords in bright silks and velvets, their household retainers in gold-threaded tabards, and burly men-at-arms with the glint of chain mail beneath their tunics. He found a space near the back wall and claimed it. The few who started to protest took one look at his wide shoulders and determined face and held their peace.

Broch glanced around. "Fah! I've never seen so many strutting peacocks," he said in disdain. "We have no place among them."

"Not yet."

Broch stared. "I mislike it when you speak in riddles."

"You'd like it even less if you knew what I have in mind."

"By the Great Dragon, you try my patience. I've half a mind to knock you on the head and carry you out over my shoulder."

"I wouldn't try it," Tor said with a hint of steel in his voice.

"Well, I wouldn't waste my breath. You've a head as hard as granite."

A small smile curved Tor's firm mouth, but his dark eyes were unreadable. He folded his arms across his chest and leaned against the sun-warmed stone.

Up on one of the parapets, a young woman of eighteen summers peeked down at the scene below. She was called Mouse, although her hair was not dull brown but a rich, dark auburn, and her dark-lashed eyes were the same sparkling silver-blue as the sea that pounded Airan's western shores.

Mouse was the youngest of the castle's weavers, and as quiet as her namesake. No one had called her by her given name in many years. Indeed, she doubted that any even remembered it.

Someone jostled her, and she looked up.

"Oh, it's you, Mouse. I didn't notice you there." It was Luce, a bold and pretty girl who worked in the spinning room, making yarn for the looms. Mouse moved to make room for her.

Luce leaned against the rail, her long yellow braids dangling over it. "Well, well. A fine lot of likely lads," she announced, and busied herself happily in ogling the men below.

A few ogled her back. Luce was a pretty, slender girl. With her full bosom and the enticing swing to her walk, she attracted men's attention wherever she went—but Mouse was used to going about unnoticed. At times, she thought, it was almost as if she were invisible.

Mostly she was glad of it. If no handsome youth brought her flowers and fairings, or asked her to walk out among the summer meadows, neither did she have to fear being accosted by some amorous knave. Not even the off-duty soldiers, who flirted with the serving wenches and bawdy laundresses, called out to Mouse to dally a while.

At least it gives me the freedom to wander about at my will when my work is done, she consoled herself. Mouse knew the maze of corridors and the hidden courtyards within the castle's great curtain wall as well as she knew the workings of her loom.

But still there were times when she felt lonely and odd, different from the other girls in a way that seemed obvious to everyone but herself.

Perhaps my luck will change. There might be some handsome lad among the servants of the noble visitors who will catch my eye and who will find me pleasing in return. Perhaps a lad who would sweep her away to the life of stirring adventure that filled her daydreams.

On May Day she'd joined the other maidens to go gathering hawthorn blossoms along the hedgerows. Legend said that a young woman who put a sprig of hawthorn beneath her pillow would dream of her own true love.

Mouse *had* dreamed.

In those airy fantasies, she had left the castle's gleaming towers far behind. She'd ridden through clinging silver mists and dark forests. Along high, treacherous mountain passes in the heat of day, and across wide meadows in starshine. In one, she'd stood in utter silence and watched a streak of multicolored light arc across the heavens, as the flight of a jeweled phoenix lit up the night.

Of course, the phoenix was only a legend. She knew there was no proof that it existed or ever had. There was no reason to believe that the bird in her dreams was real—any more than the black-haired man who'd accompanied Mouse on each of her dream odysseys.

Common sense said he was not real, but in her heart Mouse believed that he did exist.

Somewhere.

Why else would she have that feeling of recognition each time she slipped into her dreams to find him waiting there?

The breeze snapped red and blue banners atop the tower. It tugged loose stray wisps of Mouse's auburn hair and filled her with restlessness.

She looked out over the thatched cottages and slat-roofed buildings that nestled in the bowl of wooded hills. Once upon a time this had been a small village, but it had grown with Airan's power over the years. In the distance carved ships rode at anchor in the bay, with the bright face of the limestone cliffs beyond.

In her free time she went there, sometimes afoot, other times on the cob that Elva, the village wisewoman, kept stabled in her shed. There were plants she picked to dye her wool, or for Elva's herbal remedies. In time Mouse had come to know the overgrown trackways, the forgotten ruins and secret coves that lined the shore very well indeed.

But of the world beyond Airan, she knew little.

Was it true that there were humped animals that lived in the desert of Persiod, who drank no water and needed only air to survive? Or creatures larger than the largest ox, that swam in the cold seas beneath the shining ice-mountains of Far Islandia?

Mouse longed for adventure, for the sight of distant and exotic lands; but certainly there was no way a simple weaver could experience such things on her own. Unless the man in her dreams arrived to claim her one day, she would likely live out her life like old Elva—busy and alone.

Her quick blue gaze skimmed over the would-be suitors below, in their gold and gems, their splendid cloaks and richly embroidered tunics. They were a colorful sight against the pale stones of the courtyard. Then her eye, trained to distinguish among a great variety of hues, was caught by something unexpected: a lack of color at the very back of the cobbled court.

A tall man leaned against the stone inner wall. Here was no elegant courtier, she saw, but someone who, by the look of him, had traveled long and hard to reach Airan. His body was hard-muscled, his skin deeply bronzed by wind and weather.

Like his companion's the man's garments were simple and foreign: He was dressed all in black, except for a cloak of deep, dull green. For all that, she noticed the subtle drape of it across his wide shoulders. It had been fashioned by an expert weaver. Light glinted off the twisted silver torque he wore about his muscular throat, but his thick, dark hair was clubbed back at the nape of his neck, restrained only by a simple knotted cord.

She wondered from where he had come, and what he was doing here among this gilded company. *Perhaps he is guard to one of the princes or lords who have answered the king's summons.*

Mouse wished that she could see his face. There was something familiar about him. . . .

She examined him more closely. There was a small harp in a battered leather case slung over one shoulder. *A bard,* she realized, *come to sing for his supper.*

But his hands were strong and looked more suited to

wielding a sword than plucking harp strings. He stirred, and beneath that deceptively simple cloak, she saw the glint of a broadsword buckled to his side.

He was not only the musician and storyteller that the harp in its worn covering proclaimed, she was sure of it.

A wolf among lapdogs.

The thought caught Mouse by surprise, and she shivered.

A fanfare of trumpets shattered the air. The tramp of boots echoed from the stairs leading down into the castle's courtyard. "Make way! Make way!"

Mouse turned her attention away from the dangerous-looking stranger. The king and queen were coming to formally greet their illustrious guests. There had never been such a glorious gathering in the castle's long history.

Gilmore, High King of all the Western Lands, had invited every eligible prince and nobleman from the surrounding kingdoms to a great tournament. They had come eagerly from far and wide, spurred by rumors that the king was seeking a husband for his daughter, the beautiful Princess Camaris.

Someone jostled Mouse again from the side. Another trod on her toes. Luce elbowed them away. She grinned at Mouse.

"The princess will be hard to please if she doesn't find a husband among them. I'll wager she'll take one of those dainty princelings. She'll settle for no less."

"Hah," snorted the old woman beside them, pursing her wrinkled lips. "The queen will accept no less than the wealthiest one. And it is her that has the say in such matters."

Mouse said nothing at all, only listened.

Once again her eyes were drawn to the dark-haired man in the leather jerkin and green wool cloak. His quarter-profile was to her now, displaying a well-shaped nose and a decidedly firm chin. She caught her breath. Could it be? The resemblance to the man in her dreams was uncanny.

Turn this way! Look at me!

But he did not obey her silent call, turning away instead.

Mouse fingered the amulet she wore, taking comfort from the smooth coolness of it. It was a habit she'd had since childhood, whenever she felt uneasy. Her earliest memories were all bound up in the pretty talisman. The dark red stone on the fine silver chain had swung above her cradle from the day she was born until she was old enough to wear it around her neck. It was her dearest treasure.

Suddenly her fingers froze and she gave a small cry of dismay. The surface of the stone had turned rough and crumbly in one spot. Lifting the amulet by the chain, she cupped it in her palm. What she saw startled her.

She'd always believed the stone to be a solid piece of jasper, but she'd been wrong. A long section of the polished red surface had peeled away, like a petal separating from a tightly curled rose. Inside was something odd.

Mouse stared down at it. Prodded it with her finger. The core of the amulet felt smooth and cool, and gleamed with inner light.

It looked, she thought, like a clear quartz pebble.

Or perhaps a tear.

2

CHEERS RANG THROUGH the courtyard as the king and
queen appeared at the head of the stairs. Tor watched in
silence, assessing the royal couple as they ascended the
dais.

Gilmore was still a handsome man, but time had placed
its mark on him. The weight of responsibility had furrowed his brow and streaked his ruddy hair with silver.
He'd won the crown of Airan in battle, and gone on to
unite the Western Lands, and his peers had elected him
High King. For eighteen years he had ruled with wisdom
and dignity.

His only weakness had been his choice of queen.

Broch muttered something, and Tor leaned down to
hear. "How," the older man said, "a man so good and fair
in judgment could have taken a woman so spiteful to wife
is beyond my ken."

While he didn't know much about the details, Tor knew

that his companion had fought beside the men of Airan in the wars. Broch always spoke well of the king. But where as Gilmore was loved and respected, Queen Bryn was feared and disliked.

No one, it seemed to Tor, had anything good to say of the queen. Nor did they voice their disapproval aloud. "Perhaps," he replied quietly, "it is true what rumors say: that Queen Bryn holds him under an enchantment."

He'd heard that the king might quell the boldest knight with a word, a single glance, but bowed to his queen's slightest wishes like a lovestruck moonling.

No one would guess it by the king's manner as he rose from his throne. He looked regal and very much in command.

"In this courtyard today," he proclaimed, "I see the greatest gathering of nobles and knights that has ever assembled in all the Western Lands. You have come as my guests, hoping to win honors and prizes upon the field of tournament."

His eyes glinted in the sunshine, and the great ring upon his finger glowed darkly blue. "There is a greater prize at stake," he said softly. "One far greater than I have ever given before."

The king watched the effect of his words upon his assembled guests. He smiled, secrets shifting like mists behind his hooded eyes. He held out his battle-scarred hand, and the sapphire bearing his royal seal blazed again with light.

"Behold," he called out, "the Flower of Airan: my daughter, the Princess Camaris."

Silence fell as a vision in azure silk and cloth of gold came through the archway to join him upon the dais. A sigh went up from the assembly, like the whisper of wavelets on smooth sand. The Princess Camaris was far more lovely than any of them had dared to believe.

Her hair was as finespun as the gold threads that lined her cloak, and her eyes as amber as the topazes in her delicate diadem. She moved with exquisite grace across the dais and took her place on the smaller throne beside her father. Gems winked on her fingers and at her white throat. Her smile was small and aloof, a mere curving of her full, red mouth. If there was haughtiness and perhaps bored amusement in her expression, it only added to the sense that she was a rare treasure.

Up on the parapet, Mouse was pleased to see that the princess was wearing the cloth she'd woven for her. It suited her delicate coloring. "How beautiful Princess Camaris is! There is not a man among them who will not strive to win her hand in marriage."

Luce folded her arms. "Pretty is as pretty does! Camaris would be the better for it if the good fairies had granted her the sweetness and wisdom to go with her beauty."

Someone shushed her. King Gilmore was speaking again. "My daughter is ripe for marriage, and I would have an heir to succeed me. The man who wins the princess shall have half my kingdom as well!"

His announcement rang from the walls of the great court, stirring echoes in the hearts of the assembled men. Airan was a kingdom with fertile green fields, deep blue harbors, and misty purple mountains thickly threaded with veins of gold and silver, copper and iron. A very great prize indeed.

At the back of the courtyard, Tor leaned against the thick stone walls and smiled. His eyes shone with appreciation.

"All that, and half a kingdom, Broch," he said, eyeing the princess. "A man would risk his life for far less!"

The older man stroked his scarred chin. "There's a trick in it somewhere, mark my words. Gilmore is a canny ruler and still in his prime. He has fought hard to keep his throne. He has no intention of handing over the reins of even half his kingdom to another man!"

Tor shifted, resting his weight on the cross-handle of his unadorned sword. "Not even the High King would dare to make so public a challenge and then go back upon his word."

His black gaze scrutinized the Princess Camaris, stripping away her silks and brocades with the ease of experience. Her fair face, graceful figure, and full, sulky mouth were the stuff of fevered dreams.

The smile that Broch mistrusted spread across Tor's face. "By the Great Dragon, I've a mind to try for the prize he offers."

"Hah!" Broch shook his head. "I'd give all I own to see you decked out in jeweled chains and satin boots, like these pink-cheeked lordlings. And believe me, the Princess Camaris would demand no less of any man aspiring to her hand." His blue eyes were shrewd. "You can tell that she's one as knows her own worth."

Tor laughed. "You're a sour old man these days." He slanted a glance at his comrade. "I've never met the woman I couldn't bed and pleasure. Aye, and make her smile for days afterward, just for the remembering of it."

" 'Small dogs bark loud,' " Broch grunted.

"And large dogs bark loudest," Tor replied with a twinkle in his eye. "That old proverb does not apply to me."

"Let's see how you boast when all is said and done!" Broch narrowed his eyes. "I'll wager the Princess Camaris has as much iron in her will as you have in your sword."

"Then," Tor said, grinning broadly, "she has met her match."

Gilmore's challenge stirred his interest. The Princess Camaris stirred his loins. His face sobered. "By the gods, she's a beauty. I'll have her, kingdom or no!"

Broch sent him a sharp look. "You are too cocky by half. Gilmore did not send *you* an invitation to take part in his tournament. And if he had, what makes you think that you could meet the challenge?"

A hard light gleamed in the depths of Tor's dark eyes. He had his own reasons, and Gilmore's offer was only half of it. The gleam was gone as quickly as it had come. His bronzed hand clasped the old man's shoulder.

"How can I fail in any feat of arms? Did I not have the finest teacher in all the world?"

Broch's mouth twisted in what passed for his smile. "Aye, you did." His fingers tightened on the stout black-thorn staff he used for support. "And if the Beast of Cullen hadn't snared my thigh with his great claw, I'd best you still, you proud young pup."

Tor's voice softened. "Aye. Aye, you would."

Broch's seamed face reddened. Seeing that he had embarrassed his companion, Tor turned his attention back to the Princess Camaris. Like every other man in the chamber who didn't have one foot in the grave, Tor was smitten. And determined.

The beautiful Camaris would be his.

While he watched her, he was unaware that he was himself the object of much speculation. Luce pointed down at him.

"Look at that rude fellow smiling at the princess, as if she were a dainty sweetcake. He is not even fit to touch the hem of the princess's skirt!"

Mouse felt a tingle dance along her skin. *I wish he would look up and smile at me,* she thought, and was surprised when the other girl jumped. She hadn't realized that she'd spoken aloud.

Luce stared. "Do you? Well, I wouldn't say no, myself. Such a fine set-up man can touch my skirts anytime he pleases. Aye, and lift them as well!"

Mouse didn't say anything at all. She couldn't.

The dark-haired stranger had glanced up at the parapet, casually. For a few seconds before he turned back to his companion his gaze locked with hers. From that moment she'd been robbed of speech. Of breath.

She grasped the worn stones for support. She didn't believe in love at first sight. Mouse knew that was merely attraction, the mating lure between the sexes. Old Elva had told her so, many a time, and that she must respect the soul of the man she loved more than she did his face.

But Mouse believed that if she ever met her soul mate, she would recognize him instantly. And she recognized this man.

Perhaps he was not her true soul mate, but at any rate he was the man who had haunted her dreams in recent weeks. He had the same dark eyes alight with inner fire, the same strong nose and square, stubborn jaw. And that mouth! Oh, yes. She knew that mouth. She'd awakened from its hot kisses, tangled in her sheet and aching with need.

Closing her eyes, she tried to blend their images. It was the same man. In her dreams, though, his gleaming dark hair had been unbound, flying out behind him as he raced his night-black steed along the causeway to the castle. And in his gauntleted hand, he'd held aloft something that sparkled and shone with jeweled fire.

There was fire of a different sort in his eyes now as they gazed upon the princess. Mouse saw it, and her heart plummeted. Every man who set eyes upon Camaris was taken with the princess's beauty. No, more than that. Blinded and enchanted.

Pain gathered and swelled like a molten bubble in her chest. The man of her dreams was real. But she'd dreamed that he came to her. To *her*! Not to the Princess Camaris, who had beauty and grace and learning, and all the riches that the world could offer.

Look at me, Mouse willed him. *Over here!* Every fiber of her soul resonated with the yearning. *Look this way. Look at me! See me.*

He turned his head, frowning up at the parapet. It was as if, she thought, he'd heard her unspoken command. But his gaze passed lightly over her and returned to the princess. A flush rose up his windburned cheeks.

Mouse bit her lip. He had eyes only for Camaris.

It was too cruel.

She gathered her will and found her voice. "Who . . . who is he?"

"I don't know, but I'll find out!" Luce told her. She had made it her business to know everything about the men who entered the castle precincts.

"A handsome devil, is he not? But after all, only a

border ruffian come to see the tournament, and no more fit to mingle with the lords and princes in the courtyard below than we. I've a mind to set my cap for him, but nothing would come of it. I know a man with wanderlust in his heart. After the festivities he'll be on his way, and we'll never set eyes on him again."

You are wrong! Mouse wanted to cry out.

But she realized, with a sinking heart, that her dream was not wrong. She had only misinterpreted it, out of sheer romantic folly. He was not for her.

The black-haired stranger would go away, it was true. But he would return as she had seen, racing across the drawbridge with the wind whipping his black hair wild and free.

Her fingers pressed tightly against her amulet. The small fracture inside the quartz pebble grew. Mouse heard something crack—a small crystalline sound—and thought it was her heart. When he returned—and she had no doubt that he would—it would be to claim the Princess Camaris for his bride.

She slipped away and vanished into the shadows of the tower.

No one noticed that she was gone.

No one remembered that she had been there at all.

3

"Fetch the princess her cloak of gold wool, and the feathered cap," Queen Bryn commanded. "And do not snag it with your harsh hands!"

Mouse hurried across the tapestry-hung hall to one of the carved chests that stood between the windows, hoping she would open the right one first. The princess was suffering from a fit of the sullens, and the queen was in a rare temper.

Mouse's duties as a weaver seldom brought her into contact with the royal family, and she had rarely set foot inside the princess's private quarters. But today she had been walking by when Camaris's waiting woman had slipped and broken her arm. She'd responded to the cries for aid—and had been pressed into temporary service in the woman's place.

Kneeling before the chest, she caught her reflection and that of the princess, in the polished brass lock. What a contrast they made: the princess in burgundy cut velvet draped over yellow satin, Mouse in her simple round dress of periwinkle blue.

And not merely in our garments, she thought.

She knew she looked well enough. Her figure was neat, her features pleasing, her auburn tresses thick and shining. *But even if I were gowned in splendor, I would still be a pale moon to Camaris's sun.*

Mouse was conscious that she lacked something the princess had in abundance: the power to turn men's heads. To weave herself into their dreams, waking and sleeping.

The only weaving she could do was with flax and wool dyed with plants she gathered from the woods or along the rocky cliffs, and the reels of vibrant silk thread imported from exotic lands. From warm cloaks to keep away the cold to transparent veils shot with gold and silver, there was nothing she couldn't create.

I am more fortunate than many, she reminded herself. At least she could earn her own keep, by the intricate work of her clever fingers. She would never starve or lack a warm fire and roof over her head.

But, oh! How she would have liked to turn the head of that handsome stranger her way!

The queen paced the chamber. "Hurry, girl! The duke of Ragnor is awaiting the princess in the rose garden."

"I don't wish to walk with him in the garden." The princess shuddered. "He has yellow teeth and the face of a halibut!"

"You are a fool, Camaris! He is the most powerful ruler outside of Airan, and his coffers overflow with gold."

The princess bit her lip. "He might rule the entire world, for all I care. He would still look like a fish!"

Queen Bryn strode up and down the chamber, her eyes snapping with anger. The argument had been going on all afternoon. All because a handsome young lordling in blue velvet had caught her daughter's eye. "I will not let you throw yourself away on a mere nobody!"

Bryn glanced at the looking glass. She was in her

prime, the most powerful woman in all the civilized world. But no longer the most lovely. That title belonged to Camaris now. Ungrateful girl that she was!

Along with the spells and potions to ensure the girl's beauty, the queen had raised her daughter with one aim— to make herself alluring to men. If a woman did not inherit her own wealth and estates, it was the only way that she could hope to wield power. The queen was determined that her lovely daughter would contract a brilliant marriage.

Bryn had used her own beauty and cunning to raise herself up from her beginnings as the eldest daughter of a very minor king to her current position as the highest lady in the Western Lands. From the moment she'd first set eyes on Gilmore, she had known he was her destiny.

To that end, Bryn had schemed and plotted to ensnare him. She had even delved deeper into the Dark Arts.

A mistake, that!

A shudder ran through her frame at the memory of it. She had been unable to control the forces she'd conjured, and her body bore the scars of that terrible miscalculation. Her profile was still lovely; but beneath the scarf that shielded her throat from view was a mass of ropy purple scar, like a coiled serpent.

Her mouth curved bitterly. It was a hard thing for any woman to bear. Especially one used to wielding her great beauty as a lure—and a weapon.

But, Bryn assured herself, there were still glory and power to come, and that would be worth every sacrifice. She would not let Camaris ruin everything!

Adjusting the veil more securely, she forced herself to smile.

"Consider yourself fortunate that the duke wishes to ally himself with the kingdom of Airan. You will walk with the duke, and you will be at your most charming."

The princess leaned back upon the silken cushions. "I do not wish to wed the Duke of Ragnor. And I will not!"

"This is what comes of spoiling you." Queen Bryn

fought the urge to slap her daughter's lovely face.

Under the best of circumstances, the princess had the casual arrogance that too often accompanies beauty and wealth. But her mother wasn't blind: Camaris was as demanding as a child, and she had neither wit nor charm to recommend her. In time the attraction of her fair face would pale. And where would they be then?

Bryn was aware that her own power over the king had faded with time. Although Gilmore was still under her spell, the hold it had upon him was not as strong as it had been. She could feel him struggling to free himself from its web.

But if Camaris wed the duke, it would consolidate Bryn's power considerably. If she played her hand well, in time she would rule two kingdoms: Airan and the Western Lands through Gilmore and another, vaster one through her daughter's chosen husband.

Chosen by *her*.

It *must* happen. She must make it so! Then, even if Gilmore cast off the spell, he could never set her aside.

Her temper frayed like a raveled hem. She would allow nothing to come between her and her ambitions. Not even the king.

"I will brook no defiance in this matter! Youth and beauty fade. You must secure your position in the world before that happens." Bryn clenched her hands. "If you do not come down of your own free will, I will have the sergeant-at-arms drag you to the garden by your hair!"

Camaris went white with shock. The queen had never used such words to *her*.

Mouse hunched over the cedarwood chest, pretending she'd heard nothing of the altercation. The brass catch was hard to lift. She winced as she banged her finger against it, but succeeded on the second try.

Inside were a multitude of beautiful cloaks, each more lovely than the other. She found the one the princess wanted at the very bottom. The fabric was the same tawny shade as the princess's eyes.

Mouse shook it out and carried it to the princess. Camaris rose and stood rigidly while the cape was settled over her shoulders.

Suddenly the queen stiffened.

"Stupid girl!" She clouted Mouse across the shoulders. "See what you've done!"

Mouse was aghast. Although her hands were smooth from the oils in the wool she wove, her fingernail had snagged thread of the fine wool like a bur. She must have torn the nail on the faulty catch. As she drew her hand away, the thread pulled away with her fingers, puckering the cloth.

Bryn turned on her in a fury. "You fool!" Snatching the garment away, she flung it across the room toward the hearth, where a fire was always kept burning against the chill of the thick stone walls.

"I won't have such a clumsy cow waiting upon the princess," she said viciously. "Go back to the kitchens, or the scullery, or wherever you belong—and stay there!"

Without warning, her hand lashed out at Mouse again. She was caught off guard, and the force of the blow sent her sprawling on the floor.

For a moment Mouse couldn't hear anything at all. Then her head rang like a great brass bell, and her ear burned like a white-hot coal. The rest of her face felt numb.

No one had ever struck her before. She struggled to her feet, while anger rose like a white-hot flame within her. She tried to repress it, but felt it burning like a torch. Could almost smell the singe of it in the air.

Then she realized that the odor came from Camaris's discarded cloak. The hem of the garment was on fire. An ember had fallen out of the hearth, and little licks of flame danced along the cloth.

"Oh!" Snatching up a pitcher of water from the table, Mouse dashed it over the burning cloak. Smoke, black and pungent, filled the air. She grabbed the damp garment and held it up. The ember had burned through several folds of fabric, leaving a series of blackened holes.

"Now it is ruined beyond repair," the queen said through gritted teeth. "I could have you whipped for this!"

Mouse bit back a hot retort. It would only fetch her another blow. "The rest is still good, Your Majesty. I am handy with my needle. I could fashion it into a cape."

"You've done quite enough for one day! Get out, and take this sorry mess with you. I never want to see it again." Her eyes narrowed. "As for you, keep out of my sight. Show your face to me again, and I will have you flogged within an inch of your life!"

Mouse scooped up the scorched cloak and hurried out of the room. Her ear throbbed and buzzed like a hornets' nest, but at least she had a quantity of warm wool for her troubles. She would take it to the woman who had raised her and use it to line her cloak. Elva's cottage was across the river, beyond the village.

This will keep the old dear snug when the winds come down from the north.

In her haste, Mouse rounded the corner and collided with a tall figure coming the other way. Only his strong arm kept her from falling. She looked up into a pair of eyes as deep and black as midnight. And as impersonal as air.

The dark-haired stranger she'd seen in the courtyard! Mouse was too embarrassed to speak. He was impressive at a distance, overwhelming so near at hand. His muscles felt like steel beneath the sleeve of his black leather jerkin.

"Watch your step!" Tor exclaimed. "You might have tumbled down the stairs."

The bundled cloak was caught between them, but Mouse realized she was pressed tight against his broad chest. Was that his heart pounding, or hers?

His touch was firm, and sent heat penetrating beneath her delicate skin, racing through her to coil in her belly. She felt dizzy and closed her eyes. A great mistake. Her every sense was heightened by his nearness.

A gasp of breath, and she inhaled the heady, masculine

scent of him. Sun-warmed earth and the rich, cool green of wild grass. She colored and pulled away.

Tor released her at once. "Your pardon," he said.

She was obviously an upper servant or craftswoman, by her clothing and demeanor. A fetching little thing, small and willow-slender, with shining auburn hair plaited loosely at her nape. She smelled like wild raspberries, and her eyes were like no color he had ever seen. Hues shifted in them like the sea in sunlight, in multiple shades of silvery blue.

He flushed when she continued to stare at him. "I meant no harm, mistress." he said. "My only thought was to save you from a fall."

"I thank you, sir, for your quick action." Mouse averted her face from his level gaze. "And now I'd best be on my way."

Tor saw the scarlet mark along her cheek and the swelling purple bruise. All his gallant instincts were aroused. Was this why she'd flinched?

"By the Great Dragon! Has some scoundrel accosted you? Only say his name and I'll have his hide!"

Mouse bit her lip. "Nay, sir. I . . . I was merely clumsy and was punished for my lack of grace."

"You have a harsh mistress," Tor declared. "Her temper should be checked. Where I come from, no lady of quality would treat a servant so!"

"Alas, sir, there is none to stop her," Mouse said.

"Then you should petition the queen. Surely she must take an interest in the welfare of her household."

Mouse gave him a tight little smile. "You are mistaken. The queen's only interest is the welfare of the queen."

She clamped a hand to her mouth. She couldn't believe that she'd blurted out such a dangerous truth. *If anyone heard me . . .*

She dipped a slight curtsey and whisked herself away, down the winding staircase. Tor stared after her, frowning. The episode left him frustrated, angry, and determined to look into it further.

But by the time Mouse reached the bottom step, he had forgotten the incident entirely.

4

Mouse approached the half-timbered cottage and
ducked beneath the low door. Elva sat at the pine table
by the window, sorting through her dried herbs. Stone jars
were lined up neatly along the whitewashed wall, waiting
to be filled.

She looked up when Mouse's shadow fell over her.

"Ah, Rosaleen, my love!"

Mouse smiled. It always startled her to hear Elva call
her by her given name. No one else did. And it always
comforted her, as well. At least here in this little cottage
she was known and loved.

Her heart swelled with deep affection for the old
woman. "Blessings on you," she said in greeting. "I see
you've set two mugs out for tea."

"I knew you would come today." Elva noticed the bun-
dle beneath Mouse's arm. "What have you there, child?"

"I've brought you something. A goodly quantity of fine

wool—woven, I might add, on my own loom."

Elva's thin fingers touched the soft fabric with its intricate weave. "It's beautiful work you've done. But why have you brought it away from the castle to show me? It's a terrible risk. You'd be punished if anyone knew."

"That I won't. The queen gave it to me herself!"

"I've never heard her to be generous before." The old woman looked worried.

A dimple peeked at the corner of Mouse's mouth. "It wasn't hers. It belonged to Camaris." Shaking out the cloak with its burned hem, she told Elva the story of how she'd obtained it.

"You are so small, there is enough to line your cloak and boots, and make a shawl as well."

"My old bones will be grateful when the snows come. I've the kettle on the boil. Sit down and I'll make some tea, while you tell me all the castle gossip. Rumor says that King Gilmore means to marry off the princess."

"And a great quarrel it's provoked." Mouse folded the wool and smoothed it carefully. "The queen has her eye on the Duke of Ragnor, but Camaris wants a young and handsome prince. Not that it matters who is wanted by either, for whichever knight wins the tournament will win the hand of the princess in marriage."

Elva poured boiling water into two earthen cups. The scent of elderflower and lemon balm filled the air. "Do not be fooled. Gilmore rules the kingdom, but the queen rules him. Bryn will do whatever she must to make the duke win the tournament."

"Do you mean she will cast a spell upon the others?" Mouse was shocked.

"Nay, girl. No need of the Dark Arts to make sure the man she had chosen will be tournament champion, when simple means will do the trick. A few loyal servants willing to maudle the wine. Or stablehands willing to slip certain herbs into the feed of the other's men's horses, in return for a handful of coins."

A shiver ran up Mouse's spine. She shook it off. "I am

glad my role at the castle is a minor one. It makes life much simpler all around."

She looked up suddenly, ears pricked. A shadow had passed by the window. Rising, Mouse went to the open casement. Twice on her way to the cottage she'd had the sensation that someone was keeping pace with her along the track through the woods, but had dismissed it as her imagination. Now she leaned out the window, but there was no one in sight.

It must have been the shadow of a hawk flying by, she told herself. *Or perhaps another bird.*

Elva was lost in her own thoughts and hadn't noticed anything beyond them. For three nights her sleep had been troubled with portents of danger. Neighing horses, the clash of armor, the thunder of discord.

But last night she'd dreamed of a jeweled phoenix, flashing across the night sky like a falling star. And of Mouse's poor mother, God rest her soul.

Try as she might, she could not shake her forebodings. "You are as dear to me as if you were my own, Rosaleen. If the queen is in a foul mood, you must take care to stay out of her path. Promise me."

"Today was a rare occasion. My path rarely crosses hers." Mouse put her hand over Elva's. "Do not fear. Except for the tournament, I will keep myself busy all day in the weaver's room. I give you my word."

The old woman glanced anxiously at Mouse. She curled her hands around the mug for warmth.

I failed her mother, but I have not failed her. At least she is in no danger. My Spell of Forgetting has kept her safe.

Unseen beneath Mouse's plain bodice, another layer of petals crumbled and turned to dust.

5

THE SUN WAS slanting over the far hills when Mouse left Elva and hurried across the bridge and up the dusty road to the castle.

Perhaps it is all this talk of spells and sorcery that has me on edge, she thought.

Whatever its cause, the peace she'd felt in Elva's thatched cottage fell away as she crossed the moat and entered the castle's outer courtyard. With the commotion of housing all the nobles' guests, the morrow's tournament, and the tension between the princess and the queen, the place was buzzing like a hornets' nest. Servants were scurrying to and fro, intent on their errands.

She slipped up the stairs and into the minuscule room near the weaving chamber that she shared with Luce. Mouse opened the small chest that held her possessions and took out a folded dress. She had made it with wool that Elva had gathered from her own sheep and dyed with the dark red juice of winterberries. She'd never worn it before.

As she dressed her hair and tied it back with a matching band, Mouse knew she was doing it all in hopes that the dark-haired stranger would notice her.

Except that his name was Tor, no one knew anything about him. She imagined that as a traveling bard he would earn his supper and a place to sleep by entertaining the court with his music and then go on his way again.

Her heart beat a little faster thinking of him. She hoped very much that he would be inclined to linger. She was drawn to him like iron to lodestone. There was something about him that was more than the sum of his handsome face and wide shoulders and strong physique. More than the humor and intelligence she'd seen in his keen dark eyes.

If she closed her eyes Mouse could still imagine the wild, summery scent of him, the dizzying thrill of his nearness. He was the reason she'd made the decision to brave the queen's wrath tonight and take her usual place at the servants' table. *Chances are that she has already forgotten me,* she told herself.

Certainly Tor had. He'd passed her in the great hall twice without so much as noticing her. But she was determined that she would make him do so.

The bells rang out, announcing the hour. It was time for the company to assemble. Mouse didn't want to draw attention to herself by arriving late. She ran down a little-used stairway to a quiet courtyard. She stopped in dismay when King Gilmore stepped from the shadows. She dipped into a low curtsey, expecting him to continue on his way.

"You are in a dire hurry, lass. Do you rush to meet your handsome young lover?"

She shook her head. "Nay, Majesty. It is but love of my supper that calls me to the banqueting hall with all good speed."

He laughed. "Then be on your way. It would not do for you to arrive after the king."

She curtsied again and hurried away beneath a stone arch.

Gilmore stared after her. A pretty thing! She reminded him of someone. . . .

He spied something lying on the stones at his feet, winking like a jewel. He bent to pick it up. Only a broken bit of glass-clear quartz, and the dried petal of a rose. He wondered if the girl had dropped them. As his fingers closed over them he felt suddenly dizzy.

Flickers of memory teased him. A dark-haired woman—surely the very image of the girl, with eyes of the same silvery blue. Visions came tumbling into his mind, sensations assaulted him. The smell of woodsmoke and the leaping flames of the Beltane fire. Words of love whispered, acts of love consummated, with no other witness than the whirling stars. He saw her clearly now: the beautiful lover to whom he'd pledge his heart and troth. Her name . . . her name was . . .

Suddenly Gilmore felt caught in an invisible net. It tightened around him inexorably. He struggled, but in a matter of seconds the woman's face vanished. Everything was gone: name, images, every vestige of memory, leaving him with an aching head and pervading sense of loss.

He stood alone for some time in the silence of the courtyard, while twilight drifted down around him.

6

As Mouse entered the great hall, her heart thudded with mingled hope and fear that this time Tor might notice her. She wished that she had gowns of gold-shot sendal, exotically scented perfumes to lure his attention. Jeweled earrings to dangle from her lobes that would wink in the candlelight to catch his eye.

But as always, once she slipped into the great hall, no one seemed to remark her presence. She took a seat along one of two tables set at angles to the dais. The amulet that hung around her neck brushed against her bodice. Unnoticed, another piece of dried rose petal flaked away.

Like others with valued skills, Mouse was fed and housed by the king. The weavers' appointed place was above that of the ordinary household servants and the carvers of fine wood but below that of the jewelers, whose baubles of gold and glowing gems adorned the royal family.

The highest nobles and princes were seated at the head table, quaffing mead and wine from glass cups encased in intricate silver. Light from the torches glimmered from their embroidered robes and silk and velvet tunics and glinted from jeweled collars and hammered gold torques.

She scanned the sides of the hall, searching for Tor, but he was nowhere to be seen among the other musicians. Her disappointment was keen.

When the royal family took their places, she sighed. Camaris the golden. The princess was gowned in azure satin, decked with pearls. Her bright hair was confined in a matching snood. She was so beautiful that everyone else suffered in comparison. *What a fool I am. If Tor were here, he would not notice me at all.*

It was only when the candles beside the head table had burned low in their iron branches that Tor made his entrance. His dark hair gleamed as he bowed before the king and queen. King Gilmore leaned back on his throne, his favorite wine goblet of rock crystal and gold in his hand.

"I am told you have great skill upon the harp. You are welcome to my court, sir bard. I bid you play for us."

Tor took a place at the foot of the dais in profile to the king and placed his hands upon the harp. Notes rippled from it, dancing through the air like motes of light. He was a master harper, and he caught his listeners in a net spun of sunshine and moonbeams. He conjured up the ice-clad mountains of his homeland, shining against a sky so blue it hurt the eyes, and they felt his yearning. When he sang of Airan's heroes who had fallen in freedom's name, their blood roused to the echo of ancient war drums.

Mouse listened raptly. The music of the harp was sweet, but it was his voice that captured her heart. Deep and true, it resonated through her, stirring emotions she had never known before. Wild longings and unspoken desires that swirled like storm winds off the sea.

All her life she had lived in the shadows, moving cautiously, attracting no notice. It was something as integral to her as the color of her eyes. Yet as she listened to Tor play and sing, watched the sure movements of his hands upon the harpstrings, she wished that he would look up at her.

Only at her.

When the last lovely note died, the great hall was completely silent. A moment later it erupted in cheers. The king held up his hand, and gradually the clamor ceased. Gilmore inclined his head toward the bard. "We thank you for the gift of your music. What is your name, and from whence do you come?"

"I am called Tor," the man replied, green eyes glinting. "Like my fathers before me, I have been raised in exile, among the wild peaks of Far Islandia."

A ripple of tension ran around the room. Mouse noticed that the guards suddenly laid their hands upon their sword hilts. When Gilmore had united the Western Lands, only the hardy people of Far Islandia had refused to acknowledge him as their ruler. There was bad blood, legacy of an ancient feud, between them. Gilmore's ascent to the throne had driven the two countries further apart.

The king rubbed his beard and eyed Tor steadily. "Far Islandia has been a thorn in Airan's side for a hundred years. It breeds rebels like no other place on earth."

"Aye," Tor said softly. "It does."

Then the king smiled. Perhaps his goal of uniting their countries in friendship could begin here. "And brave men and women. I welcome you to my court, Tor of Far Islandia. Will you play another song before the hour grows late?"

"Aye, Your Majesty."

Tor surveyed the room, and his gaze fell upon Mouse, sitting with her hands folded beneath her chin. He frowned. There was something familiar about that lass. Something of importance. He struggled to recall it, then shook his head.

Try as he might, he couldn't place her.

Touching the strings again, he played a tune that wound around and around upon itself, then launched into a tender ballad. The tale of a fair maid who loved unwisely and too well. Who waited faithfully for her lover to return from war, only to find that he had wed another. And who died giving birth to his child, without his ever knowing it.

It wasn't what Tor had intended to play. In fact, it was a new song, pouring out of him—or through him—as if it came from another realm. He felt the wrenching of his heart with every word, the sorrow of the brokenhearted maid with every poignant note. It left him shaken.

The last notes echoed among the high, carved rafters like the maiden's soul ascending to heaven. No one who heard the song was untouched by it.

Except the queen, who wore a fearsome frown upon her white brow.

Gilmore gripped his empty cup in his fisted hand. He stared down into it for what seemed like a long time, then slowly lifted his head. His eyes looked dazed. "A sad song, sir bard, terrible in its power and beauty. But well worth the hearing."

He rose suddenly, every inch the king, and pulled the massive emerald off his finger. "Take this ring in payment for the pleasure you have given."

Tor rose and bowed. "I am a simple man and have no use for fine jewels."

"Then name your prize!" Gilmore commanded. "Whatever you wish shall be yours. I give you my word as High King."

A look of triumph flashed in Tor's eyes. He slanted a glance to where Broch stood along the wall. *Did I not tell you?* that gaze demanded. His mobile mouth quirked up slightly at the corners. He lifted his head and faced the king squarely.

"I ask the right to fight in the tournament tomorrow, for the hand of the your daughter in marriage."

A murmur at his audacity ran through the assemblage. It was the last thing anyone expected. Mouse put her hand to her mouth in dismay.

A muscle ticked at Gilmore's jaw. He regretted his hasty vow. "Have you lost your wits? You are a weaver of song, not a knight trained to battle!"

The queen glared icily down. "And insolent beyond forgiveness. He is not even fit to speak the name of the Princess Camaris aloud!"

Tor's voice rang out through the hall. "A bard I am, but the blood of kings runs through my veins. I am trained in the art of combat, and as skilled with sword and lance as any here."

The king scowled. "Ask me for another boon instead," he commanded.

"No, sire. I will not take back my words. Nor," Tor challenged, "can you take back yours."

The tension in the room heightened. It was true. Gilmore had given his royal oath.

Reaching out, the queen grasped her husband's wrist. Her fingers dug into his wrist. "You must deny this absurd request!"

Gilmore turned on her, his eyes glittering with anger. "You heard the man—and you heard me as well. I have pledged my word. Now we must all live with the consequences."

No one had ever heard the king speak so roughly to the queen before. Even Bryn was taken aback. She went very still. Panic fluttered inside her breast, and her knuckles blanched whiter than the sleeve of her pale silk gown. She examined Tor from head to toe. This man, whoever he was, had power. That was undeniable. She feared him.

It was a new emotion for the queen, and it rattled her. She rallied quickly and addressed her husband, gathering her robes around her as if they were protective armor.

"You will do what you must do," she said. "And let me warn you, my lord, that I shall do the same!"

Queen Bryn signaled her daughter and their waiting women, then swept off the dais and vanished behind the tapestry that hung in front of the stairs to the royal chambers. The Princess Camaris followed her, her lovely head held high.

For a moment King Gilmore looked old and ill. His kingdom had been at peace for eighteen years, but he hadn't known a moment of it in his own heart. He rubbed the bridge of his nose wearily.

Then he drew himself up, as regal as ever. "You are a fool, Tor of Far Islandia, and you shall surely die a fool's death. May God have mercy upon you."

Tor bowed. "I do not ask for mercy, Your Majesty, only your word, which you have freely given."

King Gilmore rose. "Let it be on your head, then. Your boon is granted. Tomorrow you shall fight in the tournament."

He left the dais, followed by his retainers. The princes and lords murmured among themselves, then left their places. As the hall emptied, people flowed away on either side of Tor, like a river streaming around a rock.

Broch joined him beneath one of the tall windows. "They flee from you as if you were diseased."

"Like the king, they think I am indeed a fool," Tor said with a harsh laugh. "Or a dead man."

Broch eyed his protégé. "They may be right on both counts. Tomorrow will tell the tale."

Mouse clenched her hands in frustration. In the past hour she had learned many things about dark-eyed Tor, who haunted her dreams. His singing was so beautiful it could make the angels weep. He had pride, courage, and great daring.

And it seemed that he was hell-bent on self-destruction.

She fled to her chamber and wept herself to sleep. Her dreams were comforting. She was back at Elva's cottage, snug in her bed. A woman with roses in her hair sat at a loom weaving by candlelight. In and out the shuttle darted, trailing gleaming threads of gold and silver that shaped the image of a glorious bird whose eyes glowed redder than any ruby.

Mouse smiled in her dreams.

7

Pennants waved from the grandstand where King Gilmore sat in state with his family and noble guests. The sun shone down on the already defeated, resting beneath the trees, and the two remaining combatants preparing to take up arms.

Gilmore wished the day already over. He had slept ill, assaulted by dreams. He'd been young again and filled with idealism. There had been a phoenix, his chosen symbol, blazing a rainbow of fire so bright that it dimmed the glory of the starry night. Once the bird had flown free over Airan, and sightings were common. There had been none in many years now. Perhaps it was an ill omen.

But there had also been a woman, her dark hair twined with roses and gleaming silver ribbon. She had smiled at him so sweetly, her eyes filled with love. He knew her name now: Deirdre.

Gilmore rubbed his temples. He'd wakened before

dawn, filled with emptiness and an ache so profound that he felt as if a sword had pierced his heart. Deirdre the fair. How could he have ever forgotten her?

He glanced at his queen beside him. The answer lay in her. Not in her beauty, which was still potent, nor in the charm she could still summon when she wished. It was something deeper, darker. He fought it with all his might.

Trumpets sounded, announcing that the next challenge would be starting soon. Liveried pages swarmed about the Duke of Ragnor, helping him into his full battle gear: gilded armour, a red-crested helm, and a rectangular body shield as tall as a man.

The king brooded. Old enemies were working in the background to bring Airan down. If he could no longer keep the peace by persuasion and diplomacy, he could still do so through the marriage of his daughter. An alliance with a powerful duke like Ragnor would make them back away like cringing dogs.

Now Tor, the dark stranger from Far Islandia, had loosed a cat among the pigeons.

Gilmore was distracted by the arrival of his most trusted aide. The man spoke low so that only the king could hear. "I have made the inquiries you wished, Majesty and have information you may not welcome."

The king rose. "I will walk with you, while the contestants prepare."

The queen watched them leave the grandstand. Something was wrong. Gilmore struggled against her power. She could feel it, more and more. She reached beneath the veil wound around her throat, and touched the thick scars there. A shiver ran through her. It had been several years since she'd dared to call up the Dark Forces. Much as she feared another spell might go awry, she would have to attempt to work her magic upon the king again.

Her golden gaze settled on Tor, as he mounted his steed. As far as the barbarian from Far Islandia, she had no concerns. Ragnor was a powerful warrior, despite his unfortunate appearance. He would make short work of the upstart. If only Camaris had not set her heart against him! The girl was a fool. *I shall have to work a spell on her, as well. A love spell so that when my daughter gazes at the duke he will appear to be the most handsome of men.*

Tor steadied his mount and shielded his eyes against the glare, unaware that he drew the queen's attention. Despite Broch's dire predictions, no thieves had stolen their horses and gear from the hidden grove. Beneath his black silk tunic was the finely woven chain mail, and his boots rose high on his muscled thighs. He had less protection than the duke, but the advantage of greater speed and agility.

Tor wiped away a trickle of sweat from his brow. The day was hot and the exertion of the tournament great. In the last pass, he had shattered his lance, and his opponent's horse had fallen.

The thrill of battle was upon him. Of all the eager men who had fought this day for glory, and the hand of the princess, only he and the Duke of Ragnor had vanquished all previous challengers. Now they faced each other at either side of the greensward again, each one determined to win the challenge and the hand of the Princess Camaris in marriage.

"Strike well," Broch said, handing Tor another lance. "One blow and it will all be over. Whether it's you or the other," he added grimly.

"Fear not for me! I will prevail."

The king had returned to the grandstand. Tor saluted to show his readiness and King Gilmore acknowledged the gesture. Between the royal couple, the pampered princess sat rigid with dismay, awaiting the outcome. Neither champion was to her liking.

"If looks were arrows," Broch muttered, "the princess would have slain you both ere now."

"I'll bring her 'round," Tor said with grim humor. "I shall make it my life's work."

Broch scowled. "A poor choice of careers," he said sourly.

Tor ignored the remark. Camaris looked more lovely than ever, in a cloth-of-gold gown. Emeralds and purple spinels wreathed her smooth white throat and glinted in the gold net that held her shining hair. The disdain in her face didn't daunt him. He liked a woman with spirit and fire. Taming her would be a delight.

She is proud, that one, but she will learn to love me. I will make her love me!

Determination steeled him. *By the gods, I will have her!*

Broch shook his head. "You look like a moon-calf," he said curtly.

"I feel like one in her presence. She is like the sun. She blinds me with her beauty."

"I've never yet known a lusty young fellow who didn't turn imbecile at the sight of a pretty face." Broch gave him a disgusted look. "Left to your own devices, you would choose a smoothly gilded rock over a nugget of pure gold—and all for the glitter of it."

Tor's brows knit. "You forget yourself. I'm a grown man and a warrior, not the stripling boy who came to you so long ago seeking wisdom and advice."

The older man folded his arms. "You'll get it anyway. Remember this, boy-o: The spawn of a serpent is still a snake, no matter how pretty her scales!"

He stepped away, and Tor took his place at the starting line.

King Gilmore waited for the action to begin again with concealed impatience. Where as once such a grand spectacle would have filled him with energy, now he found it displeasing. The desire for glory made heroes of men. The desire for power only made men desperate. And the desire for a beautiful woman could make the wisest man a fool.

He knew that all too well.

He glanced at his queen. He'd been battle-weary when he'd taken refuge at her father's tumbledown keep and had fallen under the spell of her beauty almost immediately. She had been trained from birth to marry well. Bryn was accomplished, and as clever and devious as any of his counselors.

There were times when he wondered what on earth had possessed him to marry her.

He turned to their daughter. Camaris pouted beside him, unhappy with the way things were going. She had set her spoiled heart on a minor prince, a handsome, delicate fellow in sky-blue silk, with hair like spun gold. He knew she didn't really believe that she would be forced to wed the victor.

She has twice her mother's beauty, but half her charm. And less than that of Bryn's intelligence.

Thank the gods!

Two of them, strong-willed, able to cloud men's minds and bent on having their way, would have been more than he could handle.

He watched Tor rein in his mount. A brave fellow, and lucky, too. Now was the moment to see how far he could take this opportunity he had grasped so eagerly.

Yes, a clever young rogue, Gilmore thought with a smile. *But he'll find that he has met his match in me, whichever way this journey ends, I will turn it to my advantage.*

Mouse watched, too, with fear. A man in a brown jerkin pushed past, treading on her toes. A moment later the cry went up: *"Stop, thief!"*

Looking back, she saw a rotund merchant sprawled on the ground at the back of the crowd. His manservant was in pursuit of the thief, but the young cutpurse had fled, melting into the crowd.

Fortunately, the soldiers on peace patrol caught him near the hot-food booths. Without a word they clapped him on the shoulder. The next moment they'd lifted him off his feet so that his toes barely touched the ground and carried him away, to the cheers of the gawking onlookers.

"That will teach you, young ruffian!"

"There's another," someone shouted. "The girl is his partner." No one else was apprehended, though. The altercation ended, and the bugles announced the start of the tournament. All eyes were drawn to the jousting field.

The crowd fell silent, and tension built. Mouse could hardly stand it. Off to the side she saw two men standing by with a litter, waiting to remove the loser's body from the field. This would likely be a battle to the death. It was whispered that the duke would settle for no less.

Everyone seemed certain of the outcome. Everyone but Mouse. She prayed that Tor would somehow emerge from the battle unscathed. The odds were against him. One of the soldiers had wanted to get up a wager as to who would win. There were no takers.

She wished that Elva were here with her, but the old woman had been called to the bedside of a farmwife in hard labor. Gripping her hands together tightly, she waited.

The signal was given. Tor spurred his horse and charged his opponent. Hooves thundered and churned clouds of dust in the still, bright air.

Mouse held her breath. She wanted to be anywhere in the kingdom but here, yet she could not look away. In the back of her mind was the secret thought that by sheer willpower, she could keep him safe. She would rather see him wed to Camaris, than dead on the field of valor.

Horses and riders came at one another full tilt. It was hard to see it for all the dust that rose up as they met in a clash that shook the ground. When it was over, one horse lay still upon the ground. Ragnor had fallen hard.

Tor stood back, waiting until the older man struggled to his feet in his heavy armor. They reached for their swords.

Steel rang on steel as they thrust and parried. The duke was strong, but the weight of his armor impeded him. Tor danced around behind him and delivered a whacking blow with the flat of his sword. The duke went sprawling in the dirt.

A great cry went up from the crowd. Tor cut the strap that held the other man's helmet and placed the point of his sword at the duke's throat. "Surrender!"

Mouse squeezed her eyes shut as the duke signaled to acknowledge his defeat.

Then Tor's voice rang out. "You have fought with honor and courage, Ragnor. Rise to fight another day."

She looked in time to see Tor hold out his hand to the vanquished man and help him to his feet. A great roar of approval went up from the crowd.

The duke's men hurried out and helped him stagger back to his pavilion, where the red flag of Ragnor fluttered. Only a few of all those gathered remained voiceless among the shouts and ovations. King Gilmore eyed the scene from beneath lowered brows, while the queen sat grim and impassive.

The princess had apparently fainted.

A great stillness settled over the company as Tor moved toward the grandstand. He crossed the dusty field of combat in silence. Even the breeze held its breath.

The slanting rays of the lowering sun turned the air golden. His dark hair gleamed like polished onyx as he removed his helm and knelt before the king.

"I have come to claim my prize, Your Majesty: the hand of your daughter in marriage."

Mouse turned away. So this was the end of it. So much for her foolish daydreams.

She tried to leave, but king's men in their chain mail stood just behind her. The path to the village was blocked by the throng. She bit her lip. There was no way to escape. The servants and villagers and guildsmen would leave when the pageant was over, and not a moment before. There was nothing she could do but stand and watch it all unfold.

A soldier crowded her. Mouse gave a squeak of dismay. "Kindly give me room to breathe," she protested.

They ignored her, and she did her best to ignore them. The light was failing fast and a pale mist was rising. Although torches were lit beside the grandstand, it was becoming difficult to see. Mouse strained her eyes for a better look at the commotion on the grandstand.

The king held up his hand and the assembly fell silent again. "You have been victorious, Tor of Far Islandia."

The Princess Camaris had come around from her swoon. She sat up and her shrill voice carried across the field. "No!" she wept hysterically. "I will not marry him! I am a *princess*! He is a commoner, an ill-bred rustic! Father, you cannot mean to force me!"

Gilmore held up his hand. "Silence!"

He looked down at Tor, long and hard. "A man who marries ill will surely live to regret it. Would you be content to wed a woman whose heart is set against you?"

"I will do aught I can to win her heart." Tor said. "I have no crown of gold or fine estates, but noble blood runs through my veins." He lifted his head proudly. "I am the grandson of Orgus, who ruled Far Islandia in olden times."

The queen gave a scornful laugh. "As are a score of others—bastards and barbarians all! You are not fit to stand in the shadow of the Princess Camaris."

Tor's black eyes glittered with anger in the circle of torchlight. "I do not intend to stand in her shadow, madam. I will stand at her side."

"Enough," King Gilmore said. "You are champion of the tournament and have earned the right to claim your prize. Is it indeed your wish to wed my daughter?"

"My most heartfelt one, sire."

"Do you swear on your soul that you will take her to wife, protect her and guard her and honor her all your days?"

"I do indeed swear, sire."

"Then your wish is granted. You shall have her hand." Gilmore gave a signal, and trumpets were raised in a bright fanfare.

Mouse gasped in alarm as she was caught beneath the arms and picked up off her feet. Two burly men-at-arms held her in their grasp.

"Let me go! Put me down!" she cried. "I have done nothing wrong."

"You'll come with us," one said curtly. Without further ado, they carried her off as if she weighed no more than a windblown leaf.

"Well, well," someone nearby said. "They've caught the thief's accomplice. Look, they're taking her away."

Mouse couldn't believe what was happening. The toes of her shoes skimmed over the warm summer grass and the dusty tournament field. The soldiers delivered her straight to the foot of the grandstand, where they released her so abruptly that she fell all in a heap in the circle of torchlight.

"Ah, here she is, Tor of Far Islandia." King Gilmore smiled coolly in the flickering light. "Your prize!"

Tor looked from the frightened girl struggling to rise to the monarch. "What trickery is this? Who is this girl?"

"No trickery at all, sir bard." Gilmore's voice was stern. "This indeed is my daughter that you see before you. Her name is Rosaleen."

Mouse was filled with confusion. "R-r-rosaleen is my name," she stammered. "But I am an orphan, the child of simple weavers. My father was killed in the wars. My mother died shortly after my birth."

The king touched the pouch at his belt, where a dried rose petal, and the small crystal stone he had found in the courtyard were hidden fast away. Memories were becoming more clear with every passing moment.

The king's face was lined with sorrow. "Your mother was Deirdre the weaver. We were hand-fasted at Beltane, before I went to battle. You have her silvery eyes and delicate features. But you got the fire in your hair from me, daughter!"

Mouse heard the ring of truth in his words. She lifted her chin. "If what you say is so, Majesty, why have you waited until now to claim me as your own?"

"The truth of your parentage has only just been revealed to me. I claim you now, before all the court and my noble visitors. You are mine."

He turned to Tor. "Come! Claim your prize, sir bard."

Tor saw the resemblance then, between the girl in the plain blue gown and the king. Rage filled him like roaring flame. "Daughter or no, this woman has nothing to do with me. It was the Princess Camaris I fought for!"

"Think back over my words. Never once was Camaris's name said by me to you."

Tor felt as if he'd been struck by a nailed fist. It was true. And it was wrong! "I will have Camaris," he said through clenched teeth.

Gilmore's eyes were cold as the northern ocean. "As I have kept my word, so must you keep yours. Tor of Far Islandia, grandson of the great Orgus, I grant you the hand of my daughter Rosaleen as reward for your valor today. You will be wed in the castle chapel tomorrow at noon."

8

Mouse STARED AT the king in horror.

The same emotion was reflected in Tor's black eyes. "I do not wish to marry her."

Unseen in the torchlight, a flush rose up Mouse's throat and covered her cheeks. She had endowed the stranger with all sorts of wonderful qualities. For her efforts, he had repudiated her before the entire court.

"Nor do I wish to wed this man," she said hotly. "I would not have him were he the last alive on the face of the entire earth."

The king rubbed his hand across his face. "Well, then. If neither of you is willing, let no more be said."

Mouse was giddy with relief. Tor held his ground. "There is still a prize to be claimed," he stormed. "I accepted the challenge—and I have won!"

Gilmore smiled, but his eyes were hooded. "Once again you misheard me. I mentioned a challenge to win the hand of the Princess Camaris. You all jumped to the conclusion that it was the tournament to which I referred. But there is another quest I had in mind for the man who would claim half my kingdom."

He snapped his fingers, and a page handed him a sealed scroll. "The challenge is here, dated a week past. I will read it to you now."

Breaking the seal with his thumbnail, he unrolled it. "The challenge I set is this: The man who will share the throne as co-regent must first complete a quest. He must find and bring to me the egg of the fiery phoenix!"

The crowd murmured like sea waves against Airan's towering cliffs. A few snickered. The king had set an impossible task, and everyone knew it.

Tor eyed him warily. "Does this creature even exist in Airan?"

"It is your task to find that out. In legend," the king said, "the home of the phoenix is in the Mystic Mountains, which divide Airan from the Eastern Lands. A rugged place, not one for the weak of heart. Both my daughters will remain safe in my care while you are on your quest. Bring me the egg of the phoenix. Then, Tor of Far Islandia, I shall grant any wish you desire. You have my word of honor."

"I am not inclined to take your words at face value," Tor snapped, "so facile are you at twisting them."

Gilmore shrugged. "Ah. I see. If the task is too difficult—if your courage fails you—then you may leave this country in peace, and none will call you coward!"

Tor was so angry that a red mist filled his vision and a muscle twitched in Tor's jaw. "If the phoenix exists, I shall find it!"

The king smiled grimly. "I shall order everything made ready for your journey. You will remain at the castle as my guest, of course, until such a time as you can set out."

"I will not stay a moment longer than is necessary," Tor said, in a voice that rang like steel. "I shall fulfill the quest you've set me and find this phoenix egg." His entire body was taut with anger. "And you will rue the day that I return!"

Mouse gasped. *He must be mad to utter such a threat!*

It was evident that others thought the same. In the stunned silence, Tor turned his back upon the king and strode away. The captain of the guards stepped out, his sword drawn and ready. Other weapons slithered from their scabbards.

In a movement so quick it seemed like a stroke of magic, Tor's own broadsword was in his hand. Battle light gleamed in his eyes, like cold stars in a January sky. He had fought against high odds before, and won.

"If my quest starts here, so be it!"

"It will end here as well," the captain said.

"No!" Gilmore thundered. "Let him pass freely, and in peace. He is still my guest and still under my oath of safety."

Tor sheathed his sword and strode away into the darkness.

In the commotion that followed, Mouse slipped through the crowd and vanished as well.

9

THE HOUR WAS late, the noble guests gone to bed, when the queen sought her husband. She found him alone in the tower, sipping from a goblet of wine.

Bryn smiled sweetly at her husband. "How clever of you, my lord! I admit I was terrified to think of my sweet Camaris wed to that oaf who came to claim her!"

Gilmore drained the wine from the silver-and-amethyst goblet. "He is not such a barbarian as you think, my dear. We might do worse for a son-in-law."

Bryn blinked, and her smile froze for several seconds. Then she rallied quickly. "He is bold, I grant you that. But on the wrong side of the blanket!" Orgus had no legitimate heirs.

The king took another gulp of mead. "There are some who would dispute that. Orgus wed Maire—but he was hand-fasted to another long before."

"I am no fool," the queen hissed. "You are reminding

me that there was another woman before me. But," she said pointedly, "you did not wed her. You wed me!"

He gazed down into his cup, seeing years past in the reflected light. "This you should know: Had I not wed you, I would have married Deirdre upon my return from the war that won me my crown."

"What, wed a *peasant*?"

"Her mother was a freeholder," Gilmore said, bristling. "I knew her from the time we were children. We fell in love. . . ."

The queen was alarmed. He should remember none of this! "And yet you said nothing to me? And yet you let the girl, Rosaleen, grow up like one of your servants inside these walls? What kind of love is that?"

"*I* cannot explain it," he replied softly. "But perhaps you can."

Bryn's eyes shone hard as diamonds, but her heart was filled with fear. The spell she had cast over Gilmore was losing its power more rapidly with every passing hour. She must find another, stronger one to hold him in thrall.

"I am but a woman. How can I hope to judge what was in your mind or heart. All these years? It has been a long day, my love" she said in honeyed tones, "and we are both weary. Seek your bed, my lord. We will speak of this another time."

Gilmore tossed back the last of his wine. "Yes. The hour is late. But it is my daughter Rosaleen I must seek out, first. I've given her a suite of rooms in the west tower. You must find servants and garments worthy of her status."

Bryn clenched her hands. "Do what you like. *I* shall never acknowledge her. Never!"

She whirled around and left Gilmore's chamber in a rustle of silk brocade. In her own quarters, she dismissed her servants and sent her ladies to their beds. When the castle was asleep, Bryn locked the door and then lit a candle and set it in the window of her bedchamber. Taking a seat in her gilded chair, she waited. It was not long before her signal was answered.

She heard the tap on the hidden door, and moved the tapestry aside to open it.

A steely-eyed knight entered, his burly shoulders brushing the sides of the narrow door. He knelt before her and kissed the hem of her gown. "Majesty!"

"Yes, yes." she said impatiently. "Rise. I have a commission for you."

"Anything you will, my lady, even though it cost me my life!"

She smiled. "Such loyalty! But be reassured. It is not your life I seek, but another's." She drummed her long nails on the seat of her gilded chair. "Rid me of the girl Rosaleen! I do not care how it is done."

10

A SICKLE MOON rode low in the black velvet sky as Tor thundered across the moor. A prudent man would have waited for morning to set out, but he had been too angry to be prudent.

Consequently, he had spent the last hour cursing and trying to maintain his bearings.

Night and weather were closing in more quickly now. One by one the stars were obliterated, as a luminous fog rose up from the valley. It was proving increasingly difficult to see the road. If he meant to seek shelter for the night, it would have to be soon.

Tor urged his black horse across the turf, sending up clods of earth, trying to outrace the humiliation of Gilmore's trickery. The king had made him a laughingstock in front of the entire court. Tor gritted his teeth.

Even Broch had scoffed at him. That had rankled. Tor had been sent to Broch for training when he was just a lad, and the older man had been like a surrogate father. He'd taught Tor the arts of swordplay and horsemanship, and had given him good counsel along the way.

"I warned you not to come to Airan in the first place," the older man had told him after the tournament. "Let us leave this accursed country before you come to grief."

Broch had been outraged when he'd realized that Tor had no intention of letting Gilmore hold the upper hand. "The king has made a fool of you once, and now you are letting him do it again. I won't accompany you on a fool's errand. There is no phoenix, and never was," he'd snorted. "It's as imaginary as your love for that haughty princess!"

And in the end, driven by anger and ambition, Tor had agreed that it was better if their paths diverged. The quest was liable to be both long and dangerous. He did not wish to put the old man in jeopardy. Broch could be more useful in other ways.

Once he reached the heights, Tor wheeled his mount and looked back the way he'd come. The great black horse whickered and pawed the air. Tiny lights glimmered where Castle Airan thrust up through the fog, looking as distant as the stars. Tor's jaw squared. He was a warrior who lived by his wits and his sword, but he was the equal of any man. The blood of kings ran through his veins. He would not forget it.

Nor would he let anyone else do so.

"I will be back to claim my true bride," he vowed to the night wind, raising his gloved fist. "And when I return, woe to the house of Gilmore! For I shall claim not merely half the kingdom, but the whole of it!"

His pride was no protection against the fog. It swept in around him, relentless as the tide. The damp gray air thickened and congealed. It was impossible to see more than a horse's length ahead. Much as he wanted to push on, Tor knew he would have to seek shelter for the night.

Fortunately, he had studied the old maps before arriving in Airan and knew the general lay of the land. If memory served, the old coast road branched down from here. It was rarely used these days, but dotted with ruined watch-towers that had guarded the coast from invaders centuries before. If he judged correctly, one of them was at the end of this downward slope. Even if it were nothing more than a pile of stones, it would provide some protection for the night.

Of course, if he was wrong, he might be heading out over the cliffs. Tor dismounted and led his horse through the undergrowth. The ground dipped sharply on the far side of the woods just ahead.

At first there was only earth beneath his boots, but after a few minutes he felt that give way to paving stones. They were crooked as a crone's teeth, but eventually they led him to his goal. The fog shifted and the tower loomed up without warning.

There was no door, only a high, open arch and the remains of rusted hinges. When Tor tried to lead his gelding into the shelter at the tower's base, the creature balked and rolled its eyes.

"Easy, old friend." He ran a hand over the beast's warm muzzle. "There's a hard storm brewing out at sea. We'll stay warm and dry enough here while we wait it out."

The horse refused to budge. "Is there some ghost or magic here that frightens you? Very well. You'll be fine in the lean-to."

Visibility was worsening, but the animal went docilely enough into the place where other horses had been stabled years before, comforted by their faded scent. After removing the saddle and pack, Tor rubbed his steed down. Suddenly the beast whinnied softly.

Tor went still. He heard it, too. The sound of another horse picking its way along the old coast road.

He drew steel and waited. Was it merely some other poor wayfarer, lost in the smothering grayness? Or had Gilmore sent someone to follow him? Someone, perhaps, who would rid the king of the man who aspired to the hand of the princess?

Sure and relentless as the lapping of waves against the

shore, the sounds came nearer. Soft jingle of harness, and muffled hooves. Tor smiled grimly. No one would be heading here without some dark purpose.

The hoofbeats slowed, then ceased. Now there was only the occasional skitter of stones along the path leading to the tower. The rider had dismounted. Fog distorted sound and made it difficult to pinpoint his exact position. Tor strained his ears to listen.

A rattle of stones startled him. Whirling toward it, he saw a shape come hurtling out of the night. As his sword flashed through the mist, he glimpsed a pale heart-shaped face filled with alarm. Tor cursed and leapt back, checking his powerful swing. Not a soldier, but a woman.

She slid down the rest of the way in a hail of tiny stones and fetched up against the base of the tower.

"I mean you no harm," she gasped.

He stifled a laugh and leaned on the hilt of his broadsword. "A good thing, then," he said, "for you would have failed utterly. What is your business abroad at such an hour, on such a foul night?"

The woman sat up warily. "I was making my way to the old coast road. When it became too difficult to see the way, I sought sanctuary here."

"Not refuge, but sanctuary?" Tor frowned. "An odd choice of words."

"I am fleeing for my life, sir."

The mist thinned suddenly around them. She stared up at him and the naked blade gripped in his hand. He froze. Who else but Rosaleen, the king's daughter?

"Is this another trick?" he asked harshly, dragging her to her feet.

"Let me go!"

Mouse swallowed around the dryness in her throat. What a cruel jest of Fate, to send her on a path straight to the man who had rejected her!

Humiliation filled her mouth like bitter tea. Tears of helpless anger stung her eyes and spilled over her thick lashes. She turned her head so that he wouldn't see them.

Tor stabbed his sword into the ground and gripped her shoulders. "Why has he sent you after me? And where are the king's soldiers?"

She shivered and pulled back at the strength in him. He could snap her like a twig. "The king has not sent me. No one has."

"Oh, you merely decided to risk your pretty neck by riding out in a fog as thick as lambswool? Tell me another lie. Spinning them seems to be the favorite pastime here in Airan."

Mouse wrenched away. "I speak truth. My life is worth nothing now. The queen is my mortal enemy. She will not let me live to see many more days."

She lifted her chin. "As for soldiers, my lord, there are none. Only myself, armed with nothing but my wits and this dagger."

Her cloak fell open, and the crystal pendant at her throat seemed to burn with a pale, elfin light. In its glow he saw her eyes, dark as sapphires. And the small dagger with a twisted silver hilt, in the grasp of her fingers. The blade shone wickedly. She could have shoved it between his ribs at any time while he questioned her, and they both knew it.

Tor stepped back warily. "Perhaps this is another trick, to earn my trust. If you are truly the king's daughter, tell me why you are treated as a servant within his castle— and why the queen wishes to see you dead."

Leaning on the hilt of his broadsword, he eyed her shrewdly and waited for an explanation. Mouse was too weary for anything but the truth. Lies would do her no good in any case.

She bit her lip. "I am indeed Gilmore's daughter, although I never knew the full story of my birth until to-day."

Elva had told her everything after Mouse had fled the scene of the tournament. "The king is wise in all things— except where it concerns his wife," Mouse said. "But the blame is not his. The queen has ensorcelled him."

Tor's eyebrows rose. "A poor sorceress, if she could not keep the king from dallying with your mother!"

"It is not as you think," she said hotly. "My mother and the king hand-fasted before he won the crown." Her mouth trembled with emotion. "Bryn is a wicked woman. After casting her spell upon the king, she was not content until she destroyed my mother. I was orphaned mere hours after my birth."

Tor was startled. "In Far Islandia magic is used only for good—for healing and growing crops and calling up fair weather. What of the princess? Is she an acolyte of the Dark Arts?"

"No." Mouse shook her head. "Camaris is a spoiled and rather foolish girl, but there is no true wickedness in her. She is merely a pawn to further the queen's great ambitions."

Spoiled and foolish? Tor bridled. Surely such words could not apply to the lovely Camaris. He thought he'd found a flaw in her story. "You are clever with your tongue, but the tale does not ring true. Why did the queen not dispose of you, as she did your mother?"

The fog swirled in around them while Mouse told him about Elva and the Spell of Forgetting. "Only Elva remembered the truth of my birth, and she kept her own counsel. I was raised as a weaver, learning on my mother's loom. When the princess admired my work, I was brought to the castle. It was pleasant enough and I was well paid for my work" Her voice hardened. "And so I would have lived out my days quite happily, had *you* not arrived in Airan!"

"A spell of forgetfulness." He smiled cynically. "How convenient for everyone concerned—especially for the king!"

"I assure you it is the least convenient for me!" Mouse sent him a resentful look from beneath her winged brows. "I would much prefer to spend the night beneath a warm roof than out here in the fog and cold!"

Tor heard the conviction in her voice. He sheathed his

sword. "I accept your tale. But it does not explain why you followed me here."

"I, follow *you*?" Mouse was furious. "It is the other way around. I came through the ravine."

He remembered it now, a wide slash of crumpled lines upon the map. "A dangerous journey."

"Not so dangerous as remaining beneath the same roof as Queen Bryn," she snapped. "Go on your way and leave me in peace, sir."

"Neither of us can go any further in this thick mist. Let us seek shelter in the tower while I decide what to do about you."

Anger flared in her eyes. "You need do nothing about me. I am off to seek my own fate. You have no part in it."

Tor's jaw squared. "Yet you just said in your own words that the blame for your troubles rests on me. You cannot have it both ways. And if I take the blame, lady, then I accept the responsibility as well."

"It's too late to argue. Come inside the tower. I've a fire started."

"Not very wise of you. The smoke will send us out coughing into the night, and the scent of burning wood will lead the soldiers here." He could smell it now that the wind had died away.

"The roof is mostly gone," she answered, "and there are no windows at all at the tower's base. The smoke will rise up high, and its scent will seem to be coming from the valley. We'll be safe enough."

She stopped suddenly and looked behind her, alert and wary. "There was another man with you. Where is he?"

"On his way south."

Mouse frowned. "Running away from danger? He didn't look to be a coward."

"He is not!" Tor said shortly. "I've sent him on an errand."

He ducked beneath the low doorway and followed her

inside. She sat down in front of the fire. It was small and did little to keep back the blackness.

Two fat turnips were roasting over it. "I have sausage and cheese as well, and a pouchful of raisins," Mouse told him. "If the hungry little ermald didn't eat them all."

He looked down and saw a tiny creature poised upon its furry white haunches. He'd seen one only in paintings. Its body resembled an ermine, but its large green eyes were very like a cat's. It gobbled up the raisin it held in its paws and vanished into the darkness.

"Oh, you've frightened it away."

Tor sat on the far side of the fire and eyed her warily. Some believed that ermalds were the spirits of those who'd lived before.

"Are you a sorceress? I'd heard that ermalds never come into the presence of humans. No one I know has ever seen one alive."

"They are very shy," Mouse said. "I used to have one as a pet when I was younger. Elva taught me how to win the confidence of shy creatures."

She handed him a portion of cheese. "I've plenty to spare. I took everything I could get my hands on when I fled the village."

"Taming ermalds and cooking turnips. You're a practical woman," he said. "But a woman traveling alone will be easy enough to track."

"I've brought boy's garb with me. My trail ends here."

She twisted her hair up atop her head, tucked it beneath the boy's cap, and tried to look tough. The effect was spoiled by the streak of ash her knuckle left across her face. She looked, Tor decided, less like a farm lad than like a mischievous urchin. He wasn't sure if he liked it or not.

"You still look like a girl. There's no disguising your delicate features." *Or those high, firm breasts.*

She saw it in his eyes before he looked away, as clearly as if he'd spoken aloud. Hot color flooded her cheeks. "I'm not a fool. I'll bind them."

"A pity."

Tor flushed. He'd said it without thinking—but it was still true. And the rest of her was lovely as well. How odd he hadn't noticed that earlier.

Mouse cupped her chin in her hand. She'd been mulling something over in her mind for some time. "You risked everything in the tournament, including your life. I am wondering why."

That took him aback. "The Princess Camaris is very beautiful."

She made a dismissive gesture. "That is no answer. It's clear to me that your strategy was all planned out long before you so much as set eyes on her."

"Ah, but the moment I saw her, my heart was lost."

Mouse was sorry she'd asked.

His gaze was coolly appraising. "Why do you think I came to Airan?"

"The others—the dukes and lords and princes—came in hopes of increasing their status and wealth." She tipped her head and surveyed him. "You have neither, so I suppose that is the reason."

"You are an annoying girl," he said shortly. "And you know nothing at all about me. Perhaps I have five thousand acres and five hundred head of cattle. As to what drew me to Airan—I decided that I should like to have a few more adventures before I settled down."

That intrigued her. "What kind of adventures have you had?"

"None of your business, my girl. You ask more questions of a stranger than is considered polite!"

"Ah." She regarded him from beneath her lashes. "You have no land or cattle. I thought not."

He fought the urge to throttle her. She was a most maddening girl!

Tor took a deep breath. If he had to put up with her for the night, he could at least get information from her, for his knowledge of Airan's more remote geography left much to be desired.

"If I will find this fabulous phoenix, I must know more about its habits. Tell me, what lies in the mountainous regions that the phoenix calls home?"

"Ho! Now who is asking the questions?" But she laughed softly when she said it. She considered how much to give away: Part of the truth, she decided, would be sufficient to prove her use to him.

"The Misted Mountains are a place of enchantment. The source of Airan's legends." Mouse laced her hands behind her neck. "They also are home to thunder giants who use lightning bolts to spear their prey, and to trolls with eyes as red as fire and teeth like rusted knives. Many an unwary traveler has been frightened to death by them."

Tor was not amused. "Do you think me a rustic, with hay between my teeth?" He stuck his knife tip into one of the turnips. It was still hard as wood. "I wouldn't nibble at your troll tales, any more than I would bite into this half-cooked root. Such stories are spun to frighten country bumpkins."

She eyed him steadily. "Then why do you believe in the phoenix?"

He hesitated again. "Because I have proof."

Reaching inside his jerkin, Tor withdrew a flat piece of leather. When he opened it, the looming shadows jumped back. The chamber at the base of the ruins was lit with sparkling, iridescent light.

"Oh!" Mouse blinked and shielded her eyes. "What is it?"

"The feather of a phoenix. It is my talisman." Tor held it reverently. "I had the story from my grandfather, Orgus, and this feather from his own hand before he died. He came to Airan on a quest in the long-ago and found one of the creatures captured in a trap he set. When he removed it from the snare, it spread its plumage, dazzling him so greatly that he let go of it. The phoenix flew away, leaving only this feather behind."

Mouse was awed. "May I touch it?"

He nodded, and she came around the fire to sit beside

him. "It is the most beautiful thing I've ever seen."

She reached out to the relic of the legendary bird. Little rainbows flickered over her slender hand. Her fingertips caressed the feather. It wasn't like anything she'd ever touched before. It felt warm and cool at the same time, and it tickled, as if hundreds of little golden bubbles danced against her skin.

"Thank you." She was enchanted. "Never in my life did I expect to see such a marvel. How did he capture it?"

"That," Tor said, "is a secret."

She pulled her hand back. "And how to find the phoenix is mine."

He placed the feather carefully inside the flat leather and tucked it away in his jerkin. Except for the glow of the small wood fire, the chamber was dark once more.

Mouse moved back to the other side of the fire. "I could aid you in your quest," she said quietly. "I know all the old legends and songs, even those that have been forgotten by all the rest." Elva had taught her, hoping to keep them alive. "You are an outlander. I doubt you have the smallest inkling of where the phoenix can be found."

"Tell me, then."

"For a price."

"Abominable girl!"

"It isn't gold I seek. I will aid you in your quest to find the phoenix if you will pledge to help me in mine."

"I might agree," Tor said, "but first you must prove to me that you have the knowledge I lack."

Mouse folded her hands and rested her chin upon them. Her eyes were like dark sapphires in the fire's glow, her hair like burnished copper.

"To find the phoenix, you must first locate Phoenix Pass. There's a rock that marks it, shaped like a woman. Legend says she was turned to stone by a basilisk, the sly reptiles that hatch from roosters' eggs. You can only look at them in a mirror," she added.

"Roosters do not lay eggs. Hens do," Tor exclaimed in

exasperation. "No more of these faradiddles. Tell me about the phoenix, and tell me true!"

"You needn't shout!"

"Tell me, sweet Rosaleen, I beg you."

His voice was gentle—but the words came through gritted teeth. She almost laughed aloud. She had him now.

"The phoenix is very shy. It makes its nest in the topmost branches of the silver rowan tree. They grow only near the summit of the tallest mountain and . . ."

"But of course," he broke in sarcastically. "It couldn't be just around the bend, lying by the side of the road."

". . . and are very difficult to find," she continued as if he hadn't spoken. "But the leaves of the tree are hammered silver, and the trunk is of purest gold. If the light is right, it can be seen from Phoenix Pass at sundown."

"And how do I find Phoenix Pass?"

Mouse couldn't restrain her smile. "You won't find it on your own. It can only be found by a virgin."

That let him out. He'd lost his virginity as a lusty lad of seventeen. Tor sent her a hard look across the low flames. "Very clever."

"Of course," Mouse offered, "I would be glad to be of assistance on your quest, in return for your vow to aid me."

He considered her thoughtfully. She had courage—and a wit as keen as a honed steel blade. A strange creature, this girl who was sired by a king and then forgotten. A fetching one, too.

"What is it, that you want?"

"You must promise to see me safely over the mountains to the Eastern Lands," she told him. Her face was aglow in the firelight. "There is a city there. A small but wonderful city called Penambra, with houses of gold-colored stone."

Elva had told her all about it. The wisewoman had visited relatives there long ago, when she was a young child, and remembered its honey-tiled roofs and gleaming domes. Mouse intended to send for Elva as soon as she was settled. "The moment my foot touches the ground in Penambra," she told Tor, "you are free of your vow."

He raised his brows. "And that is it?"

"Yes. I'll be safe there," she said confidently. "I have only to find the weavers guild, and they will take me in. I'll earn my way with my skills."

Tor's gaze was unreadable. "If you help me realize my quest, I vow that I will do everything in my power to see that you are safe and comfortably established. Word of a Far Islandian! And I will give you a dowry of gold."

Her eyes widened. "I didn't ask for gold!"

"It's the least I can do, after bringing the queen's wrath down upon you. Do we have a bargain?"

"I'd like something more than your word," she said. "Words can be twisted. Give me the phoenix feather as token of your faith. I swear that I will give it back once you've redeemed your vow."

Tor crossed his arms over his chest. "Unlike your father," he said, "my word is my bond. But I cannot give you the feather. It is a sacred trust."

He'd promised Orgus that he would give it someday to his own firstborn son.

Mouse didn't know if she could trust this black-eyed stranger. Her fingers caressed the fractured stone that was all that remained of her amulet while she decided. *I cannot leave Elva, aging and alone. I must get her away before the queen suspects that she had any part in my birth.* But first, she would have to reach the city beyond the mountains. *I will have to risk it.*

She took the silver chain from around her throat. The clear pebble shone like a ruby as it gathered the firelight. "This is all I have of value in the world," she said simply. "It is worth more to me than gold."

Mouse held it out to Tor. "Let us exchange necklaces as a token of faith. Your talisman for mine."

Tor saw the tear trapped in her eyelashes. He could not even begin to guess what it cost her to make the offer.

She was risking far more than he by exchanging tokens—
and by putting her honor and trust in him.

"My pledge is not worthy of yours, Rosaleen of Airan.
But my solemn oath goes with it. I will keep my vow to
you."

He accepted her amulet, then pulled the twisted silver
torque from around his neck.

She smiled tremulously, accepting his token. She
slipped the torque on. It was warm from his body, and
far too large. Tor reached over and bent the ends closer
to one another, forcing the twisted silver into a smaller
circle to fit her slender throat.

As his fingers brushed her skin, something passed between them. The air hummed with it, like a plucked harp
string. Mouse quickly pulled away. She still felt it, a vi-
bration in her bones. A resonance in her soul.

Tor looked down at her talisman in his hand. The chain
was far too small to go around his throat. Taking the
thong that bound his hair, he threaded the amulet onto it,
knotting the silver links to each end. "We have a pact,
Rosaleen of Airan. I give you my solemn oath that I will
help you, as you help me."

Mouse closed her eyes and sighed with relief. The silver torque seemed to throw a ring of protection around
her. It was an illusion, she knew, but it comforted her
nevertheless.

Although initially she'd been distressed to find that her
unwelcome visitor was Tor, she was glad now that he had
chanced upon her hideaway. Practical she might be, but
there was no way she could cross the mountains to safety
alone. He had a sword, a strong arm, and the courage to
wield both. Her odds had just improved greatly.

"I pledge the same to you, Tor of Far Islandia. You
have my oath as well."

She saw that the turnips were done, and she removed
them from the fire. They ate in silence while the flames
leapt up inside the black maw of the tower. Mouse fin-

ished half of hers and put the rest aside. "It will do for breakfast."

"Hold still, Rosaleen. You've a smut on your cheek."

He tried to rub it away with his thumb, but she pulled away. "You wouldn't be cleaning a lad's dirt off," she told him sharply. "And I am called Mouse, sir."

"Not," Tor said, "by me."

"Why?"

"It is not a dignified name for the daughter of a king."

She plopped down on her knapsack. "I am not a very dignified person."

Tor wrapped himself in his cloak and lay down on the other side of the banked fire. "Nor I."

Her sudden smile flashed. "Then we shall be disreputable together for the night."

A swift intake of breath and an awkward silence followed her gaffe. "That wasn't an invitation," she said in a gruff voice.

Tor hid his laughter. "I didn't take it as one. Go to sleep, Rosaleen of Airan. And sleep well."

She turned her back to him and lay unmoving in the dim glow. It was only a few minutes, however, before her breathing slowed and she was fast asleep.

Tor pondered the situation. He doubted whether the girl had thought further than the first day or two. The food she had with her would run out by then, and as far as he could tell she had no warm garments or leather boots to protect her from the cold of the high mountains.

Tor doubted she had the heart to wring a chicken's neck, much less the skill to trap even the weakest game. If he hadn't stumbled upon her, only the gods knew how long she might have survived on her own.

Not very long, he decided. *She is no more fit to survive in the wilds alone than an infant is.* And she would prove a hindrance to his own survival, no doubt about that either.

It wasn't just her knowledge of where the phoenix lived that had swayed his judgment—although he believed her.

It was something else she'd said that rang terribly true: If not for him, she would have lived out her life safely between the thick stone walls of Castle Aidan, her royal identity unknown.

By winning the tournament he had jeopardized everything that mattered to her. It was a burden he must bear for both of them.

Wrapped in her blanket, Mouse murmured something in her sleep. *She is having a nightmare,* Tor thought. He rose and went around the fire to kneel beside her.

In the glow, her hair was like dark flame spilling around her shoulders. Her lashes lay against her cheek, casting a shadow. She was really quite beautiful. And he recognized where he'd first seen her now.

The knowledge came all at once. She was the girl he'd encountered in the castle, fleeing as if her life depended upon it. If he hadn't caught her she might have hurtled down the stairs.

He reached his hand out. There was the mark of the bruise upon her smooth skin, fading to yellow. Gently, so as not to awaken her, he placed the back of his hand against her cheek.

So lovely, and so brave. Life has used her hard. She should have been born to silks and satins, not to a life of servitude to a cruel mistress.

Tor made another vow then and there. *Fair Rosaleen of Airan, I will do all in my power to see that you get everything your heart desires, and more.*

Although at the moment he didn't have a clue as to how he would bring it all about. Instead of going back to the other side of the fire, Tor wrapped himself up in his cloak and lay down beside her.

He was still awake at dawn.

11

AT HALF-LIGHT Tor saddled up their mounts. Mouse watched him place his bow and quiver of arrows within easy reach. "I hope you are as handy with them as you are with a broadsword."

"They are not for show!" he said stiffly.

Just then they both stopped and listened. The fitful wind had carried an ominous sound to their ears: men and horses in the distance. "We'd best be on our way."

She used a rock for a mounting block before he could help her. Tor swung up into the saddle, and they took off over the sand. Row upon row, the waves flashed dull silver as they crumpled and spilled onto the beach. The retreating surf washed away their hoofprints, and the roar of the sea covered the sound of their passage.

They went on for some time. The sun was rising over the hills when Mouse led him back toward the cliffs. A shadow behind a fall of giant rocks proved to be the narrow entrance to a cave.

"A shortcut," she said. "The coast curves in and out, like lace on a lady's gown, but this cavern tunnels deep. We'll save many miles this way, and no one the wiser."

Tor followed her, frowning. He wasn't fond of enclosed spaces, but he wasn't going to let this mere slip of a girl know that.

Mouse glanced at him from beneath her lashes. "It's all right," she said. "You won't feel smothered."

He muttered an oath and rode in.

It wasn't dark once he got inside. Weak sunshine filtered down through small crevices hidden from above by the wild grasses. The walls were a soft lavender-rose color and glittered as if they were covered with hoarfrost.

Once the seas had been higher, he guessed, for the first hundred yards of the cavern floor were covered by wave-packed sand. He saw small footsteps winding over it and realized they must be hers.

"You know this place well."

"Yes. Elva showed it to me. We used to ride out on the back of her cob to gather the wild mosses." She lifted her head, glancing up at the domed ceiling. Stalactites gleamed like tinted icicles.

"Beautiful, isn't? I've been coming here since I was a child."

"You're still . . ." He stopped and looked away.

Then he glanced back at Mouse, assessing her in the filtered green light. She wasn't a child. Not by any means.

She was truly quite lovely. During the long night hours he'd grown increasingly aware of it. Her breasts were high and firm, her hips and thighs softly rounded. And, he remembered keenly, her hair had smelled exactly like wild raspberries.

The ground underfoot rang as their horses left the sand and entered a long gallery hollowed from rock. Mouse led them through the forest of stone formations, some bridging the span from floor to high ceiling like fancifully carved pillars. Gradually the light dimmed as the way grew cramped.

"We must go single file from here," she said. "Stay well back. The cavern floor is slippery." *And,* Mouse thought, *you won't be able to question me further.*

Or see her face and realize that she'd never before gone so far into the winding maze of passageways.

Her heart beat a little faster. All she had guiding her now was Elva's instructions. The wisewoman had taught her a set of rhymes to get from the seashore caverns to the secluded valley far beyond the cliffs. Mouse prayed that she had memorized them well.

Tor didn't guess her secret. He fell in behind her, trusting her to lead the way. They rode in echoing silence for a long time, picking their way over the stone floor. At one point his horse almost lost its footing. It skittered sideways, but he held it in check. When he looked up Mouse had vanished.

There were several routes she could have taken. He called out to her. His voice came echoing back, ever fainter.

Cursing beneath his breath, Tor stopped and listened. The only sound was a soft sighing. He urged his horse toward it. There was an opening somewhere ahead. The closer he got to it, the more he felt the gentle breath of air moving past his face. He rounded a turn and came out into daylight.

They were in a narrow valley surrounded by sheer rock walls. The sky was a thin blue ribbon high above. Mouse was just a little way ahead, looking back over her shoulder.

"You should have made sure I was behind you," he said, with a hint of temper.

Her eyebrows rose. "Were you afraid that you were lost? I would have turned back and found you."

"No, by the gods! My concern wasn't for myself." Tor

reined in beside her. "The queen's men are after you, and you are unarmed!"

"They would never find their way through the caverns." She pointed up toward the mouth of the valley. "The trail leads up to the rim. It's long and steep. Best to rest and water the horses before we set out along it."

Since he was about to suggest the same thing, her advice annoyed him. He didn't know why. They took the horses to the stream that trickled down from the heights and let them quench their thirst.

Mouse had seen the frown flicker across his brow. "You are accustomed to giving the orders. You don't like taking them from a woman."

"In Far Islandia, women and men walk on equal footing. But I am not used to meekly bringing up the rear, as if I were a beardless stripling."

Mouse saw she'd stung his pride, and hid her smile. "We've a long way to go, and many adventures ahead of us. We'll take the lead in turn."

"I'll take it here," he said, with a mocking smile. "In case we run into any giants or basilisks or trolls along the way."

"If it makes you happy, lead the way. Give me a boost into the saddle."

Tor swept her a formal bow. "I am at your service, lady."

She expected him to lace his hands together to form a step for her to mount. Instead he stepped in close. The moment his strong hands spanned her waist, a curious shock of pleasure zinged through her.

Before she had time to think, he tossed her into the saddle as if she weighed no more than mist. Mouse clutched the reins and steadied her horse. *What power there is in him!*

She felt his tongue against her throat, and remembered how it had lain against her skin. Her heart skipped and fluttered like a startled bird, and her head was light with agreeable confusion. She looked quickly away.

Tor waited until he was sure she had command of her mount, then leapt up on his own. The moment his hands had closed upon her waist, he'd had the urge to pull her hard against him, and kiss her senseless. It left him startled and wary.

She's learned the legends from the village wisewoman. What else had she learned? Spells of enchantment? Certainly that would account for the suddenness, the potency of the urge that had almost overwhelmed him.

He feared, however, that it was something more difficult to keep at bay: the age-old lure of man to woman. And beneath that boy's garb, she was all woman.

Heat pooled in his loins. He remembered the feel of her narrow waist and delicate ribs. The feminine flare of her hips and the soft swell of her breasts. Her wild berry scent that teased his senses. And the king had offered her to him.

Tor gave himself a mental shake. He would not follow that line of thought: that way lay disaster.

He started up the narrow trail and left her to fall in behind him. The way sloped gently upward, then became considerably steeper. Ancient hardwoods gave way to dark fir forest. The heady scent of the trees filled the air.

Tor rode with an easy, masculine grace, sword at his side and his quiver and bow behind his saddle. Mouse was quite content to watch him. Dappled light brushed his wide shoulders and outlined his formidable physique. Although she was becoming tired, he looked fresh and alert as ever.

If trolls and giants do exist, she decided, *he could dispatch them with the same ease he vanquished Ragnor.*

She imagined Tor, then, his chest naked and sweat-slicked, sunlight gilding his body. It was so clear in her mind, she could almost feel the heat rising off him. Then she realized that the heat was inside her, burning deep in the pit of her belly. Her breath hitched in her throat.

Need and want poured through her, filled her to overflowing. It was not the sweet, innocent yearning of her dreams: It was a woman's throb of hot desire.

She fought against it. Only a fool would get caught in that trap. *I will not want a man who doesn't want me*, she vowed. *I value myself more highly than that!*

A shudder of mingled fear and anticipation shook her. Although she was a virgin, she knew the ways of the world. Fate had bound them together. Isolation in each other's company would serve to draw that bond tighter. The attraction she felt to him would tempt her sorely, and somewhere in the days ahead—it was inevitable—there would come an opportunity to quench her longing in his arms. She knew that she must guard against succumbing to it, fight it with all her might.

Mouse realized they'd reached the rim of the valley as they came out from the narrow defile onto a ledge. The sun was blinding and she shielded her eyes against the glare. They were in the foothills now, with the Misted Mountains rising above, their weathered summits wreathed in smoky veils.

Tor tipped his dark head back and gazed up at them. Excitement thrilled through his veins. *Somewhere in their mysterious heart, Destiny awaits.*

Mouse had ridden up beside him. She gestured to him. "Look. Over the cliff's edge."

Tor moved closer to the dizzying drop. Far below, a band of soldiers galloped along the coast road. They were heavily armed and wore the scarlet tunics of the queen's men.

And they were riding in the wrong direction.

"We've eluded them!" Mouse sighed in relief, and pushed damp tendrils of auburn hair away from her brow. She'd done it! Triumph surged through her.

Until this very moment she hadn't been quite sure that she could pull it off.

"You're worth your weight in rubies, fair Rosaleen!" Tor smiled at her, a flash of white in his tanned face.

Mouse flushed rosily. She felt that smile all the way

down to her toes. It melted her bones and made her head spin—just as it had in her dreams.

Tor's eyes kindled. "For now we dance to the king's piping. But when I ride back to Castle Airan to claim my prize, he'll whistle another tune!"

Mouse felt as if she'd been slapped. She'd been so dazzled by his smile that, for a few seconds, she'd forgotten the true purpose of their journey.

Her hands jerked on the reins. The horse sidled and reared in alarm. For a wild moment it seemed that she would be thrown from the saddle.

"Have a care!" Tor leaned across his saddle bow. He pictured her spinning out over the void, falling down and down through the cool blue air, to shatter like glass on the valley floor below.

Reaching out at an awkward angle, he grabbed her horse's bridle, and wrestled the bit down with strength and sheer willpower. The jolt of it was severe. It almost wrenched his arm out of the socket.

Again, Mouse was startled by his great strength and power. And by the pleasure it gave her.

She mistook his grimace of pain for one of anger. "I could have brought the horse under control without your interference," she said hotly.

His brows knit in a scowl. He'd risked death to save her pretty little neck, and this was the thanks he got for it!

"You little fool! Do you know how near you came to disaster?" he said.

"Much you'd care!" Mouse's voice was sharp. "You didn't value my companionship so highly yesterday."

Tor's temper flared. "Ah," he snapped, "but that was before I learned that *you* can lead me to the phoenix."

Mouse recoiled from the anger in his voice. "You are right. I am a fool! If I had any wisdom at all, I would have lost you in the caverns. Or better yet, I would never have agreed to this bargain we made!"

"With all respect, lady, it was you who suggested the bargain."

She had indeed. "At the time it was the lesser of two evils."

Nudging her horse, Mouse sent the beast galloping across the meadow. Clods of earth and mangled wildflowers flew out behind them, as she tried to outrace her wild emotions. She was so furious with herself that she was shaking with it.

Earlier, for a bright, fleeting moment, she'd forgotten something she must never forget again: it wasn't the thrill of the quest that drove Tor on, nor the desire to obtain the phoenix egg.

It was his desire for the Princess Camaris.

12

T OR THREW ANOTHER brand upon the leaping fire and held his hands out to its warmth. The ebony sky was studded with myriad diamonds, and a chill wind blew down from the mountain's crest. The stars were cold and distant, but they could not have been more remote than his companion.

Mouse sat a hundred feet away, silhouetted against the night, with her back to him. She'd been sitting there for hours.

Seven days and seven long nights they'd been traveling together now, higher and higher, into the heart of the Misted Mountains. She intrigued him greatly. With every mile, his interest in her grew. At the same time, hers seemed to wane. He didn't know what to make of her.

Rosaleen. Her name suited her. She was lovely as a rose in bloom. And just as prickly. Every time he tried to get too close, he ended up bloodied.

It wasn't that he expected to charm every woman whose path he crossed, but she had barely spoken to him for days. Her silence unnerved him. She made no comments on the weather or the beauty of the scenery, and she uttered no complaints about the tiring journey, or the cold nights. On the rare occasion when she did speak, she was civil, but that was all.

It isn't natural, he reflected. *Women are supposed to chatter.* He'd never known one who didn't. But then, he'd never known any woman quite like her.

Tor frowned into the fire. He had enough experience with women to know that he'd offended her somehow— just not enough to figure out exactly what his offense was.

There was another thing niggling at him. For the first two days the course she'd led had been sure. Today, it had seemed at times that she was wandering along without a clue to guide her. At other time, he wondered if she might be purposely leading him astray. But why?

To complicate matters there was an attraction between them. He felt it keenly. At first she was so reserved that he had believed it to be one-sided. Then he noticed how she watched from the corner of her eye when he stripped off his shirt to bathe at the edge of the stream on a hot afternoon. The way her skin flushed and her pupils widened when he smiled down at her. Ah, yes. She felt it, too. And the longer they were thrown together, the more likely it became that one of them would act upon it. Just thinking of it aroused him.

That made the situation increasingly awkward. He tried not to think about it. About *her.* Nothing must distract him from his true goal.

Once Airan and Far Islandia had been united under one crown. During the chaotic war years, a despot had wrested the kingdom of Airan away by treachery. Tor's father had gathered his army and marched to battle, pledging to bring back Airan's crown and unite the countries once again.

Instead he had perished on the battlefield in tarnished glory. Tor had come to Airan not to seek a wife, however beautiful, but to make good his father's vow.

Tor rubbed his aching shoulder. He wouldn't let his focus be diverted by anything. Not by Gilmore's trickery. *Not even,* he vowed, *by the nearness of a beautiful young woman on a starry summer night.*

Try as he might, it was an impossible task not to think of her. His thoughts circled like a hawk riding the air, and each time they came back to his companion.

And she calls the queen a sorceress! he thought. Certainly the fair Rosaleen had put some sort of spell on him.

He looked at her and felt that hot tug of desire. She was lucky that her lot had fallen in with him. After all, he wasn't the type of foul villain who would tumble a pretty maid without a by-your-leave. But then, as she'd reminded him, her predicament was one of his making.

What would have happened to her if I hadn't come along to poke a stick in the hornets' nest of the past?

She was a fetching lass, as clever as she was lovely. Likely some fortunate fellow would have taken her to wed and bed. Fathered some red-haired sons and daughters on her. She might, as she'd said, have lived out her life in a little cottage contentedly enough.

Tor's reflections gave him no satisfaction. Guilt and regret filled his heart. *She deserves far more than that.*

Indeed, if matters had stood differently between Gilmore and the girl's mother, she would have been raised as befitted a daughter of royalty. He scowled. *Poor brave girl! She's been robbed of her birthright. If the king had honored his hand-fasting with her mother, Rosaleen should have worn a golden diadem upon her brow, and robes of embroidered sendal.*

She should have worn jewels at her throat and wrists and fingers. Flowing garments of rose-colored silk, trimmed with ribbons of the same hue as her silver-blue eyes. He imagined her in them.

He imagined her out of them.

A vision of her rose before Tor, sweet and enticing. That glorious dark red hair tumbling over her bare shoulders. Her ivory limbs as smooth as satin, her breasts rosy-tipped and inviting. They would pleasure a man with their texture and taste—like the wild raspberry scent that rose so tantalizingly from her skin.

Heat smoldered in his belly, curled out along his veins at the thought of it. She was more than lovely, she was beautiful. And she was incredibly desirable. If he hadn't been blinded by rage after the tournament, he would have seen it then.

He realized that now every day spent in her company would be more difficult than the one before. The long nights would be torture.

Even at a hundred yards, Mouse felt him looking at her. She was intensely aware of him on every level. He was a magnificent man. His sculpted muscle and sinew pleased her eye, and his face pleased her even more. Those eyes, as dark and light-filled as the starry sky above her. That firm, determined mouth roused feelings in her she didn't wish to examine any closer.

Mouse imagined him in the midst of war, the muscles of his back and shoulders rippling beneath his leather armor, the flash of steel in his strong right hand.

She imagined lying naked beside him, amid a crumpled toss of linen, his sun-bronzed hand dark against the whiteness of her breast. Her body tingled as if he'd touched her bare skin.

I will not think of you anymore than I must, Tor of Far Islandia. I wish I'd never agreed to set out with you in search of the phoenix.

She rose, meaning to walk further away from the camp. A moment or two ago she'd glimpsed a falling star. There would be a better—and safer—view from there.

Suddenly her body tensed like a bow. *Yes! There it was again.*

"Tor! Come here!" Mouse called out softly. "Quickly!"

Tor jumped up in alarm and raced toward her, his sword drawn and ready. "What is it?"

"Wait! Watch."

He did. There was nothing to see but the immense stretch of velvet sky. Time slipped away like silk. Tor became aware of the utter stillness around them. Not an animal scurrying, not a single insect rustling in the darkness. Only the beating of his heart as he became attuned to her nearness.

Her beauty addled his head like mulled wine on a winter's night, and her scent rose around him in the darkness. He wondered what it was she wore that made her smell so enticing. He wondered what she would do if he gave in to the sudden and overwhelming urge to take her into his arms and kiss her breathless.

The air tingled. It seemed to Tor that invisible stars danced between them. Did she feel it, too? He held his breath as she stepped closer. Her fingers curled lightly over his wrist.

"There! Look!" Mouse whispered, shattering the spell. "Do you see it?"

A streak of scintillating light shot across the face of the dark. It vanished as quickly as it had come. "The phoenix," she said softly.

Excitement poured through Tor. Could it be? Certainly he had never witnessed anything like it before in all his travels.

"There's another!"

A shimmering golden ribbon unspooled against the blackness. It died to embers and winked out. Scant seconds later the night bloomed with light and color, closer still.

Mouse held her breath. Her whole body was trembling with the wonder of it. Tor's arm steadied her and they stood at the edge of the cliff. Watching. Waiting.

They waited for a long while, but the streak of gold didn't reappear. She became aware of Tor's breathing, the warm strength of his arm around her. The urge to lean into his embrace and see where the dangerous moment led them. Mouse knew he felt it, too.

They heard a rush of wings. Suddenly the air was on

fire over their heads. Sparks of silver and gold rained down around them. Pulsing jewels of multicolored light were everywhere.

They stood transfixed. They could barely make out the creature's shape amid the darting beams. Up and down and around, in great looping spirals the resplendent phoenix flew. Its glory dimmed the stars and dazzled their eyes.

Tor stood with his head thrown back, his dark eyes gleaming with reflected fire. His arm tightened and Mouse leaned against his shoulder, not even aware of doing so.

A fountain of sparks fell around them, bright gold and silver plumes, glowing clouds of scarlet and blue and green. Mouse blinked and held up her hand. It was too much, this brightness, like staring into the noonday sun.

The light blazed, soared up and up, then disappeared for good.

They were left standing in the darkness, while images burned like flame against the insides of their eyes.

Neither spoke for some time. They had experienced something wonderful together, and the magic of the moment held them both in thrall.

He turned to smile at her. "We've almost reached the end of our quest. Tomorrow we'll be there, at the nesting grounds of the phoenix."

"Oh," she said softly, "I wish that we would not!"

He wasn't sure if he'd heard correctly. Was that a sneeze or a sob she'd stifled? Were those tears in her eyes? Tor lifted her chin in his hand, and saw that it was. He felt a little shaky himself.

"Don't cry, Rosaleen. Hush, my sweeting."

His fingers brushed away the tear that spilled down her cheek. She swayed against him, more blinded by his nearness than she had been by the light. He inhaled the now familiar scent of her. Berries and woman and dark summer night.

He felt the rapid beating of her heart, the small shiver that rippled through her body as his embrace tightened.

All the feelings he'd suppressed so long would not be denied. Nor could hers. Warm and willing, she curved into the shelter of his arms. He pulled her close and lowered his head to hers. The moment his mouth touched hers, the high mountains and dark valley, the joyful dance of the phoenix, were all forgotten. The world fell away.

He angled his kiss and pulled her hard against him. As she curved into him, heat layered his body, rising in ever demanding waves. She trembled as he took the kiss deeper, but her arms rose up to wind around his neck. Her body felt so light—as if only his embrace kept her from lifting off the ground and floating away to the stars.

She'd dreamed this moment. Dreamed it a hundred times. The hardness of his lean body against hers, the steady thud of his heart. The warmth that poured through her, melding her to him. She kissed him. Not a tentative, fleeting kiss, but a full-mouthed, heated one. *Love me,* she whispered silently. *Love me.*

His mouth skimmed her cheek, her temple, her closed eyelids, soft as a whisper of eiderdown against them. This was what she'd longed for, the protective circle of his strong arms. The power and demand of him. She ached with the need to answer it. To plunge recklessly into the moment without regret.

Her breasts strained against him, her fingers wound in his hair. Her ardent response surprised and delighted him. And by the gods, he ached for her! He kissed her again and savored it, long and deep. His blood sang.

Cupping her face in his hands, he kissed her until they were both breathless. He was like a beggar at a feast. He wanted to consume her. This past week had been hell . . . watching the sunlight dance on her flaming hair and caress the sleek lines of her body.

His hands, so large and calloused, opened her tunic with infinite care. Every touch, every move, was filled with heat and tenderness. Her body was like silk and velvet beneath his questing hands, her passion like a flame. He warmed himself with it. He cupped her breast gently, trying to soothe the wild beating of her heart. Starlight turned her skin to alabaster, tipped her breasts with silver. She was so beautiful, so very desirable.

A wildness came over him. His breath came faster, in time to the pounding of his heart. The same fierce need coursed through her blood. As if he sensed it, his hands became less gentle, more urgent in their explorations. She arched with pleasure and moaned against his mouth. It was a sound of victory and surrender. Of her delight in her feminine allure and power, and her yielding to his passion. *Yes,* she thought, *yes!* and didn't know she spoke aloud.

He swept her off her feet and lifted her, his mouth hot on hers as he swirled her around and around beneath the stars. Her cap flew off and her hair tumbled over her shoulders, spilled across her body in a scented cloud. She laughed with delight and anticipation.

When he placed her softly on the ground, she was reeling with desire. He pulled his shirt over his head, and her hands reached out and touched his naked chest. Her fingers trailed over the chiseled muscle, down his ribs. Her mind was filled with the touch and scent and sight of him. She moved against him, wanting . . . wanting.

He lay down beside her on the mossy ground. His hands danced lightly over the curve of her breasts, and down. His mouth followed where his hands had been, and everywhere he touched, she burned with fire. Light kisses, soft nibbles. The delectable shock of his tongue against her flesh.

He stroked and caressed and explored, all the while murmuring soft words of love. He led her gently but inexorably on. Along the way she lost her garments and her inhibitions. She was clothed in moonlight and sudden sensual awareness.

The light skimming of his hands tantalized her, and she arched against his questing hands, opened herself to more. Sensations shot through her, a mingling of desires so strong, so deeply pleasurable that she could scarcely bear the joy of it. She was shocked at his boldness, and at her reckless response. Tension coiled inside her, building fast.

There was no shyness in her when he touched her intimately. She pressed against him, eager to follow where he led. She was lost in a world that he knew full well, and she trusted him to guide her. To take her to places she had never even glimpsed in her fevered night dreams. His body was fully alive to the changes in hers, his mind numb to the consequences. The need to pleasure her, to claim her for his own, grew with every moment. With every soft gasp of her breath, every beat of his heart.

Again his fingertips touched, retreated, touched again. Her scent was on him now, ripe summer and woman, and he knew he couldn't hold back much longer. He wanted to lose himself in her. The urgency to claim her almost drove all else from his mind. He struggled against the madness. Against the need. The intensity of it shook him.

Lovemaking had always been a game of giving and taking erotic pleasure. This time it was something different. He wanted her with a primal ferocity he hadn't known was in him. To give in to it would be insanity. He'd never meant this to happen. He fought for control. One wrong step and he could jeopardize everything he wanted most.

Muttering an oath, he kissed her hard, then pulled away. Whether they took this to the next step or not, the choice must be hers. If she chose to stop, he would return to the fire and lie awake the whole night through, yearning for—what might have been. But if she chose to continue—ah, then he would lead her surely through the dark woods of desire, and he would lead her deep.

She cried out in protest as he drew away. She looked up at him in confusion as the cool night air caressed her skin. She ached to be immersed in the heat and passion of him. To feel the strength of him against her and around her and in her.

He felt her need as strongly as he felt his own. She was passionate and eager, but as innocent as he was experienced—and he had already turned her life upside down.

"Tell me what you want," he said hoarsely, "but tell me now. One word and we'll end this, before it goes too far." Too far was only a heartbeat away. "Tell me now, love."

Her emotions were like a tangled skein of silk. She couldn't tell one from another, they were so entwined. She wasn't sure of anything except that she wanted him to hold her and make love to her, banish all the loneliness as his passion met hers in equal measure.

She lifted her head and her hair fell across his chest like a satin veil. He groaned as the sensation rippled through him. She was exquisite and exciting, and he couldn't breathe for wanting her. In the night silence, he imagined he could still hear the blood pumping through her veins and the wild fluttering of her heart. She parted her lips and he waited for her answer.

She was caught in the grip of desire, and almost beyond words. Intuition guided her, and she arched up against his hand with a soft little cry of need.

The instant she brushed against his fingers she lost all control. Her head arched back and her eyes closed. She didn't know if the light was real or was bursting outward from the very core of her. It pulsed in waves of heat and pleasure. She bucked and cried out in delight.

In that same split second, an incredible light exploded through the clearing, showering their bodies with tingling sparks of gold and silver. In their blinding midst was its cause: a graceful bird with fiery plumage and jeweled wings.

"The phoenix!" Tor shielded his eyes against the white hot pain of it.

As he cried out, he felt her hips buck and writhe beneath him. Felt the honeyed heat of her against his flesh. Felt her twist and pull away.

She huddled on her side, spent and still. Alone. Shame blazed through her, as the phoenix burned a lonely path across the stars. *How could I forget?* she thought wretchedly. *How could I?*

He shook his head to clear his vision and glanced down, expecting to see her face still filled with desire. Instead she was curled up on her side, eyes closed. The change in her startled him. One moment she'd been as eager as he, the next she was rolled up like a hedgehog. He bent down and lifted the heavy spill of hair away from her face.

He touched her cheek. "Rosaleen?"

She wouldn't look at him.

"What is it, love? Did I hurt you?"

"No," she whispered. *I fear I have hurt myself. I let desire lead me, not my head, and this is the result.*

He leaned down to kiss her, but she pushed him away. Her eyes opened, glittering like cold blue diamonds. "Answer me this: Do you mean to continue your quest for the phoenix egg?"

He rocked back on his heels, astounded. Here they were, on the verge of plunging into the act of love, and she stopped to ask such a thing?

"Well?" she asked in a dangerous tone.

"Of course I intend to fulfill my quest. What else are we doing here in this isolated place?"

"What else, indeed?"

I am a fool. Why did I expect anything more? It is Camaris and a kingdom he covets, not me. Never me!

The cool breeze danced over her naked flesh, with no more effect upon her now than if she had been a statue. All the heat of her passion was turned to fury.

Once again Tor reached out to her. "Rosaleen . . . !"

She jerked back as if his hand were a firebrand. "Do not call me that!"

It was her own secret name. A part of herself that she'd kept hidden from the world. She fought against the angry tears that stung her eyes. Her body had played her false, giving in to passion. He had breached her solitude and come close to doing the same to her virginity. She would not give up anything more to him.

Mouse grabbed her crumpled garments and rose. "I

gave you my solemn vow, and I must keep it. And *you* must keep your distance. Dare to touch me again and you'll feel my dagger in your ribs!"

"You're being unfair," he said hotly. "I never took anything but kisses. You gave them freely enough." *And would have eagerly granted far more.*

The unspoken words hung between them like a sword.

She turned and walked away into the darkness, all bare and slender limbs. She was stunned by what had happened. Her breasts ached with fullness for the touch of his mouth. Her loins ached to know the feel of him inside her, the shock and glory of victory and surrender. And she would die before she let him know it.

Mouse went back to the campfire, dressed hurriedly, and lay down, wrapped in misery and her blanket. She heard Tor follow her there and mill around before rolling up in his own.

He'd taught her things she'd never even guessed at. He'd brought her body arching to fulfillment, and then . . . Her hands fisted at her sides, and fresh tears stung her eyelids. He was right in his silent assumption. She would have given her innocence to him—not just willingly, but eagerly. Hungrily.

He had said the choice was hers, but he had been the one to stop. She knew why. It wasn't the distraction of the phoenix; it was the knowledge that only a virgin could actually lead him to its nest in the silver rowan tree.

She would never forgive him for it.

Tor cradled his hands behind his head and glared up at the sky. The fire crackled in its ring of stones, and his body ached with all the heat and passion that had just been thwarted by the untimely arrival of the phoenix.

He remembered what he thought she'd said earlier. Now there was no doubt in his mind. She'd wished that they hadn't found the phoenix, yet she had given him her oath to do so. Only a virgin could lead him there, according to legend. Had she for those few moment of passion, wanted him? Or had she hoped to prevent him from finding the phoenix. And if so—why?

Rolling on his side, he watched the flames burn low. He knew how to tease a maiden and make her smile, how to pleasure a woman's body until she came alive with fire and passion. But despite all the women he'd known, he hadn't a clue to the inner working of this one's mind. *Or,* he thought savagely, *her heart.*

His hands curled into fists. If he'd had them around that bloody bird a few minutes ago, he'd have wrung its bloody neck!

Well, perhaps he still would, after she led him to its nest.

If she led him to it.

13

MOUSE WAS HEAVY-EYED and silent, Tor moody as
they rode off in the morning light. He turned in the saddle
to glance back at her, and his breath caught in his chest.
Last night they had stood side by side and shared the
magical flight of the phoenix. Afterward, they'd soared in
each others arms, explored each other with a hot, greedy
passion.

Now she couldn't even bear to look at him.

Her hair was bound up and tucked beneath her boy's
cap, but the morning sun struck fire from it nevertheless.
The plain tunic she wore belted loosely around her hid
her feminine contours, but he remembered every lush
curve of her body. Their silken textures. Their heady
tastes.

He felt a dull flush rise up his face. The desire for her
was still there, but hedged with caution. He pushed the

tantalizing memories away. Last night they'd come so close . . .

Mouse felt him watching her but kept her gaze averted. She was trying not to think of it. Of him.

Once he had the phoenix egg, he would take her over the last line of mountains and down to the city Elva had described to her. Their ways would part forever.

Her horse stumbled suddenly, but she righted it. The beast was old and growing tired now, as if it had spent its last burst of energy in reaching this place. She guided it between the heaps of fallen granite that littered the mountainside, but as the hours passed they lagged further and further behind. She was a hundred yards away when Tor disappeared from sight.

Urging her mount on, she hurried to the place where she'd seen him last. She came around a pile of tumbled granite blocks, scanning the path for signs of him. There he was, at the foot of a weird formation—a spear of rock, cleaved from the face of the mountain. Wind and time had sculpted it into the semblance of a female form.

Mouse stared at it. *A woman turned to stone.*

That meant that Phoenix Pass, and the bird's nesting grounds, lay just beyond.

Tor had waited for her to catch up. He'd spied the stone formation and the narrow pass beyond it. "If your information is accurate, that pass should lead us straight down to the plateau—and to the phoenix."

"It might not yet have laid its egg," she warned him. "Unlike other birds, the phoenix broods in high summer. It might be anytime in the next two weeks."

Tor shrugged. "That doesn't matter. I'll capture the bird and take it back to Airan. Then it will be merely a matter of time."

Mouse bit her lower lip. The closer they came to their goal, the more she regretted her part in it. "That would be both cruel and unwise. The egg will only hatch within the nest of silver rowan leaves."

He shot her an annoyed look. "You seem determined

to find obstacles. I'm not a fool. I'll take the nest as well."

"You still have to catch it," she said. "It won't be easy. You saw how it dipped and plunged and streaked across the sky. Like lightning!"

He laughed. "That was at night. But during the day the phoenix sleeps. I'll have my net around it before it even opens its eyes."

She went still and pale at the thought of it.

"What's wrong? Is it the height?"

"No. I . . . I think we should turn back. It's a trap. I just remembered another part of the legend," she lied. "It says the pass is guarded by trolls."

"My friend Broch says Airan is overrun with them— but have you ever seen a single one?"

"N . . . no. But that doesn't prove anything! I'd never seen a phoenix before last night." She twisted the reins around her hands.

Tor's black eyes surveyed her keenly. "Why are you trying to turn me aside from my quest, now that we're so near its end?"

Can he read my mind? Mouse shifted the attack. "It isn't an idle question! Suppose there *are* trolls? What will we do if one attacks us?"

Tor was impatient. "If our luck holds, we won't have to find out."

He led the way, and they came through the pass without incident. The first thing they saw was three squat lumps of weathered stone. "There are your monsters," he laughed. If she squinted her eyes, they did look a bit like gnarled trolls.

Tor couldn't resist sending her a wry look. "So much for the legends."

He rode on, to the edge of a high ledge overlooking the plateau. The view was astonishing. And infuriating. The Misted Mountains were not jagged ridges set row on row. They wound around in concentric circles, like a bizarre maze.

He scanned the area to get his bearings. To one side

lay the Eastern Lands; to the other, Airan. He could clearly see Airan Castle and the river that flowed past it like molten silver. "By the gods! We could have gone out the northern gate and followed the river to its source—and reached this place by easy stages in a single day."

She shaded her eyes and saw nothing but high ridges and veiled peaks. "Impossible! There is no northern gate to the castle. And the river doesn't even flow toward the mountains!"

Tor realized that she was right. He'd stood on the castle's ramparts and looked to the Misted Mountains. There had been no river. No road.

He blinked. The terrain had shifted. The castle was gone. Nothing was there but a dead salt sea. Tor rubbed his eyes and the sea was gone. A fairy city rose against the sky, taller than the highest mountain peak, with towers of spun glass.

He knew that if he waited, the scene was likely to change yet again. "There is an enchantment upon this place. It is no wonder that strange legends abound!"

"Let's turn back!"

"The mirage can't fool me. That plateau beneath us is where the glowing streaks of light vanished last night."

She peered to where he pointed. Still nothing but swirling mist. Then something flashed with bright metallic luster. The mists parted and vanished, to reveal a grove of pines and the silver rowan tree in their midst. Its leaves shone gold in the bright sunlight.

Tor was baffled. Ahead lay nothing but a haze of mist and fog. But *she* saw something.

"The silver rowan," she breathed. The words were no sooner out than she wished she'd bitten her tongue.

"So it is true!" he said. *Only a virgin can lead the way.*

Mouse felt her heart drop. Vow or no, she couldn't go through with it. She tried to turn around, to go back the way they'd come. The pass had vanished. There was nothing but solid rock as far as the eye could see. The same magic that had led them there had closed any hope of retreat.

"Can you find the path?" he asked.

She stared at him. "Of course. It's as wide as a road."

It led down, straight and smooth, to the plateau. There was no way to go but forward. Mouse started down the track, leaving Tor to follow. He plunged down into the fog, ignoring the flickers of light and shadow seen from the corner of his eyes. There was no sense of descending, no feeling of up or down or sideways. She was his beacon, his safe guide through the enchantment, and he kept his fixed gaze upon her back.

Mouse wondered at his cautious progress. In a matter of minutes they were at the start of the pine grove. The lowest branches grazed her head as she dismounted. *There must be a way out of this predicament,* she thought with rising panic. *I must think of something!*

Tor swung down, breathing in the scent of invisible evergreens, and went to her. The moment his hand touched her shoulder, his vision cleared.

They were in a wild place. The rocks were black marble heavily veined with rose, the trees like none he'd ever seen before. Huge flowers like cups of gold, like cups of blood, turned to watch their passage. Their leaves whispered softly.

A dainty creature leapt up beside the path and bounded away in a flash. Mouse had only a glimpse of it. Just enough to see the twisted gold horn that rose from its forehead.

"Did you see that?" Mouse exclaimed. "A unicorn!"

Tor kept his hand on his sword. This was an ancient place, and fraught with magic. They came to a place where steam vents opened from the rock and the air stank of sulphur. He eyed a striped lizard sunning on a slab, its scales a shimmer of lavender and violet and stunning deep purple. Another strange reptile slithered away into the shadows, all rippling gold and silver. The wide neck frill that covered its shoulders gave the illusion of wings.

He tipped his dark head back and gazed up through the green branches. Something flashed, like a sunbeam dazzling through the shining leaves.

But the sun was shining from the opposite direction.

Was it another trick of magic? It all seemed real enough. The ground was soft beneath him and covered with a blanket of pine needles. Branches stirred in the wind, and a brightness caught his eyes. *The silver rowan.*

Its leaves danced in the heart of the pines, reflecting light. But near the very top of the tree, there was something brighter still. He shaded his eyes.

It was a nest woven of the rowan's silver leaves, and inside it was the most beautiful bird he'd ever seen. *The phoenix.* It was elegant, exquisite, with gleaming golden plumage that flickered with light. Its delicate tail feathers were so extravagantly long that they curved down over the edge of the nest, and its lovely head seemed crowned with sparkling jewels. Rainbow prisms shot from the bird like darts of colored flame.

Triumph burst through Tor. *Everything I want is within my reach.*

He looked again, in chagrin. So near and yet so far!

The trunk of the tree was smooth and gleaming as polished silver. There was no way he could climb up and snare the creature with his net while it slept.

There was only one way to do it. He unslung his bow from the saddlehorn. Plucking an arrow from his quiver, he nocked it carefully in place. Every move was slow and precise. Only a fool would rush at such a moment. Tor drew back his bow and took aim.

A second later a screaming fury struck him from behind.

"No!" Mouse shouted, pummeling him with her fists. "You mustn't kill it!"

Tor went sprawling facefirst onto the pine needles as her weight knocked him flat. The arrow went wide of its mark, whistling harmlessly through the long tail feathers of the phoenix. The creature cried out in a crystal voice and flew up toward the sun in a flurry of beating wings.

He rolled over, but Mouse straddled him. Her small hands pushed against his shoulders and her face was bright with wrath. She was magnificent.

The bird, the quest, were forgotten. He wanted her with a fierceness he'd never imagined possible. He grabbed her and rolled over so that she was beneath him. He grasped her wrists and held them fast. Held on to his own wild needs with all the willpower at his command.

"You little fool," he said harshly. "You've spoiled my best chance!"

"I only told you I would lead you to it," she said hotly. "I never said I'd let you take it! You tried to kill the phoenix."

"I didn't intend to harm it! I only meant to lodge an arrow in the tree so I could fix a rope to it from the pines and pull myself across."

Mouse bit her lip. She hadn't realized his intentions. Still, given the same chance, her reaction would have been unchanged.

"The creature is flown. But," she said firmly, "it doesn't matter. My part in this is over. I brought you here as I promised. Now you must keep your share of our bargain."

Tor released her wrists and rose to tower over her. "Do you really expect it of me?" His eyes were harder than his voice. "If you'll think back, fair Rosaleen, I never said I'd take you over the border."

Mouse recalled his words with a shock. He was right. He'd never said it. It had all been her words, her doing. She struggled to her feet, trying to think of a way to hold him to them. There was none.

"I don't need your aid," she said with scorn. "I'll find my way myself!"

Tor's mouth twisted. "No. You cannot. The city you seek does not exist. It was sacked and abandoned before you were born. There is nothing left of it but a pile of ruins."

His words hit her like stones. There was the ring of

truth in every one of them. She went white and blank with shock. "What will I do? Oh gods, what will I do?" He was sorry. He hadn't meant to be so brutal about it. "You need not fear. I will see that you are safe once this quest is ended."

"The bird has flown," she reminded him in a flat voice. "You have lost your chance because of me."

Tor lifted his head. "No. I vowed to return to Airan with the egg of the phoenix. I will find it and redeem my vow."

His arrow had gone wide, but it had still hit its intended target. The silver nest had tumbled from its lofty perch, coming to rest on the lowest branch. "The bird must return to the silver rowan to lay its egg. You told me so, yourself. I'll place the nest lower down and bide my time."

"It might be days before that happens."

"No. It will be soon." He pointed upward. A blur of gold shot across the blue sky, and a thin cry split the air above them. It was not the ringing crystal note they'd heard earlier. It was the sound of breaking glass.

Tor took out his harp and played a chord. Then his voice rang out, rich and full. The silver rowan's leaves danced.

A moment later the phoenix plummeted down. Just when it seemed it would smash into the ground, it flapped its wings and settled gently into the fallen nest.

The golden feathers were streaked in places, and looked like tarnished brass. The creature turned its jeweled head and looked at them, its grave eye glinting like a dulled ruby.

"You see?" Tor murmured. "Its time has come."

"It remembers," Mouse said sadly. "It knows what will happen to it."

He wasn't listening. "The egg will soon be laid—and thereby make my fortune. This time the king will not dare refuse me what I ask!"

Her hand tightened on his arm. "It is not the king who wants the egg," she told him. "It is the queen. He would never have asked for such a thing of his own will. While she lives, he will never be completely free of her evil spell."

"King or queen, it matters not to me. All that matters is that I claim my prize."

Mouse's throat felt dry. "Queen Bryn knows the legend in its entirety. She will mix the egg with wine and drink it down, hoping that it will restore her youth and beauty."

"What is that to you or me?" Tor shrugged. "An egg, whether chicken or firebird, is just an egg."

"Oh, no," Mouse cried. "You don't understand. There is only *one,* you see. One phoenix. One egg."

"What?"

"Don't you know the rest of the legend?" Mouse brushed at the loose auburn tendrils clinging to her cheek. Her fingers came away wet with tears.

"The phoenix lays her egg and dies, consumed in glory. The warmth of the ash incubates the egg. When the egg hatches, the phoenix is reborn."

Tor struggled with the concept. "As long as the egg hatches successfully, it is immortal? No." He shook his head. "Impossible. How can it be reborn? It is just a legend. . . ."

A tear stole down her cheek. "How can you say that? You've seen the phoenix with your own eyes. It is unique in all the world. It is as real as you or I. And when it is gone, there will be no more!"

His finger grazed her cheek. "Sweet Rosaleen, only think! There is no such thing in nature as one of anything."

She lifted tear-drenched eyes to him. "There is only one of *me!*"

14

"You are not the man I once thought you to be," Mouse said angrily.

Her tears had long since dried, and her arguments had been to no avail. Tor meant to take the bird back to Airan with them. Bryn would make her magic potion with the egg it laid—and the phoenix would become extinct.

He opened his saddlepack and withdrew something, avoiding her eyes. "And what kind of man was that?"

One to whom I gave my trust. My heart. One I thought I loved!

She felt a sharp pang of loss. "A man I could respect."

He flinched as if she'd struck him. A dark flush rose in his face. He hadn't yet done anything to deserve that.

"And what qualities do you respect, Rosaleen?"

Her chin lifted defiantly. "Honor and integrity above all else."

"I am sorry to have disappointed you so gravely." His jaw set. "But I must do what I must do."

Tor unfolded the bird snare he'd taken from his saddle-pack. He draped it over the bird and its nest and staked it down tightly. The phoenix made small sounds, like the tinkle of discordant chimes, and gazed sadly at him with an eye like frosted pink glass.

"You didn't have to do that," Mouse said angrily. "It is in no shape to fly away. See how dull its plumage is?" She touched a feather. It was limp and lusterless. The color had darkened to bronze.

"The creature might brood quietly in the nest until it lays its egg," he said, "but I'm taking no chances. I have some exploring to do. You stay here and keep watch over the phoenix. I'll find us a plump fish for dinner."

"I don't want dinner." Mouse turned her back.

"Well, I do."

Mouse leaned back against the tree and murmured comforting words to the bird. The aging phoenix rubbed its golden beak over Mouse's finger, acknowledging her presence. Then it held its graceful head aloft, waiting for the magical moment when its proud heart would burst into flames of joy, leaving nothing of its tired body but sparkling ash and a glowing rainbow egg. The moment was almost at hand.

Tor stalked off into the pine grove with a small wicker creel. There was a stream that cut through it, and he was bound to find a fine fish. But first he wanted to see more of this enchanted place.

He set off in the direction of the rocks where the lizards sunned. There were none to be found. He foraged for a while, wandering closer to a strange hummock that rose in the midst of the plateau. As he approached, he heard an odd metallic sound, like the gnashing of rusted steel. Wide, three-toed footprints covered the ground nearby, and the mound was studded with holes large enough for a man to enter. Tor gave the place a wide berth. He was curious as to what lived inside the burrows, but he had no intention of going in to find out.

I have other fish to fry.

Tor walked and walked, and always the stream seemed just ahead. A furry creature ran out across his path. It looked like an ermald—except for the tiny silver crown upon its head. Entering a clearing, he spied another lizard basking in the sun. This one was a fiery red, spangled with rose. A wide shadow passed over the ground, but when he looked up the sky was deep and clear.

Butterflies larger than his hand flitted through the dappled light, and the pinecones underfoot seemed carved from copper. When he touched them with the toe of his boot, they poofed into sparkles and vanished.

Everything on this plateau was under an enchantment. Nothing was what it seemed. "I'll be glad to get back to the real world," he said out loud.

The words were no sooner spoken than he saw the stream flowing in front of him. A large bass leapt out of the water to land at his feet. *"Dinner,"* the fish said, and winked at him.

Tor ignored it all as another bit of sorcery. "Into the water with you, my friend." He tossed the fish back. *It will have to be jerked beef tonight, and whatever roots are left in the saddlepacks.*

He looked up to plot the course of the sun. He'd been gone long enough. It was time to return. When he reached the silver rowan tree, Mouse was sitting almost exactly where he'd left her—but the stakes had been pulled up and the net lay sprawled over an empty nest. The phoenix was gone.

He walked over to her, his face set.

"I set it free," she told him defiantly.

"You were a fool," she added, "to leave me alone with the phoenix. You should have known I would release it at the first opportunity!"

"Yes, I suppose I should have."

She'd released the bird, knowing that he would hate

her for it. But where she'd expected anger, there was only coldness in his eyes. It chilled her to the bone.

Suddenly he squatted on his haunches beside the nest. "You are the fool, Rosaleen." He plunged his hand amid the silver leaves. When he pulled it out, something glowed through his fingers, showering the air with radiance.

Her face went white with shock. "The phoenix egg!" She hadn't seen it there, buried among the leaves. "Then . . . that part of the legend isn't true. It laid its egg and has flown away to die. But there is still only one phoenix. One egg."

Tor wrapped the egg in a handful of leaves and placed it in a leather bag attached to his belt, where it would stay safe and warm. "Come. There is no reason for us to tarry now. If that road cutting through to the south is not an illusion, we can reach the castle by nightfall."

Mouse stared out over the plateau to the final ridge of land. "I'll go my own way. There are other cities on the far side of the mountains where I can claim sanctuary."

Tor replied firmly, "You'll go with me, if I have to lead you all the way."

She was subdued and didn't protest as he saddled the horses. She tried to mount on her own, but her foot slipped out of the stirrup. "Help me up."

He came beside Mouse and put his hands on her waist, warm and strong. For a moment they stood close, their eyes locked. Her heart beat faster with the memory of his hands upon her bare flesh, the hot touch of his mouth. She could read nothing in his expression. He tossed her up into the saddle as if she were a sack of oats.

The moment she was in the saddle her demeanor changed. She nudged her horse and took off without warning, giving the cob its head. He gave a shout, but she was already urging the beast faster. If she had enough of a start, Tor wouldn't bother to pursue her, she was sure. Not now that he had the precious phoenix egg.

She'd read him wrong. Hoofbeats sounded behind her, gathering speed. He wasn't going to let her get away so easily. *If I can get past that mound in the distance, there will be only enough room for one horse between the rocks. He'll have to give up.*

Crouching low in the saddle, Mouse galloped across the plateau. He was gaining on her. The old cob was no match for his fiery steed. She felt her horse faltering.

Almost to the mound! She glanced over her shoulder and saw that he was almost at her flank. Suddenly the cob reared up, whinnying in fright. When it came down, one leg crumpled beneath it. In the moment before she was pitched over the horse's head, Mouse caught a glimpse of squat, gnarled bodies, heard the clash of tusk and metallic teeth. *Trolls!* She flew out of the saddle.

The trolls closed in on her, blood dripping from their serrated teeth. As she rolled into a protective ball, Tor galloped up, his sword flashing. She heard the ring of it on those fearsome teeth, the thud of it plunging through the troll bodies.

Tor leaned down from his saddle, scooped her up in front of him before she knew what was happening, and spurred his horse hard. She could only hang on tight and pray she wouldn't fall off.

Her ribs felt bruised from the strength of his arm against her. She tried to look back. "Don't!" he commanded.

They raced on. Small red birds flew up and lizards dashed for shelter. Tor didn't rein in until they reached the edge of the plateau. The horse was in a lather and Mouse was trembling from head to toe.

"That was a foolish thing to do," he said grimly. "We might both have been killed!"

"You didn't have to follow me," she said, shaking with emotion.

Tor cupped her face in one hand. His finger traced the line of her mouth. "Didn't I?"

Mouse looked away. "I don't understand you. Every time I think I know you, you change."

His voice was hard. "I am the same man I always was.

And now you must live with the consequences. Much as you loathe the sight of me, you have no choice of destination. You must ride with me—and I, fair Rosaleen, am going back to Airan."

She saw that there was nothing else to do. She lifted her chin. "I will go back for Elva's sake. And I will hold you to your word to see us safe."

He swung down and lifted her from the saddle. For a moment she was weightless in his arms. Then she was on the ground, her legs shaky.

Tor kept his arm around her until she got her balance. She was pale, her eyes wide and her mouth pink as a rose. He gritted his teeth. "By the gods, I'd should throttle you!"

"If you wished to be rid of me, you should have left me to the trolls."

His face darkened with anger. "Do you think me capable of such a thing?"

She bit her lip. "No." The admission was wrenched from her.

He opened the leather pouch to check the egg it held. As he unknotted the strings, light shone from it as before. She didn't know whether to be glad or sad.

They shared his water and what little cold food he had left. Everything she had was gone along with her poor, doomed horse. They remounted Tor's steed with Mouse riding behind. Mouse leaned her cheek against his broad back. It was awkward being so close to him, inhaling his masculine scent. His muscles rippled beneath his leather jerkin, and she could feel the power of him radiating through her.

They took the impossible shortcut and came out into a grassy meadow as the sun sank in the west. The sky turned orange and rose and gold, highlighting the familiar hills of Airan. If this wasn't another mirage, they would reach the castle before midnight.

The horse thundered on, its long legs eating up the miles. The moon rose, silver and full, to light their way.

Mouse was too exhausted and heartsick to care. She had thought Tor different from other men, but he was just the same as all the rest. Power was all he cared about and winning the hand of the princess Camaris.

Her eyes were wet. *Tears for the beautiful phoenix,* she thought. *And a few for myself.*

At last the towers of Castle Airan rose up beside the river valley, ghostly white in the luminous light. Mouse closed her eyes. She wanted to disappear into the darkness before they reached the gates: The last place on earth she wanted to be was by Tor's side when he claimed Camaris for his bride.

15

THE HOUR WAS past midnight when something awakened Elva. She went to the window that overlooked the river road and the distant hills beyond. The world was still dark, the only light that of the torches blazing on the castle's walls. Then she saw it: a glow coming up from the valley, white as the heart of pure flame. Her heart thumped with fear and hope. Gathering her cloak, she ran out of the cottage.

A group of men camping along the river road saw it, too. Broch gave them the signal. He'd been waiting for it, but never expected it this soon. "By the gods, he's done it!"

In the queen's bower at Castle Airan, Bryn awakened from a troubled sleep. Her skin prickled. She listened and heard shouts from the watchtower. She ran out of her chamber, scarcely stopping to snatch up a warm velvet cloak.

Gilmore was there in the corridor before her, still wearing his coronet and his robes of justice. There had been a council meeting tonight, from which she'd been excluded by law. It always rankled her that she could rule Gilmore through her spells, but not his kingdom. Fortunate for him, she thought viciously.

"What is it?" she said. "Are we under attack?"

"No." Gilmore rubbed his forehead. "But it is something dire, no doubt. Why else would a lone horseman be abroad at such an hour?"

They went out onto the ramparts together. A few seconds later they noticed the glow. It was far too bright for a lantern. Gilmore was puzzled, but Bryn knew what it was, even before the rider swept around the curve to face the castle. *The phoenix egg!*

And Tor, the dark warrior, come to claim Camaris for his bride.

Her eyes sparkled with mingled joy and malice. *I will have youth and beauty, but you will never have my daughter. I will see to that!*

She touched her husband's arm. "You are tired, Gilmore. You can scarce keep your eyes open. You will seek your bed and fall into a deep sleep."

Frowning, he turned away. "I will wait to see what news this messenger brings to us."

Bryn made a small sign and murmured a word beneath her breath. "You will go to bed now, and you will remember nothing of this in the morning!"

Gilmore struggled, then turned stiffly and moved away like a sleepwalker. A moment later his door closed behind him.

Bryn stilled the rapid beating of her heart. She could not keep him in her power much longer. He was fighting off her spells, starting to remember things that were best forgotten. The woman Deirdre and her daughter among them.

That was unfortunate. He was a lusty lover and an able king, and she still wanted him, even if his passion for her had waned. But once he knew the truth of what she had done so long ago, the last link between them would be snapped.

The queen shrugged and hardened her heart. All things, no matter how pleasant, must come to an end. As for Tor of Far Islandia . . .

She smiled. Camaris was not for such as him. Camaris would marry the duke—no matter her tears and tantrums—and extend Bryn's power.

She sent for her new captain of the guard. "The barbarian from Far Islandia is approaching. You will escort him to the privy chamber immediately."

"Yes, Majesty."

"When he realizes that the king is not there, he may try to escape. If he does, your own life will be forfeit."

The captain felt a shiver up his spine. He recalled what had happened to his predecessor a week earlier, in the castle dungeon. "Yes, Majesty. It will be as you say."

"I hope so," she said with a tight little smile. "For your sake."

"There is someone riding pillion with him," the man added.

She hurried to the window just as Tor and Mouse came over the bridge to the castle.

Two birds with one stone!

"The man is accompanied by a young woman," she said. "You will bring her to the presence chamber with him. You will see that they are treated with all respect."

Her eyes shone like pieces of gold. "And you will also see to it that neither leaves the room alive."

16

THE MOMENT THE gates opened and they rode beneath
the portcullis, Mouse and Tor were almost surrounded by
soldiers. His horse reared at his command, and they
backed away from the flailing hooves. Mouse clung to
him with all her strength.

"We mean you no harm," the captain of the queen's
men said. "We are an honor guard, sent to escort you to
the presence chamber."

Tor's sword swept a silver arc. "We need no escort."

Again his horse reared. "Stand back!"

The soldiers obeyed. Tor wheeled his mount and rode
up the courtyard steps and into the great hall. Sleepy-eyed
servants and guests rose from their pallets and scattered
as he entered.

They clattered past the dais and Tor dismounted at the
presence chamber, sword ready. Mouse slid down from
her perch and darted behind him to open the door. The

moment they were inside the chamber, she shut the door and slid the bolt across. Then she turned around and gasped. It wasn't King Gilmore, but Queen Bryn who stood before throne, flanked by her henchmen. Her golden eyes were filled with greed and eagerness.

"So, your quest has been successful."

"You must be the judge of that," Tor answered coolly. "It will hatch soon."

He took the pouch from inside his jerken. Light leaked from it, growing ever brighter as he opened it fully and removed the egg. The thick shell sparkled and glinted in his hand with increasing radiance.

Bryn's eyes opened wide when she saw it. *Youth and beauty will be mine once more!*

The magic she'd tried to conjure in their absence had failed her again. Now she was paying for the years she'd kept her youthful beauty through means of the Dark Arts. Her skin was increasingly furrowed, her eyes duller. She could feel herself aging minute by minute. And now, here was the chance to reverse the terrible process.

"Give me the egg," the queen commanded.

Tor closed his fingers around it. "And what will you give me in return?"

"Damn you for your impudence! Guard, seize the egg and bring it to me!"

One soldier tried to grab the egg from Tor's hand, then leapt back, howling and holding his hand aloft. The skin of his palm was singed and seared.

A hush fell over the chamber. "Perhaps you are as unaware of the legends surrounding the phoenix, as I was previously," Tor replied. "Rosaleen has related them to me. The egg cannot be taken from me. Only the person who has claimed the egg from the nest, can give it away."

He stepped closer and lowered his voice. "And now I repeat my question: If I do freely give the egg into your hands, Majesty, what shall you do with it? When the new phoenix bursts forth, will you keep it caged, a tame bird to sing within your bower?"

Her breath came rasping through cracked, dry lips, "There are caged songbirds enough to suit me already, and one is very like another."

Tor smiled grimly. "I am told that this egg is the last of its kind. The *only* one of its kind. Once it is gone, there will be no more. The phoenix, in all its unearthly beauty, will vanish forever from the world."

Bryn laughed harshly. "Why should the phoenix, with no more brains than the chickens scratching in the kitchen yard, have eternal youth and beauty? I am a queen, surely more worthy of such a gift." She threw her head back haughtily. "There are other birds in the forest. However, there is only one of *me*."

Her words echoed the ones Rosaleen had spoken to him earlier—but how different their meaning.

As he stepped closer to the queen, Mouse blocked his way. "Do not do it, I beg of you!" Her heart was a ball of hot lead inside her chest. Burning, burning.

"I have no choice," he said.

Mouse blinked away a hot sheen of tears. "We have traveled hard and long on our quest, Tor of Far Islandia. During that time I have seen your courage and knightly compassion. You risked your life for mine. And," she continued, "you risked that phoenix egg when you saved me from the trolls."

She clasped her hand upon his arm. "If actions speak louder than words, then I will use them for my guide. If you give the egg to the queen, you will destroy a creature that has done no harm to anyone, one that brings great pleasure to many with its beauty and song. And that would mean you are not the man I lo—"

She stopped and took a breath. "That you are not the man of honor and principle that I believe you to be."

His gaze was black and opaque as onyx. "You ask a great deal of me, Rosaleen. To give up the hand of a princess and half a kingdom. If I do what you ask of me, what do you offer me in return?"

Mouse shook her head sadly. "I have nothing to give you."

Tor looked down at her, his eyes dark as night. "You are wrong on two counts." His voice rose, sparked with passion. "You have much that I want, fair Rosaleen. But I am afraid that I am not the man you believe me to be."

He lifted his arm and held the egg out toward the queen.

17

MOUSE STEPPED BEFORE him. "If that is all you'd wanted of me, you could have taken me that night, with my full will and passion. I thought you turned away from me that night, because you needed a virgin to lead you to the silver rowan tree. I was wrong. You are good and true, Tor of Islandia! You cannot betray the phoenix any more than you could betray me."

His gaze locked with hers. "You truly believe I will forfeit everything I have fought for, while you boldly state you can offer nothing in return?"

She threw pride and caution to the winds. "The reason I have nothing to bestow on you is this: You already own the one thing that is mine alone to give—my heart. It is yours, Tor, now and forever."

"Enough of this folly," Bryn cried out. "Give me the egg before it is too late!" Already her knuckles were thickening, her hands curling into claws.

The egg in Tor's hand jumped suddenly. It almost bounced from his palm. As his fingers closed on the shell, a thin crack opened around its perimeter. Light spilled out from it, ever brighter. It dimmed the light of the torches and the flames leaping in the hearth.

Brynn held out her hand imperiously, and the jewels at her wrists and fingers winked like stars. "Hurry. You must give the egg to me! Only think! The hand of the princess and half the kingdom."

Tor wrenched his gaze away from Mouse. He lifted the egg high, and its brilliance banished the shadows from the darkest corner of the old hall. "Is that all?" His voice rang out. "What if I want more?"

The queen's eyed were wild and tarnished, her gnarled fingers ready to snatch the precious phoenix egg. "Anything! Ask anything of me, and it is yours! Even the crown of Airan."

The curtains behind her parted and the king stepped out. "Generous of you, wife. But the crown of Airan is not yours to give!"

Gilmore dismissed the guards. When they were gone, he bolted the door again. "I will take the egg."

"No!" the queen cried. "Come, give the egg into my hand, and you shall have Camaris to bed this very night. Only give me the egg!"

Tor held it just beyond her reach. It bounced again, and another crack opened. Suddenly Bryn could stand it no longer. She lunged and tried to grab the egg from his palm. Tor snatched it back. "How badly do you want it?"

He hurled the glimmering oval straight into the blazing fire that danced in the great hearth. The flames crackled up around it, erupting higher. Something cracked louder still. Zig-zag lines formed around the egg as it fractured and sizzled in the heat.

"No!" the queen shrieked in a blind fury. She dashed to the hearth, where she took up the fire tongs and she caught the egg, rolling it out onto the stone flags. An aura of light blossomed around it and the shell broke open in a dozen pieces.

Mouse threw herself at it, but Tor caught her in his arms. He pulled her hard against his chest and kept her pinioned there. "Do not look, for the love of God!"

Her face was buried against his shoulder, and she felt the strength of him, inhaled the warm, familiar scent of his body. Her body curved to fit his, supple as a willow. She felt the steady beat of his heart against her own.

Lightning filled the chamber, and the pungent odor of sulphur. Flames leapt up in a mighty roar. Despite the turmoil around them, Mouse felt safe in the circle of his arms. Safe as she had never felt before in her life.

"Look in the mirror, not at the fire!" he said urgently to the king.

Mouse lifted her head and glanced into the looking glass that hung over a chest. The presence chamber was reflected there—the hearth with flames leaping up to the chimney, gold and orange and red, casting their lurid glow upon the queen's ivory gown and golden hair.

But something was different. Chillingly so. Mouse blinked in disbelief. Queen Bryn was frozen in place, one hand extended greedily. From the tip of her velvet slippers to the crown of her head, she had been turned to stone. Every line of her face, every fold of her silken gown, every pucker of scar tissue on her unveiled throat was precise, as if carved by a master sculptor.

There was a scrabble of scaled legs among the logs, and Mouse saw what the others had already noticed in the looking glass: It was not a phoenix hatched from the egg, but a fierce lizard, with gold and silver scales. Its wide neck-frill covered its sinewy shoulders, and gave the illusion of wings.

With a sharp hiss, the creature turned and ran back inside the huge hearth. It vanished up the chimney in a puff of glittering smoke.

"What wizardry is this!" the king exclaimed.

"No wizardry, Majesty" Tor said, "but the cold stare of

the fire-born basilisk, which turns the unwary observer to stone."

Gilmore shook off the clinging webs of Bryn's spell and stared at what she had become. A lump of harmless stone.

Mouse blinked. "But how did you get the basilisk egg?"

Tor laughed. "I spied the basilisk on our way to the plateau, before we reached the silver rowan tree. When I went off 'fishing' I kept an eye out for it. When I returned to camp after you set the phoenix free, I brought the lizard's egg with me. By sleight of hand, I merely pretended to pull it from the phoenix nest and your nest I returned after leaving you alone."

Mouse smile up at him, her face shining. "You *knew* I would release the phoenix!"

His mouth turned up wryly. "Yes, Rosaleen. I counted on it."

He turned to the king. Gilmore looked dazed like a man awakening from a long and dreadful nightmare.

"A great evil has been removed from Airan. You have successfully concluded your quest, Tor of Far Islandia. I will stand by my word. You may claim the Princess Camaris and half my kingdom now, as is your right I will give you my blessing."

"I do not want the princess called the Flower of Airan. My desire for her was not love, but infatuation. Nor do I want half your kingdom. I ask instead for the hand of the Fairest Rose in all the world, my darling Rosaleen. It took only a few days in her company to know that she is my true heart's desire. *If*, that is, she will have me."

Tor turned to Mouse and took her face between his hands. "*Will* you have me, love?"

She threw her arms around his neck. "I will, with all my heart."

As they started to kiss, Gilmore cleared his throat loudly. "You cannot have her."

"What?" Mouse exclaimed.

"By the gods," Tor roared, "I will take her!"

"Only," the king said, "if you agree to half the kingdom as well. It goes with her, you know. And it might have been yours by right."

Gilmore saw the startlement in Tor's face. "Yes—I know who you are, grandson of the great Orgus. Your father was Loric. He was my friend. If the wars had gone differently, he might have sat upon the throne of Airan instead of I, so we have come full circle. I am weary of this crown. I will grant half my kingdom to the Princess Rosaleen, my firstborn daughter. She will hold it in her own right. The other half I will convey to you, on the day you two are wed."

He took Mouse's hand in his and joined it with Tor's. "Together, you will rule wisely, and well."

"But what of the Princess Camaris?" Mouse stammered. "She is your daughter, too."

The king smiled. "I assure you that she will be perfectly happy. She has neither the ambition nor the wits to rule. Last evening, after the queen retired to her chambers, Camaris eloped with her handsome lordling. They sailed with the tide, and will be far at sea by now. I'll settle a fine dowry upon her, along with my personal estates in the Western Lands. All the rest I leave to you."

"I don't need your kingdom," Tor said. "I am heir to Orgus's holdings. I have a manor and a thousand acres in Far Islandia."

"Keep them, with my good blessings. But do not forsake Airan." Gilmore's smile went awry. "This I humbly beg, not as a king but as a father. Do not take my daughter from me now when she is finally restored to me."

"That is entirely up to her." Tor tipped her chin up. "What do you say, my love?"

Mouse's heart was full, her joy complete. "I say that this is the happiest moment of my life!"

Tor drew her into his embrace. "Ah, love. This is only the beginning. There is so much more to come!"

Epilogue

TOR'S BRIDE LAY against him in the darkness, her auburn hair spilling over his naked chest like skeins of silk. The bells of Airan that had rung out in celebration of their wedding day were stilled, the explosions of fireworks were long over.

He cupped her breast and kissed it. She sighed and moved against him, feeling him stir to life. "You are greedy," she whispered.

"No more so than you, fair Rosaleen. How many times do you expect me to make love to you?"

She laughed softly. "As many times as you can."

"Is that a challenge? If so, I am more than up to it."

"So I see, braggart!"

He rolled over, pinning her beneath him as his mouth ravaged hers. He touched her and she parted to him, and her sweet scent filled the air like perfume. "Slow or quick?" he asked. "Rough or gentle?"

"I don't care, as long as it's thorough. And soon!"

Her teeth nipped his skin. Her legs wrapped around him and she pulled him deep inside. He took her with all the passion that was in him, urging her on to wild abandon. She arched against him, crying out his name. As she went spiraling up, her body filled with heat, with light. With him.

When it was over they lay spent and replete in each other's arms—but the light was still there. She could see it through her closed eyelids.

Mouse opened them. "Look!"

The phoenix had flown in their open casement and perched on the deep stone windowsill. Its eyes were filmed, its feathers bedraggled and dulled, but sparks flew from them, and its proud head was still lovely.

"What is it doing so far from its nesting grounds?" Tor murmured.

But Rosaleen knew. It had come to thank them. The phoenix cocked its head and gazed around the room. It spied her short cape of cloth of silver, which lay discarded on the floor along with her gown, her silk stockings, and velvet shoes.

It fluttered down to the cape and settled among the folds of cloth. Suddenly the bird's feathers took on a molten glow. Then the phoenix lifted its head and trilled a song so wondrous, so heartbreaking in its beauty, that Mouse's eyes filled with tears. As the highest note filled the bed-chamber, there was a burst of bright white light too dazzling to watch.

Heads averted, eyes covered, the lovers waited until its glory dimmed. The light died away.

"Oh! Tor!" She clasped her hand to her heart.

Of the old phoenix, nothing was left but sparkles of glowing ash, but an egg lay among the folds of her cape. It was smaller than the basilisk egg, with none of that reptile's strange and coruscating light. It glimmered gold and silver, as elegant as the phoenix that had brought it forth.

While they watched, the shell cracked and a young phoenix rose from the jagged pieces. It gazed at them with eyes of glowing ruby, then sang a song so pure, so golden, that their hearts were filled with joy.

Tor's arm went around her shoulders. "Out of nothing, everything. Just like our love for one another." He drew her against him and kissed her. As their passion bloomed again, the reborn phoenix flew out the open window and was lost among the fire of the stars.

Coming from G. P. Putnam's Sons in
March 2003

BIRTHRIGHT

Nora
Roberts

When five-thousand-year-old bones are
found at a construction site in the small town
of Woodsboro, the news draws archaeologist
Callie Dunbrook out of her sabbatical
and into a whirlwind of
adventure, danger, and romance.

0-399-14984-8

The #1 *New York Times*
Bestselling Author

NORA ROBERTS

works her phenomenal magic...

along with Jill Gregory, Ruth Ryan Langan,
and Marianne Willman